AMERICAN FOREIGN POLICY

FIFTH EDITION

To Willie,
with much thanks, for our
Moore partnership –
124/13
Bruce

AMERICAN
FOREIGN
POLICY

The Dynamics of Choice
in the 21st Century

FIFTH EDITION

BRUCE W. JENTLESON
Duke University

W · W · NORTON & COMPANY
NEW YORK · LONDON

W. W. Norton & Company has been independent since its founding in 1923, when William Warder Norton and Mary D. Herter Norton first published lectures delivered at the People's Institute, the adult education division of New York City's Cooper Union. The firm soon expanded its program beyond the Institute, publishing books by celebrated academics from America and abroad. By midcentury, the two major pillars of Norton's publishing program—trade books and college texts—were firmly established. In the 1950s, the Norton family transferred control of the company to its employees, and today—with a staff of four hundred and a comparable number of trade, college, and professional titles published each year—W. W. Norton & Company stands as the largest and oldest publishing house owned wholly by its employees.

Editor: Jake Schindel

Manuscript Editors: Traci Nagle, Patterson Lamb, Barbara Curialle, Lori Frankel, and Michael Fleming

Project Editor: Rachel Mayer

Electronic Media Editor: Toni Magyar

Editorial Assistant: Sarah Wolf

Marketing Manager, Political Science: Sasha Levitt

Production Manager: Andrew Ensor

Permissions Manager: Megan Jackson

Text Design: Jo Anne Metsch

Art Director: Rubina Yeh

Composition: Jouve

Manufacturing: R. R. Donnelley-Crawfordsville

The text of this book is composed in Minion with the display set in Bauer Bodoni.

Copyright © 2014, 2010, 2007, 2004, 2000 by W. W. Norton & Company, Inc.

Library of Congress Cataloging-in-Publication Data

Jentleson, Bruce W., 1951–

American foreign policy : the dynamics of choice in the 21st century / Bruce W. Jentleson, Duke University. – Fifth ed.

pages cm

Includes bibliographical references and index.

ISBN 978-0-393-91943-1 (pbk.)

1. United States–Foreign relations–1989-   2. United States–Foreign relations–1989—Forecasting.   3. United States–Foreign relations–21st century.   I. Title.

E840.J46 2013

327.73009'05–dc23

2013019153

W. W. Norton & Company, Inc., 500 Fifth Avenue, New York, N.Y. 10110-0017

wwnorton.com

W. W. Norton & Company Ltd., Castle House, 75/76 Wells Street, London W1T 3QT

1 2 3 4 5 6 7 8 9 0

Contents

6   *The Cold War Context: Lessons and Legacies*   167

Readings for Part I: The Context of U.S. Foreign Policy: Theory and History   215

PART

II *American Foreign Policy in the Twenty-First Century: Choices and Challenges*   285

7 *Grand Strategy for a New Era: (I) Power and Peace*   286

Maps, Boxes, Figures, and Tables

Maps

At the Source

Preface to the Fifth Edition

When we went to bed on the night of September 10, 2001, the world was already going through a historic transition. The Cold War had ended, raising hopes for the future. War, though, had not ended, as the 1990s bore tragic witness in Bosnia, Rwanda, and all too many other places. New forces of globalization were sweeping the world, bringing their own combination of progress and problems. Democracy had spread but was facing the challenges of consolidation and institutionalization at best, backsliding at worst. All this, and more, made for quite a full foreign policy agenda for the United States.

And then came September 11. Most of us will always remember where we were when we first heard about the terrorist attacks on the World Trade Center and the Pentagon. The images were piercing. The American psyche was shaken. And the foreign policy agenda was further transformed as the war on terrorism was launched. Less than two years later, claiming that it was a crucial front in the war on terrorism, the George W. Bush administration took the United States to war in Iraq.

In the years since, we have had to deal with this combination of the September 10 and September 11 agendas, plus the further issues posed as we move deeper into this new era and new century. Such are the challenges and opportunities for those who make American foreign policy—and for those who teach and study it.

American Foreign Policy: The Dynamics of Choice in the 21st Century, Fifth Edition, is intended to help those of us who are professors and students take advantage of those opportunities and meet those challenges. This book is designed as a primary text for courses on American foreign policy. Its scope encompasses both key issues of *foreign policy strategy*—of what the U.S. national interest is and which policies serve it best—and key questions of *foreign policy politics*—of which institutions and actors within the American political system play what roles and have how much influence. Formulating foreign policy strategy is the "essence of choice," the means by which goals are established and the policies to achieve them are forged. Foreign policy politics is the "process of choice," the making of foreign policy through the institutions and amid the societal influences of the American political system.

Part I of this book provides the theory and history for establishing the framework of the dynamics of choice. Chapter 1 draws on the international relations and American foreign policy literatures to introduce core concepts, pose debates over alternative explanations, and frame the "4 Ps" (Power, Peace, Prosperity, Principles) analytic approach to foreign policy strategy. The next two chapters provide the partner framework for the domestic politics of U.S. foreign policy, both the key decision-making institutions (Chapter 2) and the influential societal forces (Chapter 3). The history chapters help ensure that expressions such as "break with the past" are not taken too literally. Not only must we still cope with the legacies of the Cold War (Chapters 5, 6), but many current issues are contemporary versions of long-standing "great debates" going back to the 18th, 19th, and early 20th centuries (Chapter 4).

Part II (Chapters 7–14), substantially revised and updated, applies Part I's approach to the 21st century foreign policy agenda and the major choices the United States faces today. Chapters 7 and 8 examine overarching "grand strategy" structured within the 4 Ps framework. Chapter 9 extends the domestic politics framework laid out in Chapters 2 and 3 to the contemporary period. Chapters 10 through 14 take major country and regional approaches: China and Asia (Chapter 10), the Middle East (Chapter 11), Europe and Russia (Chapter 12), Latin America (Chapter 13), and Africa (Chapter 14). The chapters are highly comprehensive, providing students with a broad survey of key issues since the end of the Cold War. Each chapter also features its own foreign policy politics case study.

This book also includes maps, boxes, and four main types of feature boxes: *Historical Perspectives*, drawing on history to provide additional insights into current issues; *International Perspectives*, giving a greater sense of how other countries view American foreign policy; *Theory in the World*, bringing out ways in which theory and policy connect; and *At the Source*, highlighting excerpts from major speeches and other primary source materials.

We also continue to provide the text and a reader in a single volume. Supplemental readings are keyed to each chapter. These readings develop theories and concepts introduced in the text and delve more deeply into major policy debates. They include works by scholars such as John Mearsheimer, Robert Keohane, Arthur Schlesinger Jr., Walter LaFeber, John Ikenberry, and Charles Kupchan; major policy figures such as Henry Kissinger and Mikhail Gorbachev; and non-American authors from China, Russia, Europe, and India.

With this edition, we are offering a much-expanded and highly innovative coursepack, compatible with a variety of learning management systems (Blackboard, Moodle, Canvas, and others). It contains chapter reviews and vocabulary flashcards; multiple-choice quizzes to reinforce student understanding of chapter content and concepts; study questions to help spur class discussion and student thinking about key topics; and engaging video and critical-thinking exercises for further research and analysis. We are also offering a thoroughly updated Test Bank for this Fifth Edition, which can be found at wwnorton.com/instructors.

This book reflects my own belief in a "multi-integrative" approach to teaching about American foreign policy. By that I mean three things: an approach that breaks through the levels-of-analysis barriers and integrates international policy and domestic process, encompasses the full range of post–Cold War foreign policy issue areas, and "bridges the gap" between theory and practice by drawing on both perspectives. With regard to this last point, I have incorporated the perspectives and experiences gained through my own work in the policy world (at the State Department on the Policy Planning Staff, in Congress as a Senate foreign policy aide, and in other capacities) as well as from close to thirty years as a professor.

My interest in continuing to write this book is part of my commitment to teaching. Throughout my university education, I was fortunate to have some exceptional teachers. I was among the thousands of undergraduates at Cornell University who were first captivated by the study of foreign policy through Walter LaFeber's courses on diplomatic history. The late Bud Kenworthy, a superb and caring teacher in his own right, was instrumental in my realization as a senior that I wanted to pursue an academic career. When I went back to Cornell for my Ph.D., I was just as fortunate as a graduate student. Anyone who knows Theodore Lowi knows his intensity and passion for his work; these are especially evident in his teaching. Peter Katzenstein was my dissertation chair and has been a mentor in many ways, including in showing me how commitments to superior scholarship and excellent teaching can be combined.

In my years as a professor my good fortune has continued. In both his approach and his persona, the late Alexander George was a much valued mentor and colleague. Thanks also to Larry Berman, Ed Costantini, Emily Goldman, Alex Groth, Miko Nincic, the late Don Rothchild, and other colleagues at the University of California, Davis, who were partners of many years in trying to make our political science and international relations majors as rich and rewarding for our students as possible. And to Hal Brands, Alma Blount, Peter Feaver, Jay Hamilton, Ole Holsti, Tana Johnson, Bob Korstad, Judith Kelley, Anirudh Krishna, Bruce Kuniholm, Fritz Mayer, Tom Taylor, and many other valued colleagues here at Duke with whom I have been sharing similar pursuits over the past ten-plus years.

Rebecca Britton, Alexandra Pass, Kim Cole, and Sara Johnson were able research assistants on the First Edition; Seth Weinberger on the Second; Christopher Whytock, Kathryn McNabb Cochran, Christine Leach, Rachel Wald, and Tugba Gurcanlar on the Third; Marie Aberger, Sara Huff, Eric Lorber, Danielle Lupton, and Jessica Wirth on the Fourth; Katherine Canales, Jeffrey Gianattasio, Joy Liu, Anand Raghuraman, and Aneesha Sehgal on this Fifth Edition. The librarians Jean Stratford at UC Davis, Jim Cornelius at the U.S. Institute of Peace, and Catherine Shreve at Duke helped greatly in accessing sources and checking citations. Melody Johnson, Lori Renard, Fatima Mohamud, and especially Barbara Taylor-Keil provided tremendous support on the First Edition; Susanne Borchardt was of enormous help on the Second Edition; and Susan Alexander on the Third, Fourth, and Fifth. I owe many thanks to them all. Thanks also to UC Davis, Duke University, Oxford University, and the U.S. Institute of Peace for research support.

Special thanks to colleagues whose feedback as reviewers has been so helpful: Loch Johnson, Jim Lindsay, Dan Caldwell and his students, and others for the First Edition; John Barkdull, Colin Dueck, Todd Eisenstadt, Margaret Karns, Roy Licklider, Peter

Loedel, F. Ugboaja Ohaegbulam, and Jon Western (Second Edition); Charles Krupnick, Brian Lai, Alynna Lyon, Miko Nincic, Tony Payan, Rodger Payne, and Dan Caldwell and another of his classes (Third Edition); Susan Allen, Mark Cicnock, Shaheen Mozaffar, George Quester, and Reneé Scherlen (Fourth Edition); and Philip Brenner, Doug Gibler, David Houghton, Peter Katzenstein, Peter Liberman, John Masker, Miko Nincic, Richard Nolan, John Oates, Aaron Rapport, Laura Reed, Ionas Rus, and Boyka Stefanova for this edition. I also want to thank those colleagues who on a less formal basis have let me know how valuable they and their students find the book; unsolicited comments such as "my students really get a lot out of your book" mean so much.

At W. W. Norton, Roby Harrington has been there from the inception of the project and has provided the steady hand to see it through to initial completion and successive editions. Authors know that we can count on Roby to be supportive and enthusiastic yet also committed to quality and focused on getting the book done. Thanks are due also to Sarah Caldwell and Rob Whiteside on the First Edition; Avery Johnson, Andrea Haver, and especially Aaron Javsicas on the Second; Matt Arnold, Mik Awake, Pete Lesser, and Ken Barton on the Third; Aaron Javsicas, Rachel Comerford, Kate Feighery, Carly Fraser, and Dan Jost on the Fourth; and Jake Schindel, Ann Shin, and Peter Lesser on this edition. Traci Nagle, Patterson Lamb, Barbara Curialle, Lori Frankel, and Michael Fleming were extremely helpful and provided the enhancements that come with skilled copyediting.

Special thanks to my family: Adam and Katie, now young adults who continue to bring so much to my life and who are making their own marks on the world through their own work, and now also Britt and Matt, so exceptional in their own right, and young Daniel, he of the totally disarming smile; Barbara, who has been so supportive and encouraging while accomplishing so much to the benefit of so many students and community members in her own work; and the memory of my mother, Elaine, and my father, Ted, for their love, support, and understanding.

B.W.J.
March 2013
Durham, North Carolina

The Context of U.S. Foreign Policy: Theory and History

1

The Strategic Context: Foreign Policy Strategy and the Essence of Choice

Introduction: Foreign Policy in a Time of Transition

It was October 22, 1962, 7:00 P.M. A young boy sat on his living room floor watching television. President John F. Kennedy came on to warn the American public of an ominous crisis with the Soviet Union over nuclear missiles in Cuba. The boy's parents tried to look calm, but the fear in their eyes could not be masked. It seemed that the United States was on the brink of nuclear war.

The Cuban missile crisis ended up being settled peacefully, and the Cold War ultimately ended without nuclear war. For a while it seemed that the post–Cold War era was going to be a peaceful one. Indeed, when the Berlin Wall came down in 1989, and then the Soviet Union fell apart in 1991, a sense of near euphoria enveloped the West. President George H. W. Bush (1989–93) spoke of the end of the Cold War as "a time of great promise," an "unparalleled opportunity . . . to work toward transforming this new world into a new world order, one of governments that are democratic, tolerant and economically free at home and committed abroad to settling differences peacefully, without the threat or use of force."[1]

To be sure, the significance of families' being freed from the worry of an all-out nuclear war is not to be underestimated. In this regard, the end of the Cold War left the world more secure. All too soon, however, we saw that the end of the Cold War did not mean the end of war. The 1990s will be remembered for peace agreements and the advance of democracy—but also for ethnic "cleansings," civil wars, genocide, and new setbacks for democracy and human rights. It was a decade of strides toward peace and order, but also stumbles toward anarchy and chaos. For American foreign policy, it was a decade of great successes, but also dismal failures.

The 1990s also saw the emergence of the "globalization" agenda. Globalization has been hailed by many for bringing such benefits as the spread of capitalism and economic freedom to the former communist bloc and the developing world and the closer linking through technology and markets of all corners of the globe, and for building the basis for global prosperity. President Bill Clinton spoke of "the train of globalization" that "cannot be reversed" and of how global trade could "lift hundreds of millions of people out of poverty." But he also warned that globalization needed "a more human face," that it needed to address issues such as the global environment, the global AIDS crisis, and the widening gap between rich and poor nations.[2] Indeed, a powerful antiglobalization movement emerged in the 1990s. First in Seattle at the 1999 summit of the World Trade Organization and then at international economic meetings in ensuing years in various cities around the world, this movement mounted the most extensive and violent foreign policy protests since those of the anti–Vietnam War movement in the 1960s and 1970s. On this globalization agenda as well, the 1990s ended with a mixed sense of progress and problems.

Then came the tragic and shocking terrorist assault of September 11, 2001. "U.S. ATTACKED," the *New York Times* headline blared the next day in the large print used for only the most momentous events, and the newspaper went on to describe "a hellish storm of ash, glass, smoke and leaping victims" as the World Trade Center towers crashed down.[3] In Washington, D.C., the Pentagon, the fortress of American defense, was literally ripped open by the impact of another hijacked jetliner. The death tolls were staggering. The shock ran deep. A new sense of insecurity set in, for it soon became clear that this was not an isolated incident. President George W. Bush declared a "war on terrorism," which started in October 2001 in Afghanistan against Osama bin Laden, his Al Qaeda terrorist network, and the Taliban regime. But it did not end there. "It will not end," President Bush declared, "until every terrorist group of global reach has been found, stopped and defeated."[4] Less than two years later, claiming it to be a crucial front in the war on terrorism, the Bush administration took the United States to war in Iraq.

The Iraq war proved to be the most controversial foreign policy issue since the Vietnam war of the 1960s–70s. It was one of the key issues, along with the worst national and international economic crisis since the Great Depression, that helped Barack Obama win the presidency in 2008. During the presidential campaign he acknowledged both the threats American foreign policy needed to meet and the opportunities for progress. "This century's threats are at least as dangerous as and in some ways more complex than those we have confronted in the past," he declared. Terrorism, weapons of mass destruction, more wars in the Middle East, more genocide and other deadly conflicts, climate change, global pandemics, global recession, rising powers such as China, recovering ones such as Russia— these challenges comprised a full and complex agenda. Thinking of all this, though, was "not to give way to pessimism. Rather it is a call to action . . . [to] a new vision of leadership in the twenty-first century" geared toward a "common security for our common humanity."[5]

Any one of these sets of changes, plus new ones introduced by the Arab spring in 2011 and other recent developments, would be profound by itself. Dealing with the combined effects of all of them truly makes these first decades of the twenty-first century times of historic transition.

Just as each of the four most recent presidents has given different emphases to the U.S. role in this new era, so too have prominent scholars and analysts offered a range of views on its nature. Back in 1989, amid the sense of political and ideological triumph over communism, the neoconservative intellectual Francis Fukuyama envisioned "the end of history . . . and the universalization of Western liberal democracy as the final form of human government."[6] A few years later the Harvard University professor Samuel Huntington offered a much less optimistic view of a "clash of civilizations," particularly between the West and Islam, with prospects for political and military conflicts.[7] The *New York Times* columnist Thomas Friedman pointed rather to economics as the driving dynamic—to liberalism, clashing civilizations, and power politics as "the old system" and to globalization as "the new system."[8] Neo-conservatives proclaimed a "unipolar moment," in Charles Krauthammer's oft-cited phrasing, with the United States as dominant as any great power since the days of ancient Rome.[9] The Rockefeller Brothers Fund, a prominent philanthropy, stressed the importance of "nonmilitary threats to peace and security," especially global poverty and environmental degradation, and advocated a conception of "social stewardship" for addressing these issues "before they metastasize into larger threats."[10] The scholar-journalist Fareed Zakaria wrote of a "post-American world, a great transformation taking place around the world . . . creating an international system in which countries in all parts of the world are no longer objects or observers but players in their own right. It is the birth of a truly global order."[11] Charles Kupchan called it "no one's world," with no single country dominant amidst unprecedented political and ideological diversity.[12] In my own work I've used astronomy metaphors about the transition from a Ptolemaic world, with the United States at the center and others revolving around it, to a Copernican one with efforts at global governance at the center and twenty-first century nationalism giving different countries their own orbits.[13]

Whatever the differences among these perspectives, they share a common view of the importance of foreign policy. Time and again we hear voices claiming that the United States can and should turn inward and can afford to care less about and do less with the rest of the world. But for five fundamental reasons, the importance of foreign policy must not be underestimated.

First are security threats. September 11 drove these home all too dramatically. No longer was the threat "over there" in some distant corner of the globe; it had arrived right here at home. But it is not "just" terrorism. Although relations among the major powers are vastly improved from the Cold War, cooperation cannot be taken for granted, given both the policy differences that still exist and the internal political uncertainties Russia and China in particular face. Wars continue to be fought in the Middle East, and stability remains fragile in regions such as South Asia (India, Pakistan) and East Asia (the Koreas, China, and Taiwan). Weapons of mass destruction proliferate in these and other regions, and may fall into the hands of terrorists. The United States is also at risk from newer security threats, such as avian flu with its potential for millions of fatalities and other "diseases of mass destruction" (DMD). Cyber threats have become increasingly ominous not only in standard security terms but also with their unprecedented potential to disrupt daily life.

Second, the American economy is more internationalized than ever before. Whereas in 1960 foreign trade accounted for less than 10 percent of the U.S. gross domestic product (GDP), it now accounts for almost 30 percent. Job opportunities for American workers are increasingly affected by both the competition from imports and the opportunities for exports. When the Federal Reserve Board sets interest rates, in addition to domestic factors such as inflation, increasingly it also has to consider international ones, such as foreign-currency exchange rates and the likely reactions of foreign investors. Private financial markets have also become increasingly globalized. So when Asian stock markets plunged in late 1997, and when Russia's economy collapsed in mid-1998, middle-class America felt the effects, with mutual funds, college savings, and retirement nest eggs plummeting in value. And when U.S. financial markets had their meltdown in late 2008, the negative results were transmitted around the world.

Third, many other areas of policy that used to be considered "domestic" have been internationalized. The environmental policy agenda has extended from the largely domestic issues of the 1960s and 1970s to international issues such as global warming and biodiversity. The "just say no" drug policy of the 1980s was clearly not working when thousands of tons of drugs came into the United States every day from Latin America, Asia, and elsewhere. Whereas the Federal Bureau of Investigation's "Ten Most Wanted" list included mostly members of U.S.-based crime syndicates when it was first issued in 1950, by 1997 eight of the ten fugitives on the list were international criminals (and that was before 9/11 put Osama bin Laden and other terrorists at the top of the list). Public-health problems such as the spread of AIDS have to be combated globally. The rash of problems in 2007–2008 with children's toys, pet foods, and prescription drugs produced largely in China showed that product safety could no longer be just, or even mostly, a domestic regulatory issue. In these and other areas the distinctions between foreign and domestic policy have become increasingly blurred, as international forces affect spheres of American life that used to be considered domestic.

Fourth, the increasing racial and ethnic diversity of the American people has produced a larger number and wider range of groups with personal bases for interest in foreign affairs. Some forms of "identity politics" can be traced all the way back to the nineteenth century, and some were quite common during the Cold War. But more and more Americans trace their ancestry and heritage to different countries and regions and are asserting their interests and seeking influence over foreign policy toward those countries and regions.

Fifth, it is hard for the United States to uphold its most basic values if it ignores grievous violations of those values that take place outside its national borders. It is not necessary to take on the role of global missionary or world police. But it is also impossible to claim the country stands for democracy, freedom, and justice, yet say "not my problem" to genocide, repression, torture, and other horrors.

Foreign policy thus continues to press on Americans, as individuals and as a nation. The choices it poses are at least as crucial for the twenty-first century as the Cold War and nuclear-age choices were for the second half of the twentieth century.

This book has two principal purposes: (1) to provide a framework, grounded in international relations theory and U.S. diplomatic history, for foreign policy analysis; and (2) to apply that framework to the agenda for U.S. foreign policy in the post–Cold War world.

The analytic framework, as reflected in the book's subtitle, is *the dynamics of choice.* It is structured by two fundamental sets of questions that, whatever the specific foreign policy issues involved and whatever the time period being discussed, have been at the center of debate:

- questions of *foreign policy strategy*—of what the national interest is and how best to achieve it
- questions of *foreign policy politics*—of which institutions and actors within the American political system play what roles and how much influence they have.

Setting foreign policy strategy is the *essence of choice,* establishing the goals to be achieved and forging the policies that are the optimal means for achieving them. Foreign policy politics is the *process of choice,* the making of foreign policy through the political institutions and amid the societal influences of the American political system.

Part I of this book provides the theory (in this chapter and Chapters 2 and 3) and history (Chapters 4, 5, and 6) for establishing the framework of the dynamics of choice in U.S. foreign policy. Part II then applies the framework to the major foreign policy choices the United States faces in these first decades of the twenty-first century.

The Context of the International System

The United States, like all states, makes its choices of foreign policy strategy within the context of the international system. Although extensive study of international systems is more the province of international relations textbooks, two points are particularly important to our focus on American foreign policy.

Quasi anarchy

One of the fundamental differences between the international system and domestic political systems is the absence of a recognized central governing authority in the international system. This often is referred to as the *anarchic* view of international relations. Its roots go back to the seventeenth-century English political philosopher Thomas Hobbes and his classic treatise *Leviathan.* Hobbes saw international affairs as a "war of all against all." Unlike in domestic affairs, where order was maintained by a king or other recognized authority figure, no such recognized authority existed in the international sphere, according to Hobbes. Others since have taken a more tempered view, pointing to ways in which international norms, laws, and institutions have provided some order and authority and stressing the potential for even greater progress in this regard. Yet even in our contemporary era, although we have progressed beyond the "nasty, brutish," unadulterated Hobbesian world by developing international institutions like the United Nations and the International Monetary Fund—as well as a growing body of international law—the world still has nothing at the international level as weighty and authoritative as a constitution, a legislature, a president, or a supreme court. Thus, the prevailing sense is that what makes international relations "unique and inherently different from relations within states" is that "no ultimate authority exists to govern the international system. . . . As a result the existence of a 'quasi-anarchy' [*sic*] at the international level conditions state-to-state relations."[14]

System Structure

System structure is based on the distribution of power among the major states in the international system. "Poles" refer to how many major powers there are—two in a ***bipolar*** system, as during the Cold War, when the United States and the Soviet Union were the sole major powers; three or more in a ***multipolar*** system, as in the nineteenth century, when Great Britain, France, Austria-Hungary, Germany, and Russia were all major European powers.

Whatever the structure, where a state ranks in the system affects what it can do in foreign policy terms. Theorists such as Kenneth Waltz see system structure as very deterministic, making "[states'] behavior and the outcomes of their behavior predictable."[15] To know a state's structural position is thus to know its foreign policy strategy. Yet such claims can go too far, taking too rigid a view of how much is fixed and determined at the system level. For example, we know the Cold War went on for almost fifty years and that it ended peacefully. Waltz argues that this proves the stability of bipolarity and the success of deterrence policies. Yet it is worth asking whether the Cold War had to go on for fifty years: could it have been ended sooner if leaders on one or both sides pursued different policies? Or consider the Cuban missile crisis of 1962 (discussed in more detail in

Chapter 5): the bipolar-system structure raised the possibility of such a crisis but did not make either its occurrence or its successful resolution inevitable. Although it is important to take system structure into account, it should be as a context for, not a determinant of, choices of foreign policy strategy. This is especially true in the current era, because system structure is less clear than during the Cold War and earlier.

This is why the metaphor of a game of billiards, which state-structural explanations frequently use, is misleading. The essence of billiards is the predictability of how a ball will move once it has been struck; hit the cue ball at a certain angle from a certain distance with a certain force, and you can predict exactly where on the table the target ball will go, regardless of whether it is solid or striped. In international systems theory, the "hitting" is done by external threats, the "angles" are set by the state's position in the structure of the international system, and the "path" the state's foreign policy takes is predictable, regardless of the "stripes or solids" of its foreign policy priorities, domestic politics, or other characteristics. In reality, though, while states are not like "crazy balls," bouncing wherever their domestic whims might take them, they are not strictly reactive, either. Their foreign policy choices are constrained by the structure of the international system but are not determined by it. Domestic politics and institutions matter a great deal, as we discuss in Chapters 2 and 3.

The National Interest: The "4 Ps" Framework

The national interest: all of us have heard it preached. Many of us may have done some of the preaching ourselves—that U.S. foreign policy must be made in the name of the national interest. No one would argue with the proposition that following the national interest is the essence of the choices to be made in a nation's foreign policy. But defining what the national interest is and developing policies for achieving it have rarely been easy or self-evident. The political scientists Alexander George and Robert Keohane capture this dilemma in an article, noting that problems have been encountered because the concept of the national interest has "become so elastic and ambiguous . . . that its role as a guide to foreign policy is problematical and controversial." Yet they also stress the importance that the national interest can have, and needs to have, to help "improve judgments regarding the proper ends and goals of foreign policy."[16]

Our approach in this book is to establish in general analytic terms the four core goals that go into defining the U.S. national interest: Power, Peace, Prosperity, and Principles. These "4 Ps" are not strict categories in which this policy goes in one box and that one in another. Reality is never that neat. The national interest almost always combines two or more of the "4 Ps." Indeed, although sometimes all four core goals are complementary and can be satisfied through the same policy, more often they pose trade-offs and tensions, and sometimes major dissensus. The "4 Ps" framework helps us to see this complexity, to analyze how priorities are set, and to locate the corresponding debates over what American foreign policy *is* and what it *should be*—what we earlier called "the essence of choice" in foreign policy strategy.

In setting up this analytic framework, we are not pitting the U.S. national interest against the interests of the international community. Indeed, the U.S. national interest has become increasingly interrelated with the interests of the international community. This is not and likely never will be a pure one-to-one relationship in which the U.S. national interest and other international interests are fully in sync. There is much debate about just how interrelated they are. For example, the George W. Bush administration criticized the Clinton administration for allegedly pursuing a foreign policy in which "the 'national interest' is replaced with 'humanitarian interests' or the interests of 'the international community.' "[17] On the other hand, among the main criticisms of the Bush administration's own policies was that they often put the American national interest at loggerheads with the interests of others in the international community, and that this proved not to be in anyone's interest. The Obama conception of "common security for our common humanity" presented another approach posing its own debates.

For each of the "4 Ps" we lay out three main elements:

- basic conceptualization and working definition
- the most closely associated broader theory of international relations (the IR "-isms")
- representative policy strategies and illustrative examples.

Power

Power is the key requirement for the most basic goals of foreign policy: self-defense and the preservation of national independence and territory. It is also essential for deterring aggression and influencing other states on a range of issues. "Power enables an actor to shape his environment so as to reflect his interests," Samuel Huntington stated. "In particular it enables a state to protect its security and prevent, deflect or defeat threats to that security."[18] To the extent that a state is interested in asserting itself, advancing its own interests and itself being aggressive, it needs power. "The strong do what they have the power to do," the ancient Greek historian Thucydides wrote, "and the weak accept what they have to accept."[19]

Realism is the school of international relations theory that most emphasizes the objective of power. "International relations is a struggle for power," the noted Realist scholar Hans Morgenthau wrote; "statesmen think and act in terms of interest defined as power."[20] He and other Realists take a very Hobbesian view, seeing conflict and competition as the basic reality of international politics. The "grim picture" is painted by the University

1.1

of Chicago professor John Mearsheimer (Reading 1.1)*: "International relations is not a constant state of war, but it is a state of relentless security competition, with the possibility of war always in the background. . . . Cooperation among states has its limits, mainly because it is constrained by the dominating logic of security competition, which no amount of cooperation can eliminate. Genuine peace, or a world where states do not compete for power, is not likely."[21] Ultimately states can rely only on themselves for security. It is a "self-help" system—and power is critical to the self-help states need to be secure.

For Realists, consequently, four points are central. First, states pursue interests, not peace per se. If their interests are better served by war, aggression, and other such coercive means, appeals to peace as an objective won't work very well. Peace is best served by using power to affect the calculations states make. Second, political and military power remain the major currencies of power. They are crucial to a strong national defense, to credible deterrence, and to other effective means of statecraft. The particular requirements have varied dramatically over time with changes in the identity of the potential aggressor—Great Britain in early U.S. history, Germany in the two world wars, the Soviet Union during the Cold War, terrorists today—and the nature of weaponry—from muskets and a few warships to nuclear weapons, submarines, and supersonic bombers to suicide bombers and anthrax letter "bombs." But the basic strategy always has been essentially the same: to have sufficient military power to deter aggression and, if deterrence fails, to ensure the defense of the nation.

Third, economic power and other aspects of prosperity are valued by Realists less as their own international currency than as the "bullion" on which military power ultimately rests. The American economy must be kept strong and competitive primarily to provide the advanced technologies needed for next-generation weapons, and to maintain political support for a large defense budget and other global commitments. Fourth, although principles such as democracy and human rights are important, they should rarely be given priority over considerations of power. This last point emerged in the George W. Bush administration as a major difference between "neoconservatives," who stressed principles as well as power, and more traditional Realists.

The principal foreign policy strategies that follow from this line of reasoning are largely *coercive* ones. "Covenants without the sword," to go back to Hobbes, "are but words, and of no strength to secure a man at all. The bonds of words are too weak to bridle men's ambitions, avarice, anger and other passions, without the fear of some coercive power."[22] The ultimate coercive strategy of course, is *war*—"the continuation of policy by other means," in the words of the great nineteenth-century Prussian strategist Karl von Clausewitz, "an act of violence intended to compel our opponent to fulfill our will."

---

*Marginal icons indicate a related reading; readings follow each part of the book.

Starting with its own Revolutionary War and then through the nineteenth century (e.g., the Mexican-American War, the Spanish-American War) and the twentieth century (e.g., World Wars I and II, the Vietnam War, the Persian Gulf War) and into the twenty-first century with the Iraq and Afghanistan wars, the wars fought by the United States have had varying success in achieving the Clausewitzian objective of "compel[ling one's] opponent to fulfill [one's] will."

Along with a strong national defense, the best way to avoid war for Realists is through *deterrence.* The general definition of deterrence is the prevention of war by fear of retaliation. During the Cold War the United States and the Soviet Union were particularly concerned with nuclear deterrence and the avoidance of nuclear war because both sides feared that a first strike, would be met with a counter strike, despite any damage done.

Military interventions are "small wars," the uses of military force in a more limited fashion, as in the overthrow of governments considered hostile to U.S. interests and the protection or bringing to power of pro-U.S. leaders through military actions of limited scope and duration. We will see numerous historical examples (Chapter 4) as well as others during the Cold War (Chapters 5 and 6) and in the post–Cold War era (various chapters).

Another distinction in uses of military force concerns timing. *Self-defense* is military action taken in response to an attack. *Preemptive war* is used against an imminent threat—that is, you have strong basis for assessing that the target of the attack is about to attack you. *Preventive war* is used when the threat is less than imminent but you have strong basis for assessing that the threat will become much greater if you wait. These aspects of the use of force also have been subject to long-standing and especially intense debates in recent years, such as those over Iraq, humanitarian intervention, and the norm of Responsibility to Protect.

Alliances against a mutual enemy are a key component of both defense and deterrence strategies. For most of American history, alliances were formed principally in wartime. During the Cold War (officially, peacetime), the United States set up a global network of alliances, including multilateral ones such as the North Atlantic Treaty Organization (NATO), the Southeast Asia Treaty Organization (SEATO), and the Rio Treaty (with Latin American countries), as well as bilateral agreements with Japan, South Korea, Taiwan, Israel, Iran, and others. Some of these alliances and bilateral pacts have continued into the post–Cold War era; new ones have also been struck.

A related strategy is the provision of *military assistance*, such as weapons, advisers, financing, and other forms of aid, to a pro-American government or rebel group. Here too are numerous historical examples: Lend-Lease to Great Britain in 1940–41, before the United States entered World War II; military aid to anticommunist governments during the Cold War, including major violators of democracy and human rights; current military aid to antiterrorist governments, including many with poor records on democracy and human rights.

Power can be exerted through more than just military force. Diplomacy also can be used coercively. ***Coercive diplomacy*** takes a number of forms, from such low-level actions as the filing of an official protest or issuing a public condemnation, to withdrawing an ambassador and suspending diplomatic relations, to imposing ***economic sanctions*** and other, tougher measures.[23] Then there is ***covert action***, the secret operations of intelligence agencies conducted, as former secretary of state Henry Kissinger put it, to "defend the American national interest in the gray areas where military operations are not suitable and diplomacy cannot operate."[24] Although they have been especially associated with the Cold War and now with global counterterrorism, covert actions go back to early U.S. history, as when President Thomas Jefferson secretly arranged the overthrow of the pasha of Tripoli (in today's Libya) and when President James Madison authorized a secret attack into Florida, which then was still controlled by Spain.

Peace

In a certain sense, all four of the national-interest objectives are ultimately about *Peace*—for that is what power is supposed to safeguard, what prosperity is supposed to contribute to, what principles are supposed to undergird. We use it to stress ***diplomacy*** in its classic sense of "the formalized system of procedures or the process by which sovereign states . . . conduct their official relations."[25] From the very beginning, when the State Department was created as one of the original Cabinet departments and Benjamin Franklin was dispatched to France seeking support for the young nation, diplomacy has been a crucial element in U.S. foreign policy strategy. Diplomacy continues on a daily basis, with U.S. ambassadors stationed in capitals around the world and foreign ambassadors in Washington, D.C. It becomes especially important in crises, wars, and other such urgent times. Although it can also take coercive forms through economic sanctions and other measures as noted above, its methods stress negotiation.

   International Institutionalism is diplomacy's most closely associated IR "-ism". International Institutionalism views world politics as "a cultivable 'garden,'" in contrast to the Realist view of a global "'jungle.'"[26] Although it stops well short of world government, this theory emphasizes both the possibility and the value of reducing the chances of war and of achieving common interests sufficiently for the international system to be one of *world order*. International Institutionalists recognize that tensions and conflicts among nations do exist, but they see cooperation among nations as more possible and more beneficial than Realists do. Thus pursuing cooperation is neither naïve nor dangerous, but rather a rational way to reduce risks and make gains that even the most powerful state could not achieve solely on its own. To be sure, as Professor Inis Claude has written, "the problem of power is here to stay; it is, realistically, not a problem to be eliminated, but"—the key point for International Institutionalists—"a problem to be managed."[27] International Institutionalists have their own conception of power, which in contrast to that of Realists stresses diplomatic over military and other coercive means. To the extent that treaties and international institutions constrain potential aggressors, they contribute to the "general capacity of a state to control the behavior of others," which is how one international relations textbook defines power. When peace brokering is effective, it adds to the ability of the United States "to overcome obstacles and prevail in conflicts," which is another text's definition of power.[28]

Consistent with this sense that peace is achievable but not automatic, scholars such as Robert O. Keohane stress the importance of creating international institutions as the basis for "governance in a partially globalized world" (Reading 1.2). Anarchy cannot be eliminated totally, but it can be tempered or partially regulated. Indeed, it is precisely because the power and interests that Realists stress do generate conflicts that "international institutions . . . will be components of any lasting peace."[29] This also is true with regard to relations among allies. States may have friendly relations and share common interests but still have problems of collective action or coordination. International institutions provide the structure and the commitments to facilitate, and in some instances require, the fulfillment of commitments to collective action and coordination. "Institutions can provide information, reduce transaction costs, make commitments more credible, establish focal points for coordination and, in general, facilitate the operation of reciprocity."[30] In doing so international institutions help states overcome the difficulties of collective action, which can persist even when states have common interests. This is a very rational argument, not just an idealistic one. The world envisioned is not one free of tensions and conflicts. But it is one in which the prospects for achieving cooperation are greater than Realism and other power-based theories foresee. International Institutionalists also see the constraints on a state's own freedom of action that come with multilateralism as less consequential than the capacity gained to achieve shared objectives and serve national interests in ways that would be less possible unilaterally. In Part II, we explore the unilateralism-multilateralism debate and the sharp controversies it has sparked in recent years.

International institutions may be formal bodies such as the United Nations, but they also can be more informal, in what are often called "international regimes." Keohane defines international institutions both functionally and structurally, as "the rules that govern elements of world politics and the organizations that help implement those rules."[31] This definition encompasses norms and rules of behavior, procedures for managing and resolving conflicts, and the organizational bases for at least some degree of global governance, albeit well short of full global government.

We can identify five principal types of international institutions:

1. *Global security,* such as the League of Nations (unsuccessful) and the United Nations (more successful)
2. *Economic,* such as the International Monetary Fund, the World Bank, and the World Trade Organization

3. *International legal,* such as the long-standing World Court and the recently created International Criminal Court
4. *Policy area,* such as the International Atomic Energy Agency (IAEA) for nuclear nonproliferation, the World Health Organization (WHO) for global public health, and the United Nations Environmental Program (UNEP) for the global environment
5. *Regional,* such as the Organization on Security and Cooperation in Europe (OSCE) or the Organization of American States (OAS).

In none of these cases has the United States been the only state involved in establishing the institutions and organizations. But in most, if not all, the United States has played a key role.

Another type of foreign policy strategy that fits here is the *"peace broker"* role the United States has played in wars and conflicts to which it has not been a direct party. Familiar contemporary examples include the 1973–75 "shuttle diplomacy" in the Middle East by Henry Kissinger, the 1978 Camp David accord between Egypt and Israel brokered by President Jimmy Carter, and the Clinton administration's role in the 1995 Dayton accord ending the war in Bosnia. But this role, too, traces back historically, as with the peace treaty brokered by President Theodore Roosevelt ending the Russo-Japanese War, for which Roosevelt was awarded the 1906 Nobel Peace Prize.

Prosperity

Foreign policies motivated by the pursuit of *Prosperity* are those that give high priority to the national interest defined principally in economic terms. They seek gains for the American economy from policies that help provide reliable and low-cost imports, growing markets for American exports, profitable foreign investments, and other international economic opportunities. Some of these involve policies that are specifically *foreign economic* ones, such as trade policy. Others involve general relations with countries whose significance to U.S. foreign policy is largely economic, as with an oil-rich country like Saudi Arabia. Most generally they have involved efforts to strengthen global capitalism as the structure of the international economy.

Among theories that stress the economic factor in American foreign policy are two principal schools of thought. These schools share the emphasis on economics but differ on whether the prime motivator of policy is to serve the general public interest or the more particular interests of the economic elite. The first school of thought, which we dub "Economism," emphasizes the pursuit through foreign policy of general economic benefits to the nation: a favorable balance of trade, strong economic growth, a healthy macroeconomy.[32] The ultimate goal is collective prosperity, in which the interests served are those of the American people in general. This was said to have been a major part of U.S.

foreign policy in the nineteenth century, when about 70 percent of the treaties and other international agreements the United States signed were on matters related to trade and international commerce.[33] It was the basis for the creation after World War II of the General Agreement on Tariffs and Trade (GATT), the International Monetary Fund (IMF), and the World Bank as the key international economic institutions of an open, market-based free trade system. It also has been evident in recent years, as in the 1995 statement by then-secretary of state Warren Christopher that while other secretaries of state had put their main emphasis on arms control, "I make no apologies for putting economics at the top of [the U.S.] foreign policy agenda."[34]

The second school includes a number of theories, most notably theories of ***imperialism*** and ***neocolonialism***, that see American foreign policy as being dominated by and serving the interests of the capitalist class and other elites, such as multinational corporations and major banks.[35] Prosperity is sought more for the private benefit of special interests, and the ways in which it is sought are highly exploitative of other countries. The basics of this theory go back to the British economist John Hobson and his 1902 book *Imperialism*. Because the unequal distribution of wealth leaves the lower classes with limited purchasing power, capitalism creates the twin problems of underconsumption and overproduction. Thus a capitalist country needs to find new markets for its products if it is to avoid recession and depression. Although Britain and its colonialism were Hobson's primary focus, his arguments also were applicable to the United States and its more indirect neocolonialism in Latin America and parts of Asia (see Chapter 4).

While still in exile in Switzerland in 1916, the year before he would return to Russia to lead the communist revolution, Vladimir Ilyich Lenin wrote his most famous book, *Imperialism: The Highest Stage of Capitalism*. Lenin's version of imperialist theory differed from Hobson's in rejecting the possibility that capitalism could reform itself.* One reason was that, in addition to the underconsumption-overproduction problem, Lenin emphasized the pursuit of inexpensive and abundant supplies of raw materials as another key motive for capitalist expansionism. Giving the working class more purchasing power would not do anything about the lust for the iron ore, foodstuffs, and, later, oil that were so much more plentiful and so much cheaper in the colonial world (later called the Third World). Moreover, the essence of Lenin's theory was the belief that the capitalist class so dominated the political process and defined the limits of democracy that it would never

---

*Hobson believed that liberal domestic reforms were possible and would help capitalism break out of the underconsumption and overproduction cycle. Such reforms would create a more equitable distribution of wealth, bringing an increase in consumption, in the process both making the home society more equitable and alleviating the need for colonies, thus making foreign policy less imperialistic.

allow the kinds of reforms Hobson advocated. Lenin's theories and their spin-offs became the basis for many highly critical views of U.S. foreign policy during the Cold War, particularly in the Third World, such as that of Gabriel Kolko, as excerpted in the Readings. Another version of this debate has been developing within the context of globalization (Chapter 8).

In sum, their differences notwithstanding, these two schools share an emphasis on economic goals as driving forces behind U.S. foreign policy. They differ over whose prosperity is being served, but they agree on the centrality of prosperity among the "4 Ps".

Principles

The fourth core goal, *Principles*, involves the values, ideals, and beliefs that the United States has claimed to stand for in the world. As a more general theory, this emphasis on principles is rooted in **Democratic Idealism** (Reading 1.4).

Democratic Idealists hold to two central tenets about foreign policy. One is that when trade-offs have to be made, "right" is to be chosen over "might." This is said to be particularly true for the United States because of the ostensibly special role it claims as the world's greatest democracy—to stand up for the principles on which it was founded and to be more than just another player in global power politics. We find assertions of this notion of "American exceptionalism" throughout U.S. history. Thomas Jefferson, the country's first secretary of state and its third president, characterized the new United States of America as such: "the solitary republic of the world, the only monument of human rights . . . the sole depository of the sacred fire of freedom and self-government, from hence it is to be lighted up in other regions of the earth, if other regions shall ever become susceptible to its benign influence."[36] And then there was President Woodrow Wilson's famous declaration that U.S. entry into World War I was intended "to make the world safe for democracy": "We shall fight for the things which we have always carried nearest our hearts—for democracy, for the right of those who submit to authority to have a voice in their own government, for the rights and liberties of small nations, for a universal dominion of right by such a concert of free peoples as shall bring peace and safety to all nations and make the world in itself at last free." Democratic idealism was also claimed by Cold War presidents, from Democrats such as John Kennedy with his call in his inaugural address to "bear any burden, pay any price" to defend democracy and fight communism, to Republicans such as Ronald Reagan and his crusade against the "evil empire." It also was part of President George W. Bush's launching of the war on terrorism as not only a matter of security but also a war against "evil . . . the fight of all who believe in progress and pluralism, tolerance and freedom." So, too, did President Obama declare in his first inaugural address that "America is a friend of each nation and every man, woman, and child who seeks a future of peace and dignity."

The other key tenet of Democratic Idealism is that in the long run "right" makes for "might," and that in the end interests such as peace and power are well served by principles. One of the strongest statements of this view is the ***democratic peace*** theory, which asserts that promoting democracy promotes peace because democracies do not go to war against each other. To put it another way, the world could be made safe *by* democracy. For all the attention the democratic peace theory has received in the post–Cold War era, its central argument and philosophical basis trace back to the eighteenth-century political philosopher Immanuel Kant and his book *Perpetual Peace*. "If . . . the consent of the citizenry is required in order to decide that war should be declared," Kant wrote, "nothing is more natural than that they would be very cautious in commencing such a poor game. . . . But, on the other hand, in a constitution which is not republican, and under which the subjects are not citizens, a declaration of war is the easiest thing to decide upon, because war does not require of the ruler . . . the least sacrifice of the pleasure of his table, the chase, his country houses, his court functions and the like."[37] In Chapter 8, we take a closer look at democratic peace theory as well as major critiques of it.

As for serving the goal of power, Joseph Nye of Harvard University coined the term ***soft power*** to refer to the ways in which the values for which a nation stands, its cultural attractiveness, and other aspects of its reputation can have quite practical value as sources of influence.[38] This is not just a matter of what American leaders claim in their rhetoric, but of whether other governments and peoples perceive for themselves a consistency between the principles espoused and the actual policies pursued by the United States. It also depends on how well America is deemed to be living up to its ideals within its own society on issues such as race relations, protection of the environment, and crime and violence.

Given its strong and exceptionalist claims to principles, American foreign policy has often been severely criticized at home and abroad for not living up to its espoused ideals. Such critiques have been raised at various times throughout American history going back to the nineteenth and early twentieth centuries, during the Cold War, in the Middle East, and in the post–Cold War/post-9/11 era. Precisely because of the arguments that right should be chosen over might and that in the long run right makes for might, debates over how true American foreign policy is to its principles matter as more than just idealistic questions.

Table 1.1 summarizes the "4 Ps" of foreign policy strategy, highlighting differences among core national-interest goals, schools of international relations theory, principal conceptions of the international system, and principal types of policies pursued. It is important to emphasize again that these are distinctions of degree and not inflexible

TABLE 1.1 A Foreign Policy Strategy Typology

Core national interest goal	International relations theory	Conception of the international system	Main types of policies
Power	Realism	Competition for power	Coercive
Peace	International Institutionalism	World order	Diplomatic
Prosperity	Economism, Imperialism	Global capitalism	Economic
Principles	Democratic Idealism	Global spread of democracy	Political

one-or-the-other categorizations. They provide a framework for analyzing foreign policy strategy in ways that push deeper into general conceptions of the national interest and get at the "essence of choice" over what American foreign policy is and should be.

Dilemmas of Foreign Policy Choice: "4 Ps" Complementarity, Trade-offs, and Dissensus

"4 Ps" Complementarity: Optimal, but Infrequent

To the extent that all "4 Ps" can be satisfied through the same strategy—that is, they are complementary—the dilemmas of foreign policy choice are relatively easy. No major trade-offs have to be made, no strict priorities set. This does happen sometimes, as the following two cases illustrate.

THE 1990–91 PERSIAN GULF WAR The Persian Gulf War was a great victory for American foreign policy in many respects. The invasion of Kuwait by Iraq, led by Saddam Hussein, was a blatant act of aggression—one of the most naked acts of aggression since World War II. Furthermore, the Iraqis were poised to keep going, straight into Saudi Arabia, an even more strategic country given its oil production and a close U.S. ally.

But through U.S. leadership, *peace* was restored. "This will not stand," President George H. W. Bush declared. Resolutions were sponsored in the United Nations (UN) Security Council, demanding an Iraqi withdrawal and then authorizing the use of military force to liberate Kuwait. A twenty-seven-nation diplomatic coalition was built, including most of Western Europe, Japan, and much of the Arab world. A multinational military force went to war under the command of General Norman Schwarzkopf of the U.S. Army.

Operation Desert Storm, as it was named, was also a formidable demonstration of American *power*. It is important to recall how worried many military analysts were at the outset of Desert Storm about incurring high casualties, and even about the possibility that Saddam would resort to chemical or biological weapons. That the military victory came so quickly and with so few U.S. and allied casualties was testimony to the military superiority the United States had achieved. Striding tall from its Gulf War victory, American power was shown to be second to none.

Of course, this was not just about helping Kuwait. *Prosperity* also was at risk, in the form of oil. Twice before in recent decades, war and instability in the Middle East had disrupted oil supplies and sent oil prices skyrocketing. Many Americans remembered waiting in gasoline lines and watching prices escalate on a daily basis during the 1973 Arab-Israeli War and the 1979 Iranian Revolution. This time, though, because the Gulf War victory came so swiftly, disruptions to the American and global economies were minimized.

Although Kuwait couldn't claim to be a democracy, other important *principles* were at issue. One was the right of all states to be free from aggression. Another was the moral value of standing up to a dictator as brutal as Saddam Hussein. Comparisons to Adolf Hitler went too far, but Saddam was a leader who left a trail of torture, repression, and mass killings.

THE MARSHALL PLAN, 1947   The Marshall Plan was the first major U.S. foreign aid program; it provided about $17 billion to Western Europe for economic reconstruction following World War II.* This was an enormous amount of money, equivalent in today's dollars to over $175 billion, which would be *more than ten times greater* than the entire U.S. foreign aid budget. Yet the Marshall Plan passed Congress by overwhelming majorities, 69–17 in the Senate and 329–74 in the House. Compare these votes with today's politics, when much lower levels of foreign aid barely get a congressional majority.

The key reason for such strong support was that the Marshall Plan was seen as serving the full range of U.S. foreign policy goals. The communist parties in France, Italy, and elsewhere in Western Europe were feeding off the continuing economic suffering and dislocation, making worrisome political gains. The Marshall Plan thus was a component of the broader strategy of containment of communism to keep the *peace* in Western Europe.

---

*The Marshall Plan is named for Secretary of State George Marshall, who made the initial public proposal in a commencement speech at Harvard University.

It also asserted American *power*, for with the foreign aid came certain conditions, some explicit and some implicit. And in a more general sense, the United States was establishing its global predominance and leadership. The glorious nations of the Old World were now dependent on the New World former colony.

American *prosperity* was also well served. The rebuilding of European markets generated demand for American exports and created opportunities for American investments. Thus, although its motives were not strictly altruistic, the Marshall Plan was quite consistent with American *principles:* the stability of fellow Western democracies was at stake.

"4 Ps" Trade-offs: More Frequent, More Problematic

Not only are cases with "4 Ps" tensions more common, but they require much tougher choices. Trade-offs have to be made; priorities have to be set. The following two examples illustrate such choices.

CHINA, 1989: POWER AND PROSPERITY VS. PRINCIPLES   In 1989, hundreds of Chinese students staged a massive pro-democracy sit-in at Tiananmen Square in Beijing, China's capital city. As one expression of their protest, they constructed a statue resembling the American Statue of Liberty. The Communist government ordered the students to leave. They refused. The Chinese army then moved in with tanks and troops. An estimated one thousand students were killed, and tens of thousands of students and other dissidents were arrested.

In reaction to the Chinese crackdown, many in the United States called for the imposition of economic sanctions. The focus of these efforts was on revoking China's most-favored-nation (MFN) status. Essentially MFN status limits tariffs on a country's exports to the United States to a standard, low level; without MFN status, a country's exports to the United States are much less competitive, and that country's international trade will be adversely affected.* The pro-sanctions argument, which came from a bipartisan coalition in Congress and from human-rights groups, was based on *principles:* How could the United States conduct business as usual with a government that massacred its own people? These pro-democracy Chinese protesters had turned to America for inspiration. How could the United States not stand up for what it said were values and beliefs it held dear?

The George H. W. Bush administration, which was in office at the time, was willing to impose only limited economic sanctions; it would not revoke China's MFN status. Its main argument was based on *power*. The administration still considered the U.S.-Soviet

---

*It is not that the country receiving MFN is favored over others, but rather that all countries receiving MFN get the same "most favored" tariff treatment. In 2000 this terminology was changed from MFN to PNTR, or permanent normal trade relations.

rivalry to be the central issue in its foreign relations and thus gave priority to its geopolitical interests—namely, continued good relations with China. Among President Bush's critics was the Democratic presidential candidate, Bill Clinton, who castigated his opponent for coddling "the butchers of Beijing." Yet as president, Clinton also refused to revoke China's MFN status. His reasons were based more on economic considerations—*prosperity*—and the calculation of billions of dollars in potential trade and investment losses for the American economy.

Both Bush and Clinton claimed that they were not abandoning principles, that other steps were being taken to try to protect human rights and promote democracy in China. But although this justification was partly true, debate still raged over what trade-offs should be made in the name of the national interest. The requisites of Power and Prosperity pointed to one set of policies, Principles to another. Trade-offs were inevitable; choices had to be made.

GUATEMALA, 1954: PROSPERITY AND POWER VS. PRINCIPLES In 1945, Guatemala, the Central American country just south of Mexico, ended a long string of military dictatorships by holding free elections. A progressive new constitution was written, freedoms of the press and of speech were guaranteed, and workers and peasants were encouraged to organize. A number of military coups were attempted, but they were put down. In 1951, Colonel Jacobo Arbenz Guzman, a pro-reform military officer, was elected president.

One of Arbenz's highest priorities was land reform. Two percent of the population owned 70 percent of the land in Guatemala. The largest of all landholders was the United Fruit Company (UFCO), a U.S.-owned banana exporter. In March 1953, Arbenz's government included about 230,000 acres of UFCO holdings in the land being expropriated for redistribution to the peasantry. Most of this land was uncultivated, but that didn't matter to the UFCO. The compensation offered to the company by the Guatemalan government was deemed inadequate, even though it was the same valuation rate (a low one) that the UFCO had been using to limit the taxes it paid.

This wasn't just a UFCO problem, its corporate president declared: "From here on out it's not a matter of the people of Guatemala against the United Fruit Company. The question is going to be communism against the right of property, the life and security of the Western Hemisphere."[39] It was true that Arbenz had members of the Guatemalan Communist Party in his government. He also was buying weapons from Czechoslovakia, which was a Soviet satellite. Might this be the beginning of the feared Soviet "beachhead" in the Western Hemisphere?* In defending the anti-Arbenz coup d'état that it engineered in 1954 through covert CIA action, the Eisenhower administration stressed the *power*

---

*Fidel Castro had not yet come to power in Cuba. That would happen in 1959.

concerns raised by this perceived threat to containment. The evidence of links to Soviet communism was not that strong, but the standard that needed to be met was only what an earlier U.S. ambassador to Guatemala had called the "duck test": "Many times it is impossible to prove legally that a certain individual is a communist; but for cases of this sort I recommend a practical method of detection—the 'duck test.' The duck test works this way: suppose you see a bird walking around in a farmyard. The bird wears no label that says 'duck.' But the bird certainly looks like a duck. Also, he goes to the pond and you notice that he swims like a duck. Well, by this time you have probably reached the conclusion that the bird is a duck, whether he's wearing a label or not."[40]

An argument can be made that, given the Cold War, the duck test was sufficient from a power perspective. Even so, the anti-Arbenz coup was something of a "joint venture," strikingly consistent with Imperialist critiques of U.S. foreign policy (*prosperity*). The UFCO had close ties to the Eisenhower administration; the historical record shows evidence of collaboration between the company and the government; and one of the first acts of the new regime of General Carlos Castillo Armas, who was a graduate of the military-intelligence training school at Fort Leavenworth, Kansas, and whom the CIA installed in power after the coup, was to give land back to the UFCO.

The critical tension here was with *principles*. The Arbenz government had come to power through elections that, though not perfectly free and fair, were much fairer than those in most of Latin America. The military governments that ruled Guatemala for the thirty-five years following the U.S.-engineered coup were extremely brutal and showed wanton disregard for human rights, killing and persecuting tens of thousands of their own people. The U.S. role was hidden for decades but was pointedly revealed in 1999 in a shocking report by a Guatemalan historical commission, which estimated that two hundred thousand people had been killed by the U.S.-supported military regimes and provided strong evidence of U.S. complicity.[41]

"4 Ps" Dissensus: Bitter Conflicts

In other situations, the debates are less about this "P" having priority over that one than about deep dissensus over the nature of the national interest. The Iraq war that began in 2003 exemplifies this type of situation.[42]

IRAQ WAR, 2003   Going to war in Iraq, the Bush administration contended, was very much in the American national interest. American *power* was more than sufficient to win the war and to eliminate the threat posed by Saddam Hussein and his regional aggression, alleged WMD arsenal, and links to Al Qaeda and global terrorism. Moreover, the "shock and awe" that the U.S. military would bring to bear would enhance the credibility of American power within the Middle East as well as globally. *Peace* would be strengthened in a region that had known too little of it. Saddam, who had started wars against his own neighbors as well as threatened Israel, would be gone. The Arab-Israeli peace process could get back on track. Despite the immediate conflict with the United Nations, the U.S. willingness to do what needed to be done would be good for the world body in the long run.

Prosperity would not be hurt: budgetary estimates for the war purportedly showed that the United States would have to bear minimal costs. Indeed, U.S. and global prosperity would be helped by a post-Saddam regime's stabilizing effect on OPEC and global oil markets. Consistency with *principles* was claimed in that the war would dispense with a dictator who had used chemical weapons against his own people, tortured and murdered thousands of political prisoners, and committed countless other atrocities. The democracy that was to be created in Iraq would set a shining example for the rest of the Arab world.

Opponents asserted an equal claim to the U.S. national interest, as well as to the international interests at stake. The Bush administration, they said, was overestimating American *power*. American military superiority was a given, but converting this possession of power into actual influence over other countries was much more difficult than assumed. Within Iraq, winning the war would be one thing, but winning the peace quite another. The line between being a liberating force and an occupying one was going to be a lot harder to walk than the Bush administration was claiming. Terrorism would be strengthened, not weakened, both within Iraq and globally. The fallout would exacerbate, not ameliorate, the Israeli-Palestinian conflict. U.S. defiance of the UN undermined rather than buttressed the UN. *Peace* was being hurt not helped.

In addition, the opponents maintained, the budget numbers were being manipulated; the White House's leading economic advisor was fired for saying so. American *prosperity* would be damaged by the hundreds of billions of dollars that would inevitably be added to the federal budget deficit (trillions, by some later estimates). The further instability in Iraq would strengthen the forces pushing global oil prices, and the price at the pump for the average American, higher and higher. And one didn't have to defend Saddam to see how an extended military occupation could lead to the kinds of atrocities that were committed by American forces at Abu Ghraib. The Iraqi people's thirst for democracy, as shown in their first free elections, deserved praise and admiration. But all in all American *principles* were being undermined more than reinforced by the occupation.

We take up these issues and debates in more detail in Chapter 11.

Summary

Whatever the issue at hand, and whether past, present, or future, American foreign policy has been, is, and will continue to be about the *dynamics of choice*.

One set of choices is about *foreign policy strategy*. It is easy to preach about the national interest, but much harder to assess what that interest is in a particular situation.

One or more of the four core goals—*power, peace, prosperity,* and *principles*—may be involved. Not only may basic analyses differ but more often than not trade-offs have to be made and priorities set among these four Ps. In some cases the debates are over fundamentally conflicting positions. Views reflect different schools of international relations theory, carry with them alternative policy approaches, and can result in fundamentally different foreign policy strategies. This is the *essence of choice* that is inherent to every major foreign policy issue.

   We will use this framework for analyzing U.S. foreign policy strategy historically (Chapter 4), during the Cold War (Chapters 5 and 6), and in our current post–Cold War era (Part II, Chapters 7–14). First, though, we turn in Chapter 2 to foreign policy politics and lay out an analytic framework for another key dimension of American foreign policy, the *process of choice.*

Notes

[1]George H. W. Bush, "Remarks at the United States Military Academy in West Point, New York," January 5, 1993, *Public Papers of the Presidents: George Bush* (Washington, D.C.: Office of the Federal Register, National Archives and Records Administration, 1993), 2:2228–32.

[2]Bill Clinton, "Speech at the University of Nebraska," December 8, 2000, *Public Papers of the Presidents: William J. Clinton 2000–2001* (Washington, D.C.: U.S. Government Printing Office, 2002), 3:2653–61.

[3]Serge Schmemann, "U.S. Attacked: President Vows to Exact Punishment for 'Evil,'" *New York Times,* September 12, 2001, A1.

[4]George W. Bush, Address to a Joint Session of Congress and the American People, September 20, 2001, www.americanrhetoric.com/speeches/gwbush911jointsessionspeech.htm; and Bush, 2002 State of the Union Address, www.c-span.org/executive/transcript.asp?cat=current_event&code=bush_admin&year=2002 (accessed 5/8/09).

[5]Barack Obama, "Renewing American Leadership," *Foreign Affairs* 86 (July/August 2007): 2–4.

[6]Francis Fukuyama, "The End of History?" *National Interest* 16 (Summer 1989): 4.

[7]Samuel P. Huntington, "The Clash of Civilizations?" *Foreign Affairs* 72.3 (Summer 1993): 22, 28.

[8]Thomas L. Friedman, *The Lexus and the Olive Tree: Understanding Globalization* (New York: Farrar, Straus and Giroux, 1999), xviii.

[9]Charles Krauthammer, "The Unipolar Moment," *Foreign Affairs* 70 (Winter 1990–91).

[10]Laurie Ann Mazur and Susan E. Sechler, *Global Interdependence and the Need for Social Stewardship* (New York: Rockefeller Brothers Fund, 1997), 9–10.

[11]Fareed Zakaria, *The Post-American World* (New York: Norton, 2008), 1, 3.

[12]Charles A. Kupchan, *No One's World: The West, the Rising Rest and the Coming Global Turn* (New York: Oxford University Press, 2012).

[13]Bruce W. Jentleson, "The John W. Holmes Memorial Lecture: Global Governance in a Copernican World," *Global Governance* 18 (Summer 2012), and Steven Weber and Bruce W. Jentleson, *The End of Arrogance: America in the Global Competition of Ideas* (Cambridge: Harvard University Press, 2010).

[14]Robert J. Lieber, *No Common Power: Understanding International Relations* (Boston: Scott, Foresman, 1988), 5.

[15]Kenneth N. Waltz, *Theory of International Politics* (Reading, Mass.: Addison-Wesley, 1979), 72.

[16]Alexander L. George and Robert O. Keohane, "The Concepts of National Interests: Uses and Limitations," in *Presidential Decisionmaking in Foreign Policy: The Effective Use of Information and Advice*, Alexander L. George, ed. (Boulder, Colo.: Westview, 1980), 217–18.

[17]Condoleezza Rice, "Promoting the National Interest," *Foreign Affairs* 79.1 (January/February 2000): 47.

[18]Samuel Huntington, "Why International Primacy Matters," *International Security* 17.4 (Spring 1993): 69–70.

[19]Thucydides, *History of the Peloponnesian War,* R. Warner, trans. (New York: Penguin, 1972), 402.

[20]Hans J. Morgenthau, *Politics among Nations: The Struggle for Power and Peace* (New York: Knopf, 1948), 5.

[21]John J. Mearsheimer, "The False Promise of International Institutions," *International Security* 19.3 (Winter 1994/95): 9.

[22]Cited in Caleb Carr, *The Lessons of Terror* (New York: Random House, 2002), 81.

[23]Bruce W. Jentleson, "Coercive Diplomacy: Scope and Limits, Theory and Policy," in Victor Mauer and Myriam Dunn Cavelty (eds.), *The Routledge Handbook of Security Studies* (London, 2009).

[24]Cited in Loch K. Johnson, *America as a World Power: Foreign Policy in a Constitutional Framework* (New York: McGraw-Hill, 1991), 239.

[25]Alan K. Henrikson, "Diplomatic Method," in *Encyclopedia of U.S. Foreign Relations,* Bruce W. Jentleson and Thomas G. Paterson, eds. (New York: Oxford University Press, 1997), Volume II, 23.

[26]Michael W. Doyle, *Ways of War and Peace* (New York: Norton, 1997), 19.

[27]Claude, cited in Mearsheimer, "False Promise of International Institutions," 26–27.

[28]Bruce Russett and Harvey Starr, *World Politics: The Menu for Choice* (New York: Freeman, 1996), 117; K. J. Holsti, *International Politics: A Framework for Analysis* (Englewood Cliffs, N.J.: Prentice-Hall, 1988), 141.

[29]Robert O. Keohane and Lisa L. Martin, "The Promise of Institutionalist Theory," *International Security* 20.1 (Summer 1995): 50.

[30]Keohane and Martin, "The Promise of Institutionalist Theory," 42.

[31]Robert O. Keohane, "International Institutions: Can Interdependence Work?" *Foreign Policy* 110 (Spring 1998): 82.

[32]See, for example, Joan E. Spero and Jeffrey A. Hart, *The Politics of International Economic Relations* (New York: St. Martin's, 1997); and Richard N. Gardner, *Sterling-Dollar Diplomacy: The Origins and Prospects of Our International Economic Order* (New York: Columbia University Press, 1980).

[33]James M. McCormick, *American Foreign Policy and Process* (Itasca, Ill.: Peacock, 1992), 15–16.

[34]Michael Hirsh and Karen Breslau, "Closing the Deal Diplomacy: In Clinton's Foreign Policy, the Business of America Is Business," *Newsweek,* March 6, 1995, 34.

[35]See, for example, V. I. Lenin, *Imperialism: The Highest Form of Capitalism* (New York: International Publishers, 1939); John A. Hobson, *Imperialism* (London: George Allen and Unwin, 1954); and Richard J. Barnet and Ronald E. Muller, *Global Reach: The Power of the Multinational Corporations* (New York: Simon and Schuster, 1974).

[36]Cited in Robert W. Tucker and David C. Hendrickson, "Thomas Jefferson and Foreign Policy," *Foreign Affairs* 69.2 (Spring 1990): 136.

[37]Immanuel Kant, *Perpetual Peace,* cited in Michael W. Doyle, "Kant, Liberal Legacies and Foreign Affairs," in *Debating the Democratic Peace,* Michael E. Brown et al., eds. (Cambridge: MIT Press, 1997), 24–25.

[38]Joseph S. Nye, Jr., *Bound to Lead: The Changing Nature of American Power* (New York: Basic Books, 1990).

[39]Cited in James A. Nathan and James K. Oliver, *United States Foreign Policy and World Order* (Boston: Little, Brown, 1985), 176. See also Stephen Schlesinger and Stephen Kinzer, *Bitter Fruit: The Untold Story of the American Coup in Guatemala* (Garden City, N.Y.: Doubleday, 1982), and Stephen Kinzer, *Overthrow: America's Century of Regime Change, from Hawaii to Iraq* (New York: Times Books, 2006).

[40]Cited in Walter LaFeber, *Inevitable Revolutions: The United States in Central America*, 2d ed. (New York: Norton, 1993), 115–16.

[41]Mireya Navarro, "Guatemalan Army Waged 'Genocide', New Report Finds," *New York Times*, February 26, 1999, A1, A8. See also Documents on U.S. Policy in Guatemala, 1966–1996, National Security Archive Electronic Briefing Book No. 11, www.gwu.edu/~nsarchiv/NSAEBB/NSAEBB11/docs/ (accessed 5/18/09).

[42]On earlier U.S. policy toward Iraq and Saddam Hussein, including inaction when he waged chemical warfare against Iraqi Kurds in 1988, see Bruce W. Jentleson, *With Friends Like These: Reagan, Bush and Saddam, 1982–1990* (New York: Norton, 1994).

2

The Domestic Context: The Three Branches and the Process of Choice

Introduction: Dispelling the "Water's Edge" Myth

When it comes to foreign policy, according to an old saying, "politics stops at the water's edge." In other words, partisan and other political differences that characterize domestic policy are to be left behind—"at the water's edge"—when entering the realm of foreign policy, so that the country can be united in confronting foreign threats.

The example most often cited by proponents of this ideal is the consensus of the early Cold War era, that "golden age of bipartisanship." Here is "a story of democracy at its finest," as a top aide to President Harry Truman portrayed it, "with the executive branch of the government operating far beyond the normal boundaries of timidity and politics, the Congress beyond usual partisanship, and the American people as a whole beyond selfishness and complacency. All three . . . worked together to accomplish a national acceptance of world responsibility."[1] That's how foreign policy politics is supposed to be, the "water's edge" thinking goes.

In three key respects, though, this notion of politics stopping at the water's edge is a myth that needs to be dispelled. First, *historically, the domestic consensus that characterized the Cold War era was more the exception than the rule.* The common view is that divisive foreign policy politics started with the Vietnam War. But while Vietnam did shatter the Cold War consensus, it was hardly the first time that foreign policy politics hadn't stopped at the water's edge. Leading up to World War II, President Franklin Roosevelt had his own intense political battles with an isolationist Congress. In the years following World War I, President Woodrow Wilson suffered one of the worst foreign policy politics defeats ever when the Senate refused to ratify the Treaty of Versailles. We can even go back to 1794 when President George Washington, the revered "father" of the country, battled with

Congress over a treaty with Great Britain called the Jay Treaty. The bitter and vociferous attacks on the Jay Treaty for "tilting" toward Britain in its war with France were a rhetorical match for any of today's political battles. "Ruinous . . . detestable . . . contemptible," editorialized one major newspaper of the day, excoriating a treaty "signed with our inveterate enemy and the foe of human happiness." The Senate did ratify the treaty, but by a margin of only one vote. Indeed the Jay Treaty controversy was a key factor in President Washington's decision to retire to Mount Vernon instead of seeking a third term as president.

Second, *consensus has not always been a good thing.* It surely can be, in manifesting national solidarity behind the nation's foreign policy. But national solidarity is one thing, the delegitimization of dissent quite another. The most virulent example was the anticommunist witch hunt spurred by McCarthyism in the 1950s, during which accusations of disloyalty were hurled at government officials, playwrights, professors, scientists, and average citizens, often on the flimsiest of evidence. Dissent was also criminalized during both world wars, when domestic consensus was often crucial to meeting wartime challenges; nevertheless, many Americans paid a severe price in civil liberties and individual rights during these wars. The Espionage and Sedition Acts passed during World War I permitted such repressive measures as banning postal delivery of any magazine that included views critical of the war effort—restrictions "as extreme as any legislation of the kind anywhere in the world."[2] During World War II the national security rationale was invoked to uproot 120,000 Japanese Americans and put them in internment camps on the basis of their ethnicity. During the Vietnam War, shouts of "America, love it or leave it!" were aimed at antiwar critics and protesters. Consensus is not a particularly good thing when it equates dissent with disloyalty. These issues have arisen again in the context of the war on terrorism.

Third, *domestic political conflict is not necessarily bad for foreign policy.* When motivations are highly partisan, such conflict is not beneficial. But serious debate and honest disagreement can facilitate more thorough consideration of the issues. They can subject questionable assumptions to serious scrutiny and can bring about constructive compromises around a policy that serves the national interest better than anything either side originally proposed. As the former House Foreign Affairs Committee chair Lee Hamilton wrote, "Debate, creative tension and review of policy can bring about decisions and actions that stand a better chance of serving the interests and values of the American people."[3] A good example of this was the outcome of the debate about the U.S. role in helping restore democracy in the Philippines in the mid-1980s. The policy preferred by President Ronald Reagan was to continue supporting the dictator Ferdinand Marcos, even after his forces had assassinated the democratic opposition leader, Benigno Aquino, and amid mounting evidence of rampant corruption in the Marcos regime. But the U.S. Congress, led by a bipartisan coalition of Democrats and Republicans, refused to go along with a continued unconditional embrace of Marcos. It pushed for support of the pro-democracy forces led by Corazon Aquino, the widow of the slain opposition leader.

The change in American policy helped restore democracy and an important U.S. ally was made more stable. This result might not have been achieved, however, had it not been for the good that can sometimes come out of conflictual foreign policy politics.

Thus, the realities of *foreign policy politics,* the process by which foreign policy choices are made, are more complex than conventional wisdom holds. Our purpose in this chapter and the next is to provide a framework for understanding the dynamics of foreign policy politics. We do so by focusing on five sets of domestic actors: in this chapter on the *president and Congress*—and the "Pennsylvania Avenue diplomacy" that marks (and often mars) their interbranch relationship—and the policy- and decision-making processes within the *executive branch*; in Chapter 3 we focus on the pressures brought to bear by major *interest groups,* the impact of the *news media,* and the nature and influence of *public opinion generally and elections in particular.*

We provide examples and case studies to illustrate and flesh out this framework historically (Chapter 4) and in the Cold War (Chapters 5 and 6). In Chapter 9 we apply the overall framework to post–Cold War foreign policy politics. Chapters 10 through 14 include foreign policy politics case studies on such issues as China policy, counter-terrorism and civil liberties, nuclear arms control, immigration, and South Africa anti-apartheid economic sanctions.

The President, Congress, and "Pennsylvania Avenue Diplomacy"

They face each other down the length of Pennsylvania Avenue—the White House and the Capitol: connected by the avenue, but also divided by it. The avenue: a path for cooperation, but also a line of conflict. The president and Congress: a relationship very much in need of its own "diplomacy."

Theories of Presidential-Congressional Relations

Historically, and across various issue areas, presidential-congressional relations in the making of foreign policy have been characterized by four patterns:

- ■ *cooperation,* when Congress has either concurred with or deferred to the president and a largely common, coordinated policy has been pursued;
- ■ *constructive compromise,* when the two branches have bridged conflicts and come to a policy that proved better than either's original position (as in the 1980s Philippines case cited above);

■ *institutional competition,* in which the conflicts focused less on the substance of policy than on institutional prerogatives and the balance between executive discretion and congressional oversight; and

■ *confrontation,* in which the policy positions have been in substantial conflict and Pennsylvania Avenue diplomacy has shown its greatest tensions.

Two major groups of theories have been advanced to explain which patterns best fit different historical periods and specific issue areas within those periods.

One group focuses on *partisanship.* When the same political party controls both the White House and Congress, theories stressing partisan identity as the key factor contend that cooperation is the dominant pattern. When there is "divided government" with one party represented by the president and the other party controlling Congress (or at least one of the two chambers), there is more confrontation. As Table 2.1 shows, divided government was much less prevalent in the 1945–80 period (16 of 36 years, 44% of the time) than it has become in more recent years (26 of 34 years, 76%). Yet while politics has a role in the cooperation-confrontation dynamic, that dynamic does not always neatly follow the partisanship pattern. There has been cooperation across party lines, as in the "golden age of bipartisanship" when Democratic President Harry Truman and the Republican Chairman of the Senate Foreign Relations Committee, Arthur Vandenberg, worked closely together in 1947–48. Congressional Democrats largely supported President George H.W. Bush's handling of the Persian Gulf War and the end of the Cold War. And there have been plenty of instances of same-party opposition. President Eisenhower was challenged by Republican Senator Joseph McCarthy (1953–54). The isolationist Congress that FDR faced in the 1930s was a Democratic one. The Vietnam War opposition President Lyndon B. Johnson faced was also mostly from Democrats. In the early 1970s, conservative Republican senators opposed President Richard M. Nixon over détente with the Soviet Union. The first two years of Bill Clinton's presidency (1993–94), when Democrats controlled Congress, were marked by extensive criticism of his policies in Somalia, Bosnia, and Haiti. And as the Iraq War dragged on, some Republicans in Congress came to oppose President George W. Bush's policies.

Thus, while politics are very often in play, theories that emphasize *constitutional-structural* factors have more explanatory power. No one has come up with a definitive answer to the question of constitutional intent and design for presidential-congressional relations in the making of foreign policy. The Constitution left it, in one classic statement, as "an invitation to struggle for the privilege of directing American foreign policy."[4] Indeed, although we are usually taught to think of the relationship between the president and Congress as a "separation of powers," it really is much more "separate institutions sharing powers."[5] A separation of powers would mean that the president has power *a,* Congress power *b,* the president power *c,* Congress power *d,* and so on. But the actual relationship is more one in which both the president and Congress have a share of power *a,*

TABLE 2.1 Party Control of the Presidency and Congress, 1945–2014

	Presidency	Congress
1945–80		
Same Party Control (20 years)		
1945–46	Truman (D)	Democrats
1949–52	Truman (D)	Democrats
1953–54	Eisenhower (R)	Republicans
1961–63	Kennedy (D)	Democrats
1963–68	Johnson (D)	Democrats
1977–80	Carter (D)	Democrats
Divided Government (16 years)		
1947–48	Truman (D)	Republicans
1955–60	Eisenhower (R)	Democrats
1969–74	Nixon (R)	Democrats
1974–76	Ford (R)	Democrats
1981–2014		
Same Party Control (8 years)		
1993–94	Clinton (D)	Democrats
2003–06	George W. Bush (R)	Republicans
2009–10	Obama (D)	Democrats
Divided Government (26 years)		
House and Senate both with majorities of the other party:		
1987–88	Reagan (R)	Democrats
1989–92	George H.W. Bush (R)	Democrats
1995–2000	Clinton (D)	Republicans
2007–08	George W. Bush (R)	Democrats
Congress split between the two parties:		
1981–86	Reagan (R)	House: Democrats Senate: Republicans
2001–02	George W. Bush (R)	House: Republicans Senate: Democrats
2011–14	Obama (D)	House: Republicans Senate: Democrats

TABLE 2.2   Principal Foreign Policy Provisions of the Constitution

	Power granted to	
	President	**Congress**
War power	Commander in chief of armed forces	Provide for the common defense; declare war
Treaties	Negotiate treaties	Ratification of treaties, by two-thirds majority (Senate)
Appointments	Nominate high-level government officials	Confirm president's appointments (Senate)
Foreign commerce	No explicit powers, but treaty negotiation and appointment powers pertain	Explicit power "to regulate foreign commerce"
General powers	Executive power; veto	Legislative power; power of the purse; oversight and investigation

a share of power *b*, a share of power *c*, and so on—that is, the separate institutions *share powers*. This basic structural relationship is evident in five key areas of foreign policy politics (see Table 2.2)

War Powers

No domain of foreign policy politics has been debated more hotly or more recurringly than **war powers**. The distinguished historian Arthur M. Schlesinger, Jr., provides his view of what the founders intended in Reading 2.1. The Constitution designates the president as "commander in chief" but gives Congress the power to "declare war" and "provide for the common defense"—not separate powers, but each a share of the same power.

2.1

Both sides support their claims for the precedence of their share of the war power with citations from the country's founders. Presidentialists invoke the logic, developed by Alexander Hamilton in the *Federalist Papers,* that the need for an effective foreign policy was one of the main reasons the young nation needed an "energetic government" (*Federalist* 23); that "energy in the executive" was "a leading character in the definition of good government" (no. 70); and that "in the conduct of war . . . the energy of the executive is the bulwark of national security" (no. 75). Congressionalists, on the other hand, cite the proceedings of the Constitutional Convention. At James Madison's initiative, the original wording of the proposed constitution, which would have given Congress the power to "make war," was changed to "declare war." Congressionalists explain this as being intended to recognize that *how* to use military force ("make war") was appropriately a power for the commander in chief, whereas *whether* to use military force ("declare war") was for Congress to decide. Furthermore, as Madison stated in a letter to Thomas Jefferson, "the Constitution supposes what the history of all governments demonstrates, that the executive is the branch of power most interested in war, and most prone to it. It has accordingly with studied care vested the question of war in the legislature."[6]

Nor is the weight of historical precedent strictly on one side or the other. A favorite statistic cited by proponents of the presidency's war powers is that the United States has used military force more than two hundred times, yet Congress has declared war only five times—the War of 1812, the Mexican War (1846–48), the Spanish-American War (1898), World War I (1917–19), and World War II (1941–45). Perhaps another eighty-five or ninety uses of force (e.g., the 1991 Persian Gulf War, the 2001 Afghanistan War, and the 2003 Iraq War) have been through other action short of a declaration of war. All the others have been by presidents acting on their own, which presidentialists view as evidence of both the need for and the legitimacy of presidents' having such freedom of action.

This statistic, though, is somewhat deceptive. While some cases of presidents acting on their own involved extensive uses of force, many were minor military incidents generally regarded as the business of a commander in chief. Defenders of Congress's share of the war powers interpret this gross disproportion—many uses of military force yet few declarations of war—not as legitimizing the arrangement, but as emphasizing the problem. They put less emphasis on the overall numbers than on key cases like Vietnam and Iraq, in which undeclared war had major consequences.

There also is the issue of who has what powers once war has commenced. The president's commander-in-chief role means that he has principal authority over the conduct of a war—a war powers version of the "first mover" advantage. The early stages of the Vietnam War provide an example. In 1964, claiming an attack on American ships off the coast of North Vietnam, President Lyndon Johnson went to Congress asking for authority to use military force (the Tonkin Gulf Resolution, named for the body of water where the alleged incidents took place). While the evidence was thin—indeed, declassified documents showed at least one of the two alleged North Vietnamese attacks on U.S. ships not to have occurred—Congress could not turn down LBJ's request without, as *New York Times* columnist James Reston observed, "seeming to weaken and repudiate the President in an emergency." Because the president made the first move, Congress was "free in theory only."[7]

Congress's power of the purse does give it the capacity to end a war with which it disagrees. It used this power to end the Vietnam War, although only after the war had gone on for a decade. But as Professor Douglas Kriner shows, Congress has a number of options well short of cutting off funds to affect how and how long a war is conducted.[8] It can use public hearings to amplify opposition, create investigative committees to get information from the executive branch, write op-eds and give press interviews, and use other formal and informal strategies. These tools can be used by congressional supporters of a war as well as opponents—either way, Congress can have an impact that, while generally less than the president's, is still significant.

Two sets of congressional committees handle most of the work related to war powers issues: the Senate Foreign Relations Committee and the House Foreign Affairs Committee, and the Senate and House Armed Services Committees. Other committees often have important roles, such as the Senate and House Appropriations Committees, which control funding, determining the portion of the budget that will be allotted for foreign policy and national security expenditures. The Senate and House Intelligence Committees receive classified briefings from the CIA and other intelligence agencies positioning them to provide some oversight.

We will discuss war powers again later in Part I: as a historical issue in Chapter 4, as an early Cold War–era issue in Chapter 5, and as a Vietnam-era controversy over the 1973 War Powers Resolution in Chapter 6. In Part II we consider a number of recent cases and ongoing debates over war powers reform in Chapter 9.

Treaties and Other International Commitments

The basic power-sharing arrangement for treaties vests negotiating power in the president but requires that treaties be ratified by a two-thirds majority in the Senate. On the surface this appears to have worked pretty well: of the close to 2,000 treaties signed by presidents in U.S. history, only about twenty have been voted down by the Senate. But here, too, simple statistics can be misleading.

One reason is that although it may not happen often, Senate defeat of a treaty can have a huge foreign policy impact. A major example is the 1919–20 defeat of the Treaty of Versailles, on which the post–World War I peace was to be based. Although European leaders also had a hand in the Versailles Treaty, it was largely the work of President Woodrow Wilson. Through the breakup of the Austro-Hungarian Empire, the creation of new independent states such as Yugoslavia, and the founding of the League of Nations, Wilson sought to establish a new structure of peace infused with American principles and with the United States playing a more central global role. But he faced opposition in the U.S. Senate. The opposition was partly policy-based, particularly over retreating into isolationism rather than joining the League of Nations. It also was political, including rivalry between Wilson and the Republican senator Henry Cabot Lodge, chairman of the Senate Foreign Relations Committee. "We shall make reservation after reservation, amend and amend," Senator Lodge proclaimed, "until there is nothing left." For his part Wilson declared, "Anyone who opposes me . . . I'll crush! I shall consent to nothing. The Senate must take its medicine."[9] Wilson ended up the one whose health was broken by the treaty fight, suffering a debilitating stroke. And while many other factors contributed to the failure of the post–World War I peace, the U. S. retreat into isolationism bore its share of responsibility.

A more recent example is the 1998 defeat of the ***Comprehensive Test Ban Treaty (CTBT)***. The CTBT sought a total ban on the testing of nuclear weapons. Earlier treaties such as the 1963 Limited Test Ban Treaty had prohibited testing nuclear weapons in the atmosphere, under the sea, and in outer space. The CTBT extended this to underground testing and banned all other nuclear weapons testing other than simulations in computer models and other technological mechanisms.

The CTBT debate was also partly policy-substantive and partly political. In signing the treaty in 1996, President Clinton called it "the longest-sought, hardest-fought prize in arms control history."[10] Clinton sent the CTBT to the Senate for ratification in September 1997, but it was held up in the Senate Foreign Relations Committee for almost two years. Republicans had the majority in the Senate and controlled the key committees. Senator Jesse Helms (R-North Carolina), a strong CTBT opponent, used his powers as chair of the Foreign Relations Committee to block the scheduling of committee hearings on the treaty. In July 1999, all forty-five Senate Democrats issued a joint statement calling on Helms to hold hearings and allow the treaty to go to the floor for a full Senate vote. Helms still refused. Senator Byron Dorgan (D-North Dakota) turned to another Senate procedural tactic, threatening to filibuster on the Senate floor and block votes from being taken on other issues. He would put himself on the Senate floor "like a potted plant," Dorgan said. "I am sorry if I am going to cause some problems around here with the schedule. But frankly, as I said, there are big issues and there are small issues. This is a big issue. And I am flat tired of seeing small issues around this chamber every day in every way, when the big issues are bottled up in some committee and the key is held by one or two people."

When hearings were finally held, they included experts on both sides of the issue. Some of the most influential testimony came from the directors of the Sandia and Lawrence Livermore National Laboratories, where much American nuclear weapons testing was conducted. The weapons-lab directors had issued a pro-CTBT statement in 1998, expressing their view that computerized testing and other aspects of the "stockpile stewardship program" still permitted by the CTBT would suffice. But during the congressional hearings their testimony conveyed greater doubt and uncertainty. "Had the directors learned something," one scholar queried in his case study, "that made them more nervous about the adequacy of the stockpile program? Maybe they were just being typical scientists, unwilling to say that anything is 100 percent certain. . . . It is also possible that, on the contrary, they were shrewd politicians, men who understood that the treaty was going down, that the majority party on Capitol Hill was against it, and that they needed to be on the right side of the issue."

All along, public opinion was largely pro-CTBT, as much as 70 to 80 percent supportive. But the general public was less influential on this issue than activists. Public pressures did not bring any senator over to the pro-treaty side from a position of being opposed or undecided. The final vote was 48 in favor, 51 opposed; ratification would have required 67 votes in favor. Clinton blamed the defeat on "politics, pure and simple." He also had in mind the fallout from the congressional efforts to impeach him over the Monica Lewinsky scandal. Senate Majority Leader Trent Lott (R-Mississippi) maintained that "it was not about politics; it was about the substance of the treaty, and that's all it was." Undoubtedly both foreign policy strategy and foreign policy politics came into play.

Congress also has ways to influence treaties other than by defeating them. For example, it can offer advice during negotiations through the official "observer groups" that often accompany State Department negotiators. It also can try to amend or attach a "reservation" to alter the terms of a treaty, an action that can be quite controversial, since it may require the reopening of negotiations with the other country or countries.

On the other hand, presidents also have an array of strategies at their disposal to circumvent Senate objections. In particular, they can resort to mechanisms other than treaties, such as *executive agreements,* for making international commitments. Executive agreements usually do not require congressional approval, let alone the two-thirds Senate majority that treaties do. Although in theory executive agreements are supposed to be used for minor government-to-government matters, leaving major aspects of relations to treaties, the line between the two has never been particularly clear. For example, status of forces agreements (SOFAs), by which U.S. presidents agree with other countries' heads of state on the stationing of U.S. troops in those countries, are usually implemented as executive agreements. In addition, sometimes the most important foreign policy commitments are not established by treaties, executive agreements, or in any other written or legal form. Such *declaratory commitments* come from speeches and statements by presidents. This was the case, for example, with the Monroe Doctrine, which sprang from a speech by President James Monroe in 1823 to become the bedrock of U.S. foreign policy in the Western Hemisphere. So, too, with the Truman Doctrine (1947): its clarion call "to support free peoples who are resisting attempted subjugation by armed minorities or by outside pressures" became the basis for the containment strategy pursued in U.S. policy for the subsequent forty to fifty years.

Some presidents have also claimed authority to withdraw from existing treaties without going to the Senate for approval, as in 2001 when President George W. Bush withdrew from the 1972 Anti-Ballistic Missile (ABM) Treaty. His action differed from that of President John Adams, who terminated treaties with France in 1798 through an act of Congress, or that of President James Polk, who sought congressional approval for withdrawing from the Oregon Territory Treaty with Great Britain in 1846. A partial precedent came from President Jimmy Carter, who did not seek congressional approval when he ended the U.S. mutual defense treaty with Taiwan in 1978 as part of the normalization of diplomatic relations with the People's Republic of China. Still, the Bush withdrawal from the ABM treaty was hotly disputed on both policy and procedural grounds.

Appointments of Foreign Policy Officials

The standard process is that the president nominates and the Senate confirms (by a simple majority) the appointments of Cabinet members, ambassadors, and other high-level foreign policy officials. In statistical terms the confirmation rate for presidential foreign policy nominees is higher than 90 percent. Yet here, too, we must look past the numbers.

This confirmation rate does not include nominations that were withdrawn before a formal Senate vote was held. Nominations first go to the relevant committees—e.g., nominations for secretary of state and ambassadors go to the Senate Foreign Relations Committee; nominations for secretary of defense and chairman of the joint chiefs of staff go to the Senate Armed Services Committee; nominations for secretary of the treasury and certain other economic policy officials go to the Senate Finance Committee—before votes are held in the full Senate chamber. When White House congressional-liaison aides come back from Capitol Hill reporting that "the committee vote count doesn't look good" a president often decides to avoid the embarrassment of a vote and instead withdraws the nomination. This, for example, is largely what occurred with the possible nomination of UN Ambassador Susan E. Rice as secretary of state for the second Obama administration. Republican opposition was so strident that Ambassador Rice asked President Obama to take her out of consideration for the position.

Another Senate technique is to put "holds" on nominations. Under Senate rules a single senator can put a hold on a nomination—effectively stopping it in place—and can do so for almost any reason. A senator may have a genuine foreign policy difference with the nominee, or may use the hold to pressure the president on another foreign policy issue, or on an unrelated issue. Even when holds are eventually lifted, delays can be caused that complicate policy. When holds drag on too long, nominees may withdraw out of frustration.

Precisely because it is often assumed that nominees will be confirmed, the political impact can be substantial when they are not. For example, in 1989 more attention was given to former senator John Tower, President Bush's nominee for secretary of defense, than to all of the administration's other foreign policy nominations combined. Despite the expectation of smooth confirmation by his former colleagues, concerns about his personal life led to Tower being voted down. The Senate has also left its mark on some nominees in the process of confirming them. This was the fate of Paul Warnke, President Carter's choice to head the Arms Control and Disarmament Agency, who was excoriated by conservatives as too "dovish": Warnke was confirmed but never fully recovered from the wounds of his confirmation battle.

Another illustrative case was President Clinton's nomination of Anthony Lake as CIA director in 1997. Lake had been national security adviser during Clinton's first term. Although there were some substantive bases for questioning Lake's CIA nomination, based on his limited experience in intelligence matters despite a long diplomatic career, most observers felt these issues were not sufficient to disqualify him. Some leading Republican senators announced their support for Lake, and the votes to confirm him seemed to be there. But Senator Richard Shelby (R-Alabama), chair of the Senate Intelligence Committee, carried on what many saw as a vendetta, repeatedly delaying Lake's confirmation hearings, then dragging them out with demands for documents and other obstructionist tactics. Ultimately Lake asked Clinton to withdraw his nomination. His letter to Clinton went beyond his own case to raise the broader concern that "Washington has gone haywire":

> I hope that sooner rather than later, people of all political views beyond our city limits will demand that Washington give priority to policy over partisanship, to governing over "gotcha." It is time that senior officials have more time to concentrate on dealing with very real foreign policy challenges rather than the domestic wounds Washington is inflicting on itself.[11]

An example from George W. Bush's administration is the nomination of John Bolton as ambassador to the United Nations in 2005. The issue was not prior experience. Bolton had been undersecretary of state for arms control and international security in the administration's first term and assistant secretary of state for international organizations under the first President Bush. But even among other neoconservatives, Bolton was known for his sharp and derisive criticisms of multilateralism in general and of the United Nations in particular. "There's no such thing as the United Nations," he had contended in 1994 when opposing Clinton administration pro-UN policies. If the UN building in New York "lost ten stories, it wouldn't make a bit of difference."[12] The Bush administration's argument was that a tough critic such as Bolton was the right person to represent American interests and to push the UN for reform. Toughness and reform were one thing, opponents contended, but Bolton's in-your-face style and the real questions about whether he wanted a better UN or just a less important one were quite another. As one former Clinton UN official pointed out, "neither of President Bush's first two appointees to the UN post—former Ambassador and later Intelligence Chief John Negroponte and former [Republican] Senator John Danforth—were pushovers by any stretch of the imagination. They both pressed hard on the administration's agenda, yet neither was perceived to have an axe to grind."[13] Opposition in the Senate was sufficient to block Bolton's confirmation. But Bush resorted to a "recess appointment," a technicality that allowed him to appoint Bolton while the Senate was on its summer 2005 recess and have the appointment continue "temporarily" without Senate confirmation. Bolton resigned following the 2006 elections, knowing he would not be confirmed by the Democrat-controlled Senate.

None of these legislative tactics, however, applies to foreign policy officials who do not require Senate confirmation. This includes the assistant to the president for national security affairs (called the national security adviser, for short, and whose role is discussed below) and the staff of the National Security Council (NSC). Thus such major figures as Henry Kissinger, Zbigniew Brzezinski, and Condoleezza Rice, who served as national security advisers to Presidents Nixon, Carter, and George W. Bush, respectively, did not need Senate confirmation for that position. (When Kissinger was nominated by Nixon to also be secretary of state, and when Rice switched to this position, however, Senate confirmation was required.)

"Commerce with Foreign Nations"

The Constitution is more explicit in the area of foreign commerce than in other areas of foreign policy. Congress is very clearly granted the power "to regulate commerce with foreign nations." This entails much less sharing of powers than other constitutional clauses. Congress was also given the power "to lay and collect . . . duties." Duties, or tariffs, were considered akin to taxes, so like all federal revenue they started with Congress's power of the purse. Indeed, until the federal income tax was initiated in the early twentieth century, tariffs were the main source of federal revenue for much of U.S. history. Thus, presidential authority over trade policy has been more dependent on what and how much authority Congress chooses to delegate than other areas of executive responsibility.[14]

For about 150 years, Congress actually decided each tariff, item by item; one result of this was the infamous Smoot-Hawley Tariff Act of 1930, which set tariffs for more than twenty thousand items—and increased almost all of them, the classic example of protectionism. The Reciprocal Trade Agreements Act of 1934, which arose from the Smoot-Hawley disaster, delegated to the president extensive authority to cut tariffs by as much as 50 percent if he could negotiate reciprocal cuts with other countries. Although it is often assumed that the natural inclination in politics is for any institution or actor to try to maximize its own power and authority, in this instance Congress saw its own interests better served by delegating greater authority to the president. As Professor I. M. Destler astutely observes, Congress's strategy was to protect itself from going protectionist through a "pressure-diverting policy management system."[15] Congress knew it couldn't consistently resist the temptations to grant interest groups the trade protection they asked for, so by delegating authority to the executive it could claim an inability to do it rather than refusing to do it.

While the United States was economically dominant in the post–World War II international economy, both branches were generally happy with this arrangement. But beginning in the 1970s, as trade became more politically controversial the power-sharing struggles on international trade issues grew more frequent and more wrenching, Congress began to take back some of the trade policy authority it had delegated. Although policy stayed more pro–free trade than protectionist, the politics became much more contentious with issues like "fast track," trade promotion authority, and others that we discuss in later chapters.

Among the many congressional committees involved in trade policy, the key ones are the House Ways and Means Committee and the Senate Finance Committee. Even though their names do not have "trade" in them, their jurisdiction goes back to when the tariff served as a tax, and these committees initiate all tax- and revenue-authorizing legislation. The full Senate must vote on all trade treaties with the standard two-thirds ratification margin. Although the House of Representatives lacks a formal role in treaties, it usually finds a way to be involved in trade treaties—often through legislation providing the funds needed to implement such treaties, consistent with the constitutional requirement that all appropriations bills originate in the House. Trade agreements that are not formal treaties require approval by both chambers, although only by simple majority votes. Those that are executive agreements do not require congressional approval.

General Powers

The president and Congress also bring their general constitutional powers to the foreign policy struggle.

EXECUTIVE POWER   The Constitution states that "the executive power shall be vested in the President" and roughly defines this power as to ensure "that the laws be faithfully executed." In itself this is a broad and vague mandate, which presidents have invoked as the basis for a wide range of actions taken in order to "execute" foreign policy, such as executive agreements and executive orders, which are directives issued by the president for executive-branch actions not requiring legislative approval. Sometimes executive orders are issued to fill in the blanks of legislation passed by Congress. But they can also be used as a way of getting around Congress. For example, President Truman racially integrated the armed forces by issuing Executive Order No. 9981 on July 26, 1948, because he knew that segregationists in Congress would block any integration legislation.

The *veto* is the most potent executive power the Constitution gives the president. The authority to block legislation unless Congress can pass it a second time, by a two-thirds majority in both chambers, is a formidable power. It is especially so in foreign policy, where the president can tap both patriotism and fear to intimidate potential veto overrides. Thus, even amid the congressional activism and partisan battles of the 1970s and 1980s, presidential vetoes on foreign policy legislation were overridden only twice: President Nixon's veto of the 1973 War Powers Resolution and President Reagan's veto of the 1986 Anti-Apartheid Act against South Africa.

In many respects, even more important than a president's formal executive powers are the informal political powers of the office and the skills of being a practiced politician. Stories are legion of deal making with members of Congress to get one last vote to ratify a treaty or pass an important bill. President Lyndon Johnson was especially well known for this, promising representatives and senators other public works projects in exchange for key votes. So was President Reagan, who doled out funds for a new hospital in the state of one senator, a coal-fired power plant for another, and a U.S. attorney appointment for a friend of another to get Senate approval of a major 1981 arms sale to Saudi Arabia.

The most significant political power a president has may be what Theodore Roosevelt called the "bully pulpit." As Roosevelt once put it, "People used to say to me that I was an astonishingly good politician and divined what the people are going to think. . . . I did not 'divine' how the people were going to think, I simply made up my mind what they ought to think, and then did my best to get them to think it." And that was before television!

Presidents have also used "signing statements," written pronouncements of what they believe the bill being signed means, as a tactic for shaping how the law will be implemented. Experts debate whether these are constitutional—whether they fall within presidential prerogatives or violate the separation of powers. Throughout U.S. history signing statements were used occassionally, but President George W. Bush stirred controversy by notably increasing their use. They were reduced but not eliminated by President Obama.

LEGISLATIVE POWER   Professor Louis Henkin claims that there is no part of foreign policy "that is not subject to legislation by Congress."[16] That may be an overstatement, as demonstrated by the above examples of executive power. But it is true that the legislative power gives Congress a great deal of influence over foreign policy. Foreign policy legislation generally needs to pass through five stages within Congress: the writing of a bill, hearings and mark-up by the relevant committees, votes on the floors of the House of Representatives and the Senate, reconciliation of any differences between the House and Senate bills in a conference committee, and the appropriations process, in which the actual budgets are set for defense spending, foreign aid, and other items.

Much recent political science literature has corrected against the underestimation of Congress's role.[17] For example, the distinction made by James Lindsay between *substantive* and *procedural* legislation is useful for understanding that Congress can exert its foreign policy influence in a number of ways. **Substantive legislation** is policy-specific, spelling out what the details of foreign policy should or should not be. Disapproval of the 1919 Treaty of Versailles, approval of the 1947 Marshall Plan, ratification of the 1972 SALT arms-control treaty with the Soviet Union, approval of the 1993 North American Free Trade Agreement (NAFTA), approval of annual defense budgets—all are examples of substantive legislation.

Procedural legislation is more subtle and requires greater elaboration. It deals more with "the structures and procedures by which foreign policy is made. The underlying premise is that if Congress changes the decision-making process it will change the policy."[18] The 1973 War Powers Resolution is one example; it was an effort to restructure how decisions on the use of military force are made. The creation of new agencies and positions within the executive branch, so that particular policies or perspectives will have "champions," is another form of the procedural legislation strategy. Examples include the creation of the Arms Control and Disarmament Agency (ACDA) in 1961, the Office of the U.S. Trade Representative in 1974, and the Department of Homeland Security in 2001–2002. A third practice is the use of the *legislative veto,* a procedure by which certain actions taken and policies set by the president can be overridden by Congress through a resolution rather than through a bill. The key difference is that generally bills must be signed by the president to become law, so the president has the opportunity to exercise a veto, but congressional resolutions do not require a presidential signature. For this very reason, the Supreme Court severely limited the use of the legislative veto in its 1983 *INS v. Chadha* decision, which will be discussed in the next section.

Perhaps Congress's most important power is its *power of the purse:* "no money shall be drawn from the Treasury but in Consequence of Appropriation made by Law." This power gives Congress direct influence over decisions about how much to spend and what to spend it on. In addition to stipulating the total budget of, for example, the Defense Department, Congress can use its appropriations power directly to influence more basic policy decisions, by setting "conditionalities" as to how the money can or cannot be spent or "earmarking" it for specific programs or countries.

Congress also gains impact and leverage through its oversight and investigative powers. Cabinet officers and other executive branch officials are required to testify to congressional committees on a regular basis as part of the oversight process. In instances of particular concern Congress conducts its own investigations. This investigative power can be abused, as demonstrated by the 1950s anti-communist witch hunts led by Senator Joseph McCarthy (R-Wisconsin).

However, the investigative power can also be a vital check on executive abuse of power, as in the 1980s **Iran-contra** affair. This case involved a secret plan, worked out by the National Security Council aide Colonel Oliver North and other Reagan administration officials, for the United States to provide arms to Iran and the government of Ayatollah Ruhollah Khomeini in exchange for Iran's help in securing the release of American hostages being held in Lebanon by Islamist terrorists. The profits from the arms sales would then fund the anti-communist Nicaraguan "contras" (Spanish, meaning "against"). The scheme fell apart for a number of reasons, not the least of which was that it was an illegal and unconstitutional effort to circumvent congressional prohibitions. When the scheme was revealed, Congress launched its most significant investigation since the 1970s Watergate hearings that had led to the impeachment of President Nixon. "Secrecy, deception and disdain for the law" were among the findings of the congressional committees investigating the Iran-contra affair. "The United States Constitution specifies the processes by which laws and policies are to be made and executed. Constitutional process is the essence of our democracy and our democratic form of Government is the basis of our strength. . . . The Committees find that the scheme, taken as a whole . . . violated cardinal principles of the Constitution. . . . Administration officials holding no elected office repeatedly evidenced disrespect for Congress's efforts to perform its constitutional oversight role in foreign policy."[19]

Along with our earlier analytic point about Congress's role being more impactful than is often acknowledged are normative arguments about the positive nature of this impact. Members of Congress frequently have more experience and expertise on foreign policy issues than a newly elected president. Senator Richard Lugar (R-Indiana), for example, served 36 years in the Senate and was either chairman or ranking minority member of the Senate Foreign Relations Committee for many of those years, while presidents like Jimmy Carter, Ronald Reagan, Bill Clinton, George W. Bush and Barack Obama came into office with very little foreign policy experience. Members of Congress are also often in closer touch with public opinion. As Professor Michael Glennon, who served as Staff Director of the Senate Foreign Relations Committee in the 1970s, puts it, "deputy assistant secretaries of state do not fly back to Minneapolis, Little Rock and San Francisco on Thursday after-noons to attend a beanfeed—and get an earful of complaints about United States policy toward the Philippines, Israel or Nicaragua. Members of Congress do."[20]

To be sure, there is plenty of basis for criticism of how Congress plays its foreign policy role. But since that side of the analysis often gets more attention, it's important to acknowledge some of the strengths as we work through our assessments.

The Supreme Court as Referee?

It is not often that the Supreme Court gets involved in foreign policy politics. When the Court does become involved, it is usually to resolve presidential-congressional conflicts over foreign policy power sharing. But the Court generally has been unable and unwilling to take on this role.

The Court has been unable to do so because its past rulings seem to lend support to each side. For example, a very strong statement of presidential prerogatives in foreign policy was made in the 1936 case *United States v. Curtiss-Wright Export Corp.* Although the specific case was over the indictment of a company which had been selling weapons to Bolivia in violation of an arms embargo, the significance of the Court's ruling was in the general principle that the president could claim greater powers in foreign than in domestic policy because "the law of nations," and not just the Constitution, is relevant. Justice George Sutherland (who had been a U.S. Senator and member of the Senate Foreign Relations Committee) wrote the majority opinion:

> In this vast external realm, with its important, complicated, delicate and manifold problems, the President alone has the power to speak or listen as a representative of the nation. . . . The President is the sole organ of the nation in its external relations, and its sole representative with foreign nations. . . .

The President was also said to have practical advantages:

> The President, not Congress, has the better opportunity of knowing the conditions which prevail in foreign countries. He has his confidential sources of information. He has his agents in the form of diplomatic, consular and other officials. Secrecy in respect of information gathered by them may be highly necessary, and the premature disclosure of it productive of harmful results.

Thus the Court concluded:

> It is quite apparent that . . . in the maintenance of our international relations . . . [Congress] must often accord to the President a degree of discretion and freedom from statutory restriction which would not be admissible were domestic affairs alone involved.[21]

In many respects the 1952 case *Youngstown Sheet and Tube Co. v. Sawyer* became the counterpart to *Curtiss-Wright*, establishing some limits on executive power. This case involved a steel industry labor-union strike during the Korean War. The Truman administration's position was that the essential importance of steel as a component of weapons and other war material meant that a strike would immediately jeopardize the war effort. President Truman issued an executive order to seize the steel mills and keep them running based on a claim of "inherent powers" of the presidency. A few years earlier Congress had considered legislation for a general authorization of governmental seizure in times of emergency to avert strikes or other serious industrial showdowns, but had rejected it. Truman made a *Curtiss-Wright*–like claim that he nevertheless had the inherent power to take such action on an emergency basis.

By a 6–3 vote, the Supreme Court ruled against the Truman administration. Its opinion differentiated three types of situations: first, where the president acts "pursuant to an express or implied authorization by Congress, his authority is at its maximum, for it includes all that he possess in his own right plus all that Congress can delegate;" second, when the president takes action "incompatible with the expressed or implied will of Congress, his power is at its lowest ebb, for then he can rely only upon his own constitutional powers minus any constitutional powers of Congress over the matter;" and third, when the president acts and Congress has neither affirmed or denied, he still has his own constitutional powers, but some situations fall into what Justice Robert Jackson called "a zone of twilight in which he and Congress may have concurrent authority or in which the distribution is uncertain," and thus "any actual test of power is likely to depend on the imperatives of events and contemporary imponderables rather than on abstract theories of law."[22] On these types of issues, while stopping well short of asserting congressional preeminence, the Court did not accept nearly as much presidential preeminence as it had in 1936 in its *Curtiss-Wright* decision. As Justice

Robert Jackson stated, "the President might act in external affairs without congressional authority, but not that he might act contrary to an Act of Congress."

In other instances the Supreme Court and other federal courts have been unwilling even to attempt to adjudicate presidential-congressional foreign policy disputes. In the 1970s and 1980s members of Congress took the president to court a number of times over issues of war and treaty powers.[23] In most of these cases the courts refused to rule definitively one way or the other. Although there were differences in the specifics of the rulings, the cases generally were deemed to fall under the "political question" doctrine, meaning that they involved political differences between the executive and legislative branches more than constitutional issues, and thus required a political resolution between the branches, rather than a judicial remedy. In legal terminology this is called nonjusticiability. In more straightforward language, the Supreme Court told the president and Congress to work the issues out themselves.

Another key case was *INS v. Chadha* in 1983, mentioned earlier. In striking down the legislative veto as unconstitutional, the Court stripped Congress of one of its levers of power. Even so, within a year and a half of the *Chadha* decision, Congress had passed more than fifty new laws that sought to accomplish the same goals as the legislative veto while avoiding the objections raised by the Court. The constitutionality of some of these laws remains untested, but they still cast a sufficient shadow for the president not to be able to assume too much freedom of action.

Since September 11, 2001, the Court has heard a new wave of cases concerning presidential powers, civil liberties, and related issues. We discuss some of these in Chapter 11.

Executive-Branch Politics

There was a time when books on foreign policy didn't include sections on executive-branch politics. Foreign policy politics was largely seen as an *inter*branch phenomenon, not an *intra*branch one. The executive branch, after all, was the president's own branch. Its usual organizational diagram was a pyramid: the president sat atop it, the various executive-branch departments and agencies fell below. Major foreign policy decisions were made in a hierarchical, structured, and orderly manner. It was believed to be a highly *rational* process, often called a "rational actor" model.

Yet as we will see throughout this book, the dynamics of executive branch decision-making and policy implementation have tended to be less strictly hierarchical, less neatly structured, and much more disorderly than portrayed in the rational-actor model. To put it more directly, the executive branch also has its own politics.

Presidents as Foreign Policy Leaders

For all the other executive-branch actors that play major foreign policy roles, the president remains the key decision maker. The president's role is not as simple as "great man" theories of history, which go too far in attributing causality to individual leaders, suggest. But it is not just system structure—as in the billiard balls image discussed in Chapter 1—nor just domestic politics that drive foreign policy. These are constraints on the domain of choice, but ultimately there is choice—and choices are principally made by our presidents. It is wrong, as Elizabeth Saunders argues in *Leaders at War: How Presidents Shape Military Interventions*, to assume that leaders "are too idiosyncratic to study analytically, on the one hand, or assume that leaders respond to international or domestic conditions in similar ways, on the other."[24]

How well the president fulfills the foreign policy leadership role depends on a number of factors. One is the extent of *foreign policy experience and expertise* that a president brings to the office. Surprisingly, it was much more common in the eighteenth and nineteenth centuries for presidents to have had substantial prior foreign policy experience than in modern times. Four of the first six presidents had served previously as secretary of state (Thomas Jefferson, James Madison, James Monroe, and John Quincy Adams). So had two other presidents in the nineteenth century (Martin Van Buren and James Buchanan). But no president since has had that experience. And of the seven war heroes who became president, only one (Dwight Eisenhower) did so in the twentieth century; the others were in the eighteenth (George Washington) and nineteenth centuries (Andrew Jackson, William Henry Harrison, Zachary Taylor, Ulysses Grant, and Benjamin Harrison). Among recent presidents, Richard Nixon and George H. W. Bush had the most prior foreign policy experience, and Ronald Reagan, Jimmy Carter, Bill Clinton, George W. Bush, and Barack Obama had the least.

A second set of factors is *characteristics of the president as an individual*. As with any individual in any walk of life, the president's personality affects how and how well the job gets done. Although personality is rarely the sole determinant of behavior, in some cases it does have a very strong bearing. In their book on Woodrow Wilson, Alexander and Juliette George show how his unwillingness to compromise with Senate opponents on the Treaty of Versailles has been traced in part to his self-righteousness and other deep-seated personality traits.[25] Richard Nixon's personality significantly affected his policy making, particularly with regard to Vietnam. The consistent image of Nixon that comes through in both his own writing and that of biographers is of a pervasive suspiciousness: Nixon viewed opponents as enemies and political setbacks as personal humiliations, had an extreme penchant for secrecy, and seemed obsessed with concentrating and guarding power. These personality traits help explain the rigidity with which Nixon kept the Vietnam War effort going despite the evidence that it was failing, and the virtual paranoia he exhibited by putting antiwar figures on an "enemies list" and recruiting former

CIA operatives to work in secret as "plumbers" to "plug" supposed leaks. These actions, like those of the self-destructive figures of ancient Greek tragedies, led to Nixon's own downfall through the Watergate scandal.

A more cognitive approach to executive-branch decision making focuses on the president's worldview, or what a number of authors have called a ***belief system***. No president comes to the job as a "tabula rasa," with a cognitive clean slate; quite to the contrary, as Robert Jervis states, "it is often impossible to explain crucial decisions and policies without reference to the decision-makers' beliefs about the world and their images of others."[26] Doris Kearns Goodwin, biographer of numerous presidents, notes how "[w]orldviews, once formed, are difficult to change, especially for politicians. Always reacting and responding, their life largely one of movement and contact with others, politicians are nearly always bound to the concepts and images formed in their minds before taking office."[27]

Belief systems can be construed in terms of three core components:

- the analytic component of the *conception of the international system:* What is the president's view of the basic structure of the international system? Who and what are seen as the principal threats to the United States?
- the normative component of the *national interest hierarchy:* How does the president rank the core objectives of Power, Peace, Prosperity, and Principles?
- the instrumental component of a basic *strategy:* Given both the conception of the international system and the national interest hierarchy, what is the optimal strategy to be pursued?

We illustrate the importance of belief systems by contrasting those of Jimmy Carter and Ronald Reagan.* The differences in their worldviews are quite pronounced, and the connections to their respective foreign policies are clear. In 1977 when he took office, Carter was convinced that the Cold War was virtually over and that the rigid structures of bipolarity had given way to a "post-polar" world. His "4 Ps" hierarchy of the national interest put Principles and Peace at the top. His basic foreign policy strategy was noninterventionist. All these characteristics were evident in many if not most of his foreign policies. In contrast, Reagan saw the world in bipolar terms and focused much of his 1980 presidential campaign against Carter on Cold War themes. He put Power rather than Peace at the top of his national-interest hierarchy, and although he too stressed Principles, his conception was defined largely by anticommunism, in contrast to Carter's emphasis on human rights. In addition, Reagan's strategy was decidedly interventionist, in military and other respects.

---

*See Chapter 9 for belief system analysis of post–Cold War presidents.

Presidents of course are also politicians, so another important factor affecting presidential foreign policy leadership is *political calculation*. In his book *Politics and Strategy: Partisan Ambition and American Statecraft*, Peter Trubowitz shows that throughout U.S. history American grand strategy has had "as much to do with leaders' ability to govern effectively at home as it does with guaranteeing the nation's security abroad."[28] This can work in different ways. Presidents in trouble at home may focus more on foreign policy, hoping to draw on the prestige of international leadership to bolster their domestic standing. At other times, presidents feel pressured to put less emphasis on foreign policy in response to criticisms about not paying enough attention to the domestic front. The election cycle also plays a role, with foreign policy tending to be more politicized during election years. Outside of the election cycle is the steady flow of public-opinion polls, which are factored in along with the intelligence analyses and other parts of the decision-making process.

Senior Foreign Policy Advisers and Bureaucratic Politics

All presidents rely heavily on their senior foreign policy advisers. In looking at presidential advisers, we need to ask two questions. The first concerns who among the "big three"—the national security adviser, the secretary of state, and the secretary of defense—has the most influential role? The answer depends on a number of factors, including the respective relationships of these advisers with the president and their own prominence and bureaucratic skills. Henry Kissinger, who became so well known that he took on celebrity status, is the major example. A Harvard professor, Kissinger served as national security adviser in President Nixon's first term. When Nixon appointed him secretary of state in 1973, Kissinger also kept the national security adviser position, a highly unusual step that accorded him unprecedented influence. He continued to hold both positions under President Gerald Ford, until pressured to step down as national security adviser in 1975. All told, we find far more references in books on the foreign policy of that period to "Kissingerian" doctrines than to "Nixonian" or, especially, "Fordian" ones.

The other analytic question is whether *consensus or conflict* prevails among the senior advisers. Consensus does not mean perfect harmony, but a prevailing sense of teamwork and collegiality. A possible negative aspect of consensus, though, is that too much consensus among senior advisers can lead to **groupthink,** a social-psychology concept that refers to the pressures for unanimity within small groups that work against individual critical thinking.[29] Group cohesion is a good thing, but too much of it can be stifling. The result can be decisions about which the question is later asked, How did so many smart people make such a dumb decision? The Kennedy administration's decision making on the disastrous 1961 Bay of Pigs invasion of Cuba is an oft-cited example which we will discuss in Chapter 5.

As for conflict among senior advisers, we come back to Kissinger as a classic example. Kissinger clashed repeatedly with Secretary of State William Rogers while he was President Nixon's national security adviser, and with Defense Secretary James Schlesinger while he was President Ford's secretary of state. Kissinger won many of these battles, adding to his prominence. But the impact of these disagreements on foreign policy was often quite negative. Such high-level divisiveness made broader domestic consensus building much more difficult. Moreover, with so much emphasis on winning the bureaucratic war, some ideas that were good on their merits, but happened not to be Kissinger's, were dismissed, buried, or otherwise condemned to bureaucratic purgatory. As Ivo Daalder and Mac Destler sum it up in *In the Shadow of the Oval Office*, their book on national security advisers, on the one hand "Kissinger and Nixon demonstrated the great potential for power that inheres in the position of national security adviser. But their tenure also demonstrated the great potential for abuse of that power."[30]

The **national security adviser** who Daalder and Destler rate the highest is Brent Scowcroft. Scowcroft first served in this position for President Ford and then again for President George H. W. Bush. He "had a winning formula," and avoided senior adviser divisiveness by "building a relationship of great trust with the other key players in the administration." Scowcroft made sure that the **interagency process**, coordinating State and Defense and other executive branch agencies, was "open, fair, but determined." He also had a very close relationship with each president, especially President Bush, becoming his "most trusted adviser by providing a sounding board and pushing his [Scowcroft's] own ideas when he thought those best served the president's—and the nation's—interests."[31]

Bureaucratic Politics and Organizational Dynamics

Politics in the executive branch does not occur only at the senior advisory level. Political battles occur daily at every level of the bureaucracy. As Figure 2.1 shows, the foreign affairs bureaucracy is vast and complex (and this is only a partial depiction). We distinguish among five groupings: overall foreign policy responsibility, foreign economic policy, political democratization and economic development, intelligence agencies, and internationalized domestic policy.

"Where you stand depends on where you sit" is the basic dynamic of **bureaucratic politics**—i.e., the positions taken on an issue by different executive-branch departments and agencies depend on the interests of that particular department or agency. Graham Allison, among the first political scientists to develop bureaucratic politics as a model for analyzing U.S. foreign policy, defined its core dynamic as "players who focus not on a single strategic issue but on many diverse intranational problems as well; players who act in terms of no consistent set of strategic objectives but rather according to varying conceptions of national, organizational and personal goals; players who make government decisions not by a single, rational choice but by the pulling and hauling that is politics" (see Reading 2.2).[32]

2.2

FIGURE 2.1   The Foreign Affairs Bureaucracy

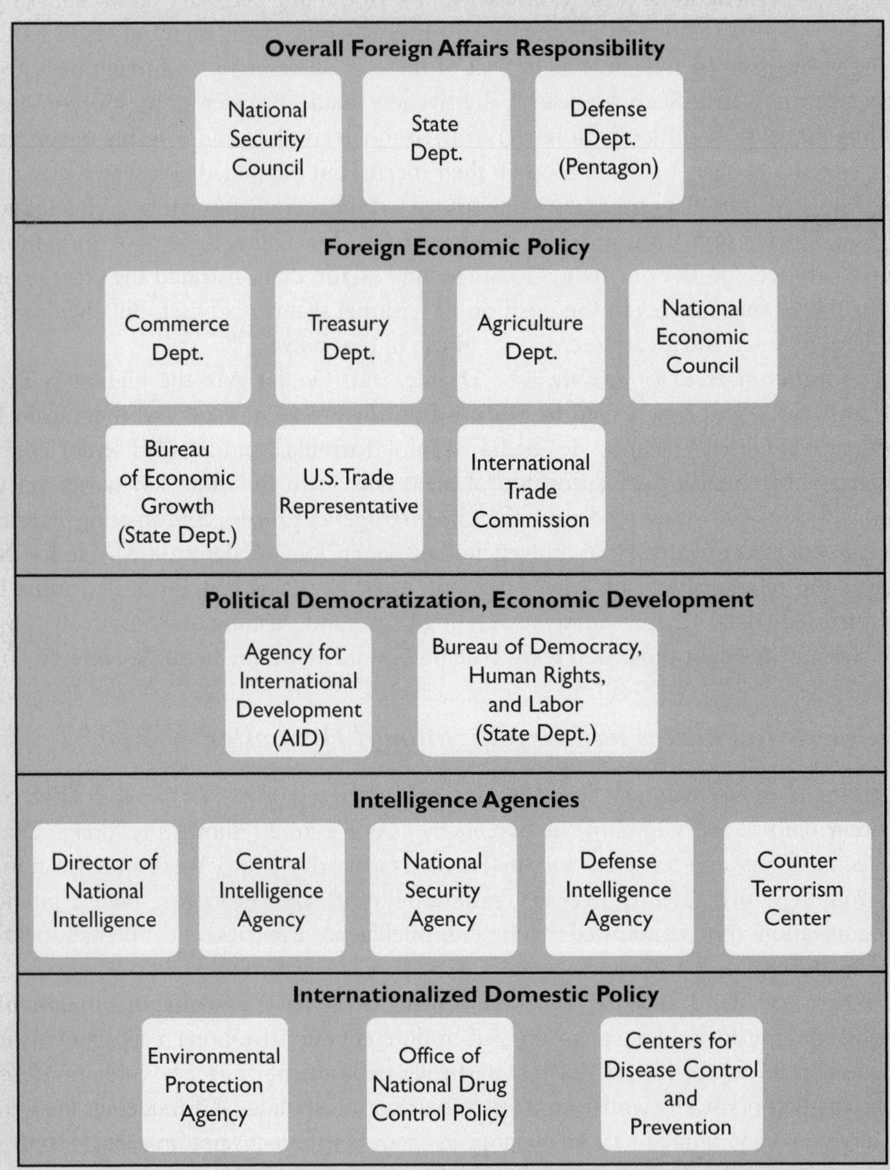

Overall Foreign Affairs Responsibility

National Security Council

State Dept.

Defense Dept. (Pentagon)

Foreign Economic Policy

Commerce Dept.

Treasury Dept.

Agriculture Dept.

National Economic Council

Bureau of Economic Growth (State Dept.)

U.S. Trade Representative

International Trade Commission

Political Democratization, Economic Development

Agency for International Development (AID)

Bureau of Democracy, Human Rights, and Labor (State Dept.)

Intelligence Agencies

Director of National Intelligence

Central Intelligence Agency

National Security Agency

Defense Intelligence Agency

Counter Terrorism Center

Internationalized Domestic Policy

Environmental Protection Agency

Office of National Drug Control Policy

Centers for Disease Control and Prevention

Another scholar, David Kozak, delineates a number of characteristics of foreign policy making highlighted by a bureaucratic politics perspective:

- The process is fragmented, nonhierarchical and nonmonolithic.
- It is best conceived of as a confederation of functional and organizational constituencies and subsystems—a bargaining arena rather than a command structure.
- Decision making requires inter- and intra-agency coordination and the integration of components.
- Decisions are driven by standard operating procedures (SOPs), incrementalism, muddling through, satisficing, compromise, and accommodation.
- Policy implementation is not automatic. It requires continuous negotiations and follow-through.[33]

Take economic sanctions as an example. The Commerce and Agriculture Departments, with their trade-promotion missions, often have opposed sanctions while the Departments of State and Defense often have supported them. This position can be disaggregated even further to bureaus within the same department or agency, which may also "stand" differently depending on where they "sit." In the 1989 Tiananmen Square case discussed in Chapter 1, the State Department's Bureau of Human Rights supported the imposition of sanctions, but the East Asia–Pacific Bureau, concerned about the overall U.S.-China relationship, opposed them.

Another example of bureaucratic politics is military ***interservice rivalry*** among the Army, Navy, Air Force, and Marines. While working together in many instances, they have been known to compete for shares of the defense budget, higher profiles in military actions, and other perceived advantages.

On top of these interest-based dynamics are the problems inherent in any large, complex bureaucracy: simply getting things done. The nineteenth-century German political philosopher Max Weber first focused on these dynamics in government as well as in other complex organizations. Often, instead of using rational processes consistent with the criteria noted earlier, bureaucracies proceed according to their own standard operating procedures and in other cumbersome ways that remind us why the term "bureaucracy" carries negative connotations.

Most of this discussion has concerned normal foreign policy decision making. In international crises, the challenges of meeting the criteria for a rational executive-branch decision-making process are even greater. The key characteristics of crises are a high level of threat against vital interests, a short time frame for decision making, and usually a significant element of surprise that the situation arose. Such situations tend to give presidents more power because they require fast, decisive action. Often they also lead presidents to set up special decision-making teams, drawing most heavily on the most trusted advisers. The Cuban missile crisis is often cited as a model of effective decision making in such a situation, which we discuss further in Chapter 5.

In sum, a rational executive-branch policy-making process is desirable but difficult to achieve. The sources of executive-branch politics are many, and the dynamics can get quite intricate. We will see these played out in ways that show both striking similarities and sharp differences over time.

Trade Policy and the Executive Branch

Trade policy involves a number of executive branch entities. The Office of the **U.S. Trade Representative (USTR)** leads trade negotiations. First established in 1962, the office has grown in importance in the years since; the head of the USTR now holds the rank of ambassador and is a member of the Cabinet. Depending on the issue area, other executive-branch actors may also be part of the negotiating team—for example, the Commerce Department on issues relating to industrial goods and technology, or the Agriculture Department on agricultural trade. The State Department may also be involved through its Bureau of Economic Growth, Energy and the Environment. On issues that may affect the environment, the Environmental Protection Agency (EPA) also plays a role.

When international financial policy is involved, the **secretary of the treasury** takes the lead role. This was one the very first Cabinet positions created in 1789 (Alexander Hamilton was the first to serve in this position). While originally largely a domestic policy position, over time it has taken on an increasingly important role in international economic policy, as in the recent international financial crises and in working with the International Monetary Fund (IMF).

The opening of markets through trade treaties and agreements does not ensure that American exporters will win the major sales. Nor is it purely a matter of economic competitiveness. All major industrial countries have government policies to promote their companies' exports, although such efforts are subject to rules established by the GATT and furthered by the WTO. The key executive-branch actors in this area are the **Export-Import Bank of the United States**, which provides credit and other financing for foreign customers to buy American exports; the **Trade and Development Agency**, which helps American companies put together business plans and feasibility studies for new export opportunities; and the **Overseas Private Investment Corporation (OPIC)**, which provides insurance and financing for foreign investments by U.S. companies that will create jobs back home and increase exports. Even though agricultural exports account for less than 10 percent of American exports, the Agriculture Department gets more than 50 percent of the export-promotion budget, reflecting interest-group politics and the power of farm constituencies. The State Department has also increased its role in export promotion as part of its post–Cold War retooling. Before assuming their embassy posts, U.S. ambassadors now go through a training course titled "Diplomacy for Global Competitiveness." Once in their posts, the U.S. ambassador to South Korea "hosted an auto show on the front lawn of his residence, displaying Buicks and Mercurys like a local used-car huckster"; the U.S. ambassador to India "won a contract for Cogentrix, a U.S. power company, with what he calls 'a lot of hugging and kissing' of Indian officials"; and the U.S. ambassador to Argentina "called in Argentine reporters to inform them that he was there as the chief U.S. lobbyist for his nation's businesses."[34]

Administrative trade remedies are actions by executive-branch agencies when relief from import competition is warranted under the rules of the international trading system. The U.S. agency that administers many of these actions is the **International Trade Commission (ITC).** The ITC is an independent regulatory agency with six members, evenly divided between Republicans and Democrats, all appointed by the president (subject to Senate confirmation). Its ability to decide cases objectively rather than politically is further aided by the seven-year length of the members' terms. The Commerce Department is also involved in some import competition cases, but because its head is a member of the president's Cabinet it is more political, and unless the ITC concurs, Commerce cannot provide import relief.

Administrative trade remedies also provide a good example of how Congress can shape policy through legislative crafting. Take the "escape clause," which was a provision within the international free trade system allowing governments to provide temporary relief to industries seriously injured by sudden increases in imports resulting from lower tariffs. The 1962 Trade Expansion Act set the criterion for escape clause relief as imports being the "major cause" of the injury suffered by an industry. This meant imports had to be *greater* than all the other causes combined, a difficult standard to meet. The 1974 Trade Act changed "major" to "substantial," which meant that the injury from imports only had to be *equal* to any of the other individual factors, a much less stringent criterion on which the ITC had to base its rulings.[35]

Summary

Foreign policy politics is the *process* by which the choices of foreign policy strategy are made. It is much more complex than the conventional wisdom depicts. Throughout American history, politics "stopping at the water's edge" has been more the exception than the rule. Relations between the president and Congress have been a mix of cooperation, confrontation, competition, and constructive compromise—a relationship very much in need of "Pennsylvania Avenue diplomacy." Along with these inter-branch politics the executive branch has its own intra-branch politics.

In the next chapter we expand our foreign policy politics framework beyond the formal political institutions to key societal actors: interest groups, the media, and public opinion.

Notes

[1] Joseph Marion Jones, *The Fifteen Weeks (February 21–June 5, 1947)* (New York: Harcourt Brace and World, 1955), 8.

[2] James M. McCormick, *American Foreign Policy and Process* (Itasca, Ill.: Peacock, 1992), 478.

[3] Quoted in Bruce W. Jentleson, "American Diplomacy: Around the World and Along Pennsylvania Avenue," in *A Question of Balance: The President, the Congress and Foreign Policy,* Thomas E. Mann, ed. (Washington, D.C.: Brookings Institution Press, 1990), 184.

[4] Edward S. Corwin, *The President: Office and Powers, 1787–1957,* 4th rev. ed. (New York: New York University Press, 1957), 171.

[5] Richard E. Neustadt, *Presidential Power: The Politics of Leadership* (New York: Wiley, 1976), 101.

[6] Cited in Arthur M. Schlesinger, Jr., *The Imperial Presidency* (New York: Atlantic Monthly Press, 1974), 17.

[7] Cited in John Byrne Cooke, *Reporting the War: Freedom of the Press from the American Revolution to the War on Terrorism* (New York: Palgrave Macmillan, 2007).

[8] Douglas A. Kriner, *After the Rubicon: Congress, Presidents and the Politics of Waging Wars* (Chicago: University of Chicago Press, 2010).

[9] Lodge quote in David Remnick, "State of the Union," *The New Yorker,* January 16, 2012, 67; Wilson quote in Nannerl O. Keohane, *Thinking about Leadership* (Princeton: Princeton University Press, 2010), 102.

[10] This section draws on Terry L. Deibel, "The Death of a Treaty," *Foreign Affairs* 81.5 (September/October 2002): 142–61.

[11] "Text of Lake's Sharply Worded Letter Withdrawing as the CIA Nominee," *New York Times,* March 18, 1997, B6. President Carter's nomination of Theodore Sorensen as CIA Director also ended up being withdrawn.

[12] Quoted in Suzanne Nossel, "Bracing for Bolton," Center for American Progress, March 8, 2005, www.americanprogress.org/issues/2005/03/b413729.html (accessed 12/15/12).

[13] Quoted in Nossel, "Bracing for Bolton."

[14] Excellent books on the executive-legislative politics of trade policy are I. M. Destler, *American Trade Politics,* 4th ed. (Washington, D.C.: Institute for International Economics, 2005); and Robert A. Pastor, *Congress and the Politics of Foreign Economic Policy, 1929–1976* (Berkeley: University of California Press, 1980).

[15] Destler, *American Trade Politics,* 4th ed., 37.

[16] Cited in McCormick, *American Foreign Policy and Process,* 268.

[17] William G. Howell and Jon C. Pevehouse, *While Dangers Gather: Congressional Checks on Presidential War Powers* (Princeton: Princeton University Press, 2007); Rebecca K. C. Hersman, *Friends and Foes: How Congress and the President Really Make Foreign Policy* (Washington, D.C.: Brookings Institution Press, 2000); Ralph G. Carter and James M. Scott, *Choosing to Lead: Understanding Congressional Foreign Policy Entrepreneurs* (Durham, N.C.: Duke University Press, 2009); James M. Lindsay, *Congress and the Politics of U.S. Foreign Policy* (Baltimore: Johns Hopkins University Press, 1994).

[18] Lindsay, *Congress and the Politics of U.S. Foreign Policy,* 102–3.

[19] U.S. Congress, *Report of the Congressional Committees Investigating the Iran-Contra Affair,* 100th Congr., 1st sess., November 1987, 11, 411, 19.

[20] Michael J. Glennon, *Constitutional Diplomacy* (Princeton: Princeton University Press, 1990), 31.

[21] *United States v. Curtiss-Wright Export Corp.* 299 U.S. 304 (1936), quoted in *Foreign Relations and National Security Law: Cases, Materials and Simulations,* Thomas M. Franck and Michael J. Glennon, eds. (St. Paul, Minn.: West Publishing, 1987), 32–37.

[22] Cited in Glennon, *Constitutional Diplomacy,* 10–11.

[23] One of these cases was *Goldwater et al. v. Carter* (1979), in which Republican senator Barry Goldwater led a suit challenging the constitutionality of President Carter's decision to terminate the Mutual Defense Treaty

with Taiwan as part of his policy of normalizing relations with the People's Republic of China. The others were four suits brought by Democratic members of Congress in the Reagan and George H. W. Bush administrations on war powers issues: *Crockett v. Reagan* (1984), on U.S. military aid and advisers in El Salvador; *Conyers v. Reagan* (1985), over the 1983 invasion of Grenada; *Lowry v. Reagan* (1987), over the naval operations in the Persian Gulf during the Iran-Iraq War; and *Dellums v. Bush* (1990), over the initial Operation Desert Shield deployment following the Iraqi invasion of Kuwait.

[24]Elizabeth N. Sanders, *Leaders at War: How Presidents Shape Military Interventions* (Ithaca, N.Y.: Cornell University Press, 2011), 2.

[25]Alexander L. George and Juliette L. George, *Woodrow Wilson and Colonel House: A Personality Study* (New York: Dover Publications, 1964).

[26]Alexander L. George, *Presidential Decisionmaking in Foreign Policy: The Effective Use of Information and Advice* (Boulder, Colo.: Westview, 1980), 10.

[27]Doris Kearns Goodwin, *Lyndon Johnson and the American Dream* (New York: Harper and Row, 1976), 258.

[28]Peter Trubowitz, *Politics and Strategy: Partisan Ambition and American Statecraft* (Princeton, N. J.: Princeton University Press, 2011), 4.

[29]See Irving L. Janis, *Groupthink: Psychological Studies of Policy Decisions and Fiascos* (Boston: Houghton Mifflin, 1982).

[30]Ivo H. Daalder and I. M. Destler, *In the Shadow of the Oval Office: Profiles of the National Security Advisers and the Presidents They Served—From JFK to George W. Bush* (New York: Simon and Schuster, 2009), 303.

[31]Daalder and Destler, *In the Shadow of the Oval Office*, 307–08.

[32]Graham T. Allison, *Essence of Decision: Explaining the Cuban Missile Crisis* (Boston: Little, Brown, 1971), 144; see also his "Conceptual Models and the Cuban Missile Crisis," *American Political Science Review* 63 (September 1969): 689–718.

[33]David C. Kozak, "The Bureaucratic Politics Approach: The Evolution of the Paradigm," in Kozak and James M. Keagle, *Bureaucratic Politics and National Security: Theory and Practice* (Boulder, Colo.: Lynne Rienner, 1988), 12.

[34]Bruce Stokes, "Team Players," *National Journal* (January 7, 1995), 10–11.

[35]I. M. Destler, *American Trade Politics*, 2d ed. (Washington, D.C.: Institute of International Economics, 1992), 142–43.

3 *The Domestic Context: Interest Groups, Media, and Public Opinion*

Introduction: Societal Actors and the Process of Choice

As the three branches seek to make policy, they not only wrestle with their own inter- and intrabranch politics, they also are influenced by actors and forces from the broader American society. When scholars such as Peter Katzenstein and Stephen Krasner characterize the American political system as a "weak state structure," a key part of what they mean is that compared to other democracies there are many more points of access for societal actors seeking to influence policy.[1] Interest groups, the media, and public opinion are the three principal sets of these societal actors.

In this chapter we lay out a basic analytic framework which we then apply historically (Chapter 4) and to the Cold War (Chapters 5 and 6). We then revisit and update this framework for post–Cold War foreign policy politics (Chapter 9) and apply it to key cases in different policy areas (Chapters 10–14).

Interest Groups and Their Influence

Interest groups are "formal organizations of people who share a common outlook or social circumstance and who band together in the hope of influencing government policy."[2] Three questions are central to understanding the foreign policy role of interest groups: (1) What are the principal types of foreign policy interest groups? (2) What are the main strategies and techniques of influence used by interest groups? (3) How much influence do interest groups have, and how much should they have?

A Typology of Foreign Policy Interest Groups

Distinctions can be made among five main types of foreign policy interest groups on the basis of differences in the nature of the interests that motivate their activity and in their forms of organization. Table 3.1 presents the typology, with some general examples.

ECONOMIC INTEREST GROUPS   This category includes multinational corporations (MNCs) and other businesses, labor unions, consumers, and other groups whose lobbying is motivated principally by how foreign policy affects the economic interests of their members.

These groups are especially active on trade and other international economic policy issues. Take the infamous 1930 Smoot-Hawley Act, which raised so many tariffs so high that it helped deepen and globalize the Great Depression. Some wondered how such a bill could ever have passed. Very easily, according to one senator who "brazenly admitted that the people who gave money to congressional campaigns had a right to expect it back in tariffs."[3] With the spread of globalization, in recent years even more groups' interests have been affected by trade and other international economic issues. Those that face economic

TABLE 3.1   A Typology of Foreign Policy Interest Groups

Type	General examples
Economic groups	AFL-CIO (organization of trade unions) National Association of Manufacturers Consumer Federation of America Major multinational corporations (MNCs)
Identity groups	Jewish Americans Cuban Americans Greek Americans African Americans
Political issue groups	Anti–Vietnam War movement Committee on the Present Danger Amnesty International World Wildlife Fund Refugees International
State and local governments	Local Elected Officials for Social Responsibility California World Trade Commission
Foreign governments	Washington law firms, lobbyists, public-relations companies (hired to promote interests of foreign governments in Washington)

competition from imports into U.S. domestic markets tend to be opposed to free trade; those that are more export-oriented tend to favor it. As recently as 1970, trade accounted for only 13 percent of the U.S. GDP. Today it amounts to almost 30 percent and comprises much more than goods and services. Companies scour the world, not just their home countries, when deciding where to build factories and make other foreign investments. Every day millions of dollars in stock investments and other financial transactions flow between New York and Frankfurt, Chicago and London, San Francisco and Tokyo. Overall, more foreign economic issues are now on the agenda, and those issues are much more politically salient than they used to be. Whereas during the Cold War most foreign economic policy issues were relegated to "low politics" status, in contrast to political and security "high politics" issues, in recent years the North American Free Trade Agreement (NAFTA), the World Trade Organization, and other international economic issues have been as hotly contested and prominent as any other foreign policy issues.

In some cases, the influence of multinational corporations (MNCs) has gone far beyond lobbying on legislation to involvment with the CIA in covert action and military coups against foreign governments that threatened their interests. We discussed one such case in Chapter 1, the 1954 covert action against the newly elected Guatemalan government that had begun nationalizing land holdings of the United Fruit Company. There were others in Latin America, going back to repeated military interventions in the early twentieth century in Mexico, Cuba, and other countries, as well as various cases during the Cold War. There also were cases in other parts of the world, such as the 1953 covert action in Iran that was a key factor in the overthrow of Prime Minister Mohammed Mossadegh, who had been planning to nationalize American and British oil companies. Oil companies are often seen as the major example of economic interest-group influence. In his book *Private Empire: ExxonMobil and American Power*, journalist Steve Coll writes of how "Exxon's empire would increasingly overlap with America's," and to the extent that they did not coincide, the Exxon CEO "would manage Exxon's global position . . . as a confident sovereign, a peer of the White House's rotating occupants."[4]

Economic sanctions are another issue on which economic interest groups have been very active. When a bipartisan coalition in Congress proposed sanctions against South Africa in the 1980s to exert pressure against apartheid, businesses with trade, investment, and finance interests lobbied against them.* In 1987–88 agricultural interests played a key role in blocking a sanctions bill which would have ended credits for agricultural exports to Iraq after Saddam Hussein used chemical weapons against the Kurds in northern Iraq. For their part, labor unions have lobbied for sanctions against countries that abuse human rights and violate fair labor practices partly on these political grounds but also as a way of protecting their own economic interests.

---

*Chapter 14 includes a case study of the domestic politics of the 1980s anti-apartheid sanctions.

IDENTITY GROUPS   These groups are motivated less by economic interests than by ethnic or religious identity. Irish Americans, Polish Americans, African Americans, Greek Americans, Vietnamese Americans—these and other ethnic identity groups have sought to influence U.S. relations with the country or region to which they trace their ancestry or heritage. The increasing racial and ethnic diversity of the American populace, resulting both from new trends in immigration and increasing empowerment of long-present minorities, is making for a larger number and wider range of groups with personal reasons for seeking to influence foreign policy. The ethnic and national origins of American immigrants in the early twenty-first century are very different from those of the early twentieth century. Whereas in 1920 87 percent of immigrants came from Europe, in 2010 it was only 8 percent. Immigration from Latin America has grown from 4 percent to 38 percent; immigration from Asia has grown from 1 percent to 40 percent; and immigration from Africa has grown from less than 1 percent to 10 percent.[5]

In his book *Foreign Attachments: The Power of Ethnic Groups in the Making of American Foreign Policy,* Professor Tony Smith makes the general argument that "the negative consequences of ethnic involvement may well outweigh the undoubted benefits this activism at times confers on America in world affairs."[6] The group often pointed to as the most powerful ethnic lobby is Jewish Americans and their principal organization, the American-Israel Public Affairs Committee (AIPAC). The book *The Israel Lobby and U.S. Foreign Policy,* by John Mearsheimer and Stephen Walt, stirred enormous controversy.[7] While they also point to evangelical Christians and other pro-Israel constituencies, Mearsheimer and Walt attribute many aspects of U.S. support for Israel and much of American Middle East policy to the influence of AIPAC and Jewish Americans. But while the Jewish-American lobby unquestionably has been quite influential, it is not nearly as powerful as they portray. This was particularly true of the Bush administration's 2003 decision to go to war in Iraq, which Mearsheimer and Walt tie to Jewish-American influence but was much more attributable to other factors (see Chapter 11). The Jewish-American lobby has also lost on some Arab-Israeli issues in part because major oil companies and arms exporters with key interests in the Arab world (i.e., economic interest groups) have exerted stronger pressure for the opposite policy. The Jewish-American community itself has been split at times, reflecting Israel's own deep political divisions on issues like the Arab-Israeli peace process. Moreover, interest group politics are not solely responsible for pro-Israel U.S. policy: both Power (the geostrategic benefits of a reliable ally in a region long known for its anti-Americanism) and Principles (Israel is the only democracy in the entire Middle East region) have also been factors.

Cuban Americans are another example of a powerful lobby. While anticommunism (Power) has been a factor in U.S. policy toward Cuba, the Cuban-American National Foundation (CANF), the lead lobbying group for the Cuban-American community—many of whom were exiled from Cuba when Fidel Castro came to power in 1959—has been a politically potent force. Its founder, Jorge Mas Canosa, became "one of the most powerful and influential lobbyists on the U.S. political scene." As journalist Tom Gjelten writes, "he mobilized his fund-raising network and this political machine to convince Washington politicians that they should serve *his* interests." Gjelten cites an interview in which Mas Canosa rather baldly states that "we have used the Americans, but we have never left the initiative for Cuban issues in the Americans' hands."[8] In a particularly far-reaching example, in the 2000 presidential election, Cuban-American opposition to the Cuba policies of the Clinton-Gore administration was a key factor in the vote in Florida being as close as it was. This led to the recount controversy and the Supreme Court ultimately stepping in to decide the election in George W. Bush's favor.

Catholic and Protestant groups have also entered the foreign policy fray on a range of issues. In the early Cold War era the Catholic Church was ardently anticommunist, supporting McCarthyism, but when the anticommunist government in El Salvador assassinated the Archbishop Oscar Romero in 1980, the Church pushed hard for restricting U.S. military aid. The Church has also strongly opposed foreign aid programs that involve support for family planning and birth control. Various Protestant groups have been active on such issues as nuclear arms control and human rights.

POLITICAL ISSUE GROUPS   This category includes groups that are organized around support or opposition to a political issue that is not principally a matter of their economic interests or group identity, but are what Joshua Busby calls "principled advocacy movements."[9] Here we draw three sub-groupings. The first comprises groups that focus on a particular issue area. Name almost any issue area and it has groups that provide expertise and advocacy: global environmental policy (World Wildlife Federation and the Sierra Club); human rights (Amnesty International and Human Rights Watch); women's rights (Women's Action for New Directions and the Women's Foreign Policy Group); refugees (InterAction and Refugees International); nuclear arms control (Arms Control Association and Ground Zero); and many others. In recent years these have fallen under the rubric of NGOs, or **nongovernmental organizations**, which are further discussed in Chapter 9.

Second are groups that have more comprehensive foreign policy agendas with particular political-ideological perspectives. For example, during the Cold War, groups such as the Council for a Livable World pushed for greater across-the-board efforts at U.S.-Soviet accommodation, while those such as the Committee on the Present Danger pushed for more hard-line policies. "Think tanks"—research institutes heavily concentrated in Washington, D.C. that conduct research and analysis that is more directly relevant to policy than university-based research—span the political-ideological spectrum. The Heritage Foundation and the American Enterprise Institute are among the most influential conservative think tanks, while the Brookings Institution and the Carnegie Endowment for International Peace are among the most influential liberal ones.

Third are broad movements such as antiwar ones. These tend to be less focused on D.C.-based lobbying than on mass demonstrations and local-level mobilization.

The anti–Vietnam War movement, while the largest in American history, was by no means the only one. The Anti-Imperialist League opposed the Spanish-American War of 1898. The America First Committee tried to keep the United States out of World War II. The 2003 Iraq war also spurred an antiwar movement.

STATE AND LOCAL GOVERNMENTS   Although they do not fit into the category of "interest groups" in the same way, and constitutional parameters and international law make the federal government the principal locus of U.S. sovereignty in the international system, state and local governments do seek to influence foreign policy as it affects their interests.[10] In the early 1980s, for example, local governments pressured the federal government to end the arms race through groups such as the Local Elected Officials for Social Responsibility, by proclamations and referenda in more than 150 cities and counties declaring themselves "nuclear-free zones," or by otherwise opposing the nuclear arms race. Conversely, states and cities with large defense industries have pressured the federal government not to cut defense spending, as the governors of Maryland and Virginia (Democrat and Republican, respectively) did during the 2013 sequestration battle. Local activism has been even greater on trade issues. In the 1980s–90s the California World Trade Commission, part of the state government, sent its own representative to the GATT trade talks in Geneva, Switzerland. Many state and local governments actually led the effort to combat apartheid in South Africa. In fact, the pressure on Congress to pass legislation on economic sanctions was strengthened because so many state and local governments, including those of California and New York City, had already imposed their own sanctions by prohibiting purchases and divesting pension-fund holdings from companies still doing business with South Africa.

FOREIGN GOVERNMENTS   It is normal diplomacy for governments to have embassies in each others' capitals. The reference here is to the American law firms, lobbyists, and public-relations companies hired by foreign governments to lobby for them. These foreign lobbyists are often former members of Congress (both Republican and Democratic), former Cabinet members, other former top executive-branch officials, and other "big guns." Indeed, by the early 1990s there were well over one thousand lobbyists in Washington who were representing foreign countries. Major controversies have arisen over foreign lobbying; one high-profile case involved Japan and, as claimed in the 1990 book *Agents of Influence*, its "manipulation" of U.S. policy through lobbyists to the point where "it threatens our national sovereignty."[11] Another striking case was that of Angola in the mid-1980s. American lobbyists were hired by both the Angolan guerrillas, to try to improve their image and win support for military aid, and by the Angolan government, to try to block aid to the guerrillas. More than $2 million was paid out by the rebels and almost $1 million by the government in just one year—a hefty sum for a poor country.

Not every issue involves all five types of interest groups, but all have at least some of these groups seeking to exert their influence.

Strategies and Techniques of Influence

Interest groups seek to influence foreign policy through many different strategies aimed at the various foreign policy actors.

INFLUENCING CONGRESSIONAL LEGISLATION   Lobbyists seek to influence legislation at each of its stages. They try to get senators and representatives to introduce and co-sponsor bills dealing with issues that affect their interests. They work with congressional staff who write the legislative language of a bill. They testify at committee hearings and seek input in the "markup" (revisions and amendments to the original bill based on the committee hearings). When bills are on their way to the House and Senate floors, lobbyists make the rounds trying to line up votes. If the House and Senate pass different versions and set up a conference committee to resolve the differences, they lobby that as well. They also try to influence the appropriations process, in which the actual amounts of money are set for defense spending, foreign aid, and other items.

INFLUENCING THE EXECUTIVE BRANCH   Interest groups try to influence executive-branch departments and agencies directly as foreign policy is formulated and implemented on a day-to-day basis. In the 1980s, AIPAC broadened its efforts from being heavily focused on Capitol Hill to working with mid-level officials in the State and Defense Departments who were involved in U.S.-Israeli relations. In trade policy there is a whole system of advisory committees through which the private sector can channel its influence to executive-branch officials who negotiate trade treaties.

Another strategy is to try to influence who gets appointed to important foreign policy positions. For example, in 1992–93 the Cuban-American National Foundation (CANF) blocked the nomination of Cuban-American Mario Baeza as assistant secretary of state for inter-American affairs because his views on how to deal with Fidel Castro were considered too moderate. In another case, Ernest LeFever, President Reagan's nominee for assistant secretary of state for human rights, was not confirmed because pro-human rights groups viewed him as more of a critic than an advocate of their cause.

INFLUENCING ELECTIONS   Interest groups also try to influence the outcomes of elections through political action committees (PACs) that steer campaign contributions to favored candidates. Sometimes this is less about party affiliation than committee assignment: for example, one study showed that almost half of the PAC contributions made by the nation's twelve largest defense contractors went to senators and representatives serving on the armed services committees and defense and military-construction subcommittees. As the cost of campaigns has gone up, so too has the need for PAC money. For members of the House who must run for re-election every two years, when one electoral fund-raising cycle ends the next one starts right away. Senators have six-year terms, but with statewide constituencies they, too, have little if any, respite from raising money. So, too, with presidential candidates who have seen the fund-raising targets for their campaigns more than double from 1980 to 1992 ($162 million to $331 million) and more than triple from 1992 to 2008 (to over $1 billion). Some of this does come from individual donors, but the bulk comes from PACs. The 2010 Supreme Court decision in the *Citizens United v. F. E. C.* case further deregulating corporate and other campaign contributions further increased the flow—more accurately, the flood—of PAC, so-called "super-PAC," and other money into politics.

INFLUENCING PUBLIC OPINION   Groups also take their efforts to influence foreign policy outside the halls of Congress and the executive branch, and not just in electoral contexts. They mobilize protests and demonstrations to show "shoulder-to-shoulder" support for their causes. This is an old tradition, going back to peace movements in the early twentieth century, and such nineteenth-century events as the Civil War veterans' march on Washington to demand payment of their pensions. The anti–Vietnam War movement was particularly known for its demonstrations on college campuses as well as in Washington. In the spring of 1970, for example, following the National Guard shooting of student protesters at Kent State University in Ohio, college campuses around the country were shut down (and final exams were canceled on many campuses) as almost half a million antiwar protesters descended on Washington. An even larger demonstration was staged in 1990 on the twentieth anniversary of "Earth Day" to pressure the government for stronger and more forward-looking policies on global environmental issues.

Especially in recent years, foreign policy interest groups have become quite astute at using the media to increase their exposure and to amplify their voices. For all the econometric models that were run and other studies that were conducted to show the damage done to the American auto industry by Japanese auto imports in the 1970s and 1980s, for example, none had the impact of the televised image of two members of Congress smashing a Toyota with a sledgehammer in front of the Capitol. Members of the anti-apartheid movement dramatized their cause by handcuffing themselves to the fence around the South African embassy in Washington, D.C., and staging other civil disobedience protests with the objective of getting coverage on the nightly television news. The anti-globalization movement of recent years has tried to use similar tactics, although violence at some of these protests has backfired by alienating broad swaths of the public.

DIRECT ACTION   NGOs often work not just to influence policy in Washington but to play direct roles themselves by providing humanitarian assistance, monitoring human rights, supervising elections, helping with economic development, and taking on countless other global responsibilities. Proponents such as Jessica Mathews, president of the Carnegie Endowment for International Peace, argue that NGOs "can outperform government in the delivery of many public services" and "are better than governments at dealing with problems that grow slowly and affect society through their cumulative effect on individuals."[12] Others see NGOs as having problems, inefficiencies, and interests that complicate and sometimes conflict with their humanitarian and other missions.[13]

CORRUPTION   Popular images of suitcases stuffed with $100 bills, exorbitant junkets, and other corrupt practices are grossly exaggerated at times. Nevertheless, there have been sufficient instances of corrupt efforts to influence foreign policy that not including it as a technique of influence would be a glaring omission. For example, Koreagate was a 1976 scandal over alleged South Korean influence-peddling in Congress to influence U.S. policy toward South and North Korea. Another example was the 1980s Pentagon defense-contract scandal involving bribes, cover-ups, and cost overruns that led to the purchase of "specially designed" $600 toilet seats and $1,000 coffee machines.

The Extent of Interest-Group Influence: Analytic and Normative Considerations

"The friend of popular governments never finds himself so much alarmed for their character and fate," James Madison warned back in *Federalist 10*, "as when he contemplates their propensity to . . . the violence of faction." Madison defined a "faction" not just as a group with a particular set of interests but as one whose interests, or "common impulse of passion," were "adverse to the rights of other citizens, or to the permanent and aggregate interests of the community."

Madison's general political concern with what we now call the extent of interest-group influence bears particularly on foreign policy for three principal reasons. First, if Americans have even the slightest sense that the nation is asking them to make the ultimate sacrifice of war for interests that are more group-specific than collectively national, the consequences for national morale and purpose can be devastating. Even in more ongoing, less dramatic areas of policy, the effects of such an impression on the overall state of democracy and conceptions of public authority can be deeply corrosive.

Second, this "capturing" of policy areas by interest groups makes change much more difficult because of the many vested interests that get ensconced.[14] This is especially a problem in foreign policy, given the many threats and challenges to which the United States must respond, including the rigors of staying competitive in the international economy. Political scientist Mancur Olson asserts that throughout history the sapping of the capacity for change and adaptation brought on by too many vested interests has brought down one empire and major power after another—a pattern into which, he warned in 1982, the United States was sinking.[15]

Third, many foreign policy issues are highly emotionally charged. The "impulses of passion" Madison warned about can be quite intense. The stakes tend to be seen not as just winning or losing, but as tests of morality and patriotism.

One oft-cited example of excessive interest-group influence is the *military-industrial complex*. Consider the warning sounded in 1961:

> The conjunction of an immense military establishment and a large arms industry is new in the American experience. The total influence—economic, political, even spiritual—is felt in every city, every statehouse, every office of the federal government. . . . We must not fail to comprehend its grave implications. Our toil, our resources and livelihood all are involved; so is the very structure of our society.
>
> In the councils of government, we must guard against the acquisition of unwarranted influence, whether sought or unsought, by the *military-industrial complex* [emphasis added]. The potential for the disastrous rise of misplaced power exists and will persist.
>
> We must never let the weight of this combination endanger our liberties or democratic processes.[16]

Sound like Abbie Hoffman or some other 1960s radical? Actually, it is from the farewell address of President (and former general) Dwight D. Eisenhower.

Some of the statistics on the Cold War military-industrial complex really are staggering. By 1970 the Pentagon owned 29 million acres of land (almost the size of New York State) valued at $47.7 billion, and had "true wealth" of $300 to $400 billion, or about six to eight times greater than the annual after-tax profits of all U.S. corporations.[17] During the Reagan defense buildup in the mid-1980s, "the Pentagon was spending an average of $28 million *an hour*."[18] One out of every sixteen American workers, 47 percent of all aeronautical engineers, more than 30 percent of mathematicians, and 25 percent of physicists either worked directly for or drew grants from the defense sector.[19]

One of the best examples of how the military-industrial complex was set up involved the B-1 bomber, a highly capable but expensive new strategic bomber whose production President Carter sought to cancel but could not, largely because of "gerrymandered subcontracting." The main contractor for the B-1 was Rockwell International, based in California. In subcontracting out the various parts of the plane, Rockwell astutely ensured that contracts would go to companies in forty-eight states: the defensive avionics to a firm in New York, the offensive avionics to one in Nebraska, the tires and wheels to Ohio, the tail to Maryland, the wings to Tennessee, and so on. To make sure they knew the score, Rockwell spent $110,000 on a study delineating the B-1's economic benefits on a state-by-state, district-by-district basis. Thus, when Carter did not include funding for the B-1 in his version of the annual defense budget, he was threatening jobs in the states and districts of a majority of the members of both the House and the Senate. Voting records show that even many liberal Democrats who were opposed to high levels of defense spending and in favor of arms control voted against Carter and added enough funding to keep the B-1 alive.[20] When Ronald Reagan became president in 1981, the B-1 production spigot was turned on full force.

Yet there is significant debate over how extensive interest-group influence is. In their review of the literature on the military-industrial complex, professors David Skidmore and Valerie Hudson conclude that the record is mixed: although there are numerous cases of significant influence, especially in weapons development and procurement, the more sweeping claims of dominance are not borne out by the empirical research.[21] Moreover, we have to go back to Madison for a note of caution about efforts to ban or otherwise "remove the causes" of interest groups: "It could never be more truly said than of [this] remedy that it was worse than the disease. Liberty is to faction what air is to fire, an aliment without which it instantly expires. But it could not be a less folly to abolish liberty, which is essential to political life, because it nourishes faction than it would be to wish the annihilation of air, which is essential to animal life, because it imparts to fire its destructive agency."[22]

Others argue along similar lines that, with the exception of issues of the utmost national security, group interests should be granted comparable legitimacy as in domestic policy. Many of the issues pushed by interest groups are actually in the broad national interest as well, such as human rights and protecting the environment, but they are not given appropriate priority within the government and need outside pressure to bring them to the fore.

In the work quoted above, Madison is more positively inclined toward efforts "to control the effects" of factions than those that would "remove their causes." Effects-controlling measures today would include such initiatives as campaign finance reform, reforms of the defense procurement process, tighter oversight of covert action, and broad general efforts to educate and engage the public. Experience, though, teaches that this is a problem for which there is no complete or enduring solution. Reform measures such as those noted above can help correct some of the worst excesses of interest-group influence. But as the American government scholars Theodore Lowi and Benjamin Ginsberg write, "there is no ideal answer. . . . Those who believe that there are simple solutions to the issues of political life would do well to ponder this problem."[23]

The Impact of the News Media

Among the many iconic quotes from Thomas Jefferson is his statement that "were it left to me to decide whether we should have government without newspapers or newspapers without government, I should not hesitate for a moment to prefer the latter."[24] As high-minded as that sounds, the reality is that the role of the press in the American democracy was controversial from the republic's earliest days. "Give to any set of men the command of the press," another of the Founders warned, and you "give them the command of the country." As constitutional scholar Geoffrey Stone recounts, in the political rivalries of those times the *Aurora,* a prominent Philadelphia newspaper, "accused even the revered George Washington of reveling in neomonarchical ceremony, dipping into the public treasury, and incompetent soldiering."[25]

While not exclusive to foreign policy, three questions have long been debated about the impact of the news media: (1) What role should the news media play? (2) How much influence do they actually have? (3) How is the balance to be struck between freedom of the press and national security?

Role of the Media Historically: Cheerleader or Critic?

In 1916, in an effort to ensure support for a just-launched military intervention into Mexico, President Woodrow Wilson stated, "I have asked the several news services to be good enough to assist the Administration in keeping this view of the expedition constantly before both the people of this country and the distressed and sensitive people of Mexico."[26] The president was asking newspapers to be his cheerleaders. The matter-of-fact tone of his statement, made in a public speech rather than leaked from a secret memo, conveys the expectation that although the press could muckrake all it wanted in domestic policy, in foreign policy, especially during wars or other crises, it was to be less free and more friendly.

In the 1930s, though, as Adolf Hitler was rising in Europe and war there began to brew, a number of major newspapers editorialized against President Franklin Roosevelt's efforts to prepare the country for the possibility of joining the war on the side of the Allies. "Americans will be told that this is their fight," a *Chicago Tribune* editorial warned. "That is not true. The frontiers of American democracy are not in Europe, Asia or Africa."[27] Once the United States was directly attacked by Japan at Pearl Harbor on December 7, 1941, the media shifted back to acting as a cheerleader. Stories and pictures of American and Allied heroism, and Nazi and Japanese evil and atrocities, filled the newspapers, and the newsreels played in movie theaters. This was "the good war," and there generally was a basis for positive reporting. Media coverage did get intentionally manipulative, however. A book called *Hollywood Goes to War* tells the story of how "officials of the Office of War Information, the government's propaganda agency, issued a constantly updated manual instructing the studios in how to assist the war effort, sat in on story conferences with Hollywood's top brass, . . . pressured the movie makers [*sic*] to change scripts and even scrap pictures when they found objectionable material, and sometimes wrote dialogue for key speeches."[28]

The news media largely carried over their role as uncritical supporters, even cheerleaders, for official policy from World War II to the Cold War. Many give credit for coining the term "Cold War" to Walter Lippmann, the leading newspaper columnist of the day. As another example, Henry Luce, owner and publisher of *Time* and *Life,* the two leading newsmagazines, personally championed South Vietnamese president Ngo Dinh Diem who came to power in 1955 and ensured favorable, even laudatory coverage for him despite his corrupt and repressive rule. Even the *New York Times* followed suit, as in a 1957 editorial titled "Diem on Democracy," in which the editors hailed Diem for being so true to democracy that "Thomas Jefferson would have no quarrel."[29]

However, as the Vietnam War continued in the 1960s and '70s, the media were the first to bring home to Americans news of how badly the war was going and how wide the credibility gap was between official accounts and the reality on the ground. More than during any other war, the press shifted from its cheerleader role. In one telling encounter, a reporter posed a tough question to an American official at a press conference. The official asked the reporter his name. "Malcolm Browne of the Associated Press," he said. "So you're Browne," the official responded, revealing a knowledge of Browne's critical reporting. "Why don't you get on the team?"[30]

During the 1990–91 Persian Gulf War, the White House and the military sought to manage news coverage with two principal goals: to limit the independence of the media coverage and to shape it to be as positive as possible. War correspondents were confined to "pools" of limited numbers and restricted to designated locations. Film footage released for TV was carefully screened to give the impression of a near-flawless bombing campaign—"smart" bombs going through ventilation shafts, high "target-kill" ratios, very few civilian sites hit. General Norman Schwarzkopf, the commanding officer of the U.S. and allied forces in the Persian Gulf, proved to be not only an excellent military strategist but also a whiz at media briefings and TV communication, which made him a new folk hero.

The media protested that, although certain restrictions were understandable during war, the measures taken during the Gulf War to control the coverage "go far beyond what is required to protect troop safety and mission security."[31] *Newsweek* called it "the propaganda war. . . . In theory, reporters in democratic societies work independent of propaganda. In practice they are treated during war as simply more pieces of military hardware to be deployed."[32] In pursuit of cheerleader coverage, the military limited the amount and accuracy of information provided to the media. It was later learned that the air campaign had not been nearly as successful as portrayed. Information revealed that only 7 percent of the bombs were precision-guided munitions, and although these did hit their targets 90 percent of the time, more than 90 percent of the bombs were conventional ones that missed their targets 75 percent of the time. Data such as these sharply contrasted with "the high-tech, never-miss image that the Pentagon carefully cultivated during the war."[33]

Media coverage during the 2003 Iraq War was even more intensive and instantaneous. The pools were replaced by a new policy of "embedding" journalists within military units, putting them directly in the field and on the march with combat troops. The six hundred "embeds" not only included reporters from the *New York Times* and the *Washington Post*, but also from *People* magazine, MTV, and local news stations;

some were also foreign correspondents. Equipped with the latest in satellite phones and other advanced communications technology, the embeds could air their television broadcasts live and file their stories on the spot and in the moment.

Some critics assessed the reporting as too uncritical and questioned whether journalistic perspective was constrained by the natural empathy that developed between the embedded journalists and the troops with whom they were stationed, who became their immediate community and were their protectors. Those who thought the reporting was too critical accused the press of overdoing the bad news, either to keep filling the "news hole" created by 24/7 coverage or from doubts about the war policy.

The other question was about the quality of press coverage. Even though journalists were on the spot, some critics felt that the coverage was like "looking through a straw," with the viewer able to see only what was within a reporter's defined and delimited field of vision. And although they were outfitted with the latest technologies, the instantaneity of reporting did not allow journalists the time they needed for reflection and insight. They were providing a huge amount of information, but giving much less emphasis—especially in television coverage—to its context, to whether its importance was brief or of more enduring significance, and to how different pieces of the story fitted together.

Howard Kurtz, the noted media critic for the *Washington Post,* summarized the key questions: "What did the media accomplish during the most intensively and instantaneously covered war in history? Did the presence of all those journalists capture the harsh realities of war or simply breed a new generation of Scud studs? Were readers and viewers well served or deluged with confusing information? And what does it portend for future wars?"[34] Such questions played out somewhat during the Afghanistan War and remain pertinent to any future military actions.

Overall, some scholars see the press-government relationship as "symbiotic," that is mutually dependent in mutually beneficial ways.[35] Reporters need the government officials who are their sources, and government officials know that, while not guaranteeing favorable reporting, good relationships with reporters may help when trying to work the "spin" of a story. Today's story is very important to a reporter, but he or she still needs to be able to get tomorrow's. Similarly, a government official angered by a story one day is constrained by tomorrow's effort to get the right spin.

Others see the relationship as having becoming less symbiotic and more one of "interdependent mutual exploitation."[36] Given that scandals, leaks, infighting, and policy failures are the news that sells—as has always been the case but which seems to be even truer today—the media have even greater incentive to play the critic role. For their part, given how campaigns never seem to end, political leaders have even greater incentive to try to get some cheerleading out there. Thus, while still interdependent, the media and the government have less common ground and can get locked into ever more concerted efforts to manipulate each other.

Cheerleader or critic? Which role have the media played? And which role should they play? These long have been and continue to be crucial questions. We take them up again in Chapter 9, including a discussion of the role of new media, such as blogs, and soft news.

Modes of Influence

Three main distinctions are made as to the modes of influence the media have on foreign policy politics: agenda setting, shaping public opinion, and direct effects on policymakers.

AGENDA SETTING   "The mass media may not be successful in telling people what to think," one classic study put it, "but the media are stunningly successful in telling their audience what to think about."[37] Television in particular has a major agenda-setting impact. Studies by the media scholar Shanto Iyengar and others show that when people are asked to identify the most significant problem facing the nation, they name something that has been on television news recently. Mass starvation was plaguing many parts of Africa in the mid-1980s, but the outside world, the United States included, was paying little attention. Yet once NBC News went to Ethiopia and broadcast footage of ravaged children and emaciated adults to millions of television viewers back in the United States, suddenly the Ethiopian famine was on the foreign policy agenda.

Of course, the equally tragic famines elsewhere in Africa, where the TV cameras did not go, did not make it onto the U.S. national agenda. Such discrepancies raise a troubling question for policy makers: If a tree falls in the woods and television doesn't cover it, did it really fall? The media play a crucial role in determining which issues receive attention and which do not. Some issues do force their way onto the agenda, and the media are largely reactive and mirroring. But other issues would get much less policy consideration if it were not for major media coverage. Conversely, there are foreign policy issues that despite their importance don't get media coverage and thus don't get on the agenda—whole "forests" may fall down with no television cameras in sight.

Newspapers also have agenda-setting impact through investigative reporting or "breaking" major news. This often comes from major papers like the *New York Times*, but not always. Back in 1992 it was *Newsday*, a lesser-known New York paper, which published the first reports and shocking photos of "ethnic cleansing" in Bosnia. Today major revelations may come from independent journalists in far-off places equipped with their own cutting-edge technology, individual activists posting on YouTube, bloggers with their own networks of sources. Still, though, it is mostly newspapers that provide steady and solid reporting, sticking with an issue and making sure that it gets on the agenda and doesn't go away.

Conscious of the media's agenda-setting power, groups have become adept at organizing protests, symbolic actions, celebrity appearances and other events orchestrated to attract media attention. With these "media events" the merits of an issue often matter less than its drama in getting it on the agenda.

SHAPING PUBLIC OPINION   In terms of substantive content, the main impact of the media on public opinion comes from what researchers call "framing" and "priming" effects.[38] The stakes involved in a particular foreign policy issue are not necessarily self-evident or part of a strictly objective reality. How an issue is presented ("framed") affects the substantive judgments people make—and the media play a key role in this framing.[39] Media coverage also prepares ("primes") the public to view a particular event or political actor a certain way, and influences the criteria by which the public judges success and failure. These framing and priming effects occur both directly through the general public's exposure to the media and indirectly through "opinion leaders"—i.e., political, business, community, educational, celebrity, and other leaders to whom the public often looks for cues.

To the extent that the media's substantive impact goes beyond these framing and priming effects, it tends to influence two kinds of foreign policy issues. One set comprises issues for which the public has little prior information and few sources other than the media. The other set includes those issues that have strong symbolic significance and are heavily emotionally charged, such as the 1979–81 Iranian hostage crisis and the 2001 terrorist attacks. *ABC News Nightline* started out as nightly coverage of just the hostage crisis and went on to be one of the top-rated news shows for the next twenty-five years. Every show would be introduced as "Day 1 of the Hostage Crisis," "Day 2 . . . ," "Day 50 . . . ," "Day 100 . . . ," all the way through "Day 444," when on January 20, 1981, the last hostages were released. The intense media coverage of the Iranian hostage crisis kept it front-and-center on the agenda, which, given the nature of the issue, also influenced the substance of public opinion. Even this didn't compare to the real-time and saturation coverage of the September 11, 2001, terrorist attacks. Virtually all Americans were glued to their television sets for days, arguably as much for the sense of community as for information.

Debate also continues over media bias. One aspect is over media objectivity. The Pew Research Center reports that the number of Americans who believe that news organizations are "politically biased in their reporting" increased from 45 percent in 1985 to 60 percent in 2005 and 77 percent by 2011.[40] The usual argument has been that this is a liberal bias. Although many still hold to this view, citing the *New York Times* and the major networks, among other media, others see a conservative bias in Fox News, newspapers owned by Rupert Murdoch, talk radio shows such as *The Rush Limbaugh Show*, and certain other media.[41] On the other side of the spectrum, critics such as Noam Chomsky see the media as part of the governing elite, no less so than politicians of both liberal and conservative stripe, and believe that while the media may be critical on particular issues they largely seek to create and maintain "manufactured consent" on the status quo.[42]

Wherever one comes down on the subject of media bias, the question is how much does this really matter? A poll by the Annenberg Public Policy Center showed 43 percent of respondents thought it was "a good thing if some news organizations have a decidedly political point of view in their coverage of the news."[43] One study found the effects of Fox News on voting patterns to be statistically insignificant. The public knows bias for what it is, the argument was made, and filters it out more than being shaped by it. Other studies have shown much greater impact, going back to the effects of framing, priming and agenda setting.

DIRECT INFLUENCE ON POLICYMAKERS   A third type of media influence is that exerted directly on policy makers. Although close and constant news coverage has many benefits, it does bring intense "real-time" pressure on policy makers. An American soldier is taken prisoner, and his face flashes on the television screen time and again, all day, all night. A terrorist incident occurs, and the video plays over and over. Often policy makers must respond with little prior notice, and in some cases may first hear about a major event on CNN rather than through official government sources. They must also respond within the immediacy of the twenty-four-hour news cycle. That makes for a very different and more difficult dynamic in key foreign policy choices than existed in the past.

Even in noncrisis situations, "What will the press think?" is regularly asked in executive-branch foreign policy meetings. Editorials and op-ed articles have a remarkable influence. Highly critical opinion pieces in major papers such as the *New York Times* and the *Washington Post*, and now on high-traffic blogs, have been known to prompt hastily called State Department meetings or to make officials rearrange their schedules in order to draft a response. Read the minutes of major foreign policy meetings, and you'll see significant attention paid to media-related issues. Check out staff rosters in the State and Defense Departments, and you'll see numerous media advisers. Look at the curricula taught at the Foreign Service Institute and the National Defense University, and you'll see courses on the role of the media. Given constantly advancing technology, these emphases will only grow with time. We come back to this dynamic in Chapter 9.

Freedom of the Press vs. National Security

How to strike a balance between freedom of the press and national security has been a recurring issue in American politics. The First Amendment guarantees freedom of the press. Yet situations can arise when the nation's security would be endangered if certain information became public. This national security rationale can be, and has been, very real; it also can be, and has been, abused.

In times of war "the press is called on to rally patriotic fervor," as John Byrne Cooke writes in his book tracing the role of the press during wartime over the course of American history (Reading 3.1).

> It is expected to be the voice of the government and the voice of the people—the voice of the country at war. If instead it challenges the government, if it questions the rationale for war, it provokes the government's impulse, already strong in times of crisis, to repress liberties in the name of security.

And, as Cooke adds, "too often the people acquiesce." He continues:

> This is the paradox that threatens the freedoms we take for granted in peacetime. In the shock of war we feel that our way of life is threatened; in response we are willing to abandon (temporarily, we think) the principles on which that way of life is founded, in the hope of regaining our security.[44]

Consider the 1961 Bay of Pigs case. The *New York Times* had uncovered information on the secret invasion of Cuba being planned by the Kennedy administration (the Bay of Pigs, or, in Spanish, *Bahia de Cochinos*, was the spot on the Cuban coast where the invading forces were to land). Under pressure from the White House, the *Times* refrained from publishing much of it. Some other papers were less restrained, but most of what appeared in the media about the plan was "designed not to alert the American public to the potentially disastrous course of its own government, but to advance the universally accepted propaganda line that Cuba under Castro was courting disaster."[45] The invasion went ahead, and it failed catastrophically—leaving many to question whether national security would have been better served had the story been more fully fleshed out and the plan unmasked.

Still, a few weeks after the Bay of Pigs, and despite his other acknowledgements of responsibility, President Kennedy delivered a very strong speech to the American Newspaper Publishers Association broadly construing the national security rationale as a constraint on freedom of the press (see "At the Source," p. 74). The Bay of Pigs may have failed, Kennedy argued, but the Cold War context of no declared war but "our way of life under attack" still held. Our enemies "have openly boasted of acquiring through our newspapers information they would otherwise hire agents to acquire." So those in the media must not only ask "Is it news?" but also "Is it in the interest of national security?"

The following year, during the Cuban missile crisis, when the United States and the Soviet Union went to the brink of nuclear war, the press again restrained some of its reporting. An ABC News correspondent even served as a secret intermediary for some tense negotiations between President Kennedy and the Soviet leader, Nikita Khrushchev. This time the outcome was more positive: the crisis was resolved, and many concluded

AT THE SOURCE

"IS IT NEWS?" OR "IS IT IN THE INTEREST OF NATIONAL SECURITY?"

Excerpts from a Speech by President John F. Kennedy

❝I do ask every publisher, every editor, and every newsman in the nation to reexamine his own standards, and to recognize the nature of our country's peril. In time of war, the Government and the press have customarily joined in an effort, based largely on self-discipline, to prevent unauthorized disclosure to the enemy. In times of clear and present danger, the courts have held that even the privileged rights of the First Amendment must yield to the public's need for national security."

Today no war has been declared—and however fierce the struggle may be, it may never be declared in the traditional fashion. Our way of life is under attack. . . .

If the press is awaiting a declaration of war before it imposes the self-discipline of combat conditions, then I can only say that no war has ever imposed a greater threat to our security. If you are awaiting a finding of 'clear and present danger,' then I can only say that the danger has never been more clear and its presence has never been more imminent. . . .

It requires a change in outlook, a change in tactics, a change in mission by the Government, by the people, by every businessman and labor leader, and by every newspaper. For we are opposed around the world by a monolithic and ruthless conspiracy that relies primarily on covert means for expanding its sphere of influence—on infiltration instead of invasion, on subversion instead of elections, on intimidation instead of free choice, on guerrillas by night instead of armies by day. . . .

The facts of the matter are that this nation's foes have openly boasted of acquiring through our newspapers information they would otherwise hire agents to acquire through theft, bribery or espionage; that details of this nation's covert preparations to counter the enemy's covert operations have been available to every newspaper reader, friend and foe alike; that the size, the strength, the location, and the nature of our forces and weapons, and our plans and strategy for their use, have all been pinpointed in the press and other news media to a degree sufficient enough to satisfy any foreign power. . . .

The newspapers which printed these stories were loyal, patriotic, responsible and well-meaning. Had we been engaged in open warfare, they undoubtedly would not have published such items. But in the absence of open warfare, they recognized only the tests of journalism and not the tests of national security. And my question tonight is whether additional tests should not now be adopted. . . .

I am asking the members of the newspaper profession and the industry in this country to reexamine their own responsibilities—to consider the degree and nature of the present danger—and to heed the duty of self-restraint which that danger imposes upon all of us.

Every newspaper now asks itself with respect to every story: 'Is it news?' All I suggest is that you add the question: 'Is it in the interest of national security?' ❞

Source: John F. Kennedy, speech to the American Newspaper Publishers Association, April 27, 1961, from *Public Papers of the Presidents, John F. Kennedy, 1961* (Washington, D.C.: U.S. Government Printing Office, 1962), 334–38.

that the restraint on full freedom of the press was justified. Historian Michael Beschloss speculates about how differently the Cuban missile crisis might have turned out if not for the "cocoon of time and privacy" that media restraint helped provide.[46] What if the television networks had broken the story on the evening news, sparking congressional and public outcry and increasing pressure on President Kennedy to take immediate but precipitous and potentially escalating action, such as an air strike? Could ExCom (Kennedy's decision-making group) have deliberated over so many days without leaks? Kennedy would not have been able to engage the diplomacy required to balance toughness with compromise if every move had been independently and immediately reported, setting off debates on radio and television talk shows.

On the other hand, there was the Vietnam War "get on the team" view noted earlier. In mid-1967, at a point when the war was going very badly, Defense Secretary Robert McNamara set up a comprehensive internal review of U.S. policy. By the end of the Johnson administration, the forty-seven-volume *History of the United States Decision-Making Process on Vietnam Policy,* which came to be called the "Pentagon Papers," had been completed. It was given highly classified status, to be kept secret and reserved for high-level government use only. But in March 1971, Daniel Ellsberg, one of the researchers and authors of the Pentagon Papers who now was a critic and opponent of the war, leaked a copy to a *New York Times* reporter. On June 13, 1971, the *Times* began publishing excerpts. The Nixon administration immediately sued to stop publication, claiming potential damage to national security. The administration also had a political agenda, fearing that the already eroding public support for the war would crumble even more. On June 30, the Supreme Court ruled 6 to 3 against the Nixon administration. The Court did not totally disregard the national security justification but ruled that the standard had not been met in this case, and that First Amendment freedom of the press rights took precedence.[47] The *Times* continued its stories on the Pentagon Papers, as did other newspapers.*

In recent years freedom of the press and national security issues have been especially controversial in the struggle against terrorism, as we will see in Chapter 10.

Public Opinion: What Is It? What Is Its Impact?

With respect to public opinion and foreign policy, our concern is with two principal questions: (1) What is the nature of public opinion? (2) How much influence does it have?

Ignorant or Sensible? The Nature of Public Opinion about Foreign Policy

To read some of the commentaries on American public opinion and foreign policy, one would think that Americans believe much more in government for the people than in government by and of the people (Reading 3.2). Walter Lippmann, the leading U.S. foreign-affairs journalist of the first half of the twentieth century, disparaged public opinion as "destructively wrong at critical junctures . . . a dangerous master of decision when the stakes are life and death."[48] The traditional view taken by leading scholars was not any more positive. "The rational requirements of good foreign policy," wrote the eminent realist Hans Morgenthau, "cannot from the outset count upon the support of a public whose preferences are emotional rather than rational."[49] George Kennan, author of the "Mr. X" telegram and the father of containment, was rather more graphic in his critique:

> But I sometimes wonder whether in this respect a democracy is not uncomfortably similar to one of those prehistoric monsters with a body as long as this room and a brain the size of a pin: he lies there in his comfortable primeval mud and pays little attention to his environment; he is slow to wrath—in fact, you practically have to whack his tail off to make him aware that his interests are being disturbed; but, once he grasps this, he lays about him with such blind determination that he not only destroys his adversary but largely wrecks his native habitat.[50]

---

*President Nixon set up the special White House unit known as the "plumbers" to "plug" any further leaks in reaction to the Pentagon Papers leak. Among the operations carried out by the "plumbers" were an illegal break-in to the offices of Daniel Ellsberg's psychiatrist, seeking information with which to discredit Ellsberg, and the 1972 June break-in at the headquarters of the Democratic National Committee in the Watergate building. These events and actions, and others uncovered later, ultimately led to an impeachment investigation against Nixon and his resignation as president on August 9, 1974.

Gabriel Almond, in *The American People and Foreign Policy,* a 1950 study long considered a classic in the field, stressed the "inattentiveness" of the vast majority of the public to foreign policy, which he attributed to the lack of "intellectual structure and factual content."[51] Others took this opinion even further, positing a historical pattern of reflexively alternating "moods" of introversion and extroversion, a sort of societal biorhythm by which every two decades or so the public shifted between internationalism and isolationism.[52]

These criticisms are built around a basic distinction between the "mass public," susceptible to all of the above and more, and the better-informed, more thoughtful, and more sophisticated "elites." The general public consistently has shown very little knowledge about foreign affairs. The following survey results illustrate general public ignorance:

- In 1964, only 58 percent of the public knew that the United States was a member of NATO, and 38 percent thought the Soviet Union was.
- In 1993, only four months after President Clinton, Israeli prime minister Yitzhak Rabin, and Palestine Liberation Organization leader Yasser Arafat announced an Arab-Israeli peace deal in a dramatic ceremony at the White House, 56 percent of Americans could not identify the group that Arafat headed.
- In 2006, three years into the Iraq War, only 37 percent of young adults could locate Iraq on a map.[53]

Within the mass public there is some variation based on levels of education and socioeconomic status. The pattern is similar to other policy areas, with higher levels of education and income correlating with greater attention to and knowledge of foreign affairs. On that basis some scholars differentiate an "attentive public" which is more knowledgeable and interested than the general public but less so than elites, and still represents a small chunk of the overall public.

Critics also focus on the mass public's overreactive tendencies. Take the "rally 'round the flag" pattern in times of crisis. On the one hand, this reaction can be quite positive in helping build consensus and national solidarity when the nation faces a serious threat. It also can be politically helpful to presidents whose popularity is boosted as part of the rallying effect. But often it becomes blind "followership," and in extremes can pose dangers to democracy by adding to the forces equating dissent with disloyalty.

Notwithstanding the evidence of low levels of knowledge and attentiveness, an alternative view sees even the mass public as much more sensible about foreign policy than it gets credit for. Elmo Roper, who founded a trailblazing public-opinion polling firm, observed in 1942 that "during my eight years of asking the common man questions about what he thinks and what he wants . . . I have often been surprised and elated to discover that, despite his lack of information, the common man's native intelligence generally brings him to a sound conclusion."[54]

Those who share the "sensible public" view stress two key points. One is that rather than being wildly and whimsically fluctuating, public opinion has been quite stable over time. Take, for example, basic attitudes toward isolationism ("stay out of world affairs") versus internationalism ("play an active role"). For the entire period from the end of World War II to the end of the Cold War (1945–90), as illustrated in Figure 3.1, despite some ups and downs the overall pro-internationalism pattern held. The same figure shows internationalism decreasing somewhat but still staying robust in the 1990s, then surging upward in the wake of 9/11 (71 percent support). Even when support for the Iraq War dropped dramatically (hovering around 30 percent), the public did not generalize this to an overall retreat from international affairs (still 69 percent in 2006). By the end of the George W. Bush administration, the combination of the strain of Iraq and other foreign policy problems, along with the economic and financial crisis, did bring the pro- and anti-internationalism figures down to 63 percent and up to 36 percent, respectively. The pro-internationalism margin increased in 2010, 67/31, but went back down again in 2012 to 61/38. On the one hand, the 38 percent saying "stay out of world affairs" was the highest number since before World War II, and the +23 percent pro-internationalism differential was the smallest since the early 1980s. On the other hand, compared to other questions on which Americans are polled, this was a substantial margin. We should pay close attention to where these numbers go in the next few years.[55]

Even with these findings, policy makers often "misread" the public, seeing it as more isolationist than it really is. A 1990s study by the Program on International Policy Attitudes (PIPA) found that 74 percent of policy makers believed that the public favored "disengagement," only 32 percent believed that the public wanted the United States to be an international leader, and only 15 percent believed that the public could be convinced to support engagement.[56] While quite out of sync with the actual opinion data, in politics perceptions often matter more than "facts." So public opinion constrains internationalist policies more than the polling data might lead one to believe it would.

On issues such as foreign aid the dynamic is especially acute. Foreign aid always has been a tough sell. Even during the Cold War support was not as high as in many other areas of foreign policy. With the end of the Cold War stripping away the main rationale and giving way to a budget-cutting fiscal climate, foreign aid became even less popular. Yet some of this was due to flawed information. A 1995 poll found 75 percent of respondents believed that too much was spent on foreign aid, with only 4 percent believing too little was spent. But whereas most people thought foreign aid accounted for 15 percent of the federal budget, in reality it is less than 1 percent. Such results inspired some hope that more accurate information might increase support. When the question was phrased differently—"Now imagine that the U.S. spends 1 percent of the Federal budget on foreign aid. Would you feel this is too little, too much or about right?"—46 percent of respondents were content that it was about right. It is not unusual, however, to agree with a hypothetical but have a very different view when confronted with actual budget amounts, especially in

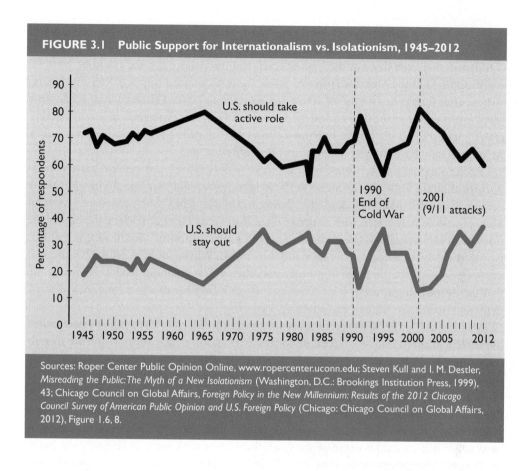

FIGURE 3.1 Public Support for Internationalism vs. Isolationism, 1945–2012

Sources: Roper Center Public Opinion Online, www.ropercenter.uconn.edu; Steven Kull and I. M. Destler, *Misreading the Public: The Myth of a New Isolationism* (Washington, D.C.: Brookings Institution Press, 1999), 43; Chicago Council on Global Affairs, *Foreign Policy in the New Millennium: Results of the 2012 Chicago Council Survey of American Public Opinion and U.S. Foreign Policy* (Chicago: Chicago Council on Global Affairs, 2012), Figure 1.6, 8.

times of fiscal constraints. Even beyond that, foreign aid still seems too "foreign" to many Americans, including some who otherwise consider themselves internationalists. Such findings limit but do not negate the general internationalism pattern.

A second point made by those who view public opinion positively is that to the extent that public views on foreign policy have changed over time, this has been less a matter of moodiness than a rational process. A study of the fifty-year period 1935–85 concluded that "virtually all the rapid shifts [in public opinion] . . . were related to political and economic circumstances or to significant events which sensible citizens would take into account. In particular, most abrupt foreign policy changes took place in connection with wars, confrontations or crises in which major policy changes in the actions of the United States or other nations quite naturally affect preference about what policies to pursue."[57] This is termed an "event-driven" process; that is to say, when the threats facing the United States or other aspects of the international situation have changed, in an altogether rational way public opinion has, too.

What, for example, was so feckless about the public turning against the Vietnam War when many people believed, and former defense secretary Robert McNamara's memoirs confirmed, that even those at the highest levels did not believe the war could be won? "It is difficult to fault the American people," wrote the army major Andrew F. Krepinevich, Jr., "when, after that long a period of active engagement, the Joint Chiefs of Staff could only offer more of the same for an indefinite period with no assurance of eventual success."[58] Indeed, had the public remained supportive of such an ill-conceived war effort, we might really have wondered about its rationality.

Public support for the use of military force is illustrative. As a general pattern, support for military force was strongest at the height of the Cold War and declined over the course of the Vietnam War and the shattering of the Cold War consensus. As John Mueller first demonstrated with a focus on the Korean and Vietnam Wars, the higher the number of U.S. casualties, the lower the levels of public support.[59] To the extent that this is true, it exhibits the logic and rationality just noted. Why would the public continue to support a policy that is incurring high casualties unless national leaders demonstrate that the overarching strategy is working and worth it (neither of which was convincingly demonstrated in the Korean and Vietnam Wars)?

Starting in the 1980s, the pattern became more mixed, embodying what I have called the "pretty prudent public." According to this assessment, public support for use of military force varies based on perceptions of what the principal policy objective was, with three general trends.[60] Public support tends to be greatest when the principal policy objective is to coerce *foreign policy restraint* of an aggressor threatening the United States, its citizens, or its interests; lowest when the principal objective is to engineer *internal political change* in another country's government; and in between for *humanitarian interventions*. While casualties decrease support, they do so with some differentiation based on the principal policy objectives. The public is most willing to sustain support, even with relatively high numbers of casualties, when force is being used for foreign policy restraint; casualties present a hindrance to public support in cases of humanitarian intervention, and an even greater hindrance in cases of internal political change.

Not only does the case evidence corroborate this assessment, but the pattern has an underlying logic based on conceptions of legitimacy and calculations of efficacy. On the first point, using force to restrain aggression has a much stronger normative claim than does trying to remake governments. Humanitarian intervention falls in between, with some situations so dire that legitimacy claims can be made even if the intervention is within a state and lacks the consent of that state's government. Regarding prospects for effectiveness, foreign policy restraint objectives have the advantage of being more readily translatable into an operational military plan. Internal political change objectives, however, tend to require strategies that are more political in nature and less suitable to an operational military plan. Humanitarian interventions fall in between on this point as well: they usually have discrete missions and objectives but are difficult to keep from crossing over into state-building.

Other factors may also come into play in any particular case. Multilateral support and burden sharing is one example; the public often wants to know that other countries are bearing some of the risks and costs. The reactions of congressional leaders, newspaper editorialists, television pundits, and other elites are also a factor. Fundamentally, the American public is hardly eager to use military force, but is not invariably opposed to it. People still lack a significant amount of information, and may not even be able to find the relevant places on a map, but they manage to show "good judgment in the use of resources" and "caution or circumspection as to danger and risk"—exactly how the dictionary defines *prudence.*

The Influence of Public Opinion on Foreign Policy

The political scientist Bruce Russett characterizes the basic public opinion–foreign policy dynamic as an interactive one. Leaders do not control the public; they cannot "persuade the populace to support whatever the leaders wish to do." Nor is the public in control, having so much impact that foreign policy basically "obeys [its] dictates." Instead, "each influences the other."[61]

This is not to say the interactive effects are symmetrical. Elites clearly have more influence on public opinion than the reverse. Research by Lawrence Jacobs and Benjamin Page, for example, finds that internationally oriented business leaders and foreign policy experts have the greatest influence both directly on policy makers and in shaping public views.[62] This is consistent with our earlier analysis of interest groups.

We can identify six principal ways that general public opinion exerts its influence:

Political Culture and Ideology   Political culture, the core values embodied in a nation's political system and the dominant self-concept to which its people hold, is an often underestimated part of politics and policy.[63] Yet it is a key part of basic judgments of "policy legitimacy" and helps define the range of options that have a real chance of gaining public support, let alone the one that gets chosen as policy.[64] In U.S. foreign policy, "American exceptionalism"—the belief that the United States has a uniqueness and special virtue that ground its foreign policy in Principles much more than the foreign policies of other countries—has been the defining aspect of the political culture. This idea can be traced all the way back to the colonial period and Massachusetts Bay Colony governor John Winthrop's "city on a Hille, the eies of all peoples upon us." While manifesting itself in various ways throughout U.S. history (see Chapter 4), and raising real questions about whether actual policy has lived up to the claims, the political potency of American exceptionalism has endured to this day. Indeed, while Americans may not think of themselves as ideological, American exceptionalism has had many of the functional characteristics of an ideology.

ANTICIPATORY PARAMETER SETTING   Public opinion imposes limits on the range of the president's policy options via presidential advisers' anticipatory assessments of which options have chance of being made to "fly" with the public and which are "nonstarters." Some of these limits go back to political culture and American exceptionalism, while some are more issue-specific. A good example of the latter is U.S. policy toward Saddam Hussein in the 1980s, before he became Public Enemy No. 1 during the Persian Gulf War. During Saddam's war with Iran, which lasted from 1980 to 1988, the Reagan administration gave Iraq extensive support on the grounds that "the enemy of my enemy is my friend." Once the Iran-Iraq War was over, and Saddam attacked the Iraqi Kurds with chemical weapons and showed other signs of aggression in the region, some in the State Department began to question whether the United States should continue aiding Iraq. But with the Iran-contra affair still in the political air, the Reagan administration flatly ruled out any shift from the pro-Saddam policy on the grounds that it risked being seen by the public as "soft on Iran." Consequently, when the internal State Department paper proposing such a shift in policy was leaked to the press, Secretary of State George Shultz "called a meeting in his office, angrily demanding to know who was responsible for the paper. . . . [The paper] was dismissed less by any analytic refutation of its strategic logic than on political grounds. . . . On the cover page, in big letters, [Shultz] had written 'NO.' "[65]

CENTRIPETAL PULL   Public opinion can also exert a centripetal pull toward the center on presidents who need to build supportive coalitions. As Miroslav Nincic has shown, this centering pull has worked on presidents whose tendencies were too far to the left and on those too far to the right to gain sufficient political support. With President Jimmy Carter, whose foreign policy reputation generally raised doubts as to whether he was "tough" enough, the public sought to balance this concern by expressing low levels of approval for Carter's Soviet policy when it was in its conciliatory phases (1977–78, most of 1979), and higher levels of support when Carter got tough (mid-1978, 1979–80). President Ronald Reagan's foreign policy reputation, in contrast, was plenty tough but raised concerns among a substantial segment of the public as to whether it was reckless and risked war. Thus, public approval of Reagan's Soviet policy fell when it was most strident and confrontational (1981–83), and then increased in late 1985 when the administration started to become more genuinely open to cooperation, peaking at 65 percent following Reagan's first summit with the Soviet leader Mikhail Gorbachev in November 1985.[66]

IMPACT ON CONGRESS   The fourth influence of public opinion is its impact on Congress. Congress is very sensitive (arguably too sensitive) to public opinion on foreign policy. It responds both to polls on specific issues and to more general assessments of whether the public really cares about foreign policy at all. The late senator Hubert H. Humphrey, a leading figure from the late 1940s to his death in 1978, excoriated many of his colleagues for being "POPPs," or what he called "public opinion poll politicians," on foreign policy.[67]

EFFECT ON DIPLOMATIC NEGOTIATIONS   Public opinion does not come into play only after a treaty or other diplomatic agreement is reached; it also can affect the actual diplomatic negotiations themselves. As in Robert Putnam's two-level games formulation, U.S. diplomats need to know, while still at the table, what terms of agreement are politically viable back home.[68] This kind of influence is not necessarily a bad thing. It can be, to the extent that it ties the negotiators' hands in ways that are politically popular but unsound in policy terms. But public opinion can also strengthen negotiators' hands as part of a "good cop–bad cop" dynamic. "I'd be more than willing to consider your proposal," a U.S. negotiator might say to his Japanese or Russian counterpart, "but the American public would never accept it."

Foreign Policy and Presidential Elections

The sixth avenue of public influence on foreign policy is through elections. Voting analysts identify three key factors in attributing significant electoral impact to a foreign policy issue: the issue must be demonstrated to be highly salient through survey questions; there must be significant differences between the positions of the Republican and Democratic candidates; and the public's awareness of these differences must be evident.[69] Three Cold War–era presidential elections fit these criteria. In 1952, with the Korean War mired in stalemate, the public had much more confidence in the Republican candidate, General Dwight D. Eisenhower, the triumphant World War II commander of U.S. forces in Europe, than in the Democratic candidate, Illinois governor Adlai Stevenson. In 1972, foreign policy was crucial in the Democratic presidential nomination process: Senator George McGovern (D-South Dakota) won the nomination largely on the basis of being the candidate most strongly opposed to the Vietnam War. But McGovern lost to President Richard Nixon in the general election. Although the Vietnam War was highly unpopular, McGovern was seen as too "dovish," whereas Nixon countered public perception of his responsibility for the war with announcements in the month before the election that "peace [was] at hand." In the 1980 election, data show that while only 38.3 percent of the public could articulate the differences between Jimmy Carter and Ronald Reagan on inflation and unemployment, 63.5 percent could do so on defense spending and 58.8 percent on relations with the Soviet Union. Moreover, the taking of American hostages in Iran was "a powerful symbol of American weakness and humiliation," for many Americans and, whether fairly or unfairly, the dominant view was "that an inability to bring the hostages home reflected directly on [Carter's] competence."[70]

The 1992 victory of Bill Clinton, who had little foreign policy experience, over George H.W. Bush, who had to his credit the peaceful ending of the Cold War and victory in the

Persian Gulf War, showed how little electoral sway foreign policy could have when the economy was especially pressing. The 2004 election between George W. Bush and John Kerry was very close, and while other factors came into play, the "rally 'round the flag" effect of 9/11 and perceptions of Bush being tougher on terrorism did contribute to Bush's margin. In the 2008 Democratic primary, Barack Obama's early opposition to the Iraq War helped him defeat Hillary Rodham Clinton, who had voted for the war as a senator. While in 2008 Obama was viewed less favorably on foreign policy than his Republican opponent John McCain, in 2012 he polled better than Mitt Romney. Foreign policy was not nearly as major a factor in that election as the economy, but this time it added to rather than detracted from Obama's victory margin.

Congressional elections are more rarely influenced by foreign policy. Even in 1970, when the Vietnam War was highly unpopular, antiwar candidates for the House and Senate did not fare that well. An exception was in 2006, when opposition to the Iraq War was a major factor in the Democrats regaining majorities in both the House and the Senate. Democrats won 31 seats in the House and took back the majority there. In the Senate they turned a 45–55 minority position into a 51–49 majority. While other factors played a role, polls showed that an anti–Iraq War stance was a major influence on voters.

Summary

This chapter has focused on the role of key societal actors—interest groups, media, and public opinion—in foreign policy politics. Table 3.2 summarizes the basic framework Chapters 2 and 3 have laid out for foreign policy politics and the *process* by which the choices of foreign policy strategy are made. The president and Congress interact as the separate institutions sharing powers that the Constitution established, forging their own

TABLE 3.2 Foreign Policy Politics and the Process of Choice	
President and Congress	Pennsylvania Avenue diplomacy
Executive-branch politics	Advisory process, decision making
Interest groups	Lobbying, other strategies of influence
News media	Cheerleader, critic
Public opinion	Influences on, influences of

"Pennsylvania Avenue diplomacy". The executive branch demonstrates its own internal politics in its advisory process and decision making. Interest groups of many types lobby and pursue other strategies of influence. The news media, traditional and new, play both cheerleader and critic roles through numerous modes of influence. Public opinion both influences and is influenced by the president and other political leaders. Ensuing chapters apply this framework, and Chapter 9 provides an update based on recent trends in foreign policy politics.

Notes

[1] Stephen D. Krasner, "United States Commercial and Monetary Policy: Unraveling the Paradox of External Strength and Internal Weakness," in Peter J. Katzenstein, ed., *Between Power and Plenty: Foreign Economic Policies of Advanced Industrial States* (Madison: University of Wisconsin Press, 1977), 51–87.

[2] Larry Berman and Bruce Murphy, *Approaching Democracy* (Englewood Cliffs, N.J.: Prentice-Hall, 1996), 408.

[3] Quoted in Robert A. Pastor, *Congress and the Politics of Foreign Economic Policy, 1929–1976* (Berkeley: University of California Press, 1980), 79.

[4] Steve Coll, *Private Empire: ExxonMobil and American Power* (New York: Penguin Press), 19.

[5] Figures for 1920 from U.S. Census Bureau, as reported in the *Washington Post*, May 25, 1998, A1; 2010 figures are from U.S. Department of Homeland Security, Office of Immigration Statistics, *Annual Flow Report: U.S. Legal Permanent Residents 2010.*

[6] Tony Smith, *Foreign Attachments: The Power of Ethnic Groups in the Making of American Foreign Policy* (Cambridge, Mass.: Harvard University Press, 2000), 2.

[7] John J. Mearsheimer and Stephen M. Walt, *The Israel Lobby and U.S. Foreign Policy* (New York: Farrar, Straus and Giroux, 2007).

[8] Tom Gjelten, *Bacardi and the Long Fight for Cuba: The Biography of a Cause* (New York: Viking, 2008), 277–78.

[9] Joshua W. Busby, *Moral Movements and Foreign Policy* (Cambridge: Cambridge University Press, 2010).

[10] Earl H. Fry, *The Expanding Role of State and Local Governments in U.S. Foreign Policy* (New York: Council on Foreign Relations Press, 1998); also Chadwick Alger, "The World Relations of Cities: Closing the Gap between Social Science Paradigms and Everyday Human Experience," *International Studies Quarterly* 34.4 (1990): 493–518; and Michael H. Shuman, "Dateline Main Street: Local Foreign Policies," *Foreign Policy* 65 (1986/87): 154–74.

[11] Pat Choate, *Agents of Influence: How Japan's Lobbyists in the United States Manipulate America's Political and Economic System* (New York: Knopf, 1990), xiv.

[12] Jessica Mathews, "Power Shift," *Foreign Affairs* 76.1 (January–February 1997): 63.

[13] Alexander Cooley and James Ron, "The NGO Scramble: Organizational Insecurity and the Political Economy of Transnational Action," *International Security* 27 (Summer 2002): 5–39.

[14] Theodore J. Lowi, *The End of Liberalism: Ideology, Policy, and the Crisis in Public Authority* (New York: Norton, 1969).

[15] Mancur Olson, *The Rise and Decline of Nations: Economic Growth, Stagflation, and Social Rigidities* (New Haven: Yale University Press, 1982).

[16] Dwight D. Eisenhower, "Farewell Address," January 1961, *Public Papers of the Presidents of the United States, Dwight D. Eisenhower* (Washington, D.C.: U.S. Government Printing Office, 1962), 8: 1035–41.

[17] Sidney Lens, *The Military-Industrial Complex* (Philadelphia: Pilgrim, 1970), 12.

[18]Charles W. Kegley, Jr., and Eugene R. Wittkopf, *American Foreign Policy: Pattern and Process,* 5th ed. (New York: St. Martin's, 1996), 302.

[19]Kegley and Wittkopf, *American Foreign Policy.*

[20]"The B-1: When Pentagon, Politicians Join Hands," *U.S. News and World Report,* July 1, 1983, 34. See also Nick Kotz, *Wild Blue Yonder: Money, Politics and the B-1 Bomber* (New York: Pantheon, 1988).

[21]David Skidmore and Valerie M. Hudson, eds., *The Limits of State Authority: Societal Groups and Foreign Policy Formation* (Boulder, Colo.: Westview, 1992), 36–38. See also Eugene Gholz, "The Curtiss-Wright Corporation and Cold War–Era Defense Procurement: A Challenge to Military-Industrial Complex Theory," *Journal of Cold War Studies* 2 (Winter 2000), 35–75.

[22]James Madison, *Federalist 10,* in *The Federalist Papers,* Clinton Rossiter, ed. (New York: New American Library, 1961), 78.

[23]Theodore J. Lowi and Benjamin Ginsberg, *American Government: Freedom and Power,* 3d ed. (New York: Norton, 1993), 540.

[24]*The Founders Constitution: Amendment I (Speech and Press), Letter from Thomas Jefferson to Edward Carrington,* January 16, 1787, http://press-pubs.uchicago.edu/founders/documents/amendI_speechs8.html.

[25]Geoffrey R. Stone, *Perilous Times: Free Speech in Wartime* (New York: W.W. Norton, 2004), 34–35.

[26]Quoted in Will Friedman, "Presidential Rhetoric, the News Media and the Use of Force in the Post–Cold War Era," paper presented to the Annual Conference of the American Political Science Association, New York, September 1994.

[27]John Byrne Cooke, *Reporting the War: Freedom of the Press from the American Revolution to the War on Terrorism* (New York: Palgrave Macmillan, 2007), 110.

[28]Clayton R. Koppes and Gregory D. Black, *Hollywood Goes to War: How Politics, Profits and Propaganda Shaped World War II Movies* (New York: Free Press, 1987), vii.

[29]James Aronson, *The Press and the Cold War* (New York: Bobbs Merrill, 1970), 186.

[30]Aronson, *Press and the Cold War,* 195.

[31]John T. Rourke, Ralph G. Carter, and Mark A. Boyer, *Making American Foreign Policy,* 2d ed. (Dubuque, Iowa: Brown and Benchmark, 1996), 362.

[32]"The Propaganda War," *Newsweek,* February 25, 1991, 38.

[33]Jerel A. Rosati, *The Politics of United States Foreign Policy* (New York: Harcourt, Brace, 1993), 507.

[34]Howard Kurtz, "For Media after Iraq, a Case of Shell Shock," *Washington Post,* April 28, 2003, A1.

[35]W. Lance Bennett and David L. Paletz, eds., *Taken by Storm: The Media, Public Opinion and U.S. Foreign Policy in the Gulf War* (Chicago: University of Chicago Press, 1994).

[36]Patrick O'Heffernan, "A Mutual Exploitation Model of Media Influence in U.S. Foreign Policy," in Bennett and Paletz, *Taken by Storm,* 232–33.

[37]Bernard C. Cohen, *The Press and Foreign Policy* (Princeton: Princeton University Press, 1963), cited in Kegley and Wittkopf, *American Foreign Policy,* 310.

[38]See Shanto Iyengar, *Is Anyone Responsible? How Television Frames Political Issues* (Chicago: University of Chicago Press, 1991); and Shanto Iyengar and Donald R. Kinder, *News That Matters: Television and American Opinion* (Chicago: University of Chicago Press, 1987).

[39]Framing is defined as "selecting and highlighting some facets of events or issues, and making the connections among them so as to promote a particular interpretation, evaluation and/or solution." Robert M. Entman, "Cascading Activation: Contesting the White House's Frame After 9/11," *Political Communication* 20 (2003): 417.

[40]1985 and 2005 statistics quoted in Alan B. Krueger, "Fair? Balanced? A Study Finds It Does Not Matter," *New York Times,* August 18, 2005; 2011 from Paul Bedard, "Pew: Public Perception of Media Bias Hits Historic High," *US News,* September 22, 2011, www.usnews.com/news/washington-whispers/articles/2011/09/22/pew-public-perception-of-media-bias-hits-historic-high.

[41]Compare Eric Alterman, *What Liberal Media? The Truth about Bias and the News* (New York: Basic Books, 2003), and Bernard Goldberg, *Bias: A CBS Insider Exposes How the Media Distort the News* (Washington, D.C.: Regnery Publishing, 2002).

[42]Edward S. Herman and Noam Chomsky, *Manufacturing Consent: The Political Economy of the Mass Media* (New York: Random House, 2002).

[43]Quoted in Richard A. Posner, "Bad News," *New York Times*, July 31, 2005.

[44]Cooke, *Reporting the War*, 1.

[45]Aronson, *Press and the Cold War*, 159.

[46]Michael R. Beschloss, *Presidents, Television, and Foreign Crises* (Washington, D.C.: Annenberg Washington Program, 1993).

[47]*New York Times Co. v. United States* (1971), cited in Franck and Glennon, eds., *Foreign Relations and National Security Law*, 863–78.

[48]Walter Lippmann, *Essays in the Public Philosophy* (Boston: Little, Brown, 1955), 20.

[49]Hans J. Morgenthau, *Politics among Nations: The Struggle for Power and Peace* (New York: Knopf, 1955), 20.

[50]George F. Kennan, *American Diplomacy, 1900–1950* (New York: Mentor, 1951), 59.

[51]Gabriel Almond, *The American People and Foreign Policy* (New York: Harcourt, Brace, 1950), 69.

[52]Frank L. Klingberg, "The Historical Alternation of Moods in American Foreign Policy," *World Politics* 4.2 (January 1952): 239–73.

[53]Lloyd A. Free and Hadley Cantril, *The Political Beliefs of Americans* (New York: Simon & Schuster, 1968), 60; Kegley and Wittkopf, *American Foreign Policy*, 265; National Geographic–Roper, "2006 Survey of Geographic Literacy." Available at www.nationalgeographic.com/roper2006/findings.html (accessed 6/2/09).

[54]Cited in Miroslav Nincic, *Democracy and Foreign Policy: The Fallacy of Political Realism* (New York: Columbia University Press, 1992), 48.

[55]Figures are from Chicago Council on Global Affairs, *Foreign Policy in the New Millennium* (2012), Figure 1.6 (p. 8), www.thechicagocouncil.org/files/Studies_Publications/POS/Survey2012/2012.aspx.

[56]Steven Kull and I.M. Destler, *Misreading the Public: The Myth of a New Isolationism* (Washington, D.C.: Brookings Institution, 1999).

[57]Benjamin I. Page and Robert Y. Shapiro, "Changes in Americans' Policy Preferences, 1935–1979," *Public Opinion Quarterly* 46.1 (1982): 34.

[58]Andrew F. Krepinevich, Jr., *The Army and Vietnam* (Baltimore: John Hopkins University Press, 1986), 270.

[59]John E. Mueller, *War, Presidents and Public Opinion* (New York: John Wiley, 1973).

[60]Bruce W. Jentleson, "The Pretty Prudent Public: Post Post-Vietnam American Public Opinion on the Use of Military Force," *International Studies Quarterly* 36.1 (March 1992), 49–74; Bruce W. Jentleson and Rebecca L. Britton, "Still Pretty Prudent: Post–Cold War American Opinion on the Use of Military Force," *Journal of Conflict Resolution* 42.4 (August 1998), 395–417.

[61]Bruce M. Russett, *Controlling the Sword* (Cambridge: Harvard University Press, 1990), 87–88.

[62]Lawrence R. Jacobs and Benjamin I. Page, "Who Influences U.S. Foreign Policy?" *American Political Science Review* 99:1 (February 2005), 107–123.

[63]Countering this trend is one of the important contributions of the constructivist school of international relations theory.

[64]Alexander L. George, *Managing U.S.-Soviet Rivalry: Problems of Crisis Prevention* (Boulder, Colo.: Westview Press, 1983), 25–27.

[65]Bruce W. Jentleson, *With Friends Like These: Reagan, Bush and Saddam, 1982–1990* (New York: Norton, 1994), 90–91.

[66]Miroslav Nincic, "The United States, the Soviet Union and the Politics of Opposites," *World Politics* 40.4 (July 1988): 452–75.

[67]Interview by author, July 20 and 22, 1977, published in Bruce W. Jentleson, ed., *Perspectives 1979* (Washington, D.C.: Close Up Foundation, 1979), 273–79.

[68]Robert Putnam, "Diplomacy and Domestic Politics: The Logic of Two-Level Games," *International Organization* 42.3 (Summer 1988): 427–60.

[69]John H. Aldrich, John L. Sullivan, and Eugene Borgida, "Foreign Affairs and Issue Voting: Do Presidential Candidates 'Waltz Before a Blind Audience'?" *American Political Science Review* 83 (March 1989): 123–42.

[70]Samuel L. Popkin, *The Reasoning Voter* (Chicago: University of Chicago Press, 1991), 111.

4 The Historical Context: Great Debates in American Foreign Policy, 1789–1945

Introduction: "What Is Past Is Prologue"

The words "What is past is prologue" are inscribed on the base of the National Archives building in Washington, D.C. For all the ways that today's world is new and different, we can learn much from history. The particular choices debated for U.S. foreign policy in the twenty-first century clearly differ in many ways from past agendas. But for all the changes, we still wrestle with many of the same core questions of foreign policy strategy and foreign policy politics that have been debated for more than two hundred years of American history.

To provide part of this important historical context, this chapter examines recurring "great debates" from pre–Cold War history (1789–1945) that are most relevant to U.S. foreign policy in the post–Cold War era. Six of these "great debates" deal with foreign policy strategy:

- the overarching debate over isolationism vs. internationalism, encompassing considerations of Power, Peace, Principles, and Prosperity
- Power and Peace debates over how big a military the United States should have and how much to spend on defense
- how true U.S. foreign policy has been to its democratic Principles
- whether U.S. foreign policy has been imperialistic (Prosperity)
- relations with Latin America as a key case exemplifying the competing tensions among the "4 Ps"
- U.S. emergence as a Pacific power and its relations with the countries of Asia as another key case

Three others deal with foreign policy politics:

■ recurring "Pennsylvania Avenue diplomacy" struggles between the president and Congress over going to war
■ tensions between considerations of national security and the constitutional guarantees of civil liberties
■ interest-group pressures and other political battles over free trade vs. protectionism

Brief Historical Chronology

Before getting to the great debates as analytic history, we present a brief chronology of key events and actions in American foreign policy from 1776 to 1945. The following section lays out a timeline of major events and their foreign policy significance traced through five historical periods: the Revolutionary War and the consolidation of independence, 1776–1800; expansion and preservation, 1801–65; global emergence, 1865–1919; isolationist retreat, 1919–41; and World War II, 1941–45.[1]

The Revolutionary War and the Consolidation of Independence, 1776–1800

The first major ally the new nation had was France. Many historians think the American Revolution would have failed had it not been for the support—money, supplies, and army and navy units—that the French king Louis XVI provided. Why did France do this? The main factor was the "enemy of my enemy is my friend" calculation stemming from French-British wars and rivalry.

Independence did not guarantee security for the newly minted United States of America. Tensions with Britain continued. The Jay Treaty managed to avoid another war with Britain but had other controversial provisions, as discussed in Chapter 2. Relations with France also had become tense amid the upheaval of the French Revolution. It was with these and other issues in mind that George Washington urged isolationism from Europe's conflicts as he left office in 1796.

Tensions with France grew worse during John Adams's presidency, coming close to war and prompting the passage of the Alien and Sedition Acts. Although these laws protected against subversive activities by the French and their sympathizers they were also quite repressive of civil liberties.

Date	Event	Foreign Policy Significance
1776	Declaration of Independence	Revolutionary War, support from France
1781	Articles of Confederation	Failed effort at creating a union
1783	Treaty of Paris	Britain defeated
1787	Constitution ratified	United States of America created
1789	George Washington, first president	Thomas Jefferson, first secretary of state
1796	Jay Treaty	United States avoids another war with Britain, but other provisions controversial
1796	Washington's Farewell Address	Warns against entangling alliances
1798	Alien and Sedition Acts	National security–civil liberties tension

Expansion and Preservation, 1801–65

On the one hand, this was a period of expansion of the size of the United States: The **Louisiana Purchase**, negotiated with France and capitalizing on Napoleon's need for money to finance his effort to conquer Europe, doubled the size of the country. The 1846–48 war with Mexico led to the annexation of Texas and the acquisition of California and other western territories. Numerous wars were fought with the Native Americans. The prevailing view of the times was that this territorial expansion was the United States' "manifest destiny," an expression coined in 1845.

This era also saw the expansion of American influence beyond territorial acquisitions. President Thomas Jefferson dispatched the navy against the Barbary pirates, who had been attacking American commercial shipping in the Mediterranean Sea. Although such forays into European affairs were still limited, the United States became more assertive within the Western Hemisphere. The Monroe Doctrine warned European powers to stay out in terms that, though affirming the independence of other nations, also were used to justify American dominance and numerous military interventions.

But for all this expansion, the very existence of the nation was twice threatened. The British came close to winning the War of 1812, even invading the nation's capital, Washington, D.C., and burning down the White House. When the election of Abraham Lincoln as president brought the issue of slavery to a head, civil war ensued. With some leverage from its cotton trade, the Confederacy tried to get Britain on its side. France tried to take advantage by invading Mexico and installing a new monarch, Emperor Napoleon III. The Civil War ended in 1865, and the Union was preserved.

Date	Event	Foreign Policy Significance
1803	Louisiana Purchase from France	Doubles size of the United States
1803–5	Military action against Barbary pirates in Mediterranean	Early presidential use of force
1812–14	War of 1812 vs. Great Britain	Aug. 24–25, 1814: Washington, D.C. burned, White House included
1823	Monroe Doctrine proclaimed	U.S. hegemony in Western Hemisphere
1845	Manifest destiny proclaimed	Basis for U.S. expansion across the continent
1846–48	War with Mexico	Texas, other territories annexed
1853–54	Commodore Perry's voyage to Japan	Some commercial and other relations established
1860	Abraham Lincoln elected president	Southern states secede, form Confederacy, seek European support and recognition

Date	Event	Foreign Policy Significance
1861–65	Civil War	Nation's future at risk
1863	France conquers Mexico	Seeks foothold in North America
1865	Civil War ends	United States reunited

Global Emergence, 1865–1919

Post–Civil War Reconstruction as well as economic cycles of boom and bust engendered some further isolationism. Additional restrictions were imposed on immigration, and on Asians in particular. Trade policy was largely protectionist, as with the 1890 tariff, which we discuss in the free trade–protectionism great debate later in the chapter.

Victory in the ***Spanish-American War*** left the United States with what the historian Walter LaFeber called a "new empire." American forces, sent in part to "liberate" Cuba from the Spanish, stayed to occupy it over almost three decades. The war spread as far as the Philippines, which was acquired as the first U.S. colony. As noted in Chapter 2, the United States took a number of actions to build on its efforts to dominate Latin America (constructing the Panama Canal, issuing the Roosevelt Corollary, occupying Nicaragua and Haiti, intervening in the Mexican Revolution). The "Open Door policy" represented a major foray into China, followed by "Dollar Diplomacy" and other efforts.

World War I began in 1914, but the United States did not enter until 1917, when the threat became sufficiently direct to overcome isolationism. American forces made substantial contributions to the Allied victory. President Woodrow Wilson played a lead role in the peace agreements, including the creation of the League of Nations.

The ***Russian Revolution*** occurred in 1917, bringing the communists (Bolsheviks) to power and creating the Union of Soviet Socialist Republics (USSR).

Date	Event	Foreign Policy Significance
1882	Chinese Exclusion Act passed	Severely limits Chinese immigration
1890	McKinley tariff passed	Protectionism

Date	Event	Foreign Policy Significance
1898	Spanish-American War	United States occupies Cuba, Philippines becomes U.S. colony, other Pacific territories acquired from Spain
1899	Secretary of State Hay's "Open Door" policy	United States competes with European powers for access and influence in China
1903	Panama Canal construction begins	President Theodore Roosevelt supports Panamanian independence from Colombia, strikes deal on canal
1904	Roosevelt Corollary	Reassertion of Monroe Doctrine including claim of right to intervene militarily
1905	Roosevelt's diplomacy helps end Russo-Japanese War	Roosevelt wins Nobel Peace Prize
1909	Occupation of Nicaragua	Maintained for most of period until 1933
1909–12	President Taft's "Dollar Diplomacy"	Emphasis on economic interests in Latin America and China
1910–17	Mexican Revolution	U.S. involvement includes occupation of Veracruz, military pursuit of Pancho Villa
1914	World War I begins; Britain and France vs. Germany and Austria-Hungary	United States declares neutrality

Date	Event	Foreign Policy Significance
1915	United States occupies Haiti	Maintains until 1934
1916	United States occupies Dominican Republic	Maintains until 1924
1917	German hostilities against United States increase, including submarine warfare and pursuing alliance with Mexico	President Wilson proposes and Congress approves declaration of war, joins Britain-France alliance
1917	Bolshevik (Communist) revolution in Russia	Union of Soviet Socialist Republics (USSR) formed
1918	United States part of anti-Bolshevik military intervention in Russia	Intervention fails
1918	World War I ends	U.S. troops return, isolationist calls for "return to normalcy"
1919	Paris peace conference, Treaty of Versailles	President Wilson plays lead role, including creation of League of Nations

Isolationist Retreat, 1919–41

These decades were dominated by a retreat back into isolationism. The U.S. Senate rejected membership in the League of Nations. Fears of communism and Soviet influence were exploited in the Red Scare violations of civil liberties. Efforts were made to guarantee security by passing a treaty, the Kellogg-Briand Pact, simply outlawing war.

The 1929 stock market crash set off the ***Great Depression***, the nation's worst economic crisis up to that point. One of the more counterproductive reactions was the passage of the Smoot-Hawley Tariff, worsening the Depression at home and furthering its spread globally.

Although the Depression was his main concern upon being elected president, Franklin Delano Roosevelt (FDR) sought to improve relations with Latin America and to initiate diplomatic relations with the USSR. His efforts to focus on the rise of Adolf Hitler and Nazism in Germany, though, were constrained by the Neutrality Acts passed by Congress.

World War II began with the German invasion of Poland in September 1939. Even when Hitler attacked Britain and conquered France the next year, isolationism still prevailed in the United States. FDR sought to change this attitude with his Four Freedoms speech and the Atlantic Charter he signed with Prime Minister Winston Churchill of Britain. But it took the Japanese attack on Pearl Harbor for political support finally to be sufficient for the United States to enter World War II.

Date	Event	Foreign Policy Significance
1919	U.S. Senate rejects Versailles Treaty	League of Nations membership rejected, Wilson's global leadership discredited
1920	Palmer raids, anticommunist "Red Scare"	National security–civil liberties tension
1921–22	Washington Conference limiting navies	United States, Great Britain, France, Italy, Japan involved
1928	Kellogg-Briand Pact outlawing war	France-U.S.–led mix of diplomacy and isolationism
1929	U.S. stock market crash	Great Depression
1930	Smoot-Hawley Tariff	Imposes high tariffs and protectionism; exacerbates Great Depression
1933	Good Neighbor policy set by President Franklin Delano Roosevelt	Major shift toward Latin America, including ending most military occupations
1933	Diplomatic recognition of USSR	First diplomatic relations since communist revolution

Date	Event	Foreign Policy Significance
1933	Adolf Hitler and Nazi party come to power in Germany	Road to World War II
1935	Congress imposes Neutrality Acts	Tensions rising in Europe, but acts are passed despite FDR's objections
1936	Spanish Civil War	Francsico Franco comes to power; rules as dictator for almost forty years
1938	Munich Agreement with Hitler signed by Britain and France	Appeasement of Hitler; fails and sets precedent constraining diplomacy
1939	World War II begins with Hitler's invasion of Poland	United States stays out of the war
1940	Britain under massive air attacks, "blitz"	United States stays out of the war
1940	Hitler conquers France	United States stays out of the war
1940	Lend-Lease and other aid to Britain, USSR	Some assistance to the Allies against Hitler
1940	Congress approves military draft	First peacetime draft in U.S. history
1940	FDR elected to third term	Promises to keep U.S. out of the war, but increasingly supportive of Britain
1941	FDR inaugural address; "Four Freedoms"	Addresses global U.S. role based on core values and principles
1941	FDR and British Prime Minster Winston Churchill issue Atlantic Charter	Solidifies U.S.-British alliance and vision for world order

Date	Event	Foreign Policy Significance
December 7, 1941	Japan attacks Pearl Harbor	Congress declares war the next day
December 11, 1941	Germany declares war on United States	United States now fully enters World War II

World War II, 1941–45

With isolationism having constrained the nation's preparation for war and the Pearl Harbor attack having devastated the naval fleet, America faced enormous challenges entering World War II. Overcoming them took the collective efforts of government, the military, business, and ordinary people. No wonder many refer to World War II as the "good war." It did, though, have aspects that brought shame, such as the internment of over one hundred thousand Japanese Americans in camps on allegations of questionable loyalty based solely on their ethnicity.

Along with winning the war, initiatives were taken to build the peace that would follow. A new international economic system was designed, seeking to avoid protectionism and other impediments to global prosperity. The United Nations was created as a basis for global security. The Big Three—FDR, Winston Churchill, and the Soviet leader Josef Stalin—negotiated territorial and other issues in a mix of cooperation and fundamental tensions that would set the stage for the Cold War.

Date	Event	Foreign Policy Significance
1942	Initial Japanese victories in the Pacific	General Douglas MacArthur forced to flee the Philippines
1942	Internment in the United States of over one hundred thousand Japanese Americans	National security–civil liberties tension
1942	Battle of Midway (June)	U.S. victory; starts to turn the tide of the war

Date	Event	Foreign Policy Significance
1942	Manhattan Project stepped up	Development of the world's first atomic bomb
1942	Germany invades USSR (September)	In November, Soviets retake key city of Stalingrad
1942	U.S. and British troops land in North Africa against German occupation	Victory by May 1943
1943	FDR and Churchill meet in Casablanca, Morocco	Wartime summit
1943	French General Charles de Gaulle forms Free French Forces	French resistance to Nazi occupation intensifies
1943	Italian dictator Benito Mussolini forced to resign, then executed	Hitler ally ousted
1943	FDR, Churchill, and the Soviet dictator Josef Stalin meet in Tehran, Iran	Wartime summit and postwar planning
1944	June 6, D-Day	Allied landing at Normandy pushes German forces back
1944	Bretton Woods (New Hampshire) conference, attended by delegates from forty-four countries	Planning postwar international economic system
1944	FDR elected to fourth term	First time in U.S. history (as was his election to a third term)
1945	Yalta conference (FDR, Churchill, Stalin)	Postwar planning
1945	April 12, FDR dies	Vice President Harry Truman becomes president

Date	Events	Foreign Policy Significance
1945	May 8, V-E day	Victory in Europe
1945	Germany divided into four occupation zones	United States, British, French, Soviet
1945	United Nations created	U.S. leadership role in creating the UN
1945	August 6–9, United States drops atomic bombs on Japanese cities Hiroshima and Nagasaki	First uses of nuclear weapons
1945	August 15, V-J day	Japan surrenders

Great Debates over Foreign Policy Strategy

Isolationism vs. Internationalism

Should the United States seek to minimize its involvement in world affairs, to isolate itself from the rest of the world? Or should it take an active, internationalist role? Which strategy would best serve the national interest in all of its "4 Ps" components?

Contrary to many traditional histories, the United States was never fully *isolationist*. From the very beginning the Founders knew that this new nation needed a foreign policy, needed to find foreign support where it could, needed to be able to trade, and generally needed to have at least some involvement in the world. Their strategy, though, was to stay out of the "Old World" European rivalries, machinations, and wars. This was what President George Washington articulated in his famous 1796 farewell address. "Steer clear of permanent alliances with any portion of the foreign world," he urged the young nation as he left office and handed the reins to President John Adams (see "At the Source," p. 102). Temporary alliances were fine—Washington knew how important the alliance with France had been to winning the Revolutionary War against Britain. French loans had kept the new nation solvent, and French military support was so extensive that at the decisive battle of Yorktown there were actually more French soldiers than Americans fighting against the British. But the best way for the United States to preserve its own peace, according to its first president, was to avoid getting "entangled" in the affairs of Europe. "Europe has a set of primary interests which to us have none or a very remote relation," Washington stated. Those interests lead its nations to "be engaged in frequent controversies, the causes of which are essentially foreign to our concerns." Moreover, "foreign influence is one of the most baneful foes of republican government," Washington cautioned with regard to the impact on the principles of the nascent American democracy. So the United States should take advantage of its "detached and distant situation" across the Atlantic Ocean, which made it physically possible to avoid such entanglements.

As far as foreign trade was concerned, Washington and his successors pursued it to the extent that it contributed to Prosperity, but sought to develop these commercial relations with as little political connection as possible. In his first inaugural address in 1801, President Thomas Jefferson reaffirmed "entangling alliances with none" while also calling for "peace, commerce and honest friendship with all nations." The goal was to extend commercial relations more than political ones. About 70 percent of the treaties and other international agreements the United States signed in the nineteenth century were on matters related to trade and commerce.[2] Nor did isolationism preclude assertions of U.S. power and interests in its own hemisphere, as through the Monroe Doctrine. What isolationism did mean most essentially was staying out of the various wars Europe fought in the nineteenth century.

Many view the Spanish-American War of 1898 as marking the beginning of the emergence of the United States as a world power. The Americans won the war, defeating a European power, and for the first time gained a far-flung colony of their own: the Philippines. Theodore Roosevelt, as a "Rough Rider" during the Spanish-American War and as president from 1901 to 1908, embodied the new and more muscular spirit of internationalism. Isolationism was no longer in the national interest, as Roosevelt saw it. "The increasing interdependence and complexity of international political and economic relations," he explained, "render it incumbent on all civilized and orderly powers to insist on the proper policing of the world."[3]

President Woodrow Wilson was also inclined toward internationalism, although his emphasis was more on Principles than Power. Yet the old tradition of noninvolvement in Europe's wars was still strong enough that when **World War I** broke out in Europe, the Wilson administration tried to stay out. Even the usually sober *New York Times* editorialized as to how the nations of Europe had "reverted to the condition of savage tribes roaming the forests and falling upon each other in a fury of blood and carnage to achieve the ambitious designs of chieftains clad in skins and drunk with mead."[4] It was only after the threat to U.S. interests became undeniably direct that the futility of trying to stay isolated became evident. When the "Zimmermann telegram," a secret German message to Mexico in early 1917 proposing an alliance against the United States, was intercepted, the United States learned that the Germans were offering to help Mexico "reconquer the lost

AT THE SOURCE
AT THE SOURCE

GEORGE WASHINGTON'S FAREWELL ADDRESS

❝ History and experience prove that foreign influence is one of the most baneful foes of republican government. . . . Excessive partiality for one foreign nation and excessive dislike of another cause those whom they actuate to see danger only on one side and serve to veil and even second the arts of influence on the other. . . .

The great rule of conduct for us in regard to foreign nations is, in extending our commercial relations to have as little political connection as possible. So far as we have already formed engagements let them be fulfilled with perfect good faith. Here let us stop.

Europe has a set of primary interests which to us have none or a very remote relation. Hence she must be engaged in frequent controversies, the causes of which are essentially foreign to our concerns. Hence, therefore, it must be unwise for us to implicate ourselves by artificial ties in the ordinary vicissitudes of her politics or the ordinary combinations and collisions of her friendships or enmities.

Our detached and distant situation invites and enables us to pursue a different course. . . . Why forego the advantages of so peculiar a situation? . . . Why, by interweaving our destiny with that of any part of Europe, estrange our peace and prosperity in the toils of European ambition, rivalship, interest, humor or caprice?

It is our true policy to steer clear of permanent alliances with any portion of the foreign world, so far, I mean, as we are at liberty to do it. . . .

Taking care always to keep ourselves to suitable establishments on a respectable defensive posture, we may safely trust to temporary alliances for extraordinary emergencies. . . .

There can be no greater error than to expect or calculate upon real favors from nation to nation. It is an illusion which experience must cure, which a just pride ought to discard. . . . ❞

Source: George Washington, "Farewell Address," September 17, 1796, reprinted in *Congressional Record*, 106th Cong., 1st sess., February 22, 1999, S1673.

[Mexican] territory in Texas, New Mexico and Arizona." German U-boats had opened up unrestricted submarine warfare and had sunk three U.S. merchant ships. Isolation was no longer possible; the world's war had come home to the United States.

However, immediately after the war, isolationism reasserted itself over what role the United States should play in building the peace. The League of Nations would create a "community of power" and provide a structure of peace, the internationalist President Wilson argued, with the collective security commitment embodied in Article X of the League Covenant destroying "the war-breeding alliance system and the bad old balance of power."[5] His isolationist opponents argued that it was precisely this kind of commitment that would obligate the United States to go to war to defend other League members and that would entangle Americans in other countries' problems. This was a time not "to make the world safe for democracy," as Wilson aspired to do, but for a "return to normalcy," back to the way things were before the war. The isolationists prevailed as the Senate refused to ratify U.S. membership in the League of Nations.

For the next two decades, Congress refused to budge from a strongly isolationist foreign policy. Interestingly, although their specific reasons for being isolationist differed, both the left and the right political wings feared the reverberations at home if the United States went to war again. As **World War II** brewed in Europe, conservatives such as Robert E. Wood, chairman of Sears, Roebuck and head of the America First Committee, argued that entry into the war against Hitler would give President Franklin Roosevelt the opportunity to "turn the New Deal into a permanent socialist dictatorship." At the other end of the political spectrum, socialists such as Norman Thomas feared that war would provide justification for repression that "would bring fascist dictatorship to America."[6] Congress even came very close to passing the **Ludlow Amendment**, a proposed constitutional amendment that would have required a national referendum before any decision to go to war.

As Henry Kissinger's book *Diplomacy* (Reading 4.1) recounts, FDR tried taking his case directly to the American people, as with his 1937 "quarantine of aggressor nations" speech:

> The very foundations of civilization are seriously threatened. . . . If those things come to pass in other parts of the world, let no one imagine that America will escape, that it will continue tranquilly and peacefully to carry on. . . . When an epidemic of physical disease starts to spread, the community approves and joins in a quarantine of the patients in order to protect the health of the community against the spread of the disease. . . . The peace-loving nations must make a concerted effort in opposition to those violations of treaties and those ignorings of humane instincts which today are creating a state of international anarchy and instability from which there is no escape through mere isolation or neutrality.

His appeal, however, fell flat. The public still did not see the connection between what was happening "over there" and American interests and security. A public-opinion poll taken the week *after* Hitler invaded Poland in September 1939 showed 94 percent of Americans opposed to declaring war.

In 1940, with FDR running for reelection to an unprecedented third term, even the fall of France to Hitler's armies was not enough to break through the isolationism of American politics. With Britain also about to fall, and Prime Minister Winston Churchill urging the United States to provide support, FDR resorted to an "end run" around Congress to provide some support through the famous "destroyers-for-bases" deal.*[7]

FDR pushed again following his reelection. "This assault has blotted out the whole pattern of democratic life in an appalling number of independent nations, great and small," he told Congress and the American people in his January 1941 "Four Freedoms" speech, referring to Hitler's conquests in Europe. "And the assailants are still on the march, threatening other nations, great and small. Therefore, as your President, performing my constitutional duties to 'give to the Congress information on the state of the union,' I find it unhappily necessary to report that *the future of our country and our democracy are overwhelmingly involved in events far beyond our borders* [emphasis added]."[8] Still, it wasn't until December 7, 1941, when the Japanese launched a surprise attack on Pearl Harbor, that the politics changed and the United States joined the effort to restore world peace. The full national mobilization that ultimately occurred during World War II stands as a monumental example of what the United States is capable of achieving.

Even then, however, FDR worried during the closing months of the war that "anybody who thinks isolationism is dead in this country is crazy. As soon as this war is over, it may well be stronger than ever."[9] Indeed, once victory was achieved there was a rapid demobilization, another yearning to "bring the boys home" and get back to normal— only to be confronted by the threats of the Cold War.

Power, Peace: How Big a Military, How Much for Defense?

For the United States to maximize its Power and to pursue Peace, how big a military is required? How much needs to be spent on defense? These issues have been hotly contested throughout American history.

This is evident even in the Constitution. On the one hand, the Constitution provides for the creation of an army and a navy. On the other, it dedicates both the Second Amendment, the right of states to have their own militias, and the Third Amendment, the prohibition on "quartering" of troops in private homes without the owner's permission, to checks on the national military. Nor was much done initially with the constitutional provisions authorizing a standing army and navy. Building more than a few naval frigates was too expensive for the young country. And when President Washington proposed a permanent peacetime draft in 1790, Congress rejected it.

---

*Under this agreement, the U.S. Navy provided the British navy with fifty destroyer warships in exchange for the rights to British military bases in the Western Hemisphere. The "end run" came from the deal's being made as an executive agreement not requiring any congressional approval.

But the risks of a weak military were quickly made evident. By 1798 the United States was on the verge of war with its former ally and patron, France. President John Adams got Congress to authorize increases in the army and the navy, and George Washington came out of retirement to take command. War was avoided through a combination of successful diplomacy and displays of naval strength. Still, the British navy used its superiority over the next decade to harass American merchant ships with continual blockades and impressment (seizing) of sailors. In the 1807 *Chesapeake* affair, tensions escalated to an attack on an American naval ship. Secretary of the Treasury Albert Gallatin expressed the sense of vulnerability in these years, warning that the British "could land at Annapolis, march to the city [Washington, D.C.], and re-embark before the militia could be collected to repel [them]."[10] Gallatin's warning proved all too prophetic when, during the War of 1812, the British did march on Washington and burned down much of the capital city, including the White House. To fight the War of 1812, the U.S. Army had to be more than tripled in size from its standing level of about twelve thousand troops (see Table 4.1). Once the war was over, the army was rapidly demobilized.

The same pattern of low troop levels, massive mobilization, and rapid demobilization was played out even more dramatically during the Civil War. When the war broke out, the Union Army had only about sixteen thousand troops. President Abraham Lincoln mobilized the state militias and took unilateral action without prior budget approval from Congress to rapidly enlarge both the army and the navy. He also instituted the first military draft in U.S. history. Through these and other measures the Union forces grew to almost 1 million. Then, in the decade following the end of the Civil War in 1865, the army decreased to twenty-five thousand troops.

In the late nineteenth century, the main debate was over building up a larger and more modern navy. There was general consensus that the army could be kept small; another direct attack on the United States by Britain or another European power now seemed

TABLE 4.1 Wartime Mobilization, Peacetime Demobilization

	Prewar troop levels	Wartime mobilization	Postwar demobilization
War of 1812	12,000	36,000	n/a
Civil War, 1861–65	16,000	1,000,000	25,000
World War I, 1917–18	130,000	2,000,000	265,000
World War II, 1941–45	175,000	8,500,000	550,000

Note: Figures are for the army only and are approximate.

highly unlikely. The real competition with the Europeans was on the high seas. The greatness of a nation, argued the navy captain Alfred Thayer Mahan in his seminal book *The Influence of Sea Power upon History* (1890), depends on a strong navy capable not just of its own coastal defense but of command of the seas. Congress was sufficiently persuaded by Mahan and others to fund enough naval construction to make the U.S. Navy the seventh largest in the world by 1893. Yet there were also critics. Some objected to Mahan's naval buildup as draining resources from domestic priorities. Others warned that the new sense of power would make the pull toward the pursuit of empire irresistible.

When World War I came, because of the new navy buildup, the United States was better prepared on the seas than on land. The United States entered the war with only 130,000 soldiers in its army. One of the first actions Congress took was passage of the Selective Service Act of 1917, reviving the military draft. At its World War I peak the army comprised over 2 million soldiers.

Yet President Wilson also realized that "it is not [just] an army that we must shape and train for war, it is a nation"—including its economy. Indeed, during World War I Wilson requested and Congress approved powers over the economy that, in the view of the noted historians Samuel Eliot Morison and Henry Steele Commager, were "more extensive than those possessed by any other ruler in the Western world."[11] The president was empowered to seize and operate factories, to operate all systems of transportation and communication, to allocate food and fuel, to set industrial production schedules, and to fix prices. To exercise these vast and unprecedented economic regulatory powers, Wilson set up a host of new executive-branch agencies. The War Shipping Board was charged with keeping merchant shipping going and with building two ships for each one sunk by German U-boats. The Food Board supervised both food production and consumption, setting rules for "Wheatless Mondays" and "Meatless Tuesdays" to ensure enough food surplus to help feed the Allies. The War Industries Board regulated virtually every production and investment decision made by private companies, from the number of automobiles rolling off Henry Ford's assembly lines, to the number of colors on typewriter ribbons (reduced from 150 to 5 to free up carbon and other chemicals for the war effort), to cutting down the length of the upper parts of shoes (to save leather for uniforms and supplies). Wilson was even able to impose new taxes on consumption and to increase existing income, inheritance, and corporate taxes, all with relatively little political opposition.

Yet once the war ended, this vast governmental economic bureaucracy was disbanded, as was the military. The army shrank to 265,000 troops by 1920. As part of the naval arms-control treaties signed at the 1921–22 Washington Naval Conference with the four other major naval powers (Britain, France, Italy, and Japan), the U.S. Navy scrapped, sank, or decommissioned about 2 million tons of ships, including thirty-one major warships.

The mobilization-demobilization pattern recurred with World War II. The army started at about 175,000 troops and grew to almost 8,500,000 by 1945. The navy amassed another 3,400,000 sailors and a fleet of 2,500 warships. President Roosevelt's wartime powers over the economy were even more extensive than his New Deal ones. He created the War Production Board (WPB), which mobilized and allocated industrial facilities and plants; the War Manpower Commission, which had sweeping authority to mobilize labor to meet the WPB's production goals; and the Office of Price Administration, which set prices and rationed goods even for such staples as meat, sugar, tires, and gasoline. The fiats these and other agencies could issue went so far as prohibiting the pleasure driving of automobiles, cutting the production of consumer durable goods by almost 30 percent, imposing wage and price controls, passing major tax increases, and taking other measures deemed necessary for "forging a war economy."[12]

The overall scope of the economic effort involved in World War II dwarfed that of any previous period in American history. The number of civilian employees of the federal government climbed from 1 million to 3.8 million. Annual budget expenditures soared from $9 billion to $98.4 billion. All told, the federal government spent nearly twice as much between 1940 and 1945 as it had in the preceding 150 years. The Manhattan Project, the program that developed the atomic bomb, itself involved expenditures of more than $2 billion, the employment of more than 150,000 people, and the building of new cities in Los Alamos, New Mexico; Oak Ridge, Tennessee; and Hanford, Washington—all with the utmost secrecy, so much so that little was known even by Vice President Harry Truman, let alone Congress.

Once Hitler was defeated and Japan had surrendered, however, the calculation of how big a military was needed and how much should be budgeted for defense was made anew. By 1948 most of the wartime economic agencies had been dismantled. The army was down to 550,000 troops. The navy also was being scaled back. But the Cold War yet again raised questions of how big a military and how much funding were necessary to ensure the peace and maintain U.S. power.

Principles: True to American Democratic Ideals?

Theories of **American exceptionalism**, which hold that the United States has a uniqueness and special virtue that ground its foreign policy in Principles much more than the policies of other countries, can be traced back throughout American history (see "Theory in the World," p. 109).[13] The question, though, is whether American foreign policy has been as true to these values historically as it has claimed.

American exceptionalism was evoked early on in a poem by David Humphreys, a protégé of George Washington:

> All former empires rose, the work of guilt,
> On conquest, blood or usurpation built;
> But we, taught wisdom by their woes and crimes,

Fraught with their lore, and born to better times;
Our constitutions form'd on freedom's base,
Which all the blessings of all lands embrace;
Embrace humanity's extended cause,
A world of our empire, for a world of our laws . . . [14]

Yes, America was to be an empire, but it would not be built like the Old World ones on "guilt, . . . conquest, blood or usurpation." It instead would serve "humanity's extended cause."

The same themes were developed further in the mid-nineteenth century in the concept of **manifest destiny**. As the term was originally coined in 1845, it referred to the "right" claimed for the United States "to overspread and to possess the whole continent which Providence has given us for the development of the great experiment of liberty and federated self government."[15] The immediate reference was to continental expansion and specific territorial disputes, including the immediate one with Mexico that resulted in the 1846–48 war and the annexation of Texas.

Again, though, manifest destiny was said not to be just typical self-interested expansionism, but rather based on principles and thus also in the interest of those over whom the United States was expanding, such as Native Americans and Mexicans. Toward the end of the nineteenth century, when the United States pretty much had finished its continental territorial expansion, manifest destiny was invoked in a similar spirit as part of the justification for the Spanish-American War and the acquisition of colonies and quasi colonies in the Pacific and the Caribbean.

For Woodrow Wilson, the main reason for fighting World War I was "to make the world safe for democracy." His message to Congress requesting a declaration of war was heavily laden with appeals to Principles (see "At the Source," p. 111). "Our motive will not be revenge or the victorious assertion of the physical might of the nation," Wilson proclaimed, "but only the vindication of right." And so too was the postwar order to be built on democratic principles and ideals.[16] Many of Wilson's Fourteen Points dealt with self-determination for various central and eastern European peoples and nations that had been subjugated in the Austro-Hungarian and Ottoman (Turkish) Empires. Despite some compromises with Britain and France, which had little interest in dismantling their own empires, a "mandate" system was established under the League of Nations that was supposed to begin the process of decolonization in Africa, the Middle East, and Asia. Whatever the resistance of European leaders, as foreign policy expert Strobe Talbott recounts, the European people hailed Wilson "as the most powerful and honored man on the earth."

Placards . . . at every stop along Wilson's way through France, Britain and Italy proclaimed him "the Champion of the Rights of Man," "the Founder of the Society of Nations," "the God of Peace," "the Savior of Humanity," and "the Moses from Across the Atlantic." Crowds cheered and threw flowers as he passed. Streets and squares were renamed after him.[17]

THEORY IN THE WORLD

THEORIES OF AMERICAN EXCEPTIONALISM

We can trace the image of the United States as a *city on a hill,* often invoked by American leaders, back to the colonial days. It was John Winthrop, governor of the Massachusetts Bay Colony, who declared in 1630 that "wee shall be as a Citty upon a Hill, the eies of all people are upon us."* This image and related others evincing the theory that the United States was to play a highly principled role in the world that would be good for both Americans and for others have had a long and influential history in American foreign policy.

Three important points about this link between theory and policy: First, the evidence of the theory-policy link is strong. American exceptionalism theory has had significant impact on American foreign policy over many years and under many presidents. We provide some historical examples in this chapter, and we will see the dynamic also in the Cold War (Chapters 5 and 6) as well as throughout Part II.

Second, the nature of the impact has varied, leading to a wide range of policies. Along the internationalism-isolationism dimension discussed earlier in this chapter, the exceptionalist self-image at times has fostered moralistic interventionism and at other times has fed retreat from those deemed less worthy. "American exceptionalism not only celebrates the uniqueness and special virtues of the United States, but also elevates America to a higher moral plane than other countries. . . . [E]xceptionalism can stimulate both crusading interventionism and complacent withdrawal from world affairs . . . the attendant American determination to spread American ideals around the world . . . [and] an excuse to remain smug and content in an isolationist cocoon, well protected from 'corrupt' or 'inferior' foreigners."†

Third is the normative analysis of whether actual policies have been consistent with the claims to virtue. We take this up in the discussion of consistency, contradictions, and cover stories.

*Cited in Loren Baritz, *City on a Hill: A History of Ideas and Myths in America* (New York: Wiley, 1964), 3.
†Tami R. Davis and Sean M. Lynn-Jones, " 'Citty Upon a Hill,' " *Foreign Policy* (Spring 1987): 20–21.

As for World War II, the case for the values at stake in the war against Hitler and Nazism was about as incontrovertible as is possible. Underlying the political and strategic issues were what FDR called the *Four Freedoms*: freedom of religion, freedom of speech, freedom from fear, and freedom from want. The *Atlantic Charter*, a joint statement by FDR and Churchill issued before the United States entered the war (August

1941), pledged to "respect the right of all peoples to choose the form of government under which they will live; and . . . to see sovereign rights and self-government restored to those who have been forcibly deprived of them."[18] The latter was a reference to those countries in Europe overrun by Hitler's Germany. The former was ostensibly about the colonial world and was something from which Churchill soon backed off. Although FDR was sincere at the time, with the onset of the Cold War the United States also did not fully or speedily follow through.

The basis for debate over how true to its Principles the United States has been historically is threefold: questions of consistency, of contradictions, and of cover stories. The question of consistency allows for acknowledgment that there has been some practicing of what is preached, but less than has been claimed. We saw this in the Mexican War, in which the U.S. claim to be liberating Texas was seen quite differently by Mexico. The condemnation by a Mexican leader of "the degenerate sons of Washington" for their "dissimulation, fraud, and the basest treachery" is a nineteenth-century echo of the "why do they hate us" question asked in the twenty-first century in the wake of the September 11, 2001, terrorist attacks (see "International Perspectives," p. 113). Through much of the nineteenth and early twentieth centuries, the United States was more opposed to than supportive of social and political revolutions against undemocratic governments in Latin America. We will see this, for example, in our discussion of U.S. relations with Latin America. We can also see it in the case of the Philippines, where after gaining colonial control, 125,000 American troops fought to put down the pro-independence Filipino forces in what has been called "one of the ugliest wars in American history," with battles that took a death toll of more than 5,000 Americans and 200,000 Filipinos.[19] The "Manifesto Protesting the United States' Claim of Sovereignty over the Philippines," issued in 1899 by Emilio Aguinaldo, leader of the Filipino independence movement, challenged the stated intentions of the United States in getting involved in the Philippine war in the first place.

Elements of racism found in a number of aspects of U.S. foreign policy also stand in contradiction to the ideals Americans espoused. This racism goes back to the African slave trade and the foreign policy importance given to protecting those trade routes. It also goes to the core of manifest destiny. "White Americans had not inherited the fabled empty continent," writes historian Michael Hunt, referring to the massive killings and displacement of Native Americans. "Rather, by their presence and policies, they had emptied it."[20] Similarly, the Mexican War was "fought with clear racial overtones."[21] These racial attitudes were captured by the poet James Russell Lowell: "Mexicans wor'nt human beans," just "the sort o'folks a chap could kill an' never dream on't after."[22] In another example, even if one were to concede a degree of benevolence in the paternalism, a sense of racial superiority was undeniable in President William McKinley's justification for making the Philippines a U.S. colony: that "we could not leave [the Filipinos] to themselves—they were unfit for self-government, and they would soon

AT THE SOURCE

AT THE SOURCE

MAKING THE WORLD SAFE FOR DEMOCRACY

❝ It is a war against all nations. . . . The challenge is to all mankind. Each nation must decide for itself how it will meet it. . . . We must put excited feeling away. Our motive will not be revenge or the physical might of the nation, but only the vindication of right, of human right, of which we are only a single champion. . . .

With a profound sense of the solemn and even tragic character of the step I am taking and of the grave responsibilities which it involves, but in unhesitating obedience to what I deem my constitutional duty, I advise the Congress to declare the recent course of the Imperial German Government to be in fact nothing less than war against the government and people of the United States. . . .

We are accepting this challenge of hostile purpose because we know that in such a government, following such methods, we can never have a friend; and that in the presence of its organized power, always lying in wait to accomplish we know not what purpose, there can be no assured security for the democratic governments of the world. . . . *The world must be made safe for democracy* [emphasis added]. . . .

It is a distressing and oppressive duty, Gentlemen of the Congress, which I have performed in thus addressing you. There are, it may be, many months of fiery trial and sacrifice ahead of us. . . . But the right is more precious than the peace, and we shall fight for the things we have always carried nearest our hearts—for democracy, for the rights and liberties of small nations, for a universal dominion of right by such a concert of free peoples as shall bring peace and safety to all nations and make the world itself at last free. To such a task we can dedicate our lives and our fortunes, everything that we are and everything that we have, with the pride of those who know that the day has come when America is privileged to spend her blood and her might for the principles that gave her birth and happiness and the peace which she has treasured. God helping her, she can do no other. ❞

Source: Woodrow Wilson, "Address to Joint Session of Congress," April 2, 1917, reprinted in *Papers of Woodrow Wilson*, Arthur S. Link, ed. (Princeton: Princeton University Press, 1966), 41: 519–27.

have anarchy over there worse than Spain's was . . . [so] there was nothing left for us to do but take them all, and to educate the Filipinos and uplift and civilize them as our fellow-men."[23]

In addition, there have been times when principles have been less a genuine driving force than something of a cover story for other objectives. This was the case, for example, with Panama and the Panama Canal in the early years of the twentieth century. Until then, Panama had been a rebellious province of Colombia. And until then, U.S. efforts to acquire the rights to build a canal across the Panamanian isthmus had been stymied by the unwillingness of the Colombian government to agree to the terms the United States demanded. So although President Theodore Roosevelt could cite the historical basis for Panama's claim to independence, the landing of U.S. troops to support the revolt had far more to do with the willingness of the Panamanian leaders to make a deal for a canal. Less than a month after Panama had declared its independence, Teddy Roosevelt had a treaty with terms even more favorable to the United States than the ones the Colombian legislature had rejected the year before.

Prosperity: U.S. Imperialism?

Those who see U.S. foreign policy as historically imperialistic focus particularly on the late nineteenth and early twentieth centuries, a key period in what historian Walter LaFeber calls the "new empire" (see Reading 4.2). An 1898 editorial in the *Washington Post* evoked—indeed, lauded—the temper of the times:

> A new consciousness seems to have come upon us—the consciousness of strength—and with it a new appetite, the yearning to show our strength. . . . Ambition, interest, land hunger, pride, the mere joy of fighting, whatever it may be, we are animated by a new sensation. . . . The taste of Empire is in the mouth of the people. . . . It means an Imperial policy, the Republic, renascent, taking her place with the armed nations.[24]

One gets a different view, however, from Mark Twain's parody of the "Battle Hymn of the Republic":

> Mine eyes have seen the orgy of the launching of the sword;
> He is searching out the hoardings where the strangers' wealth is stored;
> He has loosed his fateful lightning, and with woe and death has scored;
> His lust is marching on.[25]

Consistent with theories of imperialism as examined in Chapter 1, the growing U.S. interest in foreign markets was in part a consequence of the severe economic crises of this period (there were depressions in 1873–78 and 1893–97), which set off the problems of underconsumption and overproduction. "We have advanced in manufactures, as in agriculture," Secretary of State William M. Evans stated in 1880, "until we are being forced outward by the irresistible pressure of our internal development." The United States needed new markets or, as an economist of the day warned, "we are certain to be smothered in our own grease."[26]

INTERNATIONAL PERSPECTIVES
INTERNATIONAL PERSPECTIVES

NINETEENTH-CENTURY CRITICS

Mexican War, 1846–48

66 The annexation of the department of Texas to the United States, projected and consummated by the tortuous policy of the cabinet of the Union, does not yet satisfy the ambitious desires of the degenerate sons of Washington. The civilized world already has recognized in that act all the marks of injustice, iniquity, and the most scandalous violation of the rights of nations. Indelible is the stain which will forever darken the character for virtue falsely attributed to the people of the United States. . . . To the United States it has been reserved to put into practice dissimulation, fraud and the basest treachery, in order to obtain possession, in the midst of peace, of the territory of a friendly nation, which generously relied upon the faith of promises and the solemnity of treaties. 99

—Mexican general Francisco Mejia

Spanish-American War, 1898, and Philippine War, 1899–1902

66 It is distinctly stated that the naval and field forces of the United States had come to give us our liberty, by subverting the bad Spanish Government. And I hereby protest against this unexpected act of the United States claiming sovereignty over these Islands. My relations with the United States did not bring me over here from Hong Kong to make war on the Spaniards for their benefit, but for the purpose of our own liberty and independence. 99

—Emilio Aguinaldo

Sources: Available at www.dmwv.org/mexwar/documents/mejia.htm; www.msc.edu.ph/centennial/ag 990105.html (accessed 12/24/12).

Those new markets were sought out principally in Latin America. U.S. exports to Latin America increased more than 150 percent between 1900 and 1914. Investments in plantations, mining, manufacturing, banking, and other industries shot up at an even faster pace. And the flag seemed to be following the dollar. As shown by Map 4.1 on page 115, during this era the United States launched numerous military interventions in Latin America. In many instances these actions clearly were taken in defense of the foreign investments and other economic interests of American corporations and financiers.

By 1913, for example, the United Fruit Company (UFCO) owned more than 130,000 acres of plantations (bananas and other fruits) in Central America—and it was in significant part to defend the economic interests of UFCO that the U.S. Marines went into Nicaragua (1909–10, 1912–25) and Honduras (1924–25). So too with other American corporations and the military interventions in Haiti (1915–34) and the Dominican Republic (1916–24).

In Cuba, which was "liberated" from Spain in the Spanish-American War only to be put under U.S. domination, the pattern was even more pronounced. Though formally allowing Cuba independence, the United States insisted that the **Platt Amendment** be attached to the Cuban constitution, granting the United States the right to intervene to, among other things, protect the property of U.S. corporations.* And the Marines did so on a number of occasions. The Platt amendment also gave the United States the power to veto treaties between Cuba and other governments as another way of giving U.S. interests special status. These measures made conditions as favorable as possible for American business: U.S. investments in Cuba increased from $50 million in 1896 to $220 million in 1913, and Cuban exports to the United States grew from $31 million in 1900 to $722 million in 1920.[27]

The other side of the debate, questioning the imperialist analysis, makes two principal arguments. One is based on counterexamples that are said to show that U.S. foreign policy has not consistently been geared to the defense of American capitalist interests. One such example is from early in the **Mexican Revolution**, when Woodrow Wilson refused to recognize the military government of General Victoriano Huerta despite pressures from U.S. corporations with some $1.5 billion in Mexican investments. "I . . . am not the servant of those who wish to enhance the value of their Mexican investments," Wilson declared.[28]

The other argument is based on alternative explanations. This argument doesn't deny that American foreign policy has had its expansionist dimension but attributes it less to Prosperity than to other factors, such as Power and Principles. For example, a Power-based alternative explanation of the U.S. military interventions in Latin America acknowledges that capitalist interests were well served, but emphasizes political and military factors as the driving forces. Similarly, although the Panama Canal had unquestionable economic value, some would argue that what really motivated Teddy Roosevelt was the linking up of the Atlantic and Pacific fleets of the U.S. Navy and the confirmation of the U.S.'s status as an emerging global power.

---

*This amendment was named for its principal congressional sponsor, Senator Orville Platt. This was not, however, a case of Congress's imposing something the executive branch didn't want. Secretary of War Elihu Root worked closely with Senator Platt in writing the amendment. See Thomas G. Paterson, J. Gary Clifford, and Kenneth J. Hagan, *American Foreign Relations: A History to 1920*, Vol. 1 (Lexington, Mass.: Heath, 1995), 254–55.

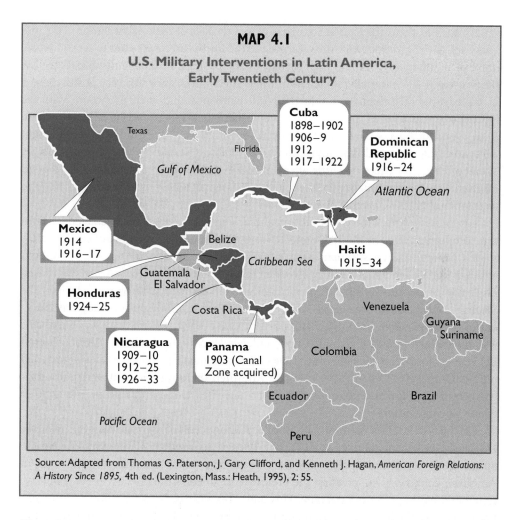

MAP 4.1

U.S. Military Interventions in Latin America, Early Twentieth Century

Cuba
1898–1902
1906–9
1912
1917–1922

Texas

Florida

Gulf of Mexico

Dominican Republic
1916–24

Atlantic Ocean

Mexico
1914
1916–17

Belize

Haiti
1915–34

Guatemala
El Salvador

Caribbean Sea

Honduras
1924–25

Costa Rica

Venezuela

Guyana
Suriname

Nicaragua
1909–10
1912–25
1926–33

Panama
1903 (Canal
Zone acquired)

Colombia

Ecuador

Brazil

Pacific Ocean

Peru

Source: Adapted from Thomas G. Paterson, J. Gary Clifford, and Kenneth J. Hagan, *American Foreign Relations: A History Since 1895,* 4th ed. (Lexington, Mass.: Heath, 1995), 2: 55.

Key Case: U.S. Relations with Latin America—Good Neighbor or Regional Hegemon?

As discussed earlier, U.S. relations with Latin America warrant special focus as a historical case providing numerous examples of the competing tensions among the "4 Ps." As the richest and most powerful country in the Western Hemisphere, was the United States to be the regional hegemon—the dominant country lording over its sphere of influence— exerting its Power largely as it saw fit, managing hemispheric Peace but on its own terms, and dominating economically for the sake of its own Prosperity? Or was the United States to be the good neighbor, true to its Principles, a benefactor to those in its hemispheric neighborhood who had less and were less powerful, promoting democracy and respecting their equal rights and privileges as sovereign nations?

For the most part the United States has played the role of regional hegemon. This role goes back to the Monroe Doctrine's warning to the European powers not to seek to recolonize or in other ways "extend their system to any position of this hemisphere" (see "At the Source," p. 117). Initially, some Latin American countries saw this very positively as a U.S. pledge to help them maintain their independence, and even proposed "that the Doctrine be transformed into a binding inter-American alliance." But "[Secretary of State John Quincy] Adams said no. He emphasized that the Doctrine was a unilateral American statement and that any action taken under it would be for the United States alone to decide."[29] There was little altruism in this policy, or even straightforward good neighborliness; it was much more the self-interest of a regional power seeking to preserve its dominant position against outside challenges.

For the rest of the nineteenth century there were quite a few outside challenges from the European powers. In the 1840s and 1850s Britain and the United States contested for rights to build a transisthmian canal across Central America. In a particularly bold episode, during the American Civil War, France sought to install its own hand-picked nobleman, Archduke Ferdinand Maximilian, as Napoleon III, emperor of Mexico. The Spanish-American War was largely about getting Spain not only out of Cuba but totally out of the hemisphere. Yet the U.S. support for Cuba's effort to end Spain's colonial rule was one thing, support for genuine Cuban independence quite another. U.S. troops stayed in Cuba for four years after the war (1898–1902) and then, as noted earlier, reintervened repeatedly in 1906–9, 1912, and 1917–22. And then there was the Platt amendment—what clearer manifestation of hegemony could there be than writing oneself into another country's constitution?

In 1904 President Theodore Roosevelt pronounced his corollary to the Monroe Doctrine (see "At the Source," p. 117). The **Roosevelt Corollary** claimed for the United States the "international police power" to intervene when instability within a Latin American country risked creating the pretext (e.g., to collect debts or protect property) for an Old World power to intervene. This policy became the basis for a host of interventions and extended military occupations in Cuba, the Dominican Republic, Haiti, Mexico, and Nicaragua. U.S. troops stayed in Haiti for almost twenty years, and in Cuba and Nicaragua on and off for twenty-five.

President Franklin Roosevelt sought to pursue a much different approach to Latin America than his cousin Theodore and most of his other predecessors. A few years before becoming president, FDR had written an article in *Foreign Affairs* that was quite critical of U.S. interventionism in Latin America. "Never before in our history," he wrote, "have we had fewer friends in the Western Hemisphere than we have today. . . . The time has come when we must accept not only certain facts but many new principles of a higher law, a newer and better standard in international relations. . . . [N]either from the argument of financial gain, nor from the sound reasoning of the Golden Rule, can our policy,

AT THE SOURCE

THE MONROE DOCTRINE (1823) AND
THE ROOSEVELT COROLLARY (1904)
Monroe Doctrine

66 The American continents, by the free and independent condition which they have assumed and maintained, are henceforth not to be considered as subjects for future colonization by any European powers. . . .

In the wars of the European powers in matters relating to themselves, we have never taken any part, not does it comport with our policy so to do. It is only when our rights are invaded or seriously menaced that we resent injuries or make preparations for our defense. With the movements in this hemisphere, we are of necessity more immediately connected, and by causes which must be obvious to all enlightened and impartial observers. . . .

We should consider any attempt on [the Europeans'] part to extend their system to any portion of this hemisphere as dangerous to our peace and safety. With the existing colonies or dependencies of any European power, we have not interfered and shall not interfere. But with the Governments who have declared their independence and maintained it, and whose independence we have, on great consideration and on just principles acknowledged, we could not view any interposition for the purpose of oppressing them, or controlling in any other manner their destiny, by any European power in any other light than as the manifestations of an unfriendly disposition toward the United States. 99

Roosevelt Corollary

66 It is not true that the United States feels any land hunger or entertains any projects as regards the other nations of the Western Hemisphere save such as are for their welfare. All that this country desires is to see the neighboring countries stable, orderly and prosperous. Any country whose people conduct themselves well can count upon our hearty friendship. If a nation shows that it knows how to act with reasonable sufficiency and decency in social and political matters, if it keeps order and pays its obligations, it need fear no interference from the United States. Chronic wrongdoing, or an impotence which results in the general loosening of the ties of civilized society, may in America, as elsewhere, ultimately require intervention by some civilized nation, and in the Western Hemisphere the adherence of the United States to the Monroe Doctrine may force the United States, however reluctantly, in

flagrant cases of such wrongdoing or impotence, to the exercise of an international police power. . . .

It is a mere truism to say that every nation, whether in America or anywhere else, which desires to maintain its freedom, its independence, must ultimately realize that the right of such independence can not be separated from the responsibility of making good use of it. . . .”

Sources: James Monroe, “Seventh Annual Message,” December 2, 1823, *The Writings of James Monroe* Stanislaus Murray Hamilton, ed. (New York: Putnam, 1912), 6: 325–42; Theodore Roosevelt, “Fourth Annual Message,” December 16, 1904, *A Compilation of the Messages and Papers of the Presidents* (New York: Bureau of National Literature, 1923), 14: 6894–930.

or lack of policy, be approved.”[30] We want to be the “good neighbor,” FDR proclaimed once elected, “the neighbor who resolutely respects himself and because he does so, respects the rights of others—the neighbor who respects the sanctity of his agreements in and with a world of neighbors.”[31] To demonstrate this new approach, FDR repealed the Platt amendment, withdrew the Marines from Nicaragua and Haiti, settled a long-standing oil dispute with Mexico, signed bilateral trade treaties as well as treaties of nonaggression and conciliation with a number of Latin American countries, and became the first U.S. president to visit South America. As World War II approached, FDR also struck a number of mutual security deals, including affirming a Monroe Doctrine–like commitment at the 1938 Pan-American Conference to resist any foreign intervention in the hemisphere.

Regional hegemon or good neighbor? Not only did the historical record feed this debate, but as we will see in the next chapter, the onset of the Cold War made it even more controversial.

Key Case: The United States as a Pacific Power

Trade and commerce (Prosperity) first took the United States across the Pacific to Asia. In the 1840s American ships were sailing to China with cotton and returning with tea. The Treaty of Wangxia, the first trade treaty with China, was signed in 1844. Close to a decade later (1853) Commodore Matthew C. Perry sailed into Tokyo Harbor and “opened up” Japan. “Our steamships can go from California to Japan in eighteen days,” President Millard Fillmore stated in the letter delivered to the Japanese rulers by Commodore Perry. “I am delighted that our two countries should trade with each other, for the benefit both of Japan and the United States.”[32]

But it was never really just trade and commerce (Prosperity) that the United States was after. America's sense of moral mission (Principles) was also at work. Interestingly, it cut both ways. On the one hand was the U.S. desire to liberalize and democratize these societies. "The thirty millions of Japan," wrote one author at the time of Commodore Perry's expedition, "await the key of the western Democrat to open their prison to the sun-light of social interchange."[33] On the other hand were fear and animosity toward the Orient and its culture, the view that "there were in conflict two great types of civilization, . . . Eastern and Western, inferior and superior."[34]

The Power motive was also at work. The historian Thomas Paterson and his colleagues describe it thus: "Perry saw his Japanese expedition as but one step toward a U.S. empire in the Pacific. . . . Eventually, the commodore prophesied, the American people would 'extend their dominion and their power, until they shall have brought within their mighty embrace the Islands of the great Pacific, and place the Saxon race upon the eastern shores of Asia.' "[35] Asia was yet another region for competition with the Europeans, who had the advantage of colonies and experience but who lacked the U.S. geographic advantage of being a Pacific as well as an Atlantic country. The United States acquired Hawaii, Samoa, and other Pacific island territories in an effort to develop that advantage further, as later it acquired the Philippines. The United States also began maintaining a military presence in the region, thanks to Captain Mahan's "new Navy." The ***Open Door policy*** of the 1890s, contrary to self-justifying claims of intending to help China against the encroachments of European colonialism, actually was a self-interested demand made on the major European powers that the United States not be closed out of spheres of trade and influence in China.

At the same time that the United States was extending its influence in Asia and the Pacific, so too was Japan. As but one example of the emerging rivalry, Japan initially refused to recognize the U.S. annexation of Hawaii, asserting its own claim based on the larger number of immigrants to Hawaii from Japan than from any other country. The antagonism subsided somewhat when, at the invitation of the Japanese government in 1904, President Theodore Roosevelt successfully mediated an end to the Russo-Japanese War.* Yet when the Japanese didn't get everything they wanted and blamed Roosevelt for reasons of domestic politics and national honor, the first anti-American demonstrations in Japanese history broke out. Relations improved sufficiently by 1908 for the Root-Takahira Agreement to be signed, mutually recognizing the status quo in the Asia-Pacific region.

By World War I, suspicions and tensions over commercial competition and naval rivalry were again running high. The wartime alliance against Germany superseded these

---

*For his efforts Roosevelt was awarded the 1905 Nobel Peace Prize; he was the first American president to win that esteemed recognition.

tensions for a while, and the Washington Naval Conference of 1921–22 worked out naval arms-control agreements (also involving the European powers). But political forces at home were making Japan increasingly militaristic and expansionist. In 1931 Japan took the bold and provocative step of invading Manchuria, against which neither the United States nor the League of Nations responded effectively. U.S.–Japanese tensions mounted through the 1930s, culminating in the attack on Pearl Harbor on December 7, 1941.

U.S. relations with China went through even more extreme fluctuations as China began what would become more than a half-century of revolution. The Chinese revolution in its various stages would be anti-foreigner, pro-democracy, anti–indigenous warlords, anti–Japanese occupation, and Marxist. The United States had to grapple with how best to defend American interests and stand up for American ideals as its relationship with China shifted from friendship and even emulation to antipathy. In 1921 the Nationalist pro-republic revolutionary leader Sun Yat-sen appealed for assistance to the United States as "the champion of liberalism and righteousness, whose disinterested friendship and support of China in her hour of distress has been demonstrated to us more than once." Three years later, though, Sun expressed his disappointment not only at how little support had come, but in the United States's having joined with other foreign powers to intervene in China over an economic dispute. "We might well have expected that an American Lafayette would fight on our side in this good cause. In the twelfth year of our struggle towards liberty there comes not a Lafayette but an American Admiral with more ships of war than any other nation in our waters."[36] The Nationalists soon thereafter struck their alliance with the communists of Mao Zedong. This alliance was short-lived and gave way to renewed civil war. But although the United States resumed its friendship with the Nationalists in 1928, the 1931 invasion of Manchuria by Japan made the limits of this support abundantly clear.

By the time World War II broke out, American interests in Asia and the Pacific had been developing for close to a century.

Great Debates in Foreign Policy Politics

Going to War

Americans have a tendency to think that only since the trauma of the Vietnam War has the nation experienced political controversy and uncertainty regarding whether to go to war. Yet as we discussed in Chapter 2, no domain better fits the "invitation to struggle" characterization of the foreign policy provisions of the Constitution than war powers. A closer look at the historical record shows that decisions on going to war have rarely come easily or readily; time and again they have been the subject of intense political debate, in early versions of the contentious Pennsylvania Avenue diplomacy between the president and Congress.

In the ***War of 1812***, for example, it took almost three weeks after President James Madison's request for a declaration of war for Congress to approve it. Even then, the votes were far from unanimous—79 to 49 in the House, 19 to 13 in the Senate—and closely followed party and regional lines. Opposition in the New England states was so strong that state leaders initially withheld both money and troops. Although myths later developed about the war's being a "glorious triumph," the historian Donald Hickey takes the view that "Mr. Madison's war" was a "futile and costly struggle in which the United States had barely escaped dismemberment and disunion." Hickey also quotes Thomas Jefferson that the War of 1812 "arrested the course of the most remarkable tide of prosperity any nation ever experienced."[37]

Controversy and interbranch maneuvering characterized the politics that led up to the ***Mexican War*** of 1846–48. The key issue in this war was the annexation of Texas, the "lone star republic," which had declared its independence from Mexico in 1836. In the 1840s, knowing that Congress was divided on the issue and thus was not likely to authorize a troop commitment to defend the annexation against the Mexicans, President John Tyler sought to make war secretly. Word leaked, however, prompting Senator Thomas Hart Benton, a leading politician of the day, to denounce Tyler's actions as "a crime against God and man and our own Constitution . . . a piece of business which belonged to Congress and should have been referred to them." President Tyler next tried the treaty route, proposing a treaty of annexation to the Senate. But the ratification vote in the Senate fell short of the two-thirds margin needed. Tyler then pulled a deft legislative maneuver by which he re-introduced the annexation proposal in the form of a joint resolution. A joint resolution must be approved by both the House and the Senate but requires only a majority vote in each house. Although denounced as "an undisguised usurpation of power and violation of the Constitution," it worked—Texas was annexed as the twenty-eighth state.[38]

Mexico responded by breaking off diplomatic relations with the United States. The new president, James K. Polk, Jr., who had defeated Tyler in the 1844 elections, "stampeded Congress" into a declaration of war by sending American troops into an area of disputed land where "Mexican units who, operating no doubt on their own theory of defensive war, supposed themselves repelling an invasion of Mexico." Many in Congress "had the uneasy feeling that the President had put something over on them."[39] But political considerations then were no different than today: when forced to vote one way or the other, elected representatives were reluctant to go on record against declaring war on a country whose troops, however provoked, had fired on American troops.

Among those who had that uneasy feeling was a first-term representative from Illinois named Abraham Lincoln. "Allow the President to invade a neighboring nation, whenever he shall deem it necessary," Representative Lincoln wrote at the time, "and you allow him to make war at [his] pleasure. Study to see if you fix *any limit* to his power in this respect."[40] Many a member of Congress would invoke Lincoln's views a century and a quarter later in the context of the Vietnam War.

The Spanish-American War of 1898 began with quite a bit of fervor, especially among expansionists in Congress and as whipped up by the "yellow journalism" of the newspaper tycoon William Randolph Hearst. The primary precipitating incident was the bombing of the battleship U.S.S. *Maine,* allegedly by Spain, killing 266 Americans in Havana Harbor, Cuba. Spurred by rallying cries such as "Remember the *Maine,* To Hell with Spain," Congress declared war. Thousands of young men enlisted in what was dubbed "a splendid little war." But although it took only four months of fighting before Spain sued for peace, the death toll was much heavier than expected. For many, this was no more "splendid" than other wars, as movingly conveyed in a letter to the editor of the *San Francisco Examiner* from the widow of a fallen soldier:

> You men who clamored for war, did you know what it would mean to the women of our country, when strife and bloodshed should sweep o'er the land; when the shouts of victory would but ineffectually drown the moans of the women who mourned for the lives of those that were given to make that victory possible? . . .
>
> To you who will celebrate our nation's success, when your spirits are raised in triumph and your songs of thanksgiving are the loudest, remember that we, who sit and weep in our closed and darkened homes, have given our best gifts to our country and our flag.
>
> Patriotism, how many hearts are broken in thy cause?[41]

As we saw earlier in this chapter, U.S. entry into World War I came almost three years after the war had started, and only after German U-boats and other direct threats to U.S. security drove home the point that isolationism was no longer possible. Germany, as President Wilson made the case, had "thrust" war upon the United States. In this context of a clear and present danger Congress approved a declaration of war by wide margins, 82 to 6 in the Senate and 373 to 50 in the House. The country pulled together, enlisting in droves under the rallying cry "Johnny Get Your Gun" and doing whatever was necessary for the war effort. Yet what was supposed to be "the war to end all wars" proved not to be so. More people died in World War I than in all the wars fought the world over in the preceding century. The American death toll was 116,516, with more than twice that many wounded.

No wonder the pattern of going to war reluctantly repeated itself in World War II. It was only after the direct attack by Japan on **Pearl Harbor**—a day of "infamy," as FDR called it—that the United States entered a war that had been raging for more than two years in Europe and even longer than that in Asia. Some historians, noting that the initial declaration of war passed by Congress was only against Japan, still wonder whether the United States would have gone to war against Germany had Hitler not declared war against the United States a few days later.

Americans came to know World War II as the "good war," in the author Studs Terkel's phrase. But the "good war" took a heavy toll, including more than one million American soldiers killed or wounded. The belief in the justness and righteousness of the cause against Hitler and Nazism and against Japanese aggression—in Peace, Power, Principles, and Prosperity all being at stake—kept public support solid despite such high casualties. Compared with earlier and later wars, however, this one was very much the historical exception.

National Security vs. the Bill of Rights

Another major recurring foreign policy politics debate has been over the tension between the demands and exigencies of safeguarding the nation's security, and the guarantees of individual rights and civil liberties ensconced in the Bill of Rights. "Perhaps it is a universal truth," James Madison wrote in a letter to Thomas Jefferson in 1798, "that the loss of liberty at home is to be charged to provisions against danger, real or pretended, from abroad."[42] How far can the justification of national security be taken, even with respect to what Madison meant by "real" danger from abroad, let alone as a rationale for "pretended" ones?

Madison himself fought bitterly against the repressive *Alien and Sedition Acts* passed by Congress and signed by President John Adams in 1798. On their face these laws were protection against subversive activities by the French and their sympathizers at a time when the United States and France were on the verge of war. But in reality they were intended to silence the opponents of war—whose leaders were none other than Madison and Jefferson—by limiting their freedom of speech and of the press. The acts represented a "loss of liberty" in the name of a "danger from abroad" which, though not fully "pretended," also was not as real as it was made out to be.

In the name of saving the Union, over the course of the Civil War, President Lincoln took a number of actions that infringed on the Bill of Rights and other civil liberties. He suspended *habeas corpus* and claimed authority to arrest without warrant persons suspected of "disloyal" practices. He banned "treasonable" correspondence from being delivered by the U.S. Post Office. He censored newspapers. He seized property. He proclaimed martial law. To those who criticized such actions as going too far, Lincoln responded that "measures otherwise unconstitutional might become lawful by becoming indispensable to the preservation of the Constitution through the preservation of the Nation." Yet he also stressed that these must be temporary powers. "The Executive power itself would be greatly diminished," he stated in 1864, "by the cessation of actual war."[43]

The *Espionage and Sedition Acts* of 1917–18, passed during World War I, were "as extreme as any legislation of the kind anywhere in the world." They made it illegal to "willfully utter, print, write or publish any disloyal, profane, scurrilous or abusive language about the United States, its form of government, the Constitution, soldiers and sailors, the flag or uniform of the armed forces . . . or by word or act oppose the cause of the United States."[44] Quite the broad prohibition! Ads were placed in the *Saturday Evening Post* and other mass-circulation magazines urging readers to report to the government "the man who spreads pessimistic stories . . . cries for peace or belittles our effort to win the war."[45] The postmaster general refused to deliver any magazine that included critical views. Schools dropped German from their curricula. German books were taken off the shelves of public libraries. Some cities banned dachshunds from their streets. Restaurants and snack bars stopped serving sauerkraut and started calling hamburgers "liberty steaks." All told, about two thousand people were prosecuted and eight hundred convicted of violations of the Espionage and Sedition Acts. The most prominent was Eugene V. Debs, leader of the Socialist party, who as a candidate for president in 1912 had received about 6 percent of the vote. Debs was given a twenty-year prison sentence for giving a speech against the war—and while still in prison during the 1920 presidential election received nearly one million votes!

The Supreme Court justices Oliver Wendell Holmes and Louis Brandeis, two giants in the Court's history, wrestled with this balance between national security and civil liberties. Justice Holmes defended the constitutionality of the Espionage and Sedition Acts with a famous analogy: "The most stringent protection of free speech," Holmes wrote, "would not protect a man in falsely shouting 'fire' in a theater and causing a panic." Holmes argued that the same general principle applied but the key was to determine in any particular instance "whether the words are used in such circumstance and are of such a nature as to create a clear and present danger that they will bring about the substantive evils that Congress has a right to prevent." Something that might not meet the "clear and present danger" test in times of peace may meet it in times of war: "When a nation is at war many things that might be said in time of peace are such a hindrance to its effort that their utterance will not be endured so long as men fight." Justice Brandeis concurred in his opinion but expressed concerns that the clear and present danger test was too easy to pass. In one case in which a man was convicted for distributing pro-German press reports, Brandeis criticized what he saw as "an intolerant majority, swayed by passion or by fear, . . . prone . . . to stamp as disloyal opinions with which it disagrees." Holmes and Brandeis, however, were in the minority in qualifying their approval of the statutes with these concerns.[46]

World War I ended and the German enemy was defeated, but a new enemy had arisen with the 1917 Communist revolution in Russia. During the **Red Scare** of 1919–20, the Wilson administration, led by Attorney General A. Mitchell Palmer, grossly overreacted to fears of internal subversion linked to "world communism" with heavy-handed repression and blatant disregard for civil liberties. "The blaze of revolution," Palmer propounded, was "eating its way into the home of the American workman, its sharp tongues of revolutionary heat . . . licking the altars of churches, leaping into the belfry of the school bell, crawling into the sacred corners of American homes, burning up the foundations of society."[47] Claiming the wartime Sedition Act as authority, on the night of January 2, 1920, Palmer sent his agents sweeping into meeting halls, offices, and homes all over the country, arresting about four thousand people as alleged communists, many even without warrants. The "Palmer raids" were so extreme that Congress almost impeached the attorney general. But it didn't, and Palmer kept up his anticommunist attacks. The Supreme Court largely supported these policies, although with strong dissents from Justice Brandeis. As his biographer recounts, Brandeis felt that restrictions on civil liberties made necessary by war "would be entirely inappropriate in peace . . . when the nation's survival was not at stake. . . . [D]uring a war 'all bets are off.' But not otherwise."[48]

Perhaps the most profound violation of civil liberties in the name of national security came during World War II with the internment of 120,000 Japanese Americans in prison camps. On February 19, 1942, about three months after the Japanese attack on Pearl Harbor, President Franklin Roosevelt issued Executive Order 9066, uprooting people of Japanese ethnicity from their homes, jobs, and communities and banishing them to fenced-in prison camps, in the name of the war effort. "A Jap's a Jap!" proclaimed one general. "It makes no difference whether he's an American or not." In reality, though, not only were the vast majority of Japanese Americans loyal and patriotic citizens of the United States, once they were allowed in 1943 to join the military more than seventeen thousand Japanese Americans volunteered. "Even though my older brother was living in Japan," one Japanese American stated, "I told my parents that I was going to enlist because America was my country."[49] One unit, the Japanese-American 442nd Regimental Combat Team, fought with such valor as to amass more than eighteen thousand individual decorations, more than any other unit of its size and duration.[50]

At the time of the ***Japanese-American internments***, very few voices were raised in protest in government, the media, or society at large. The Supreme Court even ruled that FDR's executive order was constitutional.[51] Not until more than thirty years later was a law passed as an official apology, providing some monetary compensation to those Japanese Americans who had been interned and to their families. Although this was an important act of repentance and retribution, it hardly made up for the thousands of lives damaged or destroyed. The Bill of Rights was trampled insofar as it pertained to Japanese Americans, in the name of national security.

Thus, repeatedly, between 1789 and 1945 tensions arose between considerations of national security and fundamental guarantees provided in the Bill of Rights. Repeatedly, the latter were overtaken by the former. And, repeatedly, the criticisms and outrage that followed were severe. Yet, as we will see in the next chapter, the pattern was repeated during the Cold War and, as we will see in Chapters 9 and 11, is being repeated again in the context of the war on terrorism.

Free Trade vs. Protectionism

A member of Congress from Detroit smashing a Toyota with a sledgehammer in front of the Capitol dome in the late 1970s; Ross Perot warning in 1992–93 of the "giant sucking sound" of jobs leaving the U.S. that the passage of NAFTA (the North American Free Trade Agreement) would set off; outcries in 2006 over an Arab company's running some U.S. seaports: recent decades have been full of controversies over trade and other international economic policies. But although it is true that this recent discord contrasts with the prevailing pro–free trade consensus of 1945–71, most of the rest of American history has seen extensive interest-group pressure and other political conflict over ***free trade*** vs. ***protectionism.***

In the first half of the nineteenth century, divisions over the tariff issue largely followed regional lines. Northern industrialists seeking protection from foreign competition for their "infant industries" and northern and western farmers who produced primarily for the domestic market favored high tariffs on imported goods. Northeastern merchants, whose economic interests lay in import and export businesses, and southern plantation owners, whose cotton and tobacco crops were in high demand in Europe, favored low tariffs in order to facilitate international trade. Indeed, although slavery clearly was the most contentious issue, the Civil War was also fed by these fundamental differences over trade policy.

In the late nineteenth century not only was the tariff the primary foreign policy issue of the day, tariff policy was one of the defining differences between the Democratic and Republican parties. In those days the Democrats were predominately in support of free trade while the Republicans were so protectionist as to proclaim high tariffs as one of the "plain and natural rights of Americans."[52] When President Grover Cleveland, a Democrat, managed to get a tariff reduction bill through the House, the Republican-controlled Senate killed it. The Republicans rode their protectionist position to a major victory in the 1888 elections, with Benjamin Harrison defeating Cleveland for president and Republicans winning majorities in both the House and the Senate.

Yet the Republican-controlled Congress and the new Republican president also fought over trade issues. The most significant battle centered on the Harrison administration's proposal for authority to negotiate reciprocity treaties. A reciprocity treaty involves an agreement with another country for mutual reductions in tariffs. The Senate was willing to go along with this since it would still be a player through its treaty-ratification authority. But the House, which has no constitutional authority over treaties, was concerned about being left out of the ball game. It took extensive negotiations—seven days of Republican party caucuses, according to the leading historian of the period—to get the House to agree even to a compromise version.[53] The Congress and president did agree, though, on higher tariffs, and passed these in the McKinley Tariff Act (named for William McKinley, then the chair of the House Ways and Means Committee).

Politics in those days was extremely volatile. Democrats took control of both the House and the Senate in the 1890 midterm elections, and Grover Cleveland won back the White House in 1892, becoming the only president ever to win two nonconsecutive terms. Since Democratic victories were in large part attributable to the political pendulum's having swung back toward antitariff sentiment, Cleveland made major tariff reductions one of his highest priorities. But with special interests exerting extensive pressure, by the time his antitariff bill passed the Senate it had 634 amendments. It still reduced tariffs, but by much less than the president had wanted.

In 1896, in yet another swing of the political pendulum, Republican William McKinley was elected president and the Republicans regained control of Congress. Ironically, President McKinley now pushed Congress for an even greater delegation of authority to negotiate trade treaties than that which Representative McKinley had opposed as inimical to the Constitution. McKinley won the authority, but although he and his successors would use this authority to negotiate eleven trade treaties over the next decade, not a single one was ever ratified.[54] In 1909 Congress took back the reciprocal trade treaty authority and did not regrant it to the president for another quarter-century, until after the 1930 *Smoot-Hawley* protectionist tariff had worked its disastrous effects, including contributing to the Great Depression.

With these lessons in mind, Congress ceded much of its authority to set tariffs to the president in the ***Reciprocal Trade Agreements Act*** (**RTAA**) of 1934. The RTAA, called "a revolution in tariff making" by one historian,[55] delegated to the president authority to cut tariffs on his own by as much as 50 percent if he could negotiate reciprocal cuts with other countries. This laid the basis for a fundamental shift away from protectionism and toward free trade, a shift that was further manifested following World War II, when the United States played a key role in setting up the General Agreement on Tariffs and Trade as the basis for an international system of free trade.

Summary

In studying history, we see that change often is more readily apparent than continuity. In so many ways the twenty-first century and its foreign policy challenges are vastly different from those of even the recent past, let alone those of the eighteenth, nineteenth, and early twentieth centuries. Yet many of the foreign policy choices we debate today are, at their core, about the same fundamental questions that have been debated over two centuries of U.S. history.

Can the United States best fulfill its national interest in all its components through isolationism or internationalism? How big a military and how much defense spending are needed to ensure U.S. Power and ensure the Peace? How true to its democratic

Principles does U.S. foreign policy need to be? Are those who criticize U.S. foreign policy as imperialistic right? How are we to assess the record of relations in such major regions as Latin America and Asia? Every one of these questions of foreign policy strategy has a long history that provides important context for current foreign policy choices.

The same is true with regard to the three historical debates over foreign policy politics examined in this chapter. Struggles between the president and Congress over decisions to go to war are hardly just a post-Vietnam matter; they go back a long way in U.S. history. The profoundly difficult trade-offs between the demands of national security and the constitutional guarantees of civil liberties have been demonstrated all too many times in U.S. history. And the interest-group pressures over free trade vs. protectionism were at least as intense in the late nineteenth century as in the late twentieth century.

It is therefore crucial that as we consider the foreign policy challenges today, we not only seek to understand what is new about the world today but also seek to learn from the prologue that is the past.

In the next chapter we will look at the Cold War and the more recent historical context it provides to our analysis of today's challenges.

Notes

[1] For a fuller diplomatic history, see such authors as Walter LaFeber, *The American Age: U.S. Foreign Policy at Home and Abroad, 1750–Present* (New York: Norton, 1996); Walter A. McDougall, *Promised Land, Crusader State: The American Encounter with the World since 1776* (Boston: Houghton Mifflin, 1997); Walter Russell Mead, *Special Providence: American Foreign Policy and How It Changed the World* (New York: Knopf, 2001); Thomas G. Paterson, J. Gary Clifford, and Kenneth J. Hagan, *American Foreign Relations: A History Since 1895* (Lexington, Mass.: D.C. Health, 1995); also the timelines in Bruce W. Jentleson and Thomas G. Paterson, *Encyclopedia of U.S. Foreign Relations,* Appendix 1: Chronology of U.S. Foreign Relations (compiled by Kurk Dorsey), vol. 4 (New York; Oxford University Press, 1997), and Knowledge Rush, www.knowledgerush .com/kr/encyclopedia/Timeline_of_United-States_diplomatic_history.

[2] James M. McCormick, *American Foreign Policy and Process* (Itasca, Ill.: Peacock, 1992), 15–16.

[3] Cited in John Gerard Ruggie, "The Past as Prologue? Interests, Identity and American Foreign Policy," *International Security* 21.4 (Spring 1997): 89–90.

[4] Richard J. Barnet, *The Rockets' Red Glare: War, Politics and the American Presidency* (New York: Simon & Schuster, 1990), 142.

[5] Woodrow Wilson, "An Address to a Joint Session of Congress," in Ray Stannard Baker and William E. Dodd, eds., *The Public Papers of Woodrow Wilson,* (New York: Harper and Brothers, 1927), 5: 6–16.

[6] Both cited in Barnet, *Rockets' Red Glare,* 200.

[7] Robert Shogan, *Hard Bargain: How FDR Twisted Churchill's Arm, Evaded the Law, and Changed the Role of the American Presidency* (New York: Scribner's, 1995).

[8] Franklin D. Roosevelt, 1941 State of the Union Address, www.americanrhetoric.com/speeches/ fdrthefourfreedoms.htm (accessed 6/6/09).

[9]Arthur M. Schlesinger, Jr., "Back to the Womb? Isolationism's Renewed Threat," *Foreign Affairs* 74.4 (July/August 1995): 4.

[10]Quoted in Paul A. Varg, *Foreign Policies of the Founding Fathers* (Baltimore: Penguin, 1970), 192.

[11]Samuel Eliot Morison and Henry Steele Commager, *The Growth of the American Republic* (New York: Oxford University Press, 1940), 2: 471.

[12]Richard Polenberg, *War and Society: The United States, 1941–1945* (New York: Lippincott, 1972), 5.

[13]There are also domestic-policy versions of American exceptionalism. See Seymour Martin Lipset, *American Exceptionalism: A Double-Edged Sword* (New York: Norton, 1996).

[14]Cited in Anders Stephanson, *Manifest Destiny: American Expansionism and the Empire of Right* (New York: Hill and Wang, 1995), 19.

[15]The term was first used by John L. O'Sullivan, editor of the *Democratic Review*. O'Sullivan was an interesting character, the descendant of "a long line of Irish adventurers and mercenaries," known among other things for being involved in failed plots to annex Cuba, and said by his friend, the writer Nathaniel Hawthorne, to be a "bizarre" fellow. Stephanson, *Manifest Destiny,* xi–xii.

[16]Woodrow Wilson, "Address to Joint Session of Congress," April 2, 1917, reprinted in Arthur S. Link, ed., *Papers of Woodrow Wilson* (Princeton: Princeton University Press, 1966), 519–27.

[17]Strobe Talbott, *The Great Experiment: The Story of Ancient Empires, Modern States and the Quest for a Global Nation* (New York: Simon & Schuster, 2008), 151.

[18]Atlantic Charter, joint statement by President Roosevelt and Prime Minister Churchill, August 14, 1941, in U.S. Department of State, *Foreign Relations of the United States: 1941, Vol. 1: General, the Soviet Union* (Washington, D.C.: U.S. Government Printing Office, 1958), 367–69.

[19]Thomas G. Paterson, J. Gary Clifford, and Kenneth J. Hagan, *American Foreign Relations: A History to 1920* (Lexington, Mass.: Heath, 1995), 233.

[20]Michael Hunt, *Ideology and U.S. Foreign Policy* (New Haven: Yale University Press, 1987), 53.

[21]Thomas Bortelsmann, "Race and Racism," in *Encyclopedia of U.S. Foreign Relations,* Bruce W. Jentleson and Thomas G. Paterson, eds. (New York: Oxford University Press, 1997), 3: 451–52.

[22]Cited in Alexander DeConde, "Ethnic Groups," in *Encyclopedia of U.S. Foreign Relations,* Jentleson and Paterson, eds., 2: 111.

[23]Cited in Walter LaFeber, *The American Age: United States Foreign Policy at Home and Abroad,* 2d ed. (New York: Norton, 1994), 213.

[24]Cited in Morison and Commager, *Growth of the American Republic,* 324.

[25]Cited in Paterson, Clifford, and Hagan, *American Foreign Relations: A History to 1920,* 229, from Hugh Deane, *Good Deeds and Gunboats* (San Francisco: China Books and Periodicals, 1990), 65.

[26]Both cited in Paterson, Clifford, and Hagan, *American Foreign Relations: A History to 1920,* 175.

[27]Paterson, Clifford, and Hagan, *American Foreign Relations: A History to 1920,* 254–57.

[28]Quoted in Paterson, Clifford, and Hagan, *American Foreign Relations: A History to 1920,* 262–63.

[29]Gaddis Smith, "Monroe Doctrine," in *Encyclopedia of U.S. Foreign Relations,* Jentleson and Paterson, eds., 3: 159–67.

[30]Franklin D. Roosevelt, "Our Foreign Policy: A Democratic View," *Foreign Affairs* 6.4 (July 1928): 584.

[31]Cited in Peter W. Rodman, *More Precious Than Peace: The Cold War and the Struggle for the Third World* (New York: Scribner's 1994), 38.

[32]Quoted in Paterson, Clifford, and Hagan, *American Foreign Relations: A History to 1920,* 133.

[33]Quoted in Akira Iriye, *Across the Pacific: An Inner History of American–East Asian Relations* (New York: Harcourt, Brace, 1967), 23.

[34]Iriye, *Across the Pacific,* 60.

[35]Paterson, Clifford, and Hagan, *American Foreign Relations: A History to 1920,* 135.

[36]Both quotes given in Iriye, *Across the Pacific,* 147–48.

[37]Donald R. Hickey, *The War of 1812: A Forgotten Conflict* (Urbana: University of Illinois Press, 1989), 305, 309.

[38]Arthur M. Schlesinger, Jr., *The Imperial Presidency* (New York: Atlantic Monthly Press, 1974), 51–52.

[39]Schlesinger, *The Imperial Presidency,* 53.

[40]Schlesinger, *The Imperial Presidency,* 54 (emphasis in original).

[41]The letter is from Mrs. Pauline O'Neill, wife of Captain William "Bucky" O'Neill. Captain O'Neill had been the mayor of Prescott in the territory of Arizona. Hailed in a newspaper of the day as "the most many-sided man Arizona had produced," he joined Teddy Roosevelt's fabled "Rough Riders" and was killed in the battle for Kettle Hill, outside Santiago, Cuba. Pauline O'Neill, letter published in the *San Francisco Examiner,* August 7, 1897, in the collection of the Sharlott Hall Museum, Prescott, Arizona.

[42]S. Padover, ed., *The Complete Madison* (New York: Harper, 1953), 258.

[43]Quoted in Schlesinger, *The Imperial Presidency,* 71, 75.

[44]Morison and Commager, *Growth of the American Republic,* 478.

[45]Cited in Barnet, *Rockets' Red Glare,* 158.

[46]Lewis J. Paper, *Brandeis* (Englewood Cliffs, N.J.: Prentice-Hall, 1983), 282–83.

[47]Paterson, Clifford, and Hagan, *American Foreign Relations: A History to 1920,* 324.

[48]Paper, *Brandeis,* 283. On these cases Justice Holmes was much less supportive of Brandeis.

[49]Both quoted in Jerel A. Rosati, *The Politics of United States Foreign Policy* (New York: Harcourt, Brace, 1993), 476–78.

[50]Ronald Smothers, "Japanese-Americans Recall War Service," *New York Times,* June 19, 1995, A8.

[51]*Korematsu v. United States* (1944), cited in Thomas M. Franck and Michael J. Glennon, eds., *Foreign Relations and National Security Law: Cases, Materials and Simulations* (St. Paul, Minn.: West, 1987), 43–53.

[52]Tom E. Terrill, *The Tariff, Politics and American Foreign Policy, 1874–1901* (Westport, Conn.: Greenwood, 1973), 199.

[53]Terrill, *The Tariff,* 172.

[54]Robert A. Pastor, *Congress and the Politics of Foreign Economic Policy, 1929–1976* (Berkeley: University of California Press, 1980), 75.

[55]Sidney Ratner, cited in Pastor, *Congress and the Politics of Foreign Economic Policy,* 92.

5   *The Cold War Context: Origins and First Stages*

Introduction: "Present at the Creation"

"Present at the Creation" is how Dean Acheson, secretary of state in the early days of the Cold War, titled his memoirs. At the outset of the Cold War, Americans felt they were confronting threats as dangerous and challenges as profound as any they had ever before faced in history. Moreover, the United States was no longer merely pursuing its own foreign policy; it was being looked to as a world leader, a "superpower." It had been a leader in World War II, but only after overcoming isolationism, and even then only for a period that, as dire as it was, lasted less than four years. The Cold War, though, would go on for more than four decades. And so years later, when Acheson wrote his memoirs, he chose a title that reflected his generation's sense of having created its own new era.[1]

During World War II the United States and the Soviet Union had been allies. President Franklin D. Roosevelt, the British prime minister Winston Churchill, and the Soviet leader Josef Stalin were known as the Big Three. The Soviets were second only to the British as beneficiaries of American Lend-Lease economic assistance during the war, receiving more than $9 billion worth of food, equipment, and other aid. Even Stalin's image as a ruthless dictator who viciously purged his own people in the 1930s was "spun" more favorably to the amiable "Uncle Joe." Yet fundamentally, the American-Soviet wartime alliance was another instance of the "enemy-enemy-friend" maxim. "I can't take communism," was how FDR put it, "but to cross this bridge I'd hold hands with the Devil."[2] After the war was over and the common enemy, Nazi Germany, had been vanquished, would the alliance continue? Should it?

Different views on these questions are reflected in the debate over the origins of the **Cold War.** This debate is marked by two main schools of thought, the orthodox and the revisionist. The *orthodox* view puts principal responsibility squarely on the shoulders of Josef Stalin and the Soviet Union.[3] This view has been strengthened by revelations in recent years from Soviet and other archives. "We now know," the historian John Lewis Gaddis contends, that "as long as Stalin was running the Soviet Union, a cold war was unavoidable." The Soviets used the Red Army to make Eastern Europe their own sphere of influence. They sought to subvert governments in Western Europe. They blockaded West Berlin in an effort to force the United States, France, and Britain out. In Asia they supported the Chinese communists and helped start the Korean War. They supported communist parties in Southeast Asia and Latin America, and within African anticolonial movements; indeed, one of the fundamental tenets of Soviet communist ideology was to aid revolution everywhere. And in the United States they ran a major spy ring trying, among other things, to steal the secret of the atomic bomb.

In the *revisionist* view of the origins of the Cold War, the United States bears its own significant share of the responsibility.[4] Some revisionists see the United States as seeking its own empire, for reasons of both Power and Prosperity. Its methods may have been less direct and more subtle, but its objectives nevertheless were domination to serve American grand ambitions. In citing evidence for U.S. neo-imperialist ambitions, these critics point as far back as the 1918–19 U.S. "expeditionary force" that, along with European forces, intervened in Russia to try to reverse the Russian Revolution. Other revisionists see the problem more as one of U.S. miscalculation. They maintain that the Soviets were seeking little more than to ensure their own security by preserving Poland and Eastern Europe as a *cordon sanitaire* to prevent future invasions of Soviet soil. What transpired in those early post–World War II years, these revisionists argue, was akin to the classic "security dilemma," often present in international politics, in which each side is motivated less by aggression than by the fear that the other side cannot be trusted, and thus sees its own actions as defensive while the other side sees them as offensive. Had U.S. policy been more focused on reassurance and cooperation, rather than deterrence and containment, there might not have been a Cold War.

With this debate in mind, this chapter and the next analyze the dynamics of foreign policy choice for the United States as played out during the Cold War, with regard to both foreign policy strategy and foreign policy politics. Doing so will provide a deeper understanding of the Cold War itself and the contemporary context to go with the historical one (from Chapter 4) for the challenges and choices that face the United States in the post–Cold War era.

Peace: International Institutionalism and the United Nations

Work on the United Nations (UN) was begun well before World War II was over. One of the primary reasons that World War I had not turned out to be "the war to end all wars," as Woodrow Wilson and other leaders had hoped, was the weakness of the League of Nations. Franklin Roosevelt and other world leaders felt they had learned from that experience, and this time intended to create a stronger global body as the basis for a stable peace.

The Original Vision of the United Nations

The grand hope for the **United Nations,** as articulated by FDR's secretary of state, Cordell Hull, was that "there would no longer be need for spheres of influence, for alliances, for balance of power, or any other special arrangements through which, in the unhappy past, nations strove to safeguard their security or promote their interests."[5] Their vision was of "one world" and a peace that was broad and enduring.

This was quintessential *International Institutionalism,* a vision of international relations in which the national interest of the United States, as well as the national interests of other nations, would be served best by multilateral cooperation through international institutions—a world that could be, in the metaphors cited in Chapter 1, the "cultivable garden" of peace, not necessarily the "global jungle" of power. The United States, more than any other country, saw the world in these terms and pushed for the creation of the UN. It was in San Francisco on June 26, 1945, that the UN Charter was signed (with fifty-one original signatories). New York City was chosen as the location for UN headquarters.

The lesson drawn from the failure of the **League of Nations** was not that the International Institutionalist strategy was inherently flawed, but that the post–World War I version of it had two crucial errors. One was U.S. nonmembership. FDR knew that American membership was key to the UN and that the UN was necessary to prevent the United States from reverting to isolationism. U.S. membership in the UN was "an institutional tripwire," as political scientist John Ruggie calls it, "that would force American policymakers to take positions on potential threats to international peace and security . . . not simply to look the other way, as they had done in the 1930s."[6] FDR was determined not to make the same political mistakes that Woodrow Wilson had made. Roosevelt worked closely with Congress, including giving a major role in the U.S. delegation to the San Francisco Conference to senior Republicans such as Senator Arthur Vandenberg of

Michigan. He also used his "fireside chats" and other political techniques to ensure that public opinion supported the UN. All this work paid off: the Senate vote on U.S. membership in the UN was 89–2, and public-opinion polls showed that 66 percent of Americans favored U.S. membership and only 3 percent were opposed (31 percent were uncertain).

Responding to the second error of post–World War I internationalism, world leaders strove to ensure that the UN would be a stronger institution than the League had been. Having the United States as a member was part of this plan, but so was institutional design. The League had allocated roughly equal powers to its Assembly, comprising all member nations, and to its Council, made up of permanent seats for the four "great powers" that were League members (Britain, France, Italy, and Japan) and four seats to be rotated among other member nations; all seats on the Council were equally powerful. In contrast, the UN gave its Security Council much greater authority than its General Assembly. The UN Security Council could authorize the use of military force, order the severance of diplomatic relations, impose economic sanctions, and take other actions and make them binding on member states. And the five permanent members of the Security Council—the United States, the Soviet Union, Britain, France, and China—were made particularly powerful, being given the power to veto any Security Council action.

The UN Charter even envisioned a standing UN military force. Article 43 of the charter had called on "all Members . . . to make available to the Security Council, on its call and with special agreement or agreements . . . [to be] negotiated as soon as possible . . . armed force, assistance and facilities . . . necessary for the purpose of maintaining international peace and security." This standing force was to be directed by a Military Staff Committee, consisting of the chiefs of staff of the armed forces of the permanent members of the Security Council. The Military Staff Committee would directly advise the Security Council and be in operational charge of the military forces. No Article 43 agreements were ever concluded, however. Over the years the UN has raised temporary military forces for particular missions such as peacekeeping, but it has never had a permanent standing military of its own. In this and other respects, although making important contributions, the UN did not prove able to provide the institutional infrastructure for a "one world" peace.

The Scaled-Back Reality

One reason the UN was unable to ensure peace was the political ambivalence of a number of countries, including the United States, that wanted an international institution strong enough to help keep the peace but not so strong as to threaten state supremacy or sovereignty. Although Roosevelt and Truman administration officials had helped write the Article 43 provision into the UN Charter, many in Congress saw it as a step too far toward "world government." They supported the UN, but not that much, and had the power of the purse and other legislative authority to ensure that no American troops would be put under any sort of permanent UN command. Congress demonstrated similar reticence with the

Genocide Convention ("convention" is used here as a synonym for treaty) and the Universal Declaration of Human Rights (UDHR). The goals of preventing genocide and promoting human rights obviously were nonobjectionable. But the U.S. Senate refused for years to ratify the Genocide Convention and gave only selective recognition to the UDHR because these documents ostensibly risked giving the UN and international courts jurisdiction over American domestic affairs in a manner that threatened American sovereignty. We will come back to this issue of international institutions versus national sovereignty in Part II of this book, for it has resurfaced as a major debate in post–Cold War foreign policy. The point here is that this issue was present even in the original grand vision of the UN.

The other, more important reason that the UN fell short of its original vision was the onset of the Cold War and the resultant priority given to considerations of Power. Even before the UN Charter was signed, U.S.–Soviet tensions had flared over the future of Poland and other states of Eastern Europe. It also was only weeks after the signing of the UN Charter that the United States dropped the world's first atomic bombs on Japan. President Harry Truman defended his A-bomb decision as the only alternative to a major and risky invasion, but some critics believed it was less about getting Japan to surrender and establishing peace than about demonstrating American military might so as to intimidate the Soviet Union.[7] Whichever interpretation one took, the tensions that arose during this time demonstrated the limits of the UN for managing key international events and actions. This weakness was confirmed by the 1946 controversy over the **Baruch Plan.** Named for Truman's adviser Bernard Baruch, the plan was a U.S. proposal to the UN Atomic Energy Commission for establishing international control of nuclear weapons. The Soviet Union rejected the Baruch Plan. Some cited this as evidence that Stalin's intentions were not peaceful. Others assessed the Baruch Plan as one-sided and actually intended to spur a rejection.[8]

In other ways as well, instead of a unifying institution the UN became yet another forum for the competition between the United States and the Soviet Union and their respective allies. They differed over who should be secretary-general. They disagreed on which countries would be admitted to the General Assembly. Each used its veto so many times that the Security Council was effectively paralyzed. At one point, following the October 1949 communist triumph in the Chinese civil war, the Soviets boycotted the Security Council in protest of its decision to allow Jiang Jieshi (Chiang Kai-shek) and his anticommunist Nationalist government, which had fled to the island of Taiwan, to continue to hold China's UN seat. In fact, one of the few times the Security Council did act decisively in these early years was in June 1950, when communist North Korea invaded South Korea, setting off the Korean War: The United States took advantage of the Soviet boycott of the Security Council to get a resolution passed creating a UN-sponsored military force to defend South Korea.

Americans often view the United Nations as more hostile than friendly. In later chapters, we address this idea as it pertains to the contemporary era. During the early Cold War era, though, as the "International Perspectives" box on page 136 shows, the UN was quite supportive of American foreign policy. Even so, as an international institution it was not

INTERNATIONAL PERSPECTIVES
INTERNATIONAL PERSPECTIVES

SUPPORT FOR THE UNITED STATES
IN THE UN GENERAL ASSEMBLY, 1946–60

This table compares U.S. and Soviet success rates on votes in the UN General Assembly from 1946 to 1960. Two sets of issues are disaggregated: Cold War issues and other international affairs issues. On Cold War issues the American position was supported in 94.3 percent of General Assembly votes, compared with only 6.1 percent for the Soviet position. On other issues the margin was closer but still favored the United States, 55.1 percent to 50.3 percent for successes and the even larger margin of only 28.6 percent of votes that passed the General Assembly despite U.S. opposition but 40 percent for the Soviets (this takes abstentions into account). The overall scores were 60.3 percent success and 25.3 percent failure for the United States, and 44.5 percent success and 47.2 percent failure for the Soviets.

Percentage of votes in the UN General Assembly, 1946–60*

	UNITED STATES		SOVIET UNION	
	Success	Failure	Success	Failure
Cold War issues	94.3%	3.2%	6.1%	91.4%
Other issues	55.1	28.6	50.3	40.0
All issues	60.3	25.3	44.5	47.2

*Differences from 100 percent are votes in which the United States and the Soviet Union abstained.
Source: Edward T. Rowe, "The United States, the United Nations and the Cold War," *International Organization* 25.1 (Winter 1971): 62.

strong enough to end the global game of "spheres of influence . . . alliances . . . balance of power" and make the break with that "unhappy past" envisioned by Secretary of State Hull and other UN founders. This was not the peace that was supposed to be.

Power: Nuclear Deterrence and Containment

A "one world" peace had its attractions, but was unrealistic—power had to be met with power. Some argued that this should have been foreseen even before World War II was over, and that FDR had conceded too much at the Yalta summit on issues such as the future of Poland. Now more than ever, in the classic Realist dictum presented back in Chapter 1, American foreign policy had to be based on interests defined in terms of power.

For all the other policy changes that emerged over the course of the Cold War, two basic doctrines of Power that developed in these early years remained the core of U.S. strategy. One was **nuclear deterrence.** Bernard Brodie's *Strategy in the Missile Age* (Reading 5.1) was one of the first and most influential books developing nuclear deterrence doctrine. The standard definition of deterrence is the prevention of attack through the fear of retaliation. On the one hand, deterrence is more than just the capacity to defend oneself sufficiently to prevent defeat. On the other hand, it is less than **compellence,** which means getting another state to take a particular action that it otherwise would not.[9] Although the use of deterrence strategy goes far back in history, the nuclear age gave it greater centrality. As devastating as the 1941 Japanese attack on Pearl Harbor had been, the United States managed to absorb it and recover from it. But nuclear weapons, so much more destructive than anything the world had ever seen, changed the world's security landscape. The single atomic bomb (A-bomb) dropped on Hiroshima instantly killed 130,000 people, one-third of the city's population; another 70,000 died later of radiation poisoning and other injuries. As the United States thought about its own national security in the nuclear age, its leaders realized that a strong and resilient defense, though still necessary, was no longer sufficient. Any attack with nuclear weapons or that could lead to the use of nuclear weapons had to be deterred before it began. This capacity for deterrence required a strong military, and especially nuclear weapons capability, and also had political, psychological, and perceptual dimensions. The deterrence "formula" was a combination of capabilities and intentions, both the capacity to retaliate and the will to do so. The requisites for meeting this nuclear deterrence formula changed over time, but the basic strategy of preventing attack through fear of retaliation stayed the same. Its development is a striking example of theory shaping policy, as we elaborate in "Theory in the World" on page 138.

Containment was the other basic doctrine developed during the early Cold War. In February 1946, George F. Kennan, then a high-ranking U.S. diplomat in Moscow, sent a "long telegram" back to Washington in which he sounded the alarm about the Soviet Union. A version of the long telegram later appeared in the prestigious journal *Foreign Affairs* as "The Sources of Soviet Conduct," with authorship attributed to an anonymous "X" (Reading 5.2). Kennan's analysis of Stalin and his Soviet Union was that "there can never be on Moscow's side any sincere assumption of a community of interests between the Soviet Union and powers which are regarded as capitalist." American strategy therefore had to seek the "patient but firm and vigilant containment of Russian expansive tendencies." The Soviet Union was seeking "to make sure that it has filled every nook and cranny available to it in the basin of world power." Kennan recommended a policy of "containment," whereby the United States would counter any attempt by the Soviets to expand their sphere of influence or to spread communism beyond their own borders. Only sustained containment had a chance of bringing about "the gradual mellowing of

5.1

5.2

THEORY IN THE WORLD

THE "WIZARDS OF ARMAGEDDON" AND
COLD WAR NUCLEAR DETERRENCE

Cold War nuclear deterrence doctrine is a particularly strong example of theory shaping policy. Its development involved a "small group of theorists [who] would devise and help implement a set of ideas that would change the shape of American defense policy," and with the highest stakes of possibly meaning "the difference between peace and total war." These theorists were seen as "the wizards of Armageddon," a group impressive in its intellect, developing sophisticated and mysterious theories and strategies, geared to avoiding the horrors of nuclear war.*

The nuclear age changed the nature of deterrence. Whereas in the past, countries could strategize to win wars if deterrence failed, nuclear war could not be won. Scholars and strategists who had studied naval fleets, armies, and even air power now had to develop theories and policies geared more to deterring than to winning wars. "Total nuclear war is to be avoided at all costs," Bernard Brodie wrote. "[S]uch a war, even if we were extraordinarily lucky, would be too big, too all-consuming to permit the survival even of those final values, like personal freedom, for which alone one could think of waging it."†

Brodie and his colleagues were a colorful group. Brodie had been a political science professor at Yale; he "hardly seemed the type to become the pioneer of nuclear strategy . . . short, with glasses . . . awkward . . . badly dressed." Then there was Albert Wohlstetter, a mathematician, up until then "a rather otherworldly figure," in the home-building business. He would later become a professor at the University of Chicago, where among his students would be Paul Wolfowitz, a leading neoconservative in the George W. Bush administration.‡ Wohlstetter's main work was on the need for assured second-strike capabilities, that is, ensuring that even in a case of surprise attack or other Soviet first strike, the surviving American nuclear forces would still be sufficient to credibly threaten retaliation severe enough to destroy the Soviet Union. This was less to fight a nuclear war than to strengthen deterrence through fear of retaliation even as a second strike.

Most colorful of all was Herman Kahn, a physicist, "brazenly theatrical, long-winded, overflowing with a thousand and one ideas."§ Kahn's concern was whether the threat to retaliate could ever be sufficiently credible to convince the other side that America would do it even at the risk of annihilating the human race. He speculated on whether the United States needed a "Doomsday machine" that would be programmed for automatic massive nuclear retaliation without the human factor—the president or anyone else—coming back into the decision. He too argued that this would strengthen deterrence, make nuclear war less likely. The Doomsday machine and Kahn became the basis for the 1962 movie *Dr. Strangelove,* directed by Stanley Kubrick and starring Peter Sellers, controversial at the time and later a film classic.

The leading think tank for these and other nuclear theoretician-strategists was the RAND Corporation. RAND was the Pentagon's main semi-external think tank. Its location near the beaches of Santa Monica, California, provided a setting at once conducive to big thinking yet in its serenity starkly contrasting with scenarios of nuclear war and deterrence. RAND had extensive influence in every administration during this era, especially the Kennedy administration, when Defense Secretary Robert S. McNamara brought RAND scholars into government as part of his team of "defense intellectuals." The wizards now had responsibility for helping avoid Armageddon.

*Fred Kaplan, *The Wizards of Armageddon* (New York: Simon & Schuster, 1983), 11.
†See Reading 5.1.
‡Kaplan, *Wizards of Armageddon,* 11–12, 94.
§Kaplan, *Wizards of Armageddon,* 220.

Soviet power," Kennan argued; it might even reveal the internal contradictions of their system to the point that the Soviet Union would "break up."[10]

The Formative Period, 1947–50

Both deterrence and containment were evident in Truman administration foreign policies. The **Truman Doctrine,** proclaimed in March 1947, was essentially a U.S. commitment to aid Greece and Turkey against Soviet and Soviet-assisted threats. The U.S. aid was economic, not military, and it totaled only about $400 million. But the significance, as President Truman stressed in his historic speech to Congress and the nation, was much more sweeping (see "At the Source," p. 140). This was not just another foreign policy issue involving a couple of important but minor countries. It was a defining moment in history with significance for the fate of the entire post–World War II world. And the United States was the only country that could provide the necessary leadership.

A few months later the **Marshall Plan** was announced in a commencement speech at Harvard University by Secretary of State George Marshall (see "At the Source," p. 140). Most of Western Europe still had not recovered economically from the devastation of World War II. In France, Italy, and elsewhere, communist parties were gaining support by capitalizing on economic discontent. To meet this threat to containment, the Marshall

AT THE SOURCE

THE TRUMAN DOCTRINE AND THE MARSHALL PLAN
Truman Doctrine

66 At the present moment in world history nearly every nation must choose between alternative ways of life. The choice too often is not a free one.

One way of life is based upon the will of the majority, and is distinguished by free institutions, representative government, free elections, guaranties of individual liberty, freedom of speech and religion, and freedom from political oppression.

The second way of life is based upon the will of a minority forcibly imposed upon the majority. It relies upon terror and oppression, a controlled press and radio, fixed elections, and the suppression of personal freedoms.

I believe that it must be the policy of the United States to support free peoples who are resisting attempted subjugation by armed minorities or by outside pressures. . . .

Should we fail to aid Greece and Turkey in this fateful hour, the effect will be far-reaching to the West as well as to the East. . . . 99

Marshall Plan

66 In considering the requirements for the rehabilitation of Europe, the physical loss of life, the visible destruction of cities, factories, mines and railroads was correctly estimated, but it has become obvious during recent months that this visible destruction was probably less serious than the dislocation of the entire fabric of European economy.

The truth of the matter is that Europe's requirements for the next three or four years of foreign food and other essential products—principally from America—are so much greater than her present ability to pay that she must have substantial additional help or face economic, social, and political deterioration of a very grave character. The remedy lies in breaking the vicious circle and restoring the confidence of the European people in the economic future of their own countries and of Europe as a whole. . . .

It is logical that the United States should do whatever it is able to do to assist in the return of normal economic health in the world, without which there can be no political stability and no assured peace. Our policy is directed not against any country or doctrine but against hunger, poverty, desperation, and chaos. Its purpose should be the revival of a working economy in the world so as to permit the emergence of political and social conditions in which free institutions can exist. **"**

Sources: Harry Truman, "Special Message to the Congress on Greece and Turkey: The Truman Doctrine," March 12, 1947, in *Documents on American Foreign Relations* (Princeton: Princeton University Press for the World Peace Foundation, 1947), 19: 6–7; George Marshall, "European Initiative Essential to Economic Recovery," speech made June 5, 1947, at Harvard University, reprinted in *Department of State Bulletin* 16 (June 15, 1947), 1159.

Plan pledged enormous amounts of money, the equivalent of over $60 billion today, as U.S. economic assistance to the countries of Western Europe. Thus began the first major U.S. Cold War foreign-aid program.

The creation of the ***North Atlantic Treaty Organization (NATO)*** in 1949 marked the first peacetime military alliance in American history. To the Truman Doctrine's political-diplomatic commitments and the Marshall Plan's economic assistance, NATO added the military commitment to keep U.S. troops in Europe and the ***collective defense*** pledge that the United States would defend its European allies if they were attacked. Article 5 of the NATO treaty affirmed this pledge of collective defense: "The Parties agree that an armed attack against one or more of them in Europe or North America shall be considered an attack against them all" (see "At the Source," p. 142). This included the commitment to use nuclear weapons against the Soviet Union, even if the attack was on Europe but not directly on the United States. All this was quite a change from earlier American foreign policy, such as George Washington's "beware entangling alliances" and 1930s isolationism. The 82–13 Senate vote ratifying the NATO treaty made clear that this was a consensual change.

Yet within months the Soviet threat became even more formidable. Reports emerged in August 1949 that the Soviet Union now also had nuclear weapons. This came as a surprise to the American public and even to the Truman administration. Could the Soviets really have achieved this on their own? Were spies at work stealing America's nuclear secrets? Although the answers to these questions were unclear at the time, what was certain was that the U.S. nuclear monopoly was broken, and thus the requirements of nuclear deterrence were going to have to be recalculated.

At virtually the same time, the threat to containment grew worse as the Cold War was extended from Europe to Asia. On October 1, 1949, the People's Republic of China was proclaimed by the Chinese communists, led by Mao Zedong and Zhou Enlai, who had won China's civil war. Now China, the world's most populous country, joined the Soviet

AT THE SOURCE

THE NORTH ATLANTIC TREATY

❝ The Parties to this Treaty . . . seek to promote stability and well-being in the North Atlantic area. . . .

Art. 3. In order more effectively to achieve the objectives of this Treaty, the Parties, separately and jointly, by means of continuous and effective self-help and mutual aid, will maintain and develop their individual and collective capacity to resist armed attack. . . .

Art. 5. The Parties agree that an armed attack against one or more of them in Europe or North America shall be considered an attack against them all; and consequently they agree that, if such an armed attack occurs, each of them, in exercise of the right of individual or collective self-defense recognized by Article 51 of the Charter of the United Nations, will assist the Party or Parties, [taking] such actions as it deems necessary, including the use of armed force, to restore and maintain the security of the North Atlantic area. . . . ❞

Signed in 1949 by twelve founding members: Belgium, Canada, Denmark, France, Iceland, Italy, Luxembourg, the Netherlands, Norway, Portugal, the United Kingdom, and the United States.

Source: *Department of State Bulletin* 20.507 (March 20, 1949).

Union, the world's largest, as communism's giant powers. "Red China," for many Americans, seemed an even more ominous enemy than the Soviet Union.

These developments prompted a reassessment of U.S. strategy. *NSC-68,* a seminal security-planning paper developed in early 1950 by President Truman's National Security Council, called for three important shifts in U.S. strategy (see "At the Source," p. 143). First, there needed to be a *globalization* of containment. The threat was not just in Europe and Asia, but everywhere: "the assault on free institutions is world-wide now."[11] This meant that U.S. commitments had to be extended to span the globe. Allies needed to be defended, vital sea lanes protected, and access to strategic raw materials maintained. Part of the rationale was also psychological: the concern that a communist gain anywhere would be perceived more generally as the tide turning in communism's favor and thus would hurt American credibility.

Second, NSC-68 proposed a *militarization* of containment. The Truman Doctrine and the Marshall Plan were largely diplomatic and economic measures. What was needed now

AT THE SOURCE
AT THE SOURCE

NSC-68

❝ The fundamental design of those who control the Soviet Union and the international communist movement . . . calls for the complete subversion or forcible destruction of the machinery of government and structure of society in the countries of the non-Soviet world and their replacement by an apparatus and structure subservient to and controlled from the Kremlin. To that end Soviet efforts are now directed toward the domination of the Eurasian land mass. The United States, as the principal center of power in the non-Soviet world and bulwark of opposition to Soviet expansion, is the principal enemy whose integrity and vitality must be subverted or destroyed by one means or another if the Kremlin is to achieve its fundamental design.

The Soviet Union is developing the military capacity to support its design for world domination. . . .

A more rapid build-up of political, economic, and military strength and thereby of confidence in the free world than is now contemplated is the only course which is consistent with progress toward achieving our fundamental purpose. The frustration of the Kremlin design requires the free world to develop a successfully functioning political and economic system and a vigorous political offensive against the Soviet Union. These, in turn, require an adequate military shield under which they can develop. It is necessary to have the military power to deter, if possible, Soviet expansion, and to defeat, if necessary, aggressive Soviet or Soviet-directed actions of a limited or total character. . . . Unless our combined strength is rapidly increased, our allies will tend to become increasingly reluctant to support a firm foreign policy on our part and increasingly anxious to seek other solutions, even though they are aware that appeasement means defeat. . . .

The whole success of the proposed program hangs ultimately on recognition by this Government, the American people, and all free peoples, that the cold war is in fact a real war in which the survival of the free world is at stake. ❞

Source: Text of memorandum no. NSC-68, from U.S. Department of State, *Foreign Relations of the United States 1950*, 1: 237–39.

was a broad and extensive military buildup: a global ring of overseas military bases, military alliances beyond NATO, and a substantial increase in defense spending. The latter had to be pursued, the NSC-68 strategists stressed, even if it meant federal budget deficits and higher taxes.

The third step called for by NSC-68 was the development of the **hydrogen bomb.** As destructive as the atomic bomb was, a hydrogen bomb (or H-bomb) would be vastly more destructive. The Soviets had developed the A-bomb much sooner than anticipated, so the development of the H-bomb was deemed necessary to maintain nuclear deterrence. Some policy makers believed that the United States should pursue nuclear arms–control agreements with the Soviet Union before crossing this next threshold of a nuclear arms race. But NSC-68 dismissed the prospect of the Soviets' being serious about arms-control negotiations.

NSC-68 was never formally approved. Its recommendations were tough, both strategically and politically, and thus stirred debate within the Truman administration. All that debate became largely moot, though, when the Korean War broke out a few months later. Now there could be little doubt that, as President Truman stated, "communism was acting in Korea just as Hitler, Mussolini, and the Japanese had acted 10, 15, and 20 years earlier."[12] The Korean War lasted three years and ended largely in stalemate. Its lessons were mixed, on the one hand reinforcing the view of the communist threat as globalized, while on the other showing the difficulties of land wars in Asia. It was also during this time that the United States first got involved in another part of Asia, Vietnam, sending aid to the French as they sought to maintain their colonial control against nationalist-communist independence forces led by Ho Chi Minh.

Intensification, 1950s to the Early 1960s

Over the rest of the 1950s and into the 1960s the Cold War intensified in virtually every global region. In Europe, West Germany was brought into NATO, not only to strengthen the NATO alliance, but also to address concerns rooted deep in European historical memories about Germany's rising again. In addition to "keeping the Americans in" and "the Soviets out," by integrating Germany into the U.S.-dominated alliance, NATO also was intended, with World Wars I and II in mind, to "keep the Germans down."[13] The Soviets' response, though, was to formalize their military alliance in Eastern Europe through the Warsaw Pact. The Soviets also demonstrated their determination to maintain their bloc when in 1956 they invaded Hungary to put down a political revolution that threatened communist control. The Soviet invasion left thousands dead and even more imprisoned. Despite much rhetoric from Secretary of State John Foster Dulles about not just the containment but the "rollback" of communism, NATO and the United States did nothing significant to aid the Hungarian freedom fighters.

In 1952 the United States ended the military occupation it had maintained in Japan since the end of World War II. Defense agreements were signed for U.S. troops and bases to be maintained there, both to help defend Japan and as part of the overall containment strategy in Asia. Japan had by then begun functioning as a democracy under a constitution written largely by U.S. officials and including provisions that renounced war and that permanently limited the size and scope of the Japanese military to "self-defense forces." As with Germany, the U.S. strategy in Japan was to finish the business of World War II and start the business of the Cold War, in which these former U.S. enemies were now allies against the Soviet Union, China, and world communism.

As mentioned in the preceding section, this period was also when the United States began its involvement in Vietnam. The United States provided some aid to the French, for whom Vietnam was still a colony, and then stepped up its involvement following the French defeat in 1954. The American concern was not only Vietnam itself: Vietnam was the original case on which the domino theory was based. "You have a row of dominoes set up," as President Eisenhower stated at a 1954 press conference. "You knock over the first one, and what will happen to the last one is the certainty that it will go over very quickly. So you could have a beginning of a disintegration that would have the most profound influences."[14] Throughout this period the United States got more and more involved in Vietnam. Also in Asia, the United States and its allies created the Southeast Asia Treaty Organization (SEATO), somewhat modeled after NATO, to be the Asian link in the chain of alliances with which Eisenhower and Dulles sought to ring the globe.

In the Middle East, the Baghdad Pact was set up in 1955; within a year it included Iran, Iraq, Pakistan, Turkey, and Great Britain, with the United States as a de facto but not formal member. Iraq withdrew from the group in 1958 following a radical coup against its monarchy; the rest of the alliance continued, albeit weakened, under the title Central Treaty Organization (CENTO). Containment was also manifested in Iran in 1953 in the U.S.-led covert action to bring the shah of Iran back to power and depose Prime Minister Mohammed Mossadegh, and in Lebanon in 1958 with the intervention of U.S. Marines in support of the pro-American government against its more radical domestic foes. The Lebanon case was made into a more general precedent, under the rubric of the Eisenhower Doctrine, of U.S. willingness to provide military support to any state in the Middle East against "overt armed aggression from any nation controlled by international communism."[15]

In Latin America, Cold War opposition to Soviet influence was cast as the contemporary follow-up to the Monroe Doctrine. The major challenge came in Cuba in 1958–59 with the revolution led by Fidel Castro. As in Vietnam and elsewhere, the Cuban revolution was a mix of nationalism, anti-imperialism, and communism. Historians continue to debate whether the absolute antagonism that developed between Castro's Cuba and the United States was inevitable, or whether some modus vivendi could have been worked out. Whatever chance there may have been for something other than adversarial relations was gone after the disastrous 1961 Bay of Pigs invasion. The Eisenhower administration planned and the Kennedy administration launched this covert project, in which the United States trained, supplied, and assisted Cuban exiles in an attempted invasion of Cuba aimed at overthrowing Castro. The invasion failed miserably, embarrassing the United States, leaving Castro in power, and intensifying hatred and fear on both sides.*

As for nuclear-deterrence doctrine, this period saw a number of developments. For a while the Eisenhower administration pursued the doctrine of ***massive retaliation,*** by which it threatened to resort to nuclear weapons to counter any Soviet challenge anywhere of any kind. This doctrine was not very credible, though: If a threat was made and delivered on, there would be nuclear war; if a threat was made and not delivered on, its credibility would be undermined, as in the case of the boy who cried wolf. It was also quite risky, especially as the Soviets kept pace with and even seemed poised to overtake the U.S. nuclear program. The Soviets beat the Americans into space in 1957 with the launching of the *Sputnik* satellite. That same year they also tested their first intercontinental ballistic missile (ICBM), which meant that they now had the capacity to overcome large distances and reach U.S. territory with a nuclear attack. This led to great fears of a "missile gap," a Soviet advantage in nuclear weapons, and prompted a massive U.S. nuclear buildup during the Kennedy administration.

In October 1962 the Cuban missile crisis brought the United States and the Soviet Union to the brink of nuclear war.[16] The Soviet decision to base nuclear missiles in Cuba was a daring and by most accounts reckless move. The Soviets defended it as an attempt to equalize the imbalance caused by the massive U.S. nuclear buildup under Kennedy and the stationing of U.S. nuclear forces close to Soviet borders at bases in Turkey and other NATO countries in Europe. For its part, Cuba saw this new Soviet commitment as a way to guarantee that there would not be another Bay of Pigs invasion. Whatever the claims, the effect was to bring the world dangerously close to nuclear war.

In the end the crisis was managed effectively.† Nuclear war was averted. The prevailing assessments, especially at the time, was that the Soviets had backed down, so the United States "won." But the world had come so close—too close—to nuclear war. Although many viewed the Cuban and Soviet actions that started the crisis as confirmation of U.S. global-containment and nuclear-deterrence doctrines, the dangerous dynamics of a situation that could have had catastrophic consequences drove home, as never before, the risks of the Cold War.

Principles: Ideological Bipolarity and the Third World "ABC" Approach

One of the primary differences between the Cold War and other historical great-power struggles was that the Cold War was not just between rival nations but also between opposing ideologies. This "ideological bipolarity" can be seen in the Truman Doctrine,

---

*See p. 156 for further discussion of the Bay of Pigs as an example of flawed foreign policy decision-making.
†See p. 157 for further discussion of the Cuban Missile Crisis.

the Marshall Plan, and many other official pronouncements. There was not much doubt then in general, and there is even less now, about the evils of Soviet communism. Almost immediately after World War II, the Soviets had shown in Poland and elsewhere in Eastern Europe that they had little interest in allowing democracy. In this respect containment was consistent with American principles. The controversy, though, was less about what the United States opposed than whom it supported, and how it did so.

This wasn't so much a problem in Western Europe, where genuinely democratic leaders and political parties emerged (although in countries such as Italy, where the Communist party had major electoral strength, the CIA did covertly seek to manipulate elections). But quite a few in the "Third World" (the term commonly used during the Cold War in reference to Asia, Africa, the Middle East, and Latin America) dictators garbed themselves in the rhetoric of freedom and democracy, though they only met an "ABC" definition of democracy—"anything but communism." It is naive to expect the United States to support only regimes that are considered good at heart and pure in practice. But the ABC rationale was used repeatedly, as if there could be only two options, the communists or the other guy, whoever he might be and whatever his political practices. Moreover, the criteria by which leaders, parties, and movements were deemed communist were often quite subjective, if not manipulative.

Support for "ABC Democrats"

Vietnam is a good example of the U.S. support for an "ABC" leadership. There is much historical debate over whether a relationship could have been worked out with Ho Chi Minh, the Vietnamese leader who was both nationalist and communist. During World War II Ho had worked with the Allies against the Japanese occupation of Vietnam, even receiving arms and aid from the United States. After the war he made appeals to Washington for help, based on America's professed anticolonialism, against France's effort to reestablish its own colonial rule. He even cited the American Declaration of Independence in proclaiming Vietnam's independence in 1945. There was no question that Ho was a communist; he believed in social revolution at home and received support from the Soviet Union and the Chinese communists. Yet when some experts suggested that as a nationalist, and like Tito in Yugoslavia,* Ho would not inevitably make his country a mere communist satellite, such thinking was summarily rejected. It wasn't so much that there was evidence to the contrary as that, as put in a 1949 State Department cable to the U.S. consulate in Hanoi, the "question of whether Ho was as much nationalist as

---

*Josip Broz, better known as Tito, was a communist who led the Yugoslav partisans against Nazi Germany and became Yugoslavia's dictator after the war. In 1948, Tito broke with Stalin and the other members of the Warsaw Pact and began to develop independent ties to the West.

Commie was irrelevant."[17] His communism was all that mattered. Indeed, much later, Melvin Laird, who had been ardently pro-war while a Republican congressman in the 1960s and as secretary of defense in the Nixon administration, acknowledged that "had we understood the depth of his [Ho Chi Minh's] nationalism, we might have been able to derail his communism early on."[18]

Thus the United States threw its support to one Vietnamese "ABC democrat" after another. In 1949, as their alternative to Ho Chi Minh, the French reinstalled Emperor Bao Dai. He was neither a democrat (he bore the title "emperor") nor a nationalist (having sat on the throne during the Japanese occupation in World War II) and he had little credibility with his own people. Internal State Department documents showed that Bao Dai was recognized as a French colonial puppet, but U.S. support for him was rationalized as the only alternative to "Commie domination."[19]

In 1954 the Vietnamese had won their war for independence and the French were forced to withdraw. Two nations, North and South Vietnam, were established, with Ho and the communists in control of the north and the anticommunists in control of the south. This partition was supposed to be temporary, with unification and general elections to be held within a few years. The Eisenhower administration's search for someone who could be built up as a nationalist alternative to Ho turned up Ngo Dinh Diem. Diem was not communist, but his "nationalist" credentials were more made in America through the publicity campaigns on his behalf than earned in the Vietnamese colonial struggles, in which he played a little role. He was also a Catholic in a largely Buddhist country. Diem's rule was highly authoritarian—opposing political parties were abolished, press censorship strictly enforced, Buddhists brutally repressed. He gave extensive power to his brother Ngo Dinh Nhu, by most accounts a shadowy and sinister figure. When a seventy-three-year-old Buddhist monk set himself on fire to protest the regime's repression, Nhu's wife made a sneering remark about Buddhist "barbecues."[20] Indeed, by 1963 Diem was so unpopular that the Kennedy administration had a hand in the coup that brought him down and killed him. Thus, in this case the cycle of contradicting principles ran its course—support an ally in the name of democracy who is at best an ABC democrat, but kill him off when it becomes clear that he is not the solution, and may even be part of the problem.

In Latin America generally, U.S. policy in the early Cold War was summed up in this comment about support for the Nicaraguan dictator Anastasio Somoza: "He may be an S.O.B., but he's our S.O.B."[21] This was the basis for U.S. support of Cuban dictator Fulgencio Batista. At a black-tie reception in early 1955 Vice President Richard Nixon toasted the Batista regime for its "competence and stability." CIA Director Allen Dulles paid a visit shortly thereafter. Yet Batista was known to be "a cruel and lazy tyrant [who] whiled away his time playing canasta and watching horror films, [and] put sadists in charge of the police."[22] The U.S. supported his political repression and torture even when they were directed against noncommunist elements of the opposition.

The ***Alliance for Progress***, established in 1961 by the Kennedy administration, initially was heralded as a shift away from this approach and toward promotion of democracy. "Our Alliance for Progress is an alliance of free governments," President Kennedy proclaimed, "and it must work to eliminate tyranny from a hemisphere in which it has no rightful place."[23] While JFK was pointing his rhetorical finger at Cuba and Fidel Castro, the social and economic elites and the militaries in much of the rest of Latin America, seeing their own oligarchic interests threatened by political and economic reforms, undermined "la Alianza." Military coups ousted reformist governments in the early 1960s in Argentina, Brazil, Ecuador, Honduras, and elsewhere. Although the coup makers invoked anticommunism and containment, in most cases this was a transparent rationalization. Yet the United States largely bought it. In fact, in the case of Brazil, U.S. "enthusiasm" for the coup "was so palpable that Washington sent its congratulations even before the new regime could be installed."[24] The pro-American stance of these regimes (Power) was more important than their being nondemocratic (Principles).

To be sure, some people genuinely believed that communism was so bad that support for "anybody but a communist" and "anything but communism" was consistent with American principles, at least in relative terms and given an imperfect world. One of the problems with this defense, however, was the inclusion of more moderate socialists and nationalists in the "irredeemable communists" category. No doubt this attitude was due in part to the intolerance of ideological bipolarity: it recognized no third way. The ABC attitude also reflected a calculation that, in the event of conflicts between Power and Principles in the U.S. national interest, Principles were to give way.

CIA Covert Action

Questions about consistency with Principles also were raised by CIA covert action seeking the overthrow of anti-American governments, including democratically chosen ones. A commission established by President Eisenhower provided the following recommendation: "Another important requirement is an aggressive covert psychological, political and paramilitary organization more effective, more unique, and if necessary, more ruthless than that employed by the enemy. No one should be permitted to stand in the way of the prompt, efficient and secure accomplishment of this mission. It is now clear that we are facing an implacable enemy. . . . There are no rules in such a game. Hitherto acceptable norms of human conduct do not apply."[25]

One of the cases in which this strategy was applied, in Guatemala in 1954, was discussed in Chapter 1 as an example of "4 Ps" tensions and trade-offs. Another case was that of Iran in 1953. In this case, as we saw earlier in this chapter, the target was the Iranian prime minister Mohammed Mossadegh, who had begun both to nationalize foreign-owned oil companies (Prosperity) and to develop closer relations with the Soviet Union (Power). The United States supported the exiled shah, and the CIA assisted royalist forces in a plot to return the shah to power. The plot succeeded, albeit with a "wave of repression" and "a purge of the armed forces and government bureaucracy" that "continued for more than a year, silencing all sources of opposition to the new regime." In the years following the coup the CIA helped establish and train the shah's new secret police, known as SAVAK. Over the next twenty to twenty-five years, SAVAK "became not just an externally directed intelligence agency but also a powerful, feared and hated instrument of domestic repression"—not exactly a practitioner of democratic principles.[26]

Prosperity: Creation of the Liberal International Economic Order

Along with the dangers of isolationism and appeasement, one of the other lessons that U.S. leaders had learned from the 1920s and 1930s concerned the dangers of trade protectionism and other "beggar-thy-neighbor" economic policies. These policies hurt global prosperity as well as that of the United States. They also contributed to the political instabilities that ultimately led to World War II. Thus one of the other major components of postwar U.S. policy was the creation of the *liberal international economic order (LIEO).* The term "liberal" as used in this context means a relatively open, market-based, free-trade system with a minimum of tariffs and other government-initiated trade barriers, and with international economic relations worked out through negotiations. The opposite of liberalism in this context is not conservatism, as in the domestic-policy context, but protectionism.

The Major International Economic Institutions

As set up in the 1940s, the LIEO had three principal components: (1) a free trade system under the rubric of the *General Agreement on Tariffs and Trade (GATT);* (2) an international monetary system, based on fixed exchange rates and the gold standard, and overseen by the *International Monetary Fund (IMF);* and (3) an international lending and aid system under the International Bank for Reconstruction and Development, also known as the *World Bank.*

The establishment of GATT did not bring about instantaneous free trade. Exceptions were made—for example, for agriculture, which for political and other reasons was much harder to open up to free trade. There were loopholes, as for labor-intensive industries such as shoes and textiles, which were allowed some, albeit not total, protection. And trade disputes continued. The success of GATT was in keeping the arrow pointed in the direction of free trade, in providing a mechanism for managing trade disputes so as to prevent their escalation to trade wars, and in moving the world gradually toward freer trade through periodic "rounds" of negotiations.

Protectionism had generated another insidious practice: the competitive manipulation of currencies. The fixed exchange rates of the IMF system sought to eliminate this form of destructive economic competition and help provide the monetary stability essential for global economic growth. The basic gold-standard exchange rate was set at $36 per ounce of gold. Countries whose international payments were not in balance (i.e., they imported more than they exported) could get some assistance from the IMF but also had to meet stringent IMF guidelines called "conditionalities" for economic and other reforms in order to get that assistance.

The World Bank later would grow into a major source of aid for developing countries, but initially it was focused more on European reconstruction. As of 1955, even though the U.S. Marshall Plan had ceased, about half of World Bank loans were going to industrialized countries; by 1965 this was down to one-fourth, and by 1967 virtually all lending was going to Third World development projects. The World Bank itself was chartered to lend only to governments, but over time it added an affiliate, the International Finance Corporation, that made loans to private enterprises involved in development projects.

Critiques: Economic Hegemony? Neo-Imperialism?

Although in these and other respects the LIEO did provide broad economic benefits internationally, critics point out that it largely reinforced American economic dominance, or *economic hegemony.* Voting rights in both the IMF and the World Bank were proportional to capital contributions, which meant that, as the largest contributor of funds, the United States had a correspondingly large voting share. In GATT negotiations, American positions prevailed more often than not. Indeed, the emphasis on free markets, open trade, and minimal government intervention in the economy also fit American laissez-faire economic ideology. With Europe and Japan still recovering and rebuilding from World War II, the United States dominated the world economy. Thus, while other countries benefited from the LIEO, it helped maintain American economic hegemony to go with American diplomatic dominance and military superiority.

Another critique focuses on corporate interests as driving U.S. policy. This point is often stressed by revisionists in the debate over the origins of the Cold War. Critics cite cases such as Guatemala, where U.S. policy followed the interests of the United Fruit Company, and Iran, where big oil companies were eager to see the shah restored to power, knowing he would return property to them that had been nationalized under Mossadegh. Even in Vietnam, where intrinsic U.S. economic interests were more limited, the fear was that the fall of a succession of communist "dominoes" would undermine global capitalism. So, too, the Marshall Plan is explained as an effort to rebuild European markets in order to generate demand for American exports and investments, thereby overcoming the underconsumption-overproduction dilemma and averting a depression. The deciding factor in the formation of U.S. foreign policy, in this view, was the private interests of multinational corporations, big banks, and the other captains of global capitalism.

Foreign Policy Politics and the Cold War Consensus

The main pattern in U.S. foreign policy politics during this period was the "Cold War consensus." This consensus was marked by three fundamental components: presidential dominance over Congress, a vast expansion of the executive-branch foreign and defense policy bureaucracy, and a fervent anticommunism sentiment pervading public opinion, culminating in the scourge of McCarthyism.

Pennsylvania Avenue Diplomacy: A One-Way Street

The term *spirit of bipartisanship* was coined during this period to describe the strong support for the foreign policies of President Truman, a Democrat, from the Republican-majority Congress, led by the Senate Foreign Relations Committee chair, Arthur Vandenberg. What made this support especially striking was the extent of the foreign commitments being made—declaring U.S. willingness "to support free peoples everywhere" (the Truman Doctrine), spending billions of dollars in foreign aid (the Marshall Plan), joining a military alliance during peacetime for the first time in U.S. history (NATO)—all as a matter of consensus and presidential-congressional cooperation.

Before crumbling over the Vietnam War in the Johnson and Nixon administrations, this foreign policy bipartisanship lasted through almost every conceivable Pennsylvania Avenue combination: a Democratic president supported by a Republican Congress (Truman, 1947–48), a Republican president supported by a Democratic Congress (Eisenhower, 1955–60), a Republican president and a Republican Congress (Eisenhower, 1953–54), and Democratic presidents and Democratic Congresses (Truman 1949–52, Kennedy 1961–63, and Johnson 1963 to about 1966). One prominent theory of the day spoke of "one President but two presidencies": the domestic policy one, in which the president succeeded in getting his proposals through Congress only 40 percent of the time, and the foreign policy one, in which the president's success rate was 70 percent.[27]

One of the reasons for this presidential dominance was that, although the Cold War was not a war per se, the fearsome nature of the Soviet threat and the overhanging danger of nuclear war were seen as the functional and moral equivalents of war. Given these exigencies, the presidency had the greater institutional capacity to conduct foreign affairs. Only the presidency possessed the information and expertise necessary for understanding the world, could move with the necessary speed and decisiveness in making key decisions, and had the will and the capacity to guard secrecy. Almost everywhere the president went, the "button" (the code box for ordering a nuclear attack) went with him—and it was conceivable that he would have less time to make a decision about whether to press it than it typically takes Congress to have a quorum call. For its part, Congress was seen as too parochial to pay sufficient attention to world affairs, too amateur to understand them, and too slow and unwieldy in its procedures to respond with the necessary dispatch. Even its own foreign policy leaders had expressed strong doubts about its foreign policy competence. Congress "has served us well in our internal life," wrote Senator J. William Fulbright, the longest-serving chair of the Senate Foreign Relations Committee in American history, but "the source of an effective foreign policy under our system is Presidential power." Fulbright went on to propose that the president be given "a measure of power in the conduct of our foreign affairs that we [i.e., the Congress] have hitherto jealously withheld."[28] Fulbright's counterpart, House Foreign Affairs Committee Chair Thomas (Doc) Morgan, went even further, saying that he had a "blanket, all-purpose decision rule: support all executive branch proposals."[29]

Three areas of foreign policy show how in the basic relationship of separate institutions sharing powers, the presidency now had the much larger share.

WAR POWERS   In the Korean War, Truman never asked Congress for a declaration of war. He claimed that the resolution passed by the UN Security Council for "urgent military measures . . . to repel the attack" provided him with sufficient authority to commit U.S. troops. Moreover, this wasn't really a war, Truman asserted, just "a police action." There is little doubt that Congress would have supported the president with a declaration of war if it had been asked. But in not asking, Truman set a new precedent for presidential assertion of war powers. This "police action" lasted three years, involved a full-scale military mobilization, incurred more than fifty thousand American casualties, and ended in stalemate.

In January 1951 Truman announced his intention to send the first divisions of U.S. ground troops to be stationed in Europe as part of NATO. Here he argued that he was merely fulfilling international responsibilities that Congress had previously approved (in this instance by Senate ratification of the NATO treaty in 1949) and thus did not need any further congressional approval. Congressional opposition to the NATO deployment was greater than in the Korean War case but still was not strong enough to pass anything more than a nonbinding resolution urging, but not requiring, the president to obtain congressional approval for future NATO deployments.

The trend continued under President Eisenhower, although with some interesting twists. In 1955 a crisis was brewing over threats by China against Taiwan. Unlike Truman, Eisenhower did go to Congress for formal legislative authorization, but he did so with a very open-ended and highly discretionary resolution authorizing him to use military force if and when he deemed it necessary as the situation developed. This kind of anticipatory authorization was very different from declaring war or taking other military action against a specific country. Yet Eisenhower's request was approved by overwhelming margins: 83–3 in the Senate and 410–3 in the House. House Speaker Sam Rayburn (D-Texas) even remarked, "If the President had done what is proposed here without consulting Congress, he would have had no criticism from me."[30]

In 1957 Eisenhower requested and got a very similar anticipatory authorization for a potential crisis in the Middle East. Here the concern was Soviet gains of influence amid increasing radicalism and instability in a number of Arab countries. Once again by lop-sided votes, Congress authorized the president "to employ the armed forces of the United States as he deems necessary . . . [against] international communism."[31]

COVERT ACTION   We find scattered examples of covert action throughout U.S. history. In 1819, for example, President James Monroe took covert action aimed against Spain in the Spanish territory of Florida and kept it secret from Congress. In World War II the Office of Strategic Services (OSS) played a key role in the war effort. But it was only with the onset of the Cold War that the CIA was created as the first permanent intelligence agency in U.S. history and that covert action was undertaken on a sustained, systematic basis.

Here we see another pattern of disproportionate power sharing, and again as much because of congressional abdication as because of presidential usurpation. It was Congress that created the CIA as part of the National Security Act of 1947 and the Central Intelligence Agency Act of 1949. The latter legislation included a provision authorizing the CIA to "perform such other functions and duties related to intelligence affecting the national security"—i.e., covert operations. The members of congressional oversight committees were charged with keeping an eye on these covert operations. But most senators and representatives who served on these committees during the early Cold War saw themselves more as boosters and protectors than as checkers and balancers. The "black budget" procedure, whereby funds are appropriated to the CIA without its having to provide virtually any details of its programs and accounts, was set up with a congressional wink and nod.

INTERNATIONAL COMMITMENTS   Another manifestation of presidential dominance was the increased use of executive agreements rather than treaties for making significant international commitments.[32] If we compare 1789 to 1945 with the first three post–World War II decades (1945–76), we see two major trends. One is a huge overall increase in U.S. international commitments, from 2,335 in the one-hundred-fifty-plus-year period to 7,420 in the thirty-plus-year period, for annual averages of 15 before 1945 and 239 after. This skyrocketing overall number demonstrates how much more extensive U.S. international involvements had become. Second, a trend within these numbers shows more and more frequent use of executive agreements rather than treaties. Whereas the 1789–1945 breakdown is 843 treaties and 1,492 executive agreements (i.e., executive agreements as 64 percent of the total), for 1945–76 it was 437 and 6,983 respectively

(94 percent).[33] This increase in the proportion of U.S. commitments represented by executive agreements shows how much presidents were trying to reduce Congress's role in the making of foreign policy.[34]

Note that many executive agreements dealt with technicalities and details of relations and were pursuant to statutes passed by Congress, so some of the statistical difference is accounted for simply by the sheer increase in technicalities and details that had to be worked out. But some of the pattern is due to the fact that, the greater the policy significance of the issue, the more likely were Cold War–era presidents to use executive agreements rather than treaties. Military and diplomatic matters, for example, were more than 50 percent more likely to take the form of executive agreements than were economic, transportation, communications, or cultural-technical matters. Among the significant political-military commitments made by executive agreements were the placement of U.S. troops in Guatemala (1947) and in mainland China in support of Jiang Jieshi (1948); the establishment of U.S. bases in the Philippines (1947); the sending of military missions to Honduras (1950) and El Salvador (1957); security pledges to Turkey, Pakistan, and Iran (1959); and an expanded security commitment to Thailand (1962).[35]

In sum, Pennsylvania Avenue had become a one-way street in terms of foreign policy politics during the first half of the Cold War. The arrow pointed down the avenue, away from Capitol Hill and toward the White House.

Executive-Branch Politics and the Creation of the "National Security State"

To exercise his expanded powers the president needed larger, stronger, and more numerous executive-branch departments and agencies. Again, we can draw a parallel with the expansions of the executive branch during World Wars I and II. But this time the expansion was even farther reaching and longer lasting; it created the "national security state."[36]

One of the first steps in this process was the formation in 1947 of the **National Security Council (NSC)**. The original purpose of the NSC was to provide a formal mechanism for bringing together the president's principal foreign policy advisers.* The NSC originally had only a small staff, and the national security adviser was a low-profile position. Few people can even name Truman's or Eisenhower's national security advisers. But beginning in the Kennedy administration, and peaking with Henry Kissinger in the Nixon

---

*The standing members of the NSC were the president, the vice president, the secretary of state, and the secretary of defense. The national security adviser, the CIA director, and the chair of the Joint Chiefs of Staff were technically defined as advisers. Depending on the issue at hand, other Cabinet officials such as the attorney general and the secretary of the treasury may also be included in NSC meetings. The same has been true for political officials such as the White House chief of staff.

administration, the national security adviser became even more powerful and prominent than the secretary of state in the making of U.S. foreign policy.

The ***Department of Defense (DOD)*** was created in 1949 to combine the formerly separate Departments of War (created in 1789) and the Navy (separated from the Department of War in 1798). During World War II, the ***Joint Chiefs of Staff*** had been set up to coordinate the military services. In 1947 the position of secretary of defense was created, but each military service still had its own Cabinet-level secretary. But even this proved to be inadequate coordination and consolidation, and the DOD was established with the army, navy, and air force and a newly created chair of the Joint Chiefs of Staff all reporting to the secretary of defense, who by law had to be a civilian. Measured in terms of both personnel and budget, the DOD was and is the largest Cabinet department. And its headquarters, the Pentagon, is the largest government office building.

The Central Intelligence Agency (CIA) was also created during this period, as noted earlier in this chapter. In addition, a number of other intelligence agencies were created, including the National Security Agency (1952) and the Defense Intelligence Agency (1961).

The State Department itself was vastly expanded. It grew from pre–World War II levels of about one thousand employees in Washington and two thousand overseas to about seven thousand and twenty-three thousand, respectively. It also added new bureaus and functions, notably the Policy Planning Staff established in 1949 with George Kennan ("X") as its first director, charged with strategic planning.

A number of other foreign policy–related agencies were also created during this time: the Economic Cooperation Administration to administer the Marshall Plan; the Agency for International Development (AID), in charge of distributing foreign aid; the Arms Control and Disarmament Agency (ACDA) to monitor and negotiate arms-control agreements; the U.S. Information Agency (USIA) to represent U.S. policies abroad; the U.S. Trade Representative (USTR) to conduct international trade negotiations; and others.

It is important to stress that this vast expansion of the executive branch was made largely with the consent of Congress. Some presidents did exploit, manipulate, and exceed the intended congressional mandates. But to appreciate fully the politics of the Cold War era, we need to take into account both seizings by presidential usurpation and cedings by congressional abdication.

FLAWED EXECUTIVE-BRANCH DECISION MAKING: THE BAY OF PIGS, 1961　The 1961 ***Bay of Pigs*** debacle is one of the most frequently cited cases of flawed executive-branch decision making.[37] It involved a U.S.-engineered invasion of Cuba by exiled forces seeking to overthrow Fidel Castro. (The Bay of Pigs was where they landed on the Cuban coast.) Not only did the invasion fail miserably, but major questions were raised about how the Kennedy administration could have believed that it had any chance of succeeding. Many of the assumptions on which the plan was based were exceedingly weak. For example, the cover story that the United States played no role in the invasion had already been contradicted by press reports that anti-Castro rebels were being trained by the CIA, and the planners asserted that the Cuban people were ready to rise up, even though Castro had come to power less than two years earlier and was still widely seen by his people as a great liberator. Despite these obvious warning signs, a groupthink dynamic dominated the policy-making process. Arthur Schlesinger, Jr., a noted historian and at the time a special assistant to President Kennedy, later explained that he felt that "a course of objection would have accomplished little save to gain me a name as a nuisance."[38]

CIA intelligence failures also contributed to the Bay of Pigs fiasco. A report by the CIA's own inspector general, written in the immediate aftermath but declassified only in 1998, stressed the agency's "failure to subject the project, especially in its latter frenzied stages, to a cold and objective appraisal. . . . Timely and objective appraisal of the operation in the months before the invasion, including study of all available intelligence, would have demonstrated to agency officials that the clandestine paramilitary operation had almost totally failed." The report also criticized the "failure to advise the President, at an appropriate time, that success had become dubious and to recommend that the operation be therefore cancelled."[39] President Kennedy's own comment summed it up best: "How could I have been so stupid to let them go ahead?"[40]

SUCCESSFUL CRISIS DECISION MAKING: THE CUBAN MISSILE CRISIS, 1962   On the other hand, the case most often cited as a model of effective decision making is the 1962 ***Cuban missile crisis.***[41] Having learned from the Bay of Pigs, President Kennedy set up a process and structure that were more deliberate in their pace and deliberative in their consideration of options. He went outside normal bureaucratic channels and established a special crisis decision-making team, called ExCom, with members drawn from his own Cabinet and former high-ranking foreign policy officials of previous administrations, such as Dean Acheson, secretary of state under Truman. Robert Kennedy also was a key player, an unusual foreign policy crisis role for an attorney general, but a logical one for the brother of the president.

In one sense the reason the decision-making process worked so well in this case was that formal structures were adapted and modified. The ExCom process gets much of the credit for bringing the superpowers back from the brink of nuclear war and for the successful resolution of the crisis. President Kennedy himself also gets an important share of the credit: no structure like ExCom can be established, and no decision-making process can function effectively, unless the president provides the mandate and the leadership.

It also was out of the Cuban missile crisis that bureaucratic politics and other important theories of intra–executive branch politics were developed. This analytic paradigm was based on Graham Allison's 1971 book, *The Essence of Decision: Explaining the Cuban Missile Crisis.*[42] As recounted and analyzed by Allison and others who followed, much of what transpired during the Cuban missile crisis was quite inconsistent with the traditional rational-actor model (described in Chapter 2 and Reading 2.2) of hierarchical, orderly, and structured decision making and policy implementation. Further research has raised doubts about a number of the case "facts" first stated by Allison.[43] However, as Richard Betts notes, "other chilling examples have turned up" of dangerously dysfunctional bureaucratic politics during this crisis.[44] Bureaucratic problems were still there, even if they were not as bad as originally depicted and were ultimately transcended by the effectiveness of the ExCom structure and presidential leadership.

Interest Groups, the Media, and Public Opinion: Benefits and Dangers of Consensus

Clearly there are benefits when presidents are able to count on public, interest-group, and even media support for their foreign policies. But consensus, when taken too far, also poses dangers and has disadvantages.

THE MEDIA AS CHEERLEADERS   The news media largely carried over their role as uncritical supporters, even cheerleaders, for official policy from World War II to the Cold War. To the extent that there was media criticism and pressure, it was for the president to take a tougher stand. Indeed, the news media played a significant role in the shaping of Cold War attitudes. Walter Lippmann, the leading newspaper columnist of the day, is often given credit for coining the term "Cold War." Henry Luce, owner and publisher of *Time* and *Life,* the two leading newsmagazines, personally championed South Vietnamese president Diem and ensured favorable, even laudatory coverage for him. Even the *New York Times* followed suit, as in a 1957 editorial titled "Diem on Democracy" in which the editors hailed Diem for being so true to democracy that "Thomas Jefferson would have no quarrel."[45]

In the Bay of Pigs case, the media actually had prior information about the planned invasion but for the most part refrained from publishing it. What did appear in the media about the plan was "designed not to alert the American public to the potentially disastrous course of its own government, but to advance the universally accepted propaganda line that Cuba under Castro was courting disaster."[46] Although some of the postmortems were self-critical, others were more "expressions of sadness that the job was 'bungled,' that it did not 'succeed'—and that a well-meaning President *got caught* and got a 'bloody nose.' "[47] A few weeks after the Bay of Pigs, and despite his other acknowledgements of responsibility, President Kennedy delivered a very strong speech to the American Newspaper Publishers Association broadly construing the national security rationale as a constraint on freedom of the press (see "At the Source," p. 159).

AT THE SOURCE
AT THE SOURCE

"IS IT NEWS?" OR "IS IT IN THE INTEREST OF NATIONAL SECURITY?"
Excerpts from a Speech by President John F. Kennedy

❝I do ask every publisher, every editor, and every newsman in the nation to reexamine his own standards, and to recognize the nature of our country's peril. In time of war, the Government and the press have customarily joined in an effort, based largely on self-discipline, to prevent unauthorized disclosure to the enemy. In times of clear and present danger, the courts have held that even the privileged rights of the First Amendment must yield to the public's need for national security.

Today no war has been declared—and however fierce the struggle may be, it may never be declared in the traditional fashion. Our way of life is under attack. . . .

If the press is awaiting a declaration of war before it imposes the self-discipline of combat conditions, then I can only say that no war has ever imposed a greater threat to our security. If you are awaiting a finding of 'clear and present danger,' then I can only say that the danger has never been more clear and its presence has never been more imminent. . . .

It requires a change in outlook, a change in tactics, a change in mission by the Government, by the people, by every businessman and labor leader, and by every newspaper. For we are opposed around the world by a monolithic and ruthless conspiracy that relies primarily on covert means for expanding its sphere of influence—on infiltration instead of invasion, on subversion instead of elections, on intimidation instead of free choice, on guerrillas by night instead of armies by day. . . .

The facts of the matter are that this nation's foes have openly boasted of acquiring through our newspapers information they would otherwise hire agents to acquire through theft, bribery or espionage; that details of this nation's covert preparations to counter the enemy's covert operations have been available to every newspaper reader, friend and foe alike; that the size, the strength, the location, and the nature of our forces and weapons, and our plans and strategy for their use, have all been pinpointed in the press and other news media to a degree sufficient enough to satisfy any foreign power. . . .

The newspapers which printed these stories were loyal, patriotic, responsible and well-meaning. Had we been engaged in open warfare, they undoubtedly would not have published such items. But in the absence of open warfare, they recognized only the tests of journalism and not the tests of national security. And my question tonight is whether additional tests should not now be adopted. . . .

I am asking the members of the newspaper profession and the industry in this country to reexamine their own responsibilities—to consider the degree and nature of the present danger—and to heed the duty of self-restraint which that danger imposes upon all of us.

Every newspaper now asks itself with respect to every story: 'Is it news?' All I suggest is that you add the question: 'Is it in the interest of national security?'"

Source: John F. Kennedy, speech to the American Newspaper Publishers Association, April 27, 1961, from *Public Papers of the Presidents, John F. Kennedy, 1961* (Washington, D.C.: U.S. Government Printing Office, 1962), 334–38.

INTEREST GROUPS   Foreign policy interest groups were relatively few in number and mostly supportive of the government during the early Cold War. There were some protest movements, such as the nuclear disarmament movement in the late 1950s. But more common, and more influential, were groups in favor of Cold War policies.

If anything, some of these groups were more assertive and more anticommunist than official policy. The "China lobby" strongly sided with Jiang Jieshi and Taiwan, criticizing various administrations for not "unleashing" Jiang to retake mainland China. Another example hails from the early 1960s when, in the wake of the Cuban missile crisis, Kennedy explored a "mini-détente" with the Soviets. He was attacked quite stridently when he gave a June 1963 commencement speech at American University proposing that the United States "re-examine our attitude" toward the Soviet Union. He continued that the United States should "not be blind to our differences—but let us also direct our attention to our common interests and to the means by which those differences can be resolved."[48] Later that year when Kennedy announced a $250 million sale of grain to the Soviet Union, even agricultural interest groups were unwilling to breach their anticommunism. "We oppose this action," ten Republican members of the House Agriculture Committee stated, "because we believe the vast majority of American farmers, like the vast majority of all Americans, are unwilling to sell out a high moral principle, even for solid gold."[49] At the same time a group called the Committee to Warn of the Arrival of Communist Merchandise on the Local Business Scene was operating in forty-seven states, harassing merchants who dared to sell Polish hams or other "commie" products.[50]

PUBLIC OPINION   Public opinion was grounded firmly in the Cold War consensus. Internationalism prevailed over isolationism—65 percent to 8 percent in a typical poll.

Eighty percent of Americans expressed support for NATO. Containment was ranked second by the public among all national objectives, domestic policy included.

Consensus, though, when taken too far, can breed intolerance, suspicion, and repression. This is what happened during the late 1940s and early 1950s. First, the revealingly named House Un-American Activities Committee (HUAC) launched a series of investigations claiming that communists had infiltrated American government and society. It would be affirmed much later, after the fall of the Soviet Union and the opening of Soviet archives, that some of these allegations in fact were true. Soviet spies did steal secrets for building the atomic bomb. They also operated within the State Department and other U.S. government agencies.[51] But the manner in which early Cold War anticommunism was pursued, the wide net cast, and the arbitrariness of so many of the accusations took a profound toll on civil liberties and created an environment inimical to the openness of a democratic society. The standards for the "clear and present danger" test set by Justices Holmes and Brandeis (see Chapter 4) did not require the danger to be all that clear or all that present for national security to be invoked as the basis for limiting—indeed, violating—civil liberties. This was especially the case with McCarthyism.

Senator Joseph McCarthy, until then the relatively unknown junior Republican senator from Wisconsin, became the most rabid spokesperson and instigator in the hunt for "reds under the bed." The essence of the appeal of ***McCarthyism*** comes through in a speech the senator gave in Wheeling, West Virginia, in February 1950 (see "At the Source," p. 162). "The chips are down," McCarthy warned, not because communists were superior in any way, but because of "traitorous actions" by Americans. He pointed his finger right at the State Department—"the bright young men who are born with silver spoons in their mouths," the heart of America's foreign policy "thoroughly infested with Communists." Nor did McCarthy and his cohort stop there. One member of Congress even charged Secretary of State Dean Acheson with being "on Stalin's payroll." No less a figure than George Marshall—General Marshall, the World War II hero, former secretary of state, former secretary of defense—was accused by one reckless senator of being "a front man for traitors, a living lie."[52]

Nor was it only government that was being purged. Accusations were hurled all over American society. Hollywood blacklisted writers, actors, and directors accused of being communists even though they had not been convicted. Universities fired professors. Scientists who held jobs requiring security clearances lost their positions. The country was consumed with paranoia. Ironically, many of the accusations that were true were discredited by the broader sense of injustice and illegitimacy. And from a foreign policy perspective, McCarthyism's equation of dissent with disloyalty had a chilling effect on both those within government and outside it who might have provided constructive criticisms, alternative policy ideas, and the like. The kind of self-examination that is essential for any successful policy process was closed off.

AT THE SOURCE

AT THE SOURCE

McCARTHYISM

Excerpts from a Speech by Senator Joseph McCarthy

66 Today we are engaged in a final, all-out battle between Communistic atheism and Christianity. The modern champions of Communism have selected this as the time. And, ladies and gentlemen, the chips are down—they are truly down. . . .

Ladies and gentlemen, can there be anyone here tonight who is so blind as to say that the war is not on? Can there be anyone who fails to realize that the Communist world has said, 'The time is now'—that this is the time for the show-down between the democratic Christian world and the Communistic atheistic world?

The reason why we find ourselves in a position of impotency is not because our only powerful potential enemy has sent men to invade our shores, but rather because of the traitorous actions of those who have been treated so well by this Nation. It has not been the less fortunate or members of minority groups who have been selling this Nation out, but rather those who have had all the benefits that the wealthiest nation on earth has had to offer—the finest homes, the finest college education, and the finest jobs in Government we can give. This is glaringly true in the State Department. There the bright young men who are born with silver spoons in their mouths are the ones who have been worst. . . .

In my opinion the State Department, which is one of the most important government departments, is thoroughly infested with Communists.

I have in my hand 57 cases of individuals who would appear to be either card carrying members or certainly loyal to the Communist Party, but who nevertheless are still helping to shape our foreign policy. . . .

However the morals of our people have not been destroyed. They still exist. This cloak of numbness and apathy has only needed a spark to rekindle them. Happily, this spark has finally been supplied.99

Source: Senator Joseph McCarthy, speech given February 9, 1950, in Wheeling, W.V., from *Congressional Record*, 81st Cong., 2nd sess., February 20, 1954, 58–61.

Summary

The early Cold War years were a period of crucial choices for American foreign policy. The policies pursued in these years not only addressed the immediate issues but also became the foundations and framework for the pursuit of the "4 Ps" in the decades that followed. Containment and nuclear deterrence were the central foreign policy doctrines by which American power was exercised. The United Nations was the main political-diplomatic institutional structure for the pursuit of peace. The LIEO was the main institutional structure for the international economy and the pursuit of prosperity. Anticommunism was the dominant set of beliefs by which American principles were said to be manifested. And foreign policy politics was marked by a strong consensus, even as American political institutions underwent major changes in their structure and interrelationship.

A number of questions were raised, however, both at the time and in retrospect. Although Cold War strategy proponents stressed the complementarity among the four core national-interest objectives, critics pointed out tensions and trade-offs that pitted one objective against another: for example, strengthening the United Nations vs. maximizing American power; pursuing containment globally vs. being true to principles. Concerns were also raised about the domestic political consensus, which, for all its benefits, also had a downside in the expansion of presidential power and violations of civil liberties.

These and other issues would become more difficult and more controversial beginning in the late 1960s and continuing through the 1980s.

Notes

[1]Dean G. Acheson, *Present at the Creation: My Years at the State Department* (New York: Norton, 1969).

[2]Winston Churchill put it in very similar terms: "If Hitler invaded hell, I should at least make a favorable reference to the Devil in the House of Commons." Both quotes cited in Stephen M. Walt, *The Origins of Alliances* (Ithaca, N.Y.: Cornell University Press, 1987), 38.

[3]See, for example, Adam B. Ulam, *The Rivals: America and Russia since World War II* (New York: Viking, 1971); Arthur M. Schlesinger, Jr., "Origins of the Cold War," *Foreign Affairs* 46.1 (October 1967); John Spanier, *American Foreign Policy since World War II* (New York: Praeger, 1968).

[4]See, for example, Walter LaFeber, *America in the Cold War* (New York: Wiley, 1969); Thomas G. Paterson, *Meeting the Communist Threat: From Truman to Reagan* (New York: Oxford University Press, 1988); Melvyn P. Leffler, *A Preponderance of Power: National Security, the Truman Administration, and the Cold War* (Stanford: Stanford University Press, 1992).

[5]Cited in David Reynolds, *From World War to Cold War: Churchill, Roosevelt and the International History of the 1940s* (New York: Oxford University Press, 2006), 279.

[6]John Gerard Ruggie, "The Past as Prologue? Interests, Identity and American Foreign Policy," *International Security* 21.4 (Spring 1997): 100.

[7]Gar Alperovitz, *Atomic Diplomacy: Hiroshima and Potsdam* (New York: Simon & Schuster, 1965); Martin J. Sherwin, "The Atomic Bomb and the Origins of the Cold War: U.S. Atomic Energy Policy and Diplomacy," *American Historical Review* 78.4 (October 1973): 945–68.

[8]Martin J. Sherwin, "Baruch, Bernard Mannes," in *Encyclopedia of U.S. Foreign Relations*, Bruce W. Jentleson and Thomas G. Paterson, eds. (New York: Oxford University Press, 1997), 1: 135–36.

[9]Patrick M. Morgan, "Deterrence," in *Encyclopedia of U.S. Foreign Relations*, Jentleson and Paterson, eds., 3:10–16; Thomas Schelling, *The Strategy of Conflict* (Cambridge: Harvard University Press, 1960);

Alexander L. George, "Coercive Diplomacy: Definition and Characteristics," in *The Limits of Coercive Diplomacy,* 2d ed., Alexander L. George et al. (Boulder, Colo.: Westview, 1994), 7–12.

[10]X [George F. Kennan], "The Sources of Soviet Conduct," *Foreign Affairs* 25.4 (July 1947): 572, 575, 582.

[11]"NSC-68, A Report to the President Pursuant to the President's Directive of January 31, 1950," in U.S. Department of State, *Foreign Relations of the United States: 1950* (Washington, D.C.: U.S. Government Printing Office, 1977), 1: 240.

[12]Cited in Thomas G. Paterson, "Korean War," in *Encyclopedia of U.S. Foreign Relations,* Jentleson and Paterson, eds., 3: 30.

[13]Quote from Lord Ismay, cited in David S. Yost, *NATO Transformed: The Alliance's New Role in International Security* (Washington, D.C.: U.S. Institute of Peace Press, 1998), 52.

[14]Jonathan Nashel, "Domino Theory," in *Encyclopedia of U.S. Foreign Relations,* Jentleson and Paterson, eds., 2: 32–33.

[15]Text of the legislation as passed by Congress, cited in Seyom Brown, *The Faces of Power: Constancy and Change in United States Foreign Policy from Truman to Reagan* (New York: Columbia University Press, 1983), 124.

[16]Graham Allison, *The Essence of Decision: Explaining the Cuban Missile Crisis* (Boston: Little, Brown, 1971); Robert F. Kennedy, *Thirteen Days: A Memoir of the Cuban Missile Crisis* (New York: Norton, 1969); James Blight and David Welch, eds., *On the Brink: Americans and Soviets Re-examine the Cuban Missile Crisis* (New York: Hill and Wang, 1989); Don Munton and David A. Welch, *The Cuban Missile Crisis: A Concise History* (New York: Oxford University Press, 2007).

[17]"Telegram, Secretary of State to the Consulate at Hanoi, May 20, 1949," in U.S. Department of State, *Foreign Relations of the United States: 1949* (Washington, D.C.: U.S. Government Printing Office, 1973), 7: 29–30.

[18]Melvin R. Laird, "Iraq: Learning the Lessons of Vietnam," *Foreign Affairs* 84.6 (November/December 2005): 31.

[19]Secretary of State Dean Acheson, cited in Thomas G. Paterson, J. Gary Clifford, and Kenneth J. Hagan, *American Foreign Relations: A History Since 1895* (Lexington, Mass.: Heath, 1995), 369.

[20]Cited in Paterson, Clifford, and Hagan, *American Foreign Relations,* 405.

[21]Many attribute this quotation to President Franklin Roosevelt. Although there are doubts as to whether he actually said it, few doubt that the statement captures the essence of U.S. policy. See Robert A. Pastor, *Condemned to Repetition: The United States and Nicaragua* (Princeton: Princeton University Press, 1987), 3.

[22]Tom Gjelten, *Bacardi and the Long Fight for Cuba* (New York: Penguin, 2008), 190.

[23]"Address at a White House Reception for Members of Congress and for the Diplomatic Corps of the Latin American Republics, March 13, 1961," in *Public Papers of the Presidents: John F. Kennedy, 1961* (Washington, D. C.: U.S. Government Printing Office, 1962), 170–75.

[24]Abraham F. Lowenthal, *Partners in Conflict: The United States and Latin America* (Baltimore: Johns Hopkins University Press, 1987), 30.

[25]Report of the Hoover Commission, cited in "Get Personal," *New Republic,* September 14 and 21, 1998, 11.

[26]Mark J. Gasiorowski, "Iran," in *Encyclopedia of U.S. Foreign Relations,* Jentleson and Paterson, eds., 2: 415–16. See also James A. Bill, *The Eagle and the Lion: The Tragedy of American-Iranian Relations* (New Haven: Yale University Press, 1988); Bruce R. Kuniholm, *The Origins of the Cold War in the Near East* (Princeton: Princeton University Press, 1980); Kermit Roosevelt, *Countercoup: The Struggle for the Control of Iran* (New York: McGraw-Hill, 1979); Stephen Kinzer, *All the Shah's Men: An American Coup and the Roots of Middle East Terror* (New York: Wiley, 2003); and Kinzer, *Overthrow: America's Century of Regime Change from Hawaii to Iraq* (New York: Times Books, 2006).

[27]Aaron Wildavsky, "The Two Presidencies," *Trans-action* 3 (December 1966): 8.

[28]Senator Fulbright titled the article quoted here "American Foreign Policy in the 20th Century under an 18th-Century Constitution" (*Cornell Law Quarterly* 47 [Fall 1961]). He wrote further: "The question we face is whether our basic constitutional machinery, admirably suited to the needs of a remote agrarian republic in the eighteenth century, is adequate for the formulation and conduct of the foreign policy of a

twentieth-century nation, preeminent in political and military power and burdened with all the enormous responsibilities that accompany such power. . . . My question, then, is whether we have any choice but to modify, and perhaps overhaul, the eighteenth-century procedures that govern the formulation and conduct of American foreign policy" (1–2).

[29]Richard F. Fenno, Jr., *Congressmen in Committees* (Boston: Little, Brown, 1973), 71.

[30]Cited in James M. Lindsay, *Congress and the Politics of U.S. Foreign Policy* (Baltimore: Johns Hopkins University Press, 1994), 22.

[31]Text of the legislation as passed by Congress, cited in Brown, *Faces of Power*, 124.

[32]The main precedent for the use of executive agreements rather than treaties as a way of getting around Congress had actually been set by Franklin Roosevelt in 1940 with the "destroyers-for-bases" deal with Britain (mentioned in Chapter 3). Even among those who agreed with Roosevelt's objectives, there was some concern at the time about the precedent being set. This also was the view taken in a 1969 report by the Senate Foreign Relations Committee: "Had the president publicly acknowledged his incursion on the Senate's treaty power and explained it as an emergency measure, a damaging constitutional precedent would have been averted. Instead, a spurious claim of constitutionality was made, compounding the incursion on the Senate's authority into a precedent for future incursions." Cited in Loch K. Johnson, *America as a World Power: Foreign Policy in a Constitutional Framework* (New York: McGraw-Hill, 1991), 108–9.

[33]Based on data from Michael Nelson, ed., *Congressional Quarterly's Guide to the Presidency* (Washington, D.C.: Congressional Quarterly Press, 1989), 1104.

[34]There actually was one major effort in the early 1950s to rein in executive agreements. This was the Bricker amendment, named for its principal sponsor, Senator John W. Bricker (R-Ohio), which would have amended the Constitution to require congressional approval of all executive agreements. Support for the Bricker amendment was in part a reflection of McCarthyite distrust of the executive branch, and it too faded with the overall discrediting of McCarthyism. Indeed, until the late 1960s little was heard even about the executive's taking full advantage of the lack of any deadline in the requirement that executive agreements be reported to Congress, reporting very few of these agreements—and even those in a not particularly timely manner.

[35]Loch K. Johnson and James M. McCormick, "Foreign Policy by Executive Fiat," *Foreign Policy* 28 (Fall 1977): 121.

[36]Daniel Yergin, *Shattered Peace: The Origins of the Cold War and the National Security State* (Boston: Houghton Mifflin, 1977).

[37]See, for example, James G. Blight and Peter Kornbluh, eds., *Politics of Illusion: The Bay of Pigs Invasion Re-examined* (Boulder, Colo.: Lynne Rienner, 1997); "A Perfect Failure: The Bay of Pigs," in *Groupthink: Psychological Studies of Policy Decisions and Fiascoes*, 2d ed., Irving L. Janis (Boston: Houghton Mifflin, 1982), 14–47; Peter Wyden, *Bay of Pigs: The Untold Story* (New York: Simon & Schuster, 1979).

[38]Cited in Janis, *Groupthink*, 39.

[39]Peter Kornbluh, ed., *Bay of Pigs Declassified: The Secret CIA Report on the Invasion of Cuba* (New York: Norton, 1998).

[40]Cited in Janis, *Groupthink*, 16.

[41]Allison, *Essence of Decision*; Blight and Welch, *On the Brink*; Munton and Welch, *Cuban Missile Crisis*.

[42]Allison, *Essence of Decision*; Morton H. Halperin, *Bureaucratic Politics and Foreign Policy* (Washington, D.C.: Brookings Institution Press, 1974); Morton H. Halperin and Arnold Kanter, eds., *Readings in American Foreign Policy: A Bureaucratic Perspective* (Boston: Little, Brown, 1973); David C. Kozak and James M. Keagle, *Bureaucratic Politics and National Security: Theory and Practice* (Boulder, Colo.: Lynne Rienner, 1988). The movie *Thirteen Days*, released in 2000, had some inaccuracies but did provide a clear and vivid portrayal of the strong leadership President Kennedy provided. The movie was based on a book by the same name written by Attorney General Robert F. Kennedy, the president's brother and his main confidante during the Cuban missile crisis. See Robert F. Kennedy, *Thirteen Days* (New York: Norton, 1971).

[43]Dan Caldwell, "A Research Note on the Quarantine of Cuba, 1962," *International Studies Quarterly* 21.2 (December 1978): 625–33; Joseph F. Bouchard, *Command in Crisis: Four Case Studies* (New York: Columbia University Press, 1991); Richard K. Betts, *Soldiers, Statesmen, and Cold War Crises*, 2d ed. (New York: Columbia University Press, 1991); Scott D. Sagan, "Nuclear Alerts and Crisis Management," *International Security* 9.4 (Spring 1985): 99–139; Ernest R. May and Philip D. Zelikow, eds., *The Kennedy Tapes: Inside the White House During the Cuban Missile Crisis* (Cambridge: Harvard University Press, 1997); Sheldon M. Stern, *The Week the World Stood Still: Inside the Secret Cuban Missile Crisis* (Stanford: Stanford University Press, 2005); and Graham T. Allison and Philip Zelikow, *Essence of Decision: Explaining the Cuban Missile Crisis*, 2d ed. (New York: Longman, 1999).

[44]Richard K. Betts, "Is Strategy an Illusion?" *International Security* 25.2 (Fall 2000): 34–35; Scott D. Sagan, *The Limits of Safety: Organizations, Accidents, and Nuclear Weapons* (Princeton: Princeton University Press, 1993), chaps. 2–3.

[45]James Aronson, *The Press and the Cold War* (New York: Bobbs Merrill, 1970), 186.

[46]Aronson, *The Press and the Cold War*, 159.

[47]Aronson, *The Press and the Cold War*, 159–60.

[48]"Commencement Address at American University in Washington," June 10, 1963, in *Public Papers of the Presidents: John F. Kennedy, 1963* (Washington, D.C.: U.S. Government Printing Office, 1964), 459–64.

[49]Quoted in Bruce W. Jentleson, *Pipeline Politics: The Complex Political Economy of East-West Energy Trade* (Ithaca, N.Y.: Cornell University Press, 1986), 129.

[50]Jentleson, *Pipeline Politics*, 100.

[51]Harvey Klehr, John Earl Haynes, and Kyrill M. Anderson, *The Soviet World of American Communism* (New Haven: Yale University Press, 1998); Ronald Radosh and Joyce Milton, *The Rosenberg File* (New Haven: Yale University Press, 1997).

[52]Cited in Jerel A. Rosati, *The Politics of United States Foreign Policy* (New York: Harcourt, Brace, 1993), 285.

6 *The Cold War Context: Lessons and Legacies*

Introduction: Turbulent Decades

The 1960s, 1970s, and 1980s were turbulent decades for the United States. Foreign policy was not the only reason—the civil rights movement, the counterculture, economic change, and other forces and factors were also at work. But the setbacks, shifts, and shocks endured by American foreign policy clearly were major factors.

The Vietnam War was the most profound setback American foreign policy had suffered since the beginning of the Cold War. Many saw it as the first war the United States had ever lost. The reasons were—and still are—hotly debated. But the profundity of the loss as it affected both foreign policy strategy and foreign policy politics was undeniable.

The fate of détente with the Soviet Union—first its rise and then its fall—marked major shifts. The rise of détente challenged the dominant belief of the first quarter-century of the Cold War that minimal U.S.-Soviet cooperation was possible. This challenge was especially significant because the switch to détente was led by President Richard Nixon, who had built his political career on staunch anticommunist credentials. Although détente had some successes, its hopes and promises went largely unfulfilled. It engendered major political controversy at home. And when the Soviets invaded Afghanistan in December 1979, détente was pronounced dead.

The United States also endured tremendous economic shocks during the 1970s. Although not so bad as the Great Depression, these shocks were historically unique, for they arose from the international economy. In 1971, for the first time since 1893, the American merchandise trade balance was in deficit. Then came the oil embargo and price hikes by the Organization of Petroleum Exporting Countries (OPEC), first in 1973 and again in 1979. The assumption of cheap and reliable supplies of oil, in some respects as much a part of the bedrock of the post–World War II order as anticommunism, was being called into question. Third World countries tried to capitalize on OPEC's success in bringing the industrialized West to its knees by trying to shift the defining axis of the international system from East-West to North-South. Another major economic blow fell when Japan, the country the United States defeated and occupied after World War II, became America's main economic competitor.

The 1980s thus began amid great foreign policy uncertainty, and it, too, proved a turbulent decade. Initially, following the demise of détente and the election of Ronald Reagan, the Cold War resurged. Policies on both sides grew increasingly confrontational, the rhetoric highly antagonistic. Fears of war, even nuclear war, were rising. In 1985 the Soviets selected a new leader, Mikhail Gorbachev, who dramatically changed Soviet foreign policy. By the end of the decade the Cold War was over. How much credit for the end of the Cold War goes to Gorbachev, how much to Reagan, and how much to other actors and factors has been and continues to be debated. The Cold War did end, though, and it ended peacefully.

In this chapter we examine these and other developments in U.S. foreign policy during the second half of the Cold War, with an eye to the lessons and legacies of the Cold War.

The Vietnam War: A Profound Foreign Policy Setback

In 1995 Robert McNamara, secretary of defense under Presidents Kennedy and Johnson and one of the officials most closely associated with the **Vietnam War,** published his startling mea culpa memoir, *In Retrospect.* For almost thirty years McNamara had refused to talk about Vietnam. He had left government and gone on to be president of the World Bank and worked for nuclear arms control during the 1980s, but he stayed mum on Vietnam. Now, though, he laid out his view of the reasons for the U.S. failure in Vietnam:

- We underestimated the power of nationalism to motivate a people (in this case, the North Vietnamese and Vietcong) to fight and die for their beliefs and values. . . .
- Our misjudgments of friend and foe alike reflected our profound ignorance of the history, culture, and politics of the people in the area and the personalities and habits of their leaders.

- ■ We failed then—as we have since—to recognize the limitations of modern, high-tech military equipment, forces, and doctrine in confronting unconventional, highly motivated people's movements.

- ■ We failed to draw Congress and the American people into a full and frank discussion and debate of the pros and cons of a large-scale U.S. military involvement in Southeast Asia before we initiated the action. . . .

- ■ Underlying many of these errors lay our failure to organize the top echelons of the executive branch to deal effectively with the extraordinarily complex range of political and military issues involving the great risks and costs—including, above all else, loss of life—associated with the application of military force under substantial constraints over a long period of time.[1]

McNamara was not the only former high-level government official to express such doubts about and criticisms of Vietnam. The former secretary of state Dean Acheson later acknowledged receiving advice that there was "real danger that our efforts would fail," but decided that "having put our hand to the plow, we would not look back."[2] Dwight Eisenhower wrote of being "convinced that the French could not win" the 1945–54 colonial war, but that "the decision to give this aid was almost compulsory. The United States had no real alternative."[3] John Kennedy was said to be "skeptical of the extent of our involvement in Vietnam but unwilling to abandon his predecessor's pledge."[4] And during Lyndon Johnson's "Americanization" of the war, Vice President Hubert Humphrey, Undersecretary of State George Ball, Senator J. William Fulbright, the journalist Walter Lippmann, and all other proponents of alternative options were closed out of the decision-making process because of their misgivings. Henry Kissinger himself later described "Vietnamization," the centerpiece of his own policy, as "the operation, conceived in doubt and assailed by skepticism [that] proceeded in confusion"—but proceeded nevertheless.[5]

Some critics argued that Vietnam was a war that should not have been fought, could not have been won, and could and should have been halted at several key junctures. Others vehemently contended that it was right to have fought the war, and that it could have been won through tougher policies and greater commitment by U.S. policy makers. Leslie Gelb makes a provocative and counterintuitive argument that "the system worked" (see Reading 6.1). The one point of consensus is that Vietnam was the most profound foreign policy setback the United States suffered during the Cold War era. For American foreign policy strategy, it amounted to failure on all counts: peace was not served, power was eroded, principles were violated, prosperity was damaged. In American foreign policy politics, the Cold War consensus was shattered in terms of both its institutional structures and its societal underpinnings.

6.1

Foreign Policy Strategy: Failure on All Counts

PEACE   American casualties in Vietnam numbered more than two hundred thousand, including almost sixty thousand deaths. Vietnamese casualties were over 3 million. And the war failed to keep the dominoes from falling: communism came to Vietnam, got stronger in Laos, and spread to Cambodia.

Whether peace was achievable through the war effort is one of the main debates. Secretary McNamara believed it was not, in part because of the inherent "limitations" of modern high-tech warfare when pitted against "the power of nationalism to motivate a people to fight and die for their beliefs and values."[6] Others faulted what was not done more than what was; one general wrote that American strategy violated two of the "time-honored principles of war. . . . We lacked a clear objective and an attainable strategy of a decisive nature."[7]

The sense of the war's unwinnability was not just retrospective. Even while he was intensifying American bombing of the Vietnamese, President Nixon privately acknowledged that "there's no way to win the war. But we can't say that, of course. In fact, we have to seem to say the opposite, just to keep some bargaining leverage." At the peace negotiations with the North Vietnamese in Paris, the ultimate objective was not to win but, as Kissinger stated it, to be able "to withdraw as an expression of policy and not as a collapse."[8] This approach continued after the Treaty of Paris had been signed in 1973. The Ford administration pushed for retaliation against North Vietnamese treaty violations. But it did so less to ensure a peace than to gain a "decent interval" that might convince the global audience that the United States had not lost.[9]

POWER   All along, the main factor driving U.S. involvement in Vietnam was the belief that the credibility of American power was being tested there. A 1952 State Department memorandum delineated three reasons for "the strategic importance of Indochina": "its geographic position as key to the defense of mainland Southeast Asia," a somewhat dubious proposition; "its economic importance as a potential large-scale exporter of rice," an interest much closer to trivial than vital; and *as an example of Western resistance to Communist expansion*" (emphasis added).[10] In 1965, when the decision was made to send in American troops, President Johnson quite explicitly articulated the need to demonstrate American credibility, as it pertained to global allies and adversaries alike: "Around the globe, from Berlin to Thailand, are people whose well-being rests, in part, on the belief that they can count on us if they are attacked. To leave Vietnam to its fate would shake the confidence of all these people in the value of an American commitment and in the value of America's word."[11]

This same precept carried over into the Nixon and Ford administrations. Kissinger stated unequivocally that "the commitment of 500,000 Americans has settled the issue of the importance of Vietnam. For what is involved now is confidence in American prom-ises."[12] If the United States failed this test, President Nixon claimed, it would be perceived as "a pitiful, helpless giant" and "the forces of totalitarianism and anarchy will threaten free nations around the world."[13] On the eve of the American evacuation of Saigon in 1975, President Ford beseeched Congress in similar terms not to cut off aid, arguing that to do so "would draw into question the reliability of the United States and encourage the belief that aggression pays."[14]

The **Munich analogy,** from World War II and the failed appeasement of Adolf Hitler, was implicit and at times explicit in the thinking of American leaders (see "Historical Perspectives," p. 172). Ironically, though, nothing damaged the perception of American power more than these very policies, which were supposed to preserve it. No less a figure than Hans Morgenthau, whose books were cited in our discussion of the Realist paradigm in Chapter 1, had opposed the Vietnam War as early as 1967, precisely because he believed it would be damaging to American power. The interests at stake were not worth the com-mitments needed. On the contrary, as Morgenthau himself argued, U.S. power could best be served by developing a relationship with Ho Chi Minh that, even without converting him from communism, would "prevent such a communist revolution from turning against the interests of the United States."[15]

PRINCIPLES   During the late 1950s, then-senator John Kennedy tried to make the moral case for American responsibility: "If we are not the parents of little Vietnam, then surely we are the godparents."[16] When American troops were first sent to these distant jungles, LBJ described the action as necessary because "we remain fixed on the pursuit of freedom as a deep and moral obligation that will not let us go."[17] President Nixon turned the prin-ciples argument inward with his rebuttal to the antiwar movement: if we withdrew from Vietnam, Nixon claimed, "we would lose confidence in ourselves. . . . North Vietnam can-not defeat or humiliate the United States. Only Americans can do that."[18]

Yet nowhere did Americans feel that their foreign policy violated their principles more than in Vietnam. It needs to be acknowledged that among much of the antiwar movement there was a great deal of naiveté, wishful thinking, and rationalization. Ho Chi Minh and the Vietcong were far from being exemplary freedom fighters, Jeffersonians, or the like. The hor-rors that the communist Khmer Rouge inflicted against their own people when they came to power in Cambodia shocked the world. But only according to the Cold War "ABC" defini-tion did Presidents Ngo Dinh Diem and Nguyen Van Thieu in Vietnam, and Prime Minister Lon Nol in Cambodia, each of whom received staunch U.S. support, qualify as democrats. Moreover, the scenes of peasant villagers fleeing American aircraft spreading napalm, and incidents such as the 1968 My Lai massacre, in which U.S. soldiers killed more than five hundred innocent Vietnamese villagers, were deeply disturbing to the American national conscience.

HISTORICAL PERSPECTIVES
HISTORICAL PERSPECTIVES

THE MUNICH ANALOGY AND VIETNAM

Policy makers often reason from history, usually through analogies between current issues and seemingly similar historical ones. One of the most striking examples of such reasoning is the "Munich analogy," from World War II, which greatly influenced U.S. policy in Vietnam.

The Munich analogy generally refers to negotiations held in Munich, Germany, in September 1938 at which the British prime minister Neville Chamberlain and the French prime minister Edouard Daladier agreed to Adolf Hitler's annexation of part of Czechoslovakia to Nazi Germany in the hope that it would satisfy Hitler's expansionism. It didn't. Six months later Hitler annexed all of Czechoslovakia. His invasion of Poland soon followed, and World War II began. The lesson of history that many policy makers have drawn from this, also with regard to Vietnam, is the need to confront dictators and aggressors, using force if necessary, rather than make concessions and pursue "appeasement."

Everything I know about history told me that if I got out of Vietnam and let Ho Chi Minh run through the streets of Saigon, then I'd be doing exactly what Chamberlain did in WWII. I'd be giving a big fat reward for aggression.

—President Lyndon B. Johnson

The clearest lesson of the 1930s and '40s is that aggression feeds on aggression. I am aware that Mao and Ho Chi Minh are not Hitler and Mussolini. But we should not forget what we learned about the anatomy and physiology of aggression. We ought to know better than to ignore the aggressor's openly proclaimed intentions or to fall victim to the notion that he will stop if you let him have just one more bit or speak to him a little more gently.

—Secretary of State Dean Rusk

There are those who will say that this picture is much too dark. Like Neville Chamberlain, who in 1938 described Czechoslovakia as a little-known and faraway country, they deride the importance of South Vietnam and scoff at the suggestion that to lose one more major segment of Asia means to lose it all. Such optimists contend that we should reach an agreement with our adversaries—as Chamberlain reached an agreement with Hitler in Munich in 1938.

—President Richard M. Nixon

In 1938 the Munich agreement made Chamberlain widely popular and cast Churchill in the role of alarmist troublemaker; eighteen months later Chamberlain was finished because the Munich agreement was discredited. With the Vietnam War the problem was more complex. Rightly or wrongly—I am still thoroughly convinced rightly—we thought that capitulation or steps that amounted to it would usher in a period of disintegrating American credibility that could only accelerate the world's instability.

—National Security Advisor and Secretary of State Henry Kissinger

But looking back we think, as I am sure many of you do, that it is wise to stop aggression before the aggressor becomes strong and swollen with ambition from small successes. We think the world might have been spared enormous misfortunes if Japan had not been permitted to succeed in Manchuria, or Mussolini in Ethiopia, or Hitler in Czechoslovakia or in the Rhineland. And we think that our sacrifices in this dirty war in little Vietnam will make a dirtier and bigger war less likely.

—Senator Henry M. Jackson (D-Washington)

Sources: Johnson: Jeffrey P. Kimball, *To Reason Why: The Debate about the Causes of U.S. Involvement in the Vietnam War* (Philadelphia: Temple University Press, 1990), 43.
Rusk: Kimball, *To Reason Why*, 67.
Nixon: Richard Nixon, "Needed in Vietnam: The Will to Win," *Reader's Digest*, August 1964, 39.
Kissinger: Jeffrey Record, *Making War, Thinking History: Munich to Vietnam and Presidential Uses of Force from Korea to Vietnam* (Annapolis: Naval Institute Press, 2002), 71.
Jackson: Kimball, *To Reason Why*, 66.

PROSPERITY   Theorists of the military-industrial complex claim that the raging appetite of an economy in which defense industries were so central was a key factor leading to Vietnam. Whether or not that analysis is correct, from the more general perspective of the overall American economy, the effects of the war were quite damaging to prosperity. LBJ calculated that cutting domestic spending to finance the war would further weaken political support, but his **guns and butter strategy** of trying to keep spending up in both areas backfired. The federal budget deficit grew. "Stagflation"—simultaneous high unemployment and high inflation—set in. For the first time since 1893, the trade balance went into deficit. The economic situation got so bad that President Nixon, a Republican, imposed wage and price controls and other stringent measures typically identified with liberal, Democratic politicians. But these moves only made the economic situation worse.

Foreign Policy Politics: Shattering the Cold War Consensus

As for politics, here too the effects were paradoxical. "If I did not go into Vietnam," LBJ reflected, "there would follow in this country an endless national debate—a mean and destructive debate—that would shatter my Presidency, kill my administration, and damage our democracy. I knew that Harry Truman and Dean Acheson had lost their effectiveness from the day that the Communists took over China. I believed that the loss of China had played a large role in the rise of Joe McCarthy. And I knew that all these problems, taken together, were chickenshit compared with what might happen if we lost Vietnam."[19] The last part of his statement at least was right, but because LBJ went in, not because he stayed out.

PRESIDENTIAL-CONGRESSIONAL RELATIONS   Recall Senator Fulbright's 1961 statement, cited in Chapter 5, about the need to give the president more power. It was the same Senator Fulbright who, as chairman of the Senate Foreign Relations Committee, became one of the leading opponents of the war. By 1975 he was warning of "presidential dictatorship in foreign affairs. . . . I believe that the presidency has become a dangerously powerful office, more urgently in need of reform than any other institution in government."[20] Similarly, the historian and former Kennedy aide Arthur Schlesinger, Jr., attacked "the imperial presidency . . . out of control and badly in need of new definition and restraint."[21]

Now Congress was urged to be more assertive and less deferential. Some of its most ardent supporters even proclaimed the 1970s to be an age of "foreign policy *by* Congress."[22] Many of its members were now less parochial and more worldly, some having served earlier in their careers as State or Defense Department officials, as Peace Corps volunteers, or even as political science and international relations professors. Greater expertise was also available from the expanded and more professional staffs of congressional committees. For example, between 1960 and 1975, the staff of the Senate Foreign Relations Committee increased from 25 to 62 members, and the House Foreign Affairs Committee staff grew from 14 to 54.[23] Moreover, as Senator Fulbright wrote, only partially in jest, "whatever may be said against Congress . . . there is one thing to be said for it: It poses no threat to the liberties of the American people."[24]

Congress relied heavily on procedural legislation (defined in Chapter 2) in seeking to redress the imbalance of foreign policy powers. The ***War Powers Resolution (WPR) of 1973*** was among the most central and controversial of these procedural initiatives. No declaration of war had ever been passed for the military action in Vietnam. Presidents Johnson and Nixon both justified their actions on the basis of the 1964 ***Gulf of Tonkin Resolution,*** which Congress did pass by overwhelming margins, with an open-ended authorization to use military force.* Later Congress tried a number of ways to end the war, eventually using the power of the purse to cut off funds. The WPR was intended to increase Congress's share of the war powers for the next Vietnam. Nixon vetoed the WPR, claiming it was unconstitutional as an infringement of his presidential powers as commander in chief. But with Republicans joining Democrats in a show of bipartisanship, the necessary two-thirds margin was reached in both the House and the Senate to override his veto.

The WPR limited presidential power through two sets of provisions. One set sought to tighten up requirements for the president to consult with Congress before, or at least soon after, committing U.S. troops in any situation other than a genuine national emergency. This stipulation was intended to give Congress more say in whether initial troop commitments would be made. The other established the "sixty-day clock," by which time the president would have to withdraw U.S. forces unless Congress explicitly allowed an extension. In practice, the WPR has not worked very well, as we will discuss later in this chapter. But at the time it seemed like a significant rebalancing of the war powers.

Congress also tried to claim a larger share of other aspects of shared foreign policy powers. With respect to treaties and other international commitments, it passed legislation to clamp down on the excessive use of executive agreements. It used its investigative and supervisory powers to tighten the reins on executive-branch departments and agencies, most notably the CIA. It made frequent use of the legislative veto in policy areas such as arms sales, nuclear nonproliferation, foreign aid, and trade. All in all, Congress was trying to make Pennsylvania Avenue more of a two-way street in the 1970s.

EXECUTIVE-BRANCH POLITICS   It was from Vietnam that the ***credibility gap*** arose. The Johnson and Nixon administrations kept trying to put the best face on the war by holding back some information from the public, distorting other information, and by outright lying. The public was left doubting the credibility of its leaders. Not only did this sense of skepticism—if not cynicism—cause the public to lose faith in its leaders' truthfulness about Vietnam, it was also applied to all high-level officials in all arenas of government, and thus developed into the more generalized problem of the credibility gap.

---

*It was later revealed that at least one of the two alleged North Vietnamese attacks on U.S. naval ships, the ostensible bases for the Gulf of Tonkin Resolution, never actually occurred. See Scott Shane, "Doubts Cast on Vietnam Incident, But Secret Study Stays Classified," *New York Times,* October 31, 2005; National Security Agency, Central Security Service, "Gulf of Tonkin—11/30/2005 and 5/30/2006," www.nsa.gov/public_info/declass/gulf_of_tonkin/index.shtml (accessed 4/1/13); Paul R. Pillar, *Intelligence and U.S. Foreign Policy: 9/11, Iraq and Misguided Reform* (New York: Columbia University Press, 2011), 124–7.

SHATTERING THE COLD WAR CONSENSUS   During the early Cold War period a few protest movements had emerged, but none had had any significant impact. The anti–Vietnam War movement marked a major change in this pattern. Hundreds of thousands of demonstrators marched on Washington, not just once but repeatedly. "Teach-ins" spread on college campuses, as did sit-ins and in some instances more violent demonstrations. In one particularly tragic incident in the spring of 1970, National Guard troops fired on antiwar protesters at Kent State University in Ohio, killing four students. Although some of its excesses worked against its very goals, overall the antiwar movement was an important influence on U.S. policy in Vietnam.

As for the news media, the old "cheerleader" role that had prevailed for much of the early Cold War was supplanted by the media as "critics." As discussed in Chapter 3, it was the media that first informed Americans of how badly the Vietnam War was going and of how much of a credibility gap there was between official accounts and the actual state of the war. The *Watergate* scandal took media-government antagonism further. President Johnson and his administration had shaded the truth quite a bit, but Watergate revealed that President Nixon and his cronies had lied, covered up, and even committed crimes. Had it not been for the media, none of this might have been known. Moreover, even though Watergate wasn't a foreign policy scandal per se, among its revelations was Nixon's "enemies list," which included some journalists and leaders of the antiwar movement.

Table 6.1 shows the sharp contrasts in public opinion between the Cold War consensus and the mindset of the "Vietnam trauma." Whereas only 24 percent considered involvement in Vietnam a mistake when the United States first sent troops in 1965, by 1971 61 percent did. More generally, the public had become much less internationalist and much more isolationist, as can be seen in its low ranking of the importance of containment as a national objective and its reduced willingness to use American troops to defend non-American territory, even in Western Europe.

Clearly, a lot had changed. The shift wasn't just because of Vietnam; there were other issues on which questions were increasingly being asked about foreign policy strategy and foreign policy politics. But Vietnam in particular stood as a profound setback for American Cold War strategy and shattered the political patterns of the Cold War.

The Rise and Fall of Détente: Major Foreign Policy Shifts

Détente literally means a "relaxation of tensions." It was the principal term used to characterize efforts in the 1970s to break out of the Cold War and improve relations between the United States and the Soviet Union. But whereas at the beginning of the decade détente was heralded as the dawn of a new era, by the end of the decade these hopes had been dashed and the Cold War had resumed.

TABLE 6.1 Public Opinion from Cold War Consensus to Vietnam Trauma

	Cold War consensus	Vietnam trauma
Support internationalism	65 percent	41 percent
Support isolationism	8 percent	21 percent
Rank of containment as a national objective	2nd	7th
Supporting troops to defend Western Europe	80 percent	39 percent
Supporting troops to defend the Western Hemisphere	73 percent	31 percent
Vietnam War a mistake	24 percent	61 percent

Sources: William Watts and Potomac Associates, presented in Charles W. Kegley, Jr., and Eugene R. Wittkopf, *American Foreign Policy: Pattern and Process*, 3d ed. (New York: St. Martin's, 1987), 292; Lloyd A. Free and Hadley Cantril, *The Political Beliefs of Americans* (New York: Simon & Schuster, 1968), 52; Michael Mandelbaum and William Schneider, "The New Internationalisms: Public Opinion and American Foreign Policy," in *Eagle Entangled: U.S. Foreign Policy in a Complex World*, Kenneth A. Oye, Donald Rothchild, and Robert J. Lieber, eds. (New York: Longman, 1979), 41–42, 82; Eugene R. Wittkopf, "Elites and Masses: Another Look at Attitudes toward America's World Role," *International Studies Quarterly* 31.7 (June 1987): 131–59; Barry B. Hughes, *The Domestic Context of American Foreign Policy* (San Francisco: Freeman, 1978), 38–40.

Nixon, Kissinger, and the Rise of Détente

The principal architects of détente were President Nixon and Henry Kissinger. Kissinger served as national security advisor (1969–75) and secretary of state (1973–77). A former Harvard professor, Kissinger drew much of his strategy for détente from balance-of-power theory based on nineteenth-century Europe and the diplomacy led by Prince Metternich, the foreign minister of Austria (see "Theory in the World," p. 178).

What made the rise of détente possible were shifts in all "4 Ps", as well as in foreign policy politics.

Peace was a driving force behind détente for both the Americans and the Soviets. Both sides shared interests in stabilizing Europe, where the Cold War had originated and where it had been waged for nearly a quarter-century. It was important both substantively and symbolically that one of the first détente agreements achieved (1971) was on Berlin, the divided German city that had been the locus of recurring Cold War crises. Berlin's status

THEORY IN THE WORLD

KISSINGER'S DÉTENTE AND BALANCE-OF-POWER THEORY

The first book Henry Kissinger wrote (and the subject of his Ph.D. dissertation at Harvard) was on Prince Klemens von Metternich, the Austrian foreign minister during the first half of the nineteenth century. Metternich's diplomacy was widely credited with the peace that prevailed among the major European powers of that era (Britain, France, Russia, Prussia [most of which later became Germany], and Austria).* It is instructive to see how much Kissinger's diplomacy of détente drew on Metternich. Following are two examples:

Metternich's strategy focused on maintaining sufficient balance of power to ensure system stability rather than trying to defeat a specific foe. Metternich was a "statesman of the equilibrium, seeking security in a balance of forces," Kissinger wrote. "This was the basis of Metternich's diplomacy throughout his life. Freedom of action, the consciousness of having a greater range of choice than any possible opponent. . . ."[†] We see this in détente in the triangulation of improving relations with China at the same time that tough negotiations were being pursued with the Soviet Union. "We moved toward China," Kissinger wrote of his own diplomacy, "to shape a global equilibrium. It was not to collude against the Soviet Union but to give us a balancing position for constructive ends—to give each Communist power a stake in better relations with us."[‡] The overarching goal of détente was stability, not defeating either of the communist foes.

Kissinger also drew from Metternich the Realpolitik approach of focusing on relations between countries more than on domestic policies. "Metternich was the last diplomat of the great tradition of the eighteenth century, a 'scientist' of politics, coolly and unemotionally arranging his combinations in an age increasingly conducting policy by causes. . . . He permitted no sentimental attachments to interfere with his measures."[§] Metternich's context was the prodemocratic revolutions then gaining force in many European countries. In his own time, despite such issues as Soviet abuse of human rights, Kissinger believed that "diplomacy should be divorced . . . from a moralistic and meddlesome concern with the internal policies of other nations. Stability is the prime goal of diplomacy. . . . [I]t is threatened when nations embark on ideological or moral crusades."[**]

---

*Henry Kissinger, *A World Restored: Metternich, Castlereagh and the Problems of Peace* (New York: Houghton Mifflin, 1957).

[†]Kissinger, *A World Restored*, 270, 319.

[‡]Cited in Walter Isaacson, *Kissinger: A Biography* (New York: Simon & Schuster, 1992), 336.

[§]Kissinger, *A World Restored*, 319.

[**]Isaacson, *Kissinger*, 75.

as a divided city was not ended, but new agreements did allow increased contact between West and East Berlin, and West and East Germany more generally.

Other important agreements created the Conference on Security and Cooperation in Europe (CSCE) and led to the adoption of the ***Helsinki Accords of 1975.*** The CSCE was the first major international organization other than the UN to include countries of both Eastern and Western Europe, both NATO allies (including the United States and Canada) and Warsaw Pact members; it also included neutral countries such as Sweden and Switzerland. The Helsinki Accords were something of a trade-off. On the one hand they gave the Soviets the long sought-after recognition of territorial borders in central and Eastern Europe as drawn after World War II. On the other hand they established human rights and other democratic values as basic tenets that CSCE members agreed to respect. Although this provision was not fully binding on Moscow or other communist governments, it provided a degree of legitimization and protection for dissidents that, as we will see, nurtured the seeds of the anticommunist revolutions of 1989.

The United States and the Soviet Union had also come to recognize, especially in the wake of the Cuban missile crisis, their shared interest in working together to reduce the risks of nuclear war. This interest was clearly stated in the Basic Principles of Relations, a charterlike document signed by Nixon and the Soviet leader Leonid Brezhnev at their 1972 summit (see "At the Source," p. 180). Underlying this recognition was an important shift in nuclear deterrence doctrine (Power). As noted in Chapter 5, one reason the Soviets put nuclear missiles in Cuba was to pose a threat close to American territory as a counterweight to America's overall nuclear superiority. Even though this didn't succeed—or, arguably, precisely because it didn't succeed—the Soviets came out of the Cuban missile crisis determined to close the nuclear-weapons gap. The nuclear arms race got another kick upward. On the U.S. side, the rising costs of maintaining nuclear superiority, especially on top of the costs of the Vietnam War, were becoming more burdensome. Moreover, even if nuclear superiority were maintained, the Soviets had increased their own nuclear firepower sufficiently that security would not be assured. The dilemma was laid out in a 1967 speech by Defense Secretary McNamara: "In the larger equation of security, our 'superiority' is of limited significance. . . . Even with our current superiority, or indeed with any numerical superiority realistically attainable, the blunt inescapable fact remains that the Soviet Union could still—with its present forces—effectively destroy the United States, even after absorbing the full weight of an American first strike."[25]

The strategic situation he was describing was one of ***mutually assured destruction,*** or MAD, as it became known in a fitting acronym. Yet as paradoxical as it might sound, MAD was seen as potentially stabilizing. Since neither side could launch a "first strike" without risking devastation in a "second strike"—that is, with destruction assured to be mutual—the chances were slim that either side would resort to using nuclear weapons. Trying to break out of this situation could make the arms race endless. Both sides thus had an interest in nuclear arms control.

AT THE SOURCE

U.S.-SOVIET DÉTENTE

❝ The United States of America and the Union of Soviet Socialist Republics . . . have agreed as follows:

First. They will proceed from the common determination that in the nuclear age there is no alternative to conducting their mutual relations on the basis of peaceful coexistence. Differences in ideology and in the social systems of the USA and the USSR are not obstacles to the bilateral development of normal relations based on the principles of sovereignty, equality, non-interference in internal affairs and mutual advantage.

Second. The USA and the USSR attach major importance to preventing the development of situations capable of causing a dangerous exacerbation of their relations. Therefore, they will do their utmost to avoid military confrontations and to prevent the outbreak of nuclear war. They will always exercise restraint in their mutual relations, and will be prepared to negotiate and settle differences by peaceful means. Discussions and negotiations on outstanding issues will be conducted in a spirit of reciprocity, mutual accommodation and mutual benefit.

Both sides recognize that efforts to obtain unilateral advantage at the expense of the other, directly or indirectly, are inconsistent with these objectives. The prerequisites for maintaining and strengthening peaceful relations between the USA and the USSR are the recognition of the security interests of the Parties based on the principle of equality and the renunciation of the use or threat of force. . . .

Sixth. The Parties will continue their efforts to limit armaments on a bilateral as well as on a multilateral basis. They will continue to make special efforts to limit strategic armaments. Whenever possible, they will conclude concrete agreements aimed at achieving these purposes.

The USA and the USSR regard as the ultimate objective of their efforts the achievement of general and complete disarmament and the establishment of an effective system of international security in accordance with the purposes and principles of the United Nations.

Seventh. The USA and the USSR regard commercial and economic ties as an important and necessary element in the strengthening of their bilateral relations and thus will actively promote the growth of such ties. . . .

Ninth. The two sides reaffirm their intention to deepen cultural ties with one another and to encourage fuller familiarization with each other's cultural values. They will promote improved conditions for cultural exchanges and tourism. ❞

Source: Basic Principles of Relations, signed by the United States and the Soviet Union, May 1972, in *American Foreign Relations, 1972: A Documentary Record* (New York: New York University Press for the Council on Foreign Relations, 1976), 75–78.

Prior to the détente era there had been only a few U.S.–Soviet nuclear arms-control agreements.* Thus the signing of the first ***Strategic Arms Limitation Treaty (SALT I)*** in 1972 was highly significant as recognition that peace and stability were not achievable only through arms but also required arms control. SALT I set limits on strategic nuclear weapons according to a formula known as "essential equivalence," whereby the Soviets were allowed a larger quantity of missiles because the United States had technological advantages that allowed it to put more bombs on each missile.* The idea was that if the Soviets had a quantitative edge and the United States a qualitative one, both would be assured of deterrence. SALT I also severely limited ***anti–ballistic missile (ABM) defense systems,*** on the grounds that such defensive systems were destabilizing: if one side knew it could defend itself against nuclear attack, then mutual destruction would no longer be assured and that side might be more likely to launch a first strike.

Trade was also a major component of détente, for economic reasons (Prosperity) and because of its utility for Peace and Power objectives. With respect to the latter two, one Nixon administration report stated, "our purpose is to build in both countries a vested economic interest in the maintenance of a harmonious and enduring relationship. . . . If we can create a situation in which the use of military force would jeopardize a mutually profitable relationship, I think it can be argued that security will have been enhanced."[26] The linkages between Prosperity and Peace and Power were evident both in the cut-rate grain deal the United States offered the Soviets in 1971 in part to induce them to agree to SALT I, and in the pressure the Soviets put on North Vietnam in late 1972 to sign the Paris peace treaty in order to keep U.S. trade flowing.†

In terms of economic benefits for the United States, interests were strongest in two sectors. One was agriculture. Until the 1970s, the Soviets had been largely self-sufficient in grain. The only prior major grain deal with the United States was in 1963. But because of bad weather and bad planning, Soviet grain harvests were falling far short of their

---

*One was the Antarctic Treaty of 1959, prohibiting the testing or deployment of nuclear weapons in the South Pole area. Another was the Limited Test Ban Treaty of 1963, with Great Britain and France also signees, prohibiting nuclear-weapons testing in the atmosphere, underwater, or in outer space, and imposing some limits on underground testing.

*The technical term is MIRVs, or multiple independently targeted re-entry vehicles. Think of missiles as delivery vehicles on which nuclear bombs are loaded. A MIRVed missile is one that can hold multiple bombs, each aimed at its own target.

†According to the *Wall Street Journal*, when President Nixon announced stepped-up bombing of North Vietnam and mining of its harbors, the Soviet trade minister, Nikolai Patolichev, was meeting with the U.S. commerce secretary, Peter G. Peterson. "After hearing Mr. Nixon's tough words, he [Patolichev] turned to his host [Peterson] and said: 'Well, let's get back to business.' And a couple of days later he posed happily with the President, a clear signal to Hanoi that Moscow put its own interests first." Cited in Bruce W. Jentleson, "The Political Basis for Trade in U.S.–Soviet Relations," *Millennium: Journal of International Studies* 15 (Spring 1986): 31.

needs. Ironically, their first purchases of American grain were so huge and transacted through such clever manipulation of the markets that they garnered low prices for themselves while leaving U.S. domestic grain markets with short supplies and high inflation. The Nixon and Ford administrations worked out trade agreements for future purchases that tried to lock in the export benefits from the grain sales while insulating American markets from further inflationary effects. By 1980, American exporters supplied 80 percent of Soviet grain imports.

The other key sector was energy. As of the early 1970s the Soviet Union was second only to Saudi Arabia in the size of its oil reserves, and it was first in the world in natural gas reserves. Even before the OPEC shocks hit in late 1973, the Nixon administration assessed that "with the tremendous increases that are projected in our energy requirements by the end of this century, it may be very much in our interest to explore seriously the possibility of gaining access to, and in fact to aid in the development of energy fields as rich as those possessed by the Soviet Union."[27] After the OPEC crisis there was even more basis for this economic calculus, not least because while supporting the OPEC embargo against the United States and the Netherlands in their rhetoric, the Soviets had undercut it by quietly providing both countries with some additional oil.

The role of Principles in promoting détente was mixed. The Nixon-Kissinger approach was to give limited emphasis in their "high politics" to Soviet political and human rights dissidents and other such issues. "The domestic practices of the Soviet Union are not necessarily related to détente," which was primarily related to foreign policy, Kissinger stated in testimony to Congress. Such a position was not "moral callousness" but rather a recognition of the "limits on our ability to produce internal change in foreign countries."[28] A particularly contentious issue in this regard was the linkage between most-favored-nation (MFN) status and other trade benefits for the Soviet Union and U.S. pressures for increased emigration rights for Soviet Jews. In keeping with his view of détente as mainly about Soviet foreign policy, Kissinger preferred to leave the Soviet Jewry issue to "quiet diplomacy." Congress, however, saw it differently, and in 1974 passed the *Jackson-Vanik Amendment,* linking MFN status to a prescribed increase in emigration visas for Soviet Jews.

The Carter administration put much more emphasis on human rights in its détente strategy, in two respects. One was directly vis-à-vis the Soviet Union, as when President Carter met with Aleksandr Solzhenitsyn, the renowned Soviet author and dissident who was exiled in 1974 after decades in prison camps (gulags), and with whom President Ford and Secretary Kissinger had refused to meet. Also in a radical departure from the policies of his predecessors, Carter championed human rights with respect to the Third World. Declaring in his 1977 inaugural address that "our commitment to human rights must be absolute," Carter cut or withdrew support from such traditional "ABC" allies as the Somoza family in Nicaragua and the shah of Iran.[29]

For foreign policy politics, initially it seemed that détente might provide the basis for a new consensus. It may have appeared ironic that Richard Nixon, who had launched his political career as a staunch anticommunist, pursued détente with the Soviet Union and visited "Red" China. But there was a political logic to this seeming reversal, because someone with impeccable anticommunist credentials could be insulated from charges of being soft on communism. In any case, the public was captivated by images of President Nixon in China sharing Champagne toasts with Mao Zedong, and of Soviet leader Leonid Brezhnev donning a cowboy hat and giving a bear hug to Chuck Connors, the star of a popular American television series.

Even so, détente encountered some opposition from both ends of the political spectrum. Liberals supported its overall thrust but criticized the Nixon-Kissinger de-emphasis of human rights. Conservatives, though Nixon's longtime political comrades, were not yet ready to admit that anything other than confrontation was possible with the Soviets. They were skeptical of arms control in general and of SALT I in particular. Conservatives' main criticism of SALT I was that it gave the Soviets a potential advantage once they developed MIRV technology, breaking out of essential equivalence and gaining true superiority. And on China, Mao was still viewed as the subversive who wrote that "little red book," the most famous collection of communist principles since Lenin's *What is to be Done?*, and conservatives' real passion was to stop the "abandonment" of Taiwan.

Executive-branch politics was marked more by the personality of Henry Kissinger than by the policy of détente. Kissinger's biographers paint a picture of a man whose ego often got in the way of his brilliance.[30] Many examples can be drawn of Kissinger's penchant for bureaucratic warfare. As President Nixon's national security advisor, he tried to confine Secretary of State William Rogers to minor issues. When Nixon made Kissinger secretary of state in his second term, he allowed Kissinger to keep the national security advisor title as well. Kissinger did give up the NSC post once Gerald Ford became president, but ensured that the position went to his former deputy Brent Scowcroft. Kissinger also fought major bureaucratic battles with Defense Secretary James Schlesinger, who tended to be more hawkish on arms control and defense issues. To be sure, Kissinger won more rounds of executive-branch politics than he lost. And there is something to be said for a take-charge approach that avoids bureaucratic bogs. But some of the flaws in his policies were due to his resistance to input from other top officials, and some of the enemies he made engendered political problems that hampered his effectiveness.

Executive-branch politics during this period was also marred by a number of scandals. The CIA was especially hard hit, both in congressional hearings and in the media, with revelations and allegations ranging from assassination plots concocted against Fidel Castro and other foreign leaders to illegal spying on U.S. citizens at home, including monitoring and intercepting the mail of members of Congress. Covert actions, in the words of the Senate Select Committee on Intelligence Activities (known as the Church Committee after its chair, Senator Frank Church, a Democrat from Idaho), had been intended only as "exceptional instruments used only in rare instances," but "presidents and administrations have made excessive, and at times self-defeating, use of covert action."[31]

No doubt the greatest political scandal during these years was Watergate. The Watergate break-in occurred in June 1972, only a little more than a month after President Nixon's first major summit in Moscow. As it built up over the next two years, the Watergate scandal dominated the media and public opinion, crowding out most other news stories. And it precluded any chance Nixon had of converting his 1972 landslide re-election victory into a mandate for foreign or domestic policy. Ultimately, on August 9, 1974, it led to Nixon's resignation. Although Nixon didn't take détente down with him, his political self-destruction surely added to the problems détente faced.

Reasons for the Fall of Détente

John Lewis Gaddis argues that détente was more about stabilizing than ending American-Soviet competition. "Its purpose was not to end [the Cold War conflict] but rather to establish rules by which it would be conducted."[32] There were tensions all along, which largely were managed, until the December 1979 Soviet invasion of Afghanistan. This is the event most often cited as marking the end of détente. President Carter called it "a clear threat to peace" and warned the Soviets that unless they withdrew, "this [would] inevitably jeopardize the course of United States–Soviet relations throughout the world."[33] The U.S. government's main concern, even more than the Soviet presence in Afghanistan, was that the Soviets would not stop in Afghanistan but would continue on into the oil-rich Persian Gulf region. The **Carter Doctrine,** proclaimed in January 1980, echoed the Truman Doctrine and other cornerstones of the early Cold War: "Let our position be clear," Carter declared. "An attempt by any outside force to gain control of the Persian Gulf region will be regarded as an assault on the vital interests of the United States of America, and such an assault will be repelled by any means necessary, including military force."[34] This was much tougher talk and a more centrist policy than Carter had originally articulated and pursued.

Yet Afghanistan wasn't solely responsible for détente's fall. There were two deeper reasons. One was that all along, and for both sides, the relaxation of tensions and increased cooperation of détente did not put an end to continued competition and rivalry. Though the 1972 Basic Principles of Relations agreement (see "At the Source," p. 180) stated that "both sides recognize that efforts to obtain unilateral advantage at the expense of the other, directly or indirectly, are inconsistent" with the objectives of détente, this statement was an example of papering over rather than resolving fundamental differences. The differences are well stated by Raymond Garthoff, a scholar and former State Department official:

> The U.S. conception of détente . . . called for U.S. manipulation of incentives and penalties in bilateral relations in order to serve other policy interests . . . a strategy for managing the emergence of Soviet power by drawing the Soviet Union into the existing world order through acceptance of a code of conduct for competition that favored the United States.
>
> The Soviet conception of détente was one of peaceful coexistence, which would set aside direct conflict between the two superpowers, in order to allow socialist and anti-imperialist forces a free hand. The Soviet leadership thus saw their task as maneuvering the United States into a world no longer marked by U.S. predominance.
>
> This discrepancy led to increasing friction.[35]

For both sides the main objective still was Power much more than Peace. This fact was evident in the different ways in which each side tried to use its relations with China as leverage in great-power politics. The Soviets were trying to get U.S. support in their split with China. The Soviet-Chinese split had long been much worse than was realized in the United States. In 1969 military skirmishes took place along the Soviet-Chinese border. The Soviets even tried to find out what the U.S. reaction would be if they went to war with China. Not only was this inquiry rebuffed, but one of the strategic calculations for Nixon and Kissinger in their surprise opening to China (see "At the Source," p. 186) was to use this new relationship as leverage in U.S.-Soviet relations. They were "playing the China card," as it was dubbed, beginning the "careful search for a new relationship" and shifting emphasis from the twenty-odd most recent years of animosity to the longer "history of friendship" between the Chinese and American people. Nor were Nixon and Kissinger particularly subtle in playing the China card: it was no coincidence that their trip to China came a few months earlier in 1972 than their trip to Moscow.

The clashing conceptions of the purposes of détente were also evident in the limits of what was achieved through arms control. The best that could be said for SALT I and **SALT II** (the follow-up agreement) was that they somewhat limited the growth of nuclear arsenals. No cuts were made by either side, just limits on future growth, and there was plenty of room within those limits for new and more destructive weapons. In addition, the Soviets were discovered to have cheated in certain areas. It took seven years after SALT I was signed until Carter and Brezhnev signed SALT II. American conservatives were strongly opposed to the new treaty, and they raised the specter of the Soviets' gaining nuclear superiority and the United States' facing a "window of vulnerability." Liberals were more supportive, some only grudgingly so, as they did not think the treaty went far enough. SALT II was never ratified by the Senate, because Carter withdrew it in response to the Soviet invasion of Afghanistan.

AT THE SOURCE

THE OPENING OF RELATIONS WITH CHINA

Excerpts from a Speech by President Richard Nixon

66 The following considerations shaped this Administration's approach to the People's Republic of China.

- Peace in Asia and peace in the world require that we exchange views, not so much despite our differences as because of them. A clearer grasp of each other's purposes is essential in an age of turmoil and nuclear weapons.
- It is in America's interest, and the world's interest, that the People's Republic of China play its appropriate role in shaping international arrangements that affect its concerns. Only then will that great nation have a stake in such arrangements; only then will they endure.
- No one nation shall be the sole voice for a bloc of states. We will deal with all countries on the basis of specific issues and external behavior, not abstract theory.
- Both Chinese and American policies could be much less rigid if we had no need to consider each other permanent enemies. Over the longer term there need be no clashes between our fundamental national concerns.
- China and the United States share many parallel interests and can do much together to enrich the lives of our peoples. It is no accident that the Chinese and American peoples have such a long history of friendship.

On this basis we decided that a careful search for a new relationship should be undertaken. 99

Source: Richard M. Nixon, "U.S. Foreign Policy for the 1970s: The Emerging Structure of Peace," report to Congress, February 9, 1972, reprinted in *Department of State Bulletin* 66.1707 (March 13, 1972): 327.

Nor was it just in Afghanistan that U.S.-Soviet Third World rivalries intensified and expanded. The U.S. expectation had been that détente meant Soviet acceptance of containment, that the Soviets would step back from spreading Marxist-Leninist revolution. The Soviets, though, as Garthoff indicated, saw détente mainly as a way to avoid superpower conflict while continuing global geopolitical competition. Thus in Vietnam the Soviets pressured North Vietnam to sign the 1973 Paris peace treaty, but then aided the

North's military victory and takeover of the South in 1975. They also became much more active in Africa, supporting Marxist coups and guerrilla wars in places such as Angola and Ethiopia.

U.S. Third World policy was still mired in confusion and contradiction. On the one hand, the Nixon and Ford administrations were still intent on containment. In Chile, for example, the CIA was heavily involved in 1970–73 efforts to overthrow the socialist (but freely elected) president Salvador Allende.[36] In Angola, CIA and military aid were started for the pro-American faction battling the pro-Soviet one, but in 1976 Congress passed legislation prohibiting further aid. On these and other issues, the essence of the debate was over which "lessons of Vietnam" were the right ones: Did communism really have to be contained? Or would such efforts end up as costly quagmires?

Another, related part of the debate was over President Carter's emphasis on human rights. In Nicaragua, where the dictatorship of the Somoza family had a long record of human rights violations, the Carter administration cut back support and brought pressure for reform. Although this had some positive effects, the ensuing revolution that deposed Anastasio Somoza brought to power the Sandinistas, who were initially a mix of nationalists, socialists, Marxist-Leninists, and anti-Americans. Even though the history of U.S. imperialist domination was more the cause of the revolution than the Carter human rights policy, the policy got much of the blame. The same dynamic played out in Iran, with the fall of the shah to the virulently anti-American Islamic fundamentalist revolution led by Ayatollah Ruhollah Khomeini. Not only did the United States lose a strategically located ally when the shah fell, but the whole American psyche was deeply shaken by the November 1979 seizure of the U.S. embassy in Tehran and the taking of more than seventy Americans as hostages. Ayatollah Khomeini justified the hostage taking as action against "this great Satan— America." These developments were traumatic for Americans, who were unaccustomed to the sense of vulnerability that the Iranian hostage crisis evoked. Those shock waves— strategic, political, and psychological—were still being felt when barely a month later the Soviets invaded Afghanistan.

Amid all this, domestic politics grew more and more divisive. President Carter had a Democratic Congress, but that helped only marginally in getting congressional support. His executive branch was stricken by bitter internal politics, with National Security Advisor Zbigniew Brzezinski and Secretary of State Cyrus Vance waging their own bureaucratic war. Conservatives, now led by an organization called the Committee on the Present Danger, became increasingly active in opposition to détente. Carter also felt pressure from agricultural interest groups when he imposed grain sanctions as part of his response to the Soviet invasion of Afghanistan. General public opinion was deeply split, and increasingly confused.

Disparagements of "the decade of so-called détente" were staples of candidate Ronald Reagan's speeches. "We are blind to reality," he said on the campaign trail, "if we refuse to recognize that détente's usefulness to the Soviets is only as a cover for their traditional and basic strategy for aggression."[37] In November 1980 Reagan was elected president. The Cold War would be renewed, and then ultimately begin to end, during the Reagan presidency.

1970s Economic Shocks

The 1970s were the decade during which the myth of assured prosperity was shattered. The American economy, and the economic psyche of the American people, endured a series of shocks that recast the international economy and the U.S. position in it as less hegemonic and more uncertain than it had been in generations. Some of the fundamental sources of these new economic problems were rooted in U.S. domestic and economic policies such as LBJ's "guns and butter" and the stagflation that ensued, and President Nixon's overstimulation of the economy as part of his 1972 reelection strategy. But the focus was more on external (foreign) sources.

The Nixon Shock, 1971

On August 15, 1971, with the value of the dollar at its lowest point since World War II, President Nixon announced that the United States was unilaterally devaluing the dollar, suspending its convertibility to gold, and imposing a 10 percent special tariff on imports. These moves, which came to be known as the *Nixon shock,* were targeted principally at Europe and Japan, which were still strategic allies, but increasingly had become economic competitors. "Foreigners are out to screw us," Treasury Secretary John Connally rather indelicately put it, "and it's our job to screw them first."[38]

In more analytical terms the principal significance was threefold. First, while for the previous quarter-century the United States had been willing to grant economic concessions to its allies to help with their economic reconstruction and ensure their political stability as part of containment, now it was projecting onto them responsibility for its own economic problems. The United States was coming close, as Kissinger and others warned, to economic war with its allies.

Second, one of the key pillars of the liberal international economic order (LIEO), the international monetary system based on fixed exchange rates and the gold standard, had crumbled with the U.S. abandonment of the gold standard. The world risked descending back into competitive devaluations and other monetary manipulations. Some efforts were made to prevent such moves, first with a system of "floating" exchange rates and then of "flexible" ones, but the new reality fell well short of the stability and multilateralism of the old system.

Third, the free trade versus protectionism debate was reopened in U.S. domestic politics. Labor unions such as the AFL-CIO had generally supported free trade during the 1950s and 1960s. They had lobbied for loopholes for industries facing the toughest competition from imports (textiles, for instance) but had supported most free-trade bills. As long as the United States was running a trade surplus, more jobs were being created by exports than were being lost to imports. But with the United States running a merchandise trade deficit for the first time since 1893, labor unions shifted their politics accordingly, becoming much more protectionist.

The OPEC Shocks, 1973 and 1979

The American automobile culture was built on a steady and inexpensive supply of oil. American suburban families and college students alike took it for granted that they could drive to a nearby gas station and fill up at prices of about thirty-three cents per gallon. That all changed in October 1973, when Americans had to learn a new acronym: *OPEC (Organization of the Petroleum Exporting Countries).*

OPEC, founded in 1960, had tried oil embargoes and oil price hikes before, but they hadn't succeeded. In 1967, during the Arab-Israeli Six-Day War, two factors undermined the embargo that OPEC instituted to weaken international support for Israel. One was that some of OPEC's non-Arab members, such as Iran (a Muslim but non-Arab country) and Venezuela, didn't go along, and even stepped up their oil production. The other was that the United States at that time was still the world's largest oil producer and was able to compensate by increasing its own production by a million barrels per day. In 1973, though, the cartel held together, with all OPEC members agreeing to 25 percent production cuts, full oil embargoes targeted at the United States and the Netherlands for their support of Israel in the Yom Kippur War, and a worldwide price increase of 325 percent. U.S. oil production had been falling since 1970, and this time only a meager increase of one hundred thousand barrels per day could be mustered.

Economically, the OPEC embargo was like pouring fuel onto a fire. The stagflation, the trade imbalance, and other economic problems plaguing the American economy were made much worse. No commodity was so central to industry as oil, and no commodity was so essential to the consumer culture. Moreover, beyond the material impact, the psychological shocks were highly disorienting. The easy-in, easy-out gas stations gave way to miles-long lines. For a while gas was rationed, with fill-ups alternated daily for even-numbered and odd-numbered license plates. The ultimate insult was that it wasn't even the Soviet Union or a European power that was revealing American vulnerabilities—it was weaker, less-developed, not even "modern" countries of sheiks and shahs. Though we may condemn such thinking as arrogant, it is important to acknowledge it in order to understand the trauma of the OPEC oil shock.

If there were doubts or hopes that this was a one-time occurrence, they were shattered when the second OPEC oil shock hit in 1979 with the Iranian Revolution. Oil supplies were disrupted again. Prices were hiked. Gas lines returned, unemployment was fed, inflation skyrocketed, interest rates hit double digits, and trade deficits shot up. By the mid-1980s, oil prices actually started to come down in real terms, but the marks left by the OPEC shocks were permanent.

The North-South Conflict and Demands for an "NIEO"

Despite having 74 percent of the world's population, as of the early 1970s Third World countries accounted for only 17 percent of the global gross national product (GNP). So when OPEC successfully brought the industrialized world to heel, many Third World countries saw an opportunity to redefine international economic relations toward greater equity and justice for the developing-world "South" against the industrialized "North." They criticized the LIEO for giving inadequate attention to issues of development and for perpetuating inequalities in the global distribution of wealth. The General Agreement on Tariffs and Trade may have opened markets, but the terms of trade tended to favor the industrial exports of the developed countries over the raw materials and foodstuffs exported by the developing world. The IMF and the "conditionalities" it attached to its loans (i.e., economic, social, and other policy changes required of Third World debtor countries in exchange for receiving IMF financial assistance) were the targets of protests and riots in Third World cities. So, too, with foreign aid, which was criticized as being too little and not the right kind of development assistance.

In May 1974, at a special session of the UN General Assembly, the South put forward a "Declaration of a New International Economic Order" (see "International Perspectives," p. 191). This NIEO was intended to replace the LIEO. For the United States, this proposal threatened both its economic interests and its free-market ideology. The American economy depended on cheap commodities and raw materials, yet the NIEO demanded higher prices for raw materials and commodities in the name of "justice and equity." American multinational corporations had substantial investments in the Third World, yet the NIEO called for some form of international "regulation and supervision." The NIEO even demanded that modern science and technology be "given" to developing countries. Among proposals for "special measures in favor of the least developed" and the "full and equal participation" of developing countries in setting international economic policy were direct and indirect accusations that the United States was the source of much that was wrong with the international economy.

The NIEO declaration was formally adopted by the UN General Assembly, and some of its measures were initiated. However, it was a mostly symbolic vote. Actual economic

INTERNATIONAL PERSPECTIVES
INTERNATIONAL PERSPECTIVES

THE DECLARATION OF A
NEW INTERNATIONAL ECONOMIC ORDER (NIEO)

66 *We, the Members of the United Nations,*
Having convened a special session of the General Assembly to study for the first time the problems of raw materials and development, devoted to the consideration of the most important economic problems facing the world community . . .

Solemnly proclaim our united determination to work urgently for the establishment of a new international economic order based on equity, sovereign equality, interdependence, common interest and co-operation among all States, irrespective of their economic and social systems which shall correct inequalities and redress existing injustices, make it possible to eliminate the widening gap between the developed and the developing countries and ensure steadily accelerating economic and social development and peace and justice for present and future generations, and to that end declare . . .

It has proved impossible to achieve an even and balanced development of the international community under the existing international economic order. The gap between the developed and the developing countries continues to widen in a system which was established at a time when most of the developing countries did not even exist as independent States and which perpetuates inequality. . . .

The developing world has become a powerful factor felt in all fields of international activity. These irreversible changes in the relationship of forces in the world necessitate the active, full and equal participation of the developing countries in the formulation and application of all decisions that concern the international community. . . .

The prosperity of the international community as a whole depends upon the prosperity of its constituent parts. International co-operation for development is the shared goal and common duty of all countries. Thus the political, economic and social well-being of present and future generations depends more than ever on co-operation between all members of the international community on the basis of sovereign equality and the removal of the disequilibrium that exists between them.

The new international economic order should be founded on full respect for the following principles: . . .

The broadest co-operation of all the State members of the international community, based on equity, whereby the prevailing disparities in the world may be banished and prosperity secured for all; . . .

The necessity to ensure the accelerated development of all the developing countries, while devoting particular attention to the adoption of special measures in favour of the least developed. . . .

The right [of] every country to adopt the economic and social system that it deems to be the most appropriate for its own development and not to be subjected to discrimination of any kind as a result; . . .

Regulation and supervision of the activities of transnational corporations by taking measures in the interest of the national economies of the countries where such transnational corporations operate on the basis of the full sovereignty of those countries; . . .

Just and equitable relationship between the prices of raw materials, primary products, manufactured and semi-manufactured goods exported by developing countries and the prices of raw materials, primary commodities, manufactures, capital goods and equipment imported by them with the aim of bringing about sustained improvement in their unsatisfactory terms of trade and the expansion of the world economy; . . .

Giving to the developing countries access to the achievements of modern science and technology, and promoting the transfer of technology and the creation of indigenous technology for the benefit of the developing countries in forms and in accordance with procedures which are suited to their economies. ”

Source: "Declaration on Establishment of a New International Economic Order," *Annual Review of UN Affairs 1974* (New York: Oceana Publications, 1976), 208–12.

changes were limited, and many Third World countries fell even further behind economically. For the United States, though, here was yet another external source of disruption and challenge. Anti-UN, anti–foreign aid, and anti–Third World sentiments grew ever stronger in the U.S. Congress and among the American public.

Trade with Japan and the Rest of the World

In the 1950s and 1960s, an American child whose parent came back from a business trip might be told, "I got you just a little something as a present; it's a toy made in Japan." By the 1970s and 1980s, though, any child told that a present had come from Japan would think it was a stereo, television, or VCR—not exactly a "little" something. And his or her parents might be thinking "automobile."

In 1960 Japan's per capita income was only 30 percent of the U.S. level, about equal to that of Mexico. But between 1960 and 1970 its real GNP grew an average of more than 10 percent per year. Its merchandise exports grew even faster, and its share of world exports doubled between the mid-1960s and the mid-1980s. U.S. trade with Japan went from surplus to deficit. Indeed, the deficit with Japan was the single largest component of the overall U.S. trade deficit.

The United States had had trade disputes with allies before. In the 1960s, for example, it fought "chicken wars" and "pasta wars" with the Europeans. But the trade tensions with Japan threatened to rise to an even more intense level. Some of the criticism of Japan was little more than protectionism. Some was more legitimate, as Japan did have higher trade barriers and more unfair trade practices than the United States did. The two sets of issues that these discrepancies generated, closing U.S. import markets to Japanese exports and opening Japanese markets to U.S. exports, were distinct but interconnected, especially in their politics.

Things started to come to a head in the late 1970s over the issue of Japanese auto imports. Toyota, Nissan, and other Japanese car companies were beating Ford, General Motors, and Chrysler (the "Big Three") in both price and reputation for quality. Chrysler was losing so much money that the Carter administration and Congress put together a bailout package for the company. However, when the American auto companies and unions took their case to the ***International Trade Commission (ITC),*** the main U.S. regulatory agency on import-relief cases, the ITC ruled that the main problem was of the Big Three's own creation and denied the requests to restrict Japanese auto imports. Pressure nevertheless continued in Congress. Numerous protectionist and retaliatory bills were introduced. Some members of Congress even smashed a Toyota with a sledgehammer in front of the Capitol. In 1981 the Reagan administration negotiated a "voluntary" agreement with Japan for some limits on Japanese auto imports. "Voluntary" is in quotes because, in reality, Japan had little choice.

In part as a reflection of Japan's more prominent position in world trade, the 1970s round of GATT global trade negotiations was initiated in Tokyo, Japan's capital. Like the previous six GATT rounds of negotiations, going back to 1945, the ***Tokyo Round*** was intended to promote free trade. It went further than its predecessors, however, not only lowering tariffs but also bringing down "nontariff barriers"—various governmental policies and practices that discriminated against imports and thus impeded free trade. Examples of nontariff barriers include government procurement regulations requiring that purchases be made only from domestic suppliers, or government subsidies (such as aid and tax breaks) to exporters to make their products more competitive in global markets. Such policies were not limited to the United States; many other countries had nontariff barriers higher than those of the United States, Japan in particular. As with all GATT agreements, the strategy in the Tokyo Round was to set new rules for the whole international economic system, with all countries both making their own concessions and benefiting from those of others.

Because trade politics became so much more contentious at home over the course of the 1970s, a new U.S. legislative mechanism called ***fast-track*** was developed to help ensure passage of the Tokyo Round. In Chapter 2 we saw that the Constitution was unusually explicit in granting authority over trade to Congress, with presidential trade authority heavily subject to the limits of what Congress chooses to delegate. Fast-track authority gets its name from the guarantee that any trade agreements the president negotiates and submits to Congress will receive expedited legislative consideration within ninety days, and under a special procedural rule the vote on that agreement will be "up or down," yea or nay, with no amendments allowed. In this way Congress could allow free trade to go forward while "protecting itself," as Professor I. M. Destler insightfully put it, from the pressure of interest groups demanding special protection.[39] With fast-track authority, representatives or senators could avoid having to respond to particular concerns from lobbyists, because Congress could deal only with the package as a whole. Such concerns would therefore be deflected on to the president—and become the president's potential political liability. This worked for the Tokyo Round, which Congress passed in 1979 with large majorities in both the House and the Senate. By the mid-1990s, though, as we'll see in Chapter 8, fast-track authority unraveled amid the increased pressures of trade politics.

Reagan, Gorbachev, and the End of the Cold War

The "4 Ps" under Reagan

Ronald Reagan came into office firmly believing that American foreign policy had to be reasserted along all four dimensions of the national interest.

PEACE   Not only had détente failed to bring about peace, but as far as President Reagan and his supporters were concerned the Soviets had used it "as a cover for their traditional and basic strategy of aggression." Reagan pulled few rhetorical punches: the Soviets "lie and cheat"; they had been "unrelenting" in their military buildup; indeed, "the Soviet Union underlies all the unrest that is going on. If they weren't engaged in this game of dominoes, there wouldn't be any hot spots in the world."[40] The reference to the early Cold War domino theory was intentional, and it was telling. Reagan believed the Soviets hadn't changed one iota. Democrats such as President Carter, and even Republicans such as Nixon, Ford, and Kissinger, had been deluding themselves, and endangering the country, in thinking the Soviets had changed.

With Reagan, then, peace was not going to be achieved through negotiations. It could be achieved only through strength. "Peace through strength" was his motto.

POWER American power had to be reasserted, in a big way, and in all its aspects. The ***Reagan Doctrine*** was developed as the basis not only for taking a harder line on global containment, but also for going further than ever before toward rollback—that is, ousting communists who had come to power. Unlike Secretary of State John Foster Dulles, who failed to deliver on rollback against the 1956 Soviet invasion of Hungary, the Reagan administration provided extensive military aid, weapons, and covert action for the Afghan mujahideen fighting against the Soviets and the puppet government they set up in the Afghan capital, Kabul. The struggle was a protracted one, as Afghanistan became the Soviets' Vietnam. They suffered their own decade of defeat and demoralization, and in 1989 were forced to withdraw from Afghanistan.

Another Reagan Doctrine target was Nicaragua, where the communist-nationalist Sandinistas had triumphed. They were being opposed by the Nicaraguan contras (in Spanish, "those against"), to whom the Reagan administration supplied extensive military aid, CIA assistance, and other support. For the administration, the Nicaragua issue embodied all that was wrong with the Vietnam syndrome and Carterite moralism. The Sandinistas professed Marxism-Leninism as their ideology. They were Soviet and Cuban allies. They were running guns to comrades in El Salvador and other neighboring countries. Their heritage as a movement was rooted in anti-American songs, slogans, and versions of history. But even more than that, their very existence was deemed a challenge to the credibility of American power. "If the United States cannot respond to a threat near our own borders," Reagan asked, "why should Europeans or Asians believe that we are seriously concerned about threats to them? . . . Our credibility would collapse, our alliances would crumble."[41]

Opponents of the Reagan Nicaragua policy also invoked analogies to Vietnam, but as a quagmire to be avoided, not a syndrome to be overcome. They did not necessarily embrace the Sandinistas or deny that the United States had vital interests in the region; instead they stressed the possibilities for a negotiated settlement establishing viable terms for coexistence. As for the credibility issue, they saw this as a matter of judgment rather than resolve; what would truly be impressive would be a demonstration that the United States could distinguish a test from a trap.

The Reagan administration also had to contend with its disastrous 1982–84 military intervention in Lebanon. American troops were sent to Lebanon as part of a multilateral peacekeeping force following the June 1982 Israeli military invasion of that country. Although some initial success was achieved in stabilizing the situation, the United States was increasingly pulled into the still-raging Lebanese civil war. In October 1983 an Islamic fundamentalist terrorist group bombed the barracks of the U.S. Marine Corps in Beirut, killing 241 marines and other personnel. Within months the Reagan administration withdrew the remaining American troops. "Redeployment offshore" was the euphemism used in official pronouncements, but this could not mask the reality of retreat.

AT THE SOURCE

AT THE SOURCE

THE "WEINBERGER CRITERIA" FOR
THE USE OF MILITARY FORCE (1984)

❝ Under what circumstances, and by what means, does a great democracy such as ours reach the painful decision that the use of military force is necessary to protect our interests or to carry out our national policy? . . .

Some reject entirely the question of whether any force can be used abroad. They want to avoid grappling with a complex issue because, despite clever rhetoric disguising their purpose, these people are in fact advocating a return to post–World War I isolationism. While they may maintain in principle that military force has a role in foreign policy, they are never willing to name the circumstances or the place where it would apply.

On the other side, some theorists argue that military force can be brought to bear in any crisis. Some of the proponents of force are eager to advocate its use even in limited amounts simply because they believe that if there are American forces of *any* size present they will somehow solve the problem.

Neither of these two extremes offers us any lasting or satisfying solutions. The first—undue reserve—would lead us ultimately to withdraw from international events that require free nations to defend their interests from the aggressive use of force. . . .

The second alternative—employing our forces almost indiscriminately and as a regular and customary part of our diplomatic efforts—would surely plunge us headlong into the sort of domestic turmoil we experienced during the Vietnam War, without accomplishing the goal for which we committed our forces. . . .

I believe the postwar period has taught us several lessons, and from them I have developed *six* major tests to be applied when we are weighing the use of U.S. combat forces abroad. . . .

First, the United States should not commit forces to *combat* overseas unless the particular engagement or occasion is deemed vital to our national interest or that of our allies. . . .

Second, if we decide it *is* necessary to put *combat* troops into a given situation, we should do so wholeheartedly, and with the clear intention of winning. If we are *un*willing to commit the forces or resources necessary to achieve our objectives, we should not commit them at all. . . .

Third, if we *do* decide to commit to combat overseas, we should have clearly defined political and military objectives. And we should know precisely how our forces can accomplish those clearly defined objectives. And we should have and send the forces needed to do just that. . . .

Fourth, the relationship between our objectives and the forces we have committed—their size, composition and disposition—must be continually reassessed and adjusted if necessary. Conditions and objectives invariably change during the course of a conflict. When they do change, so must our combat requirements. . . .

Fifth, before the U.S. commits combat forces abroad, there must be some reasonable assurance that we will have the support of the American people and their elected representatives in Congress. . . .

Finally, the commitment of U.S. forces to combat should be a last resort. "

Source: Speech by Secretary of Defense Caspar Weinberger to the National Press Club, November 28, 1984, included in Richard N. Haass, *Intervention: The Use of American Military Force in the Post–Cold War Era* (Washington, D.C.: Carnegie Endowment for International Peace Press, 1994), App. C, 173–81.

The Lebanon failure prompted Defense Secretary Caspar Weinberger in November 1984 to give a speech laying out six criteria that needed to be met for future uses of U.S. military force ("At the Source," p. 196). The **Weinberger criteria** set a high threshold for when and how to use military force. The lesson being drawn from Lebanon, and indeed going back to Vietnam, was that these failures resulted because too many military commitments had been made too half-heartedly with objectives that were too vague and with too little political support, or were otherwise inconsistent with the criteria Weinberger laid out. The pronouncement of this new doctrine brought on some intra-branch tension, with Secretary of State George Shultz arguing for a more flexible approach and still being willing in certain situations to use force on a more limited basis. The Weinberger approach, though, largely prevailed. It also was the basis for the doctrine of "decisive force" developed in 1990–91 by Colin Powell, then chair of the Joint Chiefs of Staff, for U.S. strategy in the Persian Gulf War following Iraq's invasion of Kuwait (see Chapters 7 and 11).

Power considerations also were the basis for the Reagan nuclear buildup. The "window of vulnerability" that the Reaganites believed had opened up because of the combined effects of the Soviet nuclear buildup and the Carter "defense neglect" needed to be closed, and quickly. Overall defense spending went up 16 percent in 1981, and another 14 percent in 1982. Major new nuclear-weapons systems, such as the B-1 bomber, the Trident submarine, and the MX missile, whose development had been slowed by President Carter, were revived and accelerated. The go-ahead was given for deployment in

Europe of Pershing and cruise missiles, modern and more capable intermediate-range nuclear missiles. And with great fanfare the **Strategic Defense Initiative (SDI),** also known as "Star Wars," was announced as an effort to build a nationwide defense umbrella against nuclear attack.

Guiding the Reagan nuclear buildup were two main shifts in *nuclear deterrence* doctrine. First, this administration was much more skeptical of arms control than were the Nixon, Ford, or Carter administrations. Security had to be guaranteed principally by one's own defense capabilities, the Reaganites believed. They did not write off arms-control prospects totally, but at minimum they wanted more bargaining chips to bring to the table. Second, they doubted the security and stability of the MAD (mutual assured destruction) doctrine. Thus they advocated replacing MAD with NUTS(!), which stood for **nuclear utilization targeting strategy** and which constituted a nuclear war-fighting capability. Only if the United States had the capacity to fight a "limited" nuclear war would deterrence be strengthened—and would the United States be in a position to "win" should it come to that. Their defensive strategy involved SDI, which reopened the question, supposedly settled with SALT I and the ABM Treaty, of the desirability and feasibility of building a defensive shield against nuclear attacks.

However, just as a president perceived as pursuing Peace at the expense of Power (Carter) was pulled from the left toward the center, now a president perceived as excessively risking Peace in pursuit of Power (Reagan) was pulled from the right back toward the center.[42] In the early 1980s the **nuclear freeze movement** gathered strength. A 1982 rally in New York City attracted some seven hundred thousand people. Large demonstrations were also held in Western Europe, protesting Pershing and cruise missile deployments there. *The Day After,* a made-for-television movie about a nuclear war, was both indicative of and a further contributor to a widespread fear that the buildup was going too far and that things might be careening out of control. These developments slowed the Reagan nuclear buildup, but they did not stop it.

PRINCIPLES   They were "the focus of evil in the modern world," headed for "the ash bin of history." President Reagan didn't mince words in describing how he saw the Soviet Union (see "At the Source," p. 199). In a television debate during his 1984 reelection campaign, he accused his Democratic opponent, Walter Mondale, of being so misguided as to believe that the "Soviets were just people like ourselves." Reagan matched this view of the enemy as demonic with classic American exceptionalism. America was "a shining city on a hill," the "nation of destiny," the "last best hope of mankind." Even the Vietnam War (especially the Vietnam War) had been "a noble cause."[43]

In Nicaragua and elsewhere, the ostensibly principled human rights policies of the Carter administration came under scathing attack as having their own "double standards." Jeane Kirkpatrick, then a political science professor, wrote an article in 1979 strongly making this argument, which led to her appointment as Reagan's UN ambassador. How morally defensible was it, she questioned, to have cut support for Somoza in

AT THE SOURCE

AT THE SOURCE

FREEDOM VS. "TOTALITARIAN EVIL"

Excerpts from a 1982 Speech by President Ronald Reagan

66 We're approaching the end of a bloody century plagued by a terrible political invention—totalitarianism. Optimism comes less easily today, not because democracy is less vigorous, but because democracy's enemies have refined their instruments of repression. Yet optimism is in order, because day by day democracy is proving itself to be a not-at-all fragile flower. From Stettin on the Baltic to Varna on the Black Sea, the regimes planted by totalitarianism have had more than 30 years to establish their legitimacy. But none—not one regime—has yet been able to risk free elections. . . .

The decay of the Soviet experiment should come as no surprise to us. Wherever the comparisons have been made between free and closed societies—West Germany and East Germany, Austria and Czechoslovakia, Malaysia and Vietnam—it is the democratic countries that are prosperous and responsive to the needs of their people. And one of the simple but overwhelming facts of our time is this: Of all the millions of refugees we've seen in the modern world, their flight is always away from, not toward the Communist world. Today on the NATO front line our forces face east to prevent a possible invasion. On the other side of the line, the Soviet forces also face east to prevent their people from leaving. . . .

The objective I propose is quite simple to state: to foster the infrastructure of democracy, the system of a free press, unions, political parties, universities, which allows a people to choose their own way to develop their own culture, to reconcile their differences through peaceful means. . . .

No, democracy is not a fragile flower. Still it needs cultivating. If the rest of this century is to witness the gradual growth of freedom and democratic ideals, we must take action to assist the campaign for democracy. . . .

This is not cultural imperialism, it is providing the means for genuine self-determination and protection for diversity. Democracy already flourishes in countries with very different cultures and historical experiences. It would be cultural condescension, or worse, to say that any people prefer dictatorship to democracy. Who would voluntarily choose not to have the right to vote, decide to purchase government propaganda handouts instead of independent newspapers, prefer government to worker-controlled unions, opt for land to be owned by the state instead of those who till it, want government repression of religious liberty, a single political party instead of a free choice, a rigid cultural orthodoxy instead of democratic tolerance and diversity? 99

Source: Ronald Reagan, "Address to Members of the British Parliament," June 8, 1982, *Public Papers of the Presidents: Ronald Reagan, 1982* (Washington, D.C.: U.S. Government Printing Office, 1983), 742–48.

Nicaragua and the shah in Iran when the regimes that came to power in their wake (the Marxist-Leninist Sandinistas, Ayatollah Khomeini and his Islamic fundamentalists) were not just authoritarian but totalitarian? Although authoritarians weren't democratic, at least they largely limited their repression to the political sphere; totalitarian regimes sought "total" domination of the personal and political spheres of life. Therefore, Kirkpatrick contended, there *was* a moral basis to the "ABC" rule, as communists were often far more repressive than other leaders, however imperfect those others may be. This argument resquared the circle, casting Principles and Power as complementary once again. The contras were freedom fighters, nothing less than the "moral equal of our Founding Fathers."[44]

This view was hard to reconcile, though, with U.S. support for the military regime in El Salvador, which tacitly supported the mass murder of its citizens. The Salvadoran "death squads" were brutal in their tactics and sweeping in whom they defined as a communist—as but one example, they assassinated the Roman Catholic archbishop Oscar Romero in his cathedral while he was saying Mass. It was Congress, over Reagan administration objections, that attached human rights conditions to U.S. aid to El Salvador. A few years later the Salvadoran defense minister conceded that Congress's insistence on these human rights conditions made the Salvadoran military realize that "in order to receive U.S. aid, we had to do certain things."[45] Among those "certain things" was cracking down on the death squads.

PROSPERITY   It often is forgotten that during the early 1980s the American economy was so mired in the deepest recession since the Great Depression that Ronald Reagan's popularity fell as low as 35 percent. Also forgotten is the fact that for all the attacks on Democrats for deficit spending, the Reagan administration ran up greater budget deficits during its eight years than the total deficits of every previous president from George Washington to Jimmy Carter combined. And the U.S. trade deficit, which had caused alarm in the 1970s when it was running around $30 billion, went over $100 billion in 1984, and over $150 billion in 1986.

Nevertheless, the Reagan years became prosperous ones. Inflation was tamed, brought down from more than 20 percent in 1979 to less than 10 percent in 1982. The economy boomed at growth rates of over 7 percent per year. The increases in defense spending were in part responsible for this prosperity. One of candidate Reagan's most effective lines in the 1980 presidential campaign was the question posed in his closing statement in a debate with President Carter: "Are you better off now than you were four years ago?" With inflation and unemployment both running so high, most Americans answered "no." In 1984, with the economic recovery racing along, voters seemed to answer "we are now," as the revived prosperity contributed significantly to Reagan's landslide reelection victory.

Confrontational Foreign Policy Politics

Pennsylvania Avenue diplomacy broke down during the Reagan years. The dominant pattern of presidential-congressional relations was confrontational.

CONTRA AID   The politics of aid to the contras and other aspects of the Nicaragua issue were the most glaring example. The debate was extremely bitter. The National Conservative Political Action Committee circulated a letter to all senators before one crucial vote on aid to the contras, threatening that "should you vote against Contra aid, we intend to see that a permanent record is made—a roll of dishonor, a list of shame, for all to see—of your failure of resolve and vision at this crucial hour."[46] For their part, liberal groups had no less harsh words for contra supporters, making for a virulent and vitriolic debate.

The contra-aid issue also got caught in "backward" institutional power-sharing arrangements. Each branch coveted the policy instruments of the other. The policy instrument the executive branch needed most—money—was controlled by Congress. The Reagan administration did get Congress to appropriate contra aid in 1983. But the aid was defeated in 1984, then passed again in 1985 with restrictions, increased and de-restricted in 1986, cut back and re-restricted in 1987, and cut back and restricted further in 1988.

On the other side, for its preferred policy objective of a negotiated regional peace plan, Congress needed diplomatic authority and negotiating instruments of its own. But that remained the nearly exclusive authority of the executive branch, and the Reagan administration preferred to appear to support peace negotiations rather than seriously pursuing them. At one point House Speaker Jim Wright actually launched his own "alternative-track diplomacy," meeting with the Nicaraguan president, Daniel Ortega. Irrespective of the ends being pursued, this was a serious breach, for the costs and risks are substantial when any member of Congress tries to circumvent the president and become an alternative negotiating partner for a foreign leader.

The greatest breach of all was the ***Iran-contra scandal,*** which combined the Nicaragua issue with U.S. Middle East policy, particularly the problem of the American hostages taken by Iranian-supported fundamentalist terrorists in Lebanon. The basic deal, as worked out by National Security Council aide Colonel Oliver North and other Reagan administration officials, was that the United States would provide arms to Iran in exchange for Iran's help in getting the American hostages in Lebanon released; the profits from the arms sales would be used to fund the Nicaraguan contras, thereby circumventing congressional prohibitions. The scheme fell apart for a number of reasons, not the least of which was that at its core it was an illegal and unconstitutional effort to get around Congress. When the cover was broken and the scheme was revealed, Congress launched its most significant investigation since Watergate. "Secrecy, deception and disdain for the law" were among the findings of the congressional investigative committees. "The United States Constitution specifies the processes by which laws and policies are to be made and executed. Constitutional process is the essence of our democracy and our democratic form of Government is the basis of our strength. . . . The Committees find that the scheme, taken as a whole . . . violated cardinal principles of the Constitution. . . . Administration officials holding no elected office repeatedly evidenced disrespect for Congress' efforts to perform its constitutional oversight role in foreign policy."[47]

WAR POWERS   The failings of the 1973 War Powers Resolution also became increasingly apparent. As discussed earlier in this chapter, when originally passed with an override of President Nixon's veto, the WPR was regarded as finally settling the war powers issue. In practice, though, the resolution was ignored far more than it was invoked. This was true in the Ford and Carter administrations, although the cases then were few and minor, such as the 1975 *Mayaguez incident* involving the limited use of force against Cambodia to rescue an American merchant ship and its crew, and the 1980 attempt to rescue American hostages in Iran. It was especially true in the Reagan administration, when uses of force were more frequent and of greater magnitude. In addition to the 1982–84 Lebanon case, these included the 1983 invasion of Grenada, which the administration defined as a rescue mission to protect American medical students but which congressional critics claimed was an effort to overthrow the island's Marxist government; the 1986 bombing of Libya in retaliation for Libyan leader Muammar Qaddafi's involvement in terrorism against Americans; and the 1987–88 naval operations in the Persian Gulf during the Iran-Iraq War to protect Kuwait, help Iraq, and maintain safe passage for oil tankers.

One of the problems inherent in the WPR that these cases made more apparent was that it ran against institutionally rooted attitudes in both branches. For presidents, opposition to the WPR has almost been an institutionally instinctual response. The WPR's very existence, let alone its specific provisions, has been seen as an infringement on the role of the commander in chief and other aspects of the presidency's constitutional share of war powers. This was true for Presidents Ford and Carter but was especially so for President Reagan, who took a more assertive approach to the presidency.

The WPR's fundamental problem lies in the ambiguity of its legal and legislative language. Take the 1987–88 Persian Gulf naval operation as an example. The mission of the U.S. Navy was defined as a defensive one: protecting oil tankers. This was not strictly a neutral act, however; it was taking the side of Kuwait and Iraq against Iran. Sure enough, Iran launched a series of attacks, and the American naval forces counterattacked. More than one incident occurred, and there were casualties on both sides. Section 2 of the WPR, the law's statement of purpose, states that it is to apply to situations in which "imminent involvement in hostilities is clearly indicated." Yet there is no clear definition in the law of what level of attack is necessary to be considered actual "hostilities." Thus Congress had no definitive basis for challenging the Reagan administration's claim that the Kuwaiti reflagging operation was below the threshold of "hostilities," and thus did not fall under the strictures of the WPR.

Ambiguity also is inherent in Section 3 of the WPR and its provision for consultation with Congress "in every possible instance . . . before introducing U.S. armed forces into hostilities or into situations where imminent involvement in such is clearly indicated." When is consultation "possible"? Does it meet the requirement of being "before" if, as in 1986 when attacks were launched against Libya, congressional leaders are called in once the planes are on their way, but before they have dropped their bombs?

One doesn't have to be a linguist or a lawyer to see the problems that arise when these terms are left open to interpretation. It is true that the option was there when the law was written in 1973–74, and is there today for those who would rewrite it, to use tighter and more precise language. One could, for example, define "hostilities" as the firing of any first shot at a U.S. soldier, or "imminent involvement" as a U.S. soldier's being within range of an enemy's weapon—say 50 feet for a gun, 10 miles for a bomb, 100 miles for a missile. Clearly, though, such language tightening can present its own problems by taking too much discretion away from a president, straitjacketing the president's ability to formulate strategy.

With the WPR not resolving much, members of Congress resorted to lawsuits as a means of trying to rein in the president. In 1982 eleven House members filed suit, claiming that the commitment of U.S. military advisers to El Salvador without congressional consent violated the Constitution. A similar claim was made about the 1983 Grenada intervention. A third suit involved the 1987–88 Persian Gulf naval operation case. Yet in all three cases even the lower courts refused to rule and dismissed the suits. These were some of the cases referred to in Chapter 2 as falling under the "political question" doctrine and therefore being "nonjusticiable," meaning that they involved political differences between the executive and legislative branches rather than constitutional issues, and required a political resolution directly between those two branches. In other words, the courts were telling the president and Congress to work out the issues themselves.*

There were other issues over which President Reagan and Congress had less conflict, and some on which they even cooperated. The number of these common-ground issues increased in the second Reagan term, especially as the Cold War began to thaw.

---

*See Chapter 9 for analysis of more recent war powers issues.

The End of the Cold War: Why Did the Cold War End, and End Peacefully?

Just as we can't say precisely when the Cold War began, neither can we pinpoint a specific date for its end. The year 1989 was truly revolutionary, as one East European Soviet-satellite regime after another fell (see Table 6.2). Some point to November 9, 1989, the day the Berlin

TABLE 6.2 1989: Eastern Europe's Year of Revolution	
Date	**Event**
January 11	Hungarian parliament permits independent political parties for the first time under communist rule
April 5	Ban repealed on Solidarity movement in Poland
May 2	Hungary takes major steps to further open its borders with Austria, providing a route for thousands of East Germans to emigrate to West Germany
June 3	Solidarity candidates for Parliament win by huge margin in Poland
July 21	General Wojciech Jaruzelski, who had led the imposition of martial law in Poland in 1981, has no choice but to invite Solidarity to form a coalition government
October 18	Hungary adopts a new constitution for multiparty democracy
October 18	Longtime East German communist leader Erich Honecker is forced to resign, and is replaced by another, much weaker, communist
November 3	Czechoslovakia opens border for East Germans seeking to go to the West
November 9	Amid mounting protests, East Germany opens the Berlin Wall and promises free elections in 1990
November 10	Unrest in Bulgaria forces resignation of Communist Party leader Todor Zhivkov
November 24	Peaceful mass protests, dubbed the "velvet revolution" and led by the former political prisoner Vaclav Havel, overthrow the communist government of Czechoslovakia
December 6	East German government resigns
December 22–25	Protests turn violent in Romania, leading to execution of the communist leader Nicolae Ceauşescu and his wife

Wall came down, as the Cold War's end. Others cite December 25, 1991, the day the Soviet Union was officially disbanded. Others place it on other dates.

But whatever the day, few if any academics, policy makers, intelligence analysts, journalists, or other "experts" predicted that the Cold War would end when it did, or as peacefully as it did. As with the origins of the Cold War, different theories have been put forward to explain its end.[48] Here we group them into two principal categories.

U.S. TRIUMPHALISM   This theory gives the United States, and particularly President Reagan, the credit for having pursued a tough and assertive foreign policy that pushed the Soviets into collapse (see Reading 6.2). In one sense, the credit is shared by every administration from President Truman's on; they all sustained deterrence and containment and generally pursued tough Cold War strategies (albeit some administrations more than others). The cumulative effects of those policies over the decades laid the groundwork. The pressure ratcheted up by the Reagan administration in the 1980s turned the tide. In this view, the domestic and foreign policy changes undertaken by Mikhail Gorbachev, who became the leader of the Soviet Union in 1985, were more reactions to the limited options the Reagan policies left him than bold new peace initiatives.

The Soviets simply couldn't match American power as it had been rebuilt and reasserted by Reagan. SDI was a good example. For all the questioning by critics within the United States of whether it was technologically feasible, SDI sure worried the Soviets. The Kremlin feared that the Soviet economy couldn't finance the huge expenditures necessary to keep up and doubted its scientists could master the new technologies needed. So when Gorbachev showed new interest in arms control, it was less because of his heralded "new thinking" than because he finally had to admit that his country couldn't win an arms race with the United States. So too with the Intermediate Nuclear Forces (INF) Treaty in 1987, eliminating major arsenals of nuclear weapons stationed in Europe.* This was the first U.S.–Soviet arms control treaty that actually reduced nuclear weapons, rather than just limiting their future growth (as did the SALT treaties). Yet in the triumphalist view, the INF treaty never would have happened if the Reagan administration had not withstood the political pressures of the nuclear freeze movement at home and the peace movements in Western Europe and gone ahead with the Pershing and cruise missile deployments.

The Reagan Doctrine, with its rollback and containment components, stopped the tide of Soviet geopolitical gains in the Third World. In Nicaragua the Sandinistas were

*Intermediate-range nuclear missiles were those with attack ranges of between 500 and 5,500 kilometers (311 to 3,418 miles). This included most of the nuclear missiles stationed in NATO countries and those in the Soviet Union that could attack Western Europe. It did not include long-range missiles that the United States and the Soviets had aimed at each other or shorter-range and battlefield nuclear weapons in the European theater.

forced to agree to elections as part of a peace plan; sure enough, when elections were held in 1990, they lost. In El Salvador a peace accord was reached that included elections, which were also won by the pro-American side. Most significantly, the Red Army was forced to beat a retreat out of Afghanistan, with politically wrenching and demoralizing consequences back in the Soviet Union.

The triumph was also one of American principles. The fall of communism in Eastern Europe was a revolution from below, brought about by masses of people who wanted freedom and democracy. When Vaclav Havel, a playwright who had been a human rights activist and political prisoner under the communists in Czechoslovakia, became the democratically elected president of that country, he quoted Thomas Jefferson in his inaugural speech. Lech Walesa, the courageous Polish shipyard worker and leader of the Solidarity movement, who was arrested when martial law was imposed in 1981 at Moscow's behest, was elected president of Poland in 1990. Throughout most of the former Soviet bloc, and ultimately in most of the former Soviet Union itself, new constitutions were written, free elections held, an independent and free press established, and civil societies fostered. The "campaign for democracy" that Reagan had heralded in his 1982 speech (see "At the Source," p. 199) had been successful; "man's instinctive drive for freedom and self-determination," which throughout history "surfaces again and again" had done so, again.

Capitalism and its perceived promise of prosperity were also part of the appeal of the American model. Back in the late 1950s, when Soviet leader Nikita Khrushchev had threatened the West that "we will bury you," he was speaking in part about economic competition and the sense that socialism was in the process of demonstrating its superiority. The Soviet system at that time had piled up impressive rates of economic growth. But this simply reflected the suitability of command economies for the initial stages of industrialization concentrated in heavy industries such as steel; over the ensuing three decades the inefficiencies of the Soviet economy, both in itself and as a model, had become glaringly clear. Meanwhile, for all its economic problems in the 1970s, capitalism was on the rebound in the 1980s. The postcommunist governments were quick to start selling off state enterprises, opening their economies to Western foreign investment, and taking other measures to hang out the sign "open for business," capitalist style. The results were not uniformly positive—growth rates were lower than expected, unemployment was higher, and corruption was more rampant in a number of countries. But there was no going back to communist economic systems.

Overall, this view confirms the validity of the U.S. Cold War position and policies. The Soviets and their leaders really did bear most of the responsibility for the Cold War. Stalin *was* an evil megalomaniac with aspirations to global domination. Marxism-Leninism *was* an ideology with limited appeal that declined even more over time. The Soviet Union was "a state uniquely configured to the Cold War—and it has become a good deal more difficult, now that that conflict has ended, to see how it could have done so without the Soviet Union itself having passed from the scene."[49]

Reagan also had the domestic political credibility within American foreign policy politics to counter pressures from remaining Cold Warriors. As when Nixon went to China, Reagan had sufficient standing as a hard-liner to make nuclear arms-control agreements and pursue other policies that emphasized engagement over confrontation. Although his first-term policies and much of his political advocacy in the 1970s fueled dangerous escalation of the Cold War, Reagan, as the historian John Patrick Diggins concludes, "turned from escalation to negotiation," from seeking to win the Cold War to seeking to end it.[50]

GORBACHEV'S LEADERSHIP AND REVISIONIST THEORIES Just as revisionist theories of the origins of the Cold War put more blame on the United States, revisionist theories of the end of the Cold War give the United States less credit. Much more credit in these explanations goes to Gorbachev. In 1982, after eighteen years in power, the Soviet leader Leonid Brezhnev died. He was replaced first by Yuri Andropov, the former head of the KGB (the Soviet spy agency), but Andropov died in 1984. His successor, Konstantin Chernenko, an old *apparatchik* (party bureaucrat) in the Brezhnev mold, was ill during most of the time he was leader and died barely a year later. Gorbachev was a relative unknown when he came to power in 1985 but was immediately billed by no less a figure than the conservative British prime minister Margaret Thatcher as "a man we can do business with." And she didn't just mean business deals, she meant the whole foreign policy agenda.

At age fifty-one, Gorbachev was of a different generation than his predecessors (see Reading 6.3). He quickly proclaimed a "new thinking" based on **glasnost (openness)** and **perestroika (restructuring).** In terms of Soviet domestic policy *glasnost* meant greater political freedoms, including a degree of freedom of the press, the release of such leading dissidents as Andrei Sakharov,* and an end to the Communist party's "leading role" in society. *Perestroika* meant changes in the Soviet economy, allowing for more open markets with some private enterprise and foreign investment. In Soviet foreign policy, the "new thinking" was manifest in numerous initiatives aimed at reducing tensions and

6.3

---

*Andrei Sakharov was known around the world for his courageous opposition to the Soviet regime. He actually was the physicist who, earlier in his career, had developed the Soviet hydrogen bomb. But he became a leading advocate of arms control and, later, of human rights and political freedom. He was awarded the Nobel Peace Prize in 1973, but was denied permission to go to Stockholm, Sweden, to receive it. Sakharov was harassed by the KGB and, following his opposition to the Soviet invasion of Afghanistan, was put under house arrest. That was where and how he was forced to stay until Gorbachev freed him in 1986.

promoting cooperation. Gorbachev saw possibilities for mutual security rather than just continued zero-sum East-West geopolitical competition. The British scholar Archie Brown argues that if another leader had been selected, he likely would not have pursued the policies that Gorbachev did, and the Cold War thus would not have ended when it did.[51] Under Gorbachev the Soviets became much more amenable to arms control. They signed the INF treaty in 1987 and moved forward with negotiations in the Strategic Arms Reduction Talks (START), which were the successor to SALT. Although there were doubts as to whether it was more than rhetoric, Gorbachev declared the goal of eliminating all nuclear weapons by 2000. It was also Gorbachev who agreed in 1988 to the UN-mediated accord under which the Soviets withdrew their military forces from Afghanistan. And whereas Nikita Khrushchev had crushed the 1956 Hungarian Revolution and Brezhnev had done the same to the "Prague Spring" in Czechoslovakia in 1968, Gorbachev did not send a single tank into any East European country as the people in one country after another overthrew their communist governments.

So at least part of the answer to the question of why the Cold War ended when it did, and especially to the question of why it ended peacefully, is Gorbachev. Whereas the triumphalists contend that U.S. pressures and strengths left Gorbachev with little choice other than to do what he did, revisionists argue that this is too simplistic. How many other times in history have leaders responded to crises at home and declining strength abroad by choosing repression and aggression? The central concept of foreign policy choice that frames our entire discussion of U.S. foreign policy in this book also applies to other countries. Gorbachev had choices: he could have sought to put down the rebellions in Eastern Europe. This might not have worked, but he could have tried it. The popular revolutions still might have prevailed, and the Cold War still might have come to an end—but it would have been a much less peaceful end. The same argument applies to many other aspects of the Gorbachev foreign policy. The choices he made were not the only ones he had. Gorbachev not only received the Nobel Peace Prize but was deemed by one leading American scholar "the most deserving recipient in the history of the award."[52]

Nor was it only Gorbachev. Revisionists also give credit to American and European peace movements.[53] They tempered Reagan's hard-line policies, keeping him, for example, from spending even more on SDI and possibly from a direct military intervention in Nicaragua. With the Reagan policies moved back toward the center, there was more of a basis for finding common ground with the Soviets. Peace activists had also built relationships over many years with intellectuals, activists, scientists, and others within the Soviet Union. Even in the dark days of the early 1980s, Reagan's "evil empire" rhetoric notwithstanding, various groups kept up efforts to exchange ideas, maintain communications, and try to find common ground with colleagues, counterparts, and friends within the Soviet Union. Many of these counterparts came into positions of influence under Gorbachev; even those who did not were important sources of support and expertise for Gorbachev's liberalizing policies.[54]

Other international actors also deserve some of the credit. We have already mentioned the Polish dissident Lech Walesa and the Czech dissident Vaclav Havel, whose courage inspired and mobilized their peoples. So too did the courage of Pope John Paul II, the "Polish pope," whose influence was so great that the Soviets actually played a role in trying to assassinate him. A number of Western European leaders for many years had pushed more strongly for détente than the United States wanted. The West German chancellor Helmut Kohl was instrumental in the reunification of Germany following the fall of the Berlin Wall. The United Nations played such a key role in helping bring peace in Afghanistan and elsewhere that its peacekeeping units won the 1988 Nobel Peace Prize. Another Nobel Peace Prize went to Oscar Arias, the president of Costa Rica, whose peace plan was the basis for the settlements in Nicaragua and El Salvador. Principal focus on the two superpowers is warranted, but the roles of these other important international actors should not be ignored.

A further point concerns nuclear weapons and nuclear deterrence. Some revisionists take issue with any suggestion that nuclear weapons were ultimately part of the solution to the Cold War, seeing them more as a major part of the problem, causing close calls like the Cuban missile crisis and the overhanging specter of the arms race. Others give some credit to nuclear deterrence as having ensured the avoidance of a major-power war, but still argue that the ratcheting up of the nuclear arms race to ever higher levels prolonged the Cold War.

A final point distinguishes between the Soviets' having "lost" the Cold War and the United States' having "won." The assessment of the victory needs to be more nuanced, or we could draw the wrong lessons. Containment in Europe can be assessed as a successful policy, whereas aspects of Third World containment, such as the Vietnam War and support for the Nicaraguan contras, were misguided and failed. So too were various CIA covert actions, which even when they accomplished their objectives in the field had some dangerous domestic political reverberations. And some short-term successes turned out to have longer-term negative consequences—for example, in "failed states" such as Somalia and Zaire, where corrupt dictators took advantage of their "ABC" credentials to rob and repress their people, knowing that U.S. support would continue in the name of global containment; or in Afghanistan, where the void left by the Soviet defeat and the American decision to disengage once the Soviets had left was filled by the Taliban and by Osama bin Laden and his Al Qaeda terrorist organization.[55]

This debate has no single right answer. And just as we still debate the origins of the Cold War, so too we will continue to debate its end.

What we must acknowledge is how humbling the end was, or should have been, for "experts." It was not uncommon in the mid-1980s for professors to assume that any student who imagined a post–Cold War world was just young, naive, and idealistic. The Cold War was with us and, students were told, likely to have its ups and downs, its thaws and freezes, but it was not about to go away. Yet it did.

We need to bear this lack of certainty in mind as we consider the twenty-first century and think about what the possibilities may be.

Summary

Table 6.3 summarizes the main characteristics of U.S. foreign policy strategy in the early Cold War period, the Vietnam-détente-economic shocks period, and the Reagan-Gorbachev period. We can see elements of both continuity and change in the emphasis placed on and the strategies chosen for each of the "4 Ps:"

- *Peace:* pursued at first principally by creating the multilateral structure of the United Nations; during the 1970s through the bilateral superpower diplomacy of détente; then under President Reagan by reverting more to unilateral assertion of "peace through strength."
- *Power:* containment starting in Europe and then extending to Asia and more globally; the 1970s dominated by the debate over the lessons of Vietnam; the 1980s pushing for rollback through the Reagan Doctrine. Deterrence first seen as a matter of U.S. nuclear superiority to be maintained by winning the arms race; then to be ensured through arms control; then requiring a renewed arms race as a prerequisite to more effective arms control.

TABLE 6.3 U.S. Cold War Foreign Policy Strategy

	Early Cold War	Vietnam, détente, economic shocks	Reagan-Gorbachev era
Peace	United Nations	Détente	"Peace through strength"
Power	Containment, arms race	Lessons of Vietnam, arms control	Reagan doctrine, arms race–arms control
Principles	Ideological bipolarity, Third World "ABC"	Human rights	"Evil empire," "ABC"
Prosperity	LIEO	OPEC, NIEO, Japan shock	Boom and deficits

- *Principles:* the original conception of the Cold War as not simply typical great-power politics but also deeply ideological, and the attendant equation of "ABC" with democracy in the Third World; the 1970s shift to human rights and questioning of the ABC rationale; the 1980s "evil empire" ideological warfare and reversion to ABC.
- *Prosperity:* initially to be assured by the LIEO; then shaken by OPEC, the NIEO, and other 1970s economic shocks; and restored in the 1980s boom, albeit amid massive trade and budget deficits.

We also see varying patterns in the foreign policy politics of the different subperiods (Table 6.4). As long as the Cold War consensus held, Pennsylvania Avenue was largely a one-way street in the White House's favor, making for an imperial presidency. This was as much because of congressional deference as presidential usurpation. The executive branch grew dramatically in the size, scope, and number of foreign and defense policy agencies. Societal influences were limited and mostly supportive of official policy, the media included; they also included the extremism of McCarthyism. But the consensus was shattered by the Vietnam War. Other issues and factors also came into play, with the net effect of more conflictual Pennsylvania Avenue diplomacy, with a more assertive Congress, in the eyes of some a less imperial and more imperiled presidency, more divisive intra-executive-branch politics, more interest-group pressures, much more critical media, and more "dissensus" than consensus in public opinion. Foreign policy politics in the 1980s became even more contentious, to the point where many questioned whether, as the title of one prominent book put it, we had become "our own worst enemy."[56]

We now have a picture of the dynamics of foreign policy choice during the entire Cold War era, both the foreign policy strategy choices that were its essence (drawing on the

TABLE 6.4 U.S. Cold War Foreign Policy Politics

	Early Cold War	Vietnam, détente, economic shocks	Reagan-Gorbachev era
Presidency	Imperial	Imperiled	Resurgent
Congress	Deferential	Assertive	Confrontational
Executive branch	Expanding	Bureaucratic warfare	Bureaucratic warfare
Interest groups	Supportive	Oppositional	Proliferating
News media	Cheerleaders	Critics	Critics
Public opinion	Consensus, McCarthyism	"Dissensus"	Polarized

Chapter 1 framework) and the foreign policy politics that were its process (Chapters 2 and 3). Chapter 4 gave us the historical context. And looking toward Part II, Chapters 5 and 6 have provided us with the contemporary context for the foreign policy choices that the United States faces in the post–Cold War era.

Notes

[1]Robert S. McNamara, *In Retrospect: The Tragedy and Lessons of Vietnam* (New York: Times Books, 1995), 321–33.

[2]Dean G. Acheson, *Present at the Creation: My Years at the State Department* (New York: Norton, 1969), 674.

[3]Dwight D. Eisenhower, *Mandate for Change* (New York: Doubleday, 1963), 372–73.

[4]Theodore C. Sorensen, *Kennedy* (New York: Harper and Row, 1965), 639.

[5]Cited in Stanley Karnow, *Vietnam: A History* (New York: Viking, 1983), 629.

[6]McNamara, *In Retrospect*, 322.

[7]Statement by General Bruce Palmer, Jr., cited in Bruce W. Jentleson, "American Commitments in the Third World: Theory vs. Practice," *International Organization* 41.4 (Autumn 1987): 696.

[8]Both cited in Col. Harry G. Summers, Jr., "How We Lost," *New Republic*, April 29, 1985, 22.

[9]Frank Snepp, *Decent Interval: An Insider's Account of Saigon's Indecent End* (New York: Random House, 1977); Arnold Isaacs, *Without Honor: Defeat in Vietnam and Cambodia* (Baltimore: Johns Hopkins University Press, 1983).

[10]William Appleman Williams, Thomas McCormick, Lloyd Gardner, and Walter LaFeber, *America in Vietnam: A Documentary History* (Garden City, N.Y.: Anchor Books, 1985), 122.

[11]Lyndon B. Johnson, Address at Johns Hopkins University: Peace Without Conquest, April 7, 1965, *Public Papers of the Presidents: Lyndon B. Johnson, 1965* (Washington, D.C.: U.S. Government Printing Office, 1966) 1: 395.

[12]Henry A. Kissinger, "The Vietnam Negotiations," *Foreign Affairs* 47.2 (January 1969): 218–19.

[13]Richard M. Nixon, Address to the Nation on the Situation in Southeast Asia, *Public Papers of the Presidents: Richard M. Nixon, 1970* (Washington, D.C.: U.S. Government Printing Office, 1971), 409.

[14]Cited in Snepp, *Decent Interval*, 175.

[15]Hans J. Morgenthau, "To Intervene or Not Intervene," *Foreign Affairs* 45.3 (April 1967): 434.

[16]Cited in James A. Nathan and James K. Oliver, *United States Foreign Policy and World Order*, 2d ed. (Boston: Little, Brown, 1981), 322.

[17]Lyndon B. Johnson, Telephone Remarks to the Delegates to the AFL-CIO Convention, December 9, 1965, *Public Papers of the Presidents: Lyndon B. Johnson, 1965* (Washington, D.C.: U.S. Government Printing Office, 1966) 2: 1149.

[18]Richard M. Nixon, Address to the Nation on the War in Vietnam, November 3, 1969, *Public Papers of the Presidents: Richard M. Nixon, 1969* (Washington, D.C.: U.S. Government Printing Office, 1970), 908–9.

[19]Cited in Doris Kearns, *Lyndon Johnson and the American Dream* (New York: New American Library, 1976), 264. See also Larry Berman, *Planning a Tragedy: The Americanization of the War in Vietnam* (New York: Norton, 1982); and Berman, *Lyndon Johnson's War* (New York: Norton, 1989).

[20]J. William Fulbright, "Congress and Foreign Policy," in Murphy Commission, *Organization of the Government for the Conduct of Foreign Policy* (Washington, D.C.: U.S. Government Printing Office, 1975), Vol. 5, App. L, 59.

[21]Arthur M. Schlesinger, Jr., *The Imperial Presidency* (New York: Atlantic Monthly Press, 1974), 11–12.

[22]Thomas M. Franck and Edward Weisband, *Foreign Policy by Congress* (New York: Oxford University Press, 1979).

[23]I. M. Destler, Leslie H. Gelb, and Anthony Lake, *Our Own Worst Enemy: The Unmaking of American Foreign Policy* (New York: Simon & Schuster, 1984), 137.

[24]Fulbright, "Congress and Foreign Policy," 60.

[25]Speech by Secretary of Defense Robert S. McNamara, October 1967, reprinted in Bruce W. Jentleson, *Documents in American Foreign Policy: A Reader* (Davis, Calif.: University of California at Davis, 1984), 48–53.

[26]Peter G. Peterson, *U.S.-Soviet Commercial Relations in a New Era* (Washington, D.C.: U.S. Government Printing Office, 1972), 3–4.

[27]Peterson, *U.S.-Soviet Commercial Relations*, 14.

[28]Cited in Bruce W. Jentleson, *Pipeline Politics: The Complex Political Economy of East-West Energy Trade* (Ithaca, N.Y.: Cornell University Press, 1986), 142.

[29]Jimmy Carter, Inaugural Address, January 20, 1977, in *Public Papers of the Presidents: Jimmy Carter, 1977* (Washington, D.C.: U.S. Government Printing Office, 1977), 1–4.

[30]Walter Isaacson, *Kissinger: A Biography* (New York: Simon & Schuster, 1992). See also the three volumes of Kissinger's memoirs: *White House Years* (Boston: Little, Brown, 1979); *Years of Upheaval* (Boston: Little, Brown, 1982); and *Years of Renewal* (New York: Simon & Schuster, 1999).

[31]Cited in James M. McCormick, *American Foreign Policy and Process*, 2d ed. (Itasca, Ill.: Peacock, 1992), 414.

[32]John Lewis Gaddis, *The Cold War: A New History* (New York: Penguin, 2005), 198.

[33]Quoted in Gaddis Smith, *Morality, Reason and Power: American Diplomacy in the Carter Years* (New York: Hill and Wang, 1986), 223.

[34]Jimmy Carter, State of the Union Address, January 23, 1980, *Public Papers of the Presidents: Jimmy Carter, 1980–1981* (Washington, D.C.: U.S. Government Printing Office, 1981), 194–200.

[35]Raymond L. Garthoff, "Détente," in *Encyclopedia of U.S. Foreign Relations*, Bruce W. Jentleson and Thomas G. Paterson, eds. (New York: Oxford University Press, 1997), 2: 10–11.

[36]See the recently declassified documents, "New Kissinger 'Telcons' Reveal Chile Plotting at Highest Levels of U.S. Government," National Security Archive Electronic Briefing Book No. 255, www.gwu.edu/~nsarchiv/NSAEBB/NSAEBB255/index.htm (accessed 6/8/09).

[37]Cited in Bruce W. Jentleson, "Discrepant Responses to Falling Dictators: Presidential Belief Systems and the Mediating Effects of the Senior Advisory Process," *Political Psychology* 11.2 (June 1990): 371.

[38]Quoted in Seymour Hersh, *The Price of Power: Kissinger in the Nixon White House* (New York: Summit Books, 1983), 462.

[39]I. M. Destler, *American Trade Politics*, 2d ed. (Washington, D.C.: Institute of International Economics, 1992).

[40]Cited in Jentleson, "Discrepant Responses to Falling Dictators," 371.

[41]Cited in Bruce W. Jentleson, "American Diplomacy: Around the World and Along Pennsylvania Avenue," in *A Question of Balance: The President, the Congress and Foreign Policy*, Thomas E. Mann, ed. (Washington, D.C.: Brookings Institution Press, 1990), 149.

[42]Miroslav Nincic, "The United States, the Soviet Union and the Politics of Opposites," *World Politics* 40.4 (July 1988): 452–75.

[43]Cited in Jentleson, "Discrepant Responses," 372.

[44]Jentleson, "Discrepant Responses," 372.

[45]Cited in Jentleson, "American Diplomacy," 179.

[46]Cited in Jentleson, "American Diplomacy," 151.

[47]U.S. Congress, *Report of the Congressional Committees Investigating the Iran-Contra Affair*, 100th Congr., 1st sess., November 1987, 11, 411, 19.

[48]See, for example, Richard Ned Lebow and Thomas Risse-Kappen, eds., *International Relations Theory and the End of the Cold War* (New York: Columbia University Press, 1995); Richard K. Betts, ed., *Conflicts after the Cold War: Arguments on Causes of War and Peace* (New York: Macmillan, 1994); Raymond L. Garthoff, *The Great Transition: American-Soviet Relations and the End of the Cold War* (Washington, D.C.: Brookings Institution Press, 1994); and Jay Winik, *On the Brink: The Dramatic Saga of How the Reagan Administration Changed the Course of History and Won the Cold War* (New York: Simon & Schuster, 1997).

[49]John Lewis Gaddis, "The New Cold War History," lecture published by Foreign Policy Research Institute, *Footnotes* 5 (June 1998): 1–2. See also John Lewis Gaddis, *We Now Know: Rethinking Cold War History* (New York: Oxford University Press, 1997).

[50]John Patrick Diggins, "How Reagan Beat the Neocons," *New York Times*, June 11, 2004, A27.

[51]Archie Brown, "Gorbachev and the End of the Cold War," in *Ending the Cold War: Interpretations, Causation, and the Study of International Relations*, Richard K. Herrmann and Richard Ned Lebow, ed. (New York: Palgrave Macmillan, 2004), 31–57.

[52]Michael Mandelbaum, *The Ideas That Conquered the World* (New York: Public Affairs, 2002), 121.

[53]Thomas Risse-Kappen, "Did 'Peace through Strength' End the Cold War?" *International Security* 16.1 (Summer 1991): 162–88.

[54]Matthew Evangelista, *Unarmed Forces: The Transnational Movement to End the Cold War* (Ithaca, N.Y.: Cornell University Press, 1999).

[55]See Odd Arne Westad, *The Global Cold War* (Cambridge: Cambridge University Press, 2007).

[56]Destler, Gelb, and Lake, *Our Own Worst Enemy.*

Readings for Part I
The Context of
U.S. Foreign Policy:
Theory and History

Power

JOHN J. MEARSHEIMER
Realism

* * *

The sad fact is that international politics has always been a ruthless and dangerous business, and it is likely to remain that way. Although the intensity of their competition waxes and wanes, great powers fear each other and always compete with each other for power. The overriding goal of each state is to maximize its share of world power, which means gaining power at the expense of other states. But great powers do not merely strive to be the strongest of all the great powers, although that is a welcome outcome. Their ultimate aim is to be the hegemon—that is, the only great power in the system.

There are no status quo powers in the international system, save for the occasional hegemon that wants to maintain its dominating position over potential rivals. Great powers are rarely content with the current distribution of power; on the contrary, they face a constant incentive to change it in their favor. They almost always have revisionist intentions, and they will use force to alter the balance of power if they think it can be done at a reasonable price.[1] At times, the costs and risks of trying to shift the balance of power are too great, forcing great powers to wait for more favorable circumstances. But the desire for more power does not go away, unless a state achieves the ultimate goal of hegemony. Since no state is likely to achieve global hegemony, however, the world is condemned to perpetual great-power competition.

This unrelenting pursuit of power means that great powers are inclined to look for opportunities to alter the distribution of world power in their favor. They will seize these opportunities if they have the necessary capability. Simply put, great powers are primed for offense. But not only does a great power seek to gain power at the expense of other states, it also tries to thwart rivals bent on gaining power at its expense. Thus, a great power will defend the balance of power when looming change favors another state, and it will try to undermine the balance when the direction of change is in its own favor.

Why do great powers behave this way? My answer is that the structure of the international system forces states which seek only to be

From *The Tragedy of Great Power Politics* (New York: W.W. Norton, 2001).

secure nonetheless to act aggressively toward each other. Three features of the international system combine to cause states to fear one another: 1) the absence of a central authority that sits above states and can protect them from each other, 2) the fact that states always have some offensive military capability, and 3) the fact that states can never be certain about other states' intentions. Given this fear—which can never be wholly eliminated—states recognize that the more powerful they are relative to their rivals, the better their chances of survival. Indeed, the best guarantee of survival is to be a hegemon, because no other state can seriously threaten such a mighty power.

This situation, which no one consciously designed or intended, is genuinely tragic. Great powers that have no reason to fight each other— that are merely concerned with their own survival—nevertheless have little choice but to pursue power and seek to dominate the other states in the system. . . . Although it is depressing to realize that great powers might think and act this way, it behooves us to see the world as it is, not as we would like it to be. . . . The fortunes of all states—great powers and smaller powers alike—are determined primarily by the decisions and actions of those with the greatest capability. . . . For all realists, calculations about power lie at the heart of how states think about the world around them. Power is the currency of great-power politics, and states compete for it among themselves. What money is to economics, power is to international relations.

*   *   *

In contrast to liberals, realists are pessimists when it comes to international politics. Realists agree that creating a peaceful world

would be desirable, but they see no easy way to escape the harsh world of security competition and war. Creating a peaceful world is surely an attractive idea, but it is not a practical one. . . . This gloomy view of international relations is based on three core beliefs. First, realists, like liberals, treat states as the principal actors in world politics. Realists focus mainly on great powers, however, because these states dominate and shape international politics and they also cause the deadliest wars. Second, realists believe that the behavior of great powers is influenced mainly by their external environment, not by their internal characteristics. The structure of the international system, which all states must deal with, largely shapes their foreign policies. Realists tend not to draw sharp distinction between "good" and "bad" states, because all great powers act according to the same logic regardless of their culture, political system, or who runs the government. It is therefore difficult to discriminate among states, save for differences in relative power. In essence, great powers are like billiard balls that vary only in size.[2]

Third, realists hold that calculations about power dominate states' thinking, and that states compete for power among themselves. That competition sometimes necessitates going to war, which is considered an acceptable instrument of statecraft. To quote Carl von Clausewitz, the nineteenth-century military strategist, war is a continuation of politics by other means.[3] Finally, a zero-sum quality characterizes that competition, sometimes making it intense and unforgiving. States may cooperate with each other on occasion, but at root they have conflicting interests.

*   *   *

Why Americans Dislike Realism

Americans tend to be hostile to realism because it clashes with their basic values. Realism stands opposed to Americans' views of both themselves and the wider world.[4] In particular, realism is at odds with the deep-seated sense of optimism and moralism that pervades much of American society. Liberalism, on the other hand, fits neatly with those values. Not surprisingly, foreign policy discourse in the United States often sounds as if it has been lifted right out of a Liberalism 101 lecture.

Americans are basically optimists.[5] They regard progress in politics, whether at the national or the international level, as both desirable and possible. As the French author Alexis de Tocqueville observed long ago, Americans believe that "man is endowed with an indefinite faculty of improvement."[6] Realism, by contrast, offers a pessimistic perspective on international politics. It depicts a world rife with security competition and war, and holds out little promise of an "escape from the evil of power, regardless of what one does."[7] Such pessimism is at odds with the powerful American belief that with time and effort, reasonable individuals can cooperate to solve important social problems.[8] Liberalism offers a more hopeful perspective on world politics, and Americans naturally find it more attractive than the gloomy specter drawn by realism.

Americans are also prone to believe that morality should play an important role in politics. As the prominent sociologist Seymour Martin Lipset writes, "Americans are utopian moralists who press hard to institutionalize virtue, to destroy evil people, and eliminate wicked institutions and practices."[9]

This perspective clashes with the realist belief that war is an intrinsic element of life in the international system. Most Americans tend to think of war as a hideous enterprise that should ultimately be abolished from the face of the Earth. It might justifiably be used for lofty liberal goals like fighting tyranny or spreading democracy, but it is morally incorrect to fight wars merely to change or preserve the balance of power. This makes the Clausewitzian conception of warfare anathema to most Americans.[10]

The American proclivity for moralizing also conflicts with the fact that realists tend not to distinguish between good and bad states, but instead discriminate between states largely on the basis of their relative power capabilities. A purely realist interpretation of the Cold War, for example, allows for no meaningful difference in the motives behind American and Soviet behavior during that conflict. According to realist theory, both sides were driven by their concerns about the balance of power, and each did what it could to maximize its relative power. Most Americans would recoil at this interpretation of the Cold War, however, because they believe the United States was motivated by good intentions while the Soviet Union was not.

★   ★   ★

Rhetoric vs. Practice

Because Americans dislike realpolitik, public discourse about foreign policy in the United States is usually couched in the language of liberalism. . . . Behind closed doors, however, the elites who make national security policy speak mostly the language of power, not that of principle. . . . In essence, a discernible gap separates public rhetoric from the actual conduct of American foreign policy.

* * *

Still, the gap between rhetoric and reality usually goes unnoticed in the United States itself. Two factors account for this phenomenon. First, realist policies sometimes coincide with the dictates of liberalism, in which case there is no conflict between the pursuit of power and the pursuit of principle. Under these circumstances, realist policies can be justified with liberal rhetoric without having to discuss the underlying power realities. This coincidence makes for an easy sell. For example, the United States fought against fascism in World War II and communism in the Cold War for largely realist reasons. But both of those fights were also consistent with liberal principles, and thus policymakers had little trouble selling them to the public as ideological conflicts.

Second, when power considerations force the United States to act in ways that conflict with liberal principles, " spin doctors" appear and tell a story that accords with liberal ideals. . . .

How is it possible to get away with this contradiction between rhetoric and policy? Most Americans readily accept these rationalizations because liberalism is so deeply rooted in their culture. As a result, they find it easy to believe that they are acting according to cherished principles, rather than cold and calculated power considerations.[11]

Notes

[1] The balance of power is a concept that has a variety of meanings. See Inis L. Claude, Jr., *Power and International Relations* (New York: Random House, 1962), chap. 2; and

Ernst B. Haas, "The Balance of Power: Prescription, Concept, or Propaganda?" *World Politics* 5, No. 4 (July 1953), pp. 442–77. I use it to mean the actual distribution of military assets among the great powers in the system.

[2] Morgenthau is something of an exception regarding this second belief. Like other realists, he does not distinguish between good and bad states, and he clearly recognizes that external environment shapes state behavior. However, the desire for power, which he sees as the main driving force behind state behavior, is an internal characteristic of states.

[3] Carl von Clausewitz, *On War*, trans. and ed. Michael Howard and Peter Paret (Princeton, NJ: Princeton University Press, 1976), esp. books 1, 8. Also see Richard K. Betts, "Should Strategic Studies Survive?" *World Politics* 50, No. 1 (October 1997), pp. 7–33, esp. p. 8; and Michael I. Handel, *Masters of War: Classical Strategic Thought*, 3d ed. (London: Frank Cass, 2001).

[4] See Keith Shimko, "Realism, Neorealism, and American Liberalism," *Review of Politics* 54:2 (Spring 1992), 281–301.

[5] See Seymour Martin Lipset, *American Exceptionalism: A Double-Edged Sword* (New York: Norton, 1996), 51–52, 237. Also see Gabriel A. Almond, *The American People and Foreign Policy* (New York: Praeger, 1968), 50–51.

[6] Alexis de Tocqueville, *Democracy in America*, vol. II, trans. Henry Reeve (New York: Schocken Books, 1972), 38.

[7] Hans J. Morgenthau, *Scientific Man vs. Power Politics* (Chicago: University of Chicago Press, 1946), 201.

[8] See Reinhold Niebuhr, *The Children of Light and the Children of Darkness: A Vindication of Democracy and a Critique of Its Traditional Defense* (New York: Scribner's, 1944), especially 153–90.

[9] Lipset, *American Exceptionalism*, 63.

[10] See Samuel P. Huntington, *The Soldier and the State: The Theory and Practice of Civil-Military Relations* (Cambridge: Harvard University Press, 1957).

[11] The classic statement on the profound impact of liberal ideas on American thinking is Louis Hartz, *The Liberal Tradition in America: An interpretation of American Political Thought since the Revolution* (New York: Harcourt, Brace and World, 1955).

Peace

ROBERT O. KEOHANE
Governance in a Partially Globalized World

Talk of globalization is common today in the press and increasingly in political science. Broadly speaking, globalization means the shrinkage of distance on a world scale through the emergence and thickening of networks of connections—environmental and social as well as economic (Held et al. 1999; Keohane and Nye [1977] 2001). Forms of limited globalization have existed for centuries, as exemplified by the Silk Road. Globalization took place during the last decades of the nineteenth century, only to be reversed sharply during the thirty years after World War I. It has returned even more strongly recently, although it remains far from complete. We live in a partially globalized world.

Globalization depends on effective governance, now as in the past. Effective governance is not inevitable. If it occurs, it is more likely to take place through interstate cooperation and transnational networks than through a world state. But even if national states retain many of their present functions, effective governance of a partially—and increasingly—globalized world will require more extensive international institutions. Governance arrangements to promote cooperation and help resolve conflict must be developed if globalization is not to stall or go into reverse. . . . To make a partially globalized world benign, we need not just effective governance but the *right kind* of governance.

Desirable Institutions For A Partially Globalized World

. . . What political institutions would be appropriate for a partially globalized world? Political institutions are persistent and connected sets of formal and informal rules within which attempts at influence take place. In evaluating institutions, I am interested in their *consequences, functions, and procedures.* On all three dimensions, it would be quixotic to expect global governance to reach the standard of modern democracies or polyarchies, which

From "Governance in a Partially Globalized World: Presidential Address, American Political Science Association, 2000," *American Political Science Review* 95.1 (March 2001): 1–13.

Dahl (1989) has analyzed so thoroughly. Instead, we should aspire to a more loosely coupled system at the global level that attains the major objectives for which liberal democracy is designed at the national level.

Consequences

We can think of outcomes in terms of how global governance affects the life situations of individuals. In outlining these outcome-related objectives, I combine Amartya Sen's concept of capabilities with Rawls's conception of justice. Sen (1999, 75) begins with the Aristotelian concept of "human functioning." . . . [A] person's "capability set represents the freedom to achieve: the alternative functioning combinations from which this person can choose" (p. 75). Governance should enhance the capability sets of the people being governed, leading to enhancements in their personal security, freedom to make choices, and welfare as measured by such indices as the UN Human Development Index. And it should do so in a just way, which I think of in the terms made famous by Rawls (1971). Behind the "veil of ignorance," not knowing one's future situation, people should regard the arrangements for determining the distribution of capabilities as just. As a summary of indicators, J. Roland Pennock's (1966) list holds up quite well: security, liberty, welfare, and justice.

Functions

The world for which we need to design institutions will be culturally and politically so diverse that most functions of governance should be performed at local and national levels, on the principle familiar to students of federalism or of the European Union's notion of "subsidiarity." Five key functions, however, should be handled at least to some extent by regional or global institutions.

The first of these functions is to limit the use of large-scale violence. Warfare has been endemic in modern world politics, and modern "total warfare" all but obliterates the distinction between combatants and noncombatants, rendering the "hard shell" of the state permeable (Herz 1959). All plans for global governance, from the incremental to the utopian, begin with the determination, in the opening words of the United Nations Charter (1945), "to save succeeding generations from the scourge of war."

The second function is a generalization of the first. Institutions for global governance will need to limit the negative externalities of decentralized action. A major implication of interdependence is that it provides opportunities for actors to externalize the costs of their actions onto others. Examples include "beggar thy neighbor" monetary policies, air pollution by upwind countries, and the harboring of transnational criminals, terrorists, or former dictators. Much international conflict and discord can be interpreted as resulting from such negative externalities; much international cooperation takes the form of mutual adjustment of policy to reduce these externalities or internalize some of their costs (Keohane 1984). . . .

The third function of governance institutions is to provide *focal points* in coordination games. . . . In situations with a clear focal point, no one has an incentive to defect. Great efficiency gains can be made by agreeing on a single standard. . . . Actors may find it difficult, for distributional reasons, to reach such an agreement, but after an institutionalized solution has been found, it will be self-enforcing.

The fourth major function of governance institutions for a partially globalized world is to deal with system disruptions. As global networks have become tighter and more complex, they have generated systemic effects that are often unanticipated (Jervis 1997). Examples include the Great Depression (Kindleberger 1978); global climate change; the world financial crisis of 1997–98, with its various panics culminating in the panic of August 1998 following the Russian devaluation; and the Melissa and Lovebug viruses that hit the Internet in 2000. Some of these systemic effects arise from situations that have the structure of collaboration games in which incentives exist for defection. In the future, biotechnology, genetic manipulation, and powerful technologies of which we are as yet unaware may, like market capitalism, combine great opportunity with systemic risk.

The fifth major function of global governance is to provide a guarantee against the worst forms of abuse, particularly involving violence and deprivation, so that people can use their capabilities for productive purposes. Tyrants who murder their own people may need to be restrained or removed by outsiders. Global inequality leads to differences in capabilities that are so great as to be morally indefensible and to which concerted international action is an appropriate response. Yet, the effects of globalization on inequality are much more complicated than they are often portrayed. Whereas average per-capita income has vastly increased during the last forty years, cross-national inequality in such income does not seem to have changed dramatically during

the same period, although some countries have become enormously more wealthy, and others have become poorer (Firebaugh 1999). Meanwhile, inequality within countries varies enormously. Some globalizing societies have a relatively egalitarian income distribution, whereas in others it is highly unequal. Inequality seems to be complex and conditional on many features of politics and society other than degree of globalization, and effective action to enhance human functioning will require domestic as well as international efforts.

*   *   *

Procedures

Liberal democrats are concerned not only with outcomes but also with procedures. I will put forward three procedural criteria for an acceptable global governance system. The first is *accountability*: Publics need to have ways to hold elites accountable for their actions. The second is *participation*: Democratic principles require that some level of participation in making collective decisions be open to all competent adults in the society. The third is *persuasion*, facilitated by the existence of institutionalized procedures for communication, insulated to a significant extent from the use and threats of force and sanctions, and sufficiently open to hinder manipulation.

Our standards of accountability, participation, and persuasion will have to be quite minimal to be realistic in a polity of perhaps ten billion people. Because I assume the maintenance of national societies and state or state-like governance arrangements, I do not presume that global governance will benefit from consensus on deep substantive principles. Global governance will have to be limited and somewhat shallow if it is to be sustainable. Overly ambitious attempts at global governance would necessarily rely too much on material sanctions and coercion. The degree of consensus on principles—even procedural principles, such as those of accountability, participation, and persuasion—would be too weak to support decisions that reach deeply into people's lives and the meanings that they construct for themselves. The point of presenting ideal criteria is to portray a *direction*, not a blueprint. . . .

Accountability

The partially globalized world that I imagine would not be governed by a representative electoral democracy. States will remain important; and one state/one vote is not a democratic principle. National identities are unlikely to dissolve into the sense of a larger community that is necessary for democracy to thrive.

Accountability, however, can be indirectly linked to elections without a global representative democracy. . . . Nonelectoral dimensions of accountability also exist. . . . Global governance, combined with modern communications technology (including technologies for linguistic translations), can begin to generate a public space in which some people communicate with one another about public policy without regard to distance. Criticism, heard and responded to in a public space, can help generate accountability. Professional standards comprise another form of nonelectoral accountability. . . . In devising acceptable institutions for global governance, accountability

needs to be built into the mechanisms of rule making and rule implementation. . . .

Meaningful collective participation in global governance in a world of perhaps ten billion people will surely have to occur through smaller units, but these may not need to be geographically based. In the partially globalized world that I am imagining, participation will occur in the first instance among people who can understand one another, although they may be dispersed around the world in "diasporic public spheres," which Arjun Appuradai (1996, 22) calls "the crucibles of a postnational political order."

Whatever the geographical quality of the units that emerge, democratic legitimacy for such a governance system will depend on the democratic character of these smaller units of governance. It will also depend on the maintenance of sufficient autonomy and authority for these units, if participation at this level is to remain meaningful.

Persuasion and Institutions

Since the global institutions that I imagine do not have superior coercive force to that of states, the influence processes that they authorize will have to be legitimate. . . . To understand the potential for legitimate governance in a partially globalized world, we need to understand how institutions can facilitate rational persuasion. How do we design institutions of governance so as to increase the scope for reflection and persuasion, as opposed to force, material incentives, and fraud?

* * *

Insofar as the consequences and functions of institutions are not seriously degraded, institutions that encourage reflection and persuasion are normatively desirable and should be fostered.

Conclusion

The stakes in the mission I propose are high, for the world and for political science. If global institutions are designed well, they will promote human welfare. But if we bungle the job, the results could be disastrous. Either oppression or ineptitude would likely lead to conflict and a renewed fragmentation of global politics. Effective and humane global governance arrangements are not inevitable. They will depend on human effort and on deep thinking about politics.

As we face globalization, our challenge resembles that of the founders of this country: how to design working institutions for a polity of unprecedented size and diversity. Only if we rise to that challenge will we be doing our part to ensure Lincoln's "rebirth of freedom" on a world—and human—scale.

References

Firebaugh, Glen. 1999. "Empirics of World Income Inequality." *American Journal of Sociology* 104 (May): 1597–1631.

Held, David, et. al. 1999. *Global Transformation: Politics, Economic and Culture.* Stanford, Cal.: Stanford University Press.

Herz, John H. 1959. *International Politics in the Atomic Age.* New York: Columbia University Press.

Jervis, Robert. 1997. *System Effects: Complexity in Political and Social Life.* Princeton: Princeton University Press.

Keohane, Robert O. 1984. *After Hegemony; Cooperation and Discord in the World Political Economy.* Princeton: Princeton University Press.

Keohane, Robert O., and Joseph S. Nye, Jr. [1977] 2001. *Power and Interdependence.* 3rd ed. New York: Addison-Wesley.

Kindleberger, Charles P. 1973. *The World in Depresssion, 1929–1939.* Berkeley: University of California Press.

Pennock, J. Roland. 1966. "Political Development, Political Systems and Political Goods." *World Politics* 18 (April): 415–34.

Rawls, John. 1971. *A Theory of Justice.* Cambridge: Harvard University Press.

Sen, Amartya K. 1999. *Development as Freedom.* New York: Knopf.

Prosperity

The United States and World Economic Power

* * *

To understand the unique economic interests and aspirations of the United States in the world, and the degree to which it benefits or loses within the existing distribution and structure of power and the world economy, is to define a crucial basis for comprehending as well as predicting its role overseas.

* * *

The United States and Raw Materials

The role of raw materials is qualitative rather than merely quantitative, and neither volume nor price can measure their ultimate significance and consequences. The economies and technologies of the advanced industrial nations, the United States in particular, are so intricate that the removal of even a small part, as in a watch, can stop the mechanism. The

steel industry must add approximately thirteen pounds of manganese to each ton of steel, and though the weight and value of the increase is a tiny fraction of the total, a modern diversified steel industry *must* have manganese. The same analogy is true of the entire relationship between the industrial and so-called developing nations: The nations of the Third World may be poor, but in the last analysis the industrial world needs their resources more than these nations need the West, for poverty is nothing new to peasantry cut off from export sectors, and trading with industrial states has not ended their subsistence living standards. In case of a total rupture between the industrial and supplier nations, it is the population of the industrial world that proportionately will suffer the most.

* * *

It is extraordinarily difficult to estimate the potential role and value of these scarce minerals to the United States, but certain approximate definitions are quite sufficient to make the point that the future of American economic

From *The Roots of American Foreign Policy* (Boston: Beacon Press, 1969), chap. 3.

power is too deeply involved for this nation to permit the rest of the world to take its own political and revolutionary course in a manner that imperils the American freedom to use them. Suffice it to say, the ultimate significance of the importation of certain critical raw materials is not their cost to American business but rather the end value of the industries that *must* employ these materials, even in small quantities, or pass out of existence. And in the larger sense, confident access to raw materials is a necessary precondition for industrial expansion into new or existing fields of technology, without the fear of limiting shortages which the United States' sole reliance on its national resources would entail. Intangibly, it is really the political and psychological assurance of total freedom of development of national economic power that is vital to American economic growth. Beyond this, United States profits abroad are made on overseas investments in local export industries, giving the Americans the profits of the suppliers as well as the consumer. An isolated America would lose all this, and much more.

* * *

World Trade and World Misery

If the postwar experience is any indication, the nonsocialist developing nations have precious little reason to hope that they can terminate the vast misery of their masses. For in reality the industrialized nations have increased their advantages over them in the world economy by almost any standard one might care to use.

The terms of trade—the unit value or cost of goods a region imports compared to its exports—have consistently disfavored the developing nations since 1958, ignoring altogether the fact that the world prices of raw materials prior to that time were never a measure of equity. Using 1958 as a base year, by 1966 the value of the exports of developing areas had fallen to 97, those of the industrial nations had risen to 104. Using the most extreme example of this shift, from 1954 to 1962 the terms of trade deteriorated 38 percent against the developing nations, for an income loss in 1962 of about $11 billion, or 30 percent more than the financial aid the Third World received that year. Even during 1961–66, when the terms of trade remained almost constant, their loss in potential income was $13.4 billion, wiping away 38 percent of the income from official foreign aid plans of every sort.

* * *

In fact, whether intended or otherwise, low prices and economic stagnation in the Third World directly benefit the industrialized nations. Should the developing nations ever industrialize to the extent that they begin consuming a significant portion of their own oil and mineral output, they would reduce the available supply to the United States and prices would rise. And there has never been any question that conservative American studies of the subject have treated the inability of the Third World to industrialize seriously as a cause for optimism in raw materials planning. Their optimism is fully warranted, since nations dependent on the world market for the capital to industrialize are unlikely to succeed, for when prices of raw materials are high they tend to concentrate on selling more raw materials, and when prices are low their earnings are insufficient to raise capital for diversification. The United States especially gears its investments, private and public, to increasing the output of exportable minerals and agricultural commodities, instead of balanced economic development. With relatively high capital-labor intensive investment and feeding transport facilities to port areas rather than to the population, such investments hardly scratch the living standards of the great majority of the local peasantry or make possible the large increases in agricultural output that are a precondition of a sustained industrial expansion.

* * *

United States Investment and Trade

* * *

American foreign investments are unusually parasitic, not merely in the manner in which they use a minimum amount of dollars to mobilize maximum foreign resources, but also because of the United States' crucial position in the world raw-materials price structure both as consumer and exporter. This is especially true in the developing regions, where extractive industries and cheap labor result in the smallest permanent foreign contributions to national wealth. In Latin America in 1957, for example, 36 percent of United States manufacturing investments, as opposed to 56 percent in Europe and 78 percent in Canada, went for plant and equipment. And wages as a percentage of operating costs in United States manu-

facturing investments are far lower in Third World nations than Europe or Canada.[1]

* * *

Seen in this light, United States foreign aid has been a tool for penetrating and making lucrative the Third World in particular and the entire nonsocialist world in general. The small price for saving European capitalism made possible later vast dividends, the expansion of American capitalism, and ever greater power and profits. It is this broader capability eventually to expand and realize the ultimate potential of a region that we must recall when short-term cost accounting and a narrow view make costly American commitments to a nation or region inexplicable. Quite apart from profits on investments, during 1950–60 the United States allocated $27.3 billion in nonmilitary grants, including the agricultural disposal program. During that same period it exported $166 billion in goods on a commercial basis, and imported materials essential to the very operation of the American economy.[2] It is these vast flows of goods, profits, and wealth that set the fundamental context for the implementation and direction of United States foreign policy in the world.

The United States and the Price of Stability

Under conditions in which the United States has been the major beneficiary of a world economy geared to serve it, the continued, invariable American opposition to basic innovations and reforms in world economic relations is entirely predictable. Not merely resistance to stabilizing commodity and price agreements, or non-tied grants and loans, but to every imperatively needed structural change has characterized United States policy toward the Third World. In short, the United States is today the bastion of the *ancient regime,* of stagnation and continued poverty for the Third World.

* * *

The numerous American interventions to protect its investors throughout the world, and the United States ability to use foreign aid and loans as a lever to extract required conformity and concessions, have been more significant as a measure of its practice. The instances of this are too plentiful to detail here, but the remarkable relationship between American complaints on this score and the demise of objectionable local political leaders deserves more than passing reference.

* * *

In today's context, we should regard United States political and strategic intervention as a rational overhead charge for its present and future freedom to act and expand. One must also point out that however high that cost may appear today, in the history of United States diplomacy specific American economic interests in a country or region have often defined the national interest on the assumption that the nation can identify its welfare with the profits of some of its citizens—whether in oil, cotton, or bananas. The costs to the state as a whole are less consequential than the desires and profits of specific class strata and their need to operate everywhere in a manner that, collectively, brings vast prosperity to the United States and its rulers.

Today it is a fact that capitalism in one country is a long-term physical and economic impossibility without a drastic shift in the distribution of the world's income. Isolated, the United States would face those domestic backlogged economic and social problems and weaknesses it has deferred confronting for over two decades, and its disappearing strength in a global context would soon open the door to the internal dynamics which might jeopardize the very existence of liberal corporate capitalism at home.

The existing global political and economic structure, with all its stagnation and misery, has not only brought the United States billions but has made possible, above all, a vast power that requires total world economic integration not on the basis of equality but of domination. And to preserve this form of world is vital to the men who run the American economy and politics at the highest levels.

Notes

[1]Department of Commerce, *U.S. Business Investments,* 43, 65–66; *The Economist,* July 10, 1965, 167; Allan W. Johnstone, *United States Direct Investment in France* (Cambridge, 1965), 48–49; *Le Monde,* January 14–15, July 23, 1968; *Wall Street Journal,* December 12, 1967; Committee on Foreign Relations, *United States–Latin American Relations,* 388; *New York Times,* April 16, 1968. [2]Department of Commerce, *Balance of Payments,* 120, 150–51.

Principles

Tony Smith

The United States and the Global Struggle
for Democracy: Early 1990s Perspective

If the United States had never existed, what would be the status in world affairs of democracy today? Would its forces based in France, Britain, the Low Countries, and Scandinavia have survived the assaults of fascism and communism, or would one of these rival forms of mass political mobilization have instead emerged triumphant at the end of the twentieth century?

The answer is self-evident: we can have no confidence that, without the United States, democracy would have survived. To be sure, London prepared the way for Washington in charting the course of liberal internationalism; and the United States was slow to leave isolationism after 1939, while the Red Army deserves primary praise for the defeat of Nazi Germany. Yet it is difficult to escape the conclusion that since World War I, the fortunes of democracy worldwide have largely depended on American power.

The decisive period of the century, so far as the eventual fate of democracy was concerned,

came with the defeat of fascism in 1945 and the American-sponsored conversion of Germany and Japan to democracy and a much greater degree of economic liberalism. Here were the glory days of American liberal democratic internationalism (and not the 1980s, however remarkable that decade, as some believe). American leadership of the international economy—thanks to the institutions created at Bretton Woods in 1944, its strong backing for European integration with the Marshall Plan in 1947 and support for the Schuman Plan thereafter, the formation of NATO in 1949, the stability of Japanese political institutions after 1947 and that country's economic dynamism after 1950 (both dependent in good measure on American power)—created the economic, cultural, military, and political momentum that enabled liberal democracy to triumph over Soviet communism. Except perhaps for NATO, all of these developments were the product of the tenets of thinking first brought together in modern form by Woodrow Wilson, before

From *America's Mission: The United States and the Worldwide Struggle for Democracy in the 20th Century* (Princeton: Princeton University Press, 1994), chap. 1 and appendix.

being adapted to the world of the 1940s by the Roosevelt and Truman administrations.

In the moment of triumph, it should not be forgotten that for most of this century, the faith in the future expansion of democracy that had marked progressive thinking in Europe and America at the turn of the century seemed exceedingly naive. By the 1930s, democracy appeared to many to be unable to provide the unity and direction of its totalitarian rivals. Indeed, again in the 1970s, there was a resurgence of literature predicting democracy's imminent demise: its materialism, its individualism, its proceduralism (that is, the elaborate sets of rules and institutions needed to make it function), its tolerance, not to say its permissiveness—the list could be extended indefinitely—seemed to deprive it of the toughness and confidence necessary to survive in a harsh world of belligerent, ideologically driven fascist and communist states.

Fascism was essentially undone by its militarism and its racism; Soviet communism by its overcentralized economic planning and its failure to provide a political apparatus capable of dealing with the tensions of nationalism not only within the Soviet empire but inside the Soviet Union itself. By contrast, however varied the forms of government may be that rightly call themselves democratic, they have demonstrated a relative ability to accommodate class, gender, and ethnic diversity domestically through complicated institutional forms centering on competitive party systems and representative governments. As importantly, the democracies have shown an ability to cooperate internationally with one another through a variety of regimes managing the complex issues of their interdependence, despite the centrifugal force of rival state interests and nationalism. Hence, at the end of the twentieth century, democracy is unparalleled for its political flexibility, stability, legitimacy, and ability to cooperate internationally.

* * *

The most important statement on the uniqueness of American liberalism remains Alexis de Toqueville's *Democracy in America* published in 1835 (a second volume appeared in 1840). Commenting that the United States was "born free," that "the social state of the Americans is eminently democratic . . . even the seeds of aristocracy were never planted," Toqueville continues:

> There society acts by and for itself. There are no authorities except within itself; one can hardly meet anybody who would dare to conceive, much less to suggest, seeking power elsewhere. The people take part in the making of the laws by choosing the lawgivers, and they share in their application by electing the agents of the executive power; one might say that they govern themselves, so feeble and restricted is the part left to the administration, so vividly is that administration aware of its popular origin, and obedient to the fount of power. The people reign over the American political world as God rules over the universe. It is the cause and the end of all things; everything rises out of it and is absorbed back into it.[1]

Toqueville was correct to see how democratic the United States was by contrast with other countries in the 1830s, for with Andrew Jackson's election in 1828 it could rightfully call itself the first modern democracy. Yet it should be recalled that at the time of American independence there were property qualifications for the vote and that certain religious denominations, as well as women and slaves, were disfranchised. Had Toqueville arrived a decade earlier, his account might not have been so perspicacious.

* * *

It is inevitable that the meaning of liberal democracy in domestic American life should deeply mark the conduct of its foreign policy. When their policy intends to promote democracy abroad, Americans rather naturally tend to think in terms of a weak state relative to society. The result for others is a paradoxical form of "conservative radicalism": radical in that for many countries, democracy has meant an abrupt and basic political change away from the narrow-based authoritarian governments with which these people are familiar; conservative in that in fundamental ways, the Americans have not meant to disturb the traditional social power relations based on property ownership.

Here was the genius, and also the tragedy, of the American sponsorship of democracy abroad: it was genuinely innovative politically, but it was not profoundly upsetting socioeconomically. The genius of the approach was that it could be attractive to established elites abroad (provided that they had the wit to try to adapt), for whatever the hazards of introducing democracy, it promised to modernize and stabilize those regimes that could reform enough to be called democratic. The tragedy, especially in lands that were predominantly agrarian, was that these political changes (where they were accepted) were often not enough to create the cultural, economic, and social circumstances that could reinforce a democratic political order. As a result, American efforts either failed completely (as in

Central America and the Caribbean during Wilson's presidency) or created narrowly based and highly corrupt elitist forms of democracy (as in the Philippines or more recently in the Dominican Republic).

It was different when the United States occupied Japan and Germany to promote democracy in 1945. But the men and women who undertook this mission were not liberal democrats of the traditional American sort. Instead, many of them were New Dealers, for whom the prerequisites of democracy included strong labor unions, land reform, welfare legislation, notions of racial equality, and government intervention in the economy. Moreover, they had the good fortune to be working with societies that already had centralized political institutions, diversified industrial economies, and (at least in Germany) many convinced democrats awaiting deliverance from fascism and communism alike. The Americans who conceived of the Alliance for Progress in Latin America were for the most part cut of the same cloth as the New Dealers. But their power in Latin America was not nearly so great as their predecessors' had been in Germany and Japan, and the socioeconomic structures of South and Central America lacked the inherent advantages for democratizers that the former fascist powers possessed. Hence the Alliance's failure.

This New Deal outlook was not typical of the Americans who took the Philippines in 1898 or who were in power under what was deservedly called the "progressive" presidency of Woodrow Wilson. These Franklin Roosevelt Democrats were also different from liberal reformers like Jimmy Carter, who favored a strictly human-rights approach to democratization. The most interesting contrast comes with Ronald Reagan, however, whose insistence on the contribution free markets could make to democratic government shared with the New Dealers the notion that political life depends in good measure on the structure of power socioeconomically (even if the two approaches differed on the need for governmental regulation and social redistribution).

As these cases suggest, American liberal democratic internationalism varied in its agenda over time. The continuity was such, however, that we can speak of a tradition in American foreign policy, one with an agenda for action abroad tied to a firm notion of the national interest that was to have momentous consequences for world affairs in the twentieth century.

*   *   *

The irony of American liberal internationalism by late 2011 was that a framework for policy that had done so much to establish America's preeminence in world affairs between 1945 and 2001 should have contributed so significantly to its decline thereafter. . . .

During the first decade of the twenty-first century, the very forces that had allowed America to win the cold war had created the illusion that with relative ease history could now be controlled and international affairs fundamentally restructured by the expansion of the free-market democratic world into an international order of peace. Under neoconservative and neoliberal auspices, democracy was believed to have a "universal appeal" with peace-giving qualities of benefit to all peoples. A market economy both domestically and globally would compound the process of polit-ical stabilization. . . . For a "unipolar world" a global mission was conceived, as in neoliberal and neoconservative hands neo-Wilsonianism evolved into a hard ideology, the equivalent in conceptual terms to Marxism-Leninism, with a capacity to give leaders and people a sense of identity and worldwide purpose to a degree that liberalism had never before possessed.

*   *   *

Communism was dead, but "free-market democracy" was proving to be a much weaker blueprint for world order than had only recently been anticipated. As Machiavelli had counseled in his *Discourses,* "Men always commit the error of not knowing where to limit their hopes, and by trusting to these rather than to a just measure of their resources, they are generally ruined."

*   *   *

The fate of liberal internationalism thus depends for the most part on the behavior of those who guide the policies of the democratic world. If leaders in a Wilsonian persuasion could rein in the inflated self-confidence that too many of them had in the two decades after the end of the cold war with respect to the merits of an indiscriminate promotion of democratic nation- and state-building and with regard to their unquestioning support for a deregulated capitalism—if they could regain the modesty and realism that Reinhold Niebuhr called for sixty years ago and that in many respects Woodrow Wilson displayed a century ago—then liberal internationalism might continue to play a beneficent role in world politics.

The choice was for America to make, as Niebuhr had insisted in the lines of *The Irony of American History*:

> If we should perish, the ruthlessness of the foe would be only the secondary cause of the disaster. The primary cause would be that the strength of a great nation was directed by eyes too blind to see all the hazards of the struggle; and the blindness would be induced not by some accident of nature or history but by hatred and vainglory.

Note

[1] Alexis de Toqueville, *Democracy in America* (New York: Harper and Row, 1966), pt. 1, chaps. 2–3. For a modern restatement of Toqueville's insistence on American egalitarianism, see Gordon S. Wood, *The Radicalism of the American Revolution* (New York: Knopf, 1992).

The President, Congress and War Powers

ARTHUR M. SCHLESINGER, JR.
What the Founders Intended*

* * *

The Constitutional Convention had no stouter champion of Executive power than Alexander Hamilton, but even Hamilton vigorously rejected the notion that foreign policy was the personal prerogative of the President. "The history of human conduct," Hamilton wrote in the 75th Federalist, "does not warrant that exalted opinion of human virtue which would make it wise in a nation to commit interests of so delicate and momentous a kind, as those which concern its intercourse with the rest of the world, to the sole disposal of the President of the United States." Abraham Lincoln accurately expressed the purpose of the Framers with regard to the warmaking power when he wrote 60 years later that "they resolved to so frame the Constitution that no one man should hold the power of bringing this oppression upon us."

The Framers, in short, envisaged a partnership between Congress and the President in the conduct of foreign affairs with Congress, and particularly the Senate, as the senior partner. Hamilton's comment on the treatymaking power applies to the broad legislative-executive balance with regard to foreign policy: "The joint possession of the power in question, by the President and Senate, would afford a greater prospect of security than the separate possession of it by either of them."

. . . No one can doubt that the original intent of the Framers was to assure Congress the major role in the formulation of foreign policy and above all to deny Presidents the power to make war on their own. Yet the present [Nixon] administration somehow manages to champion a theory of inherent Presidential prerogative in foreign affairs that would have appalled the Founding Fathers.

This theory of Presidential supremacy has only crystallized in recent times. While early Presidents did not hesitate to use armed force without congressional authorization to protect American lives, property, and interests, they used it typically against pirates, brigands,

---

*From testimony to the U.S. Congress, Senate, Committee on Foreign Relations, Special Subcommittee on War Powers, *The War Power after 200 Years: Congress and the President at a Constitutional Impasse,* 100th Cong., 2nd session, July 13, 14, August 5, September 7, 15, 16, 20, 23 and 29, 1988, S. Rept. OCLC:19496995. Vol. 1428. Washington: U.S. G.P.O., 1989. Print. S. Hrg.; 100–1012.

revolutionaries, and tribes rather than against sovereign states. And as Judge Sofaer wrote in his notable work, "War, Foreign Affairs and Constitutional Power," "At no time did the Executive claim inherent power to initiate military action."

Nor indeed did Lincoln in 1861 or Franklin Roosevelt in 1941 claim that power. They undertook warlike and plainly unconstitutional actions because they believed that the life of the Nation was at stake and that their actions responded, in Lincoln's words, to "a popular demand and a public necessity." They rested their case not on assertions of constitutionally valid unilateral Presidential power, but rather on versions of John Locke's old doctrine of emergency prerogative beyond the Constitution.

* * *

The transfer of foreign policy warmaking power from Congress to the Executive results most of all from our situation in the world. The Republic has become a superpower. It has lived now for half a century in a state of chronic international crisis, real, imagined, and contrived. Under the pressure of incessant crisis, Congress has gladly relinquished many of its constitutional powers to the Presidency. Perhaps it has done so because the congressional record of error between the wars—from the rejection of the Versailles Treaty to the rigid neutrality legislation of the 1930's—had produced an institutional inferiority complex. Perhaps Members of Congress are intimidated by Executive claims of superior knowledge and wisdom. Perhaps they simply prefer to dodge responsibility and turn national decisions over to the President. For whatever reason, Congress has let constitutional powers slip away and Presidents now claim the warmaking power as

their personal property. It is too bad that this should be the case, for history, I believe, abundantly confirms Hamilton's proposition that the best security lies in partnership between the two branches rather than in separate possession of the warmaking power by either one of them. Neither branch, after all, is infallible. Each can benefit from the experience and counsel of the other.

It is a delusion, sedulously encouraged by the executive branch, that Presidents are necessarily wiser or even better informed than Congress. Sometimes they are; sometimes they aren't. Franklin Roosevelt was better informed than William E. Borah or Burton K. Wheeler and the isolationist leaders of the 1930's. But which body made more sense about the Vietnam War 20 years ago, the National Security Council or the majority of this particular committee?

* * *

. . . Presidents in their own self-interest should regard the requirement of congressional collaboration in foreign affairs not as a challenge to be evaded nor as a burden from which to be delivered, but as an opportunity to be embraced, the heaven-sent opportunity to give their policies a solid basis in consent. Congressional criticism alerts the President to flaws in his policy. Congressional support strengthens his hand, increases his authority, and diffuses his responsibility. As our wisest diplomat of the century, Averell Harriman, once put it, "No foreign policy will stick unless the American people are behind it. And unless Congress understands it, the American people aren't going to understand it."

But Presidents, like other people, do not always understand their own self-interest, nor can we write statutes on the kindly assumption that good and cooperative men will always reside in the White House. As the Supreme Court once said in a celebrated decision, the Republic has "no right to expect that it will always have wise and humane rules, sincerely attached to the principles of the Constitution. Wicked men, ambitious power, with hatred of liberty and contempt of law, may fill the place once occupied by Washington and Lincoln." Even nonwicked Presidents may be driven to diminish a congressional role by their own foreign policy obsessions or by the ambitions and delusions of their advisers.

* * *

On reading the Constitution, I stand with Woodrow Wilson who observed that the Constitution is "the vehicle of a nation's life" and that its meaning is determined "not by the original intentions of those who drew the paper, but by the exigencies and new aspects of life itself."

It may well be that the exact allocation of authority, as laid down by the Framers for a minor 18th century state, do not meet the needs of a 20th century superpower. But underneath that particular allocation lies a deeper principle. With regard to foreign affairs in general and to the warmaking power in particular, the Constitution commands above all a partnership between the legislative and executive branches. The terms of the partnership vary according to the pressures, political and geopolitical, of the day. That is the way it should be in a democracy. But the partnership must endure.

The vital problems of foreign policy belong in the political arena. They must be argued out before Congress and the electorate. The salient question, the question to which Congress must above all address itself is if it is to regain lost powers, must be whether the policies proposed make any sense. Neither branch of Government has a divine right to prevail over the other. Congress must understand that it cannot conduct day-to-day foreign policy. The President must understand that no foreign policy can last that is not founded on popular understanding and congressional consent, and that only a fool in the White House would take unto himself exclusively the fateful decision to enter or risk war. When we find means of making the partnership real, we remain faithful to the deeper intentions of the Framers.

Bureaucratic Politics

Graham T. Allison

Conceptual Models and the Cuban Missile Crisis

Most analysts explain (and predict) the behavior of national governments in terms of various forms of one basic conceptual model, here entitled the Rational Policy Model (Model I). In terms of this conceptual model, analysts attempt to understand happenings as the more or less purposive acts of unified national governments. For these analysts, the point of an explanation is to show how the nation or government could have chosen the action in question, given the strategic problem that it faced.

* * *

For some purposes, governmental behavior can be usefully summarized as action chosen by a unitary, rational decisionmaker: centrally controlled, conpletely informed, and value maximizing. But this simplification must not be allowed to conceal the fact that a "government" consists of a conglomerate of semi-feudal, loosely allied organizations, each with a substantial life of its own. Government leaders do sit formally, and to some extent in fact, on top of this conglomerate. But governments perceive problems through organizational sensors. Governments define alternatives and estimate consequences as organizations process information. Governments act as these organizations enact routines. Government behavior can therefore be understood according to a second conceptual model, less as deliberate choices of leaders and more as *outputs* of large organizations functioning according to standard patterns of behavior.

* * *

Model III: Bureaucratic Politics

The leaders who sit on top of organizations are not a monolithic group. Rather, each is, in his own right, a player in a central, competitive game. The name of the game is bureaucratic politics: bargaining along regularized channels among players positioned hierarchically within the government. Government behavior can thus be understood according to a third conceptual model, not as organizational outputs, but as outcomes of bargaining games. In contrast with Model I, the bureaucratic politics model sees no unitary actor but rather many actors as players who focus not on a single strategic issue but on many diverse intra-national problems as well, in terms of no consistent set of strategic objectives but rather

From *American Political Science Review* 62.3 (September 1969).

according to various conceptions of national, organizational, and personal goals, making government decisions not by rational choice but by the pulling and hauling that is politics.

* * *

The concept of national security policy as political outcome contradicts both public imagery and academic orthodoxy. Issues vital to national security, it is said, are too important to be settled by political games. They must be "above" politics. To accuse someone of "playing politics with national security" is a most serious charge. What public conviction demands, the academic penchant for intellectual elegance reinforces. Internal politics is messy; moreover, according to prevailing doctrine, politicking lacks intellectual content. As such, it constitutes gossip for journalists rather than a subject for serious investigation. Occasional memoirs, anecdotes in historical accounts, and several detailed case studies to the contrary, most of the literature of foreign policy avoids bureaucratic politics. The gap between academic literature and the experience of participants in government is nowhere wider than at this point.

* * *

Players in Positions. The actor is neither a unitary nation, nor a conglomerate of organizations, but rather a number of individual players. Groups of these players constitute the agent for particular government decisions and actions. Players are men in jobs. . . . Positions define what players both may and must do. The advantages and handicaps with which each player can enter and play in various games stem from his position. So does a cluster of obligations for the performance of certain tasks. . . .

Action as Politics. Government decisions are made and government actions emerge neither as the calculated choice of a unified group, nor as a formal summary of leaders' preferences. Rather the context of shared power but separate judgments concerning important choices determines that politics is the mechanism of choice. Note the *environment* in which the game is played: inordinate uncertainty about what must be done, the necessity that something be done, and crucial consequences of whatever is done. These features force responsible men to become active players. The *pace of the game*—hundreds of issues, numerous games, and multiple channels—compels players to fight to "get other's attention," to make them "see the facts," to assure that they "take time to think seriously about the broader issue." The *structure of the game*—power shared by individuals with separate responsibilities—validates each player's feeling that "others don't see my problem," and "others must be persuaded to look at the issue from a less parochial perspective." The *rules of the game*—he who hesitates loses his chance to play at that point, and he who is uncertain about his recommendation is overpowered by others who are sure—pressures players to come down on one side of a 51–49 issue and play. The *rewards of the game*—effectiveness, i.e., impact on outcomes, as the immediate measure of performance—encourages hard play. Thus, most players come to fight to "make the government do what is right." The strategies and tactics employed are quite similar to those formalized by theorists of international relations. . . .

Where you stand depends on where you sit. Horizontally, the diverse demands upon each player shape his priorities, perceptions, and issues. For large classes of issues, e.g., budgets and procurement decisions, the stance of a particular player can be predicted with high reliability from information concerning his seat.

The Media

JOHN BYRNE COOKE
The Press in Wartime*

Civil liberties are rarely more endangered than in wartime, and none is more at risk than freedom of the press. The press is called on to rally patriotic fervor. It is expected to be the voice of the government and the voice of the people—the voice of the country at war. If instead it challenges the government, if it questions the rationale for war, it provokes the government's impulse, already strong in times of crisis, to repress liberties in the name of security, and too often the people acquiesce. This is the paradox that threatens the freedoms we take for granted in peacetime. In the shock of war we feel that our way of life is threatened; in response we are willing to abandon (temporarily, we think) the principles on which that way of life is founded, in the hope of regaining our security.

The Founding Fathers saw government's inclination to suppress the rights of the citizens not as occasional, or rare, but constant. They trusted in freedom of speech, and of the press, to encourage a free flow of opinions, to keep the people informed and to warn them whenever their liberties were threatened from any quarter, so they might give, or withhold, the consent that is government's only legitimate source of power. Above all, the Founders trusted in the free press. In the debate over ratifying the Constitution, no right was more often proclaimed inviolable. The federalists, who wrote the Constitution and advocated its adoption, and their opponents, the anti-federalists, vied to outdo each other in championing freedom of the press as the most essential safeguard of the liberties the Revolution had been fought to secure. The heart of the constitutional debate was not what freedoms Americans held sacred—they had proclaimed these rights "unalienable" in the Declaration of Independence—but whether the government proposed by the Constitution would protect or usurp them.

The federalists declared that the government could never threaten personal freedoms because it had no power to suppress them—it would have only those powers specifically bestowed by the Constitution. This didn't satisfy a Pennsylvania anti-federalist who protested that the framers of the Constitution

---

*From *Reporting the War: Freedom of the Press from the American Revolution to the War on Terrorism* (New York: Palgrave Macmillan, 2007), Introduction.

"have made no provision for the *liberty of the press,* that grand *palladium of freedom,* and *scourge of tyrants.*"[1] Without exception, the constitutions of the states had declarations or "bills" of rights. The anti-federalists wanted such a bill in the federal Constitution. In the end they got their way, and some federalists as well agreed that affirming the most vital liberties in a bill of rights was a good thing. Even well after the Constitution was accepted as the foundation of the American government and the Bill of Rights enshrined the fundamental freedoms on which the republic was founded, James Madison felt it was important to emphasize that "among those sacred rights considered as forming the bulwark of their liberty, which the government contemplates with awful reverence and would approach only with the most cautious circumspection, there is no one of which the importance is more deeply impressed on the public mind than the liberty of the press."[2]

The First Amendment cares nothing for a fair and balanced press. It is freedom of the press as the bulwark of liberty and the scourge of tyrants that the Founders protected. To be sure, we ask more of the press than simply to oppose the government. We expect it to report the facts accurately. We expect events of the day to be set in a larger context. We expect opinion to be separated from news. We expect fairness. We expect the press to seek the truth in the welter of conflicting claims and opinions. But when government threatens the checks and balances the Founders crafted to protect the rights of the people, we expect the press to speak the truth in the face of governmental intimidation, secrecy, evasions and lies.

In the past sixty years, the integrity of the press has been threatened by the relentless commercialism of radio and television and the submersion of publishing and broadcasting enterprises into larger corporate entities who value profit over the obligations of a free press. More recently we have returned to do something closer to what the Founding Fathers had in mind, since the development of the Internet has enabled anyone with access to a computer to publish his or her opinions online for the world to read. The lasting effects of these developments on the dissemination of news and opinion are not yet fully clear. It seems certain that the role of the electronic media will only increase, and equally certain that the primary goals of the broadcast media will continue to be entertainment and profit.

Newspapers, descended from the Revolutionary weeklies and unchallenged as the principal news medium until the middle of the twentieth century, continue to exert an influence that is disproportionate to their circulation. The print media influence policymakers. They form the core of the historical archive. In the first wars of the twenty-first century, newspapers and magazines still play a leading role in commenting on government policy and criticizing it.

My purpose is to examine the relationship of the press and the national government in wartime. In each of a dozen wars—those that threatened the nation's survival or transformed America's role in the world—I have looked for examples of how the press has fulfilled its constitutional responsibility by questioning and opposing the government. I have concentrated on how opposition arose within the swell of patriotic support that characterizes the start of a war, following the story until the press is focused on the contentious issues and public debate is assured. Sometimes one printer, one newspaper, one reporter or one publisher stood out from the rest; sometimes it was helpful to follow several newspapers that collectively represented shifting attitudes in wartime.

The attitudes of different administrations have been as varied as those of the press. Some have tried to suppress opposing opinions. Others have made no efforts at repression despite being subjected to vitriolic criticism. Some controversies revive in virtually every war—you would think by now we could agree that dissent is not disloyal—while other controversies are unique to one conflict. If there is a virtue in moving quickly from one war to the next, it is in discovering the patterns that emerge in the contests between wartime governments and the press. Like the stories of the wars themselves, these are journeys of discovery, with unexpected turns and outcomes. I hope my readers will find in them, as I do, frequent reminders of the wisdom of the Founders, who protected the ability of the press to inform the ongoing debates that are the lifeblood of democracy and to sound the alarm at the first glimpse of tyranny. . . .

Notes

[1] "Centinel" Number 1 (October 5, 1787) in *The Anti-Federalist Papers and the Constitutional Convention Debate*, Ralph Ketcham, ed. (New York: New American Library, 2003), 236.

[2] James Madison, *Address of the General Assembly to the People of the Commonwealth of Virginia, 23 Jan. 1799*; Writings 6:333–336 in *The Writings of James Madison*, Gaillard Hunt, ed., 9 vols (New York: G. P. Putnam's Sons, 1900–1910). Vol. 5, Amendment I (Speech and Press), Document 21, from the University of Chicago Press website http://press-pubs.uchicago.edu/founders/documents/amendI_spechs21.html

Public Opinion

3.2

OLE R. HOLSTI

Public Opinion and Foreign Policy: Challenges to the Almond-Lippmann Consensus

* * *

The Post–World War II Consensus

The availability after World War II of growing sets of polling data and the institution of systematic studies of voting behavior, combined with the assumption of a leadership role in world affairs by the United States, served to stimulate a growth industry in analyses of public opinion. The consensus view that developed during this period of some fifteen or twenty years after the end of World War II and just prior to the Vietnam escalation centered on three major propositions:

■ Public opinion is highly volatile and thus it provides very dubious foundations for a sound foreign policy.
■ Public attitudes on foreign affairs are so lacking in structure and coherence

that they might best be described as "non-attitudes."
■ At the end of the day, however, public opinion has a very limited impact on the conduct of foreign policy.

Public Opinion Is Volatile

As noted earlier, Walter Lippmann's books of the interwar period described the mass public as neither sufficiently interested nor informed to play the pivotal role assigned to it by classical democratic theory. At the height of the Cold War thirty years later, Lippmann had become even more alarmed, depicting the mass public as not merely uninterested and uninformed, but as a powerful force that was so out of sync with reality as to constitute a massive and potentially fatal threat to effective government and policies.

The unhappy truth is that the prevailing public opinion has been destructively wrong at the critical junctures. The people have impressed a crit-

From *International Studies Quarterly* 36.4 (December 1992).

ical veto upon the judgments of informed and responsible officials. They have compelled the government, which usually knew what would have been wiser, or was necessary, or what was more expedient, to be too late with too little, or too long with too much, too pacifist in peace and too bellicose in war, too neutralist or appeasing in negotiations or too intransigent. Mass opinion has acquired mounting power in this country. It has shown itself to be a dangerous master of decision when the stakes are life and death.[1]

Similarly pessimistic conclusions and dire warnings were emerging from disparate other quarters as well. Drawing on a growing body of polling data and fearing that the American public might relapse into a mindless isolationism, because only a thin veneer of postwar internationalism covered a thick bedrock of indifference to the world, Gabriel Almond depicted public opinion as a volatile and mood-driven constraint upon foreign policy: "The undertow of withdrawal is still very powerful. Deeply ingrained habits do not die easy deaths. The world outside is still very remote for most Americans; and the tragic lessons of the last decades have not been fully digested."[2] Consequently, "Perhaps the gravest general problem confronting policy-makers is that of the instability of mass moods, the cyclical fluctuations which stand in the way of policy stability."[3]

* * *

Further support for the critics and skeptics emerged from the growing body of polling data which yielded ample evidence of the public's limited store of factual knowledge about foreign affairs. Innumerable surveys revealed such stunning gaps in information as: X percent of the American public are unaware that there is a communist government in China, Y percent

believe that the Soviet Union is a member of NATO, or Z percent cannot identify a single nation bordering on the Pacific Ocean. Such data reinforced the case of the critics and led some of them to propose measures to reduce the influence of the public. Thus, Lippmann called for stronger executive prerogatives in foreign affairs, and Bailey wondered whether the requirements of an effective foreign policy might make it necessary for the executive deliberately to mislead the public.[4]

Public Opinion Lacks Structure and Coherence

A growing volume of data on public opinion and voting behavior, as well as increasingly sophisticated methodologies, enabled analysts not only to describe aggregate results and trends, but also to delve into the structure of political beliefs. Owing to immediate policy concerns about the U.S. role in the postwar era, many of the early studies were largely descriptive, focusing on such issues as participation in international organizations and alliances, the deployment of troops abroad, security commitments, foreign aid, trade and protectionism, and the like. The underlying premise was that a single internationalist-isolationist dimension would serve to structure foreign policy beliefs, much in the way that a liberal-conservative dimension was assumed to provide coherence to preferences on domestic issues.

In a classic study based on data from the late 1950s and early 1960s, Philip Converse concluded that the political beliefs of the mass public lack a real structure or coherence.[5] Comparing responses across several domestic and foreign policy issues, he found little if any "constraint" or underlying ideological structure that might provide some coherence to political thinking. In contrast, his analyses of elites—congressional candidates—revealed substantially higher correlations among responses to various issues. Moreover, Converse found that both mass and elite attitudes on a given issue had a short half-life. Responses in 1956 only modestly predicted responses two years later, much less in 1960. These findings led him to conclude that mass political beliefs are best described as "non-attitudes." Although Converse's findings were later to become the center of an active debate, it should be emphasized that his was not a lone voice in the wilderness. His data were drawn from the National Election Studies [NES] at the University of Michigan, and his findings were only the most widely quoted of a series of studies from the NES that came to essentially the same conclusion about the absence of structure, coherence, or persistence in the political beliefs of the mass public—especially on foreign affairs.[6]

Public Opinion Has Limited Impact on Foreign Policy

The driving force behind much of the post–World War II attention to public opinion on foreign policy issues was the fear that an ill-informed and emotional mass public would serve as a powerful constraint on the conduct of American diplomacy, establishing unwise limits on policy makers, creating unrealistic expectations about what was feasible in foreign affairs, otherwise doing serious mischief to American diplomacy and, given the American role in the world, perhaps even to international stability. As Bernard Cohen demonstrated in a critical survey of the literature, however, the constraining role of public opinion was often

asserted but rarely demonstrated—or even put to a systematic test.[7]

By the middle of the 1960s a consensus in fact seemed to emerge on a third point: Public opinion has little if any real impact on policy. Or, as the point was made most pithily by one State Department official: "To hell with public opinion. . . . We should lead, and not follow."[8] The weight of research evidence cast doubt on the potency of public opinion as a driving force behind, or even a significant constraint upon, foreign policy making. For example, a classic study of the public-legislator relationship revealed that constituents' attitudes on foreign policy had less impact on members of the House of Representatives than did their views on domestic issues.[9] Cohen's research on the foreign policy bureaucracy indicated that State Department officials had a rather modest interest in public opinion, and to the extent that they even thought about the public, it was as an entity to be "educated" rather than a lodestar by which to be guided.[10] The proposition that the president has "almost a free hand" in the conduct of foreign affairs received support from other analysis, including Lipset, LaFeber, Levering, Paterson, and Graebner.[11]

*   *   *

The Renaissance of Interest in Public Opinion and Foreign Policy

Just as World War II and fears of postwar isolationism among the mass public gave rise to concern about public opinion and its impact on foreign policy, the war in Vietnam was the impetus for a renewed interest in the subject. It was a major catalyst in stimulating a reexamination of the consensus that had emerged during the two decades after World War II. * * *

[D]uring the past two decades analysts have begun to challenge important aspects of the consensus described above.

* * *

[J. E.] Mueller's study of public opinion toward the Korean and Vietnam wars posed [a] challenge to the thesis of mindless changes in public attitudes. To be sure, public support for the U.S. war effort in both conflicts eventually changed, but in ways that seemed explicable and rational, rather than random and mindless. More specifically, he found that increasing public opposition to the conflicts traced out a pattern that fit a curve of rising battle deaths, suggesting that the public used an understandable, if simple, heuristic to assess American policy.[12]

The most comprehensive challenge to the Almond-Lippmann thesis has emerged from studies conducted by Benjamin Page and Robert Shapiro. Their evidence includes all questions that have been posed by major polling organizations since the inception of systematic surveys in the 1930s. Of the more than 6000 questions, almost 20 percent have been asked at least twice, providing Page and Shapiro with a large data set to assess the degree of stability and change in mass public attitudes. Employing a cutoff point of a difference of 6 percent from one survey to another to distinguish between continuity and change, they found that mass opinion in the aggregate is in fact characterized by a good deal of stability and that this is no less true of foreign policy

than on domestic issues.[13] More important, when attitude shifts take place, they seem to be neither random nor 180 degrees removed from the true state of world affairs. Rather, changes appear to be "reasonable, event driven" reactions to the real world, even if the information upon which they are based is marginally adequate at best. They concluded that

> virtually all the rapid shifts [in public opinion] we found were related to political and economic circumstances or to significant events which sensible citizens would take into account. In particular, most abrupt foreign policy changes took place in connection with wars, confrontations, or crises in which major changes in the actions of the United States or other nations quite naturally affect preferences about what policies to pursue.[14]

* * *

Similar conclusions, supporting Page and Shapiro and casting doubt on the Almond-Lippmann thesis, have also emerged from other studies. Jentleson found that during the post-Vietnam era, variations in public support for the use of force are best explained by differences between force to coerce foreign policy restraint by others, and force to influence or impose internal political changes within another state; the former goal has received much stronger support than the latter.[15]

An interesting variant of the "rational public" thesis stipulates that the public attempts to moderate American behavior toward the USSR by expressing preferences for a conciliatory stance from hawkish administrations while supporting more assertive policies from dovish ones.[16] To the extent that one can generalize from this study focusing on the Carter and

Reagan administrations to other periods or other aspects of foreign policy, it further challenges the Almond-Lippmann thesis—indeed, it turns that proposition on its head—for it identifies the public as a source of moderation and continuity rather than of instability and unpredictability.

It is important to emphasize that none of these challenges to the Almond-Lippmann thesis is based on some newly found evidence that the public is in fact well informed about foreign affairs. Not only do polls repeatedly reveal that the mass public has a very thin veneer of factual knowledge about politics, economics, and geography; they also reveal that it is poorly informed about the specifics of conflicts, treaties, negotiations with other nations, characteristics of weapons systems, foreign leaders, and the like. Because the modest factual basis upon which the mass public reacts to international affairs remains an unchallenged—and unchallengable—fact, we are faced with a puzzle: If a generally poorly informed mass public does indeed react to international affairs in an events-driven, rational manner, what are the means that permit it to do so? Recall that a not-insignificant body of research evidence indicated that mass public attitudes lack the kind of ideological structure that would provide some coherence across specific issues and persistence through time.

* * *

Challenge #2: Do Public Attitudes Lack Structure and Coherence?

* * *

Although the more recent research literature has yet to create a consensus on all aspects of the question, there does appear to be a considerable convergence of findings on two general points relating to belief structures:

1. Even though the general public may be rather poorly informed, attitudes about foreign affairs are in fact structured in at least moderately coherent ways. Indeed, low information and an ambiguous foreign policy environment are actually likely to motivate rather than preclude some type of attitude structure.
2. A single isolationist-to-internationalist dimension inadequately describes the main dimensions of public opinion on international affairs.

An early study, based on the first of the quadrennial Chicago Council on Foreign Relations (CCFR) surveys, employed factor analysis and other methods to uncover three foreign policy outlooks: "liberal internationalism," "conservative internationalism," and "non-internationalism."[17] A comparable trichotomy ("three-headed eagle") emerged from early analyses of the data on opinion leaders generated by the Foreign Policy Leadership Project (FPLP).[18]

Others have questioned the division of foreign policy attitudes into three *types* rather than *dimensions,* and they have offered compelling evidence in support of their critiques. Chittick and Billingsley have undertaken both original and secondary analyses which indicated the need for three *dimensions,* including one that taps unilateralist-multilateralist sentiments, not three *types,* to describe adequately the foreign policy beliefs of both the mass public and leaders.[19]

A major set of contributions to the debate about how best to describe foreign policy attitudes has come from Wittkopf's exemplary secondary analyses of the CCFR surveys of both the general public and leaders.[20] His results, developed inductively from the first four CCFR surveys, revealed that with a single exception, two dimensions are necessary to describe foreign policy attitudes: "support-oppose militant internationalism" (MI) and "support-oppose cooperative internationalism" (CI). Dichotomizing and crossing these dimensions yields four types, with the quadrants labeled as *hardliners* (support MI, oppose CI), *internationalists* (support MI, support CI), *isolationists* (oppose MI, oppose CI), and *accommodationists* (oppose MI, support CI).

Support for Wittkopf's MI/CI scheme also emerges from a reanalysis of the FPLP data on American opinion leaders.[21] That study put the MI/CI scheme to a demanding test because of three major differences in the data sets: (1) The CCFR surveys were undertaken in 1974, 1978, 1982, and 1986, whereas the four FPLP studies followed two years later in each case; (2) the two sets of surveys have only a few questionnaire items in common; and (3) the MI/CI scheme was developed largely from data on the mass public, whereas the FPLP surveys focused solely on opinion leaders.

* * *

Challenge #3: Is Public Opinion Really Impotent?

* * *

Several recent quantitative studies have challenged some important foundations of the theory that, at least on foreign and defense issues, the public is virtually impotent. One element of

that thesis is that policy makers are relatively free agents on foreign policy questions because these issues pose few dangers of electoral retribution by voters: elections are said to be decided by domestic questions, especially those sometimes described as "pocketbook" or "bread and butter" issues. However, a systematic study of presidential campaigns between 1952 and 1984 revealed that in five of the nine elections during the period, foreign policy issues had "large effects." Or, as the authors put it, when presidential candidates devote campaign time and other resources to foreign policy issues, they are not merely "waltzing before a blind audience."[22]

Recent research on voting behavior has also emphasized the importance of retrospective evaluations of performance on voter choice among candidates, especially when one of them is an incumbent.[23] Because voters are perceived as punishing incumbent candidates or parties for foreign policy failures (for example, the Iran hostage episode) or rewarding them for successes (for example, the invasion of Panama to capture General Noriega), decisions by foreign policy leaders may be made in anticipation of public reactions and the probabilities of success or failure.

* * *

Finally, two major studies have measured the congruence between changes in public preferences and a broad range of policies over extended periods. The first, a study of public opinion and policy outcomes spanning the years 1960–1974, revealed that in almost two-thirds of 222 cases, policy outcomes corresponded to public preferences. The consistency was especially high (92%) on foreign policy issues. Monroe offers three possible explanations for his findings: Foreign policy issues permit more decision making by the executive, are likely to be the object of relatively less interest and influence by organized interest groups, and are especially susceptible to elite manipulation.[24] The second study covered an even longer span—1935 to 1979—which included 357 significant changes of public preferences.[25] Of the 231 instances of subsequent policy changes, 153 (66%) were congruent with changes in public preferences. There was little difference in the level of congruence for domestic (70%) and foreign policy (62%) issues.

* * *

Among the more difficult cases are those dealing with public opinion as a possible constraint on action. During the 1980s, the Reagan administration undertook a massive public relations campaign of dubious legality to generate public support for assistance to the "contra" rebels in Nicaragua,[26] but a careful analysis of surveys on the issue revealed that a majority of the public opposed American military involvement in Central America.[27] Would the Reagan administration have intervened more directly or massively in Nicaragua or El Salvador in the absence of such attitudes? Solid evidence about contemporary non-events is, to understate the case, rather hard to come by. Case studies seem to be the only way to address such questions, although even this approach is not wholly free of potential problems. Does an absence of documentary references to public opinion indicate a lack of interest by decision-makers? Alternatively, was attention to public attitudes so deeply ingrained in their working habits that it was unnecessary to make constant references to it? Are frequent references to public opinion an indication of a significant impact on decisions—or of a desire on the part

of officials to be "on record" as having paid attention to public sentiments?

* * *

Conclusion

The consensus of the mid-1960s on the nature, structure, and impact of public opinion has clearly come under vigorous challenge during the past quarter century. The Vietnam War, while not the sole causal factor in the reexamination of the conventional wisdom, was certainly a catalyst. If a new consensus has yet to emerge on all of the issues discussed above, at least it seems safe to state that the field is marked by innovative research and active debates on the implications of the results.

* * *

Notes

[1] Walter Lippmann, *Essays in the Public Philosophy* (Boston: Little, Brown, 1955), 20.

[2] Gabriel Almond, *The American People and Foreign Policy* (New York: Praeger, 1950), 85.

[3] Almond, *The American People,* 239. Almond's use of the term "mood" differs from that of Frank Klingberg. Almond refers to sudden shifts of interest and preferences, whereas Klingberg has used the term to explain American foreign policy in terms of generation-long societal swings between introversion and extraversion.

[4] Lippman, *Essays;* T. A. Bailey, *The Man in the Street: The Impact of American Public Opinion on Foreign Policy* (New York: Macmillan, 1948), 13.

[5] Philip E. Converse, "The Nature of Belief Systems in Mass Publics," in D. E. Apter, ed., *Ideology and Discontent* (New York: Free Press, 1964).

[6] A. Campbell, P. E. Converse, W. E. Miller, and D. E. Stokes, *The American Voter* (New York: Wiley, 1964).

[7] Bernard Cohen, *The Public's Impact on Foreign Policy* (Boston: Little, Brown, 1973).

[8]Quoted in Cohen, *The Public's Impact*, 62.

[9]W. E. Miller and D. E. Stokes, "Constituency Influence in Congress," *American Political Science Review* 57 (1963), 45–46.

[10]Cohen, *The Public's Impact*.

[11]S. M. Lipset, "The President, Polls, and Vietnam," *Transaction*, September/October 1966, 10–24. W. LaFeber, "American Policy-Makers, Public Opinion, and the Outbreak of Cold War, 1945–1950," in Y. Nagai and A. Inye, eds., *The Origins of Cold War in Asia* (New York: Columbia University Press, 1977); R. B. Levering, *The Public and American Foreign Policy, 1918–1978* (New York: Morrow, 1978); T. G. Paterson, "Presidential Foreign Policy, Public Opinion, and Congress: The Truman Years," *Diplomatic History* 3 (1979), 1–18; and N. A. Graebner, "Public Opinion and Foreign Policy: A Pragmatic View," in D. C. Piper and R. J. Tercheck, eds., *Interaction: Foreign Policy and Public Policy* (Washington, D.C.: American Enterprise Institute, 1983).

[12]J. E. Mueller, *War, Presidents, and Public Opinion* (New York: Wiley, 1973). During the summer of 1965, as the Johnson administration was moving toward fateful decisions regarding Vietnam, George Ball warned: "We can't win," he said, his deep voice dominating the Cabinet Room. "The war will be long and protracted, with heavy casualties. The most we can hope for is a messy conclusion. We must measure this long-term price against the short-term loss that will result from withdrawal." Producing a chart that correlated public opinion with American casualties in Korea, Ball predicted that the American public would not support a long and inconclusive war. ✻ ✻ ✻

[13]Benjamin Page and Robert Shapiro, "Foreign Policy and the Rational Public," *Journal of Conflict Resolution* 32 (1988), 211–470.

[14]Benjamin Page and Robert Shapiro, "Changes in Americans' Policy Preferences, 1935–1979," *Public Opinion Quarterly* 46 (1982), 24–42.

[15]B. W. Jentleson, "The Pretty Prudent Public: Post-Post Vietnam American Opinion on the Use of Military Force," *International Studies Quarterly* 36 (1992) 48–73.

[16]M. Nincic, "The United States, the Soviet Union, and the Politics of Opposites," *World Politics* 40 (1988), 452–750.

[17]M. Mandelbaum and W. Schneider, "The New Internationalisms," in K. A. Oye et al., eds., *Eagle Entangled: U.S. Foreign Policy in a Complex World* (New York: Longman, 1979).

[18]O. R. Holsti, "The Three-Headed Eagle: The United States and the System Change," *International Studies Quarterly* 23 (1979), 339–59; O. R. Holsti and J. N. Rosenau, "Vietnam, Consensus, and the Belief Systems of American Leaders," *World Politics* 32 (1979), 1–56; O. R. Holsti and J. N. Rosenau, *American Leadership in World Affairs: Vietnam and the Breakdown of Consensus* (London: Allen and Unwin, 1984).

[19]W. Chittick and K. R. Billingsley, "The Structure of Elite Foreign Policy Beliefs," *Western Political Quarterly* 42 (1989), 201–24. See also B. A. Barde and R. Oldendick, "Beyond Internationalism: The Case for Multiple Dimensions in Foreign Policy Attitudes," *Social Science Quarterly* 59 (1978), 732–42; and W. Chittick, K. R. Billingsly, and R. Travis, "Persistence and Change in Elite and Mass Attitudes toward U.S. Foreign Policy," *Political Psychology* 11 (1990), 385–402.

[20]E. R. Wittkopf, "On the Foreign Policy Beliefs of the American People: A Critique and Some Evidence," *International Studies Quarterly* 30 (1986), 425–45; E. R. Wittkopf, *Faces of Internationalism: Public Opinion and Foreign Policy* (Durham: Duke University Press, 1990).

[21]O. R. Holsti and J. N. Rosenau, "The Structure of Foreign Policy Attitudes among American Leaders," *Journal of Politics* 52 (1990), 94–125.

[22]J. H. Aldrich, J. I. Sullivan, and E. Bordiga, "Foreign Affairs and Issue Voting: Do Presidential Candidates 'Waltz before a Blind Audience?'" *American Political Science Review* 83 (1989), 123–41.

[23]M. Fiorina, *Retrospective Voting in American National Elections* (New Haven: Yale University Press, 1981); P. Abramson, J. H. Aldrich, and J. Rhode, *Change and Continuity in the 1988 Election* (Washington, D.C.: Congressional Quarterly, 1990).

[24]A. D. Monroe, "Consistency between Public Preferences and National Policy Decisions," *American Politics Quarterly* 7 (1979), 3–19.

[25]Benjamin Page and Robert Shapiro, "Effects of Public Opinion on Policy," *American Political Science Review* 77 (1983), 175–90.

[26]R. Parry and P. Kornbluh, "Iran-Contra's Untold Story," *Foreign Policy* 72 (1988), 3–30.

[27]R. Sobel, "Public Opinion about United States Intervention in El Salvador and Nicaragua," *Public Opinion Quarterly* 53 (1989), 114–28. See also R. H. Hinckley, *People, Polls, and Policy-Makers* (New York: Lexington, 1992).

Isolationism vs. Internationalism

HENRY KISSINGER
Franklin D. Roosevelt and the Coming of World War II

For contemporary political leaders governing by public opinion polls, Roosevelt's role in moving his isolationist people toward participation in the war serves as an object lesson on the scope of leadership in a democracy. Sooner or later, the threat to the European balance of power would have forced the United States to intervene in order to stop Germany's drive for world domination. The sheer, and growing, strength of America was bound to propel it eventually into the center of the international arena. That this happened with such speed and so decisively was the achievement of Franklin Delano Roosevelt.

All great leaders walk alone. Their singularity springs from their ability to discern challenges that are not yet apparent to their contemporaries. Roosevelt took an isolationist people into a war between countries whose conflicts had only a few years earlier been widely considered inconsistent with American values and irrelevant to American security. After 1940, Roosevelt convinced the Congress, which had overwhelmingly passed a series of Neutrality Acts just a few years before, to authorize ever-increasing American assistance to Great Britain, stopping just short of outright belligerency and occasionally even crossing that line. Finally, Japan's attack on Pearl Harbor removed America's last hesitations. Roosevelt was able to persuade a society which had for two centuries treasured its invulnerability of the dire perils of an Axis victory. And he saw to it that, this time, America's involvement would mark a first step toward permanent international engagement. During the war, his leadership held the alliance together and shaped the multilateral institutions which continue to serve the international community to this day.

No president, with the possible exception of Abraham Lincoln, has made a more decisive difference in American history. Roosevelt took the oath of office at a time of national uncertainty, when America's faith in the New World's infinite capacity for progress had been severely shaken by the Great Depression. All around him, democracies seemed to be faltering and anti-democratic governments on both the Left and the Right were gaining ground.

From *Diplomacy* (New York: Simon & Schuster, 1994), chap. 15.

* * *

America's journey from involvement in the First World War to active participation in the Second proved to be a long one—interrupted as it was by the nation's about-face to isolationism. The depth of America's revulsion toward international affairs illustrates the magnitude of Roosevelt's achievement. A brief sketch of the historical backdrop against which Roosevelt conducted his policies is therefore necessary.

In the 1920s, America's mood was ambivalent, oscillating between a willingness to assert principles of universal applicability and a need to justify them on behalf of an isolationist foreign policy. Americans took to reciting the traditional themes of their foreign policy with even greater emphasis: the uniqueness of America's mission as the exemplar of liberty, the moral superiority of democratic foreign policy, the seamless relationship between personal and international morality, the importance of open diplomacy, and the replacement of the balance of power by international consensus as expressed in the League of Nations.

All of these presumably universal principles were enlisted on behalf of American isolationism. Americans were still incapable of believing that anything outside the Western Hemisphere could possibly affect their security. The America of the 1920s and 1930s rejected even its own doctrine of collective security lest it lead to involvement in the quarrels of distant, bellicose societies. The provisions of the Treaty of Versailles were interpreted as vindictive, and reparations as self-defeating. When the French occupied the Ruhr, America used the occasion to withdraw its remaining occupying forces from the Rhineland. That Wilsonian exceptionalism had established criteria no international order could fulfill, made disillusionment a part of its very essence.

Disillusionment with the results of the war erased to a considerable extent the distinctions between the internationalists and the isolationists. Not even the most liberal internationalists any longer discerned an American interest in sustaining a flawed postwar settlement. No significant group had a good word to say about the balance of power. What passed for internationalism was being identified with membership in the League of Nations rather than with day-to-day participation in international diplomacy. And even the most dedicated internationalists insisted that the Monroe Doctrine superseded the League of Nations, and recoiled before the idea of America's joining League enforcement measures, even economic ones.

* * *

The Kellogg-Briand Pact turned into another example of America's tendency to treat principles as self-implementing. Although American leaders enthusiastically proclaimed the historic nature of the treaty because sixty-two nations had renounced war as an instrument of national policy, they adamantly refused to endorse any machinery for applying it, much less for enforcing it. President Calvin Coolidge, waxing effusive before the Congress in December 1928, asserted: "Observance of this Covenant . . . promises more for the peace of the world than any other agreement ever negotiated among the nations."[1]

Yet how was this utopia to be achieved? Coolidge's passionate defense of the Kellogg-Briand Pact spurred internationalists and supporters of the League to argue, quite reasonably, that, war having been outlawed, the concept of neutrality had lost all meaning. In their view, since the League had been designed to identify aggressors, the international community was obliged to punish them appropriately. "Does anyone believe," asked one of the proponents of this view, "that the aggressive designs of Mussolini could be checked merely by the good faith of the Italian people and the power of public opinion?"[2]

The prescience of this question did not enhance its acceptability. Even while the treaty bearing his name was still in the process of being debated, Secretary of State Kellogg, in an address before the Council on Foreign Relations, stressed that force would never be used to elicit compliance. Reliance on force, he argued, would turn what had been intended as a long stride toward peace into precisely the sort of military alliance that was so in need of being abolished.

*   *   *

To prevent America from once again being lured into war, the Congress passed three so-called Neutrality Acts between 1935 and 1937. Prompted by the Nye Report, these laws prohibited loans and any other financial assistance to belligerents (whatever the cause of war) and imposed an arms embargo on all parties (regardless of who the victim was). Purchases of nonmilitary goods for cash were allowed only if they were transported in non-American ships.[3] The Congress was not abjuring profits so much as it was rejecting risks. As the aggressors bestrode Europe, America abolished the distinction between aggressor and victim by legislating a single set of restrictions on both.

*   *   *

After his landslide electoral victory of 1936, Roosevelt went far beyond the existing framework. In fact, he demonstrated that, though preoccupied with the Depression, he had grasped the essence of the dictators' challenge better than any European leader except Churchill. At first, he sought merely to enunciate America's moral commitment to the cause of the democracies. Roosevelt began this educational process with the so-called Quarantine Speech, which he delivered in Chicago on October 5, 1937. It was his first warning to America of the approaching peril, and his first public statement that America might have to assume some responsibilities with respect to it. Japan's renewed military aggression in China, coupled with the previous year's announcement of the Berlin-Rome Axis, provided the backdrop, giving Roosevelt's concerns a global dimension:

> The peace, the freedom and the security of ninety percent of the population of the world is being jeopardized by the remaining ten percent who are threatening a breakdown of all international order and law. . . . It seems to be unfortunately true that the epidemic of world lawlessness is spreading. When an epidemic of physical disease starts to spread, the community approves and joins in a quarantine of the patients in order to protect the health of the community against the spread of the disease.[4]

Roosevelt was careful not to spell out what he meant by "quarantine" and what, if any, specific measures he might have in mind. Had the speech implied any kind of action, it would have been inconsistent with the Neutrality Acts, which the Congress had overwhelmingly approved and the President had recently signed.

Not surprisingly, the Quarantine Speech was attacked by isolationists, who demanded clarification of the President's intentions. They argued passionately that the distinction between "peace-loving" and "warlike" nations implied an American value judgment which, in turn, would lead to the abandonment of the policy of nonintervention, to which both Roosevelt and the Congress had pledged themselves. Two years later, Roosevelt described the uproar that resulted from the speech as follows: "Unfortunately, this suggestion fell upon deaf ears—even hostile and resentful ears. . . . It was hailed as war mongering; it was condemned as attempted intervention in foreign affairs; it was even ridiculed as a nervous search 'under the bed' for dangers of war which did not exist."[5]

Roosevelt could have ended the controversy by simply denying the intentions being ascribed to him. Yet, despite the critical onslaught, Roosevelt spoke ambiguously enough at a news conference to keep open the option of collective defense of some kind. According to the journalistic practice of the day, the President always met with the press off-the-record, which meant that he could neither be quoted nor identified, and these rules were respected.

*   *   *

Munich seems to have been the turning point which impelled Roosevelt to align America with the European democracies, at first politically but gradually materially as well. From then on, his commitment to thwarting the dictators was inexorable, culminating three years later in America's entry into a second world war. The interplay between leaders and their publics in a democracy is always complex. A leader who confines himself to the experience of his people in a period of upheaval purchases temporary popularity at the price of condemnation by posterity, whose claims he is neglecting. A leader who gets too far ahead of his society will become irrelevant. A great leader must be an educator, bridging the gap between his visions and the familiar. But he must also be willing to walk alone to enable his society to follow the path he has selected.

There is inevitably in every great leader an element of guile which simplifies, sometimes the objectives, sometimes the magnitude, of the task. But his ultimate test is whether he incarnates the truth of his society's values and the essence of its challenges. These qualities Roosevelt possessed to an unusual degree. He deeply believed in America; he was convinced that Nazism was both evil and a threat to American security, and he was extraordinarily guileful. And he was prepared to shoulder the burden of lonely decisions. Like a tightrope walker, he had to move, step by careful, anguishing step, across the chasm between his goal and his society's reality in demonstrating to it that the far shore was in fact safer than the familiar promontory.

On October 26, 1938, less than four weeks after the Munich Pact, Roosevelt returned to the theme of his Quarantine Speech. In a radio address to the Herald-Tribune Forum, he warned against unnamed but easily identifiable aggressors whose "national policy adopts as a deliberate instrument the threat of war."[6] Next, while upholding disarmament in principle, Roosevelt also called for strengthening America's defenses:

> . . . we have consistently pointed out that neither we, nor any nation, will accept disarmament while neighbor nations arm to the teeth. If there is not general disarmament, we ourselves must

continue to arm. It is a step we do not like to take, and do not wish to take. But, until there is general abandonment of weapons capable of aggression, ordinary rules of national prudence and common sense require that we be prepared.[7]

In secret, Roosevelt went much further. At the end of October 1938, in separate conversations with the British air minister and also with a personal friend of Prime Minister Neville Chamberlain, he put forward a project designed to circumvent the Neutrality Acts. Proposing an outright evasion of legislation he had only recently signed, Roosevelt suggested setting up British and French airplane-assembly plants in Canada, near the American border. The United States would supply all the components, leaving only the final assembly to Great Britain and France. This arrangement would technically permit the project to stay within the letter of the Neutrality Acts, presumably on the ground that the component parts were civilian goods. Roosevelt told Chamberlain's emissary that, "in the event of war with the dictators, he had the industrial resources of the American nation behind him."[8]

Roosevelt's scheme for helping the democracies restore their air power collapsed, as it was bound to, if only because of the sheer logistical impossibility of undertaking an effort on such a scale in secret. But from then on, Roosevelt's support for Britain and France was limited only when the Congress and public opinion could neither be circumvented nor overcome.

* * *

Isolationists observing Roosevelt's actions were deeply disturbed. In February 1939, before the outbreak of the war, Senator Arthur Vandenberg had eloquently put forward the isolationist case:

> True, we do live in a foreshortened world in which, compared with Washington's day, time and space are relatively annihilated. But I still thank God for two insulating oceans; and even though they be foreshortened, they are still our supreme benediction if they be widely and prudently used. . . .
>
> We all have our sympathies and our natural emotions in behalf of the victims of national or international outrage all around the globe; but we are not, we cannot be, the world's protector or the world's policeman.[9]

When, in response to the German invasion of Poland, Great Britain declared war on September 3, 1939, Roosevelt had no choice but to invoke the Neutrality Acts. At the same time, he moved rapidly to modify the legislation to permit Great Britain and France to purchase American arms.

* * *

Roosevelt had for many months been acting on the premise that America might have to enter the war. In September 1940, he had devised an ingenious arrangement to give Great Britain fifty allegedly over-age destroyers in exchange for the right to set up American bases on eight British possessions, from Newfoundland to the South American mainland. Winston Churchill later called it a "decidedly unneutral act," for the destroyers were far more important to Great Britain than the bases were to America. Most of them were quite remote from any conceivable theater of operations, and some even duplicated existing American bases. More than anything, the destroyer deal represented a pretext based on a legal opinion by Roosevelt's own appointee, Attorney General Francis Biddle—hardly an objective observer.

Roosevelt sought neither Congressional approval nor modification of the Neutrality Acts for his destroyer-for-bases deal. Nor was he challenged, as inconceivable as that seems in the light of contemporary practice. It was the measure of Roosevelt's concern about a possible Nazi victory and of his commitment to bolstering British morale, that he took this step as a presidential election campaign was just beginning. (It was fortunate for Great Britain and for the cause of American unity that the foreign policy views of his opponent, Wendell Willkie, were not significantly different from Roosevelt's.)

Concurrently, Roosevelt vastly increased the American defense budget and, in 1940, induced the Congress to introduce peacetime conscription. So strong was lingering isolationist sentiment that conscription was renewed by only one vote in the House of Representatives in the summer of 1941, less than four months before the outbreak of the war.

* * *

Few American presidents have been as sensitive and perspicacious as Franklin Delano Roosevelt was in his grasp of the psychology of his people. Roosevelt understood that only a threat to their security could motivate them to support military preparedness. But to take them into a war, he knew he needed to appeal to their idealism in much the same way that Wilson had. In Roosevelt's view, America's security needs might well be met by control of the Atlantic, but its war aims required some vision of a new world order. Thus "balance of power" was not a term ever found in Roosevelt's pronouncements, except when he used it disparagingly. What he sought was to bring about a world community compatible with America's democratic and social ideals as the best guarantee of peace.

In this atmosphere, the president of a technically neutral United States and Great Britain's quintessential wartime leader, Winston Churchill, met in August 1941 on a cruiser off the coast of Newfoundland. Great Britain's position had improved somewhat when Hitler invaded the Soviet Union in June, but England was far from assured of victory. Nevertheless, the joint statement these two leaders issued reflected not a statement of traditional war aims but the design of a totally new world bearing America's imprimatur. The Atlantic Charter proclaimed a set of "common principles" on which the President and Prime Minister based "their hopes for a better future for the world."[10] These principles enlarged upon Roosevelt's original Four Freedoms by incorporating equal access to raw materials and cooperative efforts to improve social conditions around the world.

* * *

When the Atlantic Charter was proclaimed, German armies were approaching Moscow and Japanese forces were preparing to move into Southeast Asia. Churchill was above all concerned with removing the obstacles to America's participation in the war. For he understood very well that, by itself, Great Britain would not be able to achieve a decisive victory, even with Soviet participation in the war and American material support. In addition, the Soviet Union might collapse and some compromise between Hitler and Stalin was always a possibility, threatening Great Britain with renewed isolation. Churchill saw no point in debating postwar structure before he could even be certain that there would be one.

In September 1941, the United States crossed the line into belligerency. Roosevelt's order that the position of German submarines be reported to the British Navy had made it inevitable that, sooner or later, some clash would occur. On September 4, 1941, the American destroyer *Greer* was torpedoed while signaling the location of a German submarine to British airplanes. On September 11, without describing the circumstances, Roosevelt denounced German "piracy." Comparing German submarines to a rattlesnake coiled to strike, he ordered the United States Navy to sink "on sight" any German or Italian submarines discovered in the previously established American defense area extending all the way to Iceland. To all practical purposes, America was at war on the sea with the Axis powers.[11]

Simultaneously, Roosevelt took up the challenge of Japan. In response to Japan's occupation of Indochina in July 1941, he abrogated America's commercial treaty with Japan, forbade the sale of scrap metal to it, and encouraged the Dutch government-in-exile to stop oil exports to Japan from the Dutch East Indies (present-day Indonesia). These pressures led to negotiations with Japan, which began in October 1941. Roosevelt instructed the American negotiators to demand that Japan relinquish all of its conquests, including Manchuria, by invoking America's previous refusal to "recognize" these acts.

Roosevelt must have known that there was no possibility that Japan would accept. On December 7, 1941, following the pattern of the Russo-Japanese War, Japan launched a surprise attack on Pearl Harbor and destroyed a significant part of America's Pacific fleet. On December 11, Hitler honored his treaty with Tokyo by declaring war on the United States. Why Hitler thus freed Roosevelt to concentrate America's war effort on the country Roosevelt had always considered to be the principal enemy has never been satisfactorily explained.

America's entry into the war marked the culmination of a great and daring leader's extraordinary diplomatic enterprise. In less than three years, Roosevelt had taken his staunchly isolationist people into a global war. As late as May 1940, 64 percent of Americans had considered the preservation of peace more important than the defeat of the Nazis. Eighteen months later, in December 1941, just before the attack on Pearl Harbor, the proportions had been reversed—only 32 percent favored peace over preventing triumph.[12]

Roosevelt had achieved his goal patiently and inexorably, educating his people one step at a time about the necessities before them. His audiences filtered his words through their own preconceptions and did not always understand that his ultimate destination was war, though they could not have doubted that it was confrontation. In fact, Roosevelt was not so much bent on war as on defeating the Nazis; it was simply that, as time passed, the Nazis could only be defeated if America entered the war.

That their entry into the war should have seemed so sudden to the American people was due to three factors: Americans had had no experience with going to war for security concerns outside the Western Hemisphere; many believed that the European democracies could prevail on their own, while few understood the nature of the diplomacy that had preceded Japan's attack on Pearl Harbor or Hitler's rash declaration of war on the United States. It was a measure of the United States' deep-seated isolationism that it had to be bombed at Pearl Harbor before it would enter the war in the Pacific; and that, in Europe, it was Hitler who would ultimately declare war on the United States rather than the other way around.

By initiating hostilities, the Axis powers had solved Roosevelt's lingering dilemma about how to move the American people into the war. Had Japan focused its attack on Southeast Asia and Hitler not declared war against the United States, Roosevelt's task of steering his people toward his views would have been much more complicated. In light of Roosevelt's proclaimed moral and strategic convictions, there can be little doubt that, in the end, he would have somehow managed to enlist America in the struggle he considered so decisive to both the future of freedom and to American security.

Subsequent generations of Americans have placed a greater premium on total candor by their chief executive. Yet, like Lincoln, Roosevelt sensed that the survival of his country and its values was at stake, and that history itself would hold him responsible for the results of his solitary initiatives. And, as was the case with Lincoln, it is a measure of the debt free peoples owe to Franklin Delano Roosevelt that the wisdom of his solitary passage is now, quite simply, taken for granted.

Notes

[1] Selig Adler, *The Isolationist Impulse, Its Twentieth-Century Reaction* (New York: Free Press; London: Collier-Macmillan, 1957), 214.

[2] Quoted in Adler, *The Isolationist Impulse,* 216.

[3] Ruhl J. Bartlett, ed., *The Record of American Diplomacy* (New York: Knopf, 1956), 572–77. The First Neutrality Act, signed by FDR on August 31, 1935: arms embargo; Americans not permitted to travel on ships of belligerents. The Second Neutrality Act, signed by FDR on February 29, 1936 (a week before the reoccupation of the Rhineland on March 7): extended the First Act through May 1, 1936, and added a prohibition against loans or credits to belligerents. The Third Neutrality Act, signed by FDR on May 1, 1937: extended previous acts due to expire at midnight plus "cash and carry" provisions for certain nonmilitary goods.

[4] Address in Chicago, October 5, 1937, in Franklin Roosevelt, *Public Papers* (New York: Macmillan, 1941), 1937 vol., 410.

[5] Introduction, in Roosevelt, *Public Papers,* 1939 vol., xxviii.

[6] Radio address to the Herald-Tribune Forum, October 26, 1938, in Roosevelt, *Public Papers,* 1938 vol., 564.

[7] Radio address, 565.

[8] Donald Cameron Watt, *How War Came: The Immediate Origins of the Second World War, 1938–1939* (London: William Heinemann, 1989), 130.

[9] Vandenberg speech in the Senate, "It Is Not Cowardice to Think of America First," February 27, 1939, in *Vital Speeches of the Day,* vol. v, no. 12 (April 1, 1939), 356–57.

[10] The Atlantic Charter: Official Statement on Meeting Between the President and Prime Minister Churchill, August 14, 1941, in Roosevelt, *Public Papers,* 1941 vol., 314.

[11] Fireside Chat to the Nation, September 11, 1941, in Roosevelt, *Public Papers,* 1941 vol., 384–92.

[12] Adler, *The Isolationist Impulse,* 257.

Imperialism

WALTER LAFEBER
The American "New Empire"

Some intellectuals speak only for themselves. Theirs is often the later glory, but seldom the present power. Some, however, speak not only for themselves but for the guiding forces of their society. Discovering such men at crucial junctures in history, if such a discovery can be made, is of importance and value. These figures uncover the premises, reveal the approaches, provide the details, and often coherently arrange the ideas which are implicit in the dominant thought of their time and society.

The ordered, articulate writings of Frederick Jackson Turner, Josiah Strong, Brooks Adams, and Alfred Thayer Mahan typified the expansive tendencies of their generation. Little evidence exists that Turner and Strong directly influenced expansionists in the business community or the State Department during the 1890's, but their writings best exemplify certain beliefs which determined the nature of American foreign policy. Adams and Mahan participated more directly in the shaping of expansionist programs. It is, of course, impossible to estimate the number of Americans who accepted the arguments of

these four men. What cannot be controverted is that the writings of these men typified and in some specific instances directly influenced the thought of American policy makers who created the new empire.[1]

Frederick Jackson Turner and the American Frontier

* * *

The importance of the frontier will be associated with the name of Frederick Jackson Turner as long as historians are able to indent footnotes. Yet as Theodore Roosevelt told Turner in a letter of admiration in 1894, "I think you . . . have put into definite shape a good deal of thought which has been floating around rather loosely." As has been amply shown by several scholars, a number of observers warned of the frontier's disappearance and the possible consequences of this disappearance long before Turner's epochal paper. The accelerating communication and transportation revolution, growing agrarian unrest, violent labor strikes, and the problems arising

From *The New Empire: An Interpretation of American Expansion, 1860–1898* (Ithaca, N.Y.: Cornell University Press, 1963), chaps. 2 and 7.

from increasing numbers of immigrants broke upon puzzled and frightened Americans in a relatively short span of time. Many of them clutched the belief of the closing or closed frontier in order to explain their dilemma.[2]

Turner rested the central part of his frontier thesis on the economic power represented by free land. American individualism, nationalism, political institutions, and democracy depended on this power: "So long as free land exists, the opportunity for a competency exists, and economic power secures political power." Stated in these terms, landed expansion became the central factor, the dynamic of American progress. Without the economic power generated by expansion across free lands, American political institutions could stagnate.[3]

Such an analysis could be extremely meaningful to those persons who sought an explanation for the political and social troubles of the period. Few disputed that the social upheavals in both the urban and agrarian areas of the nation stemmed from economic troubles in the international grain markets, from the frequent industrial depressions, or, as the Populists averred, from the failure of the currency to match the pace of ever increasing productivity. This economic interpretation also fitted in nicely with the contemporary measurement of success in terms of material achievement. Perhaps most important, the frontier thesis not only defined the dilemma, but did so in tangible, concrete terms. It offered the hope that Americans could do something about their problems. Given the assumption that expansion across the western frontier explained past American successes, the solution for the present crisis now became apparent: either radically readjust the political institutions to a nonexpanding society or find new areas for expansion. When Americans

seized the second alternative, the meaning for foreign policy became apparent—and immense.

With the appearance and definition of the fundamental problems in the 1880's and 1890's, these decades assumed vast importance. They became not a watershed of American history, but *the* watershed. Many writers emphasized the supremely critical nature of the 1890's, but no one did it better than Turner when he penned the dramatic final sentence of his 1893 paper: "And now, four centuries from the discovery of America, at the end of a hundred years of life under the Constitution, the frontier has gone, and with its going has closed the first period of American history." The American West no longer offered a unique escape from the intractable problems of a closed society. As another writer stated it four years after Turner's announcement in Chicago, "we are no longer a country exceptional and apart." History had finally caught up with the United States.[4]

The first solution that came to some minds suggested the opening of new landed frontiers in Latin America or Canada. Yet was further expansion in a landed sense the answer? Top policy makers, such as Secretaries of State James G. Blaine, Thomas F. Bayard, and Walter Quintin Gresham, opposed the addition of noncontiguous territory to the Union. Some Americans interpreted the labor violence of 1877, 1886, and 1894 as indications that the federal government could no longer harmonize and control the far-flung reaches of the continental empire. Labor and agrarian groups discovered they could not command the necessary political power to solve their mushrooming problems. The sprouting of such factions as the Molly Maguires, Populists, Eugene Debs' Railroad Union, and several varieties of Socialist parties raised doubts in many minds about the ameliorating and controlling qualities which had formerly been a part of the American system.

* * *

Expansion in the form of trade instead of landed settlement ultimately offered the answer to this dilemma. This solution, embodied in the open-door philosophy of American foreign policy, ameliorated the economic stagnation (which by Turner's reasoning led to the political discontent), but it did not pile new colonial areas on an already overburdened governmental structure. It provided the perfect answer to the problems of the 1890's.

* * *

Alfred Thayer Mahan

* * *

The austere, scholarly, arm-chair sailor-turned-prophet constructed a tightly knit historical justification of why and how his country could expand beyond its continental limits.

Mahan grounded his thesis on the central characteristic of the United States of his time: it was an industrial complex which produced, or would soon be capable of producing, vast surpluses. In the first paragraph of his classic, *The Influence of Sea Power upon History, 1660–1783,* Mahan explained how this industrial expansion led to a rivalry for markets and sources of raw materials and would ultimately result in the need for sea power. He summarized his theory in a postulate: "In these [two] things—production, with the necessity of exchanging products, shipping, whereby the exchange is carried on, and colonies . . .—is to be found the key to much of the history, as well as of the policy, of nations bordering upon the sea." The order is all-important. Production leads to a need for shipping, which in turn creates the need for colonies.[5]

Mahan's neat postulate was peculiarly applicable to his own time, for he clearly understood the United States of the 1890's. His concern, stated in 1890, that ever increasing production would soon make necessary wider trade and markets, anticipated the somber, depression-ridden years of post-1893. Writing three years before Frederick Jackson Turner analyzed the disappearance of the American frontier, Mahan hinted its disappearance and pointed out the implications for America's future economic and political structure. He observed that the policies of the American government since 1865 had been "directed solely to what has been called the first link in the chain which makes sea power." But "the increase of home consumption . . . did not keep up with the increase of forth-putting and facility of distribution offered by steam." The United States would thus have to embark upon a new frontier, for "whether they will or no, Americans must now begin to look outward. The growing production of the country demands it. An increasing volume of public sentiment demands it." The theoretical and actual had met; the productive capacity of the United States, having finally grown too great for its continental container and having lost its landed frontier, had to turn to the sea, its omnipresent frontier. The mercantilists had viewed production as a faculty to be stimulated and consolidated in order to develop its full capabilities of pulling wealth into the country. But Mahan dealt with a productive complex which had been stimulated by the government for years and had been centralized and coordinated by corporate managers. He was now concerned with the problem of keeping this society ongoing without the problems of under-employment and resulting social upheavals.[6]

Reversing the traditional American idea of the oceans as a barrier against European intrigue, Mahan compared the sea to "a great highway; or better, perhaps . . . a wide common, over which men pass in all directions."

* * *

To Mahan, William McKinley, Theodore Roosevelt, and Henry Cabot Lodge, colonial possessions, as these men defined such possessions, served as stepping stones to the two great prizes: the Latin-American and Asian markets. This policy much less resembled traditional colonialism than it did the new financial and industrial expansion of the 1850–1914 period. These men did not envision "colonizing" either Latin America or Asia. They did want both to exploit these areas economically and give them (especially Asia) the benefits of western, Christian civilization. To do this, these expansionists needed strategic bases from which shipping lanes and interior interests in Asia and Latin America could be protected.

* * *

President William McKinley and the Spanish-American War of 1898

* * *

The President [McKinley] did not want war; he had been sincere and tireless in his efforts to maintain the peace. By mid-March, however,

he was beginning to discover that, although he did not want war, he did want what only a war could provide: the disappearance of the terrible uncertainty in American political and economic life, and a solid basis from which to resume the building of the new American commercial empire. When the President made his demands, therefore, he made the ultimate demands; as far as he was concerned, a six-month period of negotiations would not serve to temper the political and economic problems in the United States, but only exacerbate them.

To say this is to raise another question: why did McKinley arrive at this position during mid-March? What were the factors which limited the President's freedom of choice and policies at this particular time? The standard interpretations of the war's causes emphasize the yellow journals and a belligerent Congress. These were doubtlessly crucial factors in shaping the course of American entry into the conflict, but they must be used carefully.

Influences other than the yellow press or congressional belligerence were more important in shaping McKinley's position of April 11. Perhaps most important was the transformation of the opinion of many spokesmen for the business community who had formerly opposed war. If, as one journal declared, the McKinley administration, "more than any that have preceded it, sustains . . . close relations to the business interests of the country," then this change of business sentiment should not be discounted.[7] This transformation brought important financial spokesmen, especially from the Northeast, into much the same position that had long been occupied by pro-interventionist business groups and journals in the trans-Appalachian area. McKinley's decision to intervene placated many of the same business spokesmen whom he had satisfied throughout 1897 and January and February of 1898 by his refusal to declare war.

Five factors may be delineated which shaped this interventionist sentiment of the business community. First, some business journals emphasized the material advantages to be gained should Cuba become a part of the world in which the United States would enjoy, in the words of the New York *Commercial Advertiser,* "full freedom of development in the whole world's interest." The *Banker's Magazine* noted that "so many of our citizens are so involved in the commerce and productions of the island, that to protect these interests . . . the United States will have eventually to force the establishment of fair and reasonable government." The material damage suffered by investors in Cuba and by many merchants, manufacturers, exporters, and importers, as, for example, the groups which presented the February 10 petition to McKinley, forced these interests to advocate a solution which could be obtained only through force.[8]

A second reason was the uncertainty that plagued the business community in mid-March. This uncertainty was increased by [Senator Redfield] Proctor's powerful and influential speech and by the news that a Spanish torpedo-boat flotilla was sailing from Cadiz to Cuba. The uncertainty was exemplified by the sudden stagnation of trade on the New York Stock Exchange after March 17. Such an unpredictable economic basis could not provide the spring board for the type of overseas commercial empire that McKinley and numerous business spokesmen envisioned.

Third, by March many businessmen who had deprecated war on the ground that the United States Treasury did not possess adequate gold reserves began to realize that they had been arguing from false assumptions. The heavy exports of 1897 and the discoveries of gold in Alaska and Australia brought the yellow metal into the country in an ever widening stream. Private bankers had been preparing for war since 1897. *Banker's Magazine* summarized these developments: "Therefore, while not desiring war, it is apparent that the country now has an ample coin basis for sustaining the credit operations which a conflict would probably make necessary. In such a crisis the gold standard will prove a bulwark of confidence."[9]

Fourth, antiwar sentiment lost much strength when the nation realized that it had nothing to fear from European intervention on the side of Spain. France and Russia, who were most sympathetic to the Spanish monarchy, were forced to devote their attention to the Far East. Neither of these nations wished to alienate the United States on the Cuban issue. More important, Americans happily realized that they had the support of Great Britain. The *rapprochement* which had occurred since the Venezuelan incident now paid dividends. On an official level, the British Foreign Office assured the State Department that nothing would be accomplished in the way of European intervention unless the United States requested such intervention. The British attitude made it easy for McKinley to deal with a joint European note of April 6 which asked for American moderation toward Spain. The President brushed off the request firmly but politely. On an unofficial level, American periodicals expressed appreciation of the British policy on Cuba, and some of the journals noted that a common Anglo-American approach was also desirable in Asia.[10] The European reaction is interesting insofar as it evinces the continental powers' growing realization that the United States was rapidly becoming a major force in the world. But the European governments set no limits on American dealings with Spain. McKinley could take the initiative and make his demands with little concern for European reactions.

Finally, opposition to war melted away in some degree when the administration began to emphasize that the United States enjoyed military power much superior to that of Spain. One possible reason for McKinley's policies during the first two months of 1898 might have been his fear that the nation was not adequately prepared. As late as the weekend of March 25 the President worried over this inadequacy. But in late February and early March, especially after the $50,000,000 appropriation by Congress, the country's military strength developed rapidly. On March 13 the Philadelphia *Press* proclaimed that American naval power greatly exceeded that of the Spanish forces. By early April those who feared a Spanish bombardment of New York City were in the small minority. More representative were the views of Winthrop Chanler who wrote Lodge that if Spanish troops invaded New York "they would all be absorbed in the population . . . and engaged in selling oranges before they got as far as 14th Street."[11]

As the words of McKinley's war message flew across the wires to Madrid, many business spokesmen who had opposed war had recently changed their minds, American military forces were rapidly growing more powerful, banks and the United States Treasury had secured themselves against the initial shocks of war, and the European powers were divided among themselves and preoccupied in the Far East. Business boomed after McKinley signed the declaration of war. "With a hesitation so slight as to amount almost to indifference," *Bradstreet's*

reported on April 30, "the business community, relieved from the tension caused by the incubus of doubt and uncertainty which so long controlled it, has stepped confidently forward to accept the situation confronting it owing to the changed conditions. Unfavorable circumstances . . . have hardly excited remark, while the stimulating effects have been so numerous and important as to surprise all but the most optimistic," this journal concluded.[12] A new type of American empire, temporarily clothed in armor, stepped out on the international stage after a half century of preparation to make its claim as one of the great world powers.

* * *

By 1899 the United States had forged a new empire. American policy makers and businessmen had created it amid much debate and with conscious purpose. The empire progressed from a continental base in 1861 to assured pre-eminence in the Western Hemisphere in 1895. Three years later it was rescued from a growing economic and political dilemma by the declaration of war against Spain. During and after this conflict the empire moved past Hawaii into the Philippines, and, with the issuance of the Open-Door Notes, enunciated its principles in Asia. The movement of this empire could not be hurried. Harrison discovered this to his regret in 1893. But under the impetus of the effects of the industrial revolution and, most important, *because of the implications for foreign policy which policy makers and businessmen believed to be logical corollaries of this economic change,* the new empire reached its climax in the 1890's. At this point those who possessed a sense of historical perspective could pause with Henry Adams and observe that one hundred and fifty years of American history had suddenly fallen into place. Those who preferred to peer into the dim future of the twentieth century could be certain only that the United States now dominated its own hemisphere and, as [William] Seward had so passionately hoped, was entering as a major power into Asia, "the chief theatre of events in the world's great hereafter."

Notes

[1] One of the weakest sections in the history of ideas is the relationship between the new intellectual currents and American overseas expansion during the last half of the nineteenth century. The background and some of the general factors may be found in Alfred Kazin, *On Native Grounds: An Interpretation of Modern American Prose Literature* (Garden City, N.Y., 1942, 1956); Henry Steele Commager, *The American Mind: An Interpretation of American Thought and Character since the 1880's* (New Haven, 1950, 1959); Weinberg, *Manifest Destiny;* Julius W. Pratt, "The Ideology of American Expansion," *Essays in Honor of William E. Dodd . . .* , edited by Avery Craven (Chicago, 1935).

[2] See especially Fulmer Mood, "The Concept of the Frontier, 1871–1898," *Agricultural History,* XIX (January, 1945), 24–31; Lee Benson, "The Historical Background of Turner's Frontier Essay," *Agricultural History,* XXV (April, 1951), 59–82; Herman Clarence Nixon, "The Precursors of Turner in the Interpretation of the American Frontier," *South Atlantic Quarterly,* XXVIII (January, 1929), 83–89. For the Roosevelt letter, see *The Letters of Theodore Roosevelt,* selected and edited by Elting E. Morison *et al.* (Cambridge, Mass., 1951), I, 363.

[3] Frederick Jackson Turner, *The Frontier in American History* (New York, 1947), 32, 30; see also Per Sveaas Andersen, *Westward Is the Course of Empires: A Study in the Shaping of an American Idea: Frederick Jackson Turner's Frontier* (Oslo, Norway, 1956), 20–21; Henry Nash Smith, *Virgin Land: The American West as Symbol and Myth* (New York, 1959), 240.

[4] Turner, *Frontier in American History,* 38; Eugene V. Smalley, "What Are Normal Times?" *The Forum,* XXIII (March, 1897), 98–99; see also Turner, *Frontier in American History,* 311–312. For a brilliant criticism of Turner's closed-space concepts, see James C. Malin, *The Contriving Brain and the Skillful Hand in the United States . . .* (Lawrence, Kan., 1955), the entire essay, but especially ch. xi.

[5] A. T. Mahan, *The Influence of Sea Power upon History, 1660–1783* (Boston, 1890), 53, 28. This postulate is mentioned two more times in the famous first chapter, pages 70 and 83–84.

[6] *Ibid.,* 83–84; Mahan, "A Twentieth-Century Outlook," *The Interest of America in Sea Power, Present and Future* (Boston, 1897), 220–222; Mahan, "The United States Looking Outward," *ibid.,* 21–22. In their work which traces this centralization movement, Thomas C. Cochran and William Miller call the result the "corporate society" (*The Age of Enterprise: A Social History of Industrial America* [New York, 1942], 331).

[7] Chicago *Times-Herald* quoted in Cincinnati *Commercial Tribune,* Dec. 28, 1897, 6:2. The Chicago paper was particularly close to the administration through its publisher's friendship with McKinley. The publisher was H. H. Kohlsaat. Ernest May remarks, regarding McKinley's antiwar position in 1897 and early 1898, "It was simply out of the question for him [McKinley] to embark on a policy unless virtually certain that Republican businessmen would back him" (*Imperial Democracy: The Emergence of America as a Great Power* [New York, 1961], 118). The same comment doubtlessly applies also to McKinley's actions in March and April.

[8] *Commercial Advertiser,* March 10, 1898, 6:3; *Bankers' Magazine,* LVI (April, 1898), 519–520.

[9] *Bankers' Magazine,* LVI (March, 1898), 347–348; LVI (April, 1898), 520; *Pittsburgh Press,* April 8, 1898, 4:1; *Commercial and Financial Chronicle,* April 23, 1898, 786.

[10] Dugdale, *German Documents,* II, 500–502; Porter to Sherman, April 8, 1898, France, Despatches, and Hay to Sherman, March 26, 28, 29, April 1, Great Britain, Despatches, NA, RG 59; *Public Opinion,* March 24, 1898, 360–361.

[11] Margaret Leech, *In the Days of McKinley* (New York, 1969), 176; *Philadelphia Press,* March 13, 1898, 8:3; Garraty, *Lodge,* 191.

[12] *Bradstreet's,* April 9, 1898, 234, also April 30, 1898, 272, 282.

Nuclear Deterrence Doctrine

BERNARD BRODIE
Strategy in the Missile Age

* * *

We shall be talking about the strategy of deterrence of general war, and about the complementary principle of limiting to tolerable proportions whatever conflicts become inevitable. These ideas spring from the conviction that total nuclear war is to be avoided at almost any cost. This follows from the assumption that such a war, even if we were extraordinarily lucky, would be too big, too all-consuming to permit the survival even of those final values, like personal freedom, for which alone one could think of waging it. It need not be certain that it would turn out so badly; it is enough that there is a large chance that it would.

The conceptions of deterrence and of limited war also take account of the fact that the United States is, and has long been, a status quo power. We are uninterested in acquiring new territories or areas of influence or in accepting great hazard in order to rescue or reform those areas of the world which now have political systems radically different from our own. On the other hand, as a status quo power, we are also determined to keep what we have, including existence in a world of which half or more is friendly, or at least not sharply and perennially hostile. In other words, our minimum security objectives include not only our own national independence but also that of many other countries, especially those which cherish democratic political institutions. Among the latter are those nations with which we have a special cultural affinity, that is, the countries of western Europe.

* * *

Deterrence Old and New

Deterrence as an element in national strategy or diplomacy is nothing new. Since the development of nuclear weapons, however, the term has acquired not only a special emphasis but also a distinctive connotation. It is usually the new and distinctive connotation that we have in mind when we speak nowadays of the "strategy of deterrence."

From *Strategy in the Missile Age* (Princeton: Princeton University Press, 1965), chap. 8.

The threat of war, open or implied, has always been an instrument of diplomacy by which one state deterred another from doing something of a military or political nature which the former deemed undesirable. Frequently the threat was completely latent, the position of the monitoring state being so obvious and so strong that no one thought of challenging it. Governments, like individuals, were usually aware of hazard in provoking powerful neighbors and governed themselves accordingly. Because avoidance of wars and even of crises hardly makes good copy for historians, we may infer that the past successes of some nations in deterring unwanted action by others add up to much more than one might gather from a casual reading of history. Nevertheless the large number of wars that have occurred in modern times prove that the threat to use force, even what sometimes looked like superior force, has often failed to deter.

We should notice, however, the positive function played by the failures. The very frequency with which wars occurred contributed importantly to the credibility inherent in any threat. In diplomatic correspondence, the statement that a specified kind of conduct would be deemed "an unfriendly act" was regarded as tantamount to an ultimatum and to be taken without question as seriously intended.

Bluffing, in the sense of deliberately trying to sound more determined or bellicose than one actually felt, was by no means as common a phenomenon in diplomacy as latter-day journalistic interpretations of events would have one believe. In any case, it tended to be confined to the more implicit kinds of threat. In short, the operation of deterrence was dynamic; it acquired relevance and strength from its failures as well as its successes.

Today, however, the policy of deterrence in relation to all-out war is markedly different in several respects. For one thing, it uses a kind of threat which we feel must be absolutely effective, allowing for no breakdowns ever. The sanction is, to say the least, not designed for repeating action. One use of it will be fatally too many. Deterrence now means something as a strategic policy only when we are fairly confident that the retaliatory instrument upon which it relies will not be called upon to function at all. Nevertheless, that instrument has to be maintained at a high pitch of efficiency and readiness and constantly improved, which can be done only at high cost to the community and great dedication on the part of the personnel directly involved. In short, we expect the system to be always ready to spring while going permanently unused. Surely there is something almost unreal about all this.

The Problem of Credibility

The unreality is minimal when we are talking about what we shall henceforward call "*basic deterrence*," that is, deterrence of direct, strategic, nuclear attack upon targets within the home territories of the United States. In that instance there is little or no problem of credibility as concerns our reactions, for the enemy has little reason to doubt that if he strikes us we will try to hit back. But the great and terrible apparatus which we must set up to fulfill our needs for basic deterrence and the state of readiness at which we have to maintain it create a condition of almost embarrassing availability of huge power. The problem of linking this power to a reasonable conception of its utility has thus far proved a considerable strain.

* * *

On the other hand, it would be tactically and factually wrong to assure the enemy in advance (as we tend to do by constantly assuring ourselves) that we would in no case move against him until we had already felt some bombs on our cities and airfields. We have, as we have seen, treaty obligations which forbid so far-reaching a commitment to restraint. It is also impossible for us to predict with absolute assurance our own behavior in extremely tense and provocative circumstances. If we make the wrong prediction about ourselves, we encourage the enemy also to make the wrong prediction about us. The outbreak of war in Korea in 1950 followed exactly that pattern. The wrong kind of prediction in this regard might precipitate that total nuclear war which too many persons have lightly concluded is now impossible.

Deterrence Strategy versus Win-the-War Strategies: The Sliding Scale of Deterrence

To return now to the simpler problem of basic deterrence. The capacity to deter is usually confused with the capacity to win a war. At present, capacity to win a total or unrestricted war requires either a decisive and *completely secure* superiority in strategic air power or success in seizing the initiative. Inasmuch as mere superiority in numbers of vehicles looks like a good thing to have anyway, the confusion between deterring and winning has method in it. But deterrence *per se* does not depend on superiority.

* * *

Now that we are in a nuclear age, the potential deterrence value of an admittedly inferior force may be sharply greater than it has ever been before. Let us assume that a menaced small nation could threaten the Soviet Union with only a single thermonuclear bomb, which, however, it could and would certainly deliver on Moscow if attacked. This would be a retaliatory capability sufficient to give the Soviet government pause. Certainly they would not provoke the destruction of Moscow for trivial gains, even if warning enabled the people of the city to save themselves by evacuation or resort to shelters. Naturally, the effect is greater if warning can be ruled out.

Ten such missiles aimed at ten major cities would be even more effective, and fifty aimed at that number of different cities would no doubt work still greater deterrent effect, though of course the cities diminish in size as the number included goes up. However, even when we make allowance for the latter fact, it is a fair surmise that the increase in deterrent effect is less than proportional to the increase in magnitude of potential destruction. We make that surmise on the basis of our everyday experience with human beings and their responses to punishment or deprivation. The human imagination can encompass just so much pain, anguish, or horror. The intrusion of numbers by which to multiply given sums of such feelings is likely to have on the average human mind a rather dull effect—except insofar as the increase in the threatened amount of harm affects the individual's statistical expectation of himself being involved in it.

Governments, it may be suggested, do not think like ordinary human beings, and one has to concede that the *maximum possible deterrence* which can be attained by the threat of retaliatory damage must involve a power which guarantees not only vast losses but also utter defeat. On the other hand, governments, including communistic ones, also comprise human beings, whose departure from the mold of ordinary mortals is not markedly in the direction of greater intellectualism or detachment. It is therefore likely that considerably less retaliatory destruction than that conceived under "maximum possible deterrence" will buy only slightly less deterrence. If we wish to visualize the situation graphically, we will think of a curve of "deterrence effect" in which each unit of additional damage threatened brings progressively diminishing increments of deterrence. Obviously and unfortunately, we lack all the data which would enable us to fill in the values for such a curve and thus to draw it.

If our surmises are in general correct, we are underlining the sharp differences in character between a deterrence capability and strategy on the one hand, and a win-the-war strategy and capability on the other. We have to remember too that since the winning of a war presupposes certain limitations on the quantity of destruction to one's own country and especially to one's population, a win-the-war strategy could quite conceivably be an utter impossibility to a nation striking second, and is by no means guaranteed to a nation striking first. Too much depends on what the other fellow does—how accessible or inaccessible he makes his own retaliatory force and how he makes his attack if he decides to launch one. However much we dislike the thought, a win-the-war strategy may be impossible because of circumstances outside our control.

Lest we conclude from these remarks that we can be content with a modest retaliatory capability—what some have called "minimum deterrence"—we have to mention at once four qualifying considerations, which we shall amplify later: (a) it may require a large force in hand to guarantee even a modest retaliation; (b) deterrence must always be conceived as a relative thing, which is to say it must be adequate to the variable but generally high degree of motivation which the enemy feels for our destruction; (c) if deterrence fails we shall want enough forces to fight a total war effectively; and (d) our retaliatory force must also be capable of striking first, and if it does so its attack had better be, as nearly as possible, overwhelming to the enemy's retaliatory force. Finally, we have to bear in mind that in their responses to threat or menace, people (including heads of government) do not spontaneously act according to a scrupulous weighing of objective facts. Large forces look more impressive than small ones—for reasons which are by no means entirely irrational—and in some circumstances such impressiveness may be important to us. Human beings, differing widely as they do in temperamental and psychic make-up, nevertheless generally have in common the fact that they make their most momentous decisions by what is fundamentally intuition.

* * *

The Problem of Guaranteeing Strong Retaliation

It should be obvious that what counts in basic deterrence is not so much the size and efficiency of one's striking force before it is hit as the size and condition to which the enemy thinks he can reduce it by a surprise attack—as well as his confidence in the correctness of his predictions. The degree to which the automaticity of our retaliation has been taken for granted by the public, unfortunately including most leaders of opinion and even military officers, is for those who have any knowledge of the facts both incredible and dangerous. The general idea is that if the enemy hits us, we will kill him.

* * *

Deterrence and Armaments Control

We come finally to the question of the political environment favoring the functioning of a deterrence strategy, especially with respect to the much abused and belabored subject of international control of armaments. There is a long and dismal history of confusion and frustration on this subject. Those who have been most passionate in urging disarmament have often refused to look unpleasant facts in the face; on the other hand, the government officials responsible for actual negotiations have usually been extremely rigid in their attitudes, tending to become more preoccupied with winning marginal and ephemeral advantages from the negotiations than in making real progress toward the presumed objective. There has also been confusion concerning both the objective and the degree of risk warranted by that objective.

Here we can take up only the last point. One must first ask what degree of arms control is a reasonable or sensible objective. It seems by now abundantly clear that total nuclear disarmament is not a reasonable objective. Violation would be too easy for the Communists, and the risks to the non-violator would be enormous. But it should also be obvious that the kind of bitter, relentless race in nuclear weapons and missiles that has been going on since the end of World War II has its own intrinsic dangers.

* * *

The kind of measures in which we ought to be especially interested are those which could seriously reduce on all sides the dangers of surprise attack. Such a policy would be entirely compatible with our basic national commitment to a strategy of deterrence. The best way to reduce the danger of surprise attack is to reduce on all sides the incentives to such attack, an end which is furthered by promoting measures that enhance deterrent rather than aggressive posture—where the two can be distinguished, which, if one is looking for the chance to do so, is probably pretty often. It also helps greatly to reduce the danger of accidental outbreak of total war if each side takes it upon itself to do the opposite of "keeping the enemy guessing" concerning its pacific intentions. This is accomplished not through reiterated declaration of pacific intent, which is for this purpose a worn and useless tactic, but through finding procedures where each side can assure the other through the latter's own eyes that deliberate attack is not being prepared against him.

* * *

Our over-riding interest, for the enhancement of our deterrence posture, is of course in the security of our own retaliatory force. But that does not mean that we especially desire the other side's retaliatory force to be insecure. If the opponent feels insecure, we suffer the hazard of his being more trigger-happy.

*   *   *

Stability is achieved when each nation believes that the strategic advantage of striking first is overshadowed by the tremendous cost of doing so. If, for example, retaliatory weapons are in the future so well protected that it takes more than one missile to destroy an enemy missile, the chances for stability become quite good. Under such circumstances striking first brings no advantage unless one has enormous numerical superiority. But such a situation is the very opposite of the more familiar one where both sides rely wholly or predominately on unprotected aircraft.

Technological progress could, however, push us rapidly towards a position of almost intolerable mutual menace. Unless something is done politically to alter the environment, each side before many years will have thousands of missiles accurately pointed at targets in the other's territory ready to be fired at a moment's notice. Whether or not we call it "push-button" war is a matter of our taste in phraseology, but there is no use in telling ourselves that the time for it is remote. Well before that time arrives, aircraft depending for their safety on being in the air in time will be operating according to so-called "airborne alert" and "fail-safe" patterns. Nothing which has any promise of obviating or alleviating the tensions of such situations should be overlooked.

The Sources of Containment

Mr. X [George Kennan]
The Sources of Soviet Conduct

The political personality of Soviet power as we know it today is the product of ideology and circumstances: ideology inherited by the present Soviet leaders from the movement in which they had their political origin, and circumstances of the power which they now have exercised for nearly three decades in Russia. There can be few tasks of psychological analysis more difficult than to try to trace the interaction of these two forces and the relative rôle of each in the determination of official Soviet conduct.

* * *

[T]remendous emphasis has been placed on the original Communist thesis of a basic antagonism between the capitalist and Socialist worlds. It is clear, from many indications, that this emphasis is not founded in reality. The real facts concerning it have been confused by the existence abroad of genuine resentment provoked by Soviet philosophy and tactics and occasionally by the existence of great centers of military power, notably the Nazi régime in Germany and the Japanese Government of the late 1930's, which did indeed have aggressive designs against the Soviet Union. But there is ample evidence that the stress laid in Moscow on the menace confronting Soviet society from the world outside its borders is founded not in the realities of foreign antagonism but in the necessity of explaining away the maintenance of dictatorial authority at home.

Now the maintenance of this pattern of Soviet power, namely, the pursuit of unlimited authority domestically, accompanied by the cultivation of the semi-myth of implacable foreign hostility, has gone far to shape the actual machinery of Soviet power as we know it today. Internal organs of administration which did not serve this purpose withered on the vine. Organs which did serve this purpose became vastly swollen. The security of Soviet power came to rest on the iron discipline of the party, on the severity and ubiquity of the secret police, and on the uncompromising economic monopolism of the state. The "organs of suppression," in which the Soviet leaders had sought security from rival forces, became in large measure the masters of those whom they were designed to serve. Today the major part of the structure of Soviet power is committed to the perfection of the dictatorship and to the maintenance of the concept of Russia as in a state of siege, with the enemy lowering beyond the walls. And the millions of human beings who form that part of the structure of power must defend at all costs

From *Foreign Affairs* (July 1947).

this concept of Russia's position, for without it they are themselves superfluous.

As things stand today, the rulers can no longer dream of parting with these organs of suppression. The quest for absolute power, pursued now for nearly three decades with a ruthlessness unparalleled (in scope at least) in modern times, has again produced internally, as it did externally, its own reaction. The excesses of the police apparatus have fanned the potential opposition to the régime into something far greater and more dangerous than it could have been before those excesses began.

But least of all can the rulers dispense with the fiction by which the maintenance of dictatorial power has been defended. For this fiction has been canonized in Soviet philosophy by the excesses already committed in its name; and it is now anchored in the Soviet structure of thought by bonds far greater than those of mere ideology.

II

So much for the historical background. What does it spell in terms of the political personality of Soviet power as we know it today?

Of the original ideology, nothing has been officially junked. Belief is maintained in the basic badness of capitalism, in the inevitability of its destruction, in the obligation of the proletariat to assist in that destruction and to take power into its own hands. But stress has come to be laid primarily on those concepts which relate most specifically to the Soviet regime itself: to its position as the sole truly Socialist régime in a dark and misguided world, and to the relationships of power within it.

The first of these concepts is that of the innate antagonism between capitalism and Socialism. We have seen how deeply that concept has become imbedded in foundations of Soviet power. It has profound implications for Russia's conduct as a member of international society. It means that there can never be on Moscow's side any sincere assumption of a community of aims between the Soviet Union and powers which are regarded as capitalist. It must invariably be assumed in Moscow that the aims of the capitalist world are antagonistic to the Soviet régime, and therefore to the interests of the peoples it controls. If the Soviet Government occasionally sets its signature to documents which would indicate the contrary, this is to be regarded as a tactical manœuvre permissible in dealing with the enemy (who is without honor) and should be taken in the spirit of *caveat emptor*. Basically, the antagonism remains. It is postulated. And from it flow many of the phenomena which we find disturbing in the Kremlin's conduct of foreign policy: the secretiveness, the lack of frankness, the duplicity, the wary suspiciousness, and the basic unfriendliness of purpose. These phenomena are there to stay, for the foreseeable future. There can be variations of degree and of emphasis. When there is something the Russians want from us, one or the other of these features of their policy may be thrust temporarily into the background; and when that happens there will always be Americans who will leap forward with gleeful announcements that "the Russians have changed," and some who will even try to take credit for having brought about such "changes." But we should not be misled by tactical manœuvres. These characteristics of Soviet policy, like the postulate from which they flow, are basic to the internal nature of Soviet power, and will be with us whether in the foreground or the background, until the internal nature of Soviet power is changed.

*   *   *

These considerations make Soviet diplomacy at once easier and more difficult to deal with than the diplomacy of individual aggressive leaders like Napoleon and Hitler. On the one hand it is more sensitive to contrary force, more ready to yield on individual sectors of the diplomatic front when that force is felt to be too strong, and thus more rational in the logic and rhetoric of power. On the other hand it cannot be easily defeated or discouraged by a single victory on the part of its opponents. And the patient persistence by which it is animated means that it can be effectively countered not by sporadic acts which represent the momentary whims of democratic opinion but only by intelligent long-range policies on the part of Russia's adversaries—policies no less steady in their purpose, and no less variegated and resourceful in their application, than those of the Soviet Union itself.

In these circumstances it is clear that the main element of any United States policy toward the Soviet Union must be that of a long-term, patient but firm and vigilant containment of Russian expansive tendencies. It is important to note, however, that such a policy has nothing to do with outward histrionics: with threats or blustering or superfluous gestures of outward "toughness." While the Kremlin is basically flexible in its reaction to political realities, it is by no means unamenable to considerations of prestige. Like almost any other government, it can be placed by tactless and threatening gestures in a position where it cannot afford to yield even though this might be dictated by its sense of realism. The Russian leaders are keen judges of human psychology, and as such they are highly conscious that loss of temper and of self-control is never a source of strength in political affairs. They are quick to exploit such evidences of weakness. For these

reasons, it is a *sine qua non* of successful dealing with Russia that the foreign government in question should remain at all times cool and collected and that its demands on Russian policy should be put forward in such a manner as to leave the way open for a compliance not too detrimental to Russian prestige.

* * *

IV

It is clear that the United States cannot expect in the foreseeable future to enjoy political intimacy with the Soviet régime. It must continue to regard the Soviet Union as a rival, not a partner, in the political arena. It must continue to expect that Soviet policies will reflect no abstract love of peace and stability, no real faith in the possibility of a permanent happy coexistence of the Socialist and capitalist worlds, but rather a cautious, persistent pressure toward the disruption and weakening of all rival influence and rival power.

Balanced against this are the facts that Russia, as opposed to the western world in general, is still by far the weaker party, that Soviet policy is highly flexible, and that Soviet society may well contain deficiencies which will eventually weaken its own total potential. This would of itself warrant the United States entering with reasonable confidence upon a policy of firm containment, designed to confront the Russians with unalterable counterforce at every point where they show signs of encroaching upon the interests of a peaceful and stable world.

But in actuality the possibilities for American policy are by no means limited to holding the line and hoping for the best. It is entirely possible for the United States to influence by its actions the internal developments, both within Russia and throughout the international Communist movement, by which Russian policy is largely determined. This is not only a question of the modest measure of informational activity which this government can conduct in the Soviet Union and elsewhere, although that, too, is important. It is rather a question of the degree to which the United States can create among the peoples of the world generally the impression of a country which knows what it wants, which is coping successfully with the problems of its internal life and with the responsibilities of a World Power, and which has a spiritual vitality capable of holding its own among the major ideological currents of the time. To the extent that such an impression can be created and maintained, the aims of Russian Communism must appear sterile and quixotic, the hopes and enthusiasm of Moscow's supporters must wane, and added strain must be imposed on the Kremlin's foreign policies. For the palsied decrepitude of the capitalist world is the keystone of Communist philosophy. Even the failure of the United States to experience the early economic depression which the ravens of the Red Square have been predicting with such complacent confidence since hostilities ceased would have deep and important repercussions throughout the Communist world.

By the same token, exhibitions of indecision, disunity and internal disintegration within this country have an exhilarating effect on the whole Communist movement. At each evidence of these tendencies, a thrill of hope and excitement goes through the Communist world; a new jauntiness can be noted in the Moscow tread; new groups of foreign supporters climb on to what they can only view as the band wagon of international politics, and Russian pressure increases all along the line in international affairs.

It would be an exaggeration to say that American behavior unassisted and alone could exercise a power of life and death over the Communist movement and bring about the early fall of Soviet power in Russia. But the United States has it in its power to increase enormously the strains under which Soviet policy must operate, to force upon the Kremlin a far greater degree of moderation and circumspection than it has had to observe in recent years, and in this way to promote tendencies which must eventually find their outlet in either the break-up or the gradual mellowing of Soviet power. For no mystical, Messianic movement—and particularly not that of the Kremlin—can face frustration indefinitely without eventually adjusting itself in one way or another to the logic of that state of affairs.

Thus the decision will really fall in large measure in this country itself. The issue of Soviet-American relations is in essence a test of the over all worth of the United States as a nation among nations. To avoid destruction the United States need only measure up to its own best traditions and prove itself worthy of preservation as a great nation.

Surely, there was never a fairer test of national quality than this. In the light of these circumstances, the thoughtful observer of Russian-American relations will find no cause for complaint in the Kremlin's challenge to American society. He will rather experience a certain gratitude to a Providence which, by providing the American people with this implacable challenge, has made their entire security as a nation dependent on their pulling themselves together and accepting the responsibilities of moral and political leadership that history plainly intended them to bear.

Vietnam

LESLIE H. GELB
Vietnam: The System Worked

The story of United States policy toward Vietnam is either far better or far worse than generally supposed. Our Presidents and most of those who influenced their decisions did not stumble step by step into Vietnam, unaware of the quagmire. U.S. involvement did not stem from a failure to foresee consequences.

Vietnam was indeed a quagmire, but most of our leaders knew it. Of course there were optimists and periods where many were genuinely optimistic. But those periods were infrequent and short-lived and were invariably followed by periods of deep pessimism. Very few, to be sure, envisioned what the Vietnam situation would be like by 1968. Most realized, however, that "the light at the end of the tunnel" was very far away—if not finally unreachable. Nevertheless, our Presidents persevered. Given international compulsions to "keep our word" and "save face," domestic prohibitions against "losing," and their personal stakes, our leaders did "what was necessary," did it about the way they wanted, were prepared to pay the costs, and plowed on with

a mixture of hope and doom. They "saw" no acceptable alternative.

Three propositions suggest why the United States became involved in Vietnam, why the process was gradual, and what the real expectations of our leaders were:

First, U.S. involvement in Vietnam is not mainly or mostly a story of step by step, inadvertent descent into unforeseen quicksand. It is primarily a story of why U.S. leaders considered that it was vital not to lose Vietnam by force to Communism. Our leaders believed Vietnam to be vital not for itself, but for what they thought its "loss" would mean internationally and domestically. Previous involvement made further involvement more unavoidable, and, to this extent, commitments were inherited. But judgments of Vietnam's "vitalness"—beginning with the Korean War—were sufficient in themselves to set the course for escalation.

Second, our Presidents were never actually seeking a military victory in Vietnam. They were doing only what they thought was minimally

From *Foreign Policy* 3 (Summer 1971): 140–67.

necessary at each stage to keep Indochina, and later South Vietnam, out of Communist hands. This forced our Presidents to be brakemen, to do less than those who were urging military victory and to reject proposals for disengagement. It also meant that our Presidents wanted a negotiated settlement without fully realizing (though realizing more than their critics) that a civil war cannot be ended by political compromise.

Third, our Presidents and most of their lieutenants were not deluded by optimistic reports of progress and did not proceed on the basis of wishful thinking about winning a military victory in South Vietnam. They recognized that the steps they were taking were not adequate to win the war and that unless Hanoi relented, they would have to do more and more. Their strategy was to persevere in the hope that their will to continue—if not the practical effects of their actions—would cause the Communists to relent.

Each of these propositions is explored below.

I. Ends: "We Can't Afford to Lose"

Those who led the United States into Vietnam did so with their eyes open, knowing why, and believing they had the will to succeed. The deepening involvement was not inadvertent, but mainly deductive. It flowed with sureness from the perceived stakes and attendant high objectives. U.S. policy displayed remarkable continuity. There were not dozens of likely "turning points." Each post-war President inherited pre-vious commitments. Each extended these commitments. Each administration from 1947 to 1969 believed that it was necessary to prevent the loss of Vietnam and, after 1954, South Vietnam by force to the Communists. The reasons for this varied from person to person, from bureaucracy to bureaucracy, over time and in emphasis. For the most part, however, they had little to do with Vietnam itself. A few men argued that Vietnam had intrinsic strategic military and economic importance, but this view never prevailed. The reasons rested on broader international, domestic, and bureaucratic considerations.

* * *

The *domestic* repercussions of "losing" Vietnam probably were equally important in Presidential minds. Letting Vietnam "go Communist" was undoubtedly seen as:

- opening the floodgates to domestic criticism and attack for being "soft on Communism" or just plain soft;
- dissipating Presidential influence by having to answer these charges;
- alienating conservative leadership in the Congress and thereby endangering the President's legislative program;
- jeopardizing election prospects for the President and his party;
- undercutting domestic support for a "responsible" U.S. world role; and
- enlarging the prospects for a right-wing reaction—the nightmare of a McCarthyite garrison state.

* * *

II. Means: "Take the Minimal Necessary Steps"

None of our Presidents was seeking total victory over the Vietnamese Communists. War critics who wanted victory always knew this. Those who wanted the U.S. to get out never believed it. Each President was essentially doing what he thought was minimally necessary to prevent a Communist victory during his tenure in office. Each, of course, sought to strengthen the anti-Communist Vietnamese forces, but with the aim of a negotiated settlement. Part of the tragedy of Vietnam was that the compromises our Presidents were prepared to offer could never lead to an end of the war. These preferred compromises only served to reinforce the conviction of both Communist and anti-Communist Vietnamese that they had to fight to the finish in their civil war. And so, more minimal steps were always necessary.

*   *   *

Our Presidents reacted to the pressures as brakemen, pulling the switch against both the advocates of "decisive escalation" and the advocates of disengagement. The politics of the Presidency largely dictated this role, but the personalities of the Presidents were also important. None were as ideological as many persons around them. All were basically centrist politicians.

Their immediate aim was always to prevent a Communist takeover. The actions they approved were usually only what was minimally necessary to that aim. Each President determined the "minimal necessity" by trial and error and his own judgment. They might have done more and done it more rapidly if they were convinced that: (1) the threat of a Communist takeover were more immediate, (2) U.S. domestic politics would have been more permissive, (3) the government of South Vietnam had the requisite political stability and military potential for effective use and (4) the job really would have gotten done. After 1965, however, the minimal necessity became the maximum they could get given the same domestic and international constraints.

*   *   *

III. Expectations: "We Must Persevere"

Each new step was taken not because of wishful thinking or optimism about its leading to a victory in South Vietnam. Few of our leaders thought that they could win the war in a conventional sense or that the Communists would be decimated to a point that they would simply fade away. Even as new and further steps were taken, coupled with expressions of optimism, many of our leaders realized that more—and still more—would have to be done. Few of these men felt confident about how it would all end or when. After 1965, however, they allowed the impression of "winnability" to grow in order to justify their already heavy investment and domestic support for the war.

The strategy always was to persevere. Perseverance, it seemed, was the only way to avoid or postpone having to pay the domestic political costs of failure. Finally, perseverance, it was hoped, would convince the Communists that our will to continue was firm. Perhaps, then, with domestic support for perseverance, with bombing North Vietnam, and with inflicting heavy casualties in the South, the Communists would relent. Perhaps, then, a compromise could be negotiated to save the Communists' face without giving them South Vietnam.

*   *   *

Most of our leaders saw the Vietnam quagmire for what it was. Optimism was, by and large, put in perspective. This means that many knew that each step would be followed by another. Most seemed to have understood that more assistance would be required either to improve the relative position of our Vietnamese allies or simply to prevent a deterioration of their position. Almost each year and often several times a year, key decisions had to be made to prevent deterioration or collapse. These decisions were made with hard bargaining, but rapidly enough for us now to perceive a preconceived consensus to go on. Sometimes several new steps were decided at once, but announced and implemented piece-

meal. The whole pattern conveyed the feeling of more to come.

With a tragic sense of "no exit," our leaders stayed their course. They seemed to hope more than expect that something would "give." The hope was to convince the Vietnamese Communists through perseverance that the U.S. would stay in South Vietnam until they abandoned their struggle. The hope, in a sense, was the product of disbelief. How could a tiny, backward Asian country *not* have a breaking point when opposed by the might of the United States? How could they not relent and negotiate with the U.S.?

And yet, few could answer two questions with any confidence: Why should the Communists abandon tomorrow the goals they had been paying so dear a price to obtain yesterday? What was there really to negotiate? No one seemed to be able to develop a persuasive scenario on how the war could end by peaceful means.

Our Presidents, given their politics and thinking, had nothing to do but persevere. But the Communists' strategy was also to persevere, to make the U.S. go home. It was and is a civil war for national independence. It was and is a Greek tragedy.

*   *   *

The End of the Cold War

JOHN LEWIS GADDIS
The Unexpected Ronald Reagan

* * *

It is difficult, now, to recall how far Soviet-American relations had deteriorated at the time Ronald Reagan entered the White House. Some of the responsibility for this rested with Jimmy Carter: at a time when defeat in Vietnam had severely shaken American self-confidence, when the energy crisis appeared to be demonstrating American impotence, when the military balance seemed to be shifting in the Russians' favor, and when the domestic consensus in favor of detente was rapidly dissolving, he had chosen to launch an unprecedented effort to shift the entire basis of foreign policy from power to principle.[1] Carter's timing was terrible; his implementation was haphazard and inconsistent; only his intentions were praiseworthy, and in the climate of the late 1970s, that was not enough.

But the primary responsibility for the decline of detente must rest with the Soviet Union itself, and its increasingly senescent leader, Leonid Brezhnev. Given the long-term economic and social problems that confronted it, the Kremlin needed detente even more than Washington did. And yet, Brezhnev failed to see that he had, in Carter, an American counterpart who sincerely shared that objective; instead he chose to view the administration's fumbling earnestness as a sinister plot directed against Soviet interests. As if to compound this error, Brezhnev also allowed Soviet foreign policy to get caught up in a pattern of imperial overextension like the one that had afflicted the United States in the 1950s and 1960s. For just as the Americans had felt obliged, during those years, to prevent the coming to power of Third World Marxist governments, so the Russians now believed it necessary to sustain such governments, whatever the effect on the Soviet economy, on relations with the West, or on Moscow's overall reputation in world affairs. By equating expansionism with defense, the Soviet leader made the same mistake Stalin had made in the late 1940s: he brought about what he must have most feared. Brezhnev cannot have found it reassuring to know, as he approached the end of his life, that the invasion of Afghanistan had tarnished the Soviet image in the Third World; that a new American military buildup was under way with widespread domestic support; that an unusually determined

From *The United States and the End of the Cold War* (New York: Oxford University Press, 1992), chap. 7.

NATO alliance had decided to deploy a new generation of missiles capable of striking Moscow itself; that detente was dead; and, most unsettling of all, that Ronald Reagan had become president of the United States.

* * *

The record of the Reagan years suggests the need to avoid the common error of trying to predict outcomes from attributes.[2] There is no question that the President and his advisers came into office with an ideological view of the world that appeared to allow for no compromise with the Russians; but ideology has a way of evolving to accommodate reality, especially in the hands of skillful political leadership. Indeed a good working definition of leadership might be just this—the ability to accommodate ideology to practical reality—and by that standard, Reagan's achievements in relations with the Soviet Union will certainly compare favorably with, and perhaps even surpass, those of Richard Nixon and Henry Kissinger.

Did President Reagan intend for things to come out this way? That question is, of course, more difficult to determine, given our lack of access to the archives. But a careful reading of the public record would, I think, show that the President was expressing hopes for an improvement in Soviet-American relations from the moment he entered the White House, and that he began shifting American policy in that direction as early as the first months of 1983, almost two years before Mikhail Gorbachev came to power.[3] Gorbachev's extraordinary receptiveness to such initiatives—as distinct from the literally moribund responses of his predecessors—greatly accelerated the improvement in relations, but it would be a mistake to credit him solely with the responsibility for what happened: Ronald Reagan deserves a great deal of the credit as well.

Critics have raised the question, though, of whether President Reagan was responsible for, or even aware of, the direction administration policy was taking.[4] This argument is, I think, both incorrect and unfair. Reagan's opponents have been quick enough to hold him personally responsible for the failures of his administration; they should be equally prepared to acknowledge his successes. And there are points, even with the limited sources now available, where we can see that the President himself had a decisive impact upon the course of events. They include, among others: the Strategic Defense Initiative, which may have had its problems as a missile shield but which certainly worked in unsettling the Russians; endorsement of the "zero option" in the INF [Intermediate-Range Nuclear Forces] talks and real reductions in START [the Strategic Arms Reduction Talks]; the rapidity with which the President entered into, and thereby legitimized, serious negotiations with Gorbachev once he came into office; and, most remarkably of all, his eagerness to contemplate alternatives to the nuclear arms race in a way no previous president had been willing to do.[5]

Now, it may be objected that these were simple, unsophisticated, and, as people are given to saying these days, imperfectly "nuanced" ideas. I would not argue with that proposition. But it is important to remember that while complexity, sophistication, and nuance may be prerequisites for intellectual leadership, they are not necessarily so for political leadership, and can at times actually get in the way. President Reagan generally meant precisely what he said: when he came out in favor of negotiations from strength, or for strategic arms reductions as opposed to limitations, or even for making nuclear weapons ultimately irrelevant and obsolete, he did not do so in the "killer amendment" spirit favored by geopolitical sophisticates on the right; the President may have been conservative but he was never devious. The lesson here ought to be to beware of excessive convolution and subtlety in strategy, for sometimes simple-mindedness wins out, especially if it occurs in high places.

Finally, President Reagan also understood something that many geopolitical sophisticates on the left have not understood: that although toughness may or may not be a prerequisite for successful negotiations with the Russians—there are arguments for both propositions—it is absolutely essential if the American people are to lend their support, over time, to what has been negotiated. Others may have seen in the doctrine of "negotiation from strength" a way of avoiding negotiations altogether, but it now seems clear that the President saw in that approach the means of constructing a domestic political base without which agreements with the Russians would almost certainly have foundered, as indeed many of them did in the 1970s. For unless one can sustain domestic support—and one does not do that by appearing weak—then it is hardly likely that whatever one has arranged with any adversary will actually come to anything.

There is one last irony to all of this: it is that it fell to Ronald Reagan to preside over the belated but decisive success of the strategy of containment George F. Kennan had first proposed more than four decades earlier. For what were Gorbachev's reforms if not the long-delayed "mellowing" of Soviet society that Kennan had said would take place with the passage of time? The Stalinist system that had required outside adversaries to justify its own existence now seemed at last to have passed from the scene; Gorbachev appeared to have concluded that the Soviet Union could continue to be a great power in world affairs only through the introduction of something approximating a market economy, democratic political institutions, official accountability, and respect for the rule of law at home.[6] And that, in turn, suggested an even more remarkable conclusion: that the very survival of the ideology Lenin had imposed on Russia in 1917 now required infiltration—perhaps even subversion—by precisely the ideology the great revolutionary had sworn to overthrow.

I have some reason to suspect that Professor Kennan is not entirely comfortable with the suggestion that Ronald Reagan successfully completed the execution of the strategy he originated. But as Kennan the historian would be the first to acknowledge, history is full of ironies, and this one, surely, will not rank among the least of them.

Notes

[1] The best overall treatment of Carter administration foreign policy is Gaddis Smith, *Morality, Reason, and Power: American Diplomacy in the Carter Years* (New York: Hill and Wang, 1986).

[2] See, on this point, Kenneth N. Waltz, *Theory of International Relations* (New York: Random House, 1979), 61.

[3] See Lou Cannon's account of a secret Reagan meeting with Soviet Ambassador Anatolii Dobrynin in February, 1983, in *President Reagan: The Role of a Lifetime* (New York: Simon and Schuster, 1991), 311–12.

[4] A typical example is Garry Wills, "Mr. Magoo Remembers," *New York Review of Books*, XXXVII (December 20, 1990), 3–4.

[5] Reagan's most perceptive biographer has pointed out that he was guided "both by extraordinary vision and by remarkable ignorance." [Cannon, *President Reagan*, p. 290]. The implication is that the ignorance may have made possible the vision.

[6] Or so it appeared at the time. Whether these principles will survive the pressures that now threaten to break up the Soviet Union remains to be seen.

The End of the Cold War

MIKHAIL GORBACHEV
The Soviet Union's Crucial Role

* * *

If at the first phase of the invasion into Afghanistan, Soviet leaders could nourish hopes for a favorable outcome, it became clear after two to three years that we would be stuck for a long time without any chances of resolving the matter in our favor. As the United States generously supplied the anti-Kabul opposition groups with money and weapons, Afghanistan turned into a whirlpool, sucking in and crushing our manpower and making the related huge expenditures increasingly unbearable for our country. In general, this war was one of the causes for the economic and political crisis that necessitated *perestroika*.

The situation was further worsened by our society's silent and humble reconciliation with this years-long adventure. Unlike the case of Vietnam for the United States, no strong antiwar movement appeared in the USSR. The reason was not only that the lack of *glasnost* and hard-line political pressure ruled out any massive protest. Our public was not aware of the scale of our spending and losses since it received the

strictly rationed and propaganda-processed information on actions of the so-called limited contingent of Soviet troops, "the international assistance to the friendly people of Afghanistan," and so on. Of course, rumors were bringing news about the growing number of zinc coffins with the repatriated remains of Soviet soldiers. But the public reacted limply, without emotions, as if paralyzed by some narcotic.

* * *

German Unification and the Fall of Eastern European Communism

First, let me say that unification did not proceed according to a predesigned plan and following predetermined methods and pace. A lot happened spontaneously. As always, history took its own course, frustrating the designs of politicians and diplomats. However, there was

From *Essays on Leadership* (Washington, D.C.: Carnegie Commission on Preventing Deadly Conflict, 1998).

an understanding, or, more precisely, a sense of historical inevitability in the course of events. This grew organically from the transformations that were dictated by the new thinking.

Proceeding from the growing interdependence of countries and peoples and from the fact that a universal disaster can be avoided only through collective efforts that require the balancing of interests, we placed a conscious emphasis on the removal of the military-political bloc confrontation, elimination of the Iron Curtain, and integration of the Soviet Union into European and international economic and political structures. This process was inevitably to result in the change of the political arrangement known as the Yalta agreement, which existed on our continent for half a century. Under the new conditions, East European states gained the possibility for self-determination, and it was logical to assume that sooner or later Germans would use this chance to end the half-century of national division.

Therefore, there are no bases for contending that I did not foresee Germany's unification and the collapse of the Warsaw Pact treaty, that all of that fell upon us unexpectedly, and that the Soviet leadership had to simply reconcile itself since it had neither the power nor the possibility to impede such developments.

This is false. In reality, my colleagues and I were aware of the remote consequences of our actions. Having had sufficiently complete information about the situation in our allied states of East and Central Europe—about their difficulties and the growing influence of the opposition forces—it was not hard to imagine that the weakening of the bloc's discipline and of the political control from the "flagship"

would lead to a change in power and then in foreign policy. Under these conditions, it seemed logical for us not to run counter to the inevitable, but to do all we could for the process to take place without huge disturbances and to protect to the maximum the interests of our country.

By the way, to this day, traditionalists fiercely blame me for betrayal, saying that I gave away Poland, Czechoslovakia, Hungary, etc. I always reply with a question: "Gave to whom? Poland to the Poles, Czechoslovakia to the Czechs and Slovaks. . . ." Peoples gained the possibility to decide their own destiny. For us, this was a chance to right a historical wrong and to atone for our attempts to keep these countries forcibly in the orbit of our influence (i.e., the suppression of disturbances in the German Democratic Republic [GDR] and Poland in 1953, the uprising of Hungarians in 1956, the Prague Spring of 1968, and finally, the building of the Berlin Wall, which came to symbolize the division of Europe and of the world).

I repeat, we were not naive simpletons caught in the net of our own speeches advocating the new thinking. It was not incidentally or as a result of failures and mistakes, but by intention that we gave the possibility to our allied countries to make a free choice. This was not at all easy. There were plenty of people in the Soviet Union who considered it necessary to use any means in order not to lose the fruits of the victory in the Second World War. These voices were heard not only at home. Ceaucescu was persistently addressing me and the other leaders of the Warsaw Pact countries with a demand to undertake an armed invasion into Poland to prevent the removal of the Communist party from power. One needs only to imagine the consequences of one such punitive expedition in the late 1980s to appreciate the significance of the new thinking and the foreign policy course then taken by Moscow.

* * *

Looking back, one can see blemishes and mistakes that could have been avoided. But as the saying goes, "one doesn't shake fists after the fight is over." With all the criticism deserved for the actions of the parties involved in that process, it should be acknowledged that most importantly, they withstood the test. They managed to evade bloodshed, which would have been quite possible under the circumstances, managed not to hamper the new strategic nuclear disarmament, and did not push the world back into the Cold War.

The position of the Soviet Union then played a crucial role.

* * *

PART

II

*American Foreign
Policy in the
Twenty-First
Century: Choices
and Challenges*

7 Grand Strategy for a New Era: (I) Power and Peace

Introduction: 11/9 and 9/11—Crumbling Wall, Crashing Towers

What times these are. Americans have seen soaring highs, such as the crumbling of the Berlin Wall, an event that many had hoped for but few believed would come about peacefully. Yet it did so on the fateful evening of November 9, 1989. We have also seen traumatic lows, such as the crashing down of the World Trade Center's twin towers after a terrorist attack that shocked America and much of the rest of the world on the morning of September 11, 2001. Those memorable dates, 11/9 and 9/11, have been joined by many others. We've witnessed events both uplifting and depressing; foreign policy successes and failures. We've had causes for gratification and celebration, and for criticism and mourning.

These are truly times of historic transition. The "post–Cold War era" label is very telling: we know more about what it is not than about what it is. One system has ended; another is in the process of emerging. A number of major global forces are at work, creating a new context and posing new challenges for American foreign policy.

In the second part of this book we turn to key issues that American foreign policy faces in this new era and new century. Chapters 7 and 8 provide the grand strategy "big picture" overview within the 4 Ps framework, this chapter structured around Power and Peace and the next around Prosperity and Principles. Chapter 9 applies the foreign policy politics framework developed in Part I to "politics beyond the water's edge" in the current era. Chapters 10–14 focus on particular regions—Asia and China, the Middle East, Europe and Russia, Latin America, Africa—and key foreign policy issues, and each provides an illustrative case study of foreign policy politics in action.

The Unilateralism versus Multilateralism Debate

The debate about the U.S. role in this changing world as it first emerged at the end of the Cold War was often cast in terms of unilateralism versus multilateralism. *Unilateralism* can be defined as an approach to foreign policy that emphasizes the actions a nation takes largely on its own, or when it acts with others but largely on its own terms. *Multilateralism* emphasizes acting with other nations (three or more in *multi*lateral actions and two in *bi*lateral actions) through processes that are more consultative and consensual, as structured by international institutions, alliances, and coalitions. Although the distinction is one of degree and not a strict dichotomy, the contrast is brought out in comparing the foreign policies of the Clinton and Obama administrations to those of the George W. Bush administration. As a general pattern, the Clinton and Obama approaches were largely multilateralist whenever possible and unilateral only when necessary. In contrast, the Bush approach, especially in the first term, was largely unilateralist whenever possible and multilateral only when necessary.

The Case for Unilateralism

The unilateralist foreign policy strategy is based on six main points.

UNIPOLARITY   With the end of the Cold War, the bipolar system also came to an end. The United States won; the Soviet Union didn't just lose, it collapsed. The United States was left as the sole surviving superpower. Its military superiority was vast. Its economy drove globalization. Its ideology was spreading around the world. It was, in Charles Krauthammer's classic phrase, the "unipolar moment."[1] Scholars Stephen Brooks and William Wohlforth concurred: "There has never been a system of sovereign states that contained one state with that degree of domination."[2] Comparisons were being drawn with nothing less than ancient Rome at its height—indeed, some even openly referred to an American empire.

In March 1992 a Pentagon planning document addressing the "fundamentally new situation which has been created by the collapse of the Soviet Union" was leaked to the press. The strategy it proposed was geared to ensuring that the United States would remain the dominant world power: "Our strategy must now refocus on precluding the emergence of any potential future global competitor." Part of the leadership task would be convincing other major powers that their interests would be taken care of, that the United States would "establish and protect a new order that holds the promise of convincing potential competitors that they need not aspire to a greater role or pursue a more aggressive posture to protect their legitimate interests." Lest this strategy sound too altruistic, the Pentagon also emphasized maintaining and asserting American Power in ways that would make it clear that even if other countries were not convinced of this benevolence, there wasn't a lot they could do about it: "We must maintain the mechanisms for deterring potential competitors from *even aspiring* to a larger regional or global role."[3]

The leak of this document, which was written while Dick Cheney was the secretary of defense, stirred controversy both within the United States and internationally. It fit with readings of history that stressed the risks of war amid "power transitions" when an existing great power was challenged by a rising one. It also fit Realist theories stressing **primacy**. "The maintenance of *primacy*—preponderance in the economic, military, technological, and cultural dimensions of power—is in the national interest. And although the very fact of predominance can be a source of foreign resentment, a large disparity of power is more likely to deter challenges by other would-be powers than to provoke them." **Unipolarity**, primacy theorists such as Professor Robert Lieber (Reading 7.1) contend, makes for a stable world.[4]

7.1

POWER   "Power matters," wrote Condoleezza Rice during the 2000 presidential campaign. Of the components of the national interest, it is the most important. The problem, though, as Rice and other Bush strategists saw it, was that "many in the United States are (and always have been) uncomfortable with the notions of power politics, great powers, and power balances."[5] Multilateralists in general and the Clinton administration in particular were the implied targets of this critique. The Bush team billed itself as having no such discomfort. Indeed it felt American foreign policy makers should not have such concerns. The "inescapable reality" of the post–Cold War world, the neoconservatives William Kristol and Robert Kagan asserted, is "American power in its many forms."[6] And as has been known since the time of the ancient Greek historian Thucydides, "the strong do what they have the power to do, and the weak accept what they have to accept."[7]

Although some Realists strongly opposed many of the Bush policies, particularly the war in Iraq, as diverting from and distorting power politics logic, they held to the view that power politics remained the way of the world. Foreign policy competition is an inherently stronger dynamic than is foreign policy cooperation. In John Mearsheimer's view, states have always sought and always will seek "opportunities to take advantage of one another" as well as to "work to insure that other states do not take advantage of them."[8] This is why, as Stephen Walt puts it as both an analytic point and a criticism of the Bush foreign policy, the United States must seek to maintain its primacy, but must do so "in ways that make its position of primacy acceptable to others."[9]

Even after the Iraq War and the 2007–08 financial crisis, Brooks and Wohlforth argued, the United States still "weighs more on the traditional scales of world power than has any other state in modern history." The fundamentals of power—the United States still accounts for about half of the world's defense spending and one-quarter of its economic output—were still there. And while there were reasons for concern, "they involved public policy problems that can be fixed."[10]

BENEVOLENT HEGEMONY   The United States is deemed a benign superpower, or benevolent hegemon, committed to using its power to preserve peace and promote democratic values. This vision was posed in the Bush 2002 National Security Strategy as promoting "a balance of power that favors freedom": "The United States possesses unprecedented—and unequaled—strength and influence in the world. . . .[T]his position comes with unparalleled responsibilities, obligations and opportunity. The great strength of this nation must be used to promote a balance of power that favors freedom."[11] Thus, only those who oppose peace and freedom should fear American power and dominance.

This outlook reflects in part the Realist view that international order is most possible with a dominant *hegemon.* It is also rooted in the self-conception of *American exceptionalism,* the view we've traced back through earlier historical periods that the United States is different from classical great powers in that it pursues Peace and Principles as well as Power. "The United States would lead the civilized world," as one scholar captures this view, "in the expansion and consolidation of a liberal world order."[12] It thus is in everyone's interest, or at least in the interest of the peace-loving and democratic-spirited, for the United States to assert its power and to maintain its freedom of action with minimal impingements from treaties and other multilateral obligations. It is in this sense that the argument is said to be "hard-headed," not hard-hearted—in effect, American unilateralism is multilateral in function even if not in form.

This strong linking of Power and Principles has been a defining feature of *neoconservatism.* As one author summarizes the main tenets of neoconservatism, "History had singled out the United States to play a unique role as the chief instrument for securing the advance of freedom. . . . American ideals defined America's purpose, to be achieved through the exercise of superior American power."[13] Neoconservatives such as Paul Wolfowitz held top foreign policy posts in the second Bush administration, while others such as Charles Krauthammer, William Kristol, Robert Kagan, and Joshua Muravcik exercised influence through the media and think tanks.

NATIONAL, NOT GLOBAL, INTERESTS   Unilateralists stress the distinction between the U.S. national interest and global interests. They criticize multilateralists for thinking too much in terms of "humanitarian interests" and the "international community," and too little in terms of the national interest. "There is nothing wrong with doing something that benefits all humanity," wrote Rice, "but that is, in a sense, a second-order effect" of pursuing the national interest.[14] That is to say, what is good for the world is not a sufficient goal in itself for U.S. foreign policy. Global interests may be satisfied by the pursuit of the national interest but are not in themselves a justification for major foreign policy commitments and undertakings.

It was along these lines that unilateralists criticized the Clinton administration for its position on international commitments such as the Comprehensive Test Ban Treaty, the

International Criminal Court, and the Kyoto global-warming treaty as being "so anxious to find multilateral solutions to problems that it has signed agreements that are not in America's interest."[15] This also was the essence of the critique that humanitarian military interventions are "social work," and not in most cases a sufficiently vital U.S. national interest to warrant the use of force, or especially the commitment of U.S. troops.[16]

INEFFICACY OF MULTILATERALISM   In addition to all these points about the positives of unilateralism are the negatives of multilateralism. A major downside is said to be the loss of freedom of action the United States incurs in making key foreign policy decisions subject to multilateral approval. "Subcontracting to the UN" or "giving the UN a veto over *our* foreign policy" are the stump-speech political rhetoric expressions of this point. *Prerogative encroachment* is the more analytic term; that is, acting through the UN and other multilateral institutions encroaches on the prerogatives of American power.

Moreover, unilateralists contend, multilateralism just doesn't work very well. They grant some acknowledgment to the role of international institutions such as the United Nations and the possibilities of international cooperation, but only as partial constraints on international competition and the potential for conflict. This was Mearsheimer's point when he stated that "international institutions have minimal influence on state behavior, and thus hold little promise for promoting stability in the post–Cold War world."[17] It also was a principal reason that the second Bush administration chose the unilateral route for the Iraq War.

The inherent problems of multilateralism are those of both process and impact. The process problem arises when many countries with many national interests try to act jointly. Making decisions and building consensus among such a large number of states with such disparate interests may hinder prompt action or dilute policies that need to be clear and firm. Moreover, if decisions are made on a one-country, one-vote basis, the United States is left with the same voting weight as Ecuador, Burkina Faso, Luxembourg, and other small countries. Procedures such as the veto power wielded by the United States on the UN Security Council only partially alleviate this problem.

The problem of impact is rooted in a view of international law, as expressed by John Bolton, the former undersecretary of state and later UN ambassador, as "deeply and perhaps irrevocably flawed."[18] Unilateralists have specific critiques of particular institutions and particular treaties. But even beyond these individual instances, unilateralists are highly skeptical of even best-case scenarios of the role of multilateral institutions and treaties in keeping international order and their value for American foreign policy. "Has George Bush ever met a treaty that he liked?" *The Economist* editorialized. "It is hard to avoid the suspicion that it is the very idea of multilateral cooperation that Mr. Bush objects to."[19]

CONSERVATIVE DOMESTIC POLITICS   Unilateralists raise the specter of America's own constitutional democracy being undermined by the impingements of multilateral institutions, agreements, and other aspects of global governance. This debate over safeguarding American sovereignty against multilateralism, "fought out at the confluence of constitutional theory and foreign policy," to quote Bolton again, "is *the* decisive issue facing the United States internationally."[20] On issues such as the jurisdiction of the **International Criminal Court** over American soldiers and other citizens, or U.S. troops being under foreign command in UN peacekeeping operations, the debate is said to be a constitutional one—not just a foreign policy one—about the sanctity of America's own sovereign authority.

Domestic politics also bring more baldly electoral considerations. The noted historian Arthur Schlesinger, Jr., a strong supporter of multilateralism and particularly of the UN, nevertheless noted that "there is no older American tradition in the conduct of foreign affairs" than unilateralism.[21] Unilateralism taps the self-concept of American exceptionalism in ways that have political appeal even if, as in Schlesinger's view, exceptionalism is a form of hubris that is bad for the country and for the world. Unilateralists are well positioned politically because they can claim to be more concerned with "what's good for America" than multilateralists and play to fears and prejudices about the outside world. UN-bashing in particular has great appeal for these groups, many of which are deeply influential in the conservative wing of the Republican Party. Right-wing militia groups adhere to an extreme version of this view, including paranoid theories that the UN is seeking to take over and even invade the United States.

The Case for Multilateralism

Multilateralism has its own case to make, which can also be summarized in six main points.

INTERNATIONAL INSTITUTIONALISM   Multilateralism, grounded in the International Institutionalist paradigm (Chapter 1), emphasizes the building of a system of international institutions, organizations, and regimes that provide the basis for cooperation among states to resolve tensions, settle disputes, work together in mutually beneficial ways and, above all, to avoid war.[22] With reference to the relatively peaceful end of the Cold War, International Institutionalist scholars such as John Ruggie contend that "there seems little doubt that multilateral norms and institutions have helped stabilize [the] international consequences." As for the post–Cold War world, "such norms and institutions appear to be playing a significant role in the management of a broad array of regional and global changes in the world system today."[23] According to this view we entered the post–Cold War era with international institutions that, although not without their weaknesses, were quite strong and had the potential to be made stronger.

International Institutionalists lay claim to a "realism" of their own. Their realism takes the system as it is, not as it used to be. The United States remains the strongest country, but it is neither in the U.S. interest nor even within the realm of achievability for the United States to try to maintain peace and security on its own. It often needs to be the lead actor, and at times act unilaterally, but the greatest power is the power of numbers that comes with effective multilateralism. The key strategy is one of *integration*—bringing others in rather than keeping them down. As John Ikenberry argues (Reading 7.2), peace has been most durable when the victors in war and the most powerful states have used their position and power to foster international order based on shared interests. When they have sought only to dominate—to keep others down—their power has brought some gains but not very stable or sustainable ones.[24]

With regard to the United Nations, rather than concerns about prerogative encroachment, the emphasis is on *policy enhancement.* The freedom of action the United States gives up by acting multilaterally tends to be outweighed by the capacity gained to achieve shared objectives. Part of that gain is a political version of the international trade principle of comparative advantage, whereby different nations as well as relevant international institutions and nongovernmental organizations (NGOs) all bring to bear their complementary expertises based on their own historical experiences, traditional relationships, and policy emphases. Also gained is a sharing of burdens that can help with both the politics and finances of sustaining commitments over time. Another gain is the legitimacy that can only come from a broadly multilateral effort. International norms surely "do not determine action," as Martha Finnemore aptly puts it, but they do "create permissive conditions for action."[25] Achieving broadly multilateral efforts has obstacles and pitfalls, but the potential advantages cannot be achieved by any nation, even the United States, when acting alone or even largely on its own.

This line of thinking characterized much of the Clinton administration's foreign policy:

> International cooperation will be vital for building security in the next century because many of the challenges America faces cannot be addressed by a single nation. Many U.S. security objectives are best achieved—or can only be achieved—by leveraging our influence and capabilities through international organizations, our alliances, or as a leader of an ad hoc coalition formed around a specific objective. Leadership in the United Nations and other international organizations, and durable relationships with allies and friendly nations, are critical to our security.[26]

By the time the Obama administration came into office, there was an even broader sense of the "global governance gap" between the scope of the forces driving globalization and the international community's limited policy capacity for coordination, cooperation, and collective action. Fewer and fewer issues could be dealt with primarily or even exclusively on a national basis. And more and more states were gaining seats at the table in what Fareed Zakaria called "the rise of the rest . . . an international system in which countries in all parts of the world are no longer objects or observers but players in their own right."[27] In such a world, as the Obama *2010 National Security Strategy* stated,

> We must focus American engagement on strengthening international institutions and galvanizing the collective action that can serve common interests . . . International institutions must more effectively represent the world of the 21st century, with a broader voice—and greater responsibilities—for emerging powers, and they must be modernized to more effectively generate results on issues of global interest.[28]

This is in part about the United Nations and other international organizations. It also entails state-to-state collaboration and roles for the private sector and NGOs in public-private-nonprofit partnerships as well as more informal networks. It is in this respect that we use the term *global governance* and not *world government.*

POWER-INFLUENCE CONVERSION   U.S. power still tends to be greater than any other single country, but its relative margin is less than it used to be. While U.S. military power remains vastly superior to that of any other state (or coalition of states), the military balance is much less central to overall systemic structure than during the Cold War. In a world where there is much less of a shared and overarching threat, the currency of military strength is less convertible to other forms of power and influence than when such threats were more defining.

This is where Joseph Nye's concept of soft power comes in:

> Military power remains crucial in certain situations, but it is a mistake to focus too narrowly on the military dimensions of American power. . . . Soft power is also more than persuasion or the ability to move people by argument. It is the ability to entice and attract. And attraction often leads to acquiescence or imitation. . . . If I can get you to *want* to do what I want, then I do not have to force you to do what you do *not* want to do.[29]

This is not a strictly new phenomenon; historically, the United States and other major powers have tried to use their reputations and ideologies as sources of power. But it is more important in the post–Cold War world, when power has become "less fungible, less coercive and less tangible."[30]

Achieving foreign policy objectives is not as simple as Thucydides' dictum about the powerful doing what they want makes it sound. If hard power is wielded in ways that exacerbate tensions or antagonize others, it can be even more difficult to achieve the influence that is key to effective leadership. This more nuanced view of the nature of power and the dynamics of influence is something that, as Nye put it, "unilateralists forget at their and our peril."[31] It was on this basis that the Obama administration stressed the importance of restoring America's global reputation, not as some feel-good exercise but as a pragmatic measure for enhancing American power.

Power diffusion is especially evident in the eastward and southward shift in economic dynamism. China is, of course, Exhibit A in this trend. But as Jeffrey Immelt, General Electric CEO and then-chair of the White House economic competitiveness advisory panel acknowledged, it is "the billion people joining the middle class in Asia"—not U.S. consumers—who "are the engines driving global growth."[32] And it's not just Asia. It's a bevy of countries relegated to the Third World during the Cold War. All told, whereas in 1950 the United States, Canada, and Western Europe accounted for 68 percent of global gross domestic product, projections are that by 2050 this bloc will account for less than 30 percent.

NOT-SO-BENIGN HEGEMONY The third tenet of multilateralism is a questioning of whether other nations generally share the "benevolent hegemon" view that unilateralists claim for the United States. The essence of U.S. Cold War leadership, particularly as perceived by Western European and other allies, was the overriding sense that generally they did benefit from America's pursuit of its own national interest. The United States didn't just claim that its hegemony was benign; these other nations generally saw it that way as well. Much of the Third World, though, held a far less positive view. Chapters 5 and 6 included numerous examples of "ABC" definitions of democracy, covert actions, wars, and other U.S. Cold War policies that support the assessment of historian Arne Westad that "seen from a Third World perspective, the results of America's interventions are truly dismal."[33]

Such tensions increased with the George W. Bush administration's foreign policy on a number of issues; other countries—including many U.S. allies—saw their interests as being hurt rather than helped by America's pursuit of its own interests. The Bush administration deemed it in the country's interest to use military force unilaterally, even preemptively, when necessary. Other nations and the UN not only disagreed with this stance in specific cases but were also concerned about the broader destabilizing effects, such as the undermining of international norm of nonintervention. The Bush administration opposed the Kyoto global-warming treaty, claiming it was not in U.S. interests. The countries that had signed the treaty saw their interests as hurt by the unwillingness of the world's largest producer of harmful emissions to be part of the treaty. The Bush administration unilaterally imposed tariffs on steel imports in 2002 and claimed to be acting in accord with the World Trade Organization (WTO) system. Nations whose steel industries bore the costs saw this as exploitation of U.S. economic power and contrary to the WTO's multilateral rules. Although the general critique stops short of casting the United States as a malevolent hegemon, it does not see America as benign.

NATIONAL AND GLOBAL INTERESTS Multilateralists tend to agree that if a choice has to be made, the national interest must come first. But they see the national and global interests as much more interconnected than do unilateralists. Many of the foreign policy issues the United States faces today simply cannot be solved by one nation acting alone. Even the best national environmental policies would not be sufficient to deal with global warming;

global policies are needed for a global problem. Even the tightest homeland security cannot guarantee against the global threat of terrorism; as many countries as possible must cooperate against terrorists, wherever they may be. It is basic logic that if the scope of a problem reaches beyond national boundaries, the policy strategies for dealing with it must have comparable reach. The national and global interests are more complementary and less competitive than unilateralists claim. Whatever freedom of action is given up through multilateralism, it is outweighed by the capacity gained to achieve shared objectives and serve national interests in ways that are less possible unilaterally. Where unilateralists tally losses of prerogative encroachment, multilateralists see gains of policy enhancement.

An interesting example is combating twenty-first century piracy. Over the past decade or so there have been more than 6,000 attempted acts of piracy around the world. Many of these have been in the Gulf of Aden, off the coast of Somalia, one of the main maritime routes for global commerce. Twenty thousand ships per year, carrying 12 percent of the world's daily oil supply, pass through the Gulf of Aden, which has the highest risk of piracy in the world.[34] Perhaps the most successful anti-piracy strategy has been the establishment of the multilateral Combined Task Force 151 (CTF 151). CTF 151 includes naval ships from more than 20 countries, including Australia, Bahrain, Canada, France, Germany, Japan, Pakistan, Saudi Arabia, South Korea, Turkey, the United Kingdom, and the United States. Leadership positions within CTF 151 rotate periodically among its members, emphasizing the multilateral nature of the task force. Largely because of CTF 151, at any one time there are around forty different warships patrolling the one million square miles between the Gulf of Aden and the Mozambique Channel. While this is hardly sufficient to eliminate the piracy threat entirely, it has had a significant impact.

CORRECT, NOT REJECT   The United Nations and other multilateral institutions do have problems. But the optimal strategy according to multilateralists is to correct them, not reject them. Professors Robert Keohane and Lisa Martin lay out in functional terms the theoretical basis for why international institutions develop: "Institutions can provide information, reduce transaction costs, make commitments more credible, establish focal points for coordination and, in general, facilitate the operation of reciprocity."[35] In so doing, international institutions help states overcome the difficulties of collective action which can persist even when states have common interests. This is a very rational argument that is much more pragmatically grounded than classical Wilsonian idealism. The world it envisions is not entirely free of tensions and conflicts, but the prospects for achieving cooperation and the policy benefits of doing so are greater than unilateralists are willing to acknowledge. Substantial progress has been made recently in reforming the UN, but more needs to be done and it can be done if people get past bashing the institution. The Kyoto treaty had its flaws, but the debate could have been about amending it, not discarding it. So too with the International Criminal Court, arms-control treaties and organizations, and other multilateral measures—the option exists to correct them, rather than reject them.

LIBERAL DOMESTIC POLITICS   Multilateralism has broader but less intense domestic political support than unilateralism. Public-opinion polls show, for example, that in recent years support for the United Nations more often than not has been over 50 percent. Generally, though, pro-UN groups are less likely to make this their "single-issue vote" than are anti-UN groups. Unilateralists often accuse multilateralists of being "one-worlders," with notions of a world government superseding national governments. This is a distortion, albeit one that sells politically. Multilateralists do see the value of greater capacity for global governance in terms of structures and processes for governments to work together, which is very different from governments being supplanted or superseded. Indeed, multilateralists can make their own claim to American exceptionalism with a vision of the United States as a leader in efforts to bring nations together for common purposes and common values.

Beyond the Unilateralism-Multilateralism Terms of Debate

While the unilateralism-multilateralism debate continues, the terms of the debate have gone further. As illustrated in the "Theory in the World" box below, there are, among others, Fareed Zakaria's "post-American world," Kishore Mahbubani's "Asian rise," Charles Kupchan's "no one's world," and the "Copernican world" that Steven Weber and I have portrayed. These conceptualizations bring out three emerging aspects of the twenty-first century world.

THEORY IN THE WORLD
THEORY IN THE WORLD

CONCEPTUALIZING THE TWENTY-FIRST CENTURY

66 For most of the last century, the United States has dominated global economics, politics, science and culture. For the last twenty years, that dominance has been unrivaled, a phenomenon unprecedented in modern history. We are now living through . . . 'the rise of the rest.' . . . For the first time ever, we are witnessing genuinely global growth. This is creating an international system in which countries in all parts of the world are no longer objects or observers but players in their own right. It is the birth of a truly global order. . . . We are moving into a *post-American world*, one defined and directed from many places and by many people. 99

—Fareed Zakaria

66 The rise of the West transformed the world. The rise of Asia will bring about an equally significant transformation. . . . Asia and the West have yet to reach a com-

mon understanding about the nature of this new world. The need to develop one has never been greater. . . . [T]he mental maps of the leading minds of the world, especially in the West, are trapped in the past, reluctant or unable to conceive of the possibility that they may have to change their world-view. But unless they do, they will make strategic mistakes, perhaps on a disastrous scale. ""

—Kishore Mahbubani

"" Emerging powers will want to revise, not consolidate, the international order erected under the West's watch. They have different views about the foundations of political legitimacy, the nature of sovereignty, the rules of international trade, and the relationship between state and society. As their material power increases, they will seek to recast the international order in ways that advantage their interests and ideological preferences. ""

—Charles Kupchan

"" The ancient philosopher Ptolemy believed Earth was at the center of the universe, with all the other planets, indeed the whole solar system, revolving around it. So too in the dominant twentieth-century view was the United States at the center of the international political world . . . Not anymore. The twenty-first century is better represented by the discoveries of Copernicus, in which the United States (Earth in the astronomical version) is not at the center. Although our 'gravitational pull' is still strong, it is not so strong that others orbit around us. We have seen this geopolitically . . . We see it economically . . . We see it scientifically . . . We see it in so many other walks of life. ""

—Steven Weber and Bruce Jentleson

Sources: Fareed Zakaria, *The Post-American World* (New York: Norton, 2008), 2–5; Kishore Mahbubani, *The New Asian Hemisphere: The Irresistible Shift of Global Power to the East* (New York: Public Affairs, 2008), 1–5; Charles A. Kupchan, *No One's World: The West, the Rising Rest, and the Coming Global Turn* (New York: Oxford University Press, 2012), 7–8; Steven Weber and Bruce W. Jentleson, *The End of Arrogance: America in the Global Competition of Ideas* (Cambridge, Mass.: Harvard University Press, 2010), 9–10.

POST-POLAR SYSTEM STRUCTURE Typically, the structure of the international system is defined by counting the poles of power. The nineteenth century experienced the *multipolarity* of the major European powers. They had the power to divide up the world—this colony for us and that one for you. They established the rules of the game—when to compete and when to collude against shared enemies. They controlled the global economy in classic center-periphery terms. The system didn't always work and ultimately fell apart during World War I, but the point was the same in peace or war: world politics were largely determined by the multi-poles.

The Cold War was defined by the *bipolarity* of the two superpowers. There were efforts to loosen this grip, as with the 1950s' Non-Aligned Movement, but overall the ties within each bloc (volitional or coercive) were binding. The conflict and competition between the United States and the Soviet Union, manifested in their global containment and international solidarity strategies, respectively, divided the world. The division was ideological and economic as well as geopolitical. Some leaders and states sought to escape from the bipolar structure, or at least to bend it, but they never broke it. Other issues came up and other dynamics played out, but world politics was largely determined by the bi-poles.

Some see the current era as a twenty-first-century version of multipolarity. But while this idea captures the emergence of new powers such as China, India, and Brazil, it does not sufficiently address the dynamics of today's world. Regionalism is strengthening and deepening, not only as a matter of economic relations but also through regional security institutions. Many of the 190-plus nations in the world that are emerging on the global stage after long histories of colonialism and superpower dominance are manifesting a twenty-first century version of nationalism and nonalignment. While not as aggressive or antagonistic as in other eras, they are quite assertive of national interests and identities. As one study by the International Institute for Strategic Studies put it, "countries small, medium and large are all banking more on their own strategic initiative than on formal alliances or institutional relationships to defend their interests and advance their goals."[36] While it remains true that some states matter more than others, more states matter more today than ever before.

In addition, nonstate actors, including NGOs (nongovernmental organizations), are playing more significant international roles than ever before.[37] In sheer numbers, international NGOs more than doubled in the first decade following the Cold War, and have grown even more since then. These include NGOs that play a role for the better, such as the Bill & Melinda Gates Foundation in global health policy. The nonstate actor category also includes some that play a role for the worse, such as Al Qaeda.

All told, this makes for a system that is much less tightly and hierarchically structured than pole counting conveys.

"THREE Ds" THREATS   Historically, states seeking *dominance* over each other has been the central security dynamic in international affairs: Britain-France for centuries, Spain-Britain during the maritime colonial era, World Wars I and II, and the Cold War. This type of threat still exists and must be defended and deterred against. But while today's major powers have their differences and conflicts, they are not seeking dominance over one another. Tensions between the West and Russia have grown worse, but nothing like during the Cold War. Questions remain about how peaceful China's rise will be, but most indications point to competition, not confrontation. Even geopolitics in the Middle East, rhetoric notwithstanding, are less focused on conquest than in the past.

Two other types of threats have become much more foreboding than in prior eras. One is *disruption*: transnational forces that have major disruptive effects both internationally and within domestic societies. September 11 demonstrated how a small group operating from caves in a state deemed too far away and too unimportant to worry about could breach the security of the world's most powerful country. The 1997 global financial crisis, set off by a minor currency in a small country (the Thai bhat), shook stock markets everywhere, cracked many a family nest egg, and left a foreboding sense of what could happen if the catalyst came from a major economy—which was confirmed in spades with the worldwide effects of the 2008 U.S. financial collapse and the 2011–12 euro crisis. Threats of cyberwarfare could potentially disrupt water supplies, electricity generation, home computers, personal cell phones, and other systems on which daily life so heavily relies.

Of even greater concern are the multiple mass destruction threats. We have long lived with the threat of weapons of mass destruction (WMD). For a while we could find solace in having done better than the world containing twenty or more nuclear powers that John Kennedy warned against. Of late, though, more states have acquired or seek to acquire nuclear weapons, and terrorists threaten to gain access to chemical and biological as well as nuclear weapons. Then there is the "DMD" (diseases of mass destruction) threat—for example, an avian flu pandemic for which estimates of deaths run into the millions and economic costs into the billions. "EMD," environmental mass destruction, could be even more devastating than some WMD and may be more imminent than had been assumed. Finally, identities of mass destruction ("IMD")—genocides and ethnic cleansings—kill hundreds of thousands, again and again, despite the pledge of "never again" in the wake of World War II and the Holocaust.

INSIDE-OUT POLITICS AND THE "VEGAS DILEMMA"   During the Cold War much global instability was "outside in," i.e., states' internalization of the tensions and conflicts of the U.S.-Soviet global rivalry. In today's world the dynamic is "inside out" with the increased susceptibility of international stability to threats and other disruptions that emanate outward from individual states. It may be true that "what happens in Vegas stays in Vegas," as the tag line of a recent American commercial had it, but *what happens inside states doesn't stay inside states*. Not popular uprisings against repressive governments that spill over to other countries and scramble regional geopolitics, nor failed states that become safe havens for global terrorist groups, nor mass atrocities that cause refugee flows across borders and feed into neighbors' ethnic and other conflicts, nor inadequate public health capacity to prevent disease outbreaks from becoming pandemics, nor domestic financial bubbles that burst globally, nor carbon emissions generated locally that warp climate globally. The "Vegas dilemma" is posed by the domestic locus and transnational effects of so many twenty-first-century threats.

One aspect of the problem is normative: how to balance the rights that sovereignty confers on states and the inward (to their own people) and outward (to the international community) responsibilities that come with it. But who defines responsibility? On what terms? And with what accountability? These questions are very open and highly contested. They involve historical legacies of colonialism and Cold War interventionism, substantive differences over best practices (for example, different conceptions of the proper state-market balance), and decisions about which cases get priority for norms such as the **Responsibility to Protect (R2P).**

Another aspect of the problem is strategy. Clausewitz's classic conception of war as the "politics by other means" is challenging, but the alternative politics of building states that won't fail, won't be terrorist havens, can manage ethnic and other internal identity fissures without mass violence, and strike the right balance between being friendly to American interests and responsive to their own people is even trickier. The limits of state capacity also complicate strategic choices: we can stockpile Tamiflu, but unless areas where diseases with pandemic potential break out have front-line public health capacity, that will never be enough.

Power

One of the great international dilemmas, in the contemporary era no less than at other times, is how to balance force and diplomacy. The world may reach a point at which diplomacy in the classical sense—defined by Sir Harold Nicolson as "the management of international relations by negotiation"—fully suffices for international peace, national security, and humanitarian justice.[38] But it is not there yet. Indeed, the world is much further from this ideal than was thought amid the immediate post–Cold War euphoria. The end of the Cold War has not meant the end of war, as evidenced by ethnic conflicts and genocides in Bosnia, Darfur, and other regions; and by September 11 and the subsequent operations in Afghanistan and Iraq. Thus the United States must continue to seek ways it can best strike the balance between force and diplomacy, given both the threats and opportunities of the contemporary era.

Five elements in Power-based strategies are considered below: use of military force, nuclear deterrence, terrorism deterrence, defense budget and overall strategy, and cyber-security.

Use of Military Force

Since the end of the Cold War the use of military force has come up in a number of cases:

THE "POWELL DOCTRINE" AND THE 1990–91 PERSIAN GULF WAR With the legacy of the Vietnam War in mind, as some interpreted it, the *"Powell Doctrine"* of decisive force was developed in the late 1980s and early 1990s. Named for General Colin Powell, who was Chairman of the Joint Chiefs of Staff at the time, this doctrine advocated that when military force is to be used, it should be used overwhelmingly and decisively.[39]

The Gulf War was the principal application of the Powell Doctrine. On August 2, 1990, the Iraqi army of Saddam Hussein invaded neighboring Kuwait. Although Iraq and Kuwait had a border dispute as well as some other issues, the real problem was Saddam Hussein's desire to become the dominant power in the Persian Gulf region. Indeed, his forces were poised to continue straight into Saudi Arabia, an even more strategically located country and a close U.S. ally.

The threat to vital American interests was deemed so serious that it was met by the most rapid buildup of U.S. military forces since World War II, first as a "desert shield" to protect Saudi Arabia and then as a "desert storm" to drive Saddam out of Kuwait.

The UN Security Council (UNSC) moved swiftly to impose economic sanctions against and issue diplomatic condemnations of Iraq. As the crisis wore on and Saddam remained intransigent, UNSC passed a resolution authorizing "all necessary means" to get Iraqi troops out of Kuwait, including the use of military force. The UN set a deadline of January 15, 1991 for Iraqi withdrawal from Kuwait. When the deadline passed, the multinational military force assembled under the command of General Norman Schwarzkopf of the U.S. Army went to war. *Operation Desert Storm* proved a formidable military victory. In little more than a month, Iraqi forces were defeated and forced to withdraw from Kuwait. This was achieved with few American and coalition casualties.

1990S HUMANITARIAN INTERVENTIONS[*] Starting in the 1990s, ethnic and other identity-based conflicts posed challenges that could not be met through the Powell Doctrine.

In Somalia, the United States intervened with 27,000 troops on the largely humanitarian mission of helping restore order and get food to the Somali people. This mission, launched by the George H.W. Bush administration in December 1992 and continued by the Clinton administration, ended disastrously in October 1993 when the United States abruptly withdrew after eighteen U.S. soldiers were killed in urban battles in the capital

---

[*]See also Chapter 8 for a 4 Ps discussion of genocide prevention, Chapter 12 for more on Bosnia and Kosovo, and Chapter 14 for more on Somalia and Rwanda.

city of Mogadishu. Two decades later, Somalia still was a failed state, with continuing humanitarian crises as well as security concerns about its use as a haven for terrorists, among other issues.

The war in Bosnia (1992–95) left nearly a million people dead or wounded, almost 2 million displaced, and added the term *ethnic cleansing* to the lexicon of warfare. The war involved the most massive killings in Europe since the Nazi Holocaust. Yet for more than three years, the United States did not intervene, leaving the United Nations and the European Union to lead the multilateral peacekeeping forces. When the Clinton administration finally stepped in, combining NATO bombing and a diplomatic peace-brokering role, the war ended—but only after widespread death and enormous destruction.

In Rwanda, the horrors that transpired in 1994 were more than ethnic cleansing— they were *genocide.* "In one hundred days," reported Samantha Power in her Pulitzer Prize–winning book, *"A Problem From Hell:" America and the Age of Genocide,* "some eight hundred thousand Tutsi and politically moderate Hutu were murdered. . . . The Rwandan genocide would prove to be the fastest, most efficient killing spree of the twentieth century." Yet, she continues, "the United States did almost nothing to try to stop it."[40] Nor did the UN, Europe, nor any other major actor in the international community.

In Kosovo, the United States and NATO intervened in 1999 to stop the ethnic cleansing that Serbia was perpetrating against this heavily Muslim province. The United States and NATO won, but they "won ugly."[41] Success came only after extensive killings, after scores of villages were ravaged, and after thousands became refugees. The conflict was contained and reduced, but it had not been prevented.

These and other 1990s conflicts intensified debate over the scope and limits of state sovereignty. International rules and norms were well-established for interstate conflict, when one state invades another. But when conflicts with mass killings were intrastate, the rules and norms for military action by outside parties were much less clear. Was it a violation of the rights of state sovereignty for others to intervene? Or did sovereignty also place responsibilities on states not to slaughter their own people?

The norm of sovereignty as responsibility came through very strongly in a 2001 report, *The Responsibility to Protect,* issued by the International Commission on Intervention and State Sovereignty (ICISS), an unofficial body with representatives from around the world formed in coordination with the UN and Canada and supported by American philanthropic foundations. The core doctrine of the R2P reflects the sense that individuals must be protected from mass killings and other gross violations of their rights, and that the state that is sovereign over the territory in which they reside has primary but not exclusive responsibility. If the state does not live up to that responsibility, "then coercive intervention for human protection purposes, including ultimately military intervention, by others in the international community may be warranted in extreme cases."[42]

To answer the concern that this could open the way for big powers to go on doing what they want to do, the commission was careful to distinguish its conception of the responsibility to protect from a "right to intervene." Although acknowledging the historical roots of such fears in colonialism and the Cold War, the commission was unwilling to allow such arguments to be easily invoked as rationalizations distracting from its core concern about ethnic cleansings, genocides, and other mass killings. "What is at stake here is not making the world safe for big powers, or trampling over the sovereign rights of small ones, but delivering practical protection for ordinary people at risk of their lives, because their states are unwilling or unable to protect them."[43]

If sovereignty was to be less sacrosanct, establishing criteria for justifiable intervention was essential. These efforts heavily tapped into the *just war* tradition. Though differing in some particulars, the commission stressed four factors: *force as a last resort,* when non-military options have failed or been "explored with reasonable grounds for believing" they could not succeed; *just cause,* in response to an "extreme humanitarian emergency" or comparably dire situation; *proportionality of the military means,* which should be only enough to achieve the human protection objective; and *reasonable prospects of success,* taking into account collateral damage, civilian casualties, and other factors such that "the consequences of action [are] not likely to be worse than the consequences of inaction."[44]

While ICISS was an unofficial group and its recommendations were not binding on governments, R2P became central to debates over the use of military force within the United States and at the UN—and a decade later bore especially on the case of Libya.

9/11 AND THE AFGHANISTAN WAR   The initial war in Afghanistan was as internationally consensual as wars get. The U.S. claim to be acting in self-defense was strong. The Taliban regime had been denied its country's seat in the United Nations, and only two countries in the world had granted it diplomatic recognition. It was among the world's worst oppressors of women and worst offenders against human rights. Some aspects of the U.S. strategy were debated, but the right to use force in this situation was widely accepted by the international community. The United Nations Security Council supported the use of force, and more than 170 nations joined the U.S.-led global coalition against terrorism.

Militarily, in its initial October–December 2001 phase, the Afghanistan War showed that American military power had reached even more dominant levels than were demonstrated in the Persian Gulf War. A vast new array of technologies was displayed. Special Operations forces consisting of Green Berets, other elite units, and CIA agents infiltrated enemy areas by riding on horseback in the rugged terrain with equipment to identify targets and communicate the enemy's exact location to bombers overhead. But the initial victory proved inconclusive, as the G.W. Bush and Obama administrations found out, and as we discuss further in Chapter 11.

BUSH PREEMPTION DOCTRINE AND THE IRAQ WAR   September 11 raised doubts as to whether deterrence would work against Al Qaeda and other terrorist networks. Terrorists do not have capital cities, major population centers, or regular military installations against which to threaten retaliation. To address this dilemma, the G.W. Bush administration developed a doctrine of preemption, of first military strikes against an imminent threat (see "At the Source," p. 303). President Bush made an initial statement of this doctrine in a June 2002 speech at West Point:

> For much of the last century, America's defense relied on the Cold War doctrines of deterrence and containment. In some cases, those strategies still apply. But new threats also require new thinking. Deterrence—the promise of massive retaliation against nations—means nothing against shadowy terrorist networks with no nation or citizens to defend. Containment is not possible when unbalanced dictators with weapons of mass destruction can deliver those weapons on missiles or secretly provide them to terrorist allies.[45]

The U.S. doctrine on using force, therefore, would have to shift from relying on after-the-incident retaliation to preemptive action. "If we wait for threats to fully materialize, we will have waited too long. . . . [O]ur security will require all Americans to be forward-looking and resolute, to be ready for preemptive action when necessary to defend our liberty and to defend our lives."[46]

It was partly on this basis that the Iraq War was launched in March 2003. American forces invaded with some support from other countries, such as Great Britain, but with much more controversy within the United Nations and internationally than the Persian Gulf War. "Shock and awe" was the term coined for the military strategy. The idea was to bring so much military power to bear so quickly, inflicting such heavy destruction on enemy forces as to shock and intimidate them, leaving them so materially weakened and psychologically in awe as to undermine their will to keep fighting. Within a month American and coalition forces had prevailed. But the sense of victory did not last, as we also discuss further in Chapter 11.

Broader points beyond Iraq were also raised by critics of the Bush preemption doctrine. The legal-juridical part of the argument sees preemption as a violation of international law and norms. Article 51 of the UN Charter acknowledges the inherent right of states to act in self-defense, but only "if an armed act occurs" and until the UN Security Council acts. Some would extend this to include situations in which the threat is so imminent as to be virtually certain, as long as the decision is made by the UN, not an individual country. Two pragmatic arguments have also been raised. One is whether preemptive strikes can be counted on to work. To use force decisively when using it preemptively imposes an especially demanding requirement for reliable intelligence and especially careful planning for enemy countermoves and other contingencies. There is also the dangerous precedent set. As the British scholar Lawrence Freedman writes, "The ambiguity about situations in which it [military force] might be justified means that elevating this notion

AT THE SOURCE

AT THE SOURCE

BUSH PREEMPTION DOCTRINE

Defending our Nation against its enemies is the first and fundamental commitment of the Federal Government. Today, that task has changed dramatically. Enemies in the past needed great armies and great industrial capabilities to endanger America. Now, shadowy networks of individuals can bring great chaos and suffering to our shores for less than it costs to purchase a single tank. Terrorists are organized to penetrate open societies and turn the power of modern technologies against us. . . .

The gravest danger our Nation faces lies at the crossroads of radicalism and technology. Our enemies have openly declared that they are seeking weapons of mass destruction, and evidence indicates that they are doing so with determination. The United States will not allow these efforts to succeed. We will build defenses against ballistic missiles and other means of delivery. We will cooperate with other nations to deny, contain and curtail enemies' efforts to acquire dangerous technologies. And, as a matter of commons sense self-defense, America will act against such emerging threats before they are fully formed. . . .

While the United States will constantly strive to enlist the support of the international community, we will not hesitate to act alone, if necessary to exercise our right of self-defense by acting pre-emptively against such terrorists, to prevent them from doing harm against our people and our country. . . ."

Source: George W. Bush, *National Security Strategy for the United States, 2002,* http://georgewbush -whitehouse.archives.gov/nsc/nss/2002/.

[preemption] to a security doctrine rather than an occasional stratagem by the USA creates opportunities for states that might use new-fangled notions of preemption as rationalization when embarking on old-fashioned aggression."[47] If the United States can take preemptive action in the name of its own security and on the basis of its own threat assessments and its own decision making, then why can't other countries? Why can't India or Pakistan do so in their conflict? Israel or the Arab states in theirs? Why can't Russia act against the other former Soviet republics? Or China against Taiwan? In these or other cases, a state may genuinely see preemptive action as necessary in security terms, or could still seize on the Bush Doctrine as a convenient rationalization, laying claim to the precedent for political cover. Either way, the world could end up a more dangerous place.

LIBYA 2011 AND THE RESPONSIBILITY TO PROTECT　Libya was one of the first cases in which R2P was invoked by both the UN and the United States. In February and March 2011, inspired by the "Arab Spring" revolts in neighboring Tunisia and Egypt, the Libyan people rose up against long-time brutal dictator Muammar Qaddafi. "[We will] kill the greasy rats," Qaddafi ranted, vowing to fight "until the end." Despite its traditional opposition to intervention, the Arab League called on the UN Security Council to impose a "no-fly zone" to help protect Libyans from Qaddafi air attacks. Within a few days the Security Council passed Resolution 1973 authorizing not only no-fly zones but "all necessary measures . . . to protect civilians and civilian populated areas under threat of attack" in Libya, with the only specific prohibition being of "a foreign occupation force." With this resolution as multilateral legitimization, NATO pledging to take on the largest military burden, and Arab countries such as Qatar and the United Arab Emirates quietly agreeing to join the coalition, the U.S. initiated the military action and played a significant but not singular role in the operation. Multilateral military action ended in October 2011 following Qaddafi's capture and killing by Libyan rebel forces.

While not nearly as controversial as the 2003 Iraq War, the Libyan intervention did engender debate. President Obama stressed the Principles at stake in preventing mass atrocities (see "At the Source," p. 305). Proponents, including neoconservatives and liberal interventionists in the bipartisan mix, made a Principles-Peace-Power case, emphasizing the values at stake in preventing mass atrocities, averting potentially destabilizing spillover to other Arab countries, and showing U.S. leadership. Opponents questioned whether vital interests were in fact at stake even with the humanitarian concerns, warned against overextension with the continuing Iraq and Afghanistan wars and the budget crisis, and saw too much uncertainty in a post-Qaddafi Libya, which might pose its own threats.

Beyond the particulars of the Libya case, what precedents did it set for invoking R2P in other cases where mass atrocities were threatened or perpetrated? Syria, for example, came right on the heels of the Libya intervention, with President Bashar Assad and his regime inflicting mass atrocities on the Syrian people. Yet even measures short of military intervention were blocked in the UN Security Council by Russia. The Obama administration provided some assistance to Assad's opposition, as did numerous other countries through a coalition called the Friends of Syria, but it stopped short of military intervention. As of early 2013 the situation in Syria continued to worsen. The death toll kept mounting. The flow of refugees was in the hundreds of thousands. Concerns heightened about escalation to the use of chemical weapons. Risks of spreading to a regional conflict were increasing. The implications for R2P, among other considerations, remain to be seen.

DRONES AND REMOTE-CONTROLLED WAR　Before 9/11, the American military had less than two hundred drones, or unmanned aerial vehicles (UAVs), with both surveillance and attack capabilities in its arsenal. A decade later it had more than 7,000, with

AT THE SOURCE

AT THE SOURCE

AN OBAMA DOCTRINE?

In his March 28, 2011 television address announcing U.S. military action in Libya, President Obama also articulated a broader argument about when and why the United States should use military force:

It's true that America cannot use our military force wherever repression occurs. And given the costs and risks of intervention, we must always measure our interests against the need for action. But that cannot be an argument for never acting on behalf of what's right. In this particular country—Libya—at this particular moment, we were faced with the prospect of violence on a horrific scale. We had a unique ability to stop that violence: an international mandate for action, a broad coalition prepared to join us, the support of Arab countries, and a plea for help from the Libyan people themselves. We also had the ability to stop Qaddafi's forces in their tracks without putting American troops on the ground. To brush aside America's responsibility as a leader and—more profoundly—our responsibilities to our fellow human beings under such circumstances would have been a betrayal of who we are.

Source: www.whitehouse.gov/photos-and-video/video/2011/03/28/president-obama-s-speech-libya.

names like Predator and Global Hawk. The Bush administration and even more so the Obama administration used drones both in the Iraq and Afghanistan wars and in counterterrorism operations in Pakistan, Yemen, Somalia, and elsewhere. Indeed, the Air Force is now training more pilots for the remote operation of drones than for manning fighter and bomber planes.

Proponents of drones stress both their effectiveness and justification. They see drone attacks as having the benefits of preemption in acting early but doing so on a limited scale that avoids the massive troop commitments and other aspects of the Bush Doctrine used in the Iraq case. Drones have taken out key terrorist leaders in other countries such as Baitullah Mehsud, commander of the Pakistani Taliban, and Anwar al-Awlaki, a radical cleric whose videos and Web site called for anti-American terrorism, in Yemen. Drone strikes run much lower risks of U.S. casualties than ground operations and even air strikes by manned aircraft. And they are justified both under domestic law, tracing back to the language in Congress's post-9/11 Authorization for the Use of Military Force that gave the president broad powers to combat terrorism around the world, and international law, including the right to self-defense. All told, drones are "legal, ethical and wise," according to John O. Brennan, the top counterterrorism official in Obama's first term and CIA Director in his second term.[48]

Critics raise counterpoints on all these grounds. Whatever the strategic gains from killing terrorist leaders and disrupting their operations, there have been greater costs and consequences from civilian casualties and resentments over sovereignty violations, especially in Pakistan. "When a U.S. drone missile kills a child in Yemen," a Yemeni lawyer warned on Twitter, "the father will go to war with you, guaranteed. Nothing to do with Al Qaeda."[49] The legal justifications both within the U.S. Constitution and international law have been called into question, both generally and in cases such as Awlaki, who, whatever he did or said, was an American citizen. Moreover, beyond the cases at hand, in a world where others are developing their own drone programs—China, Russia, India, Pakistan, Iran, Israel and over 40 other countries, as well as terrorist groups—the very claims being made and precedents being set may be used by others to justify their own interests and security.

Drones are now a multibillion-dollar industry, and with backpack-sized or even micro-drones within technological reach (and not just for states or organized terrorist groups but also super-empowered individuals), this is another use-of-force issue that is here to stay.

COUNTERTERRORISM SPECIAL OPERATIONS   Along with drones, U.S. strategy turned increasingly to special operations against terrorists. Special ops forces such as Navy SEALs (Sea, Air, Land), Army Green Berets, Air Force Special Tactics, and CIA operatives were used not only in the Afghanistan and Iraq wars but also more widely. The most famous Special Ops operation was the May 2011 killing of Osama bin Laden in Pakistan. An estimated 12,000 Special Ops forces are deployed on an ongoing basis around the world. They are called on for particular missions and to provide training to foreign militaries and security forces. "Out was any talk of a land invasion in the name of counterterrorism," as national security journalists Thom Shanker and Eric Schmitt write. "In was the concept of small military deployments for quick and violent unilateral action, if required, [as well as] work alongside allies and partners to contain terrorist threats within their borders, before they could become a transnational threat to American interests."[50]

Critics have raised a number of concerns about these "shadow wars." While giving credit for strategies that "respond to changing threats with creativity and agility," former Obama Pentagon official and Georgetown law professor Rosa Brooks sees problems in the lack of transparency and accountability to congressional oversight, media inquiry, and civil liberties protection. She also points out how the lines between the military and the intelligence community "have gotten fuzzy," with the CIA conducting military operations to an unprecedented extent.[51] The need for counterterrorism is likely to continue, and issues of foreign policy strategy and foreign policy politics will, if anything, grow more complex.

Nuclear Deterrence

Nuclear deterrence, a centerpiece of U.S. foreign policy during the Cold War, remains important but is less central than during that era. "Nuclear weapons now play a smaller role in our national security strategy than at any point during the nuclear era," a top Clinton administration official stated. Still, as another strategist put it, "having the most powerful weapons and deterrent plays an essential role."[52]

How much is enough? How much is too much? The Strategic Arms Reduction Treaties (START) between the United States and Russia have continued to reduce both countries' nuclear arsenals. While the 2010 START treaty calls for 50 percent reductions in nuclear missile launchers by 2017, even this leaves each side with more than 1,500 deployed long-range nuclear warheads and large numbers in reserve. Calls for deeper cuts have not just come from "doves." In a joint op-ed in the *Wall Street Journal*, former Secretaries of State Henry Kissinger and George Shultz, former Defense Secretary William Perry, and former Senate Armed Services Committee Chairman Sam Nunn called for significantly deeper cuts and a move toward "a world free of nuclear weapons."[53] Other former officials and nuclear strategy experts have been working along similar lines through Global Zero, a bipartisan coalition.[54] Jonathan Schell, whose 1988 book *The Fate of the Earth* raised concerns about nuclear war at a particularly tense period of the Cold War, has continued to stress the "singularity" of nuclear weapons. "Their singularity, from a moral point of view, lies in the fact that the use of just a few would carry the user beyond every historical benchmark of indiscriminate mass slaughter."[55] A budget argument also is made, with estimated savings of over $125 billion in the coming years, for cuts deeper than those agreed to but still short of nuclear abolition.[56]

On the other hand, many analysts share the concern that while the Soviet/Russian threat has subsided, threats from nuclear proliferation to states such as North Korea and possibly Iran, or potentially to terrorists, have increased. "Unlike the Cold War," President Bush stated in early 2001, pre-9/11, "today's most urgent threats stem not from thousands of ballistic missiles in Soviet hands, but from a small number of missiles in the hands of [the world's least responsible] states—states for whom terror and blackmail are a way of life."[57] This was the basis for pushing forward on missile defense. Weren't the risks of nuclear deterrence failing even greater with rogue states and terrorists, missile defense proponents argued, than with the Soviet Union? Spending on missile defense increased dramatically in the G.W. Bush years. The Obama administration, while less supportive, still moved programs along.

Three issues have continued to define the missile defense debate:

- Technological effectiveness: Will the system work? Tests over the years have been mixed at best. Recent technological developments have widened the range of viable missile defense systems and improved the effectiveness of existing models, but they are still well short of full certainty. There isn't much margin for misses—even "just one" nuclear weapon getting through would wreak mass destruction.

■ Cost: About $160 billion has been spent in the thirty years since missile defense got its big push in the early Reagan administration. With pressures for overall defense budget cuts, the "how much is enough, how much too much" question takes on added significance.

■ Strategic effectiveness. Even if the system works technologically, will it contribute to security? On the affirming side are arguments about the unreliability of traditional nuclear deterrence doctrine against states such as North Korea and Iran, and Al Qaeda and other terrorist groups. On the doubting side are arguments about countermeasures that would likely be pursued to get around whatever protection missile defense provides.

Terrorism Deterrence

As noted above, part of the rationale for the emphasis on preemption was the belief that deterrence does not work against terrorism. "Traditional conceptions of deterrence will not work against a terrorist enemy whose avowed tactics are wanton destruction and the targeting of innocents," was how the Bush _2002 National Security Strategy_ put it.[58] This was essentially saying that the core strategic concept of the Cold War era did not apply to the post-9/11 era. But as scholars, policy analysts, and others continued efforts to adapt deterrence to terrorism threats, a "new deterrence" emerged that, while not precluding other elements, became part of the overarching counterterrorism strategy. True, terrorists did not have a capital city that could be targeted for retaliation. But there were other ways to create deterrence by denial and deterrence by punishment. Costs could be credibly threatened against assets such as personal glory and reputation, support among Muslim populations, network cohesion and dependability, and financial assets that could be frozen and disrupted. Their calculus of chances of success could be reduced. Diplomacy, economic sanctions, the Internet and other communications techniques, and various other instruments of power would be brought into the counterterrorism strategy along with the military and intelligence ones. As one strategist put it,

> the stereotype and monolithic image of the guy with the suicide bomb on his back isn't the only type of actor in a terrorist network. It is far-flung; it is multifaceted and multifunctional. Almost every actor has something they value. And if the U.S. and its coalition partners can put those things that those actors value at risk in some way, then you have the beginnings of a deterrence approach.[59]

The _2006 National Security Strategy_ reflected this developing strategic thinking: "A new deterrence calculus combines the need to deter terrorists and supporters from contemplating a WMD [weapons of mass destruction] attack and, failing that, to dissuade them from actually conducting an attack."[60] It continued in the Obama administration. "Though terrorists are difficult to deter directly," the *2011 National Military Strategy* stated, "they may make cost/benefit calculations and are dependent on states and other stakeholders we are capable of influencing."[61]

Defense Budget and Overall Global Strategy

Defense budget cuts were the trend for the first decade or so of the post–Cold War era. From a peak of $304 billion in fiscal year (FY) 1989, the defense budget fell to $264 billion in FY 1996, a 13 percent decline. In the last years of the Clinton administration, the trend line shifted as defense spending started increasing again, although by small amounts. September 11 and the war on terrorism first brought major increases. The FY 2003 defense budget reached $405 billion. The Iraq War then pushed it up even higher, to over $660 billion in the last year of the Bush administration. The budget increased again in the first two years of the Obama administration, reaching $768 billion (FY 2011) before decreasing with the end of the Iraq War, the drawdown in Afghanistan, and cuts in the overall federal budget as part of deficit reduction.

Part of the debate concerns how to interpret statistics such as these. By some measures spending seems too high, by others it is arguably too low. Two comparisons are especially pertinent on the "too high" side. The first is U.S. defense spending over time. The FY 2003 defense budget of $405 billion was more than double the defense budget of the early Reagan years, one of the tensest times of the Cold War. The 2012 defense budget was over 82 percent greater than FY 2003 in nominal dollars and 40 percent greater in constant dollars (i.e., controlled for inflation). We can also compare America's defense budget with those of other major powers. Figure 7.1 shows how much higher U.S. defense spending is than other major power; indeed, the United States accounts for over 40 percent of world military spending and spends more than the next twenty nations combined.

Those on the "not enough" side have their own statistical interpretations. The Cold War comparisons need to be corrected for inflation. When that is done, FY 2003 spending is only 9 percent more than that of 1982, and 2007 spending is just 14 percent more than that of 1960. A further measurement supporting this view is defense spending as a percentage of the total federal budget and of the gross domestic product (GDP). Here we see actual declines: the FY 1982 figures, for example, are 25 percent of the federal budget and 5.7 percent of GDP, whereas the FY 2003 figures amount to only 18 percent of the federal budget and 3.5 percent of GDP. Even the 2009 peak of defense spending, at about 5.8 percent GDP, is less than 1989 (6.4 percent). Proponents of higher defense spending also point to China and the rapid rate of its increase in military spending.

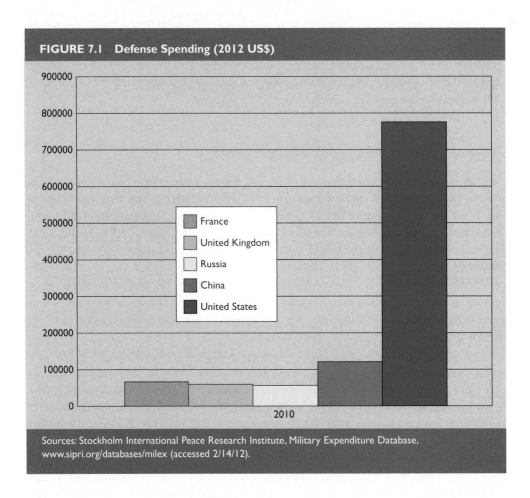

FIGURE 7.1   Defense Spending (2012 US$)

Sources: Stockholm International Peace Research Institute, Military Expenditure Database, www.sipri.org/databases/milex (accessed 2/14/12).

Whatever the defense-budget issue, pork-barrel politics often intrudes. One member of Congress slipped $250,000 into the defense budget for a study of a caffeinated chewing gum that might help sleep-deprived troops—and that is manufactured by a company in his district. Another added $5 million for retrofitting locks used on classified documents to meet stricter specifications—as manufactured by (you guessed it!) a company in his district. As Defense Secretary Robert Gates put it in 2011, the post-9/11 "no questions asked funding requests" fed into a wasteful bureaucratic "semi-feudal system—an amalgam of fiefdoms without centralized mechanisms to allocate resources."[62]

A further dimension of the debate is about whether less should be spent on defense and more on diplomacy. As of 2008, as noted earlier, there were more musicians in military bands than diplomats in the foreign service. The 7,000 soldiers that the army was estimated to add constituted more personnel than the entire existing foreign service. More than 1,100 additional foreign service officers could be hired for the cost of one C-17 military cargo plane.[63] Admiral Michael Mullen, at the time chairman of the Joint Chiefs of Staff, called for

> a whole-of-government approach to solving modern problems; that we need to reallocate roles and resources in a way that places our military as an equal among many in government. . . . If we are truly to cut oxygen from the fire of violent extremism, we must leverage every single aspect of national power—soft and hard. . . . [We need] a comprehensive approach, from diplomacy, to foreign assistance, to building partnership capacity, to building partners.[64]

Notwithstanding such statements, the DOD budget remains more than ten times greater than the State Department's.

Another part of the debate addresses the "how" and "where" of overall global defense strategy. For decades during the Cold War and its immediate aftermath, U.S. military strategy was based on the ability to fight "two-and-a-half wars" simultaneously. American forces in all their aspects—size, force, structure, deployment, weaponry—were to be maintained at levels and capabilities sufficient to pose a strong enough deterrent to prevent wars, and if necessary fight and win them. But with the lessons of the Iraq and Afghanistan wars in mind, Defense Secretary Robert Gates bluntly spoke to the "how": "Any future defense secretary who advises the president to again send a big American land army into Asia or into the Middle East or Africa should have his head examined."[65] Along these lines, the Obama defense budgets began shifting resources away from conventional warfare and traditional weapons systems such as bombers, large naval ships, and certain army combat vehicles systems, and toward intelligence and surveillance equipment, special forces, and other aspects of irregular warfare and counterinsurgency training. "The budget moves the needle closer to irregular warfare and counterinsurgency," a Pentagon spokesman said. But "it is not an abandonment of the need to prepare for conventional conflicts."[66] Where exactly that needle should be—has it gone too far toward irregular warfare? not far enough?—continues to be contested in strategic terms and on political grounds.

On the question of "where?" there was much talk of a "pivot" to Asia. This reflected rising concern about China (Chapter 10). But even with the end of the Iraq and Afghanistan wars, the Middle East remains highly unstable (Chapter 11). It could be given less relative emphasis than during the Iraq and Afghanistan wars, but would still require significant attention and resources. So, too, with other regions such as Africa, where a whole new military command (AFRICOM) had been established and security threats such as terrorism (including Al Qaeda affiliates), civil wars, mass atrocities, and piracy required their own attention and resources. Defense strategy could have its relative priorities and be pursued with appropriate budget cuts, but it still had to be global.

Cybersecurity

In 2010 the Pentagon announced that cyberspace had become "a new domain of warfare." Along with the different command structures for different regions of the world—for example, Southern Command for Latin America, Pacific Command for Asia—a new Cyber Command was created to protect the military's computer and communications systems. Hacking into the presumed-to-be-secure National Security Agency, the lead electronic surveillance intelligence agency, had been uncovered in 2008. While this incident was neutralized, when a top official asked when security would be assuredly restored, "we had to break the news to him," said one expert, "that this is never going to pass."[67]

Nor was this just about military computer systems. With day-to-day operations of public utilities, transportation, communications, banking, schools, and businesses large and small computerized and operating in cyberspace, society has become increasingly vulnerable to weapons of mass *disruption*. Attacks could come from a range of sources—terrorists, other states, or thrill-seeking hackers. According to the *2012 National Preparedness Report* there was a 650 percent increase in the number of reported cyberattacks in the United States between 2006 and 2010. The "next Pearl Harbor," Defense Secretary Leon Panetta warned, "could very well be a cyberattack that cripples our power systems, our grid, our security systems, our financial systems."[68] And while it was clear that the bombers attacking Pearl Harbor came from Japan, cyberattacks are hard to trace. Hackers can hide their identities. They may be countries, terrorist organizations, criminal gangs, or individual hackers. All this, and more, makes providing cybersecurity—and doing so while not violating citizens' rights to privacy or imposing undue costs and obstacles on normal cyber activity—very challenging.

For its part, the United States has reportedly used cyber-weapons offensively. In one notable case, the "Stuxnet" computer worm was used by the Bush and Obama administrations, along with Israel, against Iran to disrupt key machinery believed to be part of its nuclear weapons program. Proponents argued that this was a less risky strategy than a military attack, and that it might buy the time and change the calculations for diplomacy to succeed. Critics made an argument similar to the one against drones: that a dangerous precedent was being set that could come back to haunt the United States. Indeed, in early 2013, in what one security expert called "a bit of a grudge match," Iran hacked into numerous American bank computer networks.[69]

Peace

As we said in Chapter 1, while all of the national interest objectives are ultimately about Peace—that is what Power is supposed to safeguard, Prosperity to contribute to, Principles to undergird—we use it to stress diplomacy and the role of international institutions.

United Nations

UN proponents stress the institution's three unique strengths for closing or at least narrowing the globalization–global governance gap noted earlier. First is its near-global membership. Its inclusive membership makes the UN the one place where representatives of all the world's states regularly meet. As Gareth Evans, a former Australian foreign minister, put it, "[T]he world needs a center. . . . The United Nations is the only credible candidate."[70] Second, the UN Security Council (UNSC) continues to hold the international community's ultimate "seals of approval and disapproval."[71] Its resolutions are particularly important in legitimizing and mobilizing broad support for coercive measures (uses of force, sanctions) against aggressors, human rights violators, or other offending states. Third is the scope of UN programs, geared to the full global agenda, including not only peace but also economic development, the environment, human rights, and public health. Although crises such as those in Somalia, Bosnia, and Iraq get the most publicity, arguably the most meaningful work the UN does is in seeking, as stated in its Charter, "to employ international machinery for the promotion of the economic and social advancement of all peoples." It does this through specialized agencies and programs, such as UNICEF (United Nations Children's Fund), WHO (World Health Organization) and UNHCR (Office of the United Nations High Commissioner for Refugees). Susan E. Rice, the Obama administration's UN ambassador, sought to strike a balance in calling the UN

> an indispensable, if imperfect, institution. [Its diplomacy] can be slow, frustrating, complex and imperfect. . . . The UN is not a cure-all; we must be clear-eyed about the problems, challenges and frustrations of the institution. But it is a global institution that can address a tremendous range of critical American and global interests. . . . Around the world, the United Nations is performing vital, and in many areas life-saving, services. . . . Achieving the backing of an institution that represents every country in the world can give added legitimacy and leverage to our actions and facilitate our efforts to garner broad support for our policy objectives.[72]

UN SECURITY COUNCIL EXPANSION[73]   The structure of the *UNSC* reflects the global balance of power at the end of World War II. The five permanent members are the United States, Russia (formerly the Soviet Union), the United Kingdom, France, and China (the seat was held by the Republic of China [Taiwan] until 1971, and since then has been held by the People's Republic of China). In addition to their permanent seats, these states also have the power to veto any UNSC action. Ten other UNSC seats rotate among countries for two-year terms and do not carry the veto.

In recent years questions have been raised as to whether this World War II–era structure is outdated. Brian Urquhart, the former undersecretary general of the United Nations, called for a UNSC which "represent[s] the world as it is . . . not the world as it was in 1945."[74] Three main issues have been raised: Should the Security Council enlarge and add more permanent members? If so, which states? Which new members, if any, should have veto rights?

Positions are wide-ranging. To "make that body [the Security Council] more democratic, legitimate and representative," President Luiz Inácio Lula da Silva of Brazil contended, "the expansion of the Security Council must envisage the entry of developing countries as permanent members."[75] With his country's substantial financial contributions in mind, Prime Minister Junichiro Koizumi of Japan argued, "We believe that the role that Japan has played provides a solid basis for its assumption of permanent membership on the Security Council."[76] Prime Minister Manmohan Singh of India has argued his country's case on the basis of India's large population, saying that "the voice of the world's largest democracy surely cannot be left unheard on the Security Council when the United Nations is being restructured."[77] Aminu Bashir Wali, Nigeria's UN ambassador, argued, "We [Nigeria] have a track record [of doing] a lot in terms of peace and security, and we have exhibited our own commitment to the peace and security in the world. . . . Nigeria is definitely qualified."[78]

In 2005 a task force that included prominent members from the United States, other existing UNSC members, and many candidate countries was asked to come up with a proposal to put to the full UN membership. Yet even the task force could not settle on one proposal. Brent Scowcroft, the U.S. national security advisor under presidents Gerald Ford and George H. W. Bush and a UN task force member, said "for every country that people think yes, this is a power that should get it . . . Japan, Brazil, India and so forth, there are those around it who think no, it shouldn't get in."[79] The official U.S. position has been "that the long-term legitimacy and viability of the United Nations Security Council depends on its reflecting the world of the 21st century."[80] But it has not been more specific. The Obama administration did come out in favor of a permanent seat for India. But it has hedged on Brazil and others. Moreover, it is not just a U.S. decision. Regional rivalries come into play, such as those between Brazil and Argentina, China and Japan, and Nigeria and South Africa.

UN PEACE OPERATIONS   The UN had undertaken only thirteen peacekeeping missions prior to 1988, but since then more than fifty-three new missions have been initiated. The number of UN peacekeeping troops shot up from 9,570 in 1988 to 73,393 in 1994.

INTERNATIONAL PERSPECTIVES
INTERNATIONAL PERSPECTIVES

WHO PROVIDES TROOPS FOR UN PEACE OPERATIONS?

For all the peacekeeping and related missions around the world, who is providing the troops? A total of 114 countries contribute forces to UN peace operations. The top 10 countries are:

Bangladesh	8,781
Pakistan	8,216
India	7,840
Ethiopia	6,498
Nigeria	5,463
Nepal	4,462
Rwanda	3,705
Jordan	3,507
Egypt	3,095
Ghana	2,809

Source: United Nations, Ranking of Military and Policy Contributions to UN Operations, 29 Feb 2012, www.un.org/en/peacekeeping/contributors/2013/jan13_1 (accessed 4/8/13).

These numbers dropped for a few years as some peacekeeping missions were brought to a close. But they have been climbing, with more than 93,000 peacekeepers on fifteen missions in 2013. Similarly, UN peacekeeping budgets, as low as $230 million in the late 1980s, are now close to $8 billion.

While the United States pays a significant share of the peace operations budget, other countries provide the troops. Contrary to what many believe, the United States ranks 110th in the number of military troops and police provided for UN peacekeeping missions. Of the 93,244 military troops and police deployed in the fifteen UN peace operations (as of January 2013), only 117 were American. A total of 118 countries contribute forces to UN peace operations. The "International Perspectives" box above lists the top 10.

Amid the controversies over more recent failures such as Somalia and Bosnia, the UN's peacekeeping successes are often forgotten. Indeed, its record was so strong that the UN Peacekeeping Forces received the 1988 Nobel Peace Prize. The core problem has been the difference in missions between peacekeeping and peace operations. Most of the "first-generation" UN successes were situations in which the UN forces were brought in after the parties had agreed to the terms of peace, and with the consent of those parties, to ensure and facilitate the keeping of that peace; i.e., peacekeeping. Rules of engagement for peacekeeping forces are neutral and impartial: to use force only for their own self-defense, and not to interfere in the internal affairs of the parties. Cases such as Bosnia, though, were much more about peace*making* and peace *enforcing* in that the conflicts were still raging or under tenuous cease-fires, conditions in which traditional stratagems of impartiality and limited mission were not sufficient. There was no peace to be kept; it had to be imposed and enforced. To the extent that the parties had reached any agreements, they were but partial ones—holding actions, gambits, even outright deceptions. In such situations the UN's limited rules of engagement do not work very well; neutrality and impartiality can let aggressors off the hook.

Even so, there have been some successes, such as in Liberia in 2006 and Cote d'Ivoire in 2011. And some studies, such as one by the RAND Corporation, show the UN as more effective than the United States.[81] Still, the challenges posed by peace operations when the peace needs to be made and enforced, not just kept, have a long way to go to be met.

WMD Nonproliferation Regime

Nonproliferation regime refers to the treaties and international institutions seeking to prevent the **proliferation** of **weapons of mass destruction (WMD)**: nuclear, chemical and biological weapons.

NUCLEAR NONPROLIFERATION*   The first multilateral treaties preventing the proliferation of nuclear weapons began during the Cold War. In 1957 the **International Atomic Energy Agency (IAEA)** was created to ensure that, as nations develop nuclear energy, it would be used only for peaceful purposes such as nuclear power plants. In 1968 the UN General Assembly approved the **Nuclear Nonproliferation Treaty (NPT)**. The NPT allowed the five states that already had nuclear weapons—the United States, the Soviet Union, the United Kingdom, France, and China—to keep them. These states pledged to reduce their nuclear arsenals through arms-control agreements. All other states were prohibited from acquiring or developing nuclear weapons.

The NPT has had some success. Nearly 190 countries are part of it. Many fewer countries have nuclear weapons than likely would have without the NPT. But some countries have refused to sign it and have developed nuclear weapons. Among those are India and Pakistan, which successfully tested their nuclear weapons in 1998. Israel is widely believed to have

---

*Here we discuss the overall nuclear nonproliferation regime. Specific key cases are discussed in later chapters; North Korea in Chapter 10, Iran in Chapter 11.

nuclear weapons, although it has never officially stated so. Several other countries, including Iraq, North Korea, Libya, and Iran, signed the treaty but cheated on their commitments.

IAEA proponents stress that its legitimacy and relative impartiality make it the most effective institution for monitoring and actively working to combat nuclear weapons programs across the world. They cite the impact the IAEA had in cases such as Iraq in the 1990s and Iran more recently. Critics stress the limits inherent in the voluntary nature of the NPT regime and the consequent constraint of IAEA inspectors having to rely heavily on compliance and cooperation from the government of a suspected state, as well as the limits on available enforcement.

Efforts to limit nuclear testing began during the Cold War, most notably with the 1963 Limited Nuclear Test Ban Treaty. Negotiated by the United States, the Soviet Union, and the United Kingdom, and later signed by many other states, the Limited Test Ban Treaty prohibited nuclear testing in the atmosphere, underwater, and in outer space. These types of tests created the most radioactive fallout. The ban was limited, though, and still allowed underground testing and other exemptions. The CTBT is an effort to move further toward a total ban on nuclear testing.

As we discussed in Chapter 2, the failure of the Senate to ratify the CTBT in 1998 after President Clinton had signed it was among the worst foreign policy politics defeats since the rejection of Woodrow Wilson's Versailles Treaty. Although opposition to the CTBT remains, two factors may decrease it. One is the further technological advances that alleviate many of the earlier concerns about ensuring the functionality of nuclear stockpiles without necessitating actual nuclear tests. Second is the stronger linkage made by other countries between U.S. CTBT ratification and their willingness to support renewal and strengthening of the NPT. For example, the International Commission on Nuclear Nonproliferation was formed by the leaders of Japan, Australia, and other countries for "reinvigorating, at a high political level, awareness of the global need for nuclear nonproliferation and disarmament."[82]

The ***Proliferation Security Initiative (PSI)*** is a global coalition initiated by the G.W. Bush administration aimed at stopping trafficking of WMD, missiles and other delivery systems, and related materials to and from states and nonstate actors of concern. The PSI seeks to plug the holes in the NPT regime through intelligence sharing, interdiction (interception) operations, and other efforts. It was a PSI interdiction in 2003, for example, that revealed Muammar Qaddafi's efforts to build Libyan WMD. By 2012 the PSI coalition had grown to more than 90 nations.

The Nuclear Security Summit, initiated by President Obama in 2010, brought together the leaders of almost 50 nations for another set of WMD nonproliferation efforts, these principally geared to securing stockpiles of fissile material (highly enriched plutonium and other fuels and materials for nuclear bombs). While some progress has been made, estimates are that over 2 million kilograms (4.4 million pounds) of stockpiled weapons-grade nuclear material still exists, left over from decommissioned bombs and nuclear power plants. A terrorist would only need about 25 kilograms of highly enriched uranium or 8 kilograms of plutonium to make a nuclear bomb. Or, to put it another way, 100,000 new nuclear weapons could be made from the current supply of fissile material. A follow-up summit was held in Seoul, South Korea in March 2012, with an expanded number of nations and a broader agenda, including additional cooperative measures to counter the threat of nuclear terrorism.

CHEMICAL AND BIOLOGICAL NONPROLIFERATION   Many view chemical and biological weapons as even scarier than nuclear ones. One reason is that chemical and biological weapons are less expensive to produce—the "poor man's nuclear weapon," as some call them. Another is that the level of technology and military capability required for their use is much less sophisticated, so they are more accessible to terrorists. Americans experienced this in the weeks after the September 11 terrorist attacks, when anthrax-laden letters made people fearful of opening their mail. Even before this, in 1995 a cult called Aum Shinrikyo unleashed a chemical-weapons attack on a busy subway train in Tokyo. The cult had intended to kill millions of people. Although the actual death toll was limited, as a *New York Times* headline put it, the "Japanese Cult's Failed Germ Warfare Succeeded in Alerting the World."[83] Investigation of the cult found a veritable arsenal of chemical weapons, as well as labs equipped to produce lethal germs and bacteria for biological weapons.

The first major anti-chemical-weapons treaty, the Geneva Protocol, was negotiated in 1925. Its impetus was the battlefield use of chemical weapons (CW) in World War I by both sides. The Geneva Protocol prohibited the use of chemical weapons, although it did not prohibit their production or possession. Even so, chemical weapons were used subsequently—by Japan in Manchuria in the 1930s, by Italy in Ethiopia in 1935, by Egypt in Yemen in the 1960s, by both Iran and Iraq in their 1980–88 war, possibly by the Soviets in Afghanistan in their 1979–88 war, and by Iraq against its own Kurdish population in 1988. Over the course of the Cold War, both the United States and the Soviet Union built up large CW stockpiles. By the 1990s an estimated twenty other countries were believed to have chemical weapons.

The need for a new and stronger CW nonproliferation treaty was quite clear. The crucial step came with the Chemical Weapons Convention (CWC). After many years of negotiations, the CWC was completed in 1993 and came into force in 1997. As of 2012, 188 states were party to the CWC, with another two having signed but not yet ratified. The CWC bans the development, production, acquisition, stockpiling, trade, and use of chemical weapons; it calls, in effect, for the total elimination of chemical weapons. As such it has been called "the most ambitious treaty in the history of arms control."[84] It is farther-reaching than the NPT in three important respects. First, it applies to all states—no exceptions. No previous possessors are grandfathered in, as were the five major-power nuclear-weapons states in the NPT. All states are required to destroy all of their chemical weapons. Second, it has tougher and more intrusive enforcement provisions. It mandates short-notice, anytime, anywhere "challenge inspections" of sites where cheating is believed to be taking place. The Organization for the Prohibition of Chemical Weapons (OPCW) is the CWC's version of the IAEA, but it has greater authority. Third, states that do not join the treaty face automatic trade sanctions. This was a primary reason that most of the U.S. chemical industry, though not welcoming the additional regulations imposed by the CWC, calculated that American companies had more to lose if the United States was not part of the treaty and therefore supported it during the Senate ratification debate.

The key test of the CWC lies in whether these tough provisions work in practice. The challenge inspections provision remains intrusive in theory but has yet to be used in practice. A number of countries still are suspected of retaining undeclared chemical weapons stockpiles, including China, Egypt, Iran, Israel, North Korea, and Syria. Questions still remain as to whether Russia will fully follow through with eliminating its arsenal of 40,000 metric tons of chemical weapons. As with Russian "loose nukes," the concern is not only about official Russian policy but also terrorists and others gaining access to the weapons complex. The United States, which had the world's second-largest chemical weapons stockpile, still has yet to fully destroy its arsenal.

Biological weapons (also called germ warfare) have met with even less nonproliferation progress. The Biological and Toxin Weapons Convention of 1972 purported to ban them totally (development, production, stockpiling, acquisition, trade, use). Only 171 countries have signed on, and only 155 have ratified. Its monitoring, verification, and enforcement provisions and mechanisms are much weaker than those of the CWC/OPCW and the NPT/IAEA. Efforts to strengthen it have not made much progress. In mid-2001, negotiations broke up over whether the proposed changes in verification would be effective. One key issue is a greater inherent dual use issue that makes it tough to distinguish pharmaceutical or bioagricultural research from development of biological weapons. Blame for the lack of progress can be spread widely. Proposals for how to do better can be debated—keeping in mind that after months of research, interviews, and site visits, the Commission on the Prevention of Weapons of Mass Destruction assessed biological weapons to be even more of a threat than nuclear ones.[85]

International Criminal Court (ICC)

Following World War II, special international war-crimes tribunals were created to prosecute the Nazis (the Nuremberg trials) and Japanese military leaders. Nuremberg-like temporary war-crimes tribunals were set up in the 1990s to deal with atrocities committed during civil wars and ethnic conflicts in the former Yugoslavia and in Rwanda. In their wake, proposals to create a permanent International Criminal Court (ICC) gained increasing support.

The ICC was approved at a UN conference held in Rome in mid-1998. Very few countries voted against it, but the United States was one of them. Originally the Clinton administration had supported the idea of an ICC, calculating that a permanent international court would potentially enhance U.S. foreign policy in cases against aggressors, gross violators of human rights, and rogue states. It backed off, though, in part for substantive reasons but mostly for political ones. The ICC struck the chords of anti-multilateralism and leeriness about international law in American politics. The treaty would have to be ratified by the U.S. Senate, and the anticipated vote count came up well short of the two-thirds majority needed. In December 2000, just before leaving office, Clinton finally did sign the Rome Treaty, albeit far too late for him to begin a ratification process in the Senate.

The Bush administration was clear, quick, and blunt in its opposition to the ICC. Soon after taking office the administration announced that it was holding the treaty back and not sending it to the Senate. Then in May 2002 it officially rescinded the U.S. signature. The timing was deliberate: the previous month, the sixtieth country in the world had ratified the ICC treaty, the number necessary for the treaty to enter into force. As of early 2013, 121 nations had joined the ICC.

ICC proponents make three main arguments. First is that the ICC is the "missing link" in the international justice system to help achieve "justice for all," and especially deal with perpetrators of genocide, war crimes, and other crimes against humanity. The existing International Court of Justice in The Hague deals only with cases between states, not individuals. The ad hoc tribunals have had some impact but are subject to delays, uncertainties, and other deficiencies. The ICC also claims jurisdiction when national criminal-justice institutions are unwilling or unable to act. "In the prospect of an international criminal court," stated then-Secretary-General Kofi Annan, "lies the promise of universal justice."[86]

Second, the ICC can help strengthen peace processes and promote conflict resolution. Negotiators have at their disposal an array of policy instruments and incentives and disincentives in seeking cease-fires and peace settlements for conflicts that already are raging. Their hand will be strengthened if they can provide assurances to all sides that once they have laid down their arms, justice will be even-handed. This means both prosecuting those whose actions warrant it and protecting the innocent from vengeful and other politically charged prosecutions. Ideally, states should be able to create their own process of justice. In war-torn situations, though, that ideal often is not achievable, at least in the near term. As an international body, the ICC has the standing and credibility to provide the necessary assurances and thus help move peace processes along.

Third, the existence of the ICC will deter future war criminals and other aggressors. To quote the UN: "Most perpetrators of such atrocities have believed that their crimes would go unpunished. . . . Once it is clear that the international community will no longer tolerate such monstrous acts without assigning responsibility and meting out appropriate punishment—to heads of State and commanding officers as well as to the lowliest soldiers in the field or militia recruits—it is hoped that those who would incite a genocide; embark on a campaign of ethnic cleansing; murder, rape and brutalize civilians caught in armed conflict; or use children for barbarous medical experiments will no longer find willing helpers. . . . Effective deterrence is a primary objective of the International Criminal Court."[87]

Opponents make three main points. The first rejects the ICC's claim to jurisdiction over Americans on U.S. constitutional grounds. They argue that the U.S. Constitution prohibits the U.S. government from consenting to judicial proceedings against American citizens by any courts other than American ones. As stated by John Negroponte, then the Bush administration's ambassador to the United Nations, "An American judge [has] the legal and moral right, founded in our Constitution and in democratic procedures, to jail an American. But the International Criminal Court does not operate in the same democratic and constitutional context, and therefore does not have that right to deprive Americans of their freedom."[88]

Second is the concern that U.S. soldiers and diplomats, NGO workers, and others may be subjected to politically motivated charges and prosecutions. "We're the ones who respond when the world dials 911," another opponent stated, "and if you want us to keep responding you should accommodate our views."[89] The Bush administration pushed legislation through Congress linking American military aid to recipient countries that agreed to sign an exemption from ICC jurisdiction for American soldiers. Many countries resisted signing such agreements as a matter of principle, even at the risk of losing their military aid. Yet the issue remained a fundamental one for ICC opponents.

Third, some question the claim to deterrence for the ICC.[90] When so many perpetrators of ethnic cleansing and genocide are never charged, and when the prosecution of others takes so long, how strong a deterrent effect can the ICC have? To deter those who would commit war crimes, the potential consequences of such actions have to be severe and probable. In the eyes of opponents, the ad hoc tribunals have not measured up, and the ICC is not likely to, either.

Regional Organizations

As Table 7.1 shows, every region of the world has one or more regional multilateral organizations dealing with peace and security (as well as trade and other economic issues). Some were established during the Cold War, others more recently. The United States is a member of many but not all.

While some of these regional organizations are stronger than others, in almost every case they have been playing larger roles in the post–Cold War world. In later chapters we discuss each in its regional context. Here we stress three reasons for the overall pattern of stronger regional organizations.

TABLE 7.1 Major Regional Organizations

Europe
European Union (EU)*
Organization for Security and Cooperation in Europe (OSCE)

Asia
East Asia Summit **
Association of South East Asian States (ASEAN) *
ASEAN Regional Forum

Eurasia
Shanghai Cooperation Organization (SCO) *, **

Middle East
Arab League *

Africa
African Union (AU)*

Western Hemisphere
Organization of American States (OAS)
Union of South American Nations (UNASUR) *, **

Key:
*United States not a member
**Created after the Cold War

First, the sources of instability now tend to be more regionally rooted than globally trans- mitted. During the Cold War, much of the world's instability was connected to the global geopolitics of U.S.-Soviet bipolarity. In the post–Cold War era, instability tends to be more rooted in regional issues and rivalries. This has been true in the Balkans, in the Caucasus and other parts of the former Soviet Union, in Africa, in the Middle East, and in East Asia.

Second, there is increasing recognition of the interconnection between regional secu- rity and domestic instability. Ethnic conflicts, civil wars and other conflicts that start out as internal problems can draw in regional states, spread across borders, set off massive refugee migrations, and emanate other "contagion" effects.

Third, given these regional roots and effects, there is both more motivation and more need for direct cooperation among regional states themselves than in the past. On the one hand, this does mean that countries and regions must confront long histories of rivalry and even hatred. On the other hand, there can be common cultural ties, shared economic interests, and other relationships on which to try to build regional security institutions.

Preventive Diplomacy

The basic logic of preventive diplomacy seems unassailable. Act early to prevent disputes from escalating or problems from worsening.[91] Reduce tensions that, if intensified, could lead to war. Deal with today's conflicts before they become tomorrow's crises. Preventive diplomacy follows the same logic as preventive medicine: don't wait until the cancer has spread or the arteries are fully clogged. Or, as the auto mechanic says in a familiar television commercial, as he holds an oil filter in one hand and points to a seized-up engine with the other, "Pay me now or pay me later."

In one sense, preventive diplomacy involves getting at problems that are at the root of violent conflict. Economic development is one possible strategy. It is going too far to say that poverty is consistently a main cause of violent conflict. "If it were," as Gareth Evans writes, "the world, with a billion people still living on around a dollar a day, would be much more alarmingly violent than it is now." But, Evans continues, "there is every reason to accept that economic decline, low income and high unemployment are contributing conditions, either directly by fueling grievances among particular disadvantaged or excluded groups, or indirectly by reducing the relevant opportunity costs of joining a violent rebellion—or quite probably both."[92] Similar points pertain to environmental degradation. In instances where arable land, water supply and other resources are depleted, environmental issues contribute to violent conflict. In other instances, environmental issues are less of a factor in violent conflict, although are of concern in their own right, as we will see in Chapter 8.

Another aspect is that certain international strategies that may have been effective at lower levels of conflict are less likely to be so amid intensified violence. One reason for this is the classic problem of statecraft that the more extensive the objectives, the greater and usually more coercive are the strategies needed to achieve them. Consistent with both Thomas Schelling's deterrence/compellence distinction and Alexander George's work on coercive diplomacy, preventing a conflict from escalating to violence is a more limited objective than ending violence once it has begun.[93] The violence can become so indiscriminate that even humanitarian NGOs are in danger. In 2008, 260 aid workers were attacked and 122 killed while trying to carry out their work, with the highest rates in Somalia, Afghanistan, and Sudan. In this very crucial sense, options do *not* necessarily stay open. A problem can get harder down the road. When you wait, you may see a much more difficult problem than you did at first.

This point also has implications for the theory of *"ripeness."* As developed by William Zartman and others, this is an important and powerful theory.[94] The central idea is that at certain points in the life cycle of conflicts, they are more conducive to possible resolution than at others. When a situation is not "ripe," as determined in large part by the extent to which the parties to the conflict are disposed even to consider an agreement seriously, international strategies have much less chance of succeeding. But although ripeness theory is helpful in counseling prudent assessments of when and where to engage so as not to overestimate the chances of success, it sometimes gets interpreted and applied in ways that underestimate the risks and costs of waiting. Natural processes do not work in only one direction; they can move toward ripening but also toward "rotting." Crops can be left in the fields too long, as well as harvested too early; intervention may come too early, but a conflict also can deteriorate over time, grow worse, or become too far advanced.

Putting severely shattered societies back together again is enormously difficult, hugely expensive, very risky—and, very occassionally, just not possible. It is a problem, to draw again on Bill Zartman's expressive language, of "putting Humpty-Dumpty together again."[95] We have seen this situation in Somalia, where over twenty years after the UN and U.S. interventions, governments keep falling; in Haiti, where extreme poverty and political instability persist; in Bosnia, where two decades after the 1995 Dayton Accords ended the war, ethnic tensions still run high and stability is shaky; and in the Democratic Republic of Congo (DRC), where death tolls mounted even higher than in Rwanda as a consequence of both its own conflicts and the spillover from Rwanda.

In some instances, membership in international organizations has been used as preventive diplomacy leverage. The lure of membership and its benefits can be incentives for avoiding mass violence; and once a member, a country would be socialized and assisted into better domestic governance practices. This strategy has been most effective in Europe, where first the prospect and then the practice of membership in the European Union, NATO, and other organizations has helped countries such as Latvia, Hungary, and Romania manage their ethnic tensions short of mass violence.[96]

To be sure, all of these policies have difficulties. None come with guarantees. But progress has been made. According to the *Human Security Report 2012* there are fewer armed conflicts today than two decades ago.[97] Attacks on civilians in 2009 were lower than any year since 1989, the first year for which data are available. While there was a slight increase in death tolls over the previous year, the total was still much lower than back in the mid-1990s. As this report further elaborates:

> Most of today's conflict episodes are relatively short; long-lasting conflicts are increasingly the exception rather than the rule. Persistent conflicts are often very small in scale, and the higher rates of recurrence of conflict result in large part because conflicts have become more difficult to win—but not necessarily more difficult to resolve. An increasing proportion of conflicts is terminated by negotiated settlements, the majority of which prevent the recurrence of violence. We further find that even when peace deals collapse, the death toll due to subsequent fighting is dramatically reduced.[98]

Moreover, as difficult as preventive diplomacy is, the onset of mass violence transforms the nature of a conflict. A Rubicon is crossed, on the other side of which resolution and even limitation of the conflict are that much more difficult. A former Croatian militiaman who later turned himself in reflected on his own killing of seventy-two civilians and command of a death camp. "The most difficult thing is to ignite a house or kill a man for the first time," he stated, "but afterward even this becomes routine."[99] Adding revenge and retribution to other sources of tension plunges a conflict situation to a fundamentally different and more difficult depth. None of these conflicts would ever have been easy to resolve, but after all the killings, the rapes, the other war crimes, the tasks were vastly harder.

Conclusion: Power, Peace, and Strength from Within

This chapter has provided an overview of two of the key elements of U.S. grand strategy for this new era, Power and Peace. As in the past, some aspects are complementary, conducive to both aspects of the national interest being pursued, while some are more in tension, requiring trade-offs and prioritization.

While the focus of this book is foreign policy, global influence and national security also require robust and dynamic domestic foundations. There are vulnerabilities that are less about what other states seek to do to the United States than what it does or doesn't do for itself. Yet mustering this "strength from within" is proving to be a more formidable challenge than ever before.

For much of its history the United States either sat apart from or atop the world. While not as isolationist as often depicted, insulated by the oceans and blessed by a richly endowed land, it was able to selectively engage with the outside world, competing when and where it chose well into the twentieth century. During the Cold War, the United States was dominant by most every measure—economically, technologically, diplomatically, politically, and ideologically. Today, though, with insulation stripped away amidst globalization, it no longer stands apart. And with dominance chipped away by the diffusion of power and shifts in economic dynamism, it doesn't sit atop the world. This challenge has to be met without resorting to neo-isolationism: strength from within is about projecting out, not walling in. Nor will protectionism or other lashing out help: it's a matter of strengthening oneself, not weakening others; internally generating benefits, not externally imposing costs.

Notes

[1]Charles Krauthammer, "The Unipolar Moment," *Foreign Affairs* 70 (1990); Krauthammer, "The Unipolar Moment Revisited," *The National Interest* 70 (Winter 2002–2003): 5–17.

[2]Stephen G. Brooks and William Wohlforth, "American Primacy in Perspective," *Foreign Affairs* 81.4 (July/August 2002): 23.

[3]Excerpts from "Pentagon's Plan: 'Prevent the Re-Emergence of a New Rival," *New York Times*, March 8, 1992 (emphasis added).

[4]Robert J. Lieber, *The American Era: Power and Strategy for the 21st Century* (New York: Cambridge University Press, 2005), 5. See also William Wohlforth, "The Stability of a Unipolar World," *International Security* 24.1 (Summer 1999): 5–41, and Brooks and Wohlforth, "American Primacy in Perspective."

[5]Condoleezza Rice, "Promoting the National Interest," *Foreign Affairs* 79.1 (January/February 2000): 47.

[6]William Kristol and Robert Kagan, "The Present Danger," *National Interest* 59 (Spring 2000): 6.

[7]Thucydides, *History of the Peloponnesian War,* R. Warner, trans. (New York: Penguin, 1972), 402.

[8]John J. Mearsheimer, "The False Promise of International Institutions," *International Security* 19.3 (Winter 1994–95): 12.

[9]Stephen M. Walt, *Taming American Power: The Global Response to Primacy* (New York: Norton, 2005), 217.

[10]Stephen G. Brooks and William C. Wohlforth, "Reshaping the World Order," *Foreign Affairs* 88.2 (March/April 2009): 54

[11]George W. Bush, *The National Security Strategy of the United States of America,* September 17, 2002, www.informationclearinghouse.info/article2320.htm (accessed 6/30/09).

[12]Richard K. Betts, "The Soft Underbelly of American Primacy: Tactical Advantages of Terrorism," *Political Science Quarterly* 117.1 (2002): 21.

[13]Andrew J. Bacevich, *The New American Militarism: How Americans Are Seduced by War* (New York: Oxford University Press, 2005), 75. See also Stefan Halper and Jonathan Clarke, *America Alone: The Neo-Conservatives and the Global Order* (Cambridge: Cambridge University Press, 2004); and James Mann, *Rise of the Vulcans: The History of Bush's War Cabinet* (New York: Viking, 2004).

[14]Rice, "Promoting the National Interest," 47.

[15]Rice, "Promoting the National Interest," 48.

[16]Michael Mandelbaum, "Foreign Policy as Social Work," *Foreign Affairs* 75.1 (January/February 1996): 16–32.

[17]Mearsheimer, "False Promise of International Institutions," 7.

[18]John R. Bolton, "Unilateralism Is Not Isolationism," in *Understanding Unilateralism in American Foreign Relations,* Gwyn Prins, ed. (London: Royal Institute of International Affairs, 2000), 81.

[19]"Stop the World, I Want to Get Off," *The Economist,* July 28, 2001.

[20]John R. Bolton, "Should We Take Global Governance Seriously?" paper presented at the American Enterprise Institute conference, "Trends in Global Governance: Do They Threaten American Sovereignty?" April 4–5, 2000, Washington, D.C. (italics in original).

[21]Arthur M. Schlesinger, Jr., "Unilateralism in Historical Perspective," in Gwyn Prins, *Understanding Unilateralism in American Foreign Relations,* 18.

[22]Among the major works are Robert O. Keohane, *International Institutions and State Power: Essays in International Relations Theory* (Boulder, Colo.: Westview Press, 1989); Robert O. Keohane and Lisa L. Martin, "The Promise of Institutionalist Theory," *International Security* 20.1 (Summer 1995): 39–51; John Gerard Ruggie, *Winning the Peace: America and World Order in the New Era* (New York: Columbia University Press, 1996); and Stephen D. Krasner, ed. "International Regimes," special edition of *International Organization* 26.2 (Spring 1982).

[23]John Gerard Ruggie, "Multilateralism: The Anatomy of an Institution," *International Organization* 46.3 (Summer 1992): 561–98.

[24]G. John Ikenberry, *After Victory: Institutions, Strategic Restraint, and the Rebuilding of Order after Major Wars* (Princeton: Princeton University Press, 2001).

[25]Martha Finnemore, "Constructing Norms of Humanitarian Intervention," in *The Culture of National Security,* Peter J. Katzenstein, ed. (New York: Columbia University Press, 1996), 158.

[26]Bill Clinton, *A National Security Strategy for a New Century* (Washington, D.C.: U.S. Government Printing Office, 1998), 3.

[27]Fareed Zakaria, *The Post-American World* (New York: W.W. Norton, 2008):3.

[28]Barack Obama, *2010 National Security Strategy,* May 2010, 3, http://www.whitehouse.gov/sites/default/files/rss_viewer/national_security_strategy.pdf

[29]Joseph S. Nye, Jr., *The Paradox of American Power: Why the World's Only Superpower Can't Go It Alone* (New York: Oxford University Press, 2002), 8–9 (italics in original).

[30]Joseph S. Nye, Jr., *Bound to Lead: The Changing Nature of American Power* (New York: Basic Books, 1990), 188.

[31]Nye, *The Paradox of American Power*, 10.

[32]Chrystia Freeland, "GE's Immelt Speaks Out on China, exports, and competition," *Reuters*, January 21, 2011, http://blogs.reuters.com/chrystia-freeland/tag/jeff-immelt/

[33]Odd Arne Westad, *The Global Cold War* (London: Cambridge University Press, 2007), 404.

[34]James Kraska and Brian Wilson, "Fighting Pirates: the Pen and the Sword," *World Policy Journal*, 25 (Winter 2008–2009): 42–52.

[35]Robert O. Keohane and Lisa L. Martin, "The Promise of Institutionalist Theory," *International Security*, 20.1 (Summer 1995): 42.

[36]International Institute for Strategic Studies, *Strategic Survey 2010* (London, IISS, 2010), 417.

[37]Jessica T. Mathews, "Power Shift," *Foreign Affairs*, 76 (January/February 1997).

[38]Harold Nicolson, *Diplomacy* (New York: Oxford University Press, 1980; first edition 1939), 4.

[39]Colin L. Powell, "U.S. Forces: The Challenges Ahead," *Foreign Affairs*, Winter 1992-93.

[40]Samantha Power, *A Problem from Hell: America and the Age of Genocide* (New York: Basic Books, 2002), 334.

[41]Ivo H. Daalder and Michael E. O'Hanlon, *Winning Ugly: NATO's War to Save Kosovo* (Washington, D.C.: Brookings Institution Press, 2000).

[42]International Commission on Intervention and State Sovereignty (ICISS), *The Responsibility to Protect* (Ottawa: International Development Research Centre, 2001), 69.

[43]ICISS, *The Responsibility to Protect*, 11.

[44]Michael Walzer, *Just and Unjust Wars: A Moral Argument with Historical Illustrations* (New York: Basic Books, 1977); ICISS, *The Responsibility to Protect*; Simon Chesterman, *Just War or Just Peace? Humanitarian Intervention and International Law* (New York: Oxford University Press, 2003).

[45]George W. Bush, Commencement Address, U.S. Military Academy, West Point, New York, June 1, 2002, www.nytimes.com/2002/06/01/international/02PTEX-WEB.html (accessed 7/20/09).

[46]Bush, West Point speech, June 1, 2002.

[47]Lawrence Freedman, *Deterrence* (Cambridge: Polity Press, 2004), 4.

[48]Charlie Savage, "Top U.S. Security Official Says 'Rigorous Standards' Are Used for Drone Strikes," *New York Times*, April 30, 2012, http://www.nytimes.com/2012/05/01/world/obamas-counterterrorism-aide-defends-drone-strikes.html

[49]Ibrahim Mothana, "How Drones Help Al Qaeda," *New York Times*, June 13, 2012, http://www.nytimes.com/2012/06/14/opinion/how-drones-help-al-qaeda.html?emc=eta1

[50]Eric Schmitt and Thom Shanker, *Counterstrike: The Untold Story of America's Secret Campaign against Al Qaeda* (New York: Times Books, 2012), 289.

[51]Rosa Brooks, "Shadow Wars," *FP.com*, September 20, 2012, http://www.foreignpolicy.com/articles/2012/09/20/shadow_wars

[52]Michael May, "Fearsome Security: The role of Nuclear Weapons," *Brookings Review* (Summer 1995), 24.

[53]George P. Shultz, William J. Perry, Henry A. Kissinger, and Sam Nunn, "Á World Free of Nuclear Weapons," *Wall Street Journal*, January 4, 2007, posted at Friends Committee for National Legislation, http://fcnl.org/issues/nuclear/world_free_of_nuclear_weapons/

[54]Global Zero, http://www.globalzero.org/

[55]Jonathan Schell, "The Gift of Time: The Case for Abolishing Nuclear Weapons," *The Nation, February 2–9, 1998, 11–12.*

[56]Editorial, "The Bloated Nuclear Weapons Budget," *New York Times*, October 30, 2011, SR10.

[57]President Bush speech on Missile Defense, May 1, 2001, http://www.fas.org/nuke/control/abmt/news/010501bush.html (accessed 2/12/13).

[58]Schmitt and Shanker, *Counterstrike*, 14.

[59]Schmitt and Shanker, *Counterstrike*, 181.

[60]Schmitt and Shanker, *Counterstrike*, 5.

[61]Schmitt and Shanker, *Counterstrike*, 276.

[62]Charles R. Babcock, "Pentagon Budget's Stealth Spending," *Washington Post*, October 13, 1998, A1, A4; Gates quote cited in Joseph Parent, "The Wisdom of Retrenchment, *Foreign Affairs*, November/December 2011, 35.

[63]Nicholas Kristof, "Make Diplomacy, Not War," *New York Times*, August 9, 2008.

[64]John J. Kruzel, "Mullen Urges Emphasis on 'Soft Power,'" DefenseLINK, January 13, 2009, www.defenselink.mil/News/newsarticle.aspx?id=52664 (accessed 2/12/13).

[65]Thom Shanker, "Warning against Wars like Iraq and Afghanistan," *New York Times*, February 25, 2011, http://www.nytimes.com/2011/02/26/world/26gates.html/

[66]Greg Jaffe, "Short '06 Lebanon War Stokes Pentagon Debate," *Washington Post*, April 6, 2009.

[67]Ellen Nakashima, "Cyber-Intruder Sparks Massive Federal Response—and Debate over Dealing with Threats," *Washington Post*, December 10, 2011.

[68]David E. Sanger, "Mutually Assured Cyberdestruction?", *New York Times*, June 2, 2012, http://www.nytimes.com/2012/06/03/sunday-review/mutually-assured-cyberdestruction.html?emc=eta1

[69]Nicole Perlroth and Quentin Hardy, "Bank Hacks Were Work of Iranians, Officials Say," *New York Times*, January 8, 2013, B1.

[70]Quoted in Michael N. Barnett, "Bringing in the New World Order: Liberalism, Legitimacy, and the United Nations," *World Politics* 49.4 (July 1997): 541.

[71]Barnett, "Bringing in the New World Order," 543.

[72]Council on Foreign Relations, Susan Rice's Confirmation Statement, January 15, 2009, www.cfr.org/publication/18321/susan_rices_confirmation_hearing_statement.html (accessed 2/12/13).

[73]Particular thanks to Jessica Wirth, my research assistant in 2008–2009, for her work on a case study on which this section draws.

[74]Andre de Nesnera, "UN Security Council Reform May Shadow Annan's Legacy," Voice of America, November 1, 2006s, www.voanews.com/content/a-13-2006-11-01-v0a46/323974.html (accessed 2/12/13).

[75]Statement by H. E. Mr. Luiz Inácio Lula da Silva at the General Debate of the 61st Session of the United Nations General Assembly, September 19, 2006, www.un.org/webcast/ga/61/pdfs/brasil-e.pdf (accessed 2/12/13).

[76]Ministry of Foreign Affairs (Japan), "Reform of the UN Security Council: Why Japan Should Become a Member," March 2005, www.mofa.go.jp/policy/un/reform/pamph0503.pdf (accessed 2/12/13).

[77]Address by Prime Minister Manmohan Singh of India to a joint session of the U.S. Congress, Washington D.C., July 21, 2005, www.nriol.com/content/articles/article87.asp (accessed 2/12/13).

[78]Aminu Bashir Wali, "Is Makeup of Security Council About to Change?" *Diplomatic License*, Richard Roth, host, New York, October 15, 2004, http://edition.cnn.com/TRANSCRIPTS/0410/15/i_dl.01.html (accessed 2/12/13).

[79]de Nesnera, "UN Security Council Reform May Shadow Annan's Legacy."

[80]Bill Varner, "Security Council Expansion Talks at UN Get New Boost From Obama," Bloomberg.com, February 19, 2009, www.bloomberg.com/apps/news?pid=20601085&sid=aEpKLbSnxkOI&refer=europe (accessed 2/12/13).

[81]James Dobbins et al., *The UN's Role in Nation-Building: From the Congo to Iraq* (Santa Monica: Rand, 2005); James Dobbins et al., *America's Role in Nation-Building: From Germany to Iraq* (Santa Monica: Rand, 2003).

[82]Joint Statement by Gareth Evans and Yoriko Kawaguchi, New York, September 25, 2008, www.icnnd.org/reference/reports/ent/part-i.html (accessed 2/13/13).

[83]*New York Times*, May 26, 1998, A1.

[84]Joseph Cirincione, *Deadly Arsenals: Tracking Weapons of Mass Destruction* (Washington, D.C.: Carnegie Endowment for International Peace, 2002), 396.

[85]Commission on the Prevention of Weapons of Mass Destruction and Terrorism, *World at Risk* (New York: Vintage Books, 2008), xv.

[86]Kofi Annan, statement at the opening of the Preparatory Commission for the International Criminal Cases. New York, February 16, 1999, www.ngos.net/un/icc.html (accessed 2/13/13).

[87]"Rome Statute of the International Criminal Court."

[88]Statement by John D. Negroponte, U.S. Ambassador to the United Nations, July 12, 2002, www.amicc.org/docs/Negroponte_1422.pdf (accessed 2/13/13).

[89]Thomas W. Lippman, "America Avoids the Stand," *Washington Post,* July 26, 1998, C1, C4.

[90]Jack L. Snyder and Leslie Vinjamuri, "Trials and Errors: Principle and Pragmatism in Strategies of International Justice," *International Security* 28 (Winter 2003/04), 5–44.

[91]This section draws especially on Bruce W. Jentleson, *Coercive Prevention: Normative, Political, and Policy Dilemmas,* Peaceworks 35 (Washington, D.C.: U.S. Institute of Peace Press, 2000).

[92]Gareth Evans, *The Responsibility to Protect: Ending Mass Atrocity Crimes Once and For All* (Washington, D.C.: Brookings Institution Press, 2008), 91.

[93]Thomas C. Schelling, *Arms and Influence* (New Haven: Yale University Press, 1966); Alexander L. George and William E. Simmons, eds., *The Limits of Coercive Diplomacy,* 2nd ed. (Boulder, Colo.: Westview, 1994); Alexander L. George, *Forceful Persuasion* (Washington, D.C.: U.S. Institute of Peace Press, 1992).

[94]I. William Zartman, *Ripe for Resolution: Conflict and Intervention in Africa* (New York: Oxford University Press, 1989); Richard N. Haass, *Conflicts Unending: The United States and Regional Disputes* (New Haven: Yale University Press, 1992).

[95]I. William Zartman, "Putting Humpty-Dumpty Together Again," in Lake and Rothchild, eds., *International Spread of Ethnic Conflict.*

[96]Judith Kelley, *Ethnic Politics in Europe: The Power of Norms and Incentives* (Princeton: Princeton University Press, 2004).

[97]Human Security Report Project, *Human Security Report 2012* (Vancouver, Canada: Human Security Press, 2012).

[98]*Human Security Report 2012,* 165.

[99]Chris Hedges, "Croatian's Confession Describes Torture and Killing on a Vast Scale," *New York Times,* September 5, 1997, A1.

8 Grand Strategy for a New Era: (II) Prosperity and Principles

Introduction: Beyond the Globalization and Democratic Century Euphoria

Think back to those initial post–Cold War years. "If you want to understand the post–Cold War world," wrote Thomas Friedman, the Pulitzer Prize–winning columnist for the *New York Times*, "you have to start by understanding that a new international system has succeeded it—globalization. Globalization is not the only thing influencing events in the world today, but to the extent that there is a North Star and a worldwide shaping force, it is this system."[1] The U.S. economy was at the center of globalization. Many saw it as the model to emulate as other nations sought their own prosperity and all worked together for global prosperity.

That economic euphoria didn't last, especially when the 2007 global financial crisis and ensuing Great Recession hit. The global economy contracted for the first time since World War II. The drop in global trade was the steepest since the Great Depression. Within the broader critique of the Bretton Woods international economic system, the main issue was U.S. dominance. In the past the American economy had helped pull others out of economic crises, but in 2008 it was the epicenter from which the shock waves traveled. Other factors such as the euro crisis also played a role. Debates about globalization that had long been brewing intensified.

Politics, too, failed to meet early optimistic signs. In the heady days of the late 1980s and early 1990s, democracy seemed to be sweeping the world. The Berlin Wall, one of the Cold War's starkest symbols, had fallen. The Soviet Union itself crumbled. Nelson Mandela, a political prisoner of apartheid for almost thirty years, was released from prison and elected president of a post-apartheid South Africa. Military and Marxist governments fell in Latin America. It was "the end of history," as the scholar Francis

Fukuyama termed it—not just the end of the Cold War but "the universalization of Western liberal democracy as the final form of human government."[2]

As the 1990s progressed, however, horrors and inhumanity occurred on scales that many had hoped were part of the past. Ethnic "cleansing" in Bosnia was followed by genocide in Rwanda. Terror tore societies apart. Human rights were further trampled in China and elsewhere. It seemed to some, as Samuel Huntington responded to Fukuyama, that "so long as human beings exist there is no exit from the traumas of history."[3] Huntington's own "clash of civilizations" theory offered a much bleaker view of identity replacing ideology as the main source of international conflict with the main fault line between the West and the Islamic World.[4] Still others spoke of "the coming anarchy," global chaos, failed states, and the like.[5] Consequently, as the world entered what had been proclaimed the "democratic century," the record was much more mixed, the policy choices facing the United States more complicated, and the global future of democracy in the twenty-first century more uncertain than it had seemed in that initial post–Cold War euphoria.

In this chapter we provide an overview of key issues for the Prosperity and Principles dimensions of U.S. grand strategy. More specific regional and country issues are addressed in later chapters.

Prosperity

The Globalization Debate

So what is ***globalization*** anyway? What's so new and different about it? Is it a good thing or a bad thing? These and related questions can initially be addressed in terms of the dynamics and dimensions of globalization.

DEFINING GLOBALIZATION: DYNAMICS AND DIMENSIONS   The basic dynamic of globalization is the increasing interconnectedness of the world across state boundaries— an interconnectedness that affects governments, businesses, communities, and people in a wide range of policy areas. This is not totally new. As we see in "Historical Perspectives" (p. 334), past eras also had global dimensions. What makes the dynamic driving contemporary globalization unique is that it is "wider," "deeper," and "faster" than ever before. "Wider" means that it stretches beyond just the largest and richest countries of North America, Europe, and Asia to include countries and peoples in all corners of the globe. "Deeper" refers to the "thickness" of networks of interaction, that economic, cultural, and other interactions are not just individualized exchanges of goods, as in international trade, but interconnectivity linking societies and their peoples in more complex ways. The speed of these interactions is remarkable, whether it involves a few computer keystrokes that move billions of dollars from one side of the world to the other, or the instantaneous movement of news via cable and satellite telecommunications. As a 1999 UN report explained:

> Globalization is not new. Recall the early sixteenth century and the late nineteenth. . . . But the present era has distinctive features. Shrinking space, shrinking time and disappearing borders are linking people's lives more deeply, more intensely, more immediately than ever before.[6]

HISTORICAL PERSPECTIVES
HISTORICAL PERSPECTIVES

HOW "NEW" IS GLOBALIZATION?

So much is new about the current era of globalization that sometimes people lose sight of the global dimensions of past eras. This broader historical perspective is helpful in differentiating what is and isn't unique about the twenty-first century, and for drawing lessons from the past. Here are three examples.

International Finance

Wall Street giants such as Goldman Sachs have global financial networks today, but so did the Fuggers, a prominent German family in the Middle Ages. As Professor Stephen Krasner recounts: "The Fuggers controlled mines in central Europe and the Alps; had correspondents in Venice; were the dominant firm in Antwerp, the most important financial center of the time; and had branches in Portugal, Spain, Chile, Fiume, and Dubrovnik. They had agents in India and China by the end of the sixteenth century. Braudel [a leading historian] suggests that 'the empire of this huge firm was vaster than the mighty empire of Charles V and Philip II, on which as we know the sun never set.'"*

Global Public Health

Today's threats of global disease pandemics are severe, but the 1918–19 Spanish flu epidemic killed at least 50 million people, possibly even double that:

> Nearly half of all deaths in the United States in 1918 were flu-related. Some 675,000 Americans—about 6 percent of the population of 105 million and the equivalent of 2 million American deaths today—perished from the Spanish flu. . . . The highest death tolls were among young adults, ages 20–35. . . . Many deaths were never included in the pandemic's official death toll—such as the majority of victims in Africa, Latin America, Indonesia, the Pacific Islands and Russia. . . . The official estimate of 40–50 million total

deaths is believed to be a conservative extrapolation of European and American records. In fact, many historians and biologists believe that nearly a third of all humans suffered from influenza in 1918–19—and that of these, 100 million died.[†]

Immigration to the United States

The 2010 U.S. census showed that almost 70 million Americans had either been born in a foreign country or had at least one parent who had been. This was by far the highest number ever. In 1970, it was about 33 million. The previous historic high was 40 million in 1930, following a major post–World War I wave of immigration. But as a percentage of the total U.S. population, the 2010 figure was only up to 23 percent, whereas the figures for 1890 to 1930 were all above 30 percent.

The following graph shows that here, too, globalization was not a totally new phenomenon.

Percentage of Americans Born in a Foreign Country or Having at Least One Parent Who Was

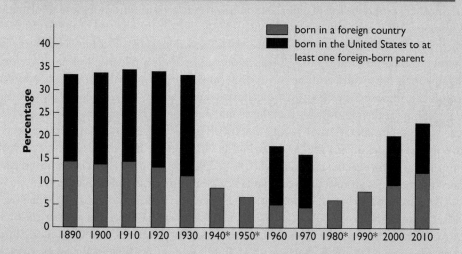

*Birthplace of parent not asked in these surveys.
Source: "Nation's Foreign-Born Population Nears 37 Million," Oct 19, 2010.
www.census.gov/newsroom/releases/archives/foreignborn_population/cb10-159.html

---

[*]Stephen D. Krasner, *Sovereignty: Organized Hypocrisy* (Princeton: Princeton University Press, 1999), 221.
[†]Laurie Garrett, "The Next Pandemic?" *Foreign Affairs* 84.4 (July/August 2005): 3, 5–6.

Today's era of globalization is also unique in its many *dimensions*. The economic dimension is arguably the most fundamental. Trade now accounts for almost 30 percent of U.S. gross domestic product (GDP), much more than in the past. Monetary policy decisions by the Federal Reserve Board used to be based almost exclusively on domestic economic factors such as inflation and unemployment, but now much greater attention is paid to the value of the dollar relative to that of other major currencies, to the impact of financial crises in other countries on U.S. growth rates, and to other international economic factors. In these and other ways globalization has both raised the salience of foreign economic policy and made the line between it and domestic economic policy less and less distinct.

A similar dynamic is evident in international finance. In the late 1990s, Roger Altman, a prominent investment banker, drew attention to the widening gap between the "awesome force of the global financial marketplace" and the more limited reach of the policies of national governments and international institutions such as the International Monetary Fund (IMF).[7] Bankers, money managers, stockbrokers, and other international financiers can choose not only among Wall Street, London, Frankfurt, and Tokyo, but also Hong Kong, Moscow, Brasília, and many other of the world's proliferated stock markets, currency markets, and other investment exchanges. Whatever their choices, it takes just one mouse click to move huge sums of money instantly—often over $2 trillion goes from one country to another in a single day.

Another key dimension of globalization involves telecommunications and information technology. News regularly moves instantaneously, 24/7, from one end of the world to the other, whether through the BBC, CNN, Al Jazeera, bloggers, or countless others. The Internet also demonstrates how globalization can be both a positive and negative force. The openness it provides and the way it undermines governmental monopolies on information can impose a check against dictators, who might be more likely to repress their people if not for their knowledge that they could not keep such repression quiet, as was evidenced by the proliferation of tweets, YouTube videos, and other social media revealing government abuses during the "Arab Spring" in 2011. Yet the Internet also facilitates problems such as terrorism: the terrorists who plotted the September 11 attacks communicated from Internet cafés around the world and even from American public libraries.

Globalization also has an important social and cultural dimension involving the flow of ideas, customs, and people. This flow is more multidirectional than many Americans realize. American products, music, movies, and other cultural influences can be found almost everywhere around the globe. McDonald's hamburgers are available in almost every major city in the world. Walk around a small village in Latin America or the Middle East and you'll see people wearing LeBron James T-shirts or New York Yankees baseball caps. In turn, American culture is much more diverse than ever before. A walk through an American city reveals many more ethnic restaurants than there were twenty years ago. More and more foreign-language movies are available online and through other sources. School calendars are written in languages such as Spanish and Vietnamese as well as in English.

Although driven in part by economics and communication, this cultural dimension especially reflects immigration patterns. It is the movement of peoples that may be the most profound dimension of globalization. Immigration into the United States has been increasing in both numbers and diversity. The most dramatic increases have come from Latin America (which accounted for 4 percent of total immigration in 1920 but 38 percent in 2010) and Asia (which grew from 1 percent of total immigration to 40 percent over the same period), while European immigration fell from 87 percent to 8 percent. Western Europe itself is much more ethnically heterogeneous due to increased immigration, especially from Africa, South Asia, and the Arab world. Other parts of the world have also seen substantial population shifts, as within Africa, where they have largely been the consequence of refugees fleeing ethnic wars and famines.

POLICY CHALLENGES   All of this poses a number of major policy dilemmas. Each of these dilemmas has its own details and specific issues, but as Joseph Stiglitz discusses (Reading 8.1), in the broadest sense all are manifestations of the challenges of "governance" amid globalization. The interconnectedness of globalization has outpaced policy capacities, creating a gap between globalization and global governance. Closing this *global governance gap* is one of the major challenges for American foreign policy and, more broadly, the international community. Global governance is not the same as global government. The latter term usually refers to ideas about making the United Nations and other international institutions into full governing structures, and creating a global constitution. Such withering of the state is highly unlikely. *Global governance* is a broader and more flexible concept:

> Governance does not mean mere government. It means the framework of rules, institutions and established practices that set limits and give incentives for the behavior of individuals, organizations and firms. . . .
>
>   Governance signifies a diverse range of cooperative problem-solving arrangements, state and nonstate, to manage collective affairs. . . . It takes place through "laws, norms and architectures," not necessarily the field of action of governments alone but rather in association with one another, with multinational bodies, with corporate and sometimes academic research entities and NGOs. Such collective activity, structured or improvised, produces governance, sometimes without governmental activity.[8]

For a while in the 1990s there was a sense that the global governance agenda was not very complex, that a ready and largely standard formula could be followed to maximize international trade and stabilize international finance for the benefit of all, and that the rest of the globalization agenda would benefit accordingly. Dubbed the *Washington consensus,* the basic formula held that countries should give the highest priority to reducing barriers to international trade and investment, cutting their own government spending, reducing government regulations, promoting privatization, and taking steps to increase economic efficiency and competitiveness to promote economic growth. This strategy relied largely on the "magic of the marketplace," which traces back to Adam Smith and his concept of the "invisible hand" by which growth would be maximized and all would benefit accordingly.

In practice, though, the magic provided fewer benefits to fewer people than advertised. In the United States and other industrialized countries, labor groups and others saw themselves as "losers," whereas others were "winners." In many developing countries, both intra-societal inequalities and the North-South income gap in the international system were seen as widening. This led to calls for "globalization with a human face":

> Inequality between countries has increased. The income gap between the fifth of the world's people living in the richest countries and the fifth in the poorest was 74 to 1 in 1997, up from 60 to 1 in 1990 and 30 to 1 in 1960. . . . Markets are neither the first nor the last word in human development. Many activities and goods that are critical to human development are provided outside the market—but these are being squeezed by the pressures of global competition. . . . When the market goes too far in dominating social and political outcomes, the opportunities and rewards of globalization spread unequally and inequitably—concentrating power and wealth in a select group of people, nations and corporations, marginalizing the others.[9]

When the 2008 economic crisis hit, the globalization debate became even more intense, particularly around the dominance of the United States.

The "democratic deficit" has posed another dilemma in global governance institutions and processes. Do institutions such as the World Trade Organization (WTO) and the International Monetary Fund (IMF) have too much power? Are they too dominated by the West and developed countries, and insufficiently representative of the global South? Should NGOs have larger roles in policy processes? The sections that follow address these issues.

Another global governance challenge has been globalization's "underside," the ways that interconnectedness has enhanced the capacity of drug traffickers, arms merchants, human traffickers, money launderers, and others involved in illegal and illicit activities. In his book *Illicit*, Moisés Naím argues that such activities are "*transforming the international system,* upending the rules, creating new players, and reconfiguring power in international politics and economics."[10] The global arms trade is a "supermarket that knows no borders and in which virtually anything can be procured for virtually anyone, so long as the buyer is prepared to pay the price." Sex slavery and other human trafficking is "booming . . . [at a] furious pace of growth." Money laundering may constitute as much as 10 percent of world GDP, facilitated by financial markets that have ended up "expand[ing] the flexibility of traffickers to invest the profits and the range of uses they can give to their capital, as well as generat[ing] many new instruments with which to move funds across the globe." Human organ trade—in kidneys, livers, and more—is fed by "forcible dona-tions" for transplants.[11]

In sum, globalization is neither wholly positive nor wholly negative. It simply *is*. Policies can shape it, but they cannot stop or reverse it. The world is too interconnected to be disconnected. The issues are closing the global governance–globalization gap in ways that best work with the dynamics and many dimensions of globalization, and deal-ing with the dilemmas posed for international trade, international finance, sustainable development, and related policy areas.

International Trade

While the post–World War II free trade system established under the Bretton Woods agreements (Chapter 5) has not collapsed, it has come under increasing strain both within the United States and internationally.

U.S. TRADE DEFICITS AND TRADE POLICY POLITICS   In 1971 the United States ran a balance-of-payments deficit for the first time since 1893. Since then, the American trade balance has been in surplus only twice, in 1973 and 1975. The trade deficit first exceeded $100 billion in 1984. In 2000 it was $377 billion; in 2005, $708 billion. While it was down to $494 billion in 2010, this largely reflected declining imports due to the Great Recession. As economic recovery began, the increase in imports exceeded the increase in exports and the 2011 trade deficit went back up to almost $560 billion. In 2012 the combination of falling global oil prices keeping the import bill down and a modest increase in exports brought the trade deficit down about 4 percent to $540 billion.

With such large and persisting deficits, it should be no surprise that trade policy has been a politically contentious area of post–Cold War U.S. foreign policy. The old free-trade consensus is not dead, but it has eroded and fractured. Indeed, the long-standing consensus on free trade theory is being challenged more than ever before, and on substan-tive policy grounds, not just for political reasons (see "Theory in the World," p. 340).

The ***North American Free Trade Agreement (NAFTA)*** was a major political test in U.S. trade policy.[12] NAFTA was originally signed in 1992 by President George H. W. Bush, and its opponents were led by the billionaire businessman Ross Perot, who was at the time an independent candidate in the 1992 presidential election and a national protest figure. The liberal wing of the Democratic Party and the neo-isolationist wing of the Republican Party were also part of the anti-NAFTA coalition. As they saw it, jobs would be lost as U.S. companies closed domestic factories and moved operations to Mexico, which had cheap labor, weak environmental regulations, and other profit-enhancing benefits. Presidential candidate Bill Clinton had given the agreement a qualified endorsement, and negotiated some additional provisions on labor and environmental standards once he was in office.

THEORY IN THE WORLD

THE FREE TRADE DEBATE

Perhaps no theory in American foreign policy has had more support over the last sixty-plus years than free trade theory.

We saw in Chapter 4 that free trade versus protectionism has been one of the great debates in American history, with policy often coming down on the protectionist side. Having learned a lesson from how much worse the 1929 Smoot-Hawley protectionist tariff made the Great Depression, Americans entered the post–World War II period with a strong pro–free trade consensus. The United States organized the international economy to be largely consistent with free trade theory (Chapter 4). It was never pure free trade, as compromises for foreign policy considerations and concessions to key domestic interest groups were made. But free trade policy was very much theory in practice until recent years, when both policies and the validity of the underlying theory have been challenged. This has had a major impact on the domestic politics of U.S. trade policy.

Free trade theory has long held that there are more winners than losers. The basic proposition goes back to the 18th and 19th century British political economists Adam Smith and David Ricardo: the aggregate benefits from the competition and specialization that free trade encourages are greater than the costs imposed on those who lose jobs and businesses to import competition. This promotion is said to still hold. According to economist Douglas Irwin, trade makes for improved resource allocation, higher productivity, and overall increases in wealth.[*] Exports accounted for more than one-fourth of U.S. economic growth in the 1990s and about 12 million jobs in the United States then. These jobs paid 13 to 18 percent higher wages than the overall average.

Four principal arguments have been raised that challenge free trade theory in ways that do not necessarily lapse into protectionism. The first is *particularistic costs vs. diffuse benefits*. In net aggregate terms, the economic benefits of free trade are greater than its costs. But the benefits are not central to people's livelihoods (for example, lower car prices) and are spread throughout the population, while costs such as lost jobs are felt by fewer people in more fundamental ways. This is what I. M. Destler calls "the root problem [of] political imbalance."[†] The number of people bearing the particularistic costs is less than the number of people getting the diffuse benefits, but the beneficiaries are more inclined to bring political pressure.

Second is *the limited capacity of free markets to facilitate economic adjustment*. The impact of factory closings on workers, families, and communities is intense and immediate. Jobs are created in more globally competitive industries, but this takes time. Federal Trade Adjustment Assistance (TAA) programs provide special government assistance to companies, workers, and communities hurt by import competition. But this program has focused more on the second A (Assistance) than the first (Adjustment): provisions such as unemployment compensation have helped with the short-term pain, but adjusting more permanently to greater global competitiveness has been much harder.

Third are *environmental issues, labor standards, and other broader social agenda issues* that are raised within U.S. politics and in the global arena. Critics fault free trade theory for leaving such factors out of its narrowly economic calculations of efficiency and wealth creation.

Fourth is the *fair trade argument*, questioning whether the playing field is level in terms of other countries being sufficiently committed to rules of openness. Fair trade supporters claim ground between free trade and protectionism, arguing that although fair trade is a less elegant theory, it is more consistent with political realities.

These arguments don't necessarily lead to a rejection of free trade theory, but they do raise important questions and critiques about how well it works in practice.

*Douglas A. Irwin, *Free Trade under Fire* (Princeton: Princeton University Press, 2002), 3.
†I. M. Destler, *American Trade Politics*, 4th ed. (Washington, D.C.: Institute for International Economics, 2005).

Clinton pushed NAFTA through congressional approval in 1993 with a coalition that drew much more support from Republicans than from Democrats. Although this amounted to a choice for free trade over protectionism, the vote was close and involved plenty of wheeling and dealing, as senators and representatives linked their votes to related trade issues and unrelated pet projects.

By 1997 trade policy politics had shifted sufficiently against trade agreements that the Clinton administration was unable to get Congress to renew its fast-track trade treaty–negotiating authority. *Fast-track authority* was first established in the 1970s (see Chapter 6) as a way of keeping trade agreements from being amended to death or unduly delayed in Congress. It guarantees that any trade agreements the president negotiates and submits to Congress under this authority will receive expedited legislative consideration within ninety days and be voted upon under the special procedural rule of an "up or down" vote—yea or nay—with no amendments allowed. Proponents saw fast-track authority as being key to the success of trade agreements over the previous two decades, as it prevented

Congress from excessively delaying or amending agreements already negotiated with other countries. Opponents, though, claimed that without some amendments, trade agreements go too far in picking winners and forsaking losers.

In 2001–2002, the Bush administration and fast-track supporters mounted another effort to renew fast-track authority. Part of their strategy was a lesson in political semantics: "fast-track" authority became *"trade promotion" authority.* The original name, with its connotation of moving quickly and not getting bogged down, had once been an advantage, but now seemed to imply a process that moved too fast and allowed too little opportunity for input. "Trade promotion" conveyed something that more people could support, something seemingly less political. It passed this time, by a solid margin in the Senate but only by a very close vote in the House. But it was not renewed in 2007.

During the Great Recession, trade policy politics became even more intense. A poll just before the 2010 congressional elections showed that only 18 percent of Americans believed that free trade creates jobs in the United States. Not only did 53 percent say free trade hurts the United States, but this sentiment spanned the ideological spectrum, with 61 percent of Tea Party respondents and 65 percent of union members agreeing.[13] Indeed, "China-bashing" television and online ads—trade with China accounted for over 50 percent of the overall trade deficit—have been used by both Republicans and Democrats in recent election campaigns. Some of the bilateral deficit was due to China manipulating its currency's exchange rate and other unfair trade practices. Some reflected the heavy investments made by American manufacturing companies (e.g., Apple) in China for lower-wage labor. The bilateral deficit also bred scapegoating, prejudice, and protectionism. While Congress went on to approve some trade agreements—including free trade agreements with South Korea, Colombia, and Panama in 2011—trade policy politics have continued to be contentious.

OIL IMPORTS   America's "oil addiction" had been causing trade problems, along with environmental and other ones, at least since 1973, the year that the first OPEC oil crisis hit. That and other oil crises, such as those prompted by the Iranian revolution in 1979 and by the Persian Gulf War 1990–91, were largely supply-side disruptions. Now, though, along with the continuing possibility of Middle East instability there is much more demand-side pressure on oil supplies and prices, reflecting the entry of India, China, and other rapidly growing countries into the global marketplace.

Over the years there have been repeated calls to reduce oil dependence and enhance *"energy security"*: from President Nixon after the 1973 OPEC crisis, from President Carter after the 1979 OPEC crisis, from President George W. Bush about America's "oil addiction," and from President Obama. With only 4 percent of the world's population, the United States accounts for 25 percent of world oil consumption. About 70 percent of this is in the transportation sector. American fuel efficiency standards for cars lag far behind those of the European countries, Japan, and many others. Yet "the lack of sustained attention to energy issues," a bipartisan task force chaired by two former secretaries of energy stressed, continues "undercutting U.S. foreign policy and national security."[14]

Recent increases in U.S. domestic oil and natural gas production have led to some projections of energy self-sufficiency. But these remain projections with lots of variables and uncertainties. True, even if U.S. oil imports don't get to zero but are significantly reduced, vulnerability to external supply disruptions will be reduced. But there really is no such thing as "energy independence." This is a politically resonant but policy-distorting term. If global oil prices ratchet up, U.S. financial markets would be affected whether or not the United States is importing lots of oil. To the extent that allies are hit by global price hikes or supply disruptions, U.S. security interests would be affected. Moreover, expanding domestic hydrocarbon production raises other issues, such as environmental concerns about global climate change and, at the local level, with the "fracking" method of natural gas production. These are among the reasons why energy security involves not just altering where oil comes from, but also shifting to alternative energy sources such as wind and solar.

THE WORLD TRADE ORGANIZATION (WTO)   The 1994 Uruguay Round trade agreement marked the transition from the General Agreement on Tariffs and Trade (GATT) discussed in Chapter 5 to the World Trade Organization (WTO). The WTO was designed as a significantly stronger multilateral institution than the GATT had been. One aspect of this strengthening is the WTO's formalization as an institution. Whereas the GATT was a set of agreements rather than an international institution per se, the WTO has full legal standing and is very much a formal organization, with more than six hundred employees at its headquarters in Geneva, Switzerland. The WTO is also more inclusive than its predecessor. As of February 2013, 158 countries were members of the WTO (accounting for over 98 percent of world trade), with 25 other countries in the process of applying for membership.

The Doha Round   In late 2001, two years after an effort to begin a new round of global trade negotiations failed amid massive anti-globalization protests at the WTO summit in Seattle, the **Doha Round** of trade negotiations (named for the capital of Qatar) was launched. The Doha Declaration, released at the first meeting, stressed the overall free trade goal of "maintain[ing] the process of reform and liberalization of trade policies." Within that goal it pledged "to ensure that developing countries, and especially the least developed among them, secure a share of the growth of world trade commensurate with their needs of economic development." It was dubbed the "Doha Development Round," reflecting a greater emphasis on the issues most affecting developing countries.

January 1, 2005, was set as the deadline for reaching an agreement. That deadline has long since passed. Limping into its second decade, the Doha Round remains deadlocked, the issues more complex and difficult than the standard free trade–protectionism dichotomy. How extensive should the special benefits be for developing countries as they seek to catch up and make up for what many see as past exploitation? What about the widening gap between the winners and losers within the United States and other developed countries, the financiers and corporate executives on one side and workers on the other? How would environmental impact be into account? These and other issues, while not entirely new, have become much more problematic, to the point where an increasing number of scholars and policy experts are questioning whether the Bretton Woods system needs to be re-assessed.

International Finance

U.S. goals for the international financial system remain fundamentally the same as when the system was set up at the end of World War II with the International Monetary Fund (IMF) as the central institution. These goals are: to help provide the monetary and financial stability necessary for global economic growth and particularly for the growth of international trade; to avoid the monetary versions of economic nationalism and protectionism that lead countries to compete more than they cooperate; and in these and other ways to contribute to international peace and stability. In recent years, however, major international financial crises have occurred one after another.

RECURRING GLOBAL FINANCIAL CRISES   The first of these post–Cold War financial crises hit Mexico in 1995. The Mexican peso collapsed, losing almost half its value in less than a month. The Mexican crisis hit home in the United States: the success of NAFTA was at stake, just a year after the hard-fought political battle to pass the agreement. Concern arose about "contagion" effects spreading to other countries in the Western Hemisphere. Working with the IMF, the Clinton administration put together a package of credits worth $50 billion, of which about $20 billion came from the United States.

The *Asian financial crisis* that struck in mid-1997 involved a number of countries. It started in Thailand and spread to Indonesia and South Korea. These "Asian tigers" had been success stories, exemplars of the newly industrialized countries that the United States hailed in the 1970s and 1980s as proof that capitalism worked better than socialism or other forms of statism. But the underside of East Asian capitalism—its speculative investments, cronyism and corruption, overconsumption of imports, and excessive debt—now burst the bubbles. U.S. interests were affected in a number of ways by this crisis. American banks and mutual funds had invested heavily in Asian markets. American companies had factories, fast-food restaurants, and other major investments at risk. American exporters lost some of their fastest-growing markets, accounting for a big chunk of the rise in the 1998–2000 trade deficit. And all three countries were political allies of the United States.

In 1998 two other major countries, Russia and Brazil, joined the list of financial crisis victims. While less foreign investment was at stake in Russia than in the Mexican and Asian cases, the Russian crisis had a "last straw" effect on investor psychology and set off a sharp drop on Wall Street. The stock market re-stabilized later in 1998, only to have Brazil—another heralded economic success story, the world's eighth-largest economy, and a potential source of contagion to other parts of Latin America—go into financial crisis in early 1999. Two years later it was Argentina, not because of a direct contagion from Brazil but as a manifestation of its own extensive fiscal and financial problems.

These crises were damaging, but they paled in comparison to the 2007–08 crisis set off by the Wall Street meltdown, which catalyzed the most severe and wide-reaching economic crisis since the Great Depression. Just as a recovery was beginning, the euro crisis hit and destabilized global financial markets again (Chapter 12). These brought the cumulative total of international financial crises to seven in just over two decades— arguably more, depending on how one counts, but even at seven this is an exceptional frequency. With the United States and Europe shifting from the "consequences end" of financial crises set off by others to being the principal causes of global crises, the fundamentals of the international financial system were called into question.

THE IMF   When a country faces a financial crisis, the IMF usually makes credit and other support available, but also insists that the recipient state agree to tight fiscal policies, outright austerity measures, and economic reforms. These and other policy guidelines are established as **conditionalities** that must be met for a country to receive IMF loans and credits. This is the financial piece of the Washington consensus discussed earlier. Critics contend that this system relied too much on "one size fits all" solutions and did not tailor strategies to different national, political, and economic contexts and structures.[15] The emphasis on **structural adjustment** policies and fiscal austerity cut deeply into employment, health, and other government services that provide a safety net for those most in need. But the medicine was considered too harsh; in the name of saving the patient it risked killing him. There must be a better way to implement reform, these critics argued, a more graduated approach that still had room for necessary social services.

During the run-up to the 2008 financial crisis, the IMF failed to provide clear warnings about the vulnerabilities within the global economy. According to its own 2011 internal report, "the IMF's ability to correctly identify the mounting risks was hindered by a high degree of groupthink, intellectual capture, a general mindset that a major financial crisis in large advanced economies was unlikely, and inadequate analytical approaches."[16] Despite earlier signs, it was not until October 2008 that the IMF announced the global financial system was at the "brink of a systematic meltdown."[17] When Iceland's banking system collapsed that December, the IMF provided a loan to a developed country for the first time since the 1970s. It went on to provide financial assistance to a number of other countries and took on a key role in the euro crisis, starting with its piece of the bailout package for Greece, the first time the IMF had lent to a eurozone country.

The IMF has also been challenged to change its internal governance to provide larger policy roles for China and other emerging economies. The U.S. voting share by which IMF policies are set was once over 40 percent, but is now down to about 17 percent. Yet with all major IMF policy decisions requiring an 85 percent majority, this still effectively gives the United States a veto. China's share has increased but is still only around 4 percent. Consider the Chinese position: It holds almost $2 trillion in hard currency reserves. It is the world's largest creditor. The United States has become the world's largest debtor. It views the 2008 global financial crisis, as do many others around the world, as largely due to American financial irresponsibility, both on Wall Street and in Washington. Its own economy has been damaged by this American profligacy. Why should the system continue to operate with most of the power to set the rules in U.S. hands? China and its fellow "BRICS" countries (*Brazil, Russia, India, China, South Africa*) are pressing for a greater voice for themselves and other developing countries.

It is in question whether these power shifts and policies are in the U.S. national interest. The dollar's role as the principal reserve currency has had benefits for the United States, including less pressure than other countries to balance its budget and trade accounts. But it has also had costs, including, in some respects, enabling rather than checking huge deficits. Some still want to maximize U.S. centrality in the IMF, as with most other considerations of power. Others see forces of change as inherent to this global era and resistance to them as counterproductive. Proponents of change think that working with and shaping these forces toward shared interests is a more useful strategy.

G-20   In the mid-1970s, the *G7 (Group of Seven)* was created by the United States and other advanced industrial states (Canada, Britain, France, Germany, Italy, and Japan) for consultation and coordination on international economic issues. The G7 was an informal but influential institution, given that it included the major economic and political powers of the day. It became the *G8* when Russia was added after the Cold War. Another institution, the *G20,* which included China, India, and a number of other developing countries, was created in 1999, but had had a less prominent role. Yet when the 2008 global economic crisis struck, the broader inclusiveness of the G20 made it the principal forum for managing this crisis. An emergency meeting was held in Washington in November 2008, and a second in London in April 2009. Although American and other Western leaders still had major roles, so too did leaders such as China's prime minister, Hu Jintao, and Brazil's president, Luis Inácio Lula da Silva. This greater assertiveness reflected the underlying economics. Even before the 2008 crisis, the original G7's share of world output, still at 65 percent as of 2003, was projected to fall to 37 percent by 2030. The major emerging economies were increasing their share from 7 percent to 32 percent.

Focusing on the shared interests of avoiding an even worse crisis, the 2008 and 2009 G20 summits produced cooperative agreements. While this was encouraging, the crisis was so severe that cooperation became a "fellowship of the lifeboat." Ensuing summits have not been highly conflictual, but they've produced less cooperation than hoped for by those who viewed the G20 as a more encompassing model for global governance.

International Development

Sustainable development has been defined as a policy approach that "meets the needs of the present without compromising the ability of future generations to meet their own needs." Its conception of "the needs of the present" has two key elements: an emphasis on issues of global inequality and "the essential needs of the world's poor, to which [*sic*] over-riding priority should be given;" and a broadening of the agenda beyond the economic aspects of development to include issues of human development and human security, such as AIDS and other global public health crises, hunger and nutrition, and education and literacy. The reference to future generations is particularly relevant to the global environment. Can it really be considered development in the positive sense of the term if the economic growth rates achieved today result from overexploitation and despoliation of natural resources that will impose major costs on and pose serious risks to future generations?

The challenges for U.S. policy and international institutions such as the World Bank are formidable. Some progress has been made; for example, as of 2010 the number of people living in extreme poverty had been cut to less than half of the 1990 rate. But of 127 developing countries, two-thirds were still ranked low or medium on the United Nations Development Program's "Human Development Index" (which includes income and such quality of life indicators as basic nutrition, health care, life expectancy, and literacy). Hunger affects almost 1 billion people including 195 million children under the age of five with stunted growth. The fastest population growth rates are in the poorest parts of the world.[18]

The standard world map shows country size measured by land mass. Now consider the alternative global maps on pages 348 and 349. Map 8.1 is drawn proportional to population size. China and India are much larger than on the standard map; so, too, are large-population countries such as Indonesia and Brazil, as well as the entire continent of Africa. The United States is smaller, as are the European countries.

Next consider Map 8.2, based on global income distribution. The United States, Japan, and Germany are much larger than on the population and land-area maps. Conversely, many of the large countries on the population map are small on the income map. The two maps together provide a graphic indication of global inequality and a sense of the way many others see the world.

MAP 8.1
ALTERNATIVE GLOBAL MAP

Global Population Patterns

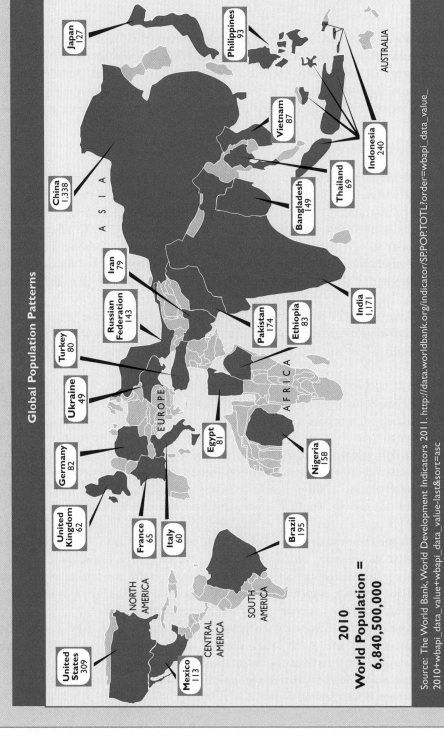

Japan 127

Philippines 93

China 1,338

Vietnam 87

Indonesia 240

AUSTRALIA

Thailand 69

Bangladesh 149

A S I A

Iran 79

Russian Federation 143

Pakistan 174

India 1,171

Turkey 80

Ethiopia 83

Ukraine 49

EUROPE

A F R I C A

Germany 82

Egypt 81

Nigeria 158

United Kingdom 62

France 65

Italy 60

NORTH AMERICA

Brazil 195

CENTRAL AMERICA

SOUTH AMERICA

United States 309

Mexico 113

**2010
World Population =
6,840,500,000**

Source: The World Bank, World Development Indicators 2011. http://data.worldbank.org/indicator/SP.POP.TOTL?order=wbapi_data_value_2010+wbapi_data_value+wbapi_data_value-last&sort=asc

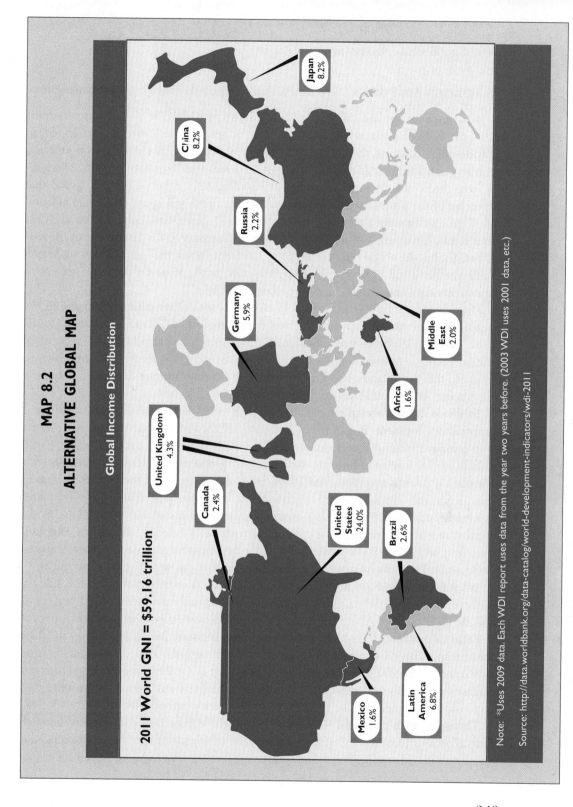

MAP 8.2
ALTERNATIVE GLOBAL MAP

Global Income Distribution

2011 World GNI = $59.16 trillion

Japan 8.2%

China 8.2%

Russia 2.2%

Germany 5.9%

Middle East 2.0%

Africa 1.6%

United Kingdom 4.3%

Canada 2.4%

United States 24.0%

Brazil 2.6%

Mexico 1.6%

Latin America 6.8%

Note: *Uses 2009 data. Each WDI report uses data from the year two years before. (2003 WDI uses 2001 data, etc.)

Source: http://data.worldbank.org/data-catalog/world-development-indicators/wdi-2011

U.S. FOREIGN AID POLICY   The debate over foreign aid runs along the following lines:

How much foreign aid should the United States provide? The United States used the end of the Cold War as a rationale to cut back, rather than reallocate, its foreign aid. In inflation-adjusted terms, the decline was close to 50 percent. U.S. aid to Central America, for example, fell from $226 million a year in the 1980s to $26 million in 1997. The politics were predictable in some respects but paradoxical in others. One poll found that 75 percent of the American public believed that too much was spent on foreign aid, and only 4 percent thought that too little was spent (17 percent thought the amount was about right). Most people thought that foreign aid accounted for 15 percent of the federal budget, but the actual figure is less than 1 percent. When the question was rephrased to ask whether a full 1 percent was too little, too much, or about right, 46 percent of respondents said "about right," and 34 percent "too little."[19]

The debate over how U.S. foreign aid compares with other countries hinges on the question of what measures to use. The total dollar amount of U.S. aid is the largest in the world. But a widely referenced standard is that foreign aid should be 0.7 percent of national income. Although only a few countries reach this level—Sweden, Norway, Denmark, the Netherlands, and Luxembourg—the average among developed nations is 0.28 percent. At about 0.15 percent, the United States ranks last.

To whom should foreign aid go? Officially U.S. policy has always favored Third World economic development. But in reality, for virtually the entire Cold War, it was a much lower priority than global containment. This is evident when we consider who received the bulk of U.S. foreign aid during the Cold War: geopolitically strategic countries such as South Vietnam in the 1960s and 1970s, Israel and Egypt since the late 1970s, and El Salvador in the 1980s. Post-9/11 geopolitical considerations have made Iraq and Afghanistan priorities. For FY 2010, as an example, Afghanistan was the largest U.S. aid recipient (economic and military combined) with $11.4 billion, followed by Pakistan, Israel, Iraq, and Egypt. Some greater priority for development is evident in analyzing economic assistance on its own, with sub-Saharan Africa as the largest regional recipient.

What form should aid take? The principal debate is over economic versus military aid. Between the end of the Cold War and 9/11, military aid decreased from 31 percent of total aid to 21 percent. After 9/11 it went back up, to over 30 percent. Another aspect of the debate is providing long-term development versus humanitarian relief. The sad fact is that humanitarian crises constantly arise and must be responded to, often entailing costs that exceed the amount budgeted for them. Yet as long as the total amount of aid does not increase significantly and substantial chunks go to military aid, humanitarian relief and economic development will be partially paired in a zero-sum calculation.

Through which channels? The "which channels" debate involves choosing between bilateral options (country to country), multilateral options (through the World Bank and other international organizations), and contracting through NGOs. About 10 percent of U.S.

aid is multilateral, whereas the average for other major donors is 33 percent. Each channel has its assets. Bilateral aid, for example, can be more specifically tailored to political considerations, while—to the extent that basic human needs and development are the priority—multilateral aid tends to be freer from politics. Should the U.S. Agency for International Development (USAID) and other government agencies be the sole administrators of their own programs? Or should they partner with NGOs? The budgetary savings of having fewer permanent staff members on the government payroll and the strengths that NGOs bring to the mission have resulted in a trend toward partnerships. Concerns have arisen, though, about ending up with too little in-house government expertise. USAID has fallen to about one-third of the staffing level it had in 1990. The Foreign Service, which also provides development experts through U.S. embassies, has also experienced shortages of trained personnel.

Should abortion and related population planning be restricted? The George W. Bush administration reverted to the Reagan administration's policy of making American aid to international population planning heavily contingent on the UN and other multilateral agencies abiding by U.S. prohibitions on funding abortion. Many other countries as well as UN officials rejected this effort to apply domestic policies (and politics) to the rest of the world as a matter of principle. They also opposed it on substantive grounds. Although U.S. policy was hardly the only cause, statistics showed that 200 million women worldwide were in need of safe and effective contraception. Estimates spoke of 70 to 80 million unwanted pregnancies annually and 150,000 maternal deaths. In one of its first actions, the Obama administration rescinded the Bush restrictions. "They have undermined efforts to promote safe and effective voluntary family planning in developing countries," stated President Obama. "For these reasons, it is right for us to rescind this policy and restore critical efforts to protect and empower women and promote global economic development."[20]

What of the role of women in development? Nicholas Kristof and Sheryl WuDunn invoke the Chinese saying "women hold up half the sky" to make the point that if nations underinvest in half the population, the prospects for progress on any formidable challenge are that much less.[21] Ending forced female labor, including sexual servitude; reducing maternal mortality; targeting economic assistance to women entrepreneurs; and providing equal legal rights to ownership and inheritance are among the principal women's empowerment policies, along with those on education. Secretary of State Hillary Clinton made these and related issues a priority during her time in office.

How effective is foreign aid? Foreign aid is more effective than it gets credit for. Villages all over the world have water and sanitation that they otherwise would not, schools have been built, jobs created, businesses started, and infrastructures built. Foreign aid does suffer from being susceptible to easy criticism. But few would argue that foreign aid is as effective as it could be and needs to be. Some critics, such as economist Jeffrey Sachs, argue that more money and better programs are needed. Some programs fail because they do not have sufficient funding and resources to be brought up to scale and perform the follow-up necessary for sustainability. Sachs also wants to deemphasize the one-size-fits-all approach and program design by outside bureaucracies, whether USAID or the World Bank. He would prefer more "clinical economics," a differential diagnosis for each country combined with more rigorous methods for monitoring and evaluation.[22] William Easterly is much more skeptical about how effective even improved foreign aid can be. *The White Man's Burden: How the West's Efforts to Aid the Rest Have Done So Much Ill and So Little Good* is the telling title of one of his books. After fifty years and over $2.3 trillion in aid, "there is shockingly little to show for it. . . . [T]he majority of places we have meddled [with] the most are in fact no better off or are even worse off than they were before."[23] Plenty of others, scholars and policy experts, have joined this debate, both in the United States and worldwide.

THE WORLD BANK   The World Bank continues to be the principal multilateral institution for fighting global poverty. It has achieved many successes but has also been plagued by failures and controversies. As with the WTO and the IMF, many critics were disillusioned with the World Bank's advocacy of the Washington consensus. A former World Bank official wrote: "To argue that developing countries need market-friendly policies, stable macroeconomic environments . . . open and transparent capital markets and equity-based corporate structures with attention to modern shareholder values is to say that you will be developed when you are developed. It is the old debate about inputs and outputs, where everything that development brings has become a necessary input to achieving it."[24]

Critics have also pointed to the need to pay more attention to corruption, political repression, and other domestic political issues in recipient countries. Traditionally, the World Bank claimed that it was apolitical, that its decisions were economic ones based on economic criteria, and that its success was to be evaluated on the basis of growth rates and other hard economic data. By the mid-1990s, though, the World Bank had begun to shift its stand, acknowledging the strong evidence that good government is a necessary part of sound economic development. This evidence was reinforced by cases such as Indonesia, a formerly vaunted success story that was undermined in large part by massive corruption.

A further issue is the extent to which donor countries are allowed to attach political conditions to their lending and voting. In theory, as a multilateral economic development institution the World Bank is supposed to be detached from the politics of the international agenda. Yet the United States, its biggest donor, has also been the country most inclined to make political linkages and attach conditions to its funding. Some of these restrictions were initiated by presidents, some imposed by Congress. When the U.S. voting share in the World Bank was over 40 percent, it was much easier for Washington to impose its position. But with its voting share at less than 17 percent and without the bloc strength of the Cold War alliances, other countries are both more willing and more able to oppose the United States. Moreover, the United States must now be concerned about precedents; in the future other countries may seek to impose political conditions on World Bank lending and get 51 percent of the vote despite U.S. opposition.

Just as the IMF directorship has been reserved for a European, the World Bank president has always been an American. The push from emerging powers and developing countries for greater inclusiveness also includes opening up these positions.

Global Public Health

There are at least three major reasons why American foreign policy needs to be concerned about global public health. First is the humanitarian dimension. It is hard to maintain a strong claim to Principles without helping prevent and treat the diseases that ravage so much of humanity. Responsibility does not fall solely on the United States, but as the richest, most powerful, and most medically advanced country in the world, America knows that it can make a significant difference.

Second is Prosperity and the importance of global public health to the fight against global poverty. Three of the eight UN Millennium Development Goals are explicitly concerned with global public health. Even the most ambitious economic development strategies cannot succeed unless global public health is improved. Extensive research conducted at the village level in a number of developing countries by Anirudh Krishna of Duke University shows that one of the key factors for families that escape from poverty is avoiding major health problems, and that one of the key factors for those who fall back into poverty is the onset of major health problems.[25]

Third is national security and considerations of Peace and Power. This point was made and concern raised about AIDS and other global infectious diseases in a landmark 2000 study by the Central Intelligence Agency: "The persistent infectious disease burden is likely to aggravate and, in some cases, may even provoke economic decay, social fragmentation, and political destabilization in the hardest hit countries in the developing and former communist worlds. . . . Infectious diseases are likely to slow socioeconomic development in the hardest hit developing and former communist countries and regions. This will challenge democratic development and transitions and possibly contribute to humanitarian emergencies and civil conflicts."[26]

GLOBAL AIDS   The figures are staggering. Since the scourge began just over 30 years ago, 30 million people have died of HIV/AIDS. Another 34 million are infected and have uncertain life prospects. This is truly, as the UN Joint Program on HIV/AIDS (UNAIDS) has called it, "a global epidemic." It is worst in sub-Saharan Africa, and the Republic of

South Africa in particular, but with alarming rates in many other regions and countries. Reading 8.2 excerpts from the 2012 UNAIDS Report.

The twofold challenge is prevention and treatment. Those who have already contracted HIV must be provided with treatment. At the same time, education and access to health care must be improved and other measures taken to prevent the further spread of HIV. Some progress has been made. By 2010 the annual death rate from AIDS was down 18 percent from its peak. HIV infection rates had also fallen somewhat. Prevention and treatment policies were having impact. The United States gets some of the credit. The President's Emergency Plan for AIDS Relief (PEPFAR) launched by the G.W. Bush administration and continued by the Obama administration substantially increased U.S. funding for combating global AIDS. UNAIDS is the coordinating body established to try to bring together the efforts of the ten separate UN agencies involved in HIV/AIDS prevention and treatment. Other donor governments, the private sector, and NGOs also are involved.

ROLE OF THE GATES FOUNDATION   A few days before a 2005 World Health Organization (WHO) meeting in Geneva, a Swiss newspaper ran the headline "The Health of the World Depends More on Bill Gates than on the WHO."[27] Though an exaggeration, it made a point. The Bill & Melinda Gates Foundation's endowment is greater than the GDP of 70 percent of the world's nations. And it has a lot less bureaucracy and a lot less politics impeding its efforts.

The foundation's global public health work includes HIV/AIDS as well as other diseases and health issues affecting the poorest countries of the world, such as malaria, tuberculosis, diarrhea, polio, and maternal and child health. Particular emphasis is placed on vaccine development and the immunization of children. Over 20 percent of children worldwide do not have access to needed vaccines. This translates to 2.4 million deaths per year. Millions more children who survive preventable diseases are left severely impaired. "The long-range effects of childhood illnesses hinder the ability of those who survive to become educated, work, or care for themselves or others. This puts a strain on their families and on the economies of developing countries."[28] The Global Alliance for Vaccination and Immunisation—a partnership of the Gates Foundation, other NGOs, the WHO, governments, and the private sector—has been making an impact through both research for vaccine development and on-the-ground immunization programs.

The Gates Foundation does have its critics. Some see it as too oriented toward "techno-fix" solutions and discovery with insufficient focus on development and delivery. It has investments in companies whose business seems to run counter to the goals of its public health programs. Some are also concerned that although its sheer size gives it some economies of scale, the foundation can crowd out other NGOs. What is clear is that the Gates Foundation is one of the key actors in global public health policy, and there is healthy debate about its optimal role.

GLOBAL PANDEMICS AND THE "DMD" THREAT   In addition to weapons of mass destruction (WMD), the world faces the threat of "DMD," or diseases of mass destruction. As bad as the 1918–19 Spanish flu epidemic was (see "Historical Perspectives," p. 334), forecasts for avian flu are even worse. In New York City, for example, where the Spanish flu killed about 33,000 people, avian flu estimates run as high as 2.8 million people becoming infected. At a possible 55 percent fatality rate, there could be close to 1.5 million deaths in New York City alone. Costs to the American economy could be as high as $600 billion. Questions still remain as to whether avian flu (the A/H5N1 strain in scientific terms) will transmit from human to human or will stay largely concentrated in birds and those who come in direct contact with them. But as with nuclear weapons and other WMD threats, the DMD policy challenge is to prevent, and if not prevent, contain, amid the uncertainties of the future. As DMD expert Laurie Garrett writes, "Nothing could happen . . . or doom may loom."[29]

The challenges of pandemics are posed to both American foreign policy and, more broadly, the international community. This was evident in 2003, with the severe acute respiratory syndrome (SARS) outbreak. SARS was first detected in China. Initially the Chinese government delayed providing the WHO access to its territory or even to its health information. Once reports leaked out through the international press and travelers, the WHO was able to respond more effectively. Also, other governments could then take action both to prevent the spread of SARS to their countries and to assist the WHO and China in containing and mitigating the outbreak.

The international challenge also was evident in 2009, with the swine flu (the H1N1 virus) outbreak, which began in Mexico and spread globally. Its impact was less than initially feared. One reason was that the flu strain was not as strong as it could have been. Another was the relatively rapid and well-coordinated response of the WHO, the U.S. *Centers for Disease Control and Prevention (CDC)*, and other governments and their key public health agencies. Even with the early warning and policy measures that helped control and mitigate the spread, there were over 250,000 cases of swine flu worldwide, with deaths in Mexico, Argentina, Spain, Britain, Ukraine, Afghanistan, Australia, Thailand, the Phillippines, the United States, and numerous other countries. In the years since, additional strands of avian flu have appeared, such as the H7N9 strand that broke out in China in early 2013.

Looking to the future, we can draw two important lessons. First, global public health is another issue in which traditional conceptions of state sovereignty collide with the interconnectedness of a global age. China's invocation of its right of sovereignty in the SARS outbreak impeded the capacity of the international community to respond. The crisis could have been much worse if the Chinese government had stuck to this position. Unless the norm of sovereignty as responsibility, not just the rights of states, continues to strengthen both in general and with specific applicability to global public health, the risks of global pandemics will be even greater. "After all," as Dr. Margaret Chan, the WHO's director general, said, "it really is all humanity that is under threat during a pandemic."[30]

Second, there are limits to any nation's capacity to deal with pandemic threats just through its own domestic policy. The "Vegas dilemma," whereby what happens inside states doesn't stay inside states (Chapter 7), pertains to pandemics as well. As with so many other globalization issues, a sound national policy is necessary but not sufficient. Avian flu and other global pandemics require global strategies. States where outbreaks may occur must have the capacity to deal with them in the early stages. Yet many of those states are developing countries with little public health capacity. Therefore, many experts advocate U.S. policies that emphasize building up the preventive and early detection capacities of other states, as well as the WHO's authority and resources as the fulcrum of global policy capacity.

Global Environmental Issues

Global environmental issues pose six types of policy challenges. First, they constitute a classic problem of "public goods" and "collective action." The renowned economist Paul Samuelson defined public goods as "collective consumption goods . . . which all enjoy in common in the sense that each individual's consumption of such a good leads to no subtraction from any other individual's consumption of that good."[31] Collective-action problems are those in which everyone would benefit by taking joint action to deal with a problem, but collective action is impeded by each waiting for the other to act first or by lack of agreement on what should be done. All countries will suffer if global warming, ozone depletion, and other global environmental problems grow worse. All countries therefore have an interest in ensuring that they do not. But it is the essence of the problem of global governance that taking such action is difficult.

Second is the balance between environmental and economic priorities. Although the treaty establishing the WTO includes environmental protection and sustainable development as goals, often there are tensions between these goals and trade promotion. The WTO claims that it gives due consideration to the environment; many environmental NGOs strongly disagree.[32] Similarly, the IMF debate concerns the fiscal austerity and export-promotion emphases of its structural adjustment policies and whether they increase pressure to adopt environmentally damaging policies. In Indonesia, for example, pressure to generate foreign exchange to pay back foreign debt led to massive burning of biologically rich tropical forests to clear land for export-oriented palm oil production.

Third, issues of North-South equity further complicate global environmental negotiations. For example, on global warming, developing countries claim a right to higher ceilings on industrial emissions. They base their claim on both economic grounds that poor countries cannot afford more sophisticated emissions-scrubbing technologies, and on the historical-justice argument that developed countries polluted heavily when they were developing during the nineteenth and early twentieth centuries.

Fourth is the problem of enforcement. As in other policy areas, once multilateral agreements are reached, norms affirmed, and actions mandated, how will fulfillment and compliance be ensured? Following the 1992 Earth Summit in Rio de Janeiro, Brazil, the UN created the Commission on Sustainable Development. Ten years later at the Johannesburg, South Africa, World Summit on Sustainable Development, the UN's own statements acknowledged how little this commission had achieved and how much it needed to be "recharged" and "revitalized."[33]

Fifth, the environment is also a peace and security issue. Not only environmentalists but also the more traditional security establishment, the Pentagon included, have conducted numerous studies about the environment as a security issue. Environmental scarcity and degradation have been sources of conflict and violence in wars, both recent and historical. The Norwegian Nobel Committee recognized this when it awarded the 2004 Peace Prize to Wangari Maathai, a Kenyan woman who started an environmental movement that, among other things, planted 30 million trees in Africa. "With this award," the Nobel committee chair stated, "we have expanded the term 'peace' to encompass environmental questions related to our beloved Earth. . . . Peace on Earth depends on our ability to secure our living environment."[34]

Sixth is the dilemma of prevention and the trade-off between immediate costs and future benefits. In his book *Collapse: How Societies Choose to Fail or Succeed,* the Pulitzer Prize–winning author Jared Diamond looks back through history at societies that brought about their own collapse because they inflicted so much environmental degradation. "How could a society," Diamond asks, "fail to have seen the dangers that seem so clear in retrospect?" Today the risks are even greater than when Easter Island or Norse Greenland collapsed because "globalization makes it impossible for societies to collapse in isolation."[35] The risk and opportunity are expressed in the subtitle of Diamond's book; failure is not inevitable and success is not guaranteed—both are dependent on the choices that societies make.

GLOBAL CLIMATE CHANGE   How strong is the scientific evidence on global climate change? Most scientists and relevant policy analysts say it is quite strong. "Warming of the climate system," states the UN Intergovernmental Panel on Climate Change (IPCC) "is unequivocal." The study by the U.S. National Research Council (Reading 8.3) concurs with this assessment. And the problem is getting worse. Unless major policy changes are implemented, there is a 50 percent chance that temperatures will rise another 5 degrees Celsius during this century; by comparison, it took thousands of years—since the last ice age—for the world to increase 5 degrees in temperature. Even a 2- to 3-degree rise would melt major glaciers and the Greenland ice sheet, and could cause 40 percent of animal species to become extinct. A 5-degree rise could raise sea levels to the point of threatening large coastal and river cities such as London, Shanghai, New York, and Tokyo, and might even wipe out whole island nations.[36] In the United States, barrier islands such as those at Cape Hatteras, North Carolina, could be threatened. So, too, could U.S. coastal areas, including heavily populated sites on the East and West Coasts as well as the Gulf of Mexico.

8.3

Some studies have focused particularly on the melting of the world's glacial ice caps. "The seemingly indestructible snows of [Mount] Kilimanjaro that inspired Ernest Hemingway's famous short story," warned a *New York Times* editorial, "may well disappear in the next 15 years."[37] The seven hundred scientists who conducted the study issued an even more dire warning: "Projected climate changes during the 21st century have the potential to lead to future large-scale and possible irreversible changes in Earth systems resulting in impacts at continental and global scales."[38] For Americans who might try to take comfort in this being relevant only to mountains in Asia or glaciers at the North and South Poles, the report went on to stress how the interlinking chain of global climate could also increase droughts in the American Midwest, floods in the Pacific Northwest, and could have other destructive effects on American life, the American economy, and the American environment.

The year 2012 had especially extreme weather, not only in the United States but globally. Table 8.1 highlights some of the climate change data.

One of the disputes among scientists has been over how much of global warming and other climate change is attributable to natural processes, which may run through self-equilibrating cycles over time, and how much is the result of human and societal practices. The evidence is stronger than ever that this is not happening *to* humans but is being done *by* humans. On a positive note, this also means that the problems can be corrected—but only through major policy shifts.

Former vice president Al Gore had a major impact on the climate change debate through his 2006 movie and book, *An Inconvenient Truth*. Gore cast the issue as having a much broader sweep and magnitude than a typical policy issue. "The relationship between human civilization and the Earth has been utterly transformed by a combination of factors, including the population explosion, the technological revolution, and a willingness to ignore the future consequences of our present actions. The underlying reality is that we are colliding with the planet's ecological system, and its most vulnerable components are crumbling as a result."[39]

Some observers disagree. The columnist George Will points to scientific predictions of global cooling in the 1970s, saying the threat of global warming is just another instance of predictions that won't come true.[40] He believes much of the data that support the prediction of global warming are exaggerated or inaccurate. He considers climate change to be a "hypothetical calamity" that distracts from "real calamities" such as the current economic situation. Other prominent critics include the economist Julian Simon, who disputed the accuracy of the evidence that scientists cited, as well as its policy implications. He claimed the limits to growth claimed by today's environmentalists would be as wrong as Thomas Malthus was about the perils of population growth. Simon's writings also reflected a sense that whatever the problems were, markets and technology would provide the fix.[41]

The 1997 United Nations Framework on Climate Change, also known as the **Kyoto treaty** after the city in Japan where key negotiations were held, has been a key part of this

TABLE 8.1 2012: Temperature Records and Other Weather Extremes

By any number of measures the year 2012 provided evidence of global warming:

- It was the hottest year ever recorded in the United States. And whereas temperature fluctuations usually are in fractions of a degree, the 55.3 degree Fahrenheit annual average was a full degree higher than the previous record in 1998.

- Local weather stations around the country recorded 34,008 daily high records and only 6,664 record lows. As recently as the 1970s highs and lows were roughly in balance.

- The 10 warmest years on record all have been within the last 15 years.

- There also were many other weather extremes including numerous tornados, Hurricane Issac in the Gulf of Mexico area, and Hurricane Sandy which did over $60 billion in damage.

And globally:

- China had its coldest winter in 30 years.

- Australia had a record heat wave.

- Pakistan had extreme flooding.

- The Middle East had a rare and vicious storm bringing rain, snow, and flooding.

- England had its wettest year since records began more than 100 years ago. Four of its five wettest years have been in the past decade.

- Rio de Janeiro had a day when the temperature reached 109.8 degrees, the hottest since records began in 1915.

Sources: Justin Gillis, "Not Even Close: 2012 Was Hottest Ever in U.S.," *New York Times*, January 8, 2013, A1, and Sarah Lyall, "Heat, Flood or Icy Cold, Extreme Weather Rages Worldwide," *New York Times*, January 10, 2013, A4.

debate. The Clinton administration signed the treaty but did not submit it to the Senate for ratification for fear that the treaty would not garner the two-thirds majority needed to pass—even with a Democratic majority in the Senate. The George W. Bush administration flatly opposed the treaty. President Bush described it as "fatally flawed," "unrealistic," and "not based on science."[42] Much of the world was highly critical of Bush's stance. Even those who agreed that countries such as China should have to meet some binding targets emphasized that the United States was by far the world's largest greenhouse gas emitter, both in total quantity and on a per capita basis. Moreover, the Bush administration's opposition to the Kyoto treaty was seen as not just a quibble about the treaty's details but as a broader manifestation of Bush's anti-multilateralist position.

Despite American opposition, the Kyoto treaty went into effect in February 2005, when it met the requirement of ratification by at least fifty-five countries, which together account for at least 55 percent of global carbon dioxide emissions. Its record has been mixed. Many countries that did sign, such as Canada, Japan, and much of Europe, have not met their targets. Policies such as **cap and trade**, whereby companies and others agree to targets for cutting emissions and can sell emissions permits to those who exceed their targets, were not working as well as projected. Still, many experts assess that the situation would have been even worse without the Kyoto treaty and that it provided a basis on which to build, particularly with studies indicating worsening climate conditions.

While pledging to make America a leader in the next round of forging a global climate change treaty, the Obama administration went to the 2009 Copenhagen climate change summit having made only limited changes in U.S. policy. Some actions were taken through executive orders, but Congress had not passed any major new legislation. While other countries also bore responsibility for the Copenhagen summit making only limited progress, the U.S. share ran counter to its claim to global leadership on this issue. Little progress was made at follow-up climate change conferences in Cancun, Mexico, in 2010, Durban, South Africa in 2011, and back in Rio in 2012.

OTHER KEY ENVIRONMENTAL ISSUES   Climate change is challenging but it isn't the only pressing global environmental issue affecting American and global Prosperity. We discuss several others here.

The World's Oceans   The acidity of world's oceans is increasing "faster than at any time in the past 300 million years."[43] Rising acidity threatens coral reefs, shellfish, and potentially the entire marine food web. These problems, along with other patterns of pollution, have raised concerns about a "global collapse" of fish species.[44] Close to 30 percent of fish species are down to 10 percent of their previous levels. This drop sets off a destructive cycle that leaves marine ecosystems more vulnerable to overfishing and less able to replenish. The world's fishing industry, at both the large-scale corporate level and the small-scale village level, is at risk.

Biodiversity   Fish species are not the only ones threatened with reduction and even extinction. The overall number and variety of plant and animal species, which scientists call *biodiversity,* is at risk. One in four land mammals faces extinction, according to a 2008 study by the International Union for Conservation of Nature (IUCN).[45] A key factor is habitat loss to development, hunting, and climate change. The good news from the study was that 5 percent of threatened mammals for which conservation measures had been taken were showing signs of recovery in the wild. The message was the same for both the problem and the solution: policy matters.

One-third of U.S. bird species are also endangered.[46] The mix of causes also included loss of habitat to development and climate change as well as wildfires and disease. In this case, too, the policy message cut both ways, with findings that herons, egrets, ducks, and other birds have benefited from wetlands conservation. Fish stocks have benefited from programs such as catch shares, initiated by the Environmental Defense Fund.

Desertification   The United Nations Convention to Combat Desertification (UNCCD) defines *desertification* as "the degradation of land in arid, semi-arid and dry sub-humid areas. It is caused primarily by human activities and climatic variations.... It occurs because dry land ecosystems, which cover over one third of the world's land area, are extremely vulnerable to over-exploitation and inappropriate land use."[47] Desertification affects almost 9 billion acres of land worldwide, or 25 percent of the Earth's terrestrial land mass. Its costs are estimated at to be more than $40 billion annually on the global scale, not including hidden costs such as the need for increased fertilizer, the loss of bio-diversity, poor health, and malnutrition. Over 250 million people are presently affected by desertification, and nearly 1 billion people in over one hundred countries are at risk. The food and health crises associated with desertification predominantly affect the world's poorest, most marginalized, and politically weakest citizens.

Deforestation   *Deforestation* is the removal of trees in forested areas, primarily by logging and/or burning. Although deforestation meets some human needs, it also has profound local and global consequences such as social conflict, extinction of plants and animals, and climate change. The leading direct causes of tropical deforestation are agricultural expansion, high levels of wood extraction, and the extension of roads and other infrastructure into forested areas. Indirect causes include increasing economic activity and associated market failures; a range of policy and institutional weaknesses and failures; the effects of technological change; low public awareness of the importance of forest areas; and human demographic factors such as population growth, population density, and migration.[48] Tropical forests are the most threatened.

More than 1.7 billion people live in the forty nations with critically low levels of forest cover, which in many cases hinders prospects for sustainable development. The number of people living in low-forest-cover countries is expected to triple to 4.6 billion by 2025, and thirteen additional countries will experience forest-resource scarcity if deforestation continues at its current pace.[49]

Air Pollution   Every year, the American Lung Association publishes a "State of the Air" report on air quality in the U.S. The 2011 report found that half of the U. S. population lives in counties with unhealthful levels of air pollution. Worldwide, the World Health Organization attributes 3.3 million premature deaths to air pollution each year. In China alone, air pollution contributed to 1.2 million premature deaths in 2010.[50] Since air is a classic example of a problem with no national boundaries, mitigating the situation calls for concerted global efforts. Moreover, reducing air-pollution levels can help reduce the global burden of illness from respiratory infections, heart disease, and lung cancer.[51]

Urbanization   The world is experiencing the largest wave of urban growth in history. More than half the human population now lives in urban areas. By 2025 the world will have eight more megacities: Asia will gain five, Latin America two, and Africa one. By 2050, Asia's urban population will double, from 1.7 billion to 3.4 billion. Africa's will triple, from 399 million to 1.2 billion, and the urban population of Latin America and the Caribbean will rise from 462 million to 648 million.[52] Though urbanization has been a historical precursor to economic growth, cities tend to concentrate poverty, slum growth, environmental degradation, and social unrest.[53]

All of these issues require global—not just U.S.—action. None of these issues are only U.S. concerns. The question is, will the United States lead or lag in such global efforts?

Principles

Here in the 21st century, as in past periods, we have been having intense debates over how much priority to give democracy promotion and human rights protection when defining the U.S. national interest (that is, how much to favor Principles over the other "Ps"). Even to the extent that Principles are given priority, the next issue is ensuring the effectiveness of policies aimed at democracy promotion and human rights protection. As we will see, U.S. policies under recent administrations have had a decidedly mixed record.

Global Democracy: Status and Prospects

When surveying the status of democracy and human rights in the world, it is necessary to take into account the successes, the limits and setbacks, and the uncertainties that remain. It's also helpful to have a historical perspective on the four "waves" through which democratization has developed in the modern world (see "Historical Perspectives," p. 363).

GLOBAL SURVEY   The annual survey done by Freedom House, which categorizes countries as free, partly free, and not free (that is, democracies that are free or partially free, and non-democracies), shows how widespread democracy has become.[54] Of 195 countries, 149 are ranked as either free (88) or partly free (61) for a combined percentage of 76 percent. This is a much higher number and a much higher percentage than in the 1980s. They include 48 countries that have made a transition to democracy since 1989, and only seven that slipped from democracy to non-democracy.

HISTORICAL PERSPECTIVES
HISTORICAL PERSPECTIVES

"WAVES" OF DEMOCRATIZATION

Many political scientists and historians see democratization as having had a number of "waves" in the modern world.*

The first wave is dated roughly from 1776 to 1933. This "long, slow wave" starts with the American Revolution, runs through the nineteenth century and greater democratization in monarchical Europe, and into the twentieth century, including the period just after World War I when Germany and parts of Eastern Europe (e.g., Czechoslovakia) were briefly democracies. The 1933–45 period was a major reversal as Nazism, other forms of fascism, and communism spread. Germany's democracy was taken over by Adolf Hitler, who went on to conquer much of Europe; Spain and Italy became fascist under Francisco Franco and Benito Mussolini, respectively. Russia, which had been a democracy for less than a year in 1917, became communist and brought most of its neighbors with it.

The second wave of democratization ran from 1945 to 1964. It included the restoration of democracy to much of Western Europe, the shift from military to democratic governments in many Latin American countries, and the establishment of democracy in a number of newly independent African states. By 1964, though, key Latin American countries such as Brazil and Argentina underwent military coups, many of which were supported by the United States according to its "ABC" (anything but communism) strategy. In Chile, where the United States had substantial involvement, the democratically elected socialist government of President Salvador Allende was overthrown in an especially violent coup. In Africa, one-man rule replaced many nascent democracies. And in Europe, a 1967 coup installed a military government in Greece, the birthplace of democracy. In 1973, of the 135 countries in the world, only 39 were democracies.

The third wave dates from 1974 to 1986. During this period Greece, Spain, and Portugal, the three major Western European countries still ruled by the military, became democratic. Other countries such as the Philippines (as we discuss later in this chapter) also overthrew dictators and became democratic. By contrast, countries such as Pakistan had military coups.

The fourth wave, starting in 1989, brought the end of communism and the emergence of democracy in much of the former Soviet Union and Soviet bloc. By 1992, 117 of 192 countries were democracies. This included many Latin American countries where the decline in U.S. "ABC" support for authoritarian leaders removed a main barrier. A number of countries that democratized in this wave subsequently experienced reversals of democracy, including Russia and some other ex-Soviet states.

> Will there be a fifth wave? This question focuses especially on Africa and the Middle East, as we see later in this chapter.
>
> *See Larry Diamond, *Developing Democracy: Toward Consolidation* (Baltimore: Johns Hopkins University Press, 1997); Samuel P. Huntington, *The Third Wave: Democratization in the Late Twentieth Century* (Norman, Okla.: University of Oklahoma Press, 1991); Robert A. Dahl, *Polyarchy: Participation and Opposition* (New Haven: Yale University Press, 1971); Philippe C. Schmitter, "The International Context of Contemporary Democratization," *Stanford Journal of International Affairs* 2.1 (1993): 1–34; Thomas Carothers, *Aiding Democracy Abroad: The Learning Curve* (Washington, D.C.: Carnegie Endowment for International Peace, 1999).

Among the new democracies are former Soviet bloc countries. Russia, though, which had moved up to partly free in the 1990s, first dropped into "not free" in 2007 and has stayed there." Also included as democracies are all the Latin American countries except Cuba. This, too, is a major historical shift: almost every country in Latin American had at least one military coup in the twentieth century. African countries have been making some progress on democratization as well. The most remarkable case is South Africa. The apartheid system had ensured the white minority's total control of the government and the economy, and condemned the black majority to oppression, injustice, and poverty. Later revelations pointed to torture and assassination plots ordered by government officials against black leaders. Yet by 1994 Nelson Mandela, a former political prisoner, had been elected president of South Africa and black majority rule was established. In the Middle East, the "Arab Spring" that began in 2011 brought down longstanding dictatorships and began an unprecedented shift toward democracy. Egypt, Tunisia, and Libya held democratic elections, Egypt's first in several generations and Tunisia and Libya's first ever.

A substantial number of countries, though, sit on the other side of the scale: 46 countries, or about 24 percent of the world, are non-democratic. Moreover, tremendous uncertainties remain as to whether the gains made in new democracies will be consolidated and institutionalized. History is replete with failed democratic revolutions—the February 1917 revolution in Russia, for example, which was trumped by Vladimir Lenin and the Bolsheviks, or the Weimar Republic of the 1920s and 1930s in Germany, which elected Adolf Hitler as chancellor.

To be sure, the problems and setbacks that feed pessimism have to be kept in perspective—after all, who believed that the successes of the early 1990s would be possible just a few years before they occurred? The lesson that endures despite the fading euphoria is that positive political change is always possible. This is a major reason that most contemporary critics find theories such as Huntington's "clash of civilizations" too deterministic. These theories suggest that states, their leaders, and their people can only play out a script inscribed over the centuries, and cannot shape their societies, political systems, or values in an evolving way.

Yet Fukuyama's "end of history" optimism also needs to be tempered. It takes nothing away from the successes achieved thus far to acknowledge that declaring democracy is not the same as consolidating and institutionalizing it. Democracy can be said to be consolidated and institutionalized in a country when governing regimes can change but the political system itself remains stable. The political change that does occur must be within the bounds of a constitutional order, and it must be peaceful, with little or limited political violence. This is the challenge facing many newly democratic countries.

We go into more detail about each region in later chapters.

DEMOCRACY PROMOTION STRATEGIES   There is no single, one-size-fits-all strategy for democracy promotion. The foreign policy challenge for the United States and other international actors is to determine the right fit and the right mix of approaches for different countries with different sets of problems, and to pursue those strategies with the right combination of international actors. This generally involves six key objectives: facilitating free and fair elections, helping build strong and accountable political institutions, establishing a free press, strengthening the rule of law, protecting human rights, and helping cultivate a robust civil society.

Facilitating Free and Fair Elections   International electoral assistance and monitoring by American and other international groups is intended to facilitate free and fair elections in newly democratizing countries. In many cases the presence of international election monitors has been a significant factor in ensuring free and fair elections. But there have been less successful cases. Research by Professor Judith Kelley points to a number of factors that affect the likelihood of effective election monitoring.[55] Some of these are tensions and trade-offs in the broader policy context that affect how hard the United States and/or other international actors press for clean elections. Others are factors within the country being monitored. Kelley, Susan Hyde, and other scholars stress the importance of getting election monitoring right, and make a number of recommendations for how to do so.[56] These include: Focus on countries already on the road to transition, where there are domestic pressures for change, and where the international community is willing to use its leverage; build capacity within the countries well prior to election dates to assemble voter rolls and ensure the secrecy of the vote; and work only with those election observer organizations that have high credibility for thorough and objective work.

Building Strong and Accountable Political Institutions   Although democratic revolutions are often personality driven, with people mobilizing around a charismatic leader, stable democracy requires strong and accountable *political institutions.* The democratization literature stresses three principal reasons that political institutionalization is important.[57] The first concerns maintaining political stability. Political systems that have built strong institutions are less dependent on and less vulnerable to the fate or whims of a particular governing regime. Second is representativeness. Political systems with strong institutions are more likely to convey a sense of genuine choice, competition, and accountability. Third is effective governance. The instability that comes with weak institutions makes it very difficult to achieve the steadiness and follow-through required to govern. In contrast, well-institutionalized democracies are more capable of governing effectively because, as the democracy scholar Larry Diamond writes, "they have more effective and stable structures for representing interests and because they are more likely to produce working legislative majorities or coalitions that can adopt and sustain policies."[58]

An important area for democratic institution-building is strengthening legislatures. To fulfill their representative functions, legislatures must develop other professional and institutional capacities to carry out such tasks as designing committee systems, developing the legal and technical expertise to draft legislation, computerizing legislative operations, communicating and servicing constituencies, and building up research and library support systems. Representative David Price (D–North Carolina), a member of the bipartisan House Democracy Assistance Commission (and a former Duke University professor of political science and public policy), states the Commission's goal as "to give parliaments in emerging democracies the necessary advice and tools to set up their governments . . . to serve not just as a model, but as a partner in the effort to strengthen democracy across the globe."[59]

Another area is civil-military relations. This is where the Pentagon has played a key role. For example, the NATO Partnership for Peace (PFP) program seeks not only to foster military cooperation but also to have western NATO militaries inculcate the principles of civilian control of the military in their ex-communist counterparts.

Local government programs are the focus of a number of USAID initiatives. An official document stressed the reasons for this focus: "Decentralization shifts responsibility for decision making to the leadership and the citizens most directly affected. Fiscal decentralization helps improve local finances, enabling local officials to better provide for their constituencies. Improvements in service delivery build public confidence in democratic processes. Accordingly, they reinforce citizen participation."[60] Among the programs cited were aid to a fishermen's association in the Philippines seeking to ban commercial trawlers from local waters, the creation of a national mayors' association in Bulgaria, and a petition drive in Mozambique to help small farmers get title to their lands.

Anticorruption initiatives are another crucial need. Corruption undermines democratization both by siphoning off scarce resources in poor countries, and by deeply delegitimizing those in power and, potentially, the political system itself. Transparency International is an NGO formed for the express purpose of fighting corruption. Each year it issues a list that ranks countries by their levels of corruption, and pressures countries to enact anticorruption reforms. One of its projects is the "Corruption Fighters' Tool Kit," which includes a range of strategies for NGOs, civil society, governments, and other actors "to demand and promote accountable and responsive public administration."[61]

Establishing Free Press   The accountability provided by a *free press* is crucial. Yet democratizing countries have mostly limited experience in this area and need outside assistance. The Vienna-based International Press Institute (www.freemedia.at), another NGO, has played an important role in this effort. It runs training programs and conferences for journalists from ex-communist and other newly democratizing countries, leads missions to assess a country's media environment, and maintains vigilance and advocates for journalists who face repression, injustice, and death threats. According to the New York–based Committee to Protect Journalists (www.cpj.org), between 1992 and 2012 971 journalists were killed. Iraq was the deadliest country for journalists (151 killed), followed by the Philippines (73), Algeria (60), Russia (54), and Pakistan (57).

Strengthening the Rule of Law   The *rule of law* means that citizens are protected by a strong constitution and other legal guarantees against arbitrary acts by the state and lawless acts by other citizens. A wide range of programs and initiatives are needed to strengthen the rule of law. These include assistance in drafting a constitution and writing other legal codes. Courts may lack the most basic infrastructure of trained judicial reporters, computers for compiling jury lists, "bench books" on how to conduct jury trials, and the like. Law school curriculums often need to be overhauled. Police forces need to be trained. Special initiatives may be needed to help women, minorities, and the disadvantaged. Education programs on the very principle of the rule of law as the basis for justice need to be undertaken. The American Bar Association's Central and East European Law Initiative (CEELI), which provided legal expertise to countries emerging from communism, is a good example of efforts to strengthen the rule of law.

Another challenge is reckoning with the past, or what is often called ***transitional justice***.[62] Many newly democratizing societies are emerging from pasts that can only be characterized as horrific: El Salvador, with its decade of civil war, right-wing "death squads," and guerrilla violence; Cambodia, where the Khmer Rouge left hundreds of thousands dead in the "killing fields"; South Africa, with generations of discrimination, oppression, and killings under the apartheid system; Chile and Argentina, where torture, arbitrary arrests, and cases of *desaparecidos* ("disappeared ones") were common under military dictatorships; Hungary, where property-rights claims must be adjudicated against confiscations made in the communist era and going back to the Nazi occupation. The public cannot just move on from such brutal pasts without some accountability, recompense, or other means of justice. The challenge is how to obtain these measures in ways that help societies move forward in their political transitions. While much of this falls to the countries themselves to determine, some U.S. State Department and USAID programs have been developed to provide expertise and other assistance during transitions.

Protecting Human Rights   Recent U.S. administrations' human rights policies have differed in their emphasis and focus on human rights violations. The Carter administration went further than its predecessors in addressing human rights violations by leaders who, although pro-American, were authoritarian and repressive—for example, Antonio Somoza in Nicaragua and the shah of Iran. The Reagan administration put its focus on communist regimes such as the Soviet Union, Cuba, and post-Somoza Marxist Nicaragua. During the G. H. W. Bush and Clinton administrations, with the Cold War over and the war on terrorism not yet begun, there was less of a pattern along pro- or anti-American lines. The pattern was revived in the G. W. Bush administration, however, with its emphasis on the "axis of evil" and other states that support terrorism. Other human rights violators were not ignored, but the emphasis was on those linked most closely to the anti-Americanism of global terrorism. The Obama administration came into office pledging to give greater priority to human rights. In practice, the administration sought to strike its own balance, as we see in later chapters regarding China, the Middle East, and elsewhere.

For many years, the UN Commission on Human Rights, which drafted the Universal Declaration of Human Rights and other human rights covenants, had been the principal UN forum in which human rights issues were raised. But it severely undermined the credibility of its own message by having gross human rights violators such as China, Cuba, Libya, Sudan, Syria, and Zimbabwe as members. Criticism did not just come from the second Bush administration; many NGOs were outraged over this "rogues' gallery of human rights abusers."[63] Reforms were made, including changing the name to the Human Rights Council, but real change has been slow at best. A UN Human Rights Council that takes its mission seriously enough to say that countries must practice what they preach could have a real impact.

NGOs such as Amnesty International and Human Rights Watch play such an important role in human rights advocacy that they are often referred to as the "conscience" of governments. Unbound by trade-offs with other foreign policy objectives and less inhibited by the formalities of traditional diplomacy, human rights NGOs can be more vocal and assertive than governments or multilateral organizations. Indeed, Amnesty International won the Nobel Peace Prize in 1977. Since then, the Internet, cell phones, and other advanced methods of communication have made it both more difficult for repressive governments to hide their human rights violations and easier for advocacy groups to communicate with their global networks of activists. The NGO role in human rights advocacy has become even more significant.

Cultivating Civil Society   A strong civil society has lots of what Harvard scholar Robert Putnam calls "*social capital*"—public-spiritedness and community involvement that goes beyond just voting. It entails other forms of civic engagement, a sense of "reciprocity and cooperation," and a shared ethic among citizens of being "helpful, respectful and trustful towards one another, even when they differ on matters of substance."[64] In many newly democratizing societies, decades of dictatorship and even longer historical traditions of authoritarianism have left little basis on which to build such practices and values. Elections won't work, political institutions won't be stable, and the rule of law won't become established unless the basic civic values of nonviolent resolution of political differences, tolerance for societal differences, and commitment to some level of political engagement provide a societal foundation.

Assessing Effectiveness Enough time has passed that assessments of the effectiveness of post–Cold War democracy promotion are being made. These assessments have been decidedly mixed. "The effects of democracy promotion programs," Thomas Carothers concludes, "are usually modestly positive, sometimes negligible and occasionally negative." He runs through many of the major program areas:

- Rule of law: "What stands out about U.S. rule-of-law assistance since the mid-1980s is how difficult and often disappointing such work is. . . . Most of the projects launched with enthusiasm—and large budgets—. . . have fallen far short of their goals."
- Legislative assistance: "The record is riddled with disappointment and failure. . . . All too often [programs] have barely scratched the surface in feckless, corrupt, patronage-ridden parliaments. . . ."
- Civil society: "Democracy promoters are starting to learn . . . just how inflated their expectations have been and how limited their capabilities to produce broad-scale change really are."[65]

In each of these areas Carothers does make some positive points: that rule-of-law programs have "help[ed] push the issue onto the agenda of governments . . . [which] in the long run may prove an important contribution"; that in some important cases legislative aid "has helped make possible significant improvement"; and that "various lines of positive evolution" and "more sophisticated programming" are seen in civil society efforts. In his conclusions he stresses that his analysis does not mean that "democracy aid does not work or is futile," rather that it is "a useful element of American foreign aid and foreign policy that is gradually gaining coherence, one that is rarely of decisive importance but usually more than a decorative add-on."[66]

A long-term perspective needs to be maintained. The U.S. democratic system was not built in a few years or few decades; it is an ongoing process, and still an imperfect one. Although impact has to be measurable, markers need to be set that allow for short- and medium-term assessment as well as a longer-term approach. One study points to the not fully tangible "enhancing [of] the resources, skills, techniques, ideas and legitimacy of civil society organizations, civic education efforts, the mass media" and other local actors as one of the main contributions of democracy-promotion programs.[67] Another study stresses that "many of the most important results of democracy promotion are psychological, moral, subjective, indirect and time-delayed."[68] Moreover, to try to build democracy without tackling poverty, the concentration of economic power, and related social inequalities is "to float on the surface of current politics, never affecting the broader structural tides beneath."[69]

Principles and Peace: The Democratic Peace Debate

According to the theory of the *democratic peace,* the United States should support the spread of democracy not just because it is the right thing to do, but also because history demonstrates that democracies do not fight wars against other democracies. This means it is in the U.S. national interest to support democratization to reduce the risks of war. The theory does not claim that democracies don't go to war at all. They have, and they do—against nondemocracies. But they don't, and they won't, it is argued, go to war against other democracies. This tenet of the democratic peace paradigm implies that right makes for might, that the world is a safer and better place to the extent that democracy spreads. For American foreign policy, the promotion of democracy is said to have the added value of serving objectives of both Peace and Principles.

Democratic peace theory has had a major influence on U.S. foreign policy in recent administrations (see "Theory in the World," p. 371). This makes it all the more important to consider the theory's validity. Below, the main arguments and evidence from proponents and critics of the theory are examined.

DEMOCRATIC PEACE THEORY   Proponents of the democratic peace theory make the sweeping claim that "the absence of war between democratic states comes as close to [*sic*] anything we have to an empirical law in international relations."[70] The empirical evidence as they present it is indeed impressive:

- Democracies have not fought any wars against each other since 1815. This encompasses 71 interstate wars involving nearly 270 participant groups.
- Since the end of World War II, democracies have been only one-eighth as likely as nondemocracies to threaten the use military force against a democracy, and only one-tenth as likely to use even limited force against each other.
- Democracies have fought numerous wars against nondemocracies, however, including World War I, World War II, and many others during the Cold War.[71]

The central tenets, logic, and philosophical basis of the democratic peace paradigm are often associated with President Woodrow Wilson. In the history of U.S. foreign policy, however, the idea can be traced all the way back to the eighteenth-century European political philosopher Immanuel Kant and his book *Perpetual Peace.* The basic argument has three components: the constraints imposed by democratic political systems, the internationalization of democratic norms, and the bonds built by trade.

THEORY IN THE WORLD

THEORY IN THE WORLD

DEMOCRATIC PEACE THEORY AND THE CLINTON AND BUSH FOREIGN POLICIES

Bill Clinton's 1994 State of the Union address sounded like a quote from the political science literature on democratic peace theory. "Democracies don't attack each other," President Clinton declared, so "ultimately the best strategy to ensure our security and to build a durable peace is to support the advance of democracy elsewhere."[*] Clinton's advisers coined the term "enlargement," playing off of Cold War "containment," to refer to the spread of global democracy and the U.S. interests this served. A major Clinton administration policy statement declared, "all of America's strategic interests—from promoting prosperity at home to checking global threats abroad before they threaten our territory—are served by enlarging the community of democratic and free-market nations."[†] Ensuring the success of democracy was posed as both a pragmatic and idealistic goal, serving Peace as well as Principles.

Many key officials of the George W. Bush administration came into office as self-styled Realists who, though not opposed to democracy, did not make its global promotion a high priority. During the 2000 presidential campaign, while serving as then governor Bush's senior foreign policy advisor, Condoleezza Rice laid out five priorities, none of which gave much weight to democracy promotion.[‡] This started to change after September 11. Bush's 2005 inaugural address went much further in invoking democratic peace logic. So too did Condoleezza Rice, now secretary of state, who wrote an op-ed tellingly titled "The Promise of Democratic Peace." "Supporting the growth of democratic institutions in all nations is not some moralistic flight of fancy," she wrote. "It is the only realistic response to our present challenges." The reasoning was that the "Fundamental character of regimes matters more today than the international distribution of power. . . . Democracy is the only assurance of lasting peace and security between states, because it is the only guarantee of freedom and justice within states."[§]

Clinton's 1994 State of the Union, Bush's 2005 inaugural, and Rice's 2005 op-ed showed exceptionally strong and direct theory-policy links. We might even have asked for footnotes!

[*]Bill Clinton, State of the Union Address, *New York Times,* January 26, 1994, A17.
[†]"A National Security Strategy of Engagement and Enlargement," reprinted in *America's Strategic Choices,* Michael E. Brown et al., eds. (Cambridge, Mass.: MIT Press, 1997), 319.
[‡]Condoleezza Rice, "Promoting the National Interest," *Foreign Affairs* 79.1 (January/February 2000): 45–62.
[§]Rice, "The Promise of Democratic Peace," *Washington Post,* December 11, 2005, B7.

Domestic Political Constraints   We have already seen how, historically, going to war is one of the recurring great debates in American politics. Kant, who was writing before the United States of America even existed with its own constitution and foreign policy, made his argument with reference to democracies in general. If "the consent of the citizens is required in order to decide that war should be declared," he wrote,

> nothing is more natural than that they would be very cautious in commencing such a poor game. . . . Among the [calamities of war] would be: having to fight, having to pay the costs of war from their own resources, having painfully to repair the devastation war leaves behind, and, to fill up the measure of evils, load themselves with a heavy national debt that would embitter peace itself and that can never be liquidated on account of constant wars in the future. But, on the other hand, in a constitution which is not republican, and under which the subjects are not citizens, a declaration of war is the easiest thing to decide upon, because war does not require of the ruler . . . the least sacrifice of the pleasure of his table, the chase, his country houses, his court functions and the like.[72]

Kant also stressed, though, that these constraints were less likely in wars against non-democracies, in which mass publics were more likely to be aroused by crusade-like appeals. Democracies' willingness to go to war against nondemocracies and their unwillingness to go to war against each other follow the same domestic political logic.

Internationalization of Democratic Norms   All democracies, no matter what their representative structure, must practice compromise and consensus-building in their domestic politics and policy. Their watchwords must be tolerance and trust, and the essence of a successful democratic system is managing, if not resolving, conflicts and tensions within society in lawful and peaceful ways. Michael Doyle, who was among the first international relations scholars to advance the democratic peace thesis, states that democracies, "which rest on consent, presume foreign republics to also be consensual, just, and therefore deserving of accommodation."[73] In contrast, nondemocracies, according to John M. Owen, "are viewed *prima facie* as unreasonable, unpredictable."[74] There is a rational logic here, not just ideology. It makes sense not to go to war against a country that you are confident won't move quickly to declare war against you. But war may become the rational choice if you fear the other country may strike preemptively or by surprise.

Bonds of Trade   This spirit of political commonality combined with the common tendency of democracies to have free-market economic systems also leads them to develop trade and other economic relations with each other. The "spirit of commerce," to use Kant's term, becomes another factor inhibiting war. The same idea is also found in the work of such other eminent political philosophers as Montesquieu, who wrote of "the natural effect" of trade "to bring about peace," and John Stuart Mill, who went even further, seeing the expansion of international trade in the mid-nineteenth century as "rapidly rendering war obsolete."[75] The basic ideas are that countries have more to lose from going to war as trade develops, and that war would be fought against people who are no longer strangers. This is said to be especially true today, because international interdependence now encompasses not just trade but investment, finance, and many other economic interconnections we discussed earlier in this chapter.

CRITIQUES AND CAVEATS Four principal arguments have been made by those who question the democratic peace theory.

A Spurious Relationship? Some scholars question whether there really is a strong relationship between states' forms of government and their likelihood of going to war against each other. These critics contend that the claim for this causal link is spurious—not valid—because of methodological problems. One problem is the way "democracy" and "war" are defined by democratic peace theorists, and how it affects the criteria for including or excluding cases. These critics examined empirical data going back to 1815 and cited a number of cases in which they claim democratic peace proponents inaccurately excluded conflicts between democracies, or miscategorized countries that fought wars as nondemocracies.[76] Among the historical examples cited are the American Civil War and Finland's siding with the Axis powers in World War II. Applying the theory to the contemporary context is problematic: many of today's wars are ethnic conflicts, civil wars, and other intrastate conflicts, yet the democratic peace theory principally addresses classical interstate wars.

A second methodological criticism is that democratic peace theorists confuse correlation with causality, mistakenly emphasizing the nature of the domestic political system as the cause of peaceful relations rather than a Realist calculation that cooperation served national interests better than conflict. For example, in response to the claim that the United States, Western Europe, and Japan didn't fight wars with each other from 1945 to 1991 because they are democracies, critics argue that a more important factor was these countries' shared security interests, which were based on the common threat from the Soviet Union. In a number of historical "near-miss" crises, democracies almost went to war against each other, but refrained based on assessments of their interests, not because the other side was a democracy. Two of these crises occurred between the United States and Great Britain in the nineteenth century, and there have been others.[77]

Trade and Peace? A second point raises doubts about how much trade actually inhibits war. On the eve of World War I, Sir Norman Angell, the foremost heir to the Kant-Montesquieu-Mill tradition, diagnosed war as "a failure of understanding" that could be corrected by the mutual familiarity and interchange bred by international commerce. Yet the fact that Germany was Britain's second largest trade partner didn't stop the two countries from going to war. In other historical cases, high levels of economic interdependence did not prevent war. Moreover, high levels of trade do not prevent other political and diplomatic conflicts. U.S.-European and U.S.-Japanese relations provide numerous examples.

Aggressive Tendencies of Democratizing States   Third, and more of a qualifying caveat than outright criticism, is that even if we accept that mature democracies may not fight with each other, states that are still undergoing democratization may be even *more* aggressive and warlike than stable nondemocracies. Transition periods are notoriously unstable, as elites and other groups compete for political influence, and the public struggles with economic difficulties, the disorientation of political change, and an uncertain future. They are quite susceptible to "belligerent nationalism" as a rallying cry and a diversion from domestic problems. According to political scientists Edward Mansfield and Jack Snyder, "like the sorcerer's apprentice, these elites typically find that their mass allies, once mobilized, are difficult to control. When this happens, war can result from nationalist prestige strategies that hard-pressed leaders use to stay astride their unmanageable political coalitions." (Reading 8.4)[78] Slobodan Milosevic in Serbia was one important example of this.

Democracy at the End of a Bayonet   The Bush administration claimed that democratization was one of the objectives of the Iraq War, citing not only the ostensible benefits for the Iraqi people but also the democratic peace logic of making this aggressive adversary into a peace-oriented friend. This claim was questioned by critics who saw the invocation of Principles as a cover for Power-based objectives. Even to the extent that democratization was a genuine priority, democracy "at the end of a bayonet" carried inherent contradictions which also reverberated for democratic peace theory, given its invocation as justification for the Iraq War.

Principles and Power: From "ABC" to "ABT"?

During the Cold War American foreign policy consistently chose Power over Principles in siding with nondemocratic but anticommunist regimes. The "ABC" definition of Third World democrats ("anything but communist") was invoked to make a Principles claim, but it was a weak one. In the context of the war on terrorism, we have seen an "ABT"— anybody but terrorists—definition.

Consider Pakistan, where General Pervez Musharraf came to power in a military coup in 1999. The Clinton administration opposed the coup as a violation of democratic principles and imposed economic sanctions on Pakistan. The Bush administration continued this policy until the September 11, 2001, terrorist attacks. At that point, Power considerations strongly overrode Principles; a close relationship with Pakistan was deemed necessary for the United States to fight the war in Afghanistan, to try to break up Al Qaeda, and to hunt for Osama bin Laden. The United States also came to see Musharraf as the best bet for blocking Islamic fundamentalists and other anti-American forces from gaining ground within Pakistan.

Although Musharraf forced out a democratic government, independent analysts acknowledged that "Pakistanis broadly welcomed [Musharraf's] overthrow of what was widely perceived as a corrupt civilian government."[79] But his own popularity soon fell. When the first post-coup legislative elections were held in October 2002, opposition groups fared better than Musharraf's political party. Among those groups were Islamic fundamentalist parties that were anti-American and called for the imposition of Islamic law.

The debate over U.S.-Pakistan relations grew more intense as Musharraf became more dictatorial and delivered less on the anti-terrorism front. Facing pressure from the United States to move back toward democracy, in October 2007 Musharraf agreed to grant amnesty to Benazir Bhutto, a two-time former prime minister living in exile, and other politicians who had been accused of political corruption. However, shortly after Bhutto returned to Pakistan, Musharraf declared a state of emergency in the country. He suspended the constitution, fired the supreme court, shut off independent and international news channels, and arrested many of his opponents. The opposition to Musharraf reached a tipping point when Bhutto was assassinated as she left a political rally on December 27, 2007. The assassination was perpetrated by Islamist extremists, but its effects reverberated against Musharraf.

Pakistan is not the only country over which this debate is playing out. The war on terrorism brought U.S. military aid and other forms of cooperation to a number of governments with questionable democratic credentials and human rights records. Many of these are Central Asian states bordering Afghanistan: Uzbekistan, Tajikistan, Turkmenistan, and Kyrgyzstan. Each has its own Islamic fundamentalist movement that is known to be or is suspected of being anti-American and having links to Al Qaeda or other global terrorist networks. "You've got to find and nullify enemy leadership," one senior Bush administration official stated. "We are going to support any viable political actor that we think will help us with counterterrorism."[80]

The Obama administration also wrestled with this dilemma. One example involved Kyrgyzstan, where ethnic violence exploded between the Kyrgyz and Uzbeks in June 2010, killing hundreds and displacing some 300,000 Uzbeks. The Obama administration exerted limited pressure, prioritizing the deals made with the Kyrgyz government for military bases that were important to the war in Afghanistan. Yemen is another example where counterterrorism cooperation has been given priority over the government's human rights abuses.

Principles, Power, Peace, and Prosperity: Preventing Genocide and Mass Atrocities

What could be more important than preventing genocide and mass atrocities? While there is plenty of blame to go around, the U.S. record on preventing genocide is not one of which to be proud (see "Historical Perspectives," p. 376). "The United States had never

HISTORICAL PERSPECTIVES
HISTORICAL PERSPECTIVES

"GENOCIDE IN THE TWENTIETH CENTURY"

It wasn't until the early 1940s that the word *genocide* appeared in *Webster's New International Dictionary*. Derived from the Greek *geno,* meaning "race" or "tribe," with the Latin *cide,* meaning "killing," it was first used to characterize Hitler's horrors against German and other European Jews.* Hitler and the Nazis killed more than 6 million Jews in gas chambers and other horrific ways in what came to be known as the Holocaust. More than two years after it had started, the United States eventually entered World War II as leader of the Allies. And even then, despite having information about the Nazi concentration camps, the war strategy did not give priority to stopping the genocide.†

Earlier in the twentieth century, during World War I, nearly 1 million Armenians were killed by the Turks. The word did not exist yet, but the actions constituted genocide. And it neither was secret nor without warning. The *Times of London* headline on October 17, 1915, read "800,000 Armenians counted destroyed." Henry Morgenthau Sr., the U.S. Ambassador to Turkey, cabled back to Washington about the "race murder" going on. But neither the United States nor Great Britain, nor any other country took serious action.‡

Amid these horrors a hero emerged. Raphael Lemkin did more than any other individual to try to generate outrage about and action against genocide. A Polish Jew, Lemkin started working on the issue in the 1920s while still a college student in Poland and continued his work as a young lawyer in the 1930s. When the Nazis invaded Poland, he was forced to flee and ended up in the United States as a law professor at Duke University. Lemkin not only coined the term *genocide* but also was the moving force behind the 1948 Convention on the Prevention and Punishment of the Crime of Genocide. This was the very first human rights treaty approved by the United Nations. Its purpose, as stated in its preamble, "recognizing that at all periods of history genocide has inflicted great losses on humanity," was "to liberate mankind from such an odious scourge." This was part of the "never again" pledge so many made in so many ways after the Nazi Holocaust.

Yet it would be almost forty years before the United States signed and ratified the Genocide Convention. No one "supported" genocide, but opponents of the treaty claimed that it would infringe on America's own sovereignty and bind American foreign policy to commitments that the United States might not want to make. Meanwhile more cases of genocide piled up: in the "killing fields" of Cambodia, where radical communists who came to power after the defeat of the U.S-backed government killed 2 million of their own people between 1975 and 1978; and in

Iraq, where Saddam Hussein used chemical weapons in 1987–88 against Iraqi Kurds.§ In the 1990s it was Bosnia, Rwanda, and Kosovo, and more recently, Darfur.

In none of these cases, historical or contemporary, was the problem a lack of information or options. "I have found," Samantha Power writes, "that in fact U.S. policymakers knew a great deal about the crimes being perpetrated. . . . And the United States did have countless opportunities to mitigate and prevent slaughter. But time and again, decent men and women chose to look away. . . . The crucial question is why."**

That question, perhaps more than any other, is worth pondering.

*Samantha Power, *"A Problem from Hell": America and the Age of Genocide* (New York: Basic Books, 2002) 42, 44.

†David S. Wyman, *The Abandonment of the Jews: America and the Holocaust, 1941–1945* (New York: Pantheon Books, 1984).

‡Power, *"A Problem from Hell,"* 9, 6.

§*The Killing Fields*, a powerful movie about Cambodia, was nominated for Best Picture at the 1984 Academy Awards. On the Iraqi Kurds, see Chapter 2 in Bruce W. Jentleson, *With Friends Like These: Reagan, Bush and Saddam, 1982–1990* (New York: Norton, 1994).

**Power, *"A Problem from Hell,"* xvi–xvii.

in its history intervened to stop genocide and had in fact rarely even made a point of condemning it as it occurred." Samantha Power makes this searing indictment in her Pulitzer Prize–winning book, *A Problem From Hell: America and the Age of Genocide.* Time and again "we all have been bystanders to genocide."[81] Each time a genocide occurred, the prevailing view was that preventing genocide was not sufficiently in the U.S. national interest to warrant the necessary action.

When Secretary of State James Baker offhandedly explained the first Bush administration's inaction while the ethnic "cleansing" mounted in the former Yugoslavia by saying, "We don't have a dog in that fight," he was, however perversely, being consistent with past U.S. foreign policy.[82] Somalia, where in 1992 mass violence also intensified, was "not a critical piece of real estate for anybody in the post–Cold War world," as a former U.S. ambassador put it.[83] In Rwanda in 1994, "in one hundred days . . . some eight hundred thousand Tutsi and politically moderate Hutu were murdered. . . . The Rwandan genocide would prove to be the fastest, most efficient killing spree of the twentieth century." Yet "the United States did almost nothing to try to stop it."[84] Neither did the UN, Europe, nor any other major actor in the international community.

The "Mother Theresa" exchange in the journal *Foreign Affairs* during the Bosnia and Rwanda crises illustrated the debate over how Power and Peace come into play. Factoring humanitarian concerns into the national interest, Michael Mandelbaum contended, is being "too much like Mother Teresa" and turns foreign policy into "social work." Stanley Hoffmann countered that the very distinction between interests and values is "largely fallacious," because "a great power has an 'interest' in world order that goes beyond strict national security concerns and its definition of world order is largely shaped by its values."[85]

Hoffman's argument taps the Peace component of the American national interest. He emphasizes the global level and the intangible yet potent ways that failures to defend basic values and confront genocide and other crimes against humanity, no matter where they occur, undermine the sense and structures of international community. Moreover, and more tangibly, these conflicts do not just feed on themselves but spread to other areas. This occurs through varying combinations of direct "contagion" (the physical movement of refugees and weapons to neighboring countries in a region), "demonstration effects" that activate and escalate other conflicts even without direct contact, and other modes of conflict diffusion.[86] This is what happened in Africa when the Rwandan conflict spread to Zaire (now Democratic Republic of Congo), and in the former Yugoslavia with the connections among the wars in Croatia, Bosnia, and Kosovo.

American Power is also more at risk than the Mandelbaum view claims. As discussed frequently in this book, power depends heavily on credibility. Weak action or inaction in the face of humanitarian crises undermines American credibility. No matter how often the no-dog-in-this-fight claim is made, American inaction is a factor. If aggressors calculate a military advantage over their internal opponents, so long as those opponents cannot count on international assistance for balance and buttressing, it should be no wonder that they choose war and violence. That is what the Serbian leader Slobodan Milosevic did in Bosnia, and because the United States, the UN, and Europe did so little to support his victims and waited so long, he did it again in Kosovo. Credibility rests on the combination of judgment and resolve. When they are brought into question by inaction in the face of humanitarian horrors, a fundamental basis of power is undermined. As Professor Donald Rothchild pointedly put it, "Inaction in the face of genocide involves costs in terms of purpose and self-esteem on the part of a great power and its people that must not be underestimated."[87]

Policy makers have a similar tendency to underestimate the economic stakes. In a sense, policy makers are no different from most people in putting greater weight on immediate costs than on anticipated ones. It often seems easier to pay tomorrow rather than today—hence the success of credit cards, and hence the failures of conflict prevention. It is only human to hope that perhaps the costs won't have to be paid, the bill won't come due, if the issue peters out or at least self-limits. But the bills have come due, with the equivalent of exorbitant interest and late fees. "The costs of remedying a situation once it gets out of control," as Sir David Hannay, the British ambassador to the United Nations stated, "[are] infinitely greater than the costs of . . . international efforts to head off such disasters before they occur."[88]

All "4 Ps" were clear in the bipartisan 2008 Genocide Prevention Task Force Report "making the case" why genocide and mass atrocities "threaten core U.S. national interests":

> Genocide and mass atrocities are a direct assault on universal human values. . . . Genocide fuels instability, usually in weak, undemocratic and corrupt states. It is in these same types of states that we find terrorist recruitment and training, human trafficking, and civil strife, all of which have damaging spillover effects for the entire world. . . .
>
> Refugee flows start in bordering countries but often spread. Humanitarian needs grow, often exceeding the capacities and resources of a generous world. . . . And the longer we wait, the more exorbitant the price tag. . . .
>
> America's standing in the world—and our ability to lead—is eroded when we are perceived as bystanders to genocide. . . .
>
> No matter how one calculates U.S. interests, the reality of our world today is that national borders provide little sanctuary from international problems. Left unchecked, genocide will undermine American security.[89]

The Obama administration acted on some of these recommendations. In its UN diplomacy it endorsed the "responsibility to protect" (R2P), as discussed in Chapter 7. R2P is an important emerging norm conditionally legitimizing military intervention and other international action to prevent genocide and mass atrocities. The administration's 2010 National Security Strategy adopted prevention of mass atrocities as part of core U.S. strategic doctrine, and made organizational changes within the State Department and the White House–led interagency executive branch policy process to give higher priority to and enhance institutional capabilities for genocide and mass atrocities prevention. In the case of Libya in 2011, the administration based the multilateral military intervention that the U.S. led on the need to prevent the brutal dictator Muammar Qaddafi from carrying out his threat to slaughter the Libyan people.

Yet there were other cases in which the tension among the 4 Ps remained. Despite the brutality and mass killings carried out by the Assad regime starting in 2011, just after the Libyan intervention was initiated, neither the United States nor the UN intervened in Syria. Principles seemed to warrant military intervention or other concerted action, but some questioned whether Principles would be well served if intervention were to further fuel the war and make the suffering worse. Similar debate revolved around Peace—would intervention end the conflict or escalate it? And Power—would U.S. credibility be enhanced and gains made by removing from power the Assad regime, which was closely allied to Iran, or would the United States be drawn into yet another Middle East conflict from which it would have trouble extricating itself?

While we don't know where and when, we can be pretty sure that more cases will arise in which potential or actual mass atrocities will challenge U.S. Principles.

Summary

With its focus on Principles and Prosperity in our current era, this chapter pairs with the previous one in providing a framework for American grand strategy in recent years and going forward.

The post–Cold War international political economy poses complex policy choices amid dynamic patterns of change. Globalization has many aspects and it is not inherently or exclusively a positive or negative force. Three things are certain, however. One is that globalization has made foreign economic and social policy issues more salient than in the past: we now hear much less "low politics" denigration of foreign economic policy issues compared with political-military ones. Second is that achieving foreign economic and social policy objectives is more complex and difficult now than when the United States enjoyed greater international economic dominance. Third is that globalization is not just a matter of trade, finance, and other economic issues, but also of the global environment and global public health.

Will the twenty-first century be a democratic one? This is one of the questions with which we began this chapter. The reasons that the answer still is uncertain should now be clear. The ancient Athenians, often credited with establishing one of the earliest democracies, chose as their patron the goddess Athena. Athena was said to have sprung forth, fully formed, from the head of Zeus, the god of gods. Democracy, however, cannot just spring forth. It must be built, painstakingly, continuously, by those who want it for their own political systems and by those whose foreign policy is served by its global spread.

Notes

[1] Thomas L. Friedman, *The Lexus and the Olive Tree: Understanding Globalization* (New York: Farrar, Straus and Giroux, 1999), xviii.

[2] Francis Fukuyama, "The End of History?" *The National Interest* 16 (Summer 1989): 3–4.

[3] Samuel P. Huntington, "No Exit—The Errors of Endism," *The National Interest* 17 (Fall 1989), 10.

[4] Samuel P. Huntington, "The Clash of Civilizations," *Foreign Affairs* 72.3 (Summer 1993): 22.

[5] Robert D. Kaplan, "The Coming Anarchy?" *Atlantic Monthly* 273 (February 1994), 44–46. Chester A. Crocker and Fen Osler Hampson with Pamela Aall, eds., *Managing Global Chaos: Sources of and Responses to International Conflict* (Washington, D.C.: U.S. Institute of Peace, 1996); I. Willam Zartman, ed., *Collapsed States: The Disintegration and Restoration of Legitimate Authority* (Boulder, Colo.: Westview Press, 1995).

[6] United Nations Development Program (UNDP), *Human Development Report 1999* (New York: Oxford University Press, 1999), 1.

[7] Roger C. Altman, "The Nuke of the 1990s," *New York Times Magazine*, March 1, 1998, 34.

[8] United Nations Development Program (UNDP), *Human Development Report 1999* (New York: Oxford University Press, 1999), 276.

[9]UNDP, *Human Development Report 1999*, 266–69.

[10]Moisés Naím, *Illicit: How Smugglers, Traffickers and Copycats Are Hijacking the Global Economy* (New York: Doubleday, 2005), 5 (italics in original).

[11]Naím, *Illicit*, 57, 88, 22, 161–62.

[12]Frederick W. Mayer, *Interpreting NAFTA: The Science and Art of Political Analysis* (New York: Columbia University Press, 1998).

[13]This data drawn from a paper by Margo Werner, a student in my Fall 2011 Politics of U.S. Foreign policy course.

[14]Council on Foreign Relations, "National Security Consequences of U.S. Oil Dependency," October 2006, www.cfr.org/publication/11683/ (accessed 7/2/09).

[15]See, for example, Joseph Stiglitz, *Globalization and Its Discontents* (New York: Norton, 2002).

[16]International Monetary Fund, Independent Evaluation Office, *IMF: Performance in the Run-Up to the Financial and Economic Crisis, IMF Surveillance in 2004–07* (International Monetary Fund, 2011), www.ieo-imf.org/ieo/files/completedevaluations/Crisis-%20Main%20Report%20%28without%20Moises%20Signature%29.pdf , p. 1 (accessed 2/14/13).

[17]BBC News, "IMF in Global 'Meltdown' Warning," October 12, 2008, http://news.bbc.co.uk/2/hi/7665515.stm (accessed 2/14/13).

[18]United Nations Development Program, *Human Development Report 2011* (New York: UN Development Program, 2011).

[19]Steven Kull and I. M. Destler, *Misreading the Public: The Myth of a New Isolationism* (Washington, D.C.: Brookings Institution Press, 1999), 113–33.

[20]Barack Obama, Statement on Rescinding the Mexico City Policy, January 23, 2009, www.whitehouse.gov/the_press_office/StatementofPresidentBarackObamaonRescindingtheMexicoCityPolicy/ (accessed 2/14/13).

[21]Nicholas D. Kristof and Sheryl WuDunn, *Half the Sky: Turning Oppression into Opportunity for Women Worldwide* (New York: Knopf, 2009).

[22]Jeffrey D. Sachs, *The End of Poverty: Economic Possibilities for Our Time* (New York: Penguin, 2005).

[23]William Easterly, *The White Man's Burden: How the West's Efforts to Aid the Rest Have Done So Much Ill and So Little Good* (New York: Penguin, 2006).

[24]Jessica Einhorn, "The World Bank's Mission Creep," *Foreign Affairs* 80.5 (September/October 2001): 31.

[25]Anirudh Krishna, *One Illness Away: Why People Become Poor and How They Escape Poverty* (New York: Oxford University Press, 2010).

[26]Central Intelligence Agency, *The Global Infectious Disease Threat and Its Implications for the United States*, National Intelligence Estimate 99-17D, January 2000, www.fas.org/irp/threat/nie99-17d.htm (accessed 2/14/13).

[27]Michael Specter, "What Money Can Buy," *The New Yorker*, October 24, 2005, 58.

[28]The Bill & Melinda Gates Foundation, "Vaccine-Preventable Diseases," www.gatesfoundation.org/topics/Pages/vaccine-preventable-diseases.aspx (accessed 2/14/13).

[29]Laurie Garrett, "The Next Pandemic?" *Foreign Affairs* 84.4 (July/August 2005): 3–4.

[30]Gardiner Harris and Lawrence K. Altman, "Managing a Flu Threat with Seasoned Urgency," *New York Times*, May 10, 2009.

[31]Paul A. Samuelson, "The Pure Theory of Public Expenditure," *Review of Economics and Statistics* 36 (November 1954): 387–89.

[32]See, for example, the WTO's "10 Common Misunderstandings about the WTO," www.wto.org/english/thewto_e/whatis_e/10mis_e/10m00_e.htm (accessed 2/15/13); Deborah James, "Free Trade and the Environment," Global Exchange, updated October 2007, www.globalexchange.org/campaigns/wto/Environment.html (accessed 2/15/13).

[33]"UN Taking First Steps towards Implementing Johannesburg Outcome," September 23, 2002. Available at www.un.org/jsummit/html/whats_new/feature_story40.html (accessed 2/15/13).

[34]Patrick E. Tyler, "Peace Prize Goes to Environmentalist in Kenya," *New York Times*, October 4, 2004, A1.

[35]Jared Diamond, *Collapse: How Societies Choose to Fail or Succeed* (New York: Viking, 2005), 23.

[36]Rajendra Pachauri, address to the World Economic Forum, Davos, Switzerland, opening session, January 23, 2008, UN Intergovernmental Panel on Climate Change, www.ipcc.ch/graphics/speeches/pachauri-davos-january-2008.pdf (accessed 2/15/13); Nicholas Stern, *The Economics of Climate Change* (Cambridge: Cambridge University Press, 2007).

[37]"A Global Warning to Mr. Bush," *New York Times*, February 26, 2001, A18.

[38]Eric Pianin, "UN Report Forecasts Crises Brought on by Global Warming," *Washington Post*, February 20, 2001, A6.

[39]Al Gore, *An Inconvenient Truth: The Planetary Emergency of Global Warming and What We Can Do About It* (New York: Rodale, 2006), 8.

[40]George F. Will, "Dark Green Doomsayers," *Washington Post*, February 15, 2009; Will, "Climate Science in a Tornado," *Washington Post*, February 27, 2009.

[41]Ed Regis, "The Doomslayer," *Wired*, February 1997, www.wired.com/wired/archive/5.02/ffsimon_pr.html (accessed 2/15/13).

[42]Chris Woodford, "Global Warming," *World at Risk: A Global Issues Sourcebook* (Washington, D.C.: Congressional Quarterly Press, 2002), 261.

[43]Editorial, "Changing the Chemistry of Earth's Oceans," *New York Times*, March 9, 2012, www.nytimes.com/2012/03/10/opinion/changing-the-chemistry-of-earths-oceans.html?_r=1&ref=oceans (accessed 2/15/13).

[44]Cornelia Dean, "Study Sees 'Global Collapse' of Fish Species," *New York Times*, November 3, 2006.

[45]International Union for Conservation of Nature, "IUCN Red List Reveals World's Mammals in Crisis," October 6, 2008, www.iucn.org/fr/propos/union/secretariat/bureaux/paco/?1695/IUCN-Red-List-reveals-worlds-mammals-in-crisis (accessed 2/15/13).

[46]*The State of the Birds*, 2009 report, March 2009, www.stateofthebirds.org/ (accessed 2/15/13).

[47]United Nations Convention to Combat Desertification, "The Problem of Land Degradation," www.unccd.int/convention/text/leaflet.php (accessed 2/15/13).

[48]Millennium Ecosystem Assessment, *Current State and Trends Assessment*, Chapter 21, Anatoly Shvidenko, Charles Victor Barber, Reidar Persson, "Forest and Woodland Systems," 587, www.millenniumassessment.org/documents/document.290.aspx.pdf (accessed 2/15/13).

[49]Millennium Ecosystem Assessment, *Current State and Trends Assessment*, Chapter 21, 613, www.millenniumassessment.org/documents/document.274.aspx.pdf (accessed 2/16/13).

[50]American Lung Association, *State of the Air 2011*, www.stateoftheair.org/2011/assets/SOTA2011.pdf (accessed 2/16/13); Edward Wong "Air Pollution Linked to 1.2 Million Premature Deaths in China," *New York Times*, April 1, 2013, A9.

[51]World Health Organization, "Air Quality and Health: Questions and Answers," www.who.int/phe/air_quality_q&a.pdf (accessed 2/16/13).

[52]United Nations Population Fund, *Fact Sheet: The World at Seven Billion*, July 2011, www.unfpa.org/webdav/site/global/shared/documents/7%20Billion/7B_fact_sheets_en.pdf (accessed 2/16/13).

[53]United Nations Population Fund, *State of World Population 2007 Report: Unleashing the Potential of Urban Growth*, Chapter 1, "The Promise of Urban Growth," June 27, 2007, www.unfpa.org/webdav/site/global/shared/documents/publications/2007/695_filename_sowp2007.eng.pdf (accessed 2/16/13).

[54]Freedom House, *Freedom in the World 2012*, www.freedomhouse.org/sites/default/files/inline_images/FIW%202012%20Booklet—Final.pdf (accessed 2/16/13). The key criteria used as measures of democracy and freedom are political rights and civil liberties. Freedom House's definition of democracy is "a political

system in which the people choose their authoritative leaders freely from among competing groups and individuals," freedom as "the opportunity to act spontaneously in a variety of fields outside the control of the government and other centers of potential domination."

[55]Judith Kelley, *Monitoring Democracy: When Election Observation Works and Why It Often Fails* (Princeton: Princeton University Press, 2012).

[56]Susan D. Hyde, *The Pseudo-Democrat's Dilemma: Why Election Monitoring Became an International Norm* (Ithaca, N.Y.: Cornell University Press, 2011).

[57]Larry Diamond, *Promoting Democracy in the 1990s: Actors and Instruments, Issues and Imperatives* (Washington, D.C.: Carnegie Commission for Preventing Deadly Conflict, 1995), 40–48.

[58]Diamond, *Promoting Democracy,* 41.

[59]"Price Named Top Democrat on International Commission," http://price.house.gov/index.php?option -com_content&task-view&id-2957&Itemid-10026c (accessed 2/16/13).

[60]USAID, *Agency Performance Report 1997,* 42, www.usaid.gov/results-and-data/progress-data/annual -performance-report (accessed 2/16/13).

[61]Transparency International, Corruption Fighters' Tool Kit, www.transparency.org/whatwedo/tools/ corruption_fighters_toolkits_introduction (accessed 2/16/13).

[62]Neil J. Kritz, ed., *Transitional Justice: How Emerging Democracies Reckon with Former Regimes* (Washington, D.C.: U.S. Institute of Peace Press, 1995).

[63]Barbara Crossette, "For First Time U.S. Is Excluded from UN Human Rights Panel," *New York Times,* May 4, 2001, A1.

[64]Robert D. Putnam, *Making Democracy Work: Civic Traditions in Modern Italy* (Princeton: Princeton University Press, 1993), 176. This section draws on an outstanding paper written by Sarah Schroeder, one of my students in Fall 1996, "How Should the United States Support Democracy Consolidation in Haiti? The Relationship between Civil Society and Political Institutions."

[65]Thomas Carothers, *Aiding Democracy Abroad: The Learning Curve* (Washington, D.C.: Carnegie Endowment for International Peace, 1999), 308, 171, 182, 251.

[66]Carothers, *Aiding Democracy Abroad,* 171, 182, 249–50, 347.

[67]Diamond, *Promoting Democracy,* 272.

[68]Carothers, *Aiding Democracy Abroad,* 340.

[69]Gideon Rose, "Democracy Promotion and American Foreign Policy: A Review Essay," *International Security* 25.2 (Winter 2000–2001), 200.

[70]Jack S. Levy, "Domestic Politics and War," in *The Origin and Prevention of Major Wars;* Robert I. Rotberg and Theodore K. Rabb, eds. (Cambridge: Cambridge University Press, 1989), 88.

[71]See, for example, Bruce Russett, *Grasping the Democratic Peace* (Princeton: Princeton University Press, 1993); John Owen, "How Liberalism Produces Democratic Peace," *International Security* 19.2 (Fall 1994): 87–125; Melvin Small and J. David Singer, "The War Proneness of Democratic Regimes," *Jerusalem Journal of International Relations* 1 (Summer 1976): 50–69.

[72]Immanuel Kant, "Perpetual Peace," cited in Michael W. Doyle, "Kant, Liberal Legacies, and Foreign Affairs," in *Debating the Democratic Peace,* Michael E. Brown et al., eds. (Cambridge, Mass.: MIT Press, 1997), 24–25.

[73]Doyle, "Kant, Liberal Legacies, and Foreign Affairs," 49.

[74]Owen, "How Liberalism Produces Democratic Peace," 96.

[75]Cited in Bruce W. Jentleson, "The Political Basis for Trade in U.S.-Soviet Relations," *Millennium: Journal of International Studies* 15 (Spring 1986): 27.

[76]David E. Spiro, "The Insignificance of the Liberal Peace," *International Security* 19.2 (Fall 1994): 50–86.

[77]Henry S. Farber and Joanne Gowa, "Politics and Peace," *International Security* 20.2 (Fall 1995): 123–46; Christopher Layne, "Kant or Cant: The Myth of the Democratic Peace," *International Security* 19.2 (Fall 1994): 5–49.

[78]Edward D. Mansfield and Jack Snyder, "Democratization and the Danger of War," *International Security* 20.1 (Summer 1995): 7; Mansfield and Snyder, *Electing to Fight: Why Emerging Democracies Go to War* (Cambridge, Mass.: MIT Press, 2005).

[79]David Rohde, "Pakistani Fundamentalists and Secular Opponents of Muhsarraf Do Well in Election," *New York Times,* October 11, 2002, A8.

[80]Mark Mazzetti, "Efforts by CIA Fail in Somalia, Officials Charge," *New York Times,* June 8, 2006, A1.

[81]Samantha Power, *"A Problem from Hell": America and the Age of Genocide* (New York: Basic Books, 2002), xv, xvii.

[82]Power, *"A Problem from Hell,"* 267.

[83]Keith B. Richburg, "Somalia Slips Back to Bloodshed," *Washington Post,* September 4, 1994, A43.

[84]Power, *"A Problem from Hell,"* 334.

[85]Michael Mandelbaum, "Foreign Policy as Social Work," *Foreign Affairs* 75.1 (January/February 1996): 16–32; Stanley Hoffman, "In Defense of Mother Theresa: Morality in Foreign Policy, *Foreign Affairs* 75.2 (March/April 1996): 172–75.

[86]Stuart Hill and Donald Rothchild, "The Contagion of Political Conflict in Africa and the World," *Journal of Conflict Resolution* 30 (December 1986): 716–35; Stuart Hill, Donald Rothchild, and Colin Cameron, "Tactical Information and the Diffusion of Peaceful Protests," in *The International Spread of Ethnic Conflict: Fear, Diffusion and Escalation,* David A. Lake and Donald Rothchild, eds. (Princeton: Princeton University Press, 1998), 61–88.

[87]Donald Rothchild, "The Logic of a Soft Intervention Strategy: The United States and Conflict Conciliation in Africa," *International Negotiation* 10 (2006): 327.

[88]Arthur M. Schlesinger, Jr., "America and the World: Isolationism Resurgent?" *Ethics and International Affairs* 10 (1996), 162–63.

[89]Genocide Prevention Task Force, *Preventing Genocide: A Blueprint for U.S. Policymakers* (Washington, D.C.: U.S. Institute of Peace, 2008), xx.

CHAPTER

9

Post–Cold War Foreign Policy Politics: Politics beyond the Water's Edge

Introduction: Diplomacy Begins at Home

"We are about to do a terrible thing to you," a Soviet official quipped toward the end of the Cold War. "We are going to deprive you of an enemy."[1] The Soviet official's remark was an astute observation of U.S. foreign policy politics. Having an Enemy (capital letter intentional) helped American presidents garner domestic political support for a strong and active foreign policy. Without the Soviet threat—indeed, without a Soviet Union at all—the U.S. foreign policy debate split wide open.

Some wanted to heed the cry, "Come home, America." Who needed foreign policy anyway? Why not just take advantage of the opportunity provided by the end of the Cold War to "put America first"? These neo-isolationists wanted to reduce America's international commitments and make them more self-centered. Their philosophy was to get beyond the old debate about whether politics should "stop at the water's edge" and just stay on America's side of the water.

The paradox of the post–Cold War era is that international affairs affect America and Americans at least as much, if not more, than during the Cold War. This was true even before the September 11, 2001, terrorist attacks on the United States. Recall the five major reasons for the continued importance of foreign policy, reasons that were first laid out in *American Foreign Policy's* first edition, published before September 11:

- ■ The United States still faces significant potential threats to its national security.
- ■ The U.S. economy is more internationalized than ever before.
- ■ Many areas of policy that used to be considered "domestic" have been internationalized.

- The increasing diversity of the American people—in race, ethnicity, religion, nationality, and heritage—makes for a larger number and wider range of groups with personal interest in foreign affairs.
- It is hard for the United States to claim to be true to its most basic values if it ignores their violation around the world.

Prior to September 11, however, none of these rationales resonated in tones that were anything close to the clarion calls of the Truman Doctrine, JFK's 1961 inaugural "Ask not" speech, or Reagan's "Tear down this wall" proclamation. But in the immediate aftermath of 9/11, there was a strong sense that Osama bin Laden and Al Qaeda were America's Enemies. This threat was exaggerated and distorted, and became especially controversial with the 2003–10 Iraq War. Moreover, the fuller foreign policy agenda laid out in Chapters 7 and 8 shows that the threats and opportunities posed by this global era go well beyond terrorism.

This chapter, drawing on the analytic framework laid out in Chapters 2 and 3, examines broad patterns of foreign policy politics since the end of the Cold War. The domestic politics of specific foreign policy issues are explored in each of the succeeding chapters: U.S.-China relations (Chapter 10); the use of torture and other civil liberties concerns during the war on terrorism (Chapter 11); nuclear arms control (Chapter 12); immigration (Chapter 13); and the anti-apartheid economic sanctions against South Africa (Chapter 14).

President, Congress, and War Powers

The post–Cold War pattern of Pennsylvania Avenue diplomacy on the use of military force has been a mix of cooperation and conflict, with the constitutional **war powers** issues remaining unresolved.

1990–91 Persian Gulf War

In 1990–91, when Saddam Hussein's forces invaded Kuwait, President George H. W. Bush proposed the initial deployment of American forces in **Operation Desert Shield** as "consistent with," not as required by, the 1973 War Powers Resolution (WPR). His report denied that hostilities were "imminent" since the use of that term would have involved the WPR. The same language game was played a few weeks later, when the deployed troops got higher salaries but not at the "hostilities" pay rate, even though the Pentagon was drawing up war plans and Bush likened Saddam to Hitler. Still, responding to Bush's televised speech to the nation, the House Majority Leader Richard Gephardt (D-Missouri) declared, "In this crisis we are not Republicans or Democrats. We are only proudly Americans. The President has asked for our support. He has it." Even traditional liberals, such as the Senate Foreign Relations Committee Chairman Claiborne Pell (D-Rhode Island), initially took the position that invoking the WPR "would upset the applecart." Instead, in early October 1990, both chambers overwhelmingly passed resolutions outside the WPR supporting Operation Desert Shield, 380–29 in the House and 96–3 in the Senate.[2]

Greater tensions with Congress emerged on November 8, 1990, when Bush announced a doubling of U.S. forces to over four hundred thousand troops and a shift in strategy to mounting "an adequate offensive military option." The issue came to a head in early January 1991. The Bush administration had won support in the UN Security Council for a resolution setting January 15 as the deadline for Iraqi withdrawal from Kuwait and authorizing any member state to use "all necessary means" after that date. Just as Truman had claimed in 1950 that the UN resolution authorizing war against North Korea after its invasion of South Korea precluded the need for a formal declaration of war by the U.S. Congress, Bush claimed that this Iraqi-withdrawal UN resolution provided comparable authorization. Bush indicated that he had no intention of invoking the WPR or asking for congressional approval before going to war. Some in the administration, however, felt it was politically risky to not go to Congress. Bush agreed to a nonbinding resolution outside of the WPR, stating that even if it was defeated, he would proceed as planned.

Congress faced criticism for being politically spineless and not taking a position one way or the other. For the Democrats in Congress, the political dilemma was particularly tough. Did economic sanctions still have a chance to get Iraq out of Kuwait? Politically, should the Democrats take a stand against the use of force as "the party of peace?" Or did they risk further reinforcing their post-Vietnam "wimp" image?

On January 11 and 12, both chambers of Congress voted on identical resolutions "to authorize the use of United States Armed Forces pursuant to United Nations Security Council Resolution 678." The resolutions passed, although by much closer votes than the earlier ones: 250–183 in the House, and 52–47 in the Senate.

On January 16, 1991, **Operation Desert Storm** was launched. The war against Iraq was on. It will never be known whether the political coalition would have held together had the war not gone as well as it did. It wasn't politically difficult to stand behind a war with so few American casualties and such a quick and overwhelming military victory. Consensual foreign policy politics held firm for the moment, but the core constitutional issues that the 1973 WPR had claimed to resolve—who had what share of the war powers—were left unresolved.

1990s Humanitarian Interventions

Somalia was Bill Clinton's first war-powers issue, and it was a disaster. The original troop commitment was made by President Bush in December 1992, with the mission defined largely as short-term humanitarian relief from starvation (Operation Provide Comfort).

The troops were sent by executive action, outside the procedures of the War Powers Resolution, but with strong bipartisan support. The Clinton administration would later be criticized for keeping the troops in Somalia and taking on the broader mission of "nation building." Had the troops been withdrawn according to the original schedule, however, the risk of reversion to chaos was high. The administration's mistake may not have been taking on the broader mission, but being inattentive to the requirements of a more effective strategy and failing to engage sufficiently with Congress to create "co-ownership" of the policy.

Once the policy started to go badly—especially in October 1993, when eighteen American soldiers were killed and one dead soldier was ignominiously dragged through the streets of Mogadishu—a political firestorm erupted on Capitol Hill, on the airwaves, and with the general public. Within hours, the president went on television to deliver a hastily prepared speech promising to withdraw the American troops. Whether or not this was the right decision, and whether the mistake was not having withdrawn the troops sooner or not having made a more concerted effort to accomplish the mission, the American political system still appeared to be fumbling the war power.

The Somalia intervention kicked off an intense political debate over whether U.S. troops should serve under foreign (i.e., non-American) command. In the United States the dominant perception of the Somalia debacle was that it was caused by the failures of UN commanders, and American soldiers paid the price with their lives. In fact, the decision to launch the commando operations that resulted in American deaths was made without the knowledge of the UN force commander. Nonetheless, the political pressure after U.S. soldiers were killed was so great that the Clinton administration not only withdrew U.S. troops from Somalia but also changed its policy on whether U.S. troops would serve under foreign command. Just a few months earlier the administration was reportedly leaning toward putting American troops under UN commanders "on a regular basis." But in the wake of Somalia it issued a major policy statement that "the United States does not support a standing UN army nor will it earmark specific military units for participation in UN operations."[3]

There is plenty to debate on this issue, but it is not true that U.S. troops have never served under foreign command. U.S. troops served under foreign command in World Wars I and II, and in some successful Cold War–era UN peacekeeping operations. They later did so in Afghanistan, under NATO command. It can still be argued that these were mostly exceptional situations, with vital U.S. interests at stake. But the record should be clear.

The September 1994 Haiti intervention went better than Somalia, but was a close call. Clinton sent the high-level team of former president Jimmy Carter, former senator Sam Nunn, and former chairman of the Joint Chiefs of Staff Colin Powell on a last-minute negotiating mission. Had the trio not succeeded in persuading the Haitian military to step down, and had the invasion brought casualties, the outcry on Capitol Hill would likely have been deafening. Other than the Congressional Black Caucus and some other liberal Democrats who had been pushing for military action, Congress was nonsupportive if not outright opposed to a Haiti intervention. And despite the consultation clause of the WPR, the Clinton administration had not bothered to come to Congress to get a resolution like the one for the Persian Gulf War.

The usual presidentialist claim of the demands of a crisis situation was not very convincing in this case, given all the advance planning and the fact that the Clinton administration had gone to the UN Security Council almost two months earlier for an "all necessary means" resolution authorizing the intervention. The real reason for not consulting Congress was that the administration was afraid it would lose. In the end, the ambiguities of the War Powers Resolution and the reluctance of Congress to act on its own allowed the president to go his own way, with plenty of criticism but few biting procedural constraints.

The politics of the deployment of U.S. troops to Bosnia as part of the NATO force after the Dayton Peace Accord in 1995 largely followed the same pattern. Congress did not stop the president from deploying the troops, but it did not support him in doing so, either. The House did pass a resolution that stated support for the troops themselves but "disowned the deployment decision."[4] The Senate resolution was more supportive, but it too contained far more caveats, criticisms, and reservations than presidents usually get when putting American troops on the ground. Moreover, to get even this much, Clinton had to state that the deployment was only for one year. Yet it was clear from the outset that this was an unrealistic timetable. Indeed, a year later the president announced that, although he would make some cuts in numbers, the troops needed to stay in Bosnia another year. A year later came yet another extension; this one was left more open-ended. Congress criticized the extensions and passed various measures affecting the deployments at the margins, but it didn't stop them.

In the Kosovo case (1999) there was neither strong and explicit congressional support nor a concerted effort to stop the military action. Support did come from numerous congressional political and foreign policy leaders, both Republican and Democrat. The Senate approved air strikes before hostilities began, but the House was "as confusing and irresolute as possible about where it stood."[5] It delayed voting on air strikes for over a month after they had begun, and when it did vote, the result was a tie. Although the resolution was nonbinding, it did have a signaling effect. Signals were further mixed by congressional approval of the president's funding request for the war and the rejection of a resolution to end the war. President Clinton said that if the war were to move to a ground campaign, he would come to Congress for its support, but the war ended without ground forces being deployed.

Some House members did try to go the judicial route with a case claiming that the president had violated the War Powers Resolution. But the courts dismissed the case on the nonjusticiability grounds cited in earlier cases (and in Chapter 2). In other words, the issue was not clearly presidential usurpation but also congressional abdication, and the evidence did not show a "sufficiently genuine impasse between the legislative and executive branches."[6]

In sum, while it was not supportive in all of these humanitarian interventions, Congress stopped short of blocking presidential action.

2001 Afghanistan War

Three days after September 11, Congress overwhelmingly approved a resolution authorizing President George W. Bush to use military force against those responsible for the terrorist attacks. The Senate approved it 98–0, the House 420–1. "I am gratified that the Congress has united so powerfully by taking this action," President Bush stated. "It sends a clear message—our people are together, and we will prevail."[7] A few weeks later this resolution became the basis for the war in Afghanistan, though it, too, was kept outside the WPR.

This was the most consensual war powers issue since the December 7, 1941, attack on Pearl Harbor and the declaration of war that brought the United States into World War II. The reason was fundamentally the same. The United States had been attacked. The Afghanistan war dragged on for over a decade—more than three times as long as World War II—but Congress did not mount a significant challenge to end it. Public opinion eventually turned against the war (see below), which influenced President Obama's decision to scale back troop levels and plan full withdrawal of combat troops by the end of 2014, but as a war powers issue it never caused major tension in executive-legislative relations.

2003 Iraq War

Congress voted for the Iraq War by smaller but still very large margins, 77–23 in the Senate and 296–133 in the House. Those voting in favor included virtually all Republicans and most Democrats. The consensus had policy, political, and process bases. In terms of policy, the context of terrorism after 9/11 and Saddam Hussein's track record—going back to his 1990 invasion of Kuwait, his 1987–88 gassing of the Kurds, and other instances of aggression and brutality—raised concerns about the threats that he posed. Intelligence reports coming from the Bush administration said that he possessed weapons of mass destruction (WMD). The Bush congressional relations strategy was to hold extensive consultations with the congressional leadership and key members, allowing them some input but mostly providing simply a sense of inclusion. As for the politics, the White House also exploited the fear of being seen as "soft." During the Cold War this had been the specter of being "soft on communism," and after September 11 it was "soft on terrorism." This was a key factor, for example, behind the three Democratic members of Congress who ran for president in 2004 (Senators John Kerry and John

Edwards and House Minority Leader Richard Gephardt) and one who would run in 2008 (Senator Hillary Rodham Clinton) voting for the Iraq War resolution.

For Senator Robert C. Byrd (D-West Virginia), though, the debate was not only about Iraq, but also, on an overall and continuing basis, about the war powers issue. Senator Byrd tried to take the debate over the October 2002 Iraq use-of-force resolution back to constitutional principles:

> Nobody will support this country in war any more strongly than will I. But here today we are being tested. . . . This is my fiftieth year in Congress. I never would have thought I would find a Senate which would lack the backbone to stand up against the stampede, this rush to war, this rush to give to the President of the United States, whatever President he is, whatever party, this rush to give a President, to put in his hands alone, to let him determine alone when he will send the sons and daughters of the American people into war, let him have control of the military forces. He will not only make war, but he will declare war. That flies in the face of this Constitution.[8]

Senator Byrd's critique concerned both presidential usurpation and congressional abdication. President Bush came under criticism from Byrd and others for the flawed and manipulated intelligence and for seeking ways to bypass the formal constitutional process of asking for a declaration of war. But the debate wasn't just about what the president took, it was also what the Congress gave up. Congress did not "assert its rights and take political responsibility," Leslie Gelb (then president of the Council on Foreign Relations) and Anne-Marie Slaughter (then dean of the Woodrow Wilson School at Princeton) wrote.[9] As a Constitution Project report suggested, Congress "should not wait for the president to ask its judgment on initiating a use of force. Instead, it should involve itself early in the decision-making process, demand and acquire relevant information, and reach a collective judgment by a roll call vote after full and public debate."[10]

As President Bush's initial claim of "mission accomplished" was increasingly called into question by events on the ground, and evidence mounted that his administration had been deceptive and manipulative in its claims for going to war, more and more early supporters of the war reassessed their positions. Representative John Murtha (D-Pennsylvania), a leading House military expert and former marine, spoke out in late 2005 against this "flawed policy wrapped in illusion. . . . Our military is suffering. The future of our country is at risk." Murtha called for a withdrawal of American troops: "It is time to bring them home."[11] Others, including some Republicans, made their own critiques.

It is rare that congressional elections turn heavily on a foreign policy issue but that is what happened in 2006. While domestic issues also came into play, opposition to the Iraq War was a major factor in the Democrats' retaking majority control of the House and Senate. The balance in the House went from 232–203, favoring the Republicans, to 233–202 for the Democrats; the Senate went from a 55–44 Republican advantage to a 51–49 Democratic majority. This was the first time the Democrats had majorities in both chambers of Congress since 1994. And in the 2008 Democratic presidential primary contest, opposition to the Iraq War was a key issue in the upset victory of then-Senator Barack Obama over then-Senator Hillary Clinton.

2011 Libya Intervention[12]

In February 2011 the Libyan people rose up against longtime dictator Muammar Qaddafi. In Tunisia and Egypt the "Arab Spring" uprisings had stayed largely peaceful, but Qaddafi threatened massive slaughter against the rebels in Libya. In response to that threat President Obama decided to use American air power, in conjunction with NATO and some Arab states, to protect the Libyan people. He made the decision with only limited consultation with Congress, informing it by letter that military action had commenced. The letter explained that strikes against military airfields and air defense systems would be "limited in their nature, duration, and scope" and that the efforts "are discrete and focused on employing unique U.S. military capabilities to set the conditions for [America's] European allies and Arab partners to carry out the measures authorized by the [UNSC] Resolution."[13] The president emphasized that no ground troops had been deployed. In early April the United States transferred control of military operations to NATO, and in a May 20 letter to Congress, President Obama stressed that the United States had "assumed a supporting role in the coalition's efforts."[14]

While few in Congress opposed the military action, some raised concerns about inadequate war powers collaboration. And not just Republicans. Senator Dick Durbin (D-Illinois), the second most powerful Senate Democrat and normally a close ally of the president, reiterated his support for U.S. involvement but stated that, "We should, as a Congress, consider it under the War Powers Resolution."[15] Other critics were not as diplomatic. Senator Jim Webb (D-Virginia) asserted, "When you have an operation that goes on for months, costs billions of dollars, where the United States is providing two-thirds of the troops, even under the NATO fig leaf, where they're dropping bombs that are killing people . . . I would say that's hostilities."

On June 24, 2011, the House defeated a bipartisan resolution that would have authorized U.S. military operations in Libya for up to a year. The bill failed 295–123 with 70 Democrats opposed in what was seen as a "symbolic blow" to the White House.[16] The same day, however, the House refrained from deserting the president completely when it rejected a bill that would have limited funding to support the intervention only.[17]

Much of the debate, as in earlier WPR cases, came down to the definition of "hostilities." The Obama administration argued that while this was a military action, "U.S. operations do not involve sustained fighting or active exchanges of fire with hostile forces, nor do they involve U.S. ground troops." Harold Koh, former Dean of the Yale Law School and the top State Department lawyer, cited as precedents past cases in which military action had not been construed as hostilities. The limited scope of the mission (protection of civilians) authorized by the UN and the support role in which U.S. forces were operating, he argued, did not constitute "full military engagement." While such arguments prevailed, it's not clear that they would have continued to do so if the military operation had not ended a few months later, when the Libyan rebels captured and killed Qaddafi.

Counterterrorism Drone Attacks

In May 2012 the *New York Times* broke a story about a "secret 'kill list'" for drone attacks against terrorist leaders in Pakistan, Yemen, and elsewhere.[18] Senior administration aides were involved in the selection process, providing intelligence and other information, with President Obama personally deciding which terrorists to target. John Brennan, then Obama's chief counterterrorism advisor, gave a speech assuring the American public that "rigorous standards" were followed. The administration, though, would not disclose much more than generalities about those standards and how they were applied in particular cases, citing the national security need for secrecy.

> We only authorize a particular operation against a specific individual if we have a high degree of confidence that the individual being targeted is indeed the terrorist we are pursuing. This is a very high bar. Of course, how we identify an individual naturally involves intelligence sources and methods, which I will not discuss.[19]

Opponents called for greater transparency and accountability to Congress. The need for secrecy is not denied, but the extent is questioned. As with other highly classified operations, there could at least be some confidential reporting to the congressional intelligence committees. Some call for fuller congressional involvement including hearings where administration officials would elaborate the criteria applied and the processes by which decisions were made. Others propose quasi-judicial or other confidential but independent review. "The U.S. is embarked on ambitious and consequential moves that will shape the security environment for years to come, whether they succeed or fail," said Steven Aftergood, a longtime analyst of issues posed by government secrecy. "Secrecy cloaks not only the operations, but their justification and rationale, which are legitimate subjects of public interest."[20] Given the increased reliance on drones as part of counterterrorism strategy and in other situations (Chapter 7), the associated war powers issues will be with us for a long time to come.

War Powers Reform

The one point of consensus is that the 1973 War Powers Resolution has not solved the problem. "Few would dispute," as the blue ribbon bipartisan National War Powers Commission wrote (Reading 9.1), "that the most important decisions our leaders make involve war. Yet after more than 200 years of constitutional history, what powers the

9.1

respective branches of government possess in making such decisions is still heavily debated."[21] Several key issues remain unresolved:

- How do we define "hostilities"? And when is involvement in them "imminent"? These questions have been hard to answer in the past, but they are even harder in an age of drone warfare.
- What are meaningful consultations with Congress? Do they have to occur prior to a presidential decision to use force? How regularly do they need to occur while military operations are under way? With whom should they be held: the full House and Senate, or principally the congressional leadership?
- Democratic and Republican presidents alike have consistently made the political calculation that it is better to limit Congress' role so as not to constrain their freedom of action. Is this reading the politics right, or would it be better politically for Congress to take some responsibility when military action is ordered and thus be less free to criticize it if/when things go bad?
- Might members of Congress with foreign policy expertise have valuable substantive policy, and not just political, input?

To be true to the Constitution, the issue of how the president and Congress share war powers must be resolved or, at least, greater agreement must be forged on the matter.

Recent Presidents as Foreign Policy Leaders

In Chapter 2 we identified two main factors—prior experience and individual belief systems—that influence how well presidents fulfill their roles as foreign policy leaders. There we applied belief systems analysis to a comparison of Presidents Jimmy Carter and Ronald Reagan. Here we apply this framework to more recent presidents: George H. W. Bush, Bill Clinton, George W. Bush, and Barack Obama.

George H. W. Bush

George H. W. Bush ranks among the presidents with the most prior foreign policy experience. He served in the military in World War II, the Navy's youngest pilot at the time, and received a medal for heroism. He was a member of the House of Representatives (1966–70), UN ambassador (1971–73), head of the first liaison office in the People's Republic of China when diplomatic relations were first established (1974–75), and CIA Director (1976–77). He also served eight years as Ronald Reagan's vice president.

In terms of the three belief system elements, Bush's conception of the international system was of the old bipolar order in transition, with the United States emerging as the most powerful country following the decline and disintegration of the Soviet Union. Although the United States needed to lead, other states and actors were also required to contribute to shaping a new world order. His national interest hierarchy put Power first and Peace second, not to the exclusion of Principles or Prosperity, but demonstrating this order of priorities in cases such as the 1989 Tiananmen Square massacre in China (see Chapter 1). In using military force he acted both unilaterally, as in the 1989 invasion of Panama to overthrown Manuel Noriega, and multilaterally, as in the 1990–91 Persian Gulf War. He was generally inclined to build coalitions in which the United States had a leadership role while also benefiting from the power and legitimacy that comes with having partners.

Bill Clinton

Bill Clinton had spent his entire political career as governor of Arkansas (1978–80, 1982–92). His foreign policy experience amounted to an overseas trade mission or two. Many attributed the foreign policy failures of his first year as president to his inexperience: "passive and changeable . . . like a cork bobbing on the waves," was one leading journalist's characterization.[22] In addition, the controversy over whether he had dodged the draft during the Vietnam War gave Clinton some personal credibility problems as commander in chief. Over the course of his presidency Clinton did gain experience and demonstrated greater foreign policy skills and savvy. In the first eighteen months of his second term, he made more foreign policy trips than in his entire first term. The percentage of people rating his foreign policy performance as excellent or good increased from 31 percent in 1994 to 55 percent in 1998. Overall, he would be better known for his domestic policy, but he did have foreign policy successes.

Clinton held to a multilateralist conception of the international system in which the United States was still the most powerful actor, but other major states and international institutions such as the UN played substantially increased roles. His national interest hierarchy gave priority to Prosperity and Principles without ignoring the other core objectives. As reflected in his 1994 State of the Union speech, he subscribed to the "democratic peace" theory discussed in Chapter 8. His strategy also combined diplomacy and force, with emphasis on the former and limited use of the latter, as in Bosnia and Kosovo. His penchant for negotiations led him to peace-brokering activism, notably in the Middle East.

George W. Bush

Like Clinton, George W. Bush had been a governor (of Texas), with the limited international agenda inherent in that office. At times during the 2000 presidential campaign this hurt Bush's candidacy. So, too, did doubts arise in his first months in office about his foreign policy competence. The strength of his foreign policy team, seasoned hands who served in his father's administration, partially compensated for this inexperience. The events of September 11 cast Bush in a new light. He was widely praised for rallying the nation at a time of crisis. In some respects his limited foreign policy experience was seen as a positive, in that he wasn't bogged down in details and nuances and got right to what many Americans saw as the fundamentals. The initial military victory in the Iraq War reinforced this sense of Bush as a strong foreign policy leader. But as the war dragged on, and more questions arose over the decision process for going to war as well as the strategies for seeking to win the peace, criticisms mounted and doubts about Bush's leadership re-emerged.

His belief system both resembled and departed from that of his father. He saw the international system as having moved from bipolarity to unipolarity, with the United States as the sole surviving superpower. Multilateralism was at most a partial component of his belief system. Even before 9/11, Bush's view was that Power needed to be put back at the top of the national interest hierarchy. Strategy needed to shift back to a greater willingness to use force and to do so unilaterally and decisively, with less concern than his father had for building coalitions. He often appeared only grudgingly willing to turn to negotiations. In his second term, especially, he also gave emphasis to the spread of freedom and democracy. This priority of Principles was different from that of his father, who was more of a classical realist and had emphasized interests over ideology. Though similar in spirit to Clinton, and in his own way tracing back to Wilsonianism, Bush was much more willing to use force in the name of democracy. Bush also gave greater weight to his religious faith as a basis for policy.

Barack Obama

Barack Obama also came to the presidency with limited foreign policy experience. Most of his political career had been at the state and local level, as a community organizer in Chicago and a state senator in the Illinois legislature. He was elected to the U.S. Senate in 2004, and held that position for only about two years before hitting the campaign trail as a presidential candidate. During the 2008 Democratic primaries, senator Hillary Clinton, then his principal opponent, attacked Obama on this point, particularly in the "3 AM Red Phone" television ad. This ad depicted the crisis hotline ringing in the middle of the night while an ominous voice questioned whether Obama had the experience needed to "protect your children."[23] The Republican presidential candidate, senator John McCain, a Vietnam War hero, pushed this attack even harder. During the campaign, Obama took a trip to the Middle East and Europe to show his capacity for statesmanship. He and his supporters stressed his extensive knowledge and sound judgment as qualities not strictly dependent on experience. This was substantially borne out in his first few years in office, as seen in the high foreign policy approval he received in public opinion polls.

Obama's conception of the international system recognizes America's central role, but places it within a heavily multilateral context. America seeks a "common security for our common humanity," he stated. The world is such that "America cannot meet the threats of this century alone, and the world cannot meet them without America. We can neither retreat from the world nor try to bully it into submission. We must lead the world, by deed and by example."[24] Cooperation with other countries is to be the norm for pragmatic, not altruistic, reasons. Though acknowledging the importance of Power, he stresses that "our power alone cannot protect us, nor does it entitle us to do as we please."[25] Obama sees American Principles as a set of ideals that "speak to aspirations shared by all people."[26] His overarching strategy is broadly encompassing including halting global climate change, achieving greater energy security, reducing global poverty, and dealing with failed and failing states.

Executive Branch Politics

Foreign policy teams and bureaucratic politics

Neither the George H. W. Bush (Bush 41) nor the Clinton administration had anything like the battles that Henry Kissinger fought with other Nixon and Ford administration officials, those between Carter's National Security Adviser Zbigniew Brzezinski and Secretary of State Cyrus Vance, or those between Reagan's Secretary of State George Shultz and Defense Secretary Caspar Weinberger. Divisive intra-executive branch politics returned in the George W. Bush (Bush 43) administration, however. Later, the Obama administration was less the "team of rivals" than some anticipated.

THE BUSH 41 TEAM   The members of the Bush 41 team had two characteristics in common.[27] They all had prior foreign policy and other governmental experience, and all were longtime friends or associates of President Bush. Secretary of State James Baker had served as White House chief of staff and secretary of the treasury in the Reagan administration, and had been friends with Bush since their early days together in Texas politics. National Security Adviser Brent Scowcroft had held the same position in the Ford administration, when his friendship with Bush began, and was a retired Air Force lieutenant colonel with a Ph.D. Defense Secretary Dick Cheney had been White House chief of staff in the Ford administration, and had been in Congress for ten years. General Colin Powell, chair of the Joint Chiefs of Staff, emerged during the Reagan administration as a top Pentagon official and served as national security adviser.

As a team, Bush and his top appointees were generally regarded as highly competent and quite cohesive. Even those who disagreed with their policies did not question their capabilities. After all the messy internal fights of prior administrations, the solidarity of the Bush team was a welcome relief. Some critics, though, voiced concerns that the group was too tightly drawn and too homogeneous. The conservative columnist William Safire remarked on the "absence of creative tension [which] has generated little excitement or innovation."[28]

THE CLINTON TEAM   While it had its supporters, the performance of the Clinton team was criticized more than the Bush 41 team. Les Aspin, Clinton's first secretary of defense, lasted less than a year, in part because he took much of the blame for the Somalia failure. Warren Christopher was a hard-working and gracious secretary of state but some felt he was not the right man for such transitional times. Sandy Berger, national security adviser in Clinton's second term, was criticized by Kissinger for being more of a "trade lawyer" than a "global strategist," approaching issues one by one and very transactionally rather than developing a so-called grand strategy.[29]

Two historic developments also occurred. First was the appointment of Madeleine Albright as the first woman secretary of state. Second was the enhanced foreign policy role played by Vice President Al Gore. Previous occupants of the office, dubbed by its first holder, John Adams, as "the most insignificant office that ever the invention of man contrived," typically did not have much of a foreign policy portfolio beyond trips to funerals of foreign dignitaries and the occasional special assignment. Gore, who had earned a reputation for foreign policy expertise while in Congress, took on much greater foreign policy responsibilities. The even greater role played by Vice President Dick Cheney in the Bush 43 administration, whatever other issues it raised, further institutionalized this more substantive vice presidential foreign policy role.

THE BUSH 43 TEAM   During the 2000 campaign the effort to earn Governor George W. Bush credit through association with an experienced foreign policy team was quite conscious. Dick Cheney and Colin Powell had served in the Bush 41 administration as secretary of defense and chairman of the Joint Chiefs of Staff, respectively, as had Condoleezza Rice, who had been a national Security Council staff specialist on the Soviet Union. Donald Rumsfeld had been the ambassador to NATO in the Nixon administration and secretary of defense in the Ford administration. This new administration had many familiar faces and presumably strong intra-administration consensus.

It wasn't long, though, before fissures became apparent. Within the first two months, the Bush 43 team already was showing "two faces . . . an ideologically conservative Pentagon and a more moderate State Department."[30] These early differences became major splits over the war in Iraq. Vice President Cheney and Defense Secretary Rumsfeld were strongly pro-war, Secretary of State Powell less so. "Bureaucratic tribalism exists in all administrations," observed Francis Fukuyama, "but it rose to pernicious levels in the Bush administration."[31] We delve into the Iraq War bureaucratic politics in Chapter 11.

THE OBAMA TEAM   When President Obama appointed Hillary Rodham Clinton, who had been his principal rival for the 2008 Democratic presidential nomination, as secretary of state there were questions about whether they could work well together. They proved to be quite collaborative, with only a few significant policy differences.[32] Obama kept Robert Gates, who had replaced Rumsfeld as Defense Secretary in the Bush administration, in that position for the first two years and this relationship also proved largely cooperative. In mid-2011 Leon Panetta, who had been the CIA Director, replaced Gates at the Pentagon and General David Petraeus, who made his name in the Iraq War, replaced Panetta at the CIA. Vice President Joseph Biden, who for many years was chairman of the Senate Foreign Relations Committee, has had a major foreign policy role, as has UN Ambassador Susan Rice. Obama's first national security adviser, Jim Jones, was replaced in 2010 by Thomas Donilon, whose experience was more in foreign policy politics and process than as a strategist.

A signature decision for the Obama team involved the May 2011 killing of Osama bin Laden. Once intelligence sources confirmed bin Laden's whereabouts in Pakistan, President Obama was presented with options. One option was to bomb the compound where bin Laden was living from the air but not send any troops in. This was seen as less risky but provided less ability to confirm that bin Laden had been killed. The other was to helicopter in a Navy SEAL team and have them capture or kill bin Laden. This was riskier, with the possibility that the troops sent in could be captured or killed, but could also prove with certainty that bin Laden had been killed. The Obama advisory team was split, with some particularly concerned that if the operation failed politically damaging comparisons would be made to President Carter's 1980 failed rescue of U.S. hostages in Iran. President Obama made the decision to go with the SEAL option. It succeeded and Obama was given a lot of credit for thoughtful analytic decision making. Of course, had the operation failed, the assessments would have been quite different.

As President Obama's second term began, a number of the changes in his foreign policy team spurred political controversy (Table 9.1). UN Ambassador Susan Rice appeared to be his first choice to succeed Hillary Clinton as secretary of state. But Republican senators such as John McCain seized on some public statements she made concerning the September 2012 attacks on the U.S. consulate in Benghazi, Libya that killed Ambassador Chris Stevens and three other Americans—the issue being the extent to which the attacks were spontaneous eruptions and the extent to which they were planned assaults by terrorist groups linked to Al Qaeda—as grounds for opposing her nomination. After Ambassador Rice withdrew from consideration, President Obama nominated Senator John Kerry, the sitting chairman of the Senate Foreign Relations Committee and someone with extensive foreign policy experience. He was readily confirmed.

Chuck Hagel, the Defense Secretary nominee, also stirred much controversy. Even though Hagel had been a Republican senator, Senate Republicans strongly opposed his appointment. The grounds cited included his opposition to the Iraq war (he had originally supported it but shifted as the war went on), questions about how supportive he was of Israel, and doubts about his views on how best to deal with the threat of Iranian nuclear proliferation. Hagel supporters stressed his military service and heroism during the Vietnam War, his moderate views on many issues, and the bipartisanship embodied in a Democratic president appointing a Republican. Hagel did end up being confirmed by the Senate, although in a close vote.

TABLE 9.1 The Obama Foreign Policy Team (second term, 2013–)	
Vice President	Joseph Biden
National Security Advisor	Thomas Donilon
Secretary of State	John Kerry
Secretary of Defense	Chuck Hagel
Chair, Joint Chiefs of Staff	General Martin Dempsey
Ambassador to the United Nations	Susan Rice
Director of National Intelligence	James Clapper
Director of the CIA	John Brennan
Secretary of Homeland Security	Janet Napolitano
Secretary of the Treasury	Jacob Lew
U.S. Trade Representative	Demetrios Marantis (acting, as of May 2013)
Director of the National Economic Council	Gene Sperling
Secretary of Commerce	Rebecca Blank (acting, as of May 2013)

A sex scandal caused Petraeus to resign as CIA Director. Obama then nominated John Brennan. Opposition to John Brennan's nomination came more from liberal groups. His support for waterboarding and torture while at the CIA during the Bush years was one issue. His support for drones and the largely secret decision-making process for their use while White House senior counterterrorism aide during the Obama first term was another. He, too, ended up being confirmed, although also with more opposition than is usually the case.

Intelligence Agencies[33]

Another key part of the executive branch, the CIA, FBI, and other intelligence agencies face a number of challenges, some of their own making. The intelligence community was found to have broken the law by violating the civil liberties of many Americans during the Cold War, a scandal which led to significant reforms following the 1970s Church Committee congressional investigations (see Chapter 6). In the latter days of the Cold War, both the CIA and the FBI had internal spy scandals. Reports also came out about the unsavory relationships the CIA maintained during the Cold War with some of its "ABC" (anything but communist) partners.

Then came 9/11. Among the many specific points made by the 9/11 Commission (known formally as the *National Commission on Terrorist Attacks Upon the United States*), was that the CIA and others were still too rooted in Cold War threats and scenarios.[34] The commission proposed a number of reforms. Some were organizational, such as the creation of an overall "czar," or Director of National Intelligence (DNI), with authority to coordinate and manage the CIA, FBI, and other intelligence agencies. Others concerned strategy and the need to commit greater resources and priority to Al Qaeda and other major threats from Islamist terrorism. Others were about mindsets, questions asked, thinking ahead of the curve, and other aspects of high-quality intelligence work that are analytic and not just organizational or budgetary. Some of the 9/11 Commission reforms have proven to be significant improvements, such as those regarding information sharing and integration of intelligence operations. Others have been less impactful; turf wars still go on within the intelligence community.[35]

Former top intelligence analyst Paul Pillar raises deeper concerns about the politicization of intelligence.[36] He sees this as a longstanding problem, citing examples throughout the Cold War of blatant pressure on intelligence officers, inconvenient analyses being ignored or distorted, and more subtle and arguably more insidious politicizations. But he sees the problem as much worse post-9/11 and especially in the Iraq War. "My corner of the intelligence community," he writes, based on his position at the time as National Intelligence Officer for the Middle East, "produced nothing during the first year of the Bush administration that could be construed as an impetus for more aggressive action against Iraq."[37] He goes further: "The war makers' posture toward intelligence went beyond mere disregard: it became one of rejection, hostility, and attempts to discredit." Pillar is also very critical of the 9/11 Commission, although other scholars such as Jordan Tama assess the Commission as less than perfect but having had significant positives.[38]

Along with Pillar's concerns about the politicization of intelligence, Professor Loch Johnson, a scholar who served on the Church Committee, gives a sense of the dilemmas involved in providing high-quality intelligence while operating within democratic principles and laws. Standing oversight mechanisms such as the congressional intelligence committees and special investigations responding to scandals, "can prove useful, leading to critical reforms, stronger oversight and, perhaps most important, changed attitudes about the CIA and other intelligence agencies." Yet, "I've also learned that high-profile investigations will not transform human nature, turning intelligence officials—or the presidents and White House aides who direct them—into angels, unsusceptible to zeal and folly."[39]

Interest Groups

In Chapter 3 we went back to James Madison's *Federalist 10* concerns about the danger of "factions": a "minority of the whole, who are united and actuated by some common impulse of passion, or of interest, adverse to the rights of other citizens, or to the permanent and aggregate interests of the community." Though groups today do not exactly match this description, they come close enough that one wonders what Madison would think about the role they play. Do they have too much influence and pull foreign policy toward the interests of particular constituencies and away from the overall national interest? Do they provide channels of influence for interests and perspectives that are otherwise insufficiently represented? Here we consider three types of interest groups prominent in foreign policy politics.

Military-Industrial-Counterterrorism-Private Contractors Complex

The fiftieth anniversary of President Eisenhower's "military-industrial complex" speech (see Chapter 3) in January 2011 prompted renewed concern about the influence of the defense industry. And not just from liberals. Speaking at the Eisenhower Library in Abilene, Kansas, Defense Secretary Robert Gates expressed his concern about continued pushes for more and more weapons systems:

> Does the number of warships we have, and are building, really put America at risk, when the U.S. battle fleet is larger than the next 13 navies combined—11 of which are our partners and allies? . . . Is it a dire threat that by 2020, the United States will have only 20 times more advanced stealth fighters than China? . . . These are the kinds of questions Eisenhower asked as commander-in-chief. They are the kinds of questions I believe he would ask today.

Secretary Gates was blunt about the barriers to cutting military spending: "What it takes is the political will and willingness, as Eisenhower possessed, to make hard choices—choices that will displease powerful people both inside the Pentagon, and out."[40] Susan Eisenhower, President Eisenhower's granddaughter, wrote an op-ed in the *Washington Post* linking the huge increase in defense spending—a 119 percent increase since 9/11, and even after subtracting the costs of the wars in Iraq and Afghanistan, still 68 percent—to the debt crisis.[41]

Christopher Preble of the libertarian Cato Institute dissected the spending on a number of major weapons systems, including the F-22 Raptor. Originally designed late in the Cold War, this became "an aircraft in search of a mission."[42] It was marred by production delays, huge cost overruns, and technical and performance problems. Yet, with production spread across forty-six states, the "iron triangle" strategy linking defense contractors, the Pentagon, and members of Congress kept production going through 2011. There are countless other examples of pork-barrel politics in the defense budget. One member of Congress slipped in $250,000 for a study of a caffeinated chewing gum that might help sleep-deprived troops—which is manufactured by a company in his district. Another added $5 million for retrofitting locks used on classified documents to meet stricter specifications—as manufactured by a company in his district.[43] As a more general indicator of how the iron triangle works, in recent years an estimated 80 percent of retiring three- and four-star military officers have taken jobs as defense industry consultants or executives, up from less than 50 percent in the mid-1990s.[44]

In the wake of 9/11 the counterterrorism industry has also grown dramatically. Billions of dollars are spent annually on the equipment, technology, and services to protect against terrorism. Some of this spending is by the federal government—not only the Pentagon but also the Department of Homeland Security, the CIA and other intelligence agencies, the Department of Health and Human Services and the Centers for Disease Control (against bioterrorism), and other departments and agencies. State and local governments as well invest in emergency preparedness at the local level. There is also spending by the private sector: it is rare to walk into an office building in any major city that does not have elaborate security checks.

The Iraq War highlighted the major increase in the government's use of private security contractors and the attendant controversies. One issue was cost. Contrary to assumptions that outsourcing saves money, the fees being paid firms such as Blackwater for providing security services were akin to the $600 toilet seats of earlier scandals. Another issue was accountability, highlighted in 2007, when Blackwater guards killed seventeen Iraqi civilians in an incident that "outraged Iraqis, put severe strain on relations between Baghdad and Washington, and served as a watershed moment in the debate surrounding private fighters in foreign war zones."[45] There is also the overarching issue of role: are private security contractors any different than mercenaries?[46] The political philosopher Max Weber stressed the authoritative control of the means of violence as a crucial defining characteristic of government. If large parts of warfare are privatized, what does that mean for the fundamental role and legitimacy of government?[47]

The Israel Lobby and Middle East Policy

As discussed in Chapter 3, there has been much debate over the "Israel lobby" and its influence on U.S. Middle East policy. *The Israel Lobby and U.S. Foreign Policy,* by John Mearsheimer and Stephen Walt, attributes many aspects of U.S. support for Israel and much of overall Middle East policy to the influence of the American-Israel Public Affairs Committee (AIPAC) and Jewish Americans. Mearsheimer and Walt contend that while the national interest does factor in somewhat, U.S. support for Israel is "due largely to the political power of the Israel lobby, a loose coalition of individuals and groups that seek to influence American foreign policy in ways that will benefit Israel." They cite a range of issues: "back[ing] Israel more or less unconditionally . . . the Israeli-Palestinian conflict, the ill-fated invasion of Iraq, and the ongoing confrontation with Iran."[48] They point to various channels for exercising that political influence: appealing to Jewish-American campaign donors and voting blocs in elections, lobbying Congress, and exerting it directly through Israel supporters who serve in prominent foreign policy positions.

Critics make three main arguments. First is over-attribution of causality for U.S policies to the Israel lobby. To the extent that U.S. policy is pro-Israel, both Power (the geostrategic benefits of a reliable ally in a region long known for its anti-Americanism) and Principles (Israel is the only democracy in the Middle East region) have also been served. With regard to the Bush administration's decision in 2003 to go to war in Iraq, which Mearsheimer and Walt tie to Jewish-American influence, other factors were much more significant, as we will see in Chapter 11.

Second is emphasis on the impact of other lobbies, such as oil companies and arms exporters with economic interests in maintaining good relations with Arab countries. One author refers to the "petro-diplomatic complex," and asks "do the Saudis have us over a barrel?"[49] Numerous policies have been pro–Saudi Arabia, including some that the Israel lobby strongly objected to, such as the 1981 sale of air defense systems (so-called AWACS) to the Saudis.

Third is ignoring splits within the Jewish-American community, reflecting Israel's own deep political splits on issues like the Arab-Israeli peace process. The lobbying group J Street was created as something of a counterbalance to AIPAC, pro-Israel but taking the view that peace with the Palestinians and other more liberal positions best serve Israel's interest. It also is the case that not all Jewish-Americans base their voting more on the Israel issue than domestic policy issues.

In recent years the Israel lobby has been the most salient in the debate over the influence of identity-based interest groups, but similar debates swirl around Cuban Americans and others.

NGOs and the Politics of Globalization

The rise of nongovernmental organizations (NGOs) has become a major part of foreign policy politics. NGOs have been particularly active on trade and other globalization issues.

A study by the scholars Margaret Keck and Kathryn Sikkink stresses four factors that make NGOs effective (Reading 9.2).[50] The first is "information politics" and the ability of NGOs to be alternative sources of credible information, using the Internet or other information technologies for timely and targeted communication of that information. National governments and international institutions are no longer exclusive sources of the "facts" and other key information about the issues of the day. Many NGOs produce their own studies, issue their own policy papers, and conduct their own press briefings. The key for them is to safeguard their reputations for credibility and avoid overstating or misstating their case.

The second factor is "symbolic politics," meaning "the ability to call upon symbols, actions or stories that make sense of a situation that is frequently far away."[51] NGOs have mastered the art of politics as theater, and global politics as global theater. They have been

9.2

adept at getting celebrity endorsements, staging events for the media that dramatize issues, and otherwise tapping into the symbols as well as the substance of issues.

The third factor is "leverage politics." In addition to generally using information and tapping into symbols, NGOs target the actors and institutions that are the greatest points of leverage on a particular issue. On some issues they focus on the United States; on others, another country's government; on yet others, the UN, the WTO, the IMF, the World Bank, or other international institutions. The NGOs' own global networks can give them the reach and flexibility to exercise this leverage.

The fourth factor is "accountability politics." NGOs have positioned themselves as the voice of the people on many issues. They are the vehicle for representing the interests and views of those outside the halls of government and corporate board rooms. This claim is one of the major reasons that NGOs are often seen as the "good guys" in the politics of globalization. Although this is often true, it is not always the case. NGOs are not strictly high-minded, altruistic actors. They have their own interests, including competition with other NGOs for prominence or funding. One study showed that "organizational insecurity, competitive pressures, and fiscal uncertainty" have become increasingly common among NGOs.[52] Nor are NGOs always effective in carrying out the goals to which they claim to aspire. In some instances their impact has been counterproductive and opportunistic.

Media Old and New

In previous chapters we've seen the role the media has played in foreign policy politics historically. How has it changed, and how is it similar, today?

Challenges to Old Media: Internet, Soft News, and Polarized News

The nature of the media has been undergoing profound change. More and more people are getting their news on the Internet, and at an accelerating rate. A 2011 study found 41 percent of Americans getting "most of their news about national and international news from the Internet," a substantial number in its own right and a dramatic jump from 24 percent just four years earlier. Among youth, the pattern is even more striking. In 2007 twice as many young people said they relied on television for news than on the Internet (68 percent versus 34 percent); by 2011, 65 percent said they primarily got their news online, as opposed to only 52 percent relying on television.[53]

The other side of this trend is reflected in the drop in newspaper readership. Daily circulation of newspapers stood at 62.3 million in 1990, and fell to 43.4 million in 2010, a decline of 30 percent.[54] Measured as sales across the industry, the decrease was almost 3 percent from 2006 to 2007, with another 2.6 percent decrease in 2008.[55] In 2009 the decline was even steeper, more than 10 percent, leaving the newspaper business facing "the greatest threat since the Depression."[56] Newspaper print circulation improved during 2010 only in the same sense that ad revenues did. Totals were still falling but not as fast as in 2008 and 2009. For the six-month period ending September 30, 2010, daily circulation was down 5 percent.[57] The situation may not be as dire for newspaper readership as a whole, though. In 2010, 37 percent of Americans said they got their news from a newspaper, including the newspaper's Web site.[58] This may indicate that although individuals are getting more and more of their news online, much of the content still comes from old media (that is, online versions of newspapers).

The Internet has also substantially enhanced the capacity of NGOs, think tanks, and other organizations to become independent sources of information, analysis, and advocacy. Nik Gowing, a journalist with the BBC, calls this development a breaking of the "information dominance" of governments, whether they are repressive regimes that would prefer to cut their people off from outside communication or democratic governments that must respond to the new dynamics of pressure.[59] Gowing was writing well before the explosive growth of the "blogosphere." In 1999 the total number of blogs was estimated at about fifty; by 2004 the estimates were 2.4 million to 4.1 million; by the end of 2011 the number had jumped to 181 million.[60]

Meanwhile, the mainstream media (MSM) have been cutting back their international coverage. In 1988 each of the major television networks spent about two thousand minutes covering international news over the course of the year; by 2000 this had declined to between eleven hundred and twelve hundred minutes. This constituted only about 9 percent of each evening news broadcast.[61] The percentage did increase in the 2000s with 9/11, the Iraq and Afghanistan Wars, and the global financial crises. As of 2012, network evening broadcasts spent 24 percent of their time on foreign policy and events. It will be interesting to see which way the trend goes.[62]

The print media have also been undergoing major changes. By the early 1990s, cutbacks were so extensive that only twenty-five of the top one hundred newspapers had at least one full-time foreign correspondent.[63] "Before September 11," wrote *Washington Post* editors Leonard Downie and Robert Kaiser, "most of the American news media gave scant coverage to the fact that the United States was the key participant in an interdependent global society, or that our economic well-being depended on foreigners, or that our population includes millions of people born in foreign lands, more every year."[64] A *Los Angeles Times* reporter expressed his concern that "you don't have editors and staff members who are conversant with the issues and with the world beyond our borders, so foreign news is easy to ignore a lot of the time."[65] Nor was this an isolated view. A survey of newspaper editors' own views found nearly two-thirds rated post–September 11 foreign news coverage as only fair or poor.[66]

These trends have intensified, as indicated in a 2008 Pew Research Center study that found almost two-thirds of American newspapers publishing less foreign news than just three years earlier. Only 10 percent of editors surveyed saw foreign news as "very essential" to their newspapers. "It's really concerning when we have two wars overseas, our economy is more global, we're competing with economies that are growing faster than ours, and our dependence on foreign oil is one of the biggest stories," commented a top Pew official.[67] The numbers have not changed drastically in recent years: an *American Journalism Review* study found that staff-produced foreign stories in eight major U.S. newspapers fell to 4 percent of content in 2010. Even when foreign news is reported, it is rarely on the front page; the same study found that only 6 percent of these foreign stories appeared on page one of major newspapers.[68]

Between 1998 and 2010, 18 American newspapers and two multinewspaper chains shut down all their foreign bureaus.[69] The Internet, while global in its reach, has its own parochial quality. Even with all the non-U.S. sites available, both official and unofficial, American Internet users get 95 percent of their news from sources published within the United States.[70]

Another part of the challenge to old media, as Matthew Baum examines in Reading 9.3, comes from "soft news." *The Daily Show with Jon Stewart* is the iconic example. The statistics on the number of younger Americans who rely on the "fake news" of *The Daily Show* or other shows in this genre, such as *The Colbert Report*, will not surprise readers of this book. That may not be such a terrible thing. Some of the points that Jon Stewart draws out through his humor are more insightful and original than the standard MSM fare. It is important to separate the empirical point of soft news having become more salient from evaluative points about the extent to which this is a "bad thing."

There also is the question of whether the media are more biased than in the past. Conservatives have long argued that the media have a liberal bias. Among those cited are major newspapers such as the *New York Times* and the *Washington Post*; television networks CBS, NBC, and ABC; National Public Radio; and public television. However some question whether the bias now tilts more in the conservative direction. The argument is that none of these outlets are as systematically and extensively politicized as Fox News or radio hosts like Rush Limbaugh. MSNBC is as self-consciously liberal as Fox News is conservative, but it has a fraction of the viewership. The op-ed page of the *Washington Post* has many more conservative columnists than liberal ones. The debate now cuts in both ideological directions within a shared view of how polarized the media have become.

Kony 2012: Case Study in Viral Social Media[71]

In March 2012, an NGO called Invisible Children posted a video on YouTube documenting the horrors inflicted by a group called the Lord's Resistance Army (LRA) led by Joseph Kony in Uganda. "In mere days," two reporters for the *New York Times* wrote, the Kony 2012 video "did what diplomats and academics have tried to do for decades: draw attention to the abuses of Joseph Kony and the Lord's Resistance Army."[72] Within a month, more than 86 million viewers had watched scenes of villages burned to the ground; indiscriminate killings of men, women, and children; and children who were coerced and brainwashed into being atrocity-inflicting soldiers.

For years, efforts had been made to focus attention and prompt action against Kony and the LRA. Congress even had passed such legislation in 2010. The Obama administration sent in military special forces in 2011. But as General Carter F. Ham, commander of American forces in Africa stated it, sitting in his office with a Kony 2012 poster on the wall, "Let's be honest, there was some constituent pressure here. Did Kony 2012 have something to do with this? Absolutely."[73]

Critics, though, argued that this social media impact also had its downsides. Arguing that the video embodies a certain "techno-utopian" approach to social activism, journalist David Rieff faults Kony 2012 as being "a new delivery system for the humanitarian wing of the old imperial enterprise." Rieff critiques both the medium *and* the message, finding the former inherently predisposed to (over)simplifying complex social phenomena, and equating the latter with a call to armed humanitarian intervention. For him, suggesting that awareness can in itself produce a solution displays a naiveté and arrogance that will likely translate into wrong-headed policies.[74] When the film was screened in northern Uganda a few weeks after its release, the dissatisfaction with its message and factual accuracy prompted such a harsh reaction that it was stopped over concerns about starting a riot.[75] The people that the film was purported to be helping reacted with both anger and violence to its very screening.

Such criticisms do not necessarily negate the arguments on the other side. They do, though, raise perspectives to be borne in mind by future activists.

Military Intervention and the "CNN Curve"

The Somalia and Bosnia humanitarian interventions in the 1990s gave rise to theories about the "CNN curve." On the front end of the curve, the spotlight intensity that is focused on such humanitarian crises is said to raise public awareness so much that it puts great pressure on officials, impelling them to precipitate military intervention too quickly and with too little fleshing out of strategy. On the back end, coverage of casualties or other major policy disasters can fuel a steep enough drop in public support to make the political pressure too much to bear without a withdrawal or other major shift in policy, even if such a move is premature or unwise as a matter of strategy.

Although the effect of CNN and new telecommunications technologies cannot be denied, it also should not be exaggerated. Journalist Warren Strobel provided one of the most insightful analyses of this dynamic. Strobel argued that the power of the media to influence a policy is inversely related to how well-grounded the policy itself is:

> It is true that U.S. government policies and actions regarding international conflict are subject to more open public review than previously in history. But policy-makers retain great power

to frame events and solicit public support—indeed, CNN at times increases this power. Put another way, if officials do not have a firm and well-considered policy or have failed to communicate their views in such a way as to garner the support of the American people, the news media will fill this vacuum (often by giving greater time and attention to the criticisms or policy preferences of its opponents).[76]

Strobel's research in Somalia and Bosnia included more than a hundred interviews with senior policy makers from both the Bush 41 and Clinton administrations, military officers and spokespersons, journalists, and others. He acknowledges that "CNN and its brethren have made leadership more difficult," and that it is television's inherent nature as a visual medium to "feed on conflict, whether political or physical, emphasizing the challenge to policy." But "when policy is well grounded, it is less likely that the media will be able to shift officials' focus. When policy is clear, reasonably constant, and well communicated, the news media follow officials rather than lead them."[77]

Public Opinion: Continuity, Change, and Uncertainty

What does the public think about foreign policy these days? As befits a period of historic transition, there is a mix of continuity with previous patterns, change from them, and uncertainty about priorities and preferences. In each of the chapters that follow we will look at public opinion on some specific issues; here our focus is on general patterns.

Overall Patterns

The long-term trends in internationalism-isolationism (Chapter 3) showed consistent preferences for internationalism with some fluctuations, including some recent narrowing of the gap. The 38 percent of Americans saying "stay out of world affairs" in the 2012 poll conducted by the Chicago Council on Global Affairs was the highest in many years, but still substantially lower than the 61 percent saying "take an active part."[78] That the gap was not narrower, given weariness from more than a decade of war and the economic crisis, shows that the American public understands that the United States has become so interconnected with the rest of the world that isolationism is not just undesirable—it is not possible.

When broken down by age groups, 52 percent of the "Millennial" generation (18–29 years old) said "stay out of world affairs."[79] This is much higher than any of the other age groups, which vary between 31 percent (60+ years old) and 39 percent (30–44 years old). While earlier surveys also found younger Americans with higher relative "stay out of world affairs" scores, there has never before been a majority; indeed, in 2009 the figure was only 39 percent, marking quite a sharp rise in just two years. Why do you and your fellow students think this is happening?

Another question about the general orientation toward internationalism comes from polls showing that the public gives higher priority to domestic issues. For example, a 2010 poll asking whether "it is more important at this time for the United States to fix problems at home or address challenges to the United States from abroad," had 91 percent of respondents saying "fix problems at home." But all this tells us is that people opt for domestic policy when given a binary choice. Especially during an economic recession, of course they would. But even in more "normal" domestic times, it's entirely logical to prioritize domestic policy unless there is a huge international crisis or major war. That domestic policy is more important does not mean foreign policy is not important.

Moreover, the public sees this foreign-domestic nexus. When given a list of foreign policy goals, four of the five with the highest "very important" ranking had a significant domestic component. These were:

- protecting the jobs of American workers, 83 percent
- reducing U.S. dependence on foreign oil, 77 percent
- containing terrorism, 64 percent
- controlling and reducing illegal immigration, 53 percent

In the top five, the only foreign policy goal without a significant domestic policy component was "preventing the spread of nuclear weapons" (72 percent).[80]

Views of the United Nations

Views of the United Nations bring out a particular aspect of the above debate. Figure 9.1 shows how strong U.S. public support was for the UN from the 1950s through the 1960s. This is consistent with the policy enhancement–prerogative encroachment analysis in Chapter 7. In those years the American public viewed the UN's role as enhancing U.S. foreign policy. The UN generally supported U.S. positions during the Cold War. The strongest example of this support was during the Korean War: On the same day that North Korea invaded South Korea, the UN Security Council ordered it to cease and withdraw, and then made the defense of South Korea a UN operation led by the United States with troops from other UN member countries. On many other issues, a pro-U.S. tilt generally characterized UN decisions. Furthermore, people felt that the UN was largely effective in achieving its programmatic goals.

The "good job"/"poor job" lines first cross in the early 1970s. The "poor job" view dominated public opinion through the mid-1980s. During this period, votes in the General Assembly were often critical of U.S. foreign policy, and criticisms of UN inefficiencies and corruption mounted. The turnaround of the late 1980s and early 1990s was prompted by peacekeeping successes in Afghanistan and elsewhere, and continued with the 1990–91 Persian Gulf War.

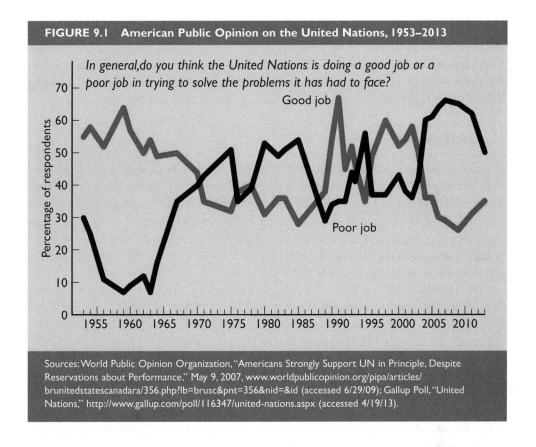

FIGURE 9.1   American Public Opinion on the United Nations, 1953–2013

In general, do you think the United Nations is doing a good job or a poor job in trying to solve the problems it has had to face?

Good job

Poor job

Percentage of respondents

Sources: World Public Opinion Organization, "Americans Strongly Support UN in Principle, Despite Reservations about Performance," May 9, 2007, www.worldpublicopinion.org/pipa/articles/brunitedstatescanadara/356.php?lb=brusc&pnt=356&nid=&id (accessed 6/29/09); Gallup Poll, "United Nations," http://www.gallup.com/poll/116347/united-nations.aspx (accessed 4/19/13).

The "poor job" gap reopened in reaction to Somalia and Bosnia. In August 1995, only 35 percent of Americans rated the UN positively, whereas 56 percent rated it negatively. Polls began to even out again in 1996 as the situation in Bosnia improved and the UN got credit for agreeing to let NATO take charge. Other factors, such as internal reforms and the election of Secretary-General Kofi Annan, also helped the "good job" rating recapture a majority.

American public opinion remained steadily supportive of the UN until the controversies of the 2003 Iraq War. Even when Americans turned against the Iraq War in subsequent years, views of the UN became even more negative. A 2009 Gallup poll still found 65 percent replying "bad job" and only 26 percent replying "good job." Some of this may be related to question wording. A 2011 poll with the question phrased as "should the U.S. cooperate with the UN" found six in ten Americans saying yes, a slight increase since 2009. Another 2011 poll asked whether the UN is an important organization, with 80 percent saying it was, and whether the U.S. should pay its dues in full and on time, with 60 percent saying yes. In this latter poll, there was a plurality in the affirmative among Republicans;

among Democrats and Independents there were majorities.[81] Along the same lines, the 2012 Chicago Council survey reported 52 percent of respondents saying the UN is effective and 46 percent saying it is ineffective. When asked whether recent efforts to strengthen the UN have been effective, 62 percent agreed.[82] Even the "good job/bad job" wording showed some limited increases in positive assessments in 2011 and 2013.

Use of Military Force

Chapter 3 discussed public support for the use of military force during the Cold War. This "pretty prudent public" pattern varied according to perceptions of the principal policy objective, with the greatest support for coercing *foreign policy restraint* on an aggressor threatening the United States, its citizens, or its interests. Support was lowest when the principal objective was to engineer *internal political change* in another country's government; and somewhere in between for *humanitarian interventions.*[83] Post–Cold War cases further illustrate the pattern.

The 1990–91 Gulf War to force Iraq to withdraw from Kuwait and prevent an invasion of Saudi Arabia (foreign policy restraint) had high levels of public support. In the build-up to the war, polls consistently showed above 60 percent support. In the early days of the war this increased to 82 percent. Even when asked whether they would continue to support the war if high casualties were incurred, 60 percent said yes. The 2003 Iraq War initially got high levels of support. The claims about weapons of mass destruction (WMD) and links to Al Qaeda, on top of Saddam Hussein's track record of aggression, framed the principal policy objective as foreign policy restraint. Over the first six weeks, when the war effort seemed to be going well, public support reached 75 percent. But within months this had slipped to 47 percent and opposition had risen to 51 percent. This was in part a reaction to the war effort starting to go badly, but more fundamentally a shift to seeing the principal objective as internal political change. By May 2006 only 32 percent of the public supported the Iraq War; by June 2008 only 25 percent did. The WMD and Al Qaeda rationales had been shown to be specious. The goal of this war was internal political change, an objective for which Americans were much less inclined to support the use of military force.

Turning to humanitarian intervention cases, initial polls regarding the operation in Somalia, which started out as the archetypal "pure" humanitarian intervention case, showed 70 percent support or higher. However, as perceptions of the mission changed to "nation-building"—i.e., internal political change—public support dropped to 47 percent, and then to 35 percent when the American soldiers were killed. This indicated much lower public tolerance for casualties when the objective was remaking governments rather than when it was restraining aggression. Bosnia was a particularly complex case, involving elements of interstate aggression, intrastate civil war, and humanitarian crisis. The American public both feared a quagmire and felt moral outrage over ethnic "cleansing." For the most part, the polls averaged in the 40–45 percent support range. Consistent with the pretty prudent public framework, polling questions that cast the use of force in terms of humanitarian objectives received higher average support (56 percent) than those that linked the use of force to internal political change (34 percent).

Public support for the war in Afghanistan was initially over 80 percent. Retaliating against Al Qaeda and the Afghan Taliban for the 9/11 attacks was very much a foreign policy restraint objective. But public support decreased over time, as the successes in weakening Al Qaeda—including the killing of Osama bin Laden—made the foreign policy restraint objective less salient, and problems within Afghanistan such as corruption and warlords made it increasingly clear that the mission had shifted to internal political change. By early 2012, 60 percent of Americans favored removing U.S. troops as soon as possible. Meanwhile, polls asking specifically about terrorism—"taking military action in countries where it [the U.S.] believes terrorists are hiding"—still got 65 percent approval.[84]

Post–September 11 Patriotism

Overall, the domestic consensus in the wake of September 11 was broader and stronger than at any point since the end of the Cold War. It was, once again, foreign policy politics with an Enemy. President Bush's popularity, which had been dipping over the summer of 2001, soared to over 80 percent. In 1999 only 7 percent of the public cited foreign policy as one of the biggest problems the United States faces, and in 2001 41 percent did. A new sense of patriotism flourished, and this sense of "recapturing the flag" was well portrayed by the journalist George Packer:

> Among the things destroyed with the twin towers was the notion, held by certain Americans ever since Vietnam, that to be stirred by national identity, carry a flag and feel grateful toward someone in uniform ought to be a source of embarrassment. The force of the blows woke us up to the fact that we are a part of a national community. This heightened awareness could be the disaster's greatest legacy.

Packer also warned, though, about the underside:

> Patriotism is as volatile as any emotion; once released, it can assume ugly forms. "I'm a patriot," said Frank Roque after being arrested for murdering a Sikh in Arizona. But in the past decade, our national disorder has been narcissism, not hysteria. Anyone who wants reform should figure out how to harness the civic passion that rose from the smoking debris. Like jet fuel, it can be used for good or ill.[85]

This new consensus has its foreign policy benefits, just as it did during the Cold War and at other points in U.S. history. It also has negative aspects for foreign policy politics, just as in the past, raising issues such as the tension between national security and civil liberties, and the narrowing of the parameters of policy debate. Just as the Vietnam War shattered the Cold War consensus, the Iraq War had a similar impact on the September 11 consensus.

Summary: Foreign Policy Politics Change and Continuity

Post–Cold War foreign policy politics show a mix of change and continuity with Cold War and historical patterns. The key elements remain the same. The president and Congress still contest war powers. Presidents' own belief systems have continued to frame the overall foreign policy strategy. The executive branch continues to have its own internal politics. Interest groups, the media, and public opinion exert their own influences. However, some aspects of that framework are markedly different than in the past; e.g., the Internet and new media.

With these general patterns in mind, we take a closer look at the foreign policy politics of particular issue areas in the chapters that follow.

Notes

[1]Quoted in Thomas McCormick, *America's Half-Century: United States Foreign Policy in the Cold War* (Baltimore: Johns Hopkins University Press, 1989), 232.

[2]Bruce W. Jentleson, "The Domestic Politics of Desert Shield: Should We Go to War? Who Should Decide?" *Brookings Review* 9 (Winter 1990–91): 22–28.

[3]Cited in Bruce W. Jentleson, "Who, Why, What and How: Debates over Post–Cold War Military Intervention," in *Eagle Adrift: American Foreign Policy at the End of the Century,* Robert J. Lieber, ed. (New York: Longman, 1997), 62–63.

[4]Pat Towell and Donna Cassata, "Congress Takes Symbolic Stand on Troop Deployment," *Congressional Quarterly Weekly Report,* December 16, 1995, 3817.

[5]Ivo H. Daalder and Michael E. O'Hanlon, *Winning Ugly: NATO's War to Save Kosovo* (Washington, D.C.: Brookings Institution Press, 2000), 161.

[6]Daalder and O'Hanlon, *Winning Ugly,* 162.

[7]"Congress Approves Resolution Authorizing Force," CNN, September 14, 2001. Available at http://archives .cnn.com/2001/US/09/15/congress.terrorism/ (accessed 7/22/09).

[8]Robert C. Byrd, remarks in the U.S. Senate, Oct. 10, 2002, *Congressional Record,* October 10, 2002, S10233 (Washington, D.C.: Government Printing Office, 2002).

[9]Leslie H. Gelb and Anne-Marie Slaughter, "No More Blank-Check Wars," *Washington Post,* November 8, 2005, A19; Gelb and Slaughter, "Declare War," *Atlantic Monthly,* November 2005, 54–56.

[10]Constitution Project, *Deciding to Use Force Abroad: War Powers in a System of Checks and Balances,* June 29, 2005, 37, www.constitutionproject.org/pdf/War_Powers_Deciding_To_Use_Force_Abroad.pdf (accessed 7/22/09).

[11]John P. Murtha, "War in Iraq," November 17, 2005, www.wagingpeace.org/articles/2005/11/17_murtha-its -time-to-bring-the-troops-home.htm (accessed 2/19/13).

[12]I draw here on research papers written for my Politics of U.S. Foreign Policy course (Fall 2011) by Chris D'Angelo and Katherine Marie Canales.

[13]"Letter from the President Regarding the Commencement of Operations in Libya." March 21, 2011, www.whitehouse.gov/the-press-office/2011/03/21/letter-president-regarding-commencement-operations- libya (accessed 2/19/13).

[14]"President Obama's Letter About Efforts in Libya," *New York Times,* www.nytimes.com/2011/05/21/ world/africa/21libya-text.html." (accessed 2/19/13)

[15]Josiah Ryan, "Durbin: Libya Conflict Requires Authorization by Congress," The Hill, http://thehill.com/ blogs/floor-action/senate/166971-durbin-libya-conflict-requires-authorization-by-congress. (accessed 2/19/13)

[16]Jennifer Steinhauer, "House Spurns Obama on Libya, but Does Not Cut Funds," *The New York Times,* June 24, 2011, A1.

[17]Steinhauer, "House Spurns Obama."

[18]Jo Becker and Scott Shane, "Secret 'Kill List' Proves a Test of Obama's Principles and Will," *New York Times,* May 29, 2012, A1.

[19]Charlie Savage, "Top U.S. Security Official Says 'Rigorous Standards' Are Used for Drone Strikes," *New York Times,* April 30, 2012, A8.

[20]Scott Shane, "U.S. Attacks, Online and From the Air, Fuel Secrecy Debate," *New York Times,* June 6, 2012, A1.

[21]The commission was chaired by two former secretaries of state, James A. Baker III and Warren Christopher. *National War Powers Commission Report* (Miller Center for Public Affairs, University of Virginia, 2008), http://millercenter.org/policy/commissions/warpowers (accessed 2/19/13).

[22]Elizabeth Drew, *On the Edge: The Clinton Presidency* (New York: Simon and Schuster, 1994), 158, 283.

[23]See this ad on YouTube, www.youtube.com/watch?v=kddX7LqgCvc (accessed 2/19/13).

[24]Barack Obama, "Renewing American Leadership," *Foreign Affairs* 4.86 (July/August 2007): 2.

[25]Barack Obama, Inaugural Address, January 20, 2009, www.nytimes.com/2009/01/20/us/politics/20text -obama.html?_r=2 (accessed 2/19/13).

[26]Barack Obama, "A World That Stands as One," Berlin, Germany, July 24, 2008, www.americanrhetoric .com/speeches/barackobamaberlinspeech.htm (accessed 2/19/13).

[27]Larry Berman and Bruce W. Jentleson, "Bush and the Post–Cold War World: Challenges for American Leadership," in *The Bush Presidency: First Appraisals,* ed. Colin Campbell and Bert A. Rockman (Chatham, N.J.: Chatham House Publishers, 1991).

[28]Berman and Jentleson, "Bush and the Post–Cold War World," 103.

[29]Elaine Sciolino, "Berger Manages a Welter of Crises in the Post–Cold War White House," *New York Times,* May 18, 1998, A9.

[30]Jane Perlez, "Bush Team's Counsel is Divided on Foreign Policy," *New York Times,* March 27, 2001, A1.

[31]Francis Fukuyama, *America at the Crossroads: Democracy, Power and the Neoconservative Legacy* (New Haven: Yale University Press, 2006), 61.

[32]"What Hillary Did Next," *The Economist,* March 24, 2012, www.economist.com/node/21551105 (accessed 2/19/13).

[33]Thanks to Professor Brent Durbin of Smith College for valuable input on this section.

[34]National Commission on Terrorist Attacks Upon the United States, *9/11 Commission Report* (New York: Norton, 2004).

[35]For sharply contrasting assessments, see Paul R. Pillar, *Intelligence and U.S. Foreign Policy: Iraq, 9/11 and Misguided Reform* (New York: Columbia University Press, 2011) and Jordan Tama, *Terrorism and National Security Reform: How Commissions Can Drive Change During Crises* (New York: Cambridge University Press, 2011).

[36]Pillar, *Intelligence and U.S. Foreign Policy.*

[37]Pillar, *Intelligence and U.S. Foreign Policy,* 31, 43.

[38]Tama, *Terrorism and National Security Reform.*

[39]Loch K. Johnson, "It's Never a Quick Fix at the CIA," *Washington Post,* August 30, 2009, www .washingtonpost.com/wp-dyn/content/article/2009/08/28/AR2009082802097.html (accessed 2/19/13).

[40]National Public Radio, "Ike's Warning of Military Expansion, 50 Years Later," January 17, 2011, www.npr .org/2011/01/17/132942244/ikes-warning-of-military-expansion-50-years-later (accessed 2/19/13).

[41]Susan Eisenhower, "Fifty Years after the Military-Industrial Complex Speech, What Eisenhower Really Meant," *Washington Post,* January 14, 2011, www.washingtonpost.com/wp-dyn/content/article/ 2011/01/14/AR2011011406229.html (accessed 2/19/13).

[42]Christopher A. Preble, *The Power Problem: How American Military Dominance Makes Us Less Safe, Less Prosperous and Less Free* (Ithaca, N.Y.: Cornell University Press, 2009), 46, 70.

[43]Charles R. Babcock, "Pentagon Budget's Stealth Spending," *Washington Post.* October 13, 1998, A4.

[44]Robert Schlesinger, "Ike's Warning and JFK's Summons," *U.S. News and World Report,* January 20, 2011, www.usnews.com/opinion/slideshows/ikes-warning-and-jfks-summons/3 (accessed 2/20/13).

[45]Ryan Devereaux, "Blackwater Guards Lose Bid to Appeal Charges in Iraqi Civilian Shooting Case," *The Guardian,* June 5, 2012, www.guardian.co.uk/world/2012/jun/05/blackwater-guards-lose-appeal-iraq -shooting (accessed 2/20/13).

[46]Jeremy Scahill, *Blackwater: The Rise of the World's Most Powerful Mercenary Army* (New York: Avalon Books, 2007).

[47]Deborah D. Avant, *The Market for Force: The Consequences of Privatizing Security* (New York: Cambridge University Press, 2005); Peter W. Singer, *Corporate Warriors: The Rise of the Privatized Military Industry* (Ithaca, N.Y.: Cornell University Press, 2008).

[48]John J. Mearsheimer and Stephen M. Walt, *The Israel Lobby and U.S. Foreign Policy* (New York: Farrar, Straus and Giroux, 2007), viii.

[49]Mitchell Bard, *The Arab Lobby: The Invisible Alliance that Undermines American Interests in the Middle East* (New York: HarperCollins, 2010), 67.

[50]Margaret E. Keck and Kathryn Sikkink, *Activists Beyond Borders: Advocacy Networks in International Politics* (Ithaca, N.Y.: Cornell University Press, 1998).

[51]Keck and Sikkink, *Activists Beyond Borders,* 16.

[52]Alexander Cooley and James Ron, "The NGO Scramble: Organizational Insecurity and the Political Economy of Transnational Action," *International Security* 27 (Summer 2002): 5–39.

[53]Pew Research Center of the People and the Press, "Internet Gains on Television as Public's Main News Source," January 4, 2011. www.people-press.org/2011/01/04/internet-gains-on-television-as-publics-main -news-source/ (accessed 2/20/13). Figures add to more than 100% because respondents could volunteer up to two main sources.

[54]Pew Research Center of the People and the Press, "The State of the News Media 2011: Newspapers By the Numbers," http://stateofthemedia.org/2011/newspapers-essay/data-page-6/ (accessed 2/20/13).

[55]Richard Pérez-Peña, "More Readers Trading Newspapers for Web Sites," *New York Times,* November 6, 2007. www.nytimes.com/2007/11/06/business/media/06adco.html (accessed 2/20/13). See also Scarborough Research, "Newspaper Audience Ratings Report 2008," referred to in Pérez-Peña, "More Readers Trading Newspapers for Web Sites."

[56]Richard Pérez-Peña, "Newspaper Circulation Falls By More Than 10%," *New York Times,* October 27, 2009, B3.

[57]Pew Research Center, "The State of the News Media 2011."

[58]Pew Research Center for the People and the Press, "Americans Spend More Time Following the News," Sept. 12, 2010, www.peoplepress.org/files/legacypdf/652.pdf (accessed 2/20/13).

[59]Nik Gowing, presentation at Managing Information Chaos, conference held at the United States Institute of Peace, Washington, D.C., March 12, 1999.

[60]Daniel W. Drezner and Henry Farrell, "Web of Influence," *Foreign Policy* 145 (November–December 2004): 32–40; Editorial, "Measuring the Blogosphere," *New York Times,* August 5, 2005; NMIncite, "Buzz in the Blogosphere: Millions more blogging and blog readers," Mar 8, 2012, www.nmincite.com/?p=6531 (accessed 2/20/13).

[61]Ken Auletta, "Annals of Communications: Battle Stations," *New Yorker,* December 10, 2001, 60–61.

[62]Pew Research Center, "State of News Media 2012."

[63]Auletta, "Annals of Communications," 61.

[64]Leonard Downie, Jr., and Robert G. Kaiser, *The News about the News: American Journalism in Peril* (New York: Knopf, 2002), 241.

[65]Cited in Downie and Kaiser, *The News about the News,* 241.

[66]Howard Kurtz, "Despite Sept. 11, Interest Still Low in Foreign News," *Washington Post,* June 10, 2002, A13.

[67]Quoted in Richard Pérez-Peña, "As Papers Struggle, News Is Cut and the Focus Turns Local," *New York Times,* July 21, 2008.

[68]Priya Kumar, "Shrinking Foreign Coverage," *American Journalism Review,* December/January 2011, www.ajr.org/article.asp?id=4998 (accessed 2/20/13).

[69]Bill Keller, "Being There." *New York Times* December 2, 2012, A29.

[70]Ethan Zuckerman, "A Small World After All?" *Wilson Quarterly,* Spring 2012, www.wilsonquarterly.com/article.cfm?AID=2153 (accessed 2/20/13).

[71]My research assistant Jeffrey Gianattasio, was particularly helpful with this section.

[72]Josh Kron and J. David Goodman, "Online, a Distant Conflict Soars to Topic No. 1," *New York Times,* March 9, 2012, A1.

[73]Jeffrey Gettleman, "In Vast Jungle, U.S. Troops Aid in Search for Kony," *New York Times,* April 29, 2012, A1.

[74]David Rieff, "The Road to Hell Is Paved with Viral Videos," *Foreign Policy,* March 14, 2012, www.foreignpolicy.com/articles/2012/03/14/the_road_to_hell_is_paved_with_viral_videos_kony_2012?page=full (accessed 2/20/13).

[75]"Kony Screening Provokes Anger in Uganda," www.youtube.com/watch?v=rU_1jnrj5VI&feature=plcp&context=C4bccaa8VDvjVQa1PpcFNqbMk5abYYIpvM2aK3xgBqd0v2NJ8XD2k%3D (accessed 2/21/13).

[76]Warren P. Strobel, "The Media and U.S. Policies toward Intervention: A Closer Look at the 'CNN Effect,'" in *Managing Global Chaos,* Chester A. Crocker and Fen Osler Hampson with Pamela A. Aall, eds. (Washington, D.C.: U.S. Institute of Peace Press, 1996), 358.

[77]Strobel, "The Media and U.S. Policies," 373–74.

[78]Chicago Council on Global Affairs, *Foreign Policy in the New Millennium* (Chicago: Chicago Council in Global Affairs, 2012), 8,

[79]Chicago Council on Global Affairs, *Foreign Policy in the New Millennium,* 9.

[80]Chicago Council on Global Affairs, *Foreign Policy in the New Millennium,* 14.

[81]Gallup Poll, "Americans Remain Critical of the United Nations," March 13, 2009, www.gallup.com/poll/116812/americansremaincriticalunitednations.aspx (accessed 2/20/13); Better World Campaign, "Index of Public Opinion on International Issues and the United Nations," May 24, 2011, www.betterworldcampaign.org/newsroom/articleseditorials/indexofpublicopinionon.html (accessed 2/20/13).

[82]Chicago Council on Global Affairs, *Foreign Policy in the New Millennium,* 24.

[83]This section draws on Bruce W. Jentleson, "The Pretty Prudent Public: Post Post-Vietnam American Public Opinion on the Use of Military Force," *International Studies Quarterly* 36.1 (March 1992): 49–74; and Bruce W. Jentleson and Rebecca L. Britton, "Still Pretty Prudent: Post–Cold War American Opinion on the Use of

Military Force," *Journal of Conflict Resolution* 42.4 (August 1998): 395–417. See also Richard C. Eichenberg, "Victory Has Many Friends: U.S. Public Opinion and the Use of Military Force," *International Security* 30.1 (Summer 2005): 140–77.

[84]Pew Research Center for People and the Press, "Most Swing Voters Favor Afghan Troop Withdrawal," April 18, 2012, www.peoplepress.org/2012/04/18/most-swing-voters-favor-afghan-troop-withdrawal/ (accessed 2/20/13); CBS News poll, November 2012, www.ropercenter.uconn.edu/data_access/tag/role_of _the_united_states_in_the_world.html (accessed 2/20/13).

[85]George Packer, "Recapturing the Flag," *New York Times Magazine*, September 30, 2001, 15–16.

CHAPTER

10 Asia's Rising Strategic Importance: Relations with China and in the Asia-Pacific Region

Introduction: China, Asia, and the 4 Ps

Over the last few years, there has been much talk of a "pivot" to Asia. The subtext is that other regions—Europe since the end of the Cold War, the Middle East with the end of the Iraq and Afghanistan wars—have become less strategically important, while the rise of China as a major power and impressive regional economic growth rates have made Asia more strategically important. As long as these are understood as shifts in relative importance, the pattern holds. Asia is more important in more ways than in prior eras. But twenty-first-century American foreign policy remains global.

China is a major focus. In the first part of this chapter we examine the overall strategic debate and key issues in U.S.-China relations. In Chapter 1 we cited the brutal 1989 Tiananmen Square crackdown as an example of trade-offs and tensions among the 4 Ps objectives. Here we focus on the overarching strategic debate and hone in on a range of issues in U.S.-China relations, examining the 4 Ps dynamics of choice even more broadly:

- *Power*: What does China's rise mean for American power globally and regionally?
- *Peace*: Can China be integrated into global and regional institutions?
- *Prosperity*: What policies should be pursued on trade and other economic issues? Who has leverage over whom?
- *Principles*: What priority should be given, and what policies pursued, for democracy promotion and human rights protection?

But it is not just China. It is the whole Asian region that is important to U.S. foreign policy. Kishore Mahbubani, Dean of the Lee Kuan Yew School of Public Policy in Singapore,

419

MAP 10.1

EAST ASIA

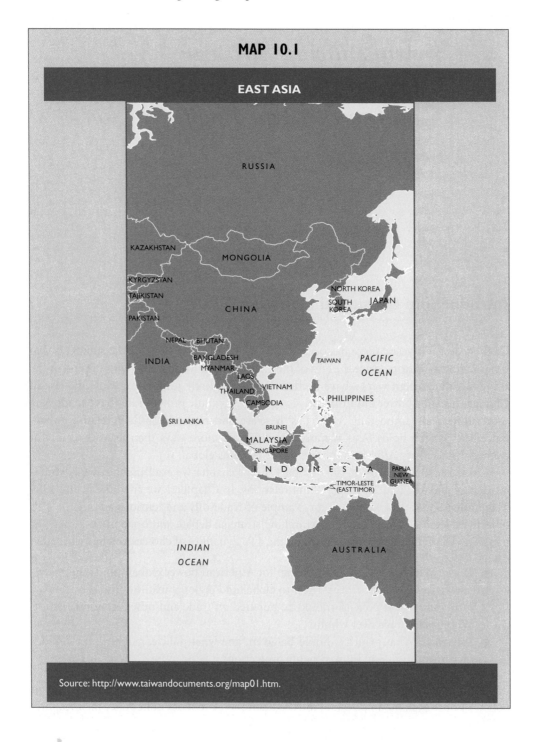

Source: http://www.taiwandocuments.org/map01.htm.

writes about the rise of Asia and "the irresistible shift of global power to the East."[1] Jeffrey Immelt, CEO of General Electric, talks of "the billion people joining the middle class in Asia"—not U.S. consumers—as "the engines driving global growth."[2] In the rest of the chapter we look at U.S. relations with Japan, North Korea, and India, as well as the role of Asian regional multilateral organizations. The foreign policy politics section is a case study of the domestic politics of the United States's China policy going back to the early Cold War, through the 1970s opening to China, and up to current controversies over trade and overall U.S.-China relations.

China: Cooperation, Competition, Confrontation?

China's emergence as a global power is evident in various indicators:

Economic: In 2011 the People's Republic of China (PRC) passed Japan as the world's second largest economy. Its average annual economic growth rate—close to 10 percent, maintained for close to a decade—was astounding. Its economic relations now span the world. Trade with Latin America has grown rapidly; for example, China replaced the United States as Brazil's largest trading partner. Trade with Africa has increased over 500 percent since 2001. China struck numerous oil and natural gas deals in the Middle East, seeking to lock up the energy supplies needed to fuel its economic growth.

Diplomatic: China has been active on many diplomatic fronts. It has improved its relations with Russia after decades of tensions going back to the Sino-Soviet split of the 1950s. It has improved its relations with India, and though tensions still remain, they are nothing like those that led to war back in 1962. It has forged a more positive identity within the East Asia region through what one expert called "remarkably adept and nuanced diplomacy, earning praise around the region."[3] At their 2012 annual summit, Chinese and European leaders "applauded the important progress achieved in the development of EU-China relations in all fields and agreed that their comprehensive strategic partnership has grown both in width and in depth."[4] China also became more of a geopolitical player in the Middle East, especially in pursuit of its oil interests. In Africa and Latin America, enhanced diplomatic relations have accompanied the growth in economic relations.

Military: China's military power and reach are growing. Its military spending has increased to become the third largest amount in the world, behind only the United States and Russia. This has included modernization of its forces and more advanced technology. China has both strengthened its regional military presence and created for the first time "blue-water navy" capacity (naval forces capable of being deployed across the oceans), giving it more of a global military presence.

Size: With 1.34 billion people, China remains the world's most populous country. And it is the fourth largest in territory with 3.7 million square miles.

China's rise is a fact. The question is, what does it mean for U.S. foreign policy? How possible is cooperation? Is competition the more prevalent mode of relations? Will the situation come to the point of confrontation?

Global Geopolitics

History and international relations theory show that tensions and war are often associated with the rise of a new great power. A. F. K. Organski has written about the dangers of ***power transitions,*** when, whether through intention or miscalculation, a rising power and the existing dominant power may go beyond competition to conflict.[5] The main historical example is Germany's rise in the 1870–1914 period, when it challenged Great Britain's dominance through rivalry and an arms race, a challenge that ultimately led to World War I. Realists such as John Mearsheimer see China's rise following a similar trajectory of not being peaceful.[6]

An alternative view, with its own basis in history and theory, predicts competition but not major conflict in China's rise. According to this concept of "peaceful contestation" China will pursue its own interests but will do so largely within the rules of the game, and will remain open to cooperation with the United States.[7] International Institutionalists stress an *integration* strategy—bringing others in rather than keeping them down. As John Ikenberry argues, and as elaborated in this chapter's Historical Perspective box (p. 423), peace has been most durable when the victors in war and the most powerful states have used their position and power to foster international order based on shared interests. When they have sought only to dominate—keep others down—their power has brought some gains but not very stable or sustainable ones.

China expert David Shambaugh conveys a sense of the internal debate within China. While Americans are familiar with their own internal foreign policy debates, we often attribute more singular, fixed positions to other countries. Yet "China's international identity is not fixed. It is fluid and a work-in-progress that remains contentious and constantly debated."[8] Scholars and policy analysts can help policymakers assess which views prevail within China. But quality analysis requires avoiding easy assumptions, whether they opt for worst-case or best-case scenarios, and instead understanding that Chinese foreign policy has its own dynamics of choice. Indeed, as Andrew Nathan and Andrew Scobell point out, "just as Americans wonder whether China's rise is good for U.S. interests or represents a looming threat, Chinese policy makers puzzle over whether the United States intends to use its power to help or hurt China."[9] Reading 10.1, from a

10.1

HISTORICAL PERSPECTIVES
HISTORICAL PERSPECTIVES

POWER AND PEACE OVER THE CENTURIES

As we face another era of major global transition, what lessons can we learn from other historical periods?

One historical perspective sees Power as the key.[*] Great-power politics has always been and always will be a competition for Power. This was true of Spain in the sixteenth century, of Britain and France in the seventeenth and eighteenth centuries, and of Germany and Japan, going back to their rise in the nineteenth century and through World War II. It was true of the Soviet Union in the Cold War. Some believe it was true of the United States, both earlier in its history and in the Cold War. Great-power competition is hard wired into the international system. Peace is inherently uncertain, a product of maintaining sufficient power to ensure one's own security and dominate others as and when necessary.

An alternative perspective sees this great-power competition as likely but not inevitable, with history showing that Peace can be achieved when the most powerful states use their power to build order through institutions and other forms of cooperation.[†] This was achieved somewhat following the Napoleonic wars, starting with the 1815 Congress of Vienna and its agreements among the major European powers to limit their competition. The peace broke down when World War I began, although it had lasted almost one hundred years. The post–World War I peace, of which President Woodrow Wilson was the principal architect, was notable in its ambition and vision but flawed in its construction. The League of Nations was too weak an institution on which to build order, especially when the United States opted out because of isolationist domestic politics. The post–World War II system, with its more numerous and stronger international institutions backed by formidable yet self-restrained American Power, proved "distinctive and unprecedented," a durable Peace that transitioned into a new era through the collapse of the Soviet Union and its empire.[‡]

[*]See, for example, John J. Mearsheimer, *The Tragedy of Great Power Politics* (New York: Norton, 2001).
[†]See, for example, G. John Ikenberry, *After Victory: Institutions, Strategic Restraint, and the Rebuilding of Order after Major Wars* (Princeton: Princeton University Press, 2001).
[‡]Ikenberry, *After Victory,* 210.

Brookings Institution study co-authored by an American and a Chinese scholar, gives a sense of the "strategic distrust" on both sides.

In its basic orientations, the U.S. policy debate has posed two principal options, generally defined as containment and engagement. *Containment* is a variation, albeit milder and more limited, of the Cold War strategy toward the Soviet Union. This strategy is short of confrontational but is firm, cautious, and attentive to threats and relative power—that is, geared to containment. It rests on the same logic as George Kennan's original 1947 formulation of containment of the Soviet Union: that the internal changes needed to make China less of a threat and more of a democracy are more likely to occur if the country's external ambitions are contained and the flaws in its domestic system thus exacerbated and exposed. Summits are acceptable, as they were for Henry Kissinger with the Soviets, but the U.S. posture should be kept strong. China may not have an inherently expansionist ideology, as did the Soviet Union, but it does have its own strong nationalism and historical sense of itself as the "middle kingdom" at the figurative center of the world. It also has been expanding its influence globally. It is rising; whether it will be a peaceful rise in significant part depends on whether U.S. policy is tough enough to check any expansionist inclination.

Those who support *engagement* take a different view of China, although not the polar opposite view. They are wary of Chinese intentions but assess them as less threatening. There are tensions, and the United States must stand by its allies and its interests, but these issues can be worked out through diplomacy and negotiations. The emphasis in engagement is on integration and diplomacy to provide structured, peaceful mechanisms for dealing with China's own concerns, and to encourage China to adopt international norms and abide by international rules. On a bilateral basis, the United States should continue with periodic summits and strategic dialogues in diplomacy, trade, and other areas of engagement. Human rights issues and democratization cannot be ignored, and other approaches should be pursued, but options other than economic sanctions are preferred.

The Clinton administration leaned more toward engagement, while the second Bush administration initially tilted more toward containment. It drew the distinction between the Clinton view of the relationship as a "strategic partnership" and its own view of "strategic competition." This outlook was revealed in Secretary of State Colin Powell's first statement (January 2001) on China: "Our challenge with China is to do what we can that is constructive, that is helpful and that is in our interest. . . . A *strategic partner* China is not, but neither is China our inevitable and implacable foe. China is a *competitor,* a potential regional rival but also a trading partner willing to cooperate in areas where our strategic interests overlap. . . . China is all of these things, but China is not an enemy, and our challenge is to keep it that way."[10] During Bush 43's second term, the U.S. view of China transitioned to that of a "responsible stakeholder." This idea recognized China's increased power and position as a stakeholder in most major global issues, but it was also a push for China to be what the United States considered more responsible in playing that role.

In Obama's first term his China policy went through two phases. Initially its strategic objectives were to emphasize and expand engagement. For example, seeking to downplay contentious issues, President Obama initially refused to meet with the Tibetan Dalai Lama. Over time, though, while still largely pro-engagement, some containment elements were accentuated. Later in his first term President Obama did meet with the Dalai Lama. He was also more assertive in regional diplomacy, supporting allies who were increasingly concerned about China's regional provocations. The "pivot" involved an increase in U.S. military deployments in Asia. Indeed, the 2012 presidential campaign was characterized by "China bashing" by both the president and his Republican challenger Mitt Romney. As the Obama administration began its second term, it toned down the campaign rhetoric while still pressing issues of concern.

Within weeks of President Obama's reelection, China made its own leadership transition. The Communist Party Congress selected Xi Jinping as the new president and Li Keqiang as the new prime minister. They were faced with a number of pressing domestic issues, as discussed below, as well as foreign policy issues.

Going beyond these general policy summaries, we consider the particular issues that continue to be key parts of U.S.-China relations.

Taiwan

From 1949, when the Chinese communist revolution triumphed, until 1971 and the Nixon-Kissinger opening to the People's Republic of China (PRC), the United States was allied to the government of Jiang Jeishi (Chiang Kai-shek) on the island of Taiwan. As part of the détente, Nixon and Kissinger established the *"one China" policy,* by which American policy supported the peaceful reunification of China. The reunification part of the policy meant that the United States ended its diplomatic recognition of Taiwan as an independent state; the peaceful part meant that it maintained its commitment to defend Taiwan if the PRC attacked. With only a few variations this has been the policy of every president, Democratic and Republican, since Nixon.

Yet it has been a difficult balance to strike, with recurring crises along the way. One of these crises came in 1995–96, when China targeted missile tests close to Taiwan as a show of force. The Clinton administration responded by deploying U.S. naval forces to deter possible Chinese aggression.[11] Another came in 2001 over the issue of arms sales to Taiwan. According to agreements going back to the 1970s and 1980s for the normalization of U.S.-China relations, the United States would continue to sell Taiwan defensive weapons but not offensive ones. Often, the line between defensive (and therefore stabilizing) and offensive (and thus potentially destabilizing) is not always inherently clear in the nature of a weapons system. Moreover, perceptions of intent and message affect assessments of a weapons system's potential use. Early in its term, for example, the G. W. Bush administration sought to strike a balance by selling some weapons to Taiwan, but not those most objectionable to China. The arms sale issue came up later in the Bush presidency and in the Obama presidency.

Concern is increasing that although this balancing act has worked for many years, it is becoming more tenuous. Pro-independence sentiment in Taiwan has grown and could lead to stronger pushes toward independence, with risks of provoking PRC retaliation. For its part, even the younger generation in PRC, which did not live through the long civil war that ended in 1949, is strikingly nationalistic on reunification. Taiwan-PRC economic ties as well as educational exchanges, transportation links, communications, and tourism have increased, exerting some influence for a cooperative resolution. But whether it is another arms sales package to Taiwan or another crisis like that of 1995–96, the Taiwan issue is likely to pose further problems for U.S.-China relations. U.S. domestic politics also come into play, as we discuss in the case study later in this chapter.

The Chinese Military

China has been increasing its military spending, modernizing its forces, and developing new capabilities. The debate is over how much and what this means for U.S. interests.

The military budget published by the Chinese government in 2012 was $106 billion. This was an 11 percent increase over the previous year. Pentagon analysis put the figure much higher, at more than $160 billion. Other studies, such as those by the RAND Corporation and the Swedish think tank SIPRI (Stockholm International Peace Research Institute), put the figure somewhere in between. Whatever the amount, it includes research on and development of modern and sophisticated weapons systems such as a new generation of stealth jet fighters, a larger submarine fleet, missile systems, and China's first aircraft carriers. China has an active force of 2.3 million soldiers, including 1.25 million ground troops, by far the world's largest.

Yet these are fractions of U.S. spending and capabilities. China's $106 billion 2012 defense budget compares to a U.S. budget of $530 billion. If the higher $160 billion estimate is used for China, the comparison should include the higher U.S. figure of close to $700 billion, including the cost of the Iraq and Afghanistan wars. In terms of weapons systems, the balance of nuclear weapons–capable intercontinental ballistic missiles is 450 for the United States to 66 for China; modern main battle tanks number 6,302 to 2,800; sixth generation tactical aircraft 3,092 to 747; nuclear-powered submarines 57 to 5, and aircraft carriers 11 to 1.[12]

China defends its increased military spending as catching up for past weaknesses and a necessity for its own legitimate national defense. The Chinese leadership vows that it will "unswervingly" pursue a foreign policy centered on ensuring "peace" and a "national defense policy solely aimed at protecting its territory and people," and that it will never seek hegemony or engage in military expansion.[13] However, the U.S.-China Economic and Security Commission, a bipartisan body—but one with a strong leaning toward conservative containment—stressed that China's "development of impressive but disturbing capabilities for military use of space and cyber warfare, and its demonstrated employment of these capabilities, suggest China is intent on expanding its sphere of control." It urged the United States to "watch these trends closely and act to protect its interests where they are threatened."[14] The Pentagon also issued its own annual report, warning that "China's leaders have yet to explain in detail the purposes and objectives of the PLA's [People's Liberation Army's] modernizing military capabilities. . . . China continues to promulgate incomplete defense expenditure figures, and engage in actions that appear inconsistent with its declaratory policies."[15] This debate also applies to strategic weaponry and whether China's increase in nuclear weapons needs to be checked by missile defense and other measures, or is still sufficiently inferior to U.S. capacity as to leave deterrence intact.

China's increasing military exchanges and cooperation raise similar ambivalence and uncertainty. It has established military ties with more than 150 countries and has military attaché offices in many of these countries. No doubt some greater influence comes with these activities and relationships. But they also have some security-enhancing aspects of shared regional and international benefit. For example, the Chinese and Indian armies have conducted joint counterterrorism exercises, and the Chinese and Japanese navies have exchanged port calls.

"Hedging," mixing containment and engagement, is one much-discussed U.S. strategy. This has appeal as a cautious strategy amid the uncertainties of Chinese military capabilities and geopolitical intentions. However, if it is perceived by the other side as threatening in its own right, the strategy may precipitate the very trends it was intended to check.

East Asian–Pacific Regional Security

During the Cold War, security in the East Asian–Pacific region was based on the U.S. military presence, which protected Japan, the Philippines, South Korea, and other states from the Russian and Chinese communist threats. The end of the Cold War meant the end of these threats. But China's increasing economic and military strength has raised additional issues for the regional balance of power. For most of the first two post–Cold War decades, China's regional diplomacy helped provide some reassurance of shared interests with its neighbors. But in recent years concerns and tensions have increased.

China-Japan relations are one area of concern. For China, the historical legacies of Japan's invasions during the 1930s and World War II remain vibrant, particularly the 1937 Nanjing massacre (also called the "rape of Nanjing"), when Japanese occupiers committed mass killings, looting, and rape. Japan has both security and economic concerns about China's growing power, as well as its own unresolved political-cultural issues of how to deal with its imperial past. In recent years disputes have erupted over nearby islands and fishing rights, and demonizing rhetoric on both sides has further strained relations. Yet there has also been significant cooperation between the two countries, including bilateral summits, increased trade, and diplomatic agreements.

Regional disputes over territorial claims in the South China Sea, the security of shipping routes, and related economic issues (including potentially major offshore oil and natural gas deposits) are another main concern. China, Taiwan, the Philippines, Indonesia, Thailand, Vietnam, Cambodia, Malaysia, Singapore, and Brunei all have coastlines along the South China Sea (see Map 10.2). Nor is it just those nations' interests at stake. About

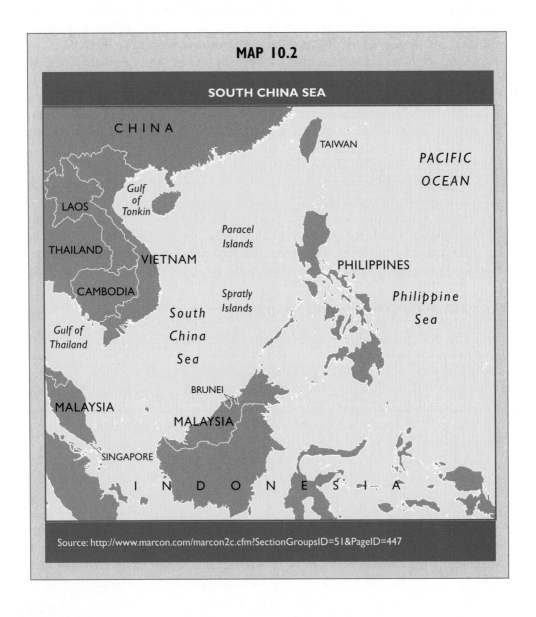

MAP 10.2

SOUTH CHINA SEA

Source: http://www.marcon.com/marcon2c.cfm?SectionGroupsID=51&PageID=447

one-third of total world trade passes through this body of water; the U.S. share is around $1.2 trillion annually. Fisheries in the South China Sea account for close to 10 percent of fish used for human consumption worldwide, worth billions of dollars to the fishing industries in the surrounding states. It also is an important area for global biodiversity.[16]

China has made claims that many of the smaller countries in the area contest. In some instances these have gone beyond diplomatic disputes to incidents at sea and other direct confrontations. Such moves set up an almost classic balancing situation for the United States, working with various countries—including U.S. allies such as the Philippines and past-enemy Vietnam—to push back against Chinese assertiveness. The balance, though, requires detering but not antagonizing China, strengthening the smaller countries' position, and creating incentives for diplomatic resolution without making China feel encircled or ganged up on. This is a tricky balance to strike. While most countries in the region feel more secure with American support, many worry about the U.S. overplaying its hand and seeking to make gains in its bilateral competition with China that could serve U.S. interests but harm theirs.

North Korea

In the 1950–53 Korean War the PRC and the United States were on opposing sides, and the conflict came dangerously close to resulting in an American invasion of China. China and North Korea remained close allies through the Cold War and remain so today. In recent years, the United States and China have both been involved with the nuclear proliferation threat posed by North Korea, which has been a mix of cooperation and differences of interests, as discussed below.

R2P and Intervention-Sovereignty

In debates over whether the international community can intervene in states to prevent mass atrocities based on the norm of the *"responsibility to protect" (R2P)*, China has most often opposed intervention and defended state sovereignty. This position is rooted in its own history, having had European powers intervene to set up their spheres of influence during the nineteenth century, and in contemporary interests on issues such as Taiwan and Tibet. China thus supported President Omar al-Bashir of Sudan in 2005 against pressures to intervene to stop the genocide his regime was committing in Darfur (a region of Sudan). Over time, though, as the Sudan conflict spread and intensified, Chinese policy put less emphasis on the intervention-sovereignty issue and more on interests such as sufficient stability to keep Sudanese oil exports flowing. China also abstained in early 2011 on the Security Council resolution authorizing the U.S.- and NATO-led intervention in Libya. While it did join Russia in vetoing UN Security Council resolutions to intervene in Syria to stop the atrocities being committed by the Bashar

Assad regime, many analysts felt that China would not have used its veto if Russia had not. So while there are significant Sino-American differences on the sovereignty-intervention balance, the Chinese position is more nuanced than it is often portrayed.[17]

U.S.-China Economic Relations

In 1989, following the Tiananmen Square massacre of Chinese students and other pro-democracy demonstrators in Beijing, the main issue in U.S.-China relations was human rights. This case was examined back in Chapter 1 as an example of "4 Ps" tensions. The first Bush administration opted to prioritize Power over Principles and imposed only limited economic sanctions. The Clinton administration came into office after heavily criticizing its predecessor for not championing democracy and human rights, but it too stopped short of serious sanctions against China. Clinton's motivation was more Prosperity than Power, given the administration's interest in rapidly growing investment in and trade with China.

In the years since, trade between the United States and China has grown exponentially, from $18 billion in 1989, to $116 billion in 2000, and $536 billion in 2012. There has been a huge imbalance within that trade relationship; indeed, over 58 percent of the U.S. trade deficit in 2012 was the bilateral deficit with China. One of the most contentious issues has been the undervaluation of the Chinese currency (the renminbi, or yuan). One of the economic effects of currency undervaluation is to make exports cheaper and thus more competitive in global markets. While economists differ as to how much the Chinese currency has been undervalued, and despite some revaluation steps, there is broad consensus that the issue remains.

The growing industry of renewable energy technologies has been another area of trade friction. In 2011 seven American solar-panel manufacturers filed a case against the Chinese solar industry claiming it violated antisubsidy and antidumping laws by selling its solar panels at artificially low prices made possible by unfair government financing and other aid. China had gained about a 50 percent share of the U.S. solar-panel market, and the case contended that China "helped its solar panel industry by providing the equivalent of billions of dollars in subsidies in the form of deeply discounted loans, land, electricity, water, and raw materials, as well as cash grants and tax breaks."[18] Three American solar-energy companies—together representing one-sixth of American manufacturing capacity in the solar sector—filed for bankruptcy, citing the plunging prices of solar technology from China. At least four of the biggest surviving companies have resorted to large layoffs in recent years and some have closed factories.

For their part, the Chinese make claims of unfair practices against the United States. For example, the U.S. government prevented the sale of the American oil company Unocal to the Chinese National Offshore Oil Company (CNOOC) on the grounds of national security. In tit-for-tat retaliation for the U.S. cases against the

Chinese solar-panel industry, the Chinese government opened up its own investigation of allegedly unfair U.S. trade practices in solar and other renewable energy industries.

The Chinese view of the 2007–09 global financial crisis was that "America is the culprit and the epicenter," with China among those most at risk as the world's largest holder of American debt and dollar currency reserves.[19] Many observers, both in China and among American analysts of the international economy, see ongoing shifts in international economic power toward China, with both strategic and economic consequences. Consider this excerpt from a story in the *Financial Times* on the global automobile market:

> At the Shanghai car show that opens Tuesday (April 2011), General Motors and PSA Peugeot Citroen will both launch global models for the first time in China, a symbol of how the car industry's center of gravity continues to shift to China, the largest car market. But it is not just about launching the new-generation Chevrolet Malibu or Citroen DS-5 first in China, to attract more Chinese buyers. When GM on Monday unveiled its Buick Envision SUV concept car, it revealed a car *designed in China, for the world.* . . . 'Five years ago, no one would have imagined that China would have surpassed the U.S. as the largest market. But now it's natural that these cars are being developed for Chinese customers *and sold globally. We will see more of this in the months and years to come.*'[20]

In the international financial system, China has been the principal purchaser of the Treasury bonds the United States has sold to finance its huge trade and budget deficits. Such sales have served some mutual interests and strengthened China as a global financial power. Its foreign exchange reserves exceed $3.4 trillion (early 2013), which is almost three times as much as the next largest country (Japan). In 2006 China did not have any banks among the world's top twenty financial institutions and the United States had seven, including the top two. By 2009 the top three banks were Chinese, while only three U.S. banks even made the list. In 2010, as an early sign of the renminbi becoming a more international currency, TPG—one of the world's largest private equity firms—created the first funds denominated entirely in Chinese currency.[21] Such shifts in global financial power underlie the greater role China has played in the G20 as well as its proposals for major changes in the international financial system.

All told, trade with China has replaced trade with Japan as the most contentious trade policy politics issue, as we will see later in this chapter.

Democratization, Human Rights and Chinese Political Stability

While Russia exemplifies the problems involved in the transition from communism to democracy, China's problems are associated with maintaining communism and resisting the transition to democracy. China is, as Edward Friedman put it, "the only major surviving communist dictatorship."[22]

The overall dilemma China faces is how to combine economic liberalization, modernization, and opening to the global economy with continuation of a closed, repressive, nondemocratic political system. Since China began its economic opening more than twenty years ago under the leadership of Deng Xiaoping, the strategy has been based on the populace being sufficiently satisfied with the economic benefits that it remains politically quiescent. This tacit bargain has not fully worked out. High economic growth rates have not brought political quiescence. Even official Chinese government statistics show that the number of protests doubled between 2006 and 2010, rising to 180,000 reported "mass incidents" in 2010 alone.[23] Some of these protests have been in rural areas, where the peasantry has been largely left out of the economic boom. Factory workers in urban areas have also protested, dissatisfied with their meager wages and benefits. And other protests have been over environmental issues. China has six of the world's ten most polluted cities. Five of its largest rivers have become too polluted to touch, let alone support village fishing industries.[24] Even before the 2003 SARS (severe acute respiratory syndrome) epidemic, China's health system was ranked 144th in the world by the World Health Organization. Its incidence of AIDS has been increasing at alarming rates, leading some experts to warn about a crisis equal to or even worse than the one in Africa.[25]

Corruption has also become more of a problem. "The linkage of money and political power is intimate," says Kenneth Lieberthal, a China expert at the Brookings Institution. "If the Chinese Communist Party were called what it really is, it would be called the Chinese Capitalist Bureaucratic Party." In 2011 the Chinese central bank estimated that from the mid-1990s to nearly 2008, some 18,000 party and government officials had transferred nearly $127 billion out of the country. Among members of the Chinese parliament, the richest seventy are said to be worth $90 billion.[26] Indeed, fighting corruption was a main theme of Xi Jinping's first speech after being named the new president in late 2012. Further, although the technologies that American and other foreign investment brought into the country have been essential to economic growth and modernization, some, such as the Internet, have aspects that bring pressure for political opening. One example of the Chinese government's fear that the Internet was undermining its monopoly on the flow of politically relevant information was the arrest of a young computer whiz "on his way back from his grandmother's funeral," without any apparent cause, other than his reputation of being able to "run circles around Beijing's Internet fire walls."[27] Soho.com, China's main Internet portal, posted a notice that "topics which damage the reputation of the state" are forbidden. It went on to warn that "if you are a Chinese national and willingly choose to break these laws, Soho.com is legally obliged to report you to the Public Security Bureau."[28]

Google and other American IT companies also have had to figure out how to operate in China. When Google first set up its Google China subsidiary in 2005, it agreed to cooperate with China's censorship laws. By 2010, though, following hacking incidents into Google account holders, Google announced that it would no longer comply with Chinese censorship laws. A series of back-and-forth moves ensued with the Chinese government revoking Google's license to operate, then re-instating it, and Google doing a mix of standing its ground (e.g., re-directing searches to its Hong Kong subsidiary) and making concessions (e.g., no longer displaying warning messages to users searching with politically sensitive phrases).

In 2012 China had an estimated 485 million Internet users, more than any other country. This included many microbloggers. In a number of domestic scandals, such as the July 2011 crash of a high-speed train that killed and injured many people despite government assurances of safety, and the October 2011 hit-and-run death of a small child while witnesses just stood by, microblogs showed their communications reach in fomenting mass protests. The government has continued to block Facebook and Twitter, cracking down even more after seeing the role they played in the 2011 "Arab Spring."

But it is not just the human rights activists who benefit from the Internet. China also has "millions of netizens in cyberspace who are extremely active and vocal" with militarist, anti-American and other fervently nationalist and right-wing views.[29] This shouldn't be surprising; right-wing militias are all over the Internet in the United States. At times this is overlooked when access to the Internet is too readily equated with pro-democratic politics.

Human rights pressures have also increased. Amnesty International and Human Rights Watch, the two major human rights NGOs, both rate China as one of the world's worst human rights violators. These groups cite numerous cases involving individual dissidents arrested, put under surveillance, and subjected to other repressive measures, as well as the Falun Gong, a partly religious and partly political movement that has faced severe governmental repression.

Another set of issues involves national and ethnic groups that seek greater autonomy from the central government in Beijing and possibly secession from China itself. March 2008 saw the largest protests since 1989 in **Tibet** against Chinese military rule and denial of autonomy or independence. The protests, of particular concern at a time when China sought to present a "harmonious image" to the rest of world at the 2008 Beijing Olympics, were squelched through violent clashes between protestors and Chinese security forces and the imposition of martial law. The global relay of the Olympic torch was met with pro-Tibet protests in many cities. The Dalai Lama's age and imminent questions of succession may make the issue even more contentious.

In July 2009, riots exploded in Xinjiang Province between the **Uighurs** and the Han, China's ethnic majority. Tensions have deep roots in this area, where the mix of ethnic and religious groups dates back centuries. Bordering eight countries, Xinjiang was a hub of trade along the Silk Road and contains thirteen principal ethnic groups, of which the Uighurs are the largest. They are Turkic Muslims. The Han Chinese population in Xinjiang has increased through Beijing's efforts to "Chinesify" the area. The riots began as a clash between Uighur and Han Chinese factory workers which intensified as retaliations and backlash spiraled between the Uighurs and Chinese security forces and between the Uighurs and the Han Chinese. With close to two hundred people killed and two thousand injured, these were the most violent clashes in China in decades.

Given these and other issues, China's weaknesses may become more of a concern to the United States and others in the international community than its strength.

Japan: Alliance in Transition

The end of the Cold War has raised new issues and dynamics for U.S.-Japan relations. The old security concern of a Soviet invasion is no longer relevant; Russia and Japan still have some territorial disputes and other issues dating from World War II, but their relations are well within the bounds of diplomacy. Nevertheless, the U.S.-Japan security alliance has continued into the post–Cold War era as, to quote the State Department, "the cornerstone of U.S. security interests in Asia and fundamental to regional stability and prosperity."[30] A new U.S.-Japan defense agreement was signed in 1997 and another in 2005. About 25,000 American troops are still based in Japan. American-Japanese cooperation has continued with regard to Taiwan, North Korea, and missile defense. Within this basic alliance, however, there are some tensions.

Trade Issues

The trade disputes that began in the 1970s grew especially heated in the 1980s but were tempered as Japan's economic problems in the 1990s eroded its image as an economic powerhouse. Still, the recent bilateral U.S.-Japan trade deficit was $63 billion, second only to the U.S. deficit with China. As long as U.S.-Japanese trade continues to run sharp imbalances, trade will be a point of contention. So, too, will banking and financial issues. The Japanese government's weakness in dealing with its own economic problems exacerbated the overall Asian financial crisis of the late 1990s. The 2008 U.S.-induced financial crisis hurt Japan along with the rest of the world, and had far greater impact than the Asian financial crisis.

Security Relations

A second set of issues concern, to borrow from the title of a popular Japanese book, *The Japan That Can Say No*—say "no," that is, to the United States, a sentiment reflecting resentments on that side of the Pacific that mirror the Japan-bashing on this side. Some in the United States feel that Japan takes advantage of American support, while some in Japan feel that the United States is domineering and Japan needs to show that its support can't be taken for granted. These sentiments have been especially strong regarding the presence of U.S. military bases in Japan, particularly on the island of Okinawa. Tensions over the continued existence of the Okinawa bases have been exacerbated over the years by incidents in which American soldiers stationed there have been charged with rape and other sexual offenses. Partly in response to such incidents, an agreement was reached in 2012 to cut the number of U.S. troops based in Okinawa by about half. Yet incidents have continued to occur, including allegations of rape and drunken assaults in late 2012.

There is also the broader issue of Japan's post–Cold War military role. The "peace constitution" written for Japan by the United States during the post–World War II occupation limited Japan's military forces strictly to self-defense. The question now is whether those limits should be loosened. As with Germany, this question reflects pressures for Japan to become a more "normal" major power amid a historical legacy of aggression and militarism. During the Persian Gulf War, this historical legacy was sufficiently strong that the Japanese Diet (the parliament) rejected a bill calling for a limited, noncombat role for the Japanese military in the war; instead, Japan confined its role to providing financial assistance. Some shift occurred during the 1990s as the Diet passed the International Peace Cooperation Law, which allows Japanese military units to serve in some UN peacekeeping missions, albeit in limited roles. In 2001 the war on terrorism posed further challenges. This time the Diet passed a bill permitting Japan to deploy a naval task force as offshore noncombat support for the United States in Afghanistan. As reported at the time,

> Flying the Rising Sun flag, a destroyer, a minesweeper and a supply ship left Japanese naval bases Sunday headed for the Indian Ocean. . . . Only a few dozen protesters gathered at the Japanese ports with anti-war banners as the ships departed following patriotic speeches from politicians and tearful families waving goodbye. But in a demonstration that not all of the old restrictions have been cast off, Japan decided against deploying a destroyer with an Aegis missile-hunting system after some lawmakers argued that to do so would violate the constitution.[31]

In the Iraq War, Japan went further, sending about eight hundred troops as part of a reconstruction and humanitarian mission—still not combat troops but for the first time since World War II a ground military presence outside its own borders.[32] Japan has taken on other military missions, as when in 2009 its navy joined an international antipiracy deployment off the coast of Somalia.

Polls show the Japanese public is split on whether to change the constitution to allow for a greater military role. One former prime minister stressed that "Japan's role in international society has largely changed from 60 years ago. We are expected, and have a responsibility, to play a greater role, and we can contribute to achieving global peace and stability by living up to that expectation."[33] The Diet set up committees to review draft amendments and draw up procedures for a national referendum on changing the constitution. The United States backs the constitutional change so that Japan can play a larger military role as part of their security alliance. "We hope and expect Japan will choose to accept more global security responsibilities in the years ahead," Secretary of Defense Robert Gates stated in 2007, a position the Obama administration has reinforced.[34]

Conservative opinion further holds that promoting a strong, secure Japan to counterbalance China is conducive to U.S. interests in the region.[35]

Another aspect of this debate concerns nuclear weapons. As the only country in the world to have had nuclear weapons dropped on its cities—Hiroshima and Nagasaki, which the United States bombed in 1945 during the last stages of World War II—Japan's foreign policy had since held to three non-nuclear principles: never to own, produce, or permit nuclear weapons on Japanese territory. But with China's military growing stronger, in part through its advanced nuclear weapons programs; with North Korea an unstable and now nuclear-armed neighbor; with the risks of Russian "loose nukes;" and amid concerns about the long-term reliability of U.S. security guarantees, some are asking whether it still is in Japan's interest to be a non-nuclear nation. "You have to wonder," a Japanese university professor speculated, "how long Japan can remain the only non-nuclear power among the major countries in the region."[36]

In 2006 Taro Aso, then the foreign minister and later the prime minister, suggested that it might be prudent for Japan to develop nuclear capability: "The reality is that it is only Japan that has not discussed possessing nuclear weapons, and all other countries have been discussing it."[37] He later clarified, noting that "Japan is capable of producing nuclear weapons. . . . But we are not saying we have plans to possess nuclear weapons." In the same speech, however, he made the argument that Japan's pacifist constitution does not forbid possession of an atomic bomb for defense.[38] The U.S. response to this shift was and remains the promise to act as Japan's nuclear shield. Secretary of State Condoleezza Rice responded to Aso by publicly pledging that the United States would retaliate swiftly and massively against aggression toward Japan, using nuclear weapons if necessary.[39]

These issues concern not just the United States but also Japan's regional neighbors. Americans often don't appreciate the extent to which anti-Japanese sentiments and fears persist in China, South Korea, the Philippines, and elsewhere in the region. These fears, which draw on the World War II experience and go back further in history, have been stirred up recently in both politics and culture.[40] With its memories of hundreds of thousands killed during the Japanese occupation of China in the 1930s and through World War II, China reacted very negatively when the Japanese Prime Minister Junichiro Koizumi visited the Yakasuni war memorial in Tokyo every year during his tenure (2001–06). South Koreans still remember the oppression of Japanese colonial rule from 1910 to 1945. Moreover, Japan and its neighbors have a number of current interests that are a mix of cooperation and competition. China and Japan are competing globally for energy supplies, yet they have enjoyed a booming two-way trade, with China surpassing the United States as Japan's top trade partner. South Korea and Japan continue military cooperation under the U.S. security umbrella yet have their own differences, including lingering territorial disputes over two islands. East Asian–Pacific regional stability thus has uncertainties involving Japan and China, which bear substantially on American interests.

Japanese Politics and Domestic Issues

When the Democratic Party of Japan (DPJ) won the 2009 national elections, it was only the second time since Japan became a democracy in 1955 that the Liberal Democratic Party (LDP) was out of power. During the DPJ's three years in power, amid internal political infighting and other factors, there were three different prime ministers. Japanese politics may have gone from too little electoral competition to too much governing instability.

Among those other factors were the March 2011 earthquake and tsunami that caused massive death and destruction, including the Fukushima nuclear power plant disaster. As an island with very limited energy resources of its own, Japan relies more heavily on nuclear power than any other country, and has planned for even more nuclear power plants. Revelations that nuclear regulators have long been "submissive to the industry" and scandals about how the disaster was handled have intensified debates over the future of nuclear power in Japan.[41] From the standpoint of other countries, there was concern that the radioactive fallout from Fukushima could have spread globally much more than it did if the winds had been stronger at the time.

The LDP came back to power in 2012, and Shinzo Abe became prime minister. Abe, who was briefly prime minister previously in 2006–07, has a reputation as an ardent nationalist and defender of Japan's historical record in relations with China and South Korea. In his first meeting with President Obama in February 2013, ties between the two countries were reaffirmed. Obama reassured Japan of support in its islands disputes with China, consistent with the longstanding defense treaty between the United States and Japan, though there was no specification of precisely what that support entailed and how unconditional it was. Prime Minister Abe also reportedly "signaled that he had reassured the Americans that he would not act rashly" towards China as well as South Korea.[42]

North and South Korea

Like Germany, Korea was split into two countries at the end of World War II. North Korea was communist and allied with the Soviet Union and later with China. South Korea was non-communist, democratic but ruled by the military at times, and allied with the United States.

Unlike East and West Germany, however, North and South Korea went to war. The war began in 1950 when the North invaded the South. The United States came to South Korea's defense with endorsement by the UN and support from other militaries. The war lasted three years and ended without either side being able to claim victory. An armistice was signed, but not a full peace treaty, and a demilitarized zone (DMZ) was created,

MAP 10.3

NORTH AND SOUTH KOREA

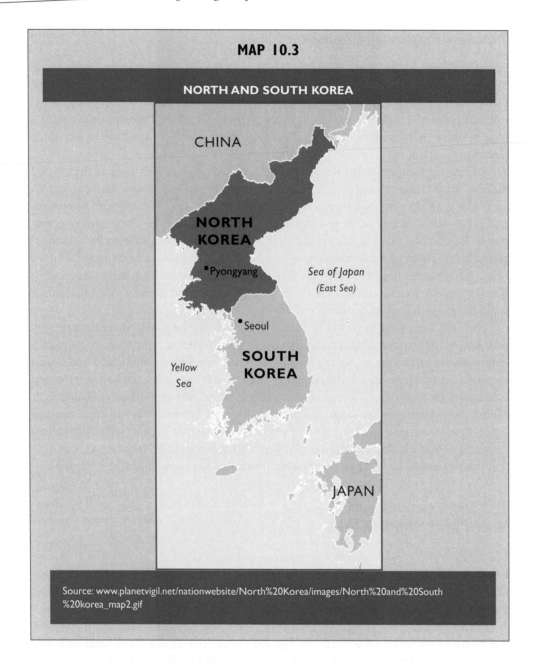

CHINA

NORTH
KOREA

•Pyongyang

Sea of Japan
(East Sea)

•Seoul

SOUTH
KOREA

Yellow
Sea

JAPAN

Source: www.planetvigil.net/nationwebsite/North%20Korea/images/North%20and%20South
%20korea_map2.gif

separating the two countries. American soldiers have been stationed at the DMZ and on bases in South Korea ever since. As of 2012 there were still about 28,000 American troops in South Korea and the DMZ.

Efforts to improve relations between South and North Korea have had numerous ups and downs over the past two decades. At times trade started to develop and borders were opened for family reunification visits, only to be followed by increased tensions. Other countries in the region also are affected, notably Japan. In the past, North Korea kidnapped Japanese citizens and fired missiles in Japan's vicinity. China, which shares a border with North Korea, fears a massive refugee flow. Food shortages, malnutrition, and starvation in North Korea—in significant part due to government policies—have stirred global humanitarian concerns. Human rights violations have also been a major issue. Control of North Korea has been handed down from father (Kim Il-sung) to son (Kim Jong-il) to grandson (Kim Jung-un), making the country a mix of communist dictatorship and monarchy.

North Korean Nuclear Proliferation

Intelligence reports in the early 1990s indicated that North Korea was diverting its ostensibly peaceful nuclear energy program to develop nuclear weapons, despite having signed the Nuclear Nonproliferation Treaty (NPT). The prospect of a nuclear-armed North Korea threatened not just South Korea but also Japan, other U.S. allies in the region, and U.S. troops stationed in these countries. Concern also arose that North Korea would sell nuclear weapons to other anti-U.S. *rogue states.* The Clinton administration pursued a strategy toward North Korea that emphasized negotiations but backed them with measures that threatened military action. The combination helped achieve a crisis-defusing agreement, called the Agreed Framework, in 1994.

In October 2002, new revelations indicated that North Korea had been cheating on the 1994 Agreed Framework and had continued nuclear-weapons development. North Korea reportedly possessed more than the one or two nuclear weapons it had when the 1994 agreement imposed its freeze, and was very close to being able to generate more. North Korea was quite provocative in its reactions to the revelations, expelling IAEA inspectors, firing up a nuclear reactor that could produce more plutonium (an essential material for nuclear bombs), and renouncing the NPT. Some believed North Korea was reacting to George W. Bush's inclusion of it in the "axis of evil" and Bush administration threats of regime change, but most experts doubted North Korea's trustworthiness and felt that another crisis was developing. **"Six-Party Talks"** were initiated in 2003 as another strategy for addressing North Korea's nuclear program among Russia, Japan, South Korea, the United States, and North Korea, with China as the host. Some diplomatic progress was made, including a September 2005 agreement on joint principles. But the crisis heated up again when North Korea conducted a series of missile tests in July 2006 and then tested a nuclear weapon in October.

Coercive diplomacy was ratcheted up. Condemnations came not only from the United States, but in stronger-than-usual terms from China and others. The UN Security Council imposed targeted economic sanctions on North Korea and threatened additional sanctions. China, the economic linchpin, reportedly applied some sanctions to energy supplies and financial relationships. The incentives of expanded aid and trade also remained on the table. The strategy seemed to be having some effect when a six-party agreement on next steps was reached in February 2007.

Over the course of 2007, some actions were taken, but key deadlines were missed. This continued into 2008, and by mid-year enough progress had been made that Secretary of State Rice agreed to meet directly with her North Korean counterpart. "We didn't get into specific timetables, but the spirit was good," Secretary Rice stated, "because people believe we have made progress."[43] That optimism did not last long, however, and was followed by border incidents and rising tensions between North and South Korea, and an apparent serious illness suffered by North Korea's leader Kim Jong-il. The debate continued. The former U.S. ambassador to the United Nations and arch-neoconservative John Bolton called for a more stringent U.S. stance toward North Korea. "They're in the classic North Korean role of deception," Bolton said in an interview. "It's like Groundhog Day; we've lived through this before." In contrast, Ambassador Christopher Hill, the lead U.S. negotiator, argued that "multilateral efforts have had a stabilizing effect. . . . Without that process we could have seen a much more dangerous counter-reaction in the region."[44]

In May 2009 events reached a new crisis point when North Korea conducted another nuclear test. The UN Security Council voted unanimously to impose another round of sanctions. Tensions were further compounded when two young American journalists, Laura Ling and Euna Lee, were sentenced to twelve years hard labor for allegedly crossing the North Korean border illegally. Former president Bill Clinton made a surprise mission to North Korea and brought the two journalists home. Over the next few months, North Korean–South Korean relations warmed a bit, including resumption of family visits, but no lasting changes took hold. To the contrary, a number of dangerous incidents occurred soon after, including a November 2010 North Korean military attack on a South Korean island that escalated tensions higher than they had been in a long time.

Things heated up again in early 2013 as North Korea conducted another nuclear test and engaged in even more saber rattling than usual. The prospects for resumption of the Six-Party Talks or other significant progress on the nuclear proliferation issue depend on three principal factors. First is internal North Korean politics. In December 2011 Kim Jong-il died and his twenty-eight-year-old son, Kim Jong-un, emerged as the new leader. His first years in power were marked by a mix of provocations (including another nuclear weapons test in February 2013), internal power struggles, and some signs of possible openings. Predicting internal politics in most states is difficult, especially so for a state as opaque as North Korea. Second is China's policy. China and the United States share interests in avoiding a major crisis that could escalate to war. But China also has interests in cooperative relations with North Korea. Third is U.S. policy. Debate continues over how "tough" to be and whether diplomacy can work.

Asian Regional Organizations

Regional organizations have traditionally been less prominent in Asia than in Europe. Although this is still true, they have been growing in both roles and numbers in recent years.

Association of Southeast Asian Nations (ASEAN) and East Asia Summit

ASEAN was established in 1967 largely to promote economic cooperation among its members, which at that time were Indonesia, Malaysia, the Philippines, Singapore, and Thailand. Security threats mostly arose from Cold War politics, and since most countries in ASEAN were U.S. allies, the United States provided the region's security. Today ASEAN includes six other nations as full members—Brunei, Indonesia, Myanmar (Burma), Cambodia, Laos, and Vietnam. ASEAN held only three summit meetings in its first twenty-five years, but it has held fourteen in the subsequent twenty years. It also created the ASEAN Regional Forum (ARF) with twenty-seven members, including the United States, China, Japan, North and South Korea, Australia, Russia, and the European Union. The ARF deals primarily with regional security issues and ASEAN Plus Three—China, Japan, and South Korea—deals with financial stability, trades, and economic policy.

Assessments of ASEAN's effectiveness as a regional organization are mixed. On regional security issues such as counterterrorism and antipiracy, it has done some fostering of regional multilateral cooperation. Its strategy of pressure with some engagement helped bring about the beginning of political liberalization in Myanmar (Burma). But it has had less impact on "hard power" regional security issues such as disputes over the South China Sea. Efforts in 2012 to develop a code of conduct for resolving such disputes under ASEAN auspices did not garner sufficient agreement. Yet ASEAN does have the Treaty of Amity and Cooperation in Southeast Asia, in which states pledge not to use force against each other.

The East Asia Summit is linked to ASEAN as an annual meeting of heads of state that began in 2005 and in which the United States first participated in 2011. Its agenda has focused on mid-level security issues such as regional coordination to prevent and contain the avian flu pandemic in 2005. More recently it has sought to tackle issues such as maritime security and nonproliferation.

Shangri-La Dialogue

The Shangri-La Dialogue is an informal conference organized by the Institute for International Strategic Studies (IISS), a London-based think tank. While not a formal regional organization, we mention it here because "the Shangri-La dialogue has rapidly become one of Asia's most important annual summits. . . . Among the reasons for its growing influence are its flexibility, the chance it offers for low-profile interaction and its targeting of ministers rather than national leaders."[45] As such, it is another example of the role that NGOs—in this case a European think tank operating in Asia—play in contemporary international affairs.

APEC

Asia also has numerous regional organizations that focus exclusively on economic matters, including Asia-Pacific Economic Cooperation (APEC). APEC was created in 1993 with members from North America (the United States, Canada, and Mexico), South America (Chile and Peru), and Asia. It focuses on liberalization of trade barriers, business facilitation, and regional economic cooperation. For many years efforts have been made to create a Free Trade Area of the Asia-Pacific (FTAAP) and more recently a Trans-Pacific Partnership (TPP). While neither has been formalized, they have been sufficiently substantive to have earned their acronyms, and may become policy in the future.

India: Relations with an Emerging Power

India-Pakistan Conflict

India and Pakistan have fought three wars and endured numerous crises since their independence from British colonial rule in 1947. India was created as a largely Hindu country, Pakistan as a largely Muslim country. In setting the boundaries, though, both sides claimed sovereignty over the state of Kashmir. Pakistan's claim was based on Kashmir's largely Muslim population, India's on the decision by the maharaja (prince) of Kashmir (a Hindu) to unite with India. Two of the India-Pakistan wars, one at independence in 1947 and the other in 1965, were fought in part over Kashmir. Both of these wars ended with cease-fires and peace plans, but neither solved the underlying conflict.

In 1999 India and Pakistan went to the brink of another war over Kashmir. This time, the crisis was compounded because both countries had nuclear weapons. Pakistan had responded to India's nuclear weapons tests in May 1998 with tests of its own, affirming what many had suspected—that both countries had been secretly developing nuclear weapons for many years. This situation gave the conflict over Kashmir much broader regional and global implications. The risk was not just another India-Pakistan war, but a nuclear war. The 1999 crisis was defused when the Clinton administration played an important peace-brokering role.

The United States traditionally had much closer relations with Pakistan than with India. During the Cold War, India was a leader of the Third World "nonaligned movement" and had close ties with the Soviet Union. Pakistan was part of the U.S. Cold War alliance system, first as a member of the Central Treaty Organization during the 1950s and then through a number of bilateral agreements. Pakistan was also a key ally in the U.S.-supported 1979–88 insurgency against the Soviet invasion of Afghanistan. The principal strains in U.S.-Pakistan relations were due to human rights and democracy concerns prompted by Pakistani military coups. A bill passed by Congress in 1985 cut off economic and military aid unless Pakistan ended its nuclear weapons program. The United States also opposed India's nuclear weapons program, but as it didn't give India foreign aid, it could not impose comparable nonproliferation pressure.

The war on terrorism pushed the United States and Pakistan closer together. Pakistan was the crucial front-line state for launching the 2001 war in Afghanistan. Within days of the September 11 attacks, General Pervez Musharraf, who became the leader of Pakistan in an October 1999 coup that the United States opposed, pledged to help the United States openly and covertly against the Taliban and Al Qaeda.

Yet in the middle of the war in Afghanistan, Kashmir heated up again. The violence intensified in and around Kashmir, then spread to Delhi, the Indian capital, where terrorists attacked the Indian parliament, killing thirteen people. India accused Pakistan of directly supporting these attacks and Pakistan responded by blaming India for its army's attacks on Pakistani soldiers along the border. Both sides began talking of and making military movements toward war. Neither side was willing to say it would not escalate to nuclear war. For a period in early 2002 the world feared the worst. A nuclear war seemed closer than at any point since the 1962 Cuban missile crisis. The G. W. Bush administration engaged in diplomacy and played an important role in bringing the crisis under control.

In November 2008, Lashkar-e-Taiba, a Pakistani terrorist group, attacked the Indian city of Mumbai (formerly known as Bombay), killing more than 160 people in a three-day siege. Although the Pakistani government was not directly implicated, it had close ties to Lashkar, Pakistan's military and intelligence services having worked with it as a guerrilla force in Kashmir. Lashkar also had ties to Al Qaeda, as reflected in statements by Osama bin Laden. He put India in the same camp as the United States and Israel, accusing them of a "Crusader-Zionist-Hindu war against Muslims."[46] Kashmir was not the only issue in the mix, but it was a major part of the tensions that brought further death and destruction and risked further escalation. Some new diplomatic overtures followed, lifting hopes that a lasting solution might be found. The possibility of another India-Pakistan crisis, though, cannot be dismissed.

India as an Emerging Global Power

10.2

Beyond India-Pakistan and Kashmir, overall U.S.-India relations have come to reflect India's status as an emerging world power with its own "grand strategy" (Reading 10.2). Five factors make India stand out.

First is its size. India is the world's second most populous country, with over 1.2 billion people, constituting about 17 percent of the world population. This makes it the world's largest democracy. And although it is a Hindu-majority country, India has the second largest Muslim population in the world (177 million, behind Indonesia and more than Pakistan).

Second is India's place in globalization. You may have firsthand experience with this if you have called a 1-800 phone number in the United States and gotten a call center operator in India. India's place in globalization goes well beyond such semi-skilled outsourcing, as it has become a major center of technological innovation in its own right. Trade with the United States, only $14.3 billion in 2000, increased to $62.8 billion by 2012. In recent years the Indian economy has had one of the world's fastest growth rates. Although this has made for substantial prosperity, economic inequality remains sharp: India now has over one hundred thousand millionaires, but the majority of the population still lives on 50 cents a day. Rates of child malnutrition are comparable to those of Bangladesh and Ethiopia.

Third is India's possession of nuclear weapons. India had been developing nuclear weapons for many years. The culminating event was its 1998 major nuclear weapons test. The Clinton administration imposed trade sanctions in response, but with little effect. The G. W. Bush administration lifted these sanctions in the wake of September 11, in large part because of the priority it gave to the war on terrorism and the partnership role India could play. In 2005, President Bush and the Indian prime minister Manmohan Singh signed an agreement whereby the United States gave de facto recognition to India's status as a nuclear weapons state. Technically, the agreement allowed trade and cooperation on civil nuclear energy, which was supposed to be prohibited to countries that had tested nuclear weapons in violation of the **Nuclear Nonproliferation Treaty (NPT).** Supporters argued that as a democracy India could be trusted more than others not to use its nuclear weapons aggressively. They also stressed the economic benefits for U.S. exports and investment in a lucrative market and the geopolitical gains from closer U.S.-India ties. Opponents contended that the NPT regime would be further weakened by the precedent that other nuclear weapons nations—for example, Pakistan or Israel—could cite. The deal did go through, winning approval of the U.S. Congress and the Indian parliament.

Fourth is India's expansion of its conventional military capabilities. A 2011 report by the Swedish think tank SIPRI named it the world's largest arms importer. This in part reflects its rivalry and tensions with China, with which it fought a border war in 1962.[47] Sea power is a particular priority, with $45 billion in projected spending on new naval vessels by 2030.[48]

Fifth is the increasingly significant global diplomatic role India has been playing. The first UN peacekeeping force sent to the former Yugoslavia in the early 1990s was headed by an Indian general. The country's candidacy for a new permanent seat on the UN Security Council was endorsed by President Obama on his 2010 trip to India. American and Indian officials now refer to their relationship as a "strategic partnership." This includes extensive defense and security cooperation as well as economic relations, joint efforts on HIV prevention, and other initiatives. Yet the United States and India disagree on some issues. On Iran, for example, India went ahead with negotiations on a major energy deal at a time when the United States was pressing for tighter economic sanctions. When the G. W. Bush administration reprimanded India, New Delhi replied by releasing a statement saying, "India and Iran are ancient civilizations whose relations span centuries. Both nations are perfectly capable of managing all aspects of their relationship with the appropriate degree of care and attention. . . . Neither country needs any guidance on the future conduct of bilateral relations. . . ."[49] India is a very nationalistic country with a strong sense of its own interests and aspirations for its own global role. "Our policy," as Prime Minister Singh stated, "seeks to . . . give us strategic autonomy in the world. Independence of our foreign policy enables us to pursue mutually beneficial cooperation with all major countries of the world."[50]

India's Democracy

India is to be admired for the ways in which its democracy functions in a country with so much poverty, such major ethnic and religious divisions, and other challenges. But these are serious problems. Business has been booming but inequality has been widening. An electrical blackout in August 2012 that affected more than half of India's population deepened concerns about the reliability of the national infrastructure. Scholar Rahul Segar excoriates Indian political leaders for "a fiscally lethal form of competitive populism and a constitutionally lethal politicization of public institutions. It is also increasingly criminal in nature, with approximately a quarter of the elected members of the national legislature facing serious criminal charges. The most immediate consequence of these trends has been a steady deterioration in the rule of law."[51]

Foreign Policy Politics Case Study: Domestic Politics of U.S. China Policy

During the Cold War, the People's Republic of China (PRC) was commonly referred to in the American political debate as "Red China." It was generally depicted as more evil and in many respects more dangerous than even the Soviet Union. The U.S. ally Jiang

Jeishi (Chiang Kai-shek) fled mainland China for the island of Taiwan in 1949 after he was defeated in the Chinese civil war by Mao Zedong and the Chinese communists. The Truman administration refused to recognize Mao's new government and stayed allied to Jiang and Taiwan. The Korean War (1950–53) came close to escalating to a direct war between the United States and the PRC.

The fervent anticommunism of McCarthyism, which had a profound impact on foreign policy politics, was especially targeted at those said to be sympathetic, or worse, to Red China. For not extending the Korean War to China, Senator Joseph McCarthy attacked President Truman as "a rather sinister monster."[52] Secretary of State Dean Acheson was accused of appeasement. The State Department Foreign Service was purged of its "China hands;" their alleged crimes included using their expertise to warn that Jiang Jeishi was going to lose, an assessment that McCarthy twisted into having plotted to defeat Jiang.

Even after Senator McCarthy was censured by the Senate, the *"China lobby"* maintained the domestic political pressure. Many viewed the China lobby as among the most powerful foreign policy interest groups of the Cold War era. It included strong supporters of Jiang Jeishi, missionaries of sects whose proselytizing in China went back to the nineteenth century, business leaders, journalists, various anticommunist groups such as the Committee to Defend America by Aiding Anti-Communist China, and numerous members of Congress. The China lobby urged maintaining a close alliance with Taiwan, keeping the PRC out of the United Nations and the China seat on the Security Council in Taiwan's hands, and quashing policy proposals that might seek improved relations with the PRC.

It seemed ironic that Richard Nixon, a key member of the China lobby at the start of his political career, was the president who initiated the "opening" to Red China, but it made political sense. Nixon's staunch anticommunist credentials made him harder to attack as "soft." So when he went to Beijing in 1972 for an official summit with Mao and Zhou Enlai, preceded by secret talks led by National Security Advisor Henry Kissinger, Nixon and his administration were more protected politically than liberal politicians would have been. Nixon and Kissinger also stressed the "strategic triangle" rationale— that good relations with China would give the United States more leverage with the Soviet Union.

Still, the China lobby was strong enough to inhibit the fuller development of U.S.-PRC relations until 1979, when President Jimmy Carter announced the normalization of relations and the establishment of diplomatic relations. The China lobby was not able to stop normalization, but it did manage to get guarantees that the United States would continue to supply Taiwan with defensive arms and other assistance. In the years since, it has continued to press for Taiwan's interests.

Beyond the Taiwan issue, the end of the Cold War changed the U.S. domestic politics of relations with China. Without the Soviet Union, the geopolitical rationale was less compelling. Issues such as human rights were now given greater priority, especially after the

May 1989 Tiananmen Square massacre. Other human rights issues were also raised, such as the use of forced prison labor, the treatment of the Dalai Lama and Tibet, and China's "one child" policy and forced sterilizations and abortions. These made for an interesting coalition of conservatives from the long-standing China lobby, liberal human rights groups such as Human Rights Watch, and the AFL-CIO and other labor unions pushing for linkages to trade. On the other side were business interests, for which the attractiveness of the China market for exports and investments was rapidly increasing. Individual companies lobbied for U.S.-China trade, as did associations such as the U.S. Chamber of Commerce, the National Association of Manufacturers, and the Business Coalition.

The politics played out in Congress and the executive branch. In Congress the splits did not strictly follow party lines. Among those on the pro–human rights side were Congresswoman Nancy Pelosi, a staunchly liberal Democrat from California who later became Speaker of the House, and Senator Jesse Helms, a staunchly conservative Republican from North Carolina. Bureaucratic politics divisions were also evident in the executive branch. I recall intense battles from when I was working in the State Department in 1993–94 between the Bureau of East Asian Affairs, concerned that trade–human rights linkages would disrupt overall U.S.-China relations, and the Bureau of Democracy, Labor and Human Rights, concerned that U.S. credibility on human rights around the world would be damaged if America didn't stand by Principles against China. Although the presidential candidate Bill Clinton had been very tough in criticizing President George H. W. Bush for coddling "the butchers of Beijing," President Clinton opted for a compromise that provided for some linkage through annual human rights reviews, but largely tilted toward the pro-trade side.

In the years since, trade and other economic relations with China have caused contention in American politics. In 2000 the issue was whether to establish normal trade relations with China on a permanent basis rather than continue the annual human rights reviews. The various China lobbies again clashed. Human rights supporters wanted the annual reviews to keep some pressure on China; pro-trade groups argued that American exporters were being handicapped because other countries did not have annual human rights reviews. The pro-trade side again prevailed. The following year the issue was China's membership in the World Trade Organization (WTO). Intense political debate arose, again on whether to seek human rights leverage through economic linkages, and with an outcome emphasizing Prosperity more than Principles.

Implicit in this debate was the calculation that the United States was the economically stronger party and could use this advantage as leverage with political issues. But by 2005 there was talk about how economically powerful China had become. China had a huge favorable balance of trade; indeed, the U.S. trade deficit with China made that with Japan pale in comparison. Once again, talk about a "red scare" in American politics arose, but this time, it was the red ink of the bilateral trade deficit. When China tried to buy a U.S. oil company, protests abounded about potential dangers to U.S. national security. Bills were introduced in Congress targeting Chinese trade policies on such issues as its currency exchange rate, pirating of computer software and other violations of intellectual property rights, and unfair labor practices. The issue of Chinese workers' rights, Thea Lee of the AFL-CIO testified to Congress, "is both a moral and economic issue, impacting the lives of Chinese workers, and the quality and composition of American jobs."[53]

Some also traced the trade imbalance to China's policy of keeping the value of its currency, the yuan, artificially low. "Alone among the world's major economies," one report stated, "China refuses to allow the *renminbi* (RMB), its currency, to respond to free market movements. China's leaders instead keep the currency trading at an artificially low level in order to suppress export prices—a deliberate violation of the rules of the International Monetary Fund, of which it is a member."[54] One Senate bill proposed an offsetting 27.5 percent tax on Chinese products. Some opponents disputed the analysis of the currency-valuation issue. Others claimed that the proposed remedy would ratchet up prices and hurt American consumers and businesses. The tax was not approved, but the issue continued to stir debate.

Security issues also have engendered a number of controversies. In 1996, reports indicated that China had been helping Pakistan develop its nuclear weapons. Policy makers on both sides acknowledged that weapons proliferation was an issue, especially China's transfer of missile and chemical-weapons technology. The debate revolved around whether to use economic sanctions to punish China for this behavior, with arguments similar to those on the human rights issue being invoked. Opponents of sanctions stressed working cooperatively within the nonproliferation treaties signed by China, whereas supporters of sanctions pointed to its breaches of those conventions. Because exports were the particular target, American high-technology companies led the antisanctions lobby.

An even hotter issue involved allegations that China had used contacts developed through military, scientific, and economic cooperation to steal secrets about American nuclear weapons design and development. Congress launched a major investigation into alleged Chinese espionage. A congressional report stated that China acquired key data on seven of the most advanced nuclear warheads in the U.S. arsenal, as well as other military and technology secrets. Focus fell on Wen Ho Lee, a Taiwanese-American scientist working at Los Alamos National Laboratory. Lee was arrested and held without bail in solitary confinement for almost a year. He pleaded guilty to a lesser charge in a plea bargain, but denied any involvement in espionage. Lee eventually won a $1.6 million settlement against the federal government and with media organizations that had run major stories on the espionage accusations.

Nevertheless, concerns remained about China's military power. Congress established the U.S.-China Economic and Security Review Commission, with a mandate to evaluate the national security effects of bilateral trade and economic relations. Though bipartisan, it tends to lean toward the conservative containment perspective.

Cyber-hacking has become a increasingly salient issue. In 2010 researchers at the University Toronto Munk School of International Affairs found evidence of Chinese hacking into computers on several continents. The data acquired included NATO documents on the Afghanistan war, Indian government documents on security issues and diplomatic relations, and personal e-mails of the Dalai Lama.[55] In February 2013 another story broke linking the Chinese military to hacking so extensive within the United States as to include Coca-Cola, The New York Times, companies involved in critical infrastructure, and government agencies.[56]

Meanwhile human rights groups have continued to raise their concerns. Tibet's cause has received added attention from the involvement of celebrities such as Brad Pitt and Sting, groups such as Students for a Free Tibet, and the series of Free Tibet concerts. In 2009, in her first major speech regarding Asia, Secretary of State Hillary Clinton said little regarding Tibet other than that the United States believes that "Tibetans . . . can enjoy religious freedom without fear of persecution." This position disappointed advocates of a free Tibet, who remembered the strong stance Clinton took on the issue as first lady and hoped the United States might actively pressure China.[57] Organizations such as Amnesty International and Human Rights Watch urged Clinton to "tell Chinese officials that China's relationship with the United States 'will depend in part on whether it lives by universally accepted human rights norms.'"[58] Their impact could be seen over the ensuing years as Secretary Clinton spoke out more on Tibet and President Obama met with the Dalai Lama.

And then there's **Taiwan.** Still. In 2008 the United States and China reached an agreement on opposing efforts for an independence referendum in Taiwan. Then-Secretary of State Condoleezza Rice warned Taiwan not to provoke China, stating that "this referendum is not going to help anyone, and, in fact, it shouldn't be held." On additional arms sales, though, traditional differences reemerged. The Bush administration had been considering a major arms sale, and intra-administration bureaucratic politics included some opposition to it. In Congress, though, the Taiwan lobby asserted itself. More than one-third of all House members were part of the Congressional Taiwan Caucus, drawn from both parties.[59] HR 6646, a bipartisan resolution, was introduced to require the executive branch to provide detailed briefings to Congress on the state of Taiwanese arms sales. Representative David Scott (D-Georgia), said that U.S. policy toward Taiwan was clear: "The United States is obligated to provide defensive military equipment to Taiwan, not just because it is right to aid our democratic friends, but also because it is the law of the land under the Taiwan Relations Act." Ed Royce (R-California), added that "the People's Republic of China continues to expand its military capabilities, amassing hundreds of short-range missiles pointed across the strait." "Now they're pointed at Taiwan."[60] Notably, the *Congressional Record* did not register any representatives as speaking out against the resolution. When the Obama administration considered its own major arms sale to Taiwan, the politics ran along similar lines.

These politics do not just involve the Chinese government and the U.S. government. "K Street" lobbyists (nicknamed for the Washington, D.C. street where many lobbyists have their offices) and public relations firms are involved on both sides. As early as the 1990s, China began a public relations campaign to promote a benign and peaceful image in the United States and around the world.[61] As part of China's political strategy for gaining approval of its permanent trade partner status, Fortune 500 companies such as Boeing, AT&T, General Motors, and General Electric—all of which sought to expand their operations into the rapidly growing Chinese market—bankrolled a successful million-dollar "China Normalization Initiative" campaign.[62] In addition, China's State Council Information Office and its Ministry of Culture launched a $7 million campaign, partly underwritten by American corporations with large investments in China, to bring a positive image of China to the United States through a traveling display of Chinese culture.[63] During the 2007 food- and product-safety scares, China put together a string of lobbyists who were "practically living on Capitol Hill." In Beijing, the government sought advice from the American public-relations giants Ogilvy and Edelman on how to convince Americans that Chinese goods were as safe as their own.[64]

On the other side of the lobbying street, Taiwan has long operated a sophisticated, well-financed public relations machine in the United States. The U.S.-China Economic and Security Commission has called the rivalry nothing less than "public opinion warfare." Citing the example of Chinese attempts to reform its image in the aftermath of the Tibetan protests before the 2008 Olympics, the commission reported that the "Chinese press published articles vigorously denouncing the actions of sympathizers for Tibet and trying to reframe the issue as an attempt by Tibetan separatists to destabilize China prior to the Olympics." It also noted that PR efforts are not confined to conventional forms of media. They include "comments to the press by Chinese officials . . . advertisements purchased in domestic or foreign publications, and actions of Chinese representatives at various international venues, including UN gatherings."[65]

In the 2010 congressional elections, for all the bitter partisanship, China bashing was one of the few areas in which Republicans and Democrats seemed to agree. For example, in just a single week of the campaign season, at least twenty-nine candidates from both sides of the aisle ran "advertisements suggesting that their opponents have been too sympathetic to China" and that American jobs had been exported to China as a result.[66] Among Democrats, Congressman Zack Space of Ohio ran an ad accusing his Republican opponent Bob Gibbs of supporting free-trade policies resulting in the loss of 91,000 Ohio jobs to China. At the end of the ad, an image of a Chinese dragon appeared and the narrator said sarcastically, "As they say in China, Xie Xie [thank you] Mr. Gibbs."[67] On the Republican side, Spike Maynard, the challenger in a House race in West Virginia, criticized incumbent Nick Rahall for supporting tax breaks for foreign companies that created wind-turbine jobs in China. Featuring Chinese music, a photo of Chairman Mao, and images of the Chinese flag, all on a red background, the ad engaged in "a familiar form of stereotyping that has quickly become acceptable again."[68]

The 2011–12 solar technology dispute discussed earlier, with the U.S. and China exchanging unfair trade practices accusations, had lobbyists on both sides. The Coalition for American Solar Manufacturing defended the American companies and their claims of unfair Chinese trade practices. A new group tried consciously not to be pro-China, stressing instead how trade restrictions would hurt the American economy by driving prices up and further damage the environment by making solar energy less price competitive. In the middle was the Solar Energy Industries Association, with members including American companies hurt by the Chinese imports and American companies that sell raw materials and factory equipment to Chinese makers of solar panels.[69]

With this history and the array of issues on the agenda, U.S.-China relations may stir even more lobbying and greater political debate in the years ahead.

Summary

While all regions of the world remain important to U.S. foreign policy, Asia is increasing in importance. Relations with China pose many uncertainties and encompass a wide range of issues, with debate manifesting different assessments of the mix of common and competing interests. American domestic politics also continue to play out on China policy. Relations with Japan are transitioning from the Cold War bases of the alliance and the intense conflicts of the 1980s and 1990s over trade issues. North Korea remains an enigma, a quite dangerous one. India is an emerging power both regionally and globally. And Asian regional organizations, while less prominent than European ones, have been growing in both roles and numbers in recent years. Power, Peace, Prosperity, and Principles all bear upon these and other key policy choices for American foreign policy.

Notes

[1]Kishore Mahbubani, *The New Asian Hemisphere: The Irresistible Shift of Global Power to the East* (New York: Public Affairs, 2008).

[2]Chrystia Freeland, "GE's Immelt Speaks Out on China, Exports, and Competition," Reuters, January 21, 2011, http://blogs.reuters.com/chrystia-freeland/tag/jeff-immelt/ (accessed 2/23/13).

[3]David Shambaugh, "China Engages Asia: Reshaping the Regional Order," *International Security* 29.3 (Winter 2004/05): 64.

[4]Council of the European Union, February 14, 2012, "Joint Press Communiqué of the 14th EU-China Summit," http://eeas.europa.eu/china/summit/summit_docs/120214_joint_statement_14th_eu_china _summit_en.pdf (accessed 2/23/13).

[5]A. F. K. Organski, *World Politics*, 2d ed. (New York: Knopf, 1968); Organski and Jacek Kugler, *The War Ledger* (Chicago: University of Chicago Press, 1981); Robert Gilpin, *War and Change in World Politics* (New York: Cambridge University Press, 1983).

[6]John J. Mearsheimer, *The Tragedy of Great Power Politics* (New York: Norton, 2001).

[7]Alistair Iaian Johnston, "Is China a Status Quo Power?" *International Security* 27.4 (Spring 2003), 5–56.

[8]David Shambaugh, "Coping with a Conflicted China," *The Washington Quarterly* 34:1 (Winter 2011), 23.

[9]Andrew J. Nathan and Andres Scobell, "How China Sees America: The Sum of Beijing's Fears," *Foreign Affairs* 91:5 (September/October 2012), 33.

[10]Confirmation Hearing by Secretary of State-Designate Colin L. Powell, January 17, 2001, http://2001 -2009.state.gov/secretary/former/powell/remarks/2001/443.htm (accessed 2/23/13).

[11]Robert S. Ross, "The 1995–96 Taiwan Straits Confrontation: Coercion, Credibility and the Use of Force," in *The United States and Coercive Diplomacy*, Robert J. Art and Patrick M. Cronin, eds. (Washington, D.C.: U.S. Institute of Peace Press, 2003), 225–73.

[12]"China's Military Rise: The Dragon's New Teeth," *The Economist*, April 7, 2012, www.economist.com/ node/21552193?frsc=dg%7Ca (accessed 2/25/13).

[13]Information Office of the State Council of the People's Republic of China, "China's National Defense in 2008," Information Office of the State Council of China, January 20, 2009, 2, http://news.xinhuanet.com/ english/2009-01/20/content_10688124.htm (accessed 2/23/13).

[14]U.S.-China Economic and Security Review Commission, *2008 Report to Congress*, November 2008, 7, www.cfr.org/china/report-congress-us-china-economic-security-review-commision-2008/p17822 (accessed 2/23/13).

[15]U.S. Department of Defense, Annual Report to Congress, *Military Power of the People's Republic of China 2008*, March 3, 2008, I, www.defenselink.mil/pubs/pdfs/China_Military_Report_08.pdf (accessed 2/23/13).

[16]These and other points in this section come from a paper by Jane Riddle, a student in my Spring 2012 Contemporary American Foreign Policy seminar.

[17]See Rosemary Foot and Andrew Walter, *China, the United States and Global Order* (New York: Cambridge University Press, 2011), Chapter 2; Thomas J. Christensen, "The Advantages of an Assertive China," *Foreign Affairs* 90 (March–April 2011), 56; Gary J. Bass, "Human Rights Last," *Foreign Policy* 185 (March–April 2011), 81–89.

[18]Keith Bradsher, "US Solar Panel Makers Say China Violated Trade Rules," *New York Times* October 19, 2011. B1.

[19]Shen Pei-Jun, "As China Sits, America Stands Off to the Side," *United Daily News*, April 8, 2009, John Yu, trans., http://watchingamerica.com/News/25220/as-china-sits-america-stands-off-to-the-side/ (accessed 2/23/13).

[20]"China's Influence on Car Design Accelerates," *Financial Times* April 18, 2011, www.ft.com/intl/cms/s/ 0/e4ee68e8-69da-11e0-89db-00144feab49a.html#axzz22P78GwIA (accessed 2/23/13).

[21]David Barboza, "TGG to Create Chinese Currency Funds," *New York Times*, August 23, 2010, www.nytimes.com/2010/08/24/business/global/24fund.html (accessed 2/23/13).

[22]Edward Friedman, "Lone Eagle, Lone Dragon? How the Cold War Did Not End," in *Eagle Rules? Foreign Policy and American Primacy in the Twenty-First Century*, Robert Lieber, ed. (Upper Saddle River, N.J.: Prentice Hall, 2001), 195.

[23]In Focus with Alan Taylor, "Rising Protests in China," *The Atlantic*, February 7, 2012, www.theatlantic .com/infocus/2012/02/rising-protests-in-china/100247/ (accessed 2/23/13).

[24]Elizabeth C. Economy, *The River Runs Black* (Ithaca, N.Y.: Cornell University Press, 2004).

[25]Minxin Pei, "Future Shock: The WTO and Political Change in China," *Policy Brief* 3 (February 2001),

Washington, D.C.: Carnegie Endowment for International Peace, www.carnegieendowment.org/files/dem.PolBrief3.pdf (accessed 2/23/13).

[26]Hannah Beech, "Murder, Lies, Abuse of Power and Other Crimes of the Chinese Century," *Time*, May 19, 2012, 20–21.

[27]Elisabeth Rosenthal, "China Detains and Isolates Liberal Computer Whiz," *New York Times*, April 21, 2001, A3.

[28]Tom Malinowski, "China's Willing Censors," *Washington Post*, April 20, 2001, A25.

[29]Shambaugh, "Coping with a Conflicted China," 21.

[30]U.S. Department of State, Bureau of East Asian and Pacific Affairs, "Background Note: Japan," October 24, 2012, www.state.gov/r/pa/ei/bgn/4142.htm (accessed 2/23/13).

[31]Peter Finn and Kathryn Tolbert, "Ex-Axis Powers Recast Foreign Military Roles," *Washington Post*, November 30, 2001, A34.

[32]Christopher W. Hughes, *Japan's Re-Emergence as a "Normal" Military Power*, International Institute for Strategic Studies, Adelphi Paper 368–69 (London: Oxford University Press, 2004); Akio Watanabe, "A Continuum of Change," *Washington Quarterly* 27.4 (Autumn 2004): 137–46.

[33]Justin McCury, "Japan Moves Towards Amending Pacifist Constitution," *The Guardian*, May 14, 2007, www.guardian.co.uk/world/2007/may/14/japan.justinmccurry (accessed 2/23/13).

[34]Thom Shanker, "Gates Urges More Japanese Action on Global Security," *New York Times*, November 9, 2007, http://www.nytimes.com/2007/11/09/world/asia/09iht-gates.8259547.html (accessed 2/23/13).

[35]Bruce Klingner, "Forging a New Era in the U.S.–Japan Alliance," Heritage Foundation, October 9, 2008, www.heritage.org/Research/AsiaandthePacific/bg2196.cfm (accessed 2/23/13).

[36]Howard W. French, "Taboo against Nuclear Arms Is Being Challenged in Japan," *New York Times*, June 9, 2002, 1.

[37]Thom Shanker and Norimitsu Onishi, "Japan Tells Rice It Will Not Seek Nuclear Weapons," *New York Times*, October 18, 2008, A1.

[38]"Japan's Nuclear Envoy says Six Party Talk on N Korea Still Possible This Year," *International Herald Tribune*, November 29, 2006, A1.

[39]Thom Shanker and Norimitsu Onishi, "Japan Tells Rice It Will Not Seek Nuclear Weapons."

[40]See, for example, Norimitsu Onishi, "Ugly Images of Asian Rivals Become Best Sellers in Japan," *New York Times*, November 19, 2005, A1.

[41]Evan Osnos, "The Fallout," *The New Yorker*, October 17, 2011, 54.

[42]Jackie Calmes, "Japan and United States Reaffirm Their Close Ties," *New York Times*. February 23, 2013, A7.

[43]Helene Cooper, "In First Meeting, Rice Presses North Korea on Nuclear Effort," *New York Times*, July 24 2008, A6.

[44]John R. Bolton, quoted in Helene Cooper, "U.S. Sees Stalling by North Korea on Nuclear Pact," *New York Times*, January 19, 2008, A1; Christopher R. Hill, Statement before the House Foreign Relations Committee: North Korea and the Status of the Six-Party Talks, February 28, 2007, http://merln.ndu.edu/archivepdf/northkorea/state/81204.pdf (accessed 2/23/13).

[45]Nick Bisley, *Building Asia's Regional Security* (London: International Institute for Strategic Studies, 2009), 44–45.

[46]Tim Weiner, "The Kashmir Connection: A Puzzle," *New York Times*, December 7, 2008, A12.

[47]For a balanced assessment of the mix of shared interests and tensions in the China-India relationship, see Jing Huang, Kanti Bajpai, and Kishore Mahbubani, "Rising Peacefully Together," *Foreign Policy* August 1, 2012, www.foreignpolicy.com/articles/2012/08/01/rising_peacefully_together?page=0,2 (accessed 2/23/13)

[48]Joshua Keating, "The Stories You've Missed in 2011: (1) India's Military Buildup," *Foreign Policy* 190 (December 2011): 11.

[49]Madhur Singh, "India and Iran: Getting Friendly?" *Time*, April 24, 2008, www.time.com/time/world/article/0,8599,1734777,00.html (accessed 2/23/13).

[50]Christopher Bodeen, "India: Foreign Policy to Stay Independent," Associated Press, January 15, 2008, www.usatoday30.usatoday.com/news/world/2008-01-15-3389222/25_x.htm (accessed 2/23/13).

[51]Rahul Sagar, "State of Mind: What Kind of Power Will India Become?" *International Affairs* 85: 4 (2009); 816.

[52]*Congressional Record* XCVII (April 19, 1951), 4261.

[53]"Human Rights in China: Improving or Deteriorating Conditions?" Testimony of Thea M. Lee, Policy Director, AFL-CIO, before the House Committee on International Relations, Subcommittee on Africa, Global Human Rights and International Operations, April 19, 2006, http://commdocs.house.gov/committees/intlrel/hfa27067.000/hfa27067_of.htm (accessed 2/23/13).

[54]U.S.-China Economic and Security Review Commission, *2008 Report to Congress,* 2.

[55]John Markoff and David Barboza, "Researchers Trace Data Theft to Intruders in China," *New York Times,* April 10, 2010, http://nytimes.com/2010/04/06/science/06cyber.html?pagewanted=all (accessed February 23, 2013)

[56]David E.Sanger, David Barboza, and Nicole Perlroth, "Chinese Army Unit Is Seen as Tied to Hacking Against U.S.," *New York Times,* February 13, 2013, A1.

[57]Hillary Clinton, "U.S.-Asia Relations: Indispensable to Our Future," remarks at the Asia Society, New York, February 13, 2009, www.state.gov/secretary/rm/2009a/02/117333.htm# (accessed 2/23/13); Matthew Lee, "Human Rights Not Focus of Clinton's China Talks," *Independent,* February 21, 2009, www .independent.co.uk/news/world/asia/human-rights-not-focus-of-clinton8217s-china-talks-1628258.html (accessed 2/23/13).

[58]Glenn Kessler, "Clinton Criticized for Not Trying to Force China's Hand," *Washington Post,* February 21, 2009, A6.

[59]Edward Wong, "Taiwan's Independence Movement Likely to Wane," *New York Times,* March 12, 2008, A8; Scott L. Kastner and Douglas R. Grob, "Legislative Foundations of U.S.-Taiwan Relations: A New Look at the Congressional Taiwan Caucus," *Foreign Policy Analysis* 5:1 (January 2009): 57–72.

[60]U.S. House of Representatives, Requiring Consultations On U.S.-Taiwan Arms Sales Talks, *Congressional Record,* September 23, 2008, http://thomas.loc.gov/cgi-bin/query/z?r110:H23SE8-0049: (accessed 2/23/13).

[61]Xu Wu, "The New 'China Lobby'? China's Government PR Effort in the U.S.," paper presented at the National Communication Association, 94th Annual Convention, November 21–24, 2008, San Diego, www.connection.ebscohost.com/c/articles/44853503/new-china-lobby-chinas-government-pr-effort-us (accessed 8/15/09).

[62]"Doing Business with Strongmen," *BusinessWeek Online,* April 22, 1996, www.businessweek.com/archives/1996/b3472069.arc.htm (accessed 2/23/13).

[63]Elisabeth Rosenthal, "China's U.S. Road Show, Aimed at Making Friends," *New York Times,* August 23, 2000, www.nytimes.com/2000/08/23/world/chinas-us-road-show-aimed-at-making-friends.html (accessed 2/23/13)

[64]Ariana Eunjung Cha, "After Silence, China Mounts Product Safety PR Offensive," *Washington Post,* July 14, 2007, http://washingtonpost.com/wp-dyn/content/article/2007/07/13/AR2007071302010.html (accessed 2/23/13).

[65]U.S.-China Economic and Security Review Commission, *2008 Report to Congress,* 154.

[66]David Chen, "China Emerges as a Scapegoat in Campaign Ads," *New York Times,* October 9, 2010, A1.

[67]Nin-Hai Tseng, "Parsing the Short-Sighted, China Bashing Midterm Ads," 29 October 2010, CNNMoney, http://finance.fortune.cnn.com/2010/10/29/parsing-the-short-sighted-china-bashing-in-midterm-ads/ (accessed 2/23/13).

[68]Adam Hanft, "Ad Attacks on China Cross the Line," 12 October 2010, *Salon,* www.salon.com/2010/10/12/ad_attacks_on_china (accessed 2/23/13).

[69]Keith Bradsher, "Trade War in Solar Takes Shape," *New York Times,* November 9, 2011, B1.

11 *War, Peace, Terrorism, Democracy: Old and New Challenges in the Middle East*

Introduction: From Hope to Tragedy, 9/13/93 to 9/11/01

On September 13, 1993, following secret talks held in Norway, the Israeli prime minister Yitzhak Rabin and the Palestine Liberation Organization (PLO) chairman Yasir Arafat shook hands on the White House lawn. With President Bill Clinton as witness, they signed an initial peace agreement. It was a beautiful late summer day: sunny, with a blue sky, full of hope and promise.

Eight years later, another late summer day that started out just as beautifully— September 11, 2001—didn't end that way. Most of us will always remember where we were when we first heard the news, when we first saw the images, when we first felt the fear. The shock of the crashing World Trade Center towers and the gashes in the walls of the Pentagon—symbols of American economic and military strength—were seared deeply into the American psyche.

More than ever before in its modern history, the United States was proven vulnerable right at home. Foreign policy usually had been about U.S. involvements "over there"—in the Middle East, in the developing world, in Europe, in Asia. Now the threat was "here," on the American side of the oceans. Not since the bloodiest battles of the U.S. Civil War (1861–65) had so many Americans been killed in conflict on a single day. Not since the War of 1812, when the British attacked Washington, D.C., and set fire to the White House, had America's own capital been attacked. Even Pearl Harbor was an attack on a military base, not on cities and civilian populations. For Americans, the sense of threat was greater than at any time since the end of the Cold War.

MAP 11.1

MIDDLE EAST

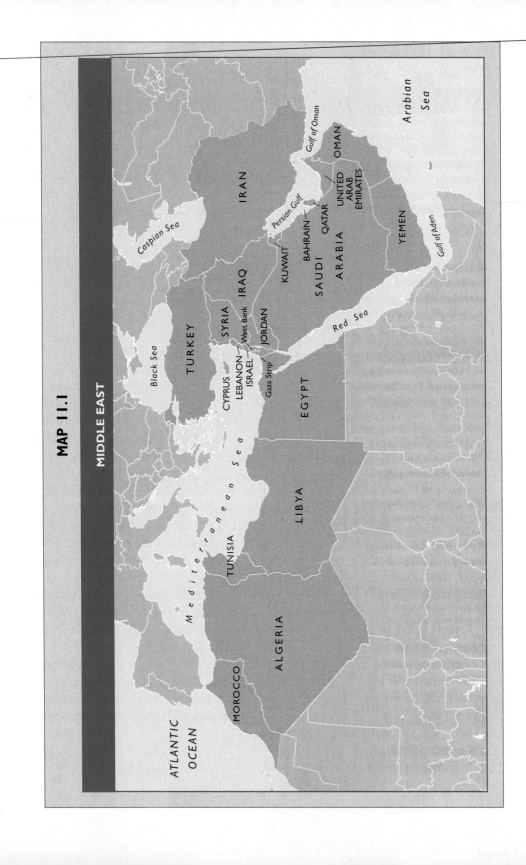

Other regions of the world grew in their own importance, but the Middle East became ever more central. Wars in Iraq and Afghanistan raised questions about whether American *Power* had been strengthened or weakened. Hopes of *Peace* were dashed amid the breakdown of the 1990s Arab-Israeli peace process, increased tensions with Iran over nuclear proliferation, and other issues. *Principles* were called into question by inconsistencies in support for democracy and alliances with authoritarian governments that risked replacing the Cold War "ABC" (anybody but communists) with "ABT" (anybody but terrorists). *Prosperity* was shaken by $140 per barrel oil prices in 2008 and continued threats to stability of supply.

Policies in this region have also raised key *foreign policy politics* issues. Some of these come through in the discussion of the Iraq War. The foreign policy politics section later in the chapter focuses on the war on terrorism's version of the national security–civil liberties "great debate."

The 1990–91 Persian Gulf War

On August 2, 1990, the Iraqi armies of Saddam Hussein invaded neighboring Kuwait. Although Iraq and Kuwait had a border dispute as well as some other issues, the real issue was Saddam Hussein's desire to become the dominant power in the Persian Gulf region. Indeed, his forces were poised to keep going straight into Saudi Arabia, an even more strategic country and a close U.S. ally.

The threat to vital American interests was deemed so serious that it was met by the most rapid buildup of U.S. military forces since World War II, first as a "desert shield" to protect Saudi Arabia and then as a "desert storm" to drive Saddam back out of Kuwait. A twenty-seven-nation coalition was built, including most of Western Europe, Japan, and much of the Arab world, and with some support even from the Soviet Union. The UN Security Council (UNSC) imposed economic sanctions and passed a resolution authorizing "all necessary means" to get Iraqi troops out of Kuwait, including the use of military force. Operation Desert Storm, launched when Saddam failed to meet the UN deadline for withdrawing from Kuwait, proved a formidable military victory.

In Chapter 1 we cited the 1990–91 Persian Gulf War as a major example of complementarity among the "4 Ps" of American foreign policy. Here we draw a number of more specific policy lessons from this war. The most immediate was that aggression was still a fact of international life. Troops marched and tanks rolled as Iraq took over Kuwait, its smaller and militarily weaker neighbor.

Second was the value of working through the UN, consistent with the policy-enhancement argument we discussed in Chapter 7. The war effort had both the benefits of UNSC legitimization and the burden-sharing of the broad multilateral coalition that sent troops, footed the bill, and provided other assistance. After the war the UN Special Commission (UNSCOM) on Iraq was created to go into Iraq and inspect and destroy Saddam's weapons of mass destruction complex.

Third was the demonstration of American military power. It is important to recall how dire many of the predictions were of the risks of going to war. But these predictions were not fulfilled, and with the help of CNN the whole world watched the vivid images of American military might and the heralded ***revolution in military affairs (RMA)***, through which mastery of electronic and information technologies gave the United States unprecedented conventional military capabilities. Although later studies indicated that the precision was not as great as was claimed at the time, the dominant sense was of a new age in which the U.S. military had superiority in the air.

Fourth was affirmation of the Powell doctrine of decisive force. Named for General Colin Powell, who at the time was chair of the Joint Chiefs of Staff, this doctrine declared that when military force is used, it should be used overwhelmingly and decisively. This was a major lesson that General Powell and others drew from the Vietnam War and its incremental approach to the use of force.

There were, however, some limits and negative aspects to the Gulf War's significance. As a military operation, for all the technological innovations the U.S. military displayed, it was fundamentally a classical strategy of armed forces against armed forces on the battlefield. But the nature of this war would prove to be more the exception than the rule. Somalia, Bosnia, Haiti, Kosovo, and the other ethnic conflicts and internal wars in which the United States became involved in the 1990s were much more politically based uses of military force, and much less battlefield-based—more like Vietnam than Desert Storm, and thus presenting different challenges for the use of military force. The 2003 Iraq War started out seemingly like Desert Storm, but winning the peace was a very different challenge from winning the war.

The UN coalition also frayed over the course of the 1990s. Economic sanctions were kept on the books but violated in practice. They also were manipulated by Saddam so that the Iraqi people were hit hard and humanitarian concerns aroused, but the regime maneuvered around them. Saddam eventually kicked out the UN inspectors, although not before they had dismantled much of his WMD capacity.

Finally, there were the lessons of the period leading up to Saddam's invasion of Kuwait, during which the United States had tilted toward Iraq in its 1980–88 war with Iran.[1] The policy was based on the greater threat posed by Iran's Islamic fundamentalists and the deep animosity of its anti-American leader, Ayatollah Ruhollah Khomeini. But the Reagan and first Bush administrations failed to see past the old adage "*the enemy of my enemy is my friend*." Indeed, the enemy of my enemy *may be* my friend, but he also may be my enemy, too. Thus it was one thing to feed the Iraqi population while it was at war with Iran, or to provide some industrial equipment, or even to share military intelligence and bolster Iraqi defensive military capabilities. It was quite another matter to loosen controls on technology and equipment with "dual uses" (both commercial and military applications). The United States (and Europe) did this to a degree that, along with Soviet aid, significantly and substantially contributed to Iraqi development of offensive military capabilities, especially its nuclear, biological, and chemical weapons. Thus, along with the lessons to be learned from how the war was fought, there were important lessons to be learned about why the war occurred.

9/11 and Its Impact

Before September 11, 2001, the post–Cold War foreign policy agenda had a long list of issues, but no single defining one, nothing like what anticommunism was during the Cold War. The war on terrorism became that defining issue for the George W. Bush administration's foreign policy.

It is true that, as Dan Caldwell states in *Vortex of Conflict,* "terrorism is as old as recorded human history." Caldwell also shows how terrorism developed in the 1990s, including (but not only) the emergence of Osama bin Laden and his **Al Qaeda** terrorist network.[2] Al Qaeda was responsible for a number of terrorist attacks on the U.S. presence abroad, including the August 1998 bombings of the American embassies in Kenya and Tanzania and the October 2000 bombing of the naval warship USS *Cole* in a harbor in Yemen. Indeed, even before the September 11 attacks, arguments were being made that terrorism had to be given higher priority in U.S. foreign policy. Consider, for example, the report of the National Commission on Terrorism, issued in June 2000:

> Terrorists attack American targets more often than those of any other country. America's preeminent role in the world guarantees that this will continue to be the case, and the threat of attacks creating massive casualties is growing. If the United States is to protect itself, if it is to remain a world leader, this nation must develop and continuously refine sound counterterrorism policies appropriate to the rapidly changing world around us. . . . International terrorists once threatened Americans only when they were outside the country. Today, international terrorists attack us on our own soil.[3]

This analysis and others like it were based in part on intelligence about bin Laden and Al Qaeda and other terrorists, as well as being grounded in three broader dynamics. First was terrorism as the "underside" of globalization. For all the benefits of the rapid and widespread movement of people, money, technology, and ideas, these trends also facilitated the operations of terrorists. Terrorists, too, could move from one corner of the globe to another. They, too, could communicate through the Internet. They, too, could visit various readily accessible Web sites and download information on various technologies, including WMD. They, too, could move their money around electronically. Terrorists operated in other eras, but globalization is part of what makes the terrorist threat that much greater today.

Second was the advantage that comes with being on the offensive and having the element of surprise on one's side. Terrorism's "tactical advantages," as the national security expert Richard Betts puts it, target "the soft underbelly of American primacy." In some situations, depending on the balance of forces and the nature of the warfare, the defense has the advantage. But with terrorism, the advantage is often with the attacker. They have the "capacity for strategic judo, the turning of the West's strength against itself.... Nineteen men from technologically backward societies did not have to rely on home-grown instruments to devastate the Pentagon and World Trade Center. They used computers and modern financial procedures with facility, and they forcibly appropriated the aviation technology of the West and used it as a weapon."[4] The openness of American society further complicates this, as we will see later in this chapter in the discussion of foreign policy politics and tensions between national security and civil liberties.

Third was the interconnection of terrorism with many aspects of U.S. policy in the Middle East and more broadly toward the Islamic world. Iran since the 1979 Islamic fundamentalist revolution; Iraq since the 1990–91 Persian Gulf War; relations with Arab governments such as Saudi Arabia and Egypt, which largely supported U.S. foreign policy but had their own instabilities and opposition (bin Laden was Saudi, and his top lieutenant Egyptian); the failure to stay engaged in Afghanistan after the defeat of the Soviets in 1988; the Arab-Israeli conflict—all these and other issues fed terrorism and turned it increasingly toward the United States as a principal target, while making strategizing against terrorism an especially complicated task.

Still, it took the 9/11 attacks on the World Trade Center and the Pentagon for the shift from *a* problem to *the* problem to occur. "We are at war," President George W. Bush told the nation in announcing the military action against the Taliban regime and the Al Qaeda terrorist network in Afghanistan. And he didn't just mean Afghanistan; the struggle was global, and it was for the long term. It was not a classical war, but it was a war nevertheless. Other foreign policy issues had to be dealt with, but there was no higher priority for the Bush administration than the war on terrorism.

Afghanistan and Pakistan

The initial war in Afghanistan was as internationally consensual as wars get. The U.S. claim to be acting in self-defense was strong. Even before 9/11 the Taliban regime had been denied its country's seat in the United Nations, and only two countries in the world had granted it diplomatic recognition. The Taliban regime was among the world's worst repressors of women and worst offenders against human rights. Some aspects of the U.S. strategy were debated, but the right to use force in this situation was widely accepted by the international community. The United Nations Security Council supported it, and over 170 nations joined the broader U.S.-led global coalition against terrorism.

Militarily, in its initial October–December 2001 phase, the ***Afghanistan war*** achieved many immediate objectives. The Taliban quickly fell. Bin Laden escaped. A vast new array of technologies was displayed. Special Operations forces, consisting of Green Berets, other elite units, and CIA agents infiltrated enemy areas, often riding on horseback in the rugged terrain yet technologically equipped to identify targets and communicate the enemy's exact location to bombers overhead. One U.S. Air Force officer called this basic equation of technology on horseback "21st-century air and space power combined with 16th-century land forces."[5]

For all the technological sophistication, though, the Afghanistan War strategy had its shortcomings. One was the reliance on local forces as a way of limiting the ground forces that the United States had to commit. The Afghan Northern Alliance, the main anti-Taliban group, was a valuable ally in many respects, but not in all. As long as its interests were consistent with those of the United States, it proved a reliable ally. But when the Northern Alliance's interests diverged from U.S. interests, it went its own way. An example of this came in the key battle of Tora Bora in December 2001. Many Al Qaeda leaders, possibly including bin Laden, were holed up in caves in this mountainous region but still managed to escape because the attacks on the caves by the Northern Alliance were poorly executed. The Northern Alliance had achieved its main objective—toppling the Taliban. Capturing Al Qaeda was less important to it than to the United States, so it was less inclined to run the risks inherent in the Tora Bora mission.

For these and other reasons, the initial victory proved inconclusive. An FBI-CIA report leaked to the press in June 2002 "concluded that the war in Afghanistan failed to diminish the threat to the United States. . . . Instead the war might have complicated counterterrorism efforts by dispersing potential attackers across a wider geographic area."[6] A few months later, Lt. General Dan McNeil, the U.S. commander in Afghanistan, forecast that it would take up to two more years to eliminate Al Qaeda and build an Afghan army strong enough to deny terrorists a future safe haven. Even this prediction proved much too optimistic. "'The Taliban and Al Qaeda are everywhere,'" a shopkeeper told an American general in May 2006.[7]

Politically, though elections were held, President Hamid Karzai squandered legitimacy through favoritism to his own ethnic group and massive corruption. "On the streets," the *New York Times* reported, "tales of corruption are as easy to find as kebab stands. Everything seems to be for sale: public offices, access to government services, even a person's freedom. . . . Transparency International, a German organization that gauges honesty in government, ranked Afghanistan 117 out of 180 countries in 2005."[8] With economic reconstruction and development also proceeding slowly and marred by corruption, opium production was one of the few "booming" areas of the Afghan economy, so much so that 90 percent of the global opiate supply was now coming from

Afghanistan. As the Bush administration left office, the situation was so bad that Admiral Mike Mullen, the chairman of the Joint Chiefs of Staff, warned that the United States was "running out of time" in Afghanistan.[9]

During the 2008 presidential campaign, Barack Obama juxtaposed his support for the Afghanistan War with his opposition to the Iraq War. Soon after taking office, he made an initial commitment to increase U.S. troops and initiated a policy review. While billed as a comprehensive review, it focused largely on different levels of additional troop commitments. From the three options proposed, the president chose the middle one of 30,000 additional troops (bringing the total to about 100,000). At the same time, it was announced that this would be a limited buildup with a drawdown of troops starting in July 2011 and a removal of all U.S. combat troops by the end of 2014. Defense Secretary Leon Panetta claimed that security gains had been made and that the timeline gave the generals on the ground "the right mix of flexibility, resources and time to continue building our progress on the ground."[10] Critics on the right called for keeping the troops in longer, questioning whether the Obama decision was more a political and civilian one than one with which the generals on the ground genuinely concurred. Others, and not just on the political left but also among many classical realists, had criticized the 2009 surge even before it started, arguing that no military strategy would make the United States any more successful than the British had been in the nineteenth century, the Soviets in the late twentieth century, or other major powers that had tried to tame Afghanistan. A former aide to top diplomat Richard Holbrooke later wrote that too much focus was on troop levels and too little on diplomacy, both regional with key surrounding countries and within Afghanistan on pursuing a political settlement through seriously exploring the possibility of negotiating with the Taliban.[11]

Relations with the Karzai government continued to be problematic. Some pressure was exerted for political reform, but not much changed. Corruption remained so rampant as to worsen the Transparency International corruption ranking to 174 out of 182 nations. For his part, Karzai pushed back against the United States, including blaming the U.S. for the continued instability. While U.S. policy clearly was not beyond criticism, Defense Secretary Panetta was prompted to fire back that President Karzai should "thank Americans for the sacrifices of those who fought and died in Afghanistan rather than level criticism at the United States."[12]

Various assessments spoke to both what had and had not been achieved. In Helmand Province, for example, whereas two years earlier farmers couldn't get to their fields of corn without risk of attack by the Taliban, the 2012 harvest had been conducted with much greater sense of safety. But among local farmers, elders, tribal leaders and others, "few expressed much faith in the ability of the Afghan government and security forces to maintain the security gains won by the huge American and British military effort there." The Pentagon's own progress report could only cite one of the Afghan Army's 23 national brigades as able to operate independently without U.S. or NATO military support.[13]

American public opinion, which at first had been highly supportive of the Afghanistan War, turned against it. Whereas initially public support was over 80 percent, and as late as 2007 over half believed the war was worth fighting, by May 2012, 67 percent said the war was not worth the costs. War-weariness was one part of this. Rising casualties were another: whereas it took nearly nine years of the Afghanistan War for the U.S. casualty count to reach 1,000, it reached 2,000 in less than the next two and a half years. So, too, was the strategic assessment by which only 30 percent felt that the war had made America safer. By mid-2012 some 82 percent felt that the troops should be withdrawn according to the 2014 deadline or sooner, with only 17 percent wanting to leave any combat troops in Afghanistan after 2014.[14]

Following his 2012 re-election, President Obama sped up the pace of the combat troop withdrawal. Debate continued over how many troops would remain and how their mission would be redefined.

At the same time there was increasing recognition that Pakistan, which was supposed to be part of the solution for stabilizing Afghanistan, had become part of the problem. The Bush administration's support for the Pakistan president, Pervez Musharraf, including over $10 billion in aid, had not produced the cooperation promised. Pakistan had become a safe haven where the Taliban rebuilt and rearmed and from which it launched attacks back into Afghanistan. It wasn't only that Pakistan had tried but had been unable to counter the Taliban. The evidence was quite strong that President Musharraf, the military, and the ISI (Pakistan's intelligence agency) had been "playing both sides of the war, the American side and the Taliban side. In return for the American billions, Pakistani forces or intelligence operatives occasionally picked off a few Al Qaeda leaders (though even that had slowed to a trickle). But they were actively supporting the Taliban and even some of the militants in the tribal regions."[15] Indeed, Pakistan's own Taliban was gaining power, as reported by the *New York Times* journalist David Sanger:

> The country is turning a blind eye as fundamentalism is taught in the schools—not just in the religious madrassas, but in the public and private schools that educate the rest of the population. . . . Take the word *collision,* which is pronounced *tay* in Urdu. The illustration [in a widely used textbook]: A picture of two airplanes flying into a burning World Trade Center. "Of all the pictures of a collision that you could find," Hoodhboy [a Pakistani critic] told me, "it's curious that they use that one in the textbook. . . . And the problem is not limited to basic readers for first-graders. Leafing through today's high school textbooks . . . [reveals that they] say little about Afghanistan or the brutal rule of the Taliban.[16]

As if these challenges were not tough enough, there also was the contentious issue of U.S. military action inside Pakistan to attack Al Qaeda and related targets. In its last months, the Bush administration had authorized using drones—unpiloted aircraft that could be operated remotely from as far away as the United States—to attack Al Qaeda and related targets inside Pakistan. The Obama administration continued this policy, substantially stepping up the number of attacks. There also were reports of some Special Operations forces crossing over from Afghanistan into Pakistan on quick, targeted missions, including the May 2011 raid that killed Osama bin Laden.

These incursions raised a number of issues. Was such action justified? Defenders traced their legitimacy back to the original 2001 retaliation against Al Qaeda for 9/11. They also viewed it as akin to "hot pursuit" tactics employed against terrorists and other fighters who had crossed over into Afghanistan to attack U.S. and NATO forces and then crossed back into Pakistan. Opponents saw the incursions as invading an ally, which violated international law and norms.

A less explicitly discussed but potentially more monumental issue was and continues to be Pakistan's nuclear weapons. If Pakistan does end up a failed state, or if radical Islamists come to power—perhaps even through their penetration of the military—and Pakistan's nuclear arsenal falls into their hands, what would, should, and could the United States do? This could be, as the military strategist Andrew Krepinevich describes the possibility, "the century's greatest crisis."[17]

Broader Global Counterterrorism

The war on terrorism "will not end," President Bush declared following 9/11, "until every terrorist group of global reach has been found, stopped and defeated." "Every day," Defense Secretary Donald Rumsfeld stated in 2003, we need to ask ourselves, "are we capturing, killing, or deterring and dissuading more terrorists than the radical clerics and madrassas are recruiting, training and deploying against us?"[18] In addition to the Afghanistan and Iraq wars, this was to be a global war on terrorism. Afghanistan was Al Qaeda's principal base but not its only one; it had developed a global network of cells. Other terrorist groups not formally affiliated but sharing goals, tactics, and enemies were also operating in countries around the world. American military commitments were made to a number of these countries where the threat was deemed the greatest: the South and Central Asian frontline states surrounding Afghanistan (Pakistan, Uzbekistan, Tajikistan, and Kyrgyzstan); Southeast Asian states with large Muslim populations and known active Al Qaeda cells and similar groups (Indonesia, Malaysia, and the Philippines); Yemen (where the October 2000 Al Qaeda attack on the USS *Cole* had occurred); Qatar (where bases were built up for attacking Iraq) and other Middle Eastern states; and Georgia (the ex-Soviet state in the Caucasus, near where Al Qaeda operatives were active in Chechnya). This list also has included Africa, both Muslim northern Africa (e.g., Morocco, Tunisia, and even the former adversary Libya) and such sub-Saharan African countries as Nigeria, Mali, and Senegal.

The Bush administration stressed that the war on terrorism was not just about security; it also claimed higher purposes, Principles as well as Power. Just as the United States fought the Cold War to ensure democracy's triumph over the communist "evil empire," so it now must fight the war on terrorism to ensure the triumph of freedom over this era's forces of evil. From the beginning, President Bush frequently used the language of "good," "evil," and "freedom." Iraq, Iran, and North Korea were named in Bush's 2002 State of the Union speech as the three principal points on the *"axis of evil."* Bin Laden and the other terrorists were, in his words, "evildoers." The war on terrorism was being fought to defeat evil and defend freedom: freedom for Afghan women, who had been so brutally repressed by the Taliban; freedom for the Iraqi people, who needed to be liberated from Saddam Hussein; freedom for Americans to live without the fear of terrorist attack; freedom for people everywhere to live without repression and fear.

Numerous political initiatives were taken to try to answer the question "Why do they hate us?" A "public diplomacy" strategy was premised on the belief that the problem was principally a communications one. The American "message" was solid—it just needed to get out more accurately and more widely. Charlotte Beers, a prominent advertising executive, was appointed undersecretary of state for public diplomacy and public affairs to take up this task. Karen Hughes, one of Bush's top campaign and political aides, later took this job. Among the initiatives to get the American message out were a new Arabic-language radio station, more engagement with moderate Islamic religious leaders, and other efforts to fare better in "the battle of ideas" that underlay and fed into much of the fundamentalism and anti-Americanism around the world.

In his last foreign policy speech as president, delivered at West Point, George W. Bush stressed the success his terrorism strategy had had. Among his points:

> We have severely weakened the terrorists. We've disrupted plots to attack our homeland. We have captured or killed hundreds of al Qaeda leaders and operatives in more than two dozen countries—including the man who masterminded the 9/11 attacks, Khalid Sheikh Mohammed. . . .
> We've helped key partners and allies strengthen their capabilities in the fight against the terrorists. We've increased intelligence-sharing with friends and allies around the world. We've provided training and support to counterterrorism partners like the Philippines, and Indonesia, and Jordan, and Saudi Arabia.[19]

Critics of the Bush strategy came to a different assessment. In their view, the credits the Bush administration claimed for its war on terrorism were classic single-column accounting, ignoring such entries in the debits column as the tripling of terrorist attacks in 2004 over 2003, and such major attacks as those in Spain in 2004, London and Amman (Jordan) in 2005, Egypt in 2006, and Israel throughout this period, as well as the growth of new terrorist groups and networks. In a June 2006 survey that asked national security experts whether the United States was winning the war on terrorism, 83 percent said no. Although Al Qaeda underestimated the effectiveness of the immediate U.S. retaliation for 9/11 that drove them out of Afghanistan, the Iraq War and other parts of the Bush strategy that fed anti-Americanism were, as one military expert put it, serving "as al-Qaeda's [sic] best recruiting tool."[20] From a democracy promotion and human rights perspective, the "ABT" (anybody but terrorists) rationale for alliances and commitments risked giving the United States bedfellows as strange as those rationalized by the "ABC" (anything but communism) rationale of the Cold War.

The Obama global counterterrorism strategy was a mix of change and continuity. A major change was in tone. Obama's message to terrorists in his 2009 inaugural address was no less tough than the Bush administration's: "We will not apologize for our way of life, nor will we waver in its defense, and for those who seek to advance their aims by inducing terror and slaughtering innocents, we say to you now that our spirit is stronger and cannot be broken; you cannot outlast us, and we will defeat you." But for the broader Muslim world, "we seek a new way forward, based on mutual interest and mutual respect."[21] He reinforced and elaborated on this message in his speech to the Turkish Parliament a little more than two months later: "We will bridge misunderstandings, and seek common ground. We will be respectful, even when we do not agree. We will convey our deep appreciation for the Islamic faith"—and, with the most emphasis—"[t]he United States is not, and never will be, at war with Islam." And in a much-heralded speech in Cairo in June 2009, he called for "a new beginning between the United States and Muslims around the world."[22] President Bush made disclaimers of his own about the U.S. attitude toward Islam, but they had not stuck. Foreign policy is about the music as well as the words, and the Obama team's assessment was that a new tone had to be struck. The term "global war on terrorism" would no longer be used. "The Administration has stopped using the phrase, and I think that speaks for itself," Secretary of State Hillary Clinton stated.[23]

The Obama strategy sought to integrate diplomatic, political, economic, and other instruments of power and influence. History shows that some terrorist movements end without having been defeated militarily—for example, by the loss of popular support, unsuccessful generational succession, or a transition into nonviolent national political processes.[24] But this was in addition to, not instead of, the use of force. Indeed, the Obama administration used drones and other military attacks against terrorist leaders and cells with much greater frequency than the Bush administration had. Targeted attacks were launched against Al Qaeda and other terrorists in Pakistan, Yemen, Somalia, and other countries—including the May 2011 killing of Osama bin Laden at his hideout in Pakistan by Navy SEALS and other Special Operations forces and intelligence operatives.

More specifically regarding the debate over drones, John O. Brennan, then the Obama administration's top counterterrorism official (and later CIA director), defended their use as "legal, ethical, wise and highly effective." They are "not the problem, they are part of the solution." In Yemen, where Al Qaeda in the Arabian Peninsula (AQAP) was behind a number of terrorist operations, "we see little evidence that these actions [the use of drones] are generating widespread anti-American sentiment or recruits for AQAP. In fact, we see the opposite. Our Yemeni partners are more eager to work with us. Yemeni citizens who have been freed from the hellish grip of AQAP are more eager, not less, to work with the Yemeni government."[25] Others took issue with these claims. Gregory Johnsen, a scholar with expertise on Yemen, cited interviews he and local journalists had conducted in Yemen that "attest to the centrality of civilian casualties [from drone attacks] in explaining Al Qaeda's rapid growth there." Micah Zenko, a Council on Foreign Relations fellow, cited this and other "downsides," including how the allure of ostensibly quick-fix, low-risk drone attacks "elevate military options above other instruments of statecraft" that are less "sexy" but potentially more effective.[26]

As much as another 9/11 or other such terrorist attacks are of concern, preventing *catastrophic terrorism*—the use of nuclear, chemical, or other weapons of mass destruction (WMD)—has remained the highest priority. This goal entails working with other nations to prevent WMD acquisition by Al Qaeda or other terrorists. It also includes efforts by the Department of Homeland Security, the FBI, the Coast Guard, and other agencies both to maximize prevention and to ensure resilience if an attack should occur.

Has all this been, as Ohio State political scientist John Mueller argues, "overblown" and "overwrought"? In Mueller's analysis the threat has been exaggerated and perspectives distorted, leading to "an ill-conceived and remarkably unreflective effort to react to an event that, however tragic and dramatic in the first instance, should have been seen to be of only limited significance at least after a few years."[27] Has the policy debate been constrained by a political correctness of not wanting to be perceived as "soft on terrorism," akin to what we saw with "soft on communism" during the Cold War?

The Iraq War

As noted earlier, despite the many ways in which the 1990–91 Persian Gulf War was a major victory, Saddam Hussein's Iraq continued to pose challenges to the United States and the United Nations. The issue came to a head post-9/11 when the Bush administration decided that the first application of the Bush doctrine on preemption was to be in Iraq (Reading 11.1). The administration debated internally whether to go to the UN Security Council for support. On March 19, 2003, President George W. Bush went on television from the Oval Office: "My fellow citizens, at this hour, American and coalition forces are in the early stages of military operations to disarm Iraq, to free its people and to defend the world from grave danger."[28] The *Iraq War* coalition had about forty countries; the main partner was Great Britain, led by Prime Minister Tony Blair. It thus was not strictly a unilateral war, but the multilateral coalition was not nearly as strong as it had been for the Persian Gulf War or the Afghanistan War. France, Germany, Russia, and Egypt were among those opposed. The "International Perspectives" box on page 469 gives a sense of the global debate.

11.1

"Shock and awe" was the term coined for the military strategy used against Iraq. The idea was to bring so much military power to bear so quickly—inflicting such heavy destruction on enemy forces as to shock and intimidate them, leaving them materially weakened and psychologically in awe—as to undermine their will to keep fighting. Within a month, American and coalition military forces had prevailed. On April 10, 2003, Bush sent a message to the Iraqi people: "This is George W. Bush, the President of the United States. At this moment, the regime of Saddam Hussein is being removed from power, and a long era of fear and cruelty is ending. American and coalition forces are now operating inside Baghdad—and we will not stop until Saddam's corrupt gang is gone. The government of Iraq, and the future of your country, will soon belong to you."[29]

The image that most conveyed the sense of great victory was that of President Bush flying onto the aircraft carrier USS *Abraham Lincoln* on May 1, "arriving in the co-pilot's seat of a Navy S-3B Viking after making two fly-bys of the carrier." The account on CNN continued: "Moments after the landing, the president, wearing a green flight suit and holding a white helmet, got off the plane, saluted those on the flight deck and shook hands with them. Above him, the tower was adorned with a big sign that read, "Mission Accomplished."[30] But the sense of victory did not last (Reading 11.2). Opponents raised three main sets of issues about the Iraq war: the validity of the rationales for going to war, the results on the ground of having won the war but perhaps not the peace, and the broader ramifications for American foreign policy.

Rationales for Going to War: Validity?

Of the various reasons that the Bush administration cited for going to war against Iraq when and how it did, two received the most emphasis and were deemed the most important. One was the WMD threat—that Saddam Hussein had weapons of mass destruction. The other was the terrorism coalition link between Al Qaeda and Saddam. Putting the two together, if Iraq were to supply WMD to Al Qaeda, "then the attacks of September the 11th would be a prelude to far greater horrors."[31] But neither of these claims proved to be true.

DID SADDAM HAVE WMD?   The WMD claim was a staple of administration speeches in the buildup to the war:

> *Vice President Cheney:* "There is no doubt that [Saddam Hussein] is amassing [WMD] to use against our friends, against our allies, and against us."[32]

> *President Bush:* "The United States of America will not permit the world's most dangerous regimes to threaten us with the world's most destructive weapons. . . . The British government has learned that Saddam Hussein recently sought significant quantities of uranium from Africa."[33]

INTERNATIONAL PERSPECTIVES
INTERNATIONAL PERSPECTIVES

SUPPORT FOR AND OPPOSITION TO THE IRAQ WAR

Support

Prime Minister Tony Blair, Great Britain: "The brutality of the repression—the death and torture camps, the barbaric prisons for political opponents, the routine beatings for anyone or their families suspected of disloyalty—are well documented. . . . We take our freedom for granted. But imagine not to be able to speak or discuss or debate or even question the society you live in. To see friends and family taken away and never daring to complain. To suffer the humility of failing courage in face of pitiless terror. That is how the Iraqi people live. Leave Saddam in place and that is how they will continue to live."

Prime Minister Silvio Berlusconi, Italy: "I'm here today to help my friend President Bush to convince everybody that this is in the interest of everybody. And if we are all united, the European Union, the United States, the Federation of Russia, everybody, all the other states under the United Nations, then Saddam Hussein will understand that he will have no other option but to reveal the arms and to destroy them."

Opposition

President Jacques Chirac, France: "Whether it concerns the necessary disarmament of Iraq or the desirable change of the regime in this country, there is no justification for a unilateral decision to resort to force. . . . No matter how events evolve now, this ultimatum challenges our view of international relations. It puts the future of a people, the future of a region and world stability at stake."

President Vladimir Putin, Russian Federation: "[The Iraq War will be a] mistake fraught with the gravest consequences which may result in casualties and destabilize the international situation in general."

Sources: "Full Text: Tony Blair's Speech," *Guardian*, March 18, 2003, www.guardian.co.uk/politics/2003/mar/18/foreignpolicy.iraq1 (accessed 3/2/13); "Bush, Italy's Berlusconi Warn Saddam to Disarm," January 30, 2003, www.america.gov/st/washfile-english/2003/January/20030130145138 jthomas@pd.state.gov0.1734735.html (accessed 3/2/13); Jacques Chirac, quoted in "In Quotes: Reaction to Bush Ultimatum," March 18, 2003, http://news.bbc.co.uk/2/hi/middle_east/2859485.stm (accessed 3/2/13); Vladimir Putin, quoted in Ron Hutcheson and Martin Merzer, "Bush Gives Saddam, Sons 48 Hours to Leave Iraq," *Stars and Stripes*, March 18, 2003, http://www.stripes.com/news/bush-gives-saddam-sons48-hours-to-leave-Iraq-1.2954 (accessed 3/2/13).

CIA Director George Tenet on the strength of the WMD evidence: "Tenet, a basketball fan who attended as many home games of his alma mater Georgetown as possible, leaned forward and threw his arms up again, 'Don't worry, it's a slam dunk!' "[34]

Secretary of State Colin Powell at the UN: "The facts and Iraq's behavior show that Saddam Hussein and his regime are concealing their efforts to produce more weapons of mass destruction. . . . Everything we have seen and heard indicates that, instead of cooperating actively with the inspectors to ensure the success of their mission, Saddam Hussein and his regime are busy doing all they possibly can to ensure that inspectors succeed in finding absolutely nothing. My colleagues, every statement I make today is backed up by sources, solid sources. These are not assertions. What we're giving you are facts and conclusions based on solid intelligence."[35]

The evidence, though, did not bear out these claims. No WMD were found. No nuclear weapons. And no significant nuclear program was left of what UN inspectors had dismantled in the 1990s and sanctions had continued to block. No significant traces of the alleged 100 to 500 tons of chemical weapons agents. The mobile lab said to be a production facility for biological weapons was more likely used for manufacturing hydrogen for military weather balloons. Far from being a "slam dunk," the WMD claims were "riddled with errors," as even a commission appointed by President Bush reported back to him.[36] Other assessments were much harsher.

Why and how were the intelligence assessments so wrong? We do need to acknowledge the inherent difficulty of getting accurate information about a secretive regime. But the chief explanation lies in the politicization of the policy process that made this case a glaring example of how bureaucratic politics and groupthink distort effective policy making.

The October 2002 **National Intelligence Estimate (NIE)** exemplifies this pattern. The official definition of an NIE is "the coordinated judgments of the Intelligence Community regarding the likely course of future events," written with the goal of providing "policymakers with the best, unvarnished and unbiased information—regardless of whether analytic judgments conform to US policy."[37] The October 2002 Iraq NIE stated that Saddam had chemical and biological weapons and that although he might not yet have nuclear weapons, he likely would within a few years.[38] But this assessment was based on some very suspect sources—for example, an Iraqi defector code-named "Curveball," who was known to have psychological problems and a drinking problem yet who was the NIE's principal source for the biological weapons intelligence.[39] Moreover, dissenting analyses were largely ignored. For example, the State Department Bureau of Intelligence and Research (INR) found that the claims of Iraqi purchases of uranium in Africa were "highly dubious"; INR and the Energy Department found that the aluminum tubes said to be for uranium enrichment "most likely are intended for conventional weapons use (artillery shells)."[40]

Some of the responsibility lies with the CIA and other intelligence agencies for failing at basic tradecraft. A Senate committee report attributed this not just to the inherent limits of discoverable information but also to groupthink:

> The Intelligence Community (IC) has long struggled with the need for analysts to overcome analytic biases, that is, to resist the tendency to see what they would expect to see in the intelligence reporting. In the case of Iraq's weapons of mass destruction (WMD) capabilities, the Committee found that intelligence analysts, in many cases, based their analysis more on their expectations than on objective evaluation of the information in the intelligence reporting. Analysts expected to see evidence that Iraq has retained prohibited weapons and that Iraq would resume prohibited WMD activities once United Nations' (UN) inspections ended. This bias that pervaded both the IC's analytic and collection communities represents "group think" . . . examining few alternatives, selective gathering of information, pressure to conform within the group or withhold criticism, and collective rationalization.[41]

But the distortions and failures also occurred at the level of top White House and Cabinet decision makers. "The war makers' posture toward intelligence went beyond mere disregard," Paul Pillar, who at the time was the principal intelligence officer for the Middle East, later wrote. "It became one of rejection, hostility and attempts to discredit." The Rumsfeld Pentagon went about "discrediting intelligence judgments rather than improving them." Vice President Cheney was the source of huge pressure to make the intelligence findings fit the premises, rather than test the premises against the intelligence. "War had become a certainty before it became an option."[42] Journalist George Packer also recounts an effort by Richard Haass, State Department Policy Planning Director, to raise concerns about going to war. "Save your breath," he was told by National Security Adviser Condoleezza Rice in June 2002. "The president has already made up his mind."[43]

SADDAM–AL QAEDA LINKS   The Bush administration also was very assertive regarding the Saddam–Al Qaeda terrorism link. "We've learned," President Bush stated, "that Iraq has trained Al Qaeda members in bomb making and poisons and gases."[44] But this claim also was based on questionable sources, including an Al Qaeda prisoner who had been "identified as a likely fabricator" by both the CIA and the Defense Intelligence Agency. Still, the Office of Special Plans—set up within the Pentagon by Defense Secretary Rumsfeld and sheltered under a nondescript title as a bastion for neoconservative appointees to provide their own intelligence analysis—kept insisting that the link existed. They approached the issue not to test a question but "to prove an assumption." They took as a given that the Saddam–Al Qaeda link was there: "the premise was true" by definition; "facts would be found to confirm it." The Pentagon neoconservatives, along with others in Vice President Cheney's office and still others "dispersed on key islands across the national security archipelago, allowed the intelligence 'product' and its effects on policy to circumvent the normal interagency process, in which the unconverted would have been among the participants and might have raised objections."[45] A former army major who was a psychiatrist assigned to interrogating prisoners at Guantánamo Bay told army investigators that "a large part of the time we were focused on trying to establish a link between Al Qaeda and Iraq and we were not being successful." This was, he testified, a factor in the move to torture: as the higher-ups grew more "frustrated," pressure increased "to resort to measures" that might get the desired answers, valid or not.[46]

The former top antiterrorism official Richard Clarke describes a conversation with Bush on September 12, 2001:

> "Look," he told us, "I know you have a lot to do and all . . . but I want you, as soon as you can, to go back over everything, everything. See if Saddam did this. See if he's linked in any way. . . ."
>
> I was once again taken aback, incredulous, and it showed. "But, Mr. President, al Qaeda did this."
>
> "I know, I know, but . . . see if Saddam was involved. Just look. I want to know any shred. . . ."
>
> "Absolutely, we will look . . . again." I was trying to be more respectful, more responsive. "But, you know, we have looked several times for state sponsorship of al Qaeda and not found any real linkages to Iraq. Iran plays a little, as does Pakistan, and Saudi Arabia, Yemen."
>
> "Look into Iraq, Saddam," the President said testily and left us.[47]

Three years later the 9/11 Commission was unequivocal in its conclusion that no evidence existed of a "collaborative operational relationship" between Saddam and Al Qaeda generally. Most especially, "We have no credible evidence that Iraq was supporting al Qaeda."[48]

Results: Winning the Peace?

Vice President Cheney said that American forces "will be greeted as liberators." "I can't say if the use of force would last five days or five weeks or five months," Defense Secretary Rumsfeld stated, "but it certainly isn't going to last any longer than that." Kenneth Adelman, a leading neoconservative commentator, predicted a "cakewalk."[49] Other Bush administration officials and supporters were no less bullish about a quick victory in Iraq. Reality proved quite different.

At a June 2003 conference outside Washington, I gave a talk in which I criticized the lack of a strategy, already becoming apparent, for how to move from having won the war to winning the peace. A colleague who worked in the government as a distinguished career national security expert berated me. "Don't assume we didn't plan," she said. A few months later when stories about "the 'Future of Iraq' project" broke in the press, I realized what she meant.[50] In fact, the State Department had devised a postwar strategy, producing a four-volume set of memos, background analyses, and strategy papers called "The Future of Iraq." The department had set up seventeen working groups on issues including the economy, the justice system, and political institutions, coordinating with over two hundred Iraqi lawyers, engineers, businesspeople, and other Iraqi nationals, as well as leading American policy experts. One of the conclusions they reached was to "prepare for a messy aftermath." Another was that Iraq "would not provide fertile ground for democracy . . . that a foreign occupying force would itself be the target of resentment and attacks—including guerrilla warfare."[51] Those running the Iraq policy, mostly a small group of officials surrounding Defense Secretary Rumsfeld and Vice President Cheney, simply ignored this report and other parts of the Future of Iraq study. Studies conducted by leading think tanks—including the Council on Foreign Relations, the Center for Strategic and International Studies, the RAND Corporation, and the U.S. Institute of Peace—were treated in the same way. It is one thing to study a report and then reject it on the basis of contrary analysis and information. That's the nature of policy choice. It's quite another, though, to dismiss studies largely because the conclusions they reach and the recommendations they make complicate or perhaps contradict policy that has already been decided.

Both groupthink and bureaucratic politics were at work on postwar strategies as well. The dominant mindset within top decision-making circles assumed postwar stability in Iraq rather than analyzing what it would take to achieve it. "There was little discussion in Washington of the aftermath of military action," the head of British intelligence reported back to Prime Minister Tony Blair after a round of meetings in Washington. As the journalist George Packer writes, on the basis of his sources within the Bush administration, "Plan A was that the Iraqi government would be quickly decapitated, security would be turned over to remnants of the Iraqi police and army, international troops would soon arrive, and most American forces would leave within a few months. There was no Plan B."[52] The Bush administration became trapped in the illogic of its own logic. "Because detailed planning for the postwar situation meant facing costs and potential problems, it weakened the case for a 'war of choice,' and was seen by the war's proponents as an 'antiwar' undertaking."[53] As a result, accounts surfaced of American officials in Iraq relying on a Lonely Planet guidebook to identify key sites that needed to be safeguarded. In another instance, a national guardsman from a small town in Rhode Island charged with organizing an Iraqi police force was given so little to work with that he sent home for his town's police manual.

One problem was security. Before the war, Army Chief of Staff General Eric Shinseki had recommended that several hundred thousand troops would be needed for stabilization and security once Saddam had been overthrown. Deputy Defense Secretary Paul Wolfowitz called this "wildly off the mark."[54] Wolfowitz's criticism was more about politics than strategy. He was trying to keep the numbers low so that the public and others would believe that the war could be won with limited commitments. Yet events showed Shinseki's number to be all too near the mark. Chaos broke out after Saddam's fall, and

American forces were far too few to respond effectively. General Shinseki was reprimanded and forced to retire. The security situation was made worse by Ambassador L. Paul Bremer III, the head of the governing structure the United States set up (the Coalitional Provisional Authority). Bremer disbanded the entire Iraqi army on the grounds that they might still be loyal to Saddam. This had the doubly negative effects of enlarging the security vacuum while further motivating the idling masses of former army officers and soldiers, who still had their weapons, to turn to terrorism, insurgency, and criminal violence.

For the first two or so years, the major security threat was from Sunni and foreign terrorists. The Iraqi population largely comprises three groups: Sunnis and Shiites—both Arab peoples but following historically conflicting branches of Islam—and Kurds, also Muslim but ethnically distinct from Iraqi Arabs and concentrated in the northern part of the country. Saddam was a Sunni; he favored the Sunnis (a minority) while repressing and at times slaughtering Shiites and Kurds. After Saddam's fall, the Shiites and Kurds gained dominance. Some Sunnis turned to terrorism against rival Iraqi groups as well as against American and other coalition forces. With the Iraqi borders exceedingly porous, in part because of the limited American forces, foreign jihadist terrorists joined the fray.

Some success stories emerged where American troops, working with Iraqi forces and political leaders, enhanced security in key cities and villages. But by early 2006 the situation was increasingly recognized as a civil war. Sunnis attacked Shiites. Shiites attacked Sunnis. Shiite factions and militias were fighting each other. Kurds also were in the picture. American casualties climbed. Iraqi casualties climbed higher. During the six weeks of full warfare, only 140 Americans died, but over 2,000 died in the three years following. Whereas only 1,300 Iraqi police and soldiers had been killed before 2005, over 2,500 died that year alone. Civilian casualties in 2005 were over 5,600, and almost triple that in 2006.[55]

The political dimension of democratic institutionalization saw some notable achievements. Since Saddam's fall, Iraq has had more and freer elections than any other Arab country. A constitution was approved. A government was elected. At each such watershed, hopes surged that democracy was taking root and political order was being established. We should not forget that many Iraqi citizens have been striving to build a better life for themselves and their families and that American soldiers, NGO workers, and others from the international community have helped, often at the risk of their own lives.

Sufficiently consolidating such progress, though, in the face of violence, disorder, and flawed policies proved difficult. Soon after each election was held and other political milestones reached, limits were evident, disappointment set in, and violence increased. Could the Sunnis, Shiites, and Kurds reach enough of a compromise for political stability? How could they share power? One of the main issues in this regard has been the militias that each group maintained as its own private army at the same time that an Iraqi

national army was getting built. The economic aspects of reconstruction also were problematic. During the prewar debate, Lawrence Lindsey, then the top Bush administration economic adviser, predicted costs of as much as $200 billion. This was the economic
equivalent of General Shinseki's point about troop needs. Like Shineski, Lindsey, too, lost
his job. Official cost projections were much lower, including the claim by Deputy Defense
Secretary Wolfowitz that much would be paid for by Iraqi oil revenues. The actual costs
of the war, though, ran much higher than even the Lindsey estimate, over $3 trillion
according to the Nobel Prize–winning economist Joseph Stiglitz.

The 2004 Abu Ghraib prison scandal, with its graphic photos and accounts of torture
by American forces, profoundly damaged American claims to the moral high ground,
also a crucial asset for winning the peace. Then in early 2006 came revelations that
American soldiers had raped and killed Iraqi civilians, including women and children, in
the Iraqi city of Haditha.

Such atrocities notwithstanding, the American military largely fulfilled its responsibilities with courage and commitment. Yet it was being stretched to and possibly beyond
the limit. By spring 2006 nearly every active-duty combat unit had been deployed to Iraq
twice, with little if any time back home. A *Military Times* poll in January 2006 found high
morale but declining support for Bush and the war effort. Only 54 percent of soldiers
polled supported President Bush's Iraq policy, and only 40 percent felt the Defense
Department civilian leaders "have my best interests at heart."[56] The National Guard and
reserves were being drawn on for an unprecedented 40 percent of the forces in Iraq. One
top general testified to Congress that this was sending the guard and reserves into "meltdown."[57] Hurricane Katrina had revealed some of the immediate consequences in 2005.
Though desperately needed at home, over three thousand Louisiana guardsmen—as well
as high-water trucks, fuel trucks, satellite phones, and much other emergency equipment—
were overseas in Iraq.

Additionally, the international coalition, never as strong as the coalitions during the
1990–91 Persian Gulf War and in Afghanistan, was eroding. The toll of the war, terrorist
retaliations, and domestic opposition together led a number of coalition members to pull
out. At home, support was weakening as well. Whereas in late 2003 nearly six in ten
Americans surveyed saw the Iraq War as worth the cost, by March 2006 only 42 percent
took this view. Approval of the Bush policy, which had been as high as 75 percent in the
"mission accomplished" days, fell to 36 percent in late 2005. Indeed, discontent over Iraq
was so deep and widespread as to be the major issue in the Democratic victory in the
2006 midterm congressional elections—one of the few times in American history that a
foreign policy issue was key to midterm congressional elections.

Rather than withdrawing from Iraq, the Bush administration made a major shift in
strategy. Dubbed the *surge,* this shift involved a buildup of another thirty thousand troops
combined with a revised counterinsurgency strategy led by General David Petraeus. As

President Bush explained in a televised speech in early 2007, "Our past efforts to secure Baghdad failed for two principal reasons: There were not enough Iraqi and American troops to secure neighborhoods that had been cleared of terrorists and insurgents . . . and there were too many restrictions on the troops we did have."[58] Another key element was building some common cause with the "Sunni Awakening," Sunni tribes who had opposed the U.S. presence in Iraq but who had grown disillusioned with the violence, radicalism, and competition for power from Al Qaeda in Iraq (AQI). The "enemy of my enemy is my friend" calculus of shared security interests was a part of this; so, too, was money, as many of the Sunnis who changed sides were put on the U.S. payroll.

The surge's effectiveness has been debated. Fred Kagan, a military historian who was one of the principal strategists behind the surge, stressed in 2008 that "violence and American casualties have dropped remarkably since the surge began last year" and that the "basic reality" the surge has created is that "Iraq is an independent, sovereign state able to negotiate on an equal basis with the United States."[59] The casualty data backed him up. U.S. soldier deaths were down almost two-thirds in 2008 compared with 2007; Iraqi civilian casualties were down about 60 percent. The number of enemy-initiated attacks fell from almost 1,500 per week to about 150; the number of foreign militants crossing into Iraq to support the insurgency fell from between eighty and ninety per week to between ten and twenty. The size of Iraq's own security forces grew from 323,000 to 589,000. Anbar Province, which had been the site of the largest number of U.S. casualties two years earlier, was now sufficiently stable to be handed back to Iraqi control. Some political progress had been made with additional rounds of elections, some Shiite-Sunni-Kurd power sharing, and other steps toward national reconciliation.

Others, such as Lawrence Korb of the Center for American Progress, wrote that although the surge may have removed Iraq from the front page of the newspapers, it had not resolved the underlying tension. "Despite recent security gains in Iraq," he said, "the surge of over 30,000 troops there has failed to meet its strategic objective—meaningful national reconciliation."[60] Political progress continued to lag, as indicated by such unmet benchmarks as disbanding militias, fulfilling the promised reintegration of Sunnis, resolving territorial and autonomy issues with the Kurds, and sharing oil revenues. Economic progress also was slow, including such basic measures as providing electricity to homes, lowering unemployment, and raising oil production.

Stephen Biddle and colleagues took a middle position. Using declassified data as well as extensive interviews with Americans and Iraqis, they posited a "synergistic interaction" between the surge strategy and the factors independently leading to the Sunni Awakening such that "both were necessary; neither was sufficient."[61] They also stressed how unique these circumstances were and noted that, because they are difficult to replicate, they cannot serve as a generalizable model for other situations such as Afghanistan.

As a candidate, Barack Obama was strongly opposed to the war. He also stressed that although in his view the war had been started irresponsibly, it still needed to be ended responsibly. By August 2010 the combat mission had ended. By the end of 2011 all U.S. troops had been withdrawn. Yet Iraq remains of questionable stability. Shiite-Sunni-Kurd tensions persist. Repression, corruption, and cronyism hamper the Iraqi government's legitimacy. Terrorist incidents continue. Clearly, winning the peace has been much more problematic than winning the war.

Ramifications: Iraq and the "4 Ps"

One point that proponents and critics agree on is that the Iraq War has never been about just Iraq. As the "Theory in the World" (p. 478) box illustrates, the issues are more broadly about America's role in the world and, in this book's terms, all "4 Ps" of the national interest. For the Bush administration and its supporters, the Iraq War was to be a "4 Ps" complementarity case. For Iraq war critics, it was riven with "4 Ps" contradictions.

Consider the points that the Bush administration and other Iraq war supporters made:

POWER   The demonstration of American military might strengthened American power. Iraq was what the Bush administration called the central front in the war on terror. The message would go out through the Middle East that the United States has the capabilities and the will to defend its interests and security when and how it sees fit. In the rest of the world, doubts about American primacy would be dispelled. The United States was Number 1. It would lead. Others needed to follow or get out of the way.

PEACE   The elimination of Saddam Hussein enhanced the prospects for peace in a region that has known too little of it. Saddam had launched wars against his neighbors (Iran, Kuwait). He had threatened Israel repeatedly, even attacking it during the 1991 Gulf War, and led efforts to block peace when Arab leaders such as Anwar Sadat had forged ahead. The United States may not have been able to find WMD, but Saddam had them before and would have sought them again; as George W. Bush stated, "With the elimination of Saddam's regime, this threat has been addressed, once and for all."[62] And although defying the United Nations in the moment, America's willingness to do what needed to be done (and which the UN kept refusing to do), including fully enforcing its own multiple resolutions, would be good for the world body in the long run.

PROSPERITY   No commodity is more economically crucial than oil. American as well as global prosperity would be served by making world oil supplies more secure. The United States would build a new economy for Iraqis based on free enterprise and opportunity. American companies would gain new investment opportunities that would also benefit average Iraqis. The new Iraqi economy would be a model for others in the region to move away from state-based to market-based systems.

THEORY IN THE WORLD
THEORY IN THE WORLD

INTERNATIONAL RELATIONS THEORY AND THE IRAQ WAR

What positions did different international relations theorists take on the Iraq war? Neoconservatives were the strongest supporters. The Iraq War was "the right war for the right reasons," Robert Kagan and William Kristol still argued in 2004:

> It is fashionable to sneer at the moral case for liberating an Iraqi people long brutalized by Saddam's rule. Critics insist mere oppression was not sufficient reason for war, and in any case that it was not Bush's reason. In fact, of course, it was one of Bush's reasons, and the moral and humanitarian purpose provided a compelling reason for a war to remove Saddam Hussein. . . . The moral case for war was linked to strategic considerations related to the peace and security of the Middle East. . . . It will continue to be the case that the war was worth fighting, and that it was necessary.

Support also came from "liberal interventionists," such as Michael Ignatieff, then both a leading scholar and journalist and later a political leader in Canada:

> If the consequence of intervention is a rights-respecting Iraq in a decade or so, who cares whether the intentions that led to it were mixed at best? . . . A lot of people who would call themselves defenders of human rights opposed intervention in Iraq for sound, prudential reasons—too risky, too costly, not likely to make America safer—but prudence also amounted to a vote for the status quo in the Middle East, and that status quo had at its heart a regime that tortured its citizens, used poison gas against its own population and executed people for the free exercise of religious faith.

The historian John Lewis Gaddis took a mixed view. He praised what he saw as

> a *grand* strategy. What appeared at first to be a lack of clarity about who was deterrable and who wasn't turned out to be a plan for transforming the entire Muslim Middle East: for bringing it, once and for all, into the modern world. There'd been nothing like this in boldness, sweep and vision since Americans took it upon themselves, more than a half century ago, to democratize Germany and Japan.

Yet he also acknowledged that "within a little more than a year and a half, the United States exchanged its long-established reputation as the principal *stabilizer* of the international system for one as its chief *destabilizer*. This was a heavy price to pay to sustain momentum, however great the need for it may have been."

Among the strongest critics were such Realist scholars as John Mearsheimer and Stephen Walt, who argued on the eve of the war:

> Both logic and historical evidence suggest a policy of vigilant containment would work, both now and in the event Iraq acquires a nuclear arsenal. . . . If the United States is, or soon will be, at war with Iraq, Americans should understand that a compelling strategic rationale is absent. This war would be one the Bush administration chose to fight but did not have to fight. . . . None of the nightmare scenarios invoked by preventive-war advocates are likely to happen.

Francis Fukuyama, one of the original neoconservatives, became another major critic of the Iraq War. Fukuyama felt that it was "very doubtful . . . that history will judge the Iraq war kindly." In his assessment, the effect of the overall war on terrorism was net negative: "Iraq has now replaced Afghanistan as a magnet, training ground, and operational base for jihadist terrorists." He also stressed the "enormous costs," including the strategic consequence that "preoccupation with Iraq limits Washington's options in other parts of the world and has distracted the attention of senior policy makers from other regions such as Asia that in the long run are likely to present greater strategic challenges." He went so far as to characterize the Bush administration's emphasis on regime change as "almost obsessive."

The historian Lloyd Gardner crystallized some of the more sweeping critiques:

> The Bush administration succeeded in using WMD to scare the nation into giving it a green light to bring down Saddam Hussein's dictatorship. . . . The real issue was never the disarmament of Iraq, but fulfilling the long-term goal of finding a "friendly" government to carry out the American global mission. . . . To get to the point where the neocons wanted to take the United States, the road led through Baghdad. . . . This ideology is married to a political economy that simply ignores—at its peril, we are discovering—any limits on the sacrifice of its own citizenry to be able to place high-tech centurions around the globe. It was all going to be so easy.

Sources: Robert Kagan and William Kristol, "The Right War for the Right Reasons," in *The Right War? The Conservative Debate on Iraq*, Gary Rosen ed. (New York: Cambridge University Press, 2005), 18–19, 35; Michael Ignatieff, "Why Are We in Iraq? (And Liberia? And Afghanistan?)," *New York Times Magazine*, September 7, 2003, 71–72; John Lewis Gaddis, *Surprise, Security and the American Experience* (Cambridge, Mass.: Harvard University Press, 2004), 94, 101 (italics in original); John J. Mearsheimer and Stephen M. Walt, "An Unnecessary War," *Foreign Policy* 134 (January–February 2003): 59, 56–57; Francis Fukuyama, *America at the Crossroads: Democracy, Power and the Neoconservative Legacy* (New Haven: Yale University Press, 2006), 2; Lloyd C. Gardner, "Present at the Culmination: An Empire of Righteousness," in *The New American Empire: A 21st-Century Teach-In on U.S. Foreign Policy*, Lloyd C. Gardner and Marilyn R. Young, eds. (New York: New Press, 2005), 3, 5, 21, 27.

PRINCIPLES   American principles were manifested in the liberation of the Iraqi people. The Bush administration had proclaimed the overarching foreign policy goal of bringing democracy to the Middle East. Positive effects could be seen in smaller but still significant moves toward democratization in Saudi Arabia, Egypt, and elsewhere.

Some counterarguments:

POWER   The Bush administration was right about one thing: Iraq had a demonstration effect—largely, though, the opposite of what was intended. It showed the limits of American power. It left American leadership in tatters. The ineffectiveness of the way the war was fought disillusioned even many supporters. Francis Fukuyama, one of the original neoconservatives but a strong opponent of the Iraq War, saw it as "very doubtful . . . that history will judge the Iraq war kindly."[63]

PEACE   As critics warned all along, the line between being a liberating force and an occupying one proved a lot harder to walk than the Bush administration wanted Americans to believe. Terrorism was strengthened both within Iraq and globally. America's reputation and credibility were dramatically diminished in many countries, particularly in the Arab world. In a global context, many of the international norms and institutions that the United States had worked for over fifty years to build up as structures of international peace and stability were severely damaged.

PROSPERITY   The Bush administration manipulated the budget numbers; the White House's leading economic adviser was fired for saying so. The American economy was weakened by the hundreds of billions added to the federal budget deficit. Some estimates projected the costs of the Iraq War as high as $3 trillion. The further instability in Iraq added to the forces pushing global oil prices, and especially the price at the pump for the average American, higher and higher. And the Iraqi people suffered through even worse economic conditions than before Saddam fell.

PRINCIPLES   The Iraqi people's thirst for democracy, as shown in their participation in their first free elections, deserves praise and admiration. But all in all, American principles have been more undermined than reinforced. The Abu Ghraib and Haditha scandals resonated around the world. So did revelations of the mistreatment of prisoners at the Guantánamo Bay prison and elsewhere in violation of the Geneva Conventions on torture. The basic trust that the United States had built up with so much of the world—what one astute foreign observer has called the "huge reservoirs of goodwill towards America among the six billion other inhabitants of this earth"—was being called into question not just by those on the side of "evil" but also by those who had looked to the United States for hope, inspiration, and leadership.[64]

Iran

During the Cold War, as discussed in Part I, the shah of Iran was a major U.S. ally. But since he was overthrown in 1979 by the Islamist revolution led by Ayatollah Ruhollah Khomeini, U.S.-Iranian relations have been tense, to say the least. The seizure of the American embassy and the taking of American hostages in November 1979 led the Carter administration to break off diplomatic relations. The Reagan administration tilted toward Iraq in the 1980–88 Iran-Iraq war, although it did undertake an ill-fated arms-for-hostages deal with Iran. The Bush administration continued the tilt toward Iraq right up until Saddam Hussein's invasion of Kuwait in 1990; even as it turned against Iraq it did not turn toward Iran.[65] Economic sanctions were ratcheted up during the Clinton administration. Relations with Iran became even tenser during the George W. Bush administration, with its "axis of evil" formulation and its threat of regime change, the Iraq War, and revelations that Iran appeared to be developing nuclear weapons in violation of its commitments under the *Nonproliferation Treaty (NPT)*. The Obama administration pursued its own mix of diplomatic engagement and coercive pressure through tighter sanctions and covert operations, such as the injection of the "Stuxnet" computer virus into Iranian nuclear technology.

Iran has insisted that its nuclear energy programs are for peaceful uses only, and that these are both consistent with the NPT and within its sovereign rights. But much of the world—the United States, the European Union, the UN Security Council, the International Atomic Energy Agency (IAEA), Israel—has disputed this. Though the evidence has yet to be definitive, it has certainly been more than suggestive.

Three main policy options have been debated for dealing with the Iranian nuclear proliferation threat: coercive diplomacy, military strikes, and grand bargaining. Coercive diplomacy has been a mix of economic sanctions and other pressures short of military force (e.g., the Stuxnet virus) combined with multilateral diplomacy to negotiate an agreement. The United States and many European countries had their own economic sanctions for a number of years. The UN Security Council first imposed multilateral sanctions on Iran in 2007, with further resolutions in ensuing years for tighter sanctions, including sanctions on purchases of Iranian oil. The "EU-3"—Britain, France, and Germany—took the lead in negotiations in the mid-2000s. In the late Bush and the Obama administrations the "P-5+1"—the five permanent members of the UN Security Council (the United States, Russia, China, Britain, France) plus Germany—took over. Other countries such as Turkey and Brazil have also been involved. The strategy has been one of carrots and sticks, to provide Iran with incentives for making a deal while also imposing costs for not doing so.

Some have called for military strikes. "Iran is right at the top of the list," Vice President Cheney told the radio host Don Imus in January 2005.[66] Cheney reportedly pushed hard within the Bush administration for attacking Iran, but President Bush resisted. The Obama administration took an all-options-on-the-table position, implying that military strikes could be resorted to. The president went a step further in a speech to the American-Israel Public Affairs Committee (AIPAC) during the 2012 election campaign, stating that "I do not have a policy of containment; I have a policy to prevent Iran from obtaining a nuclear weapon. And as I have made clear time and again during the course of my presidency, I will not hesitate to use force when it is necessary to defend the United States and its interests."[67] Advocates of the military option point to three main justifications: first, the threat to Israel, especially amid the Iranian leadership's calls for the destruction of Israel, along with denials of the Nazi Holocaust and other inflammatory rhetoric; second, broader Middle East destabilization from cascading proliferation as countries like Saudi Arabia feel the need to match the Iranian nuclear arsenal and from an Iran that would be even more aggressive behind what it might see as its nuclear shield; and third, the undermining of global nonproliferation by yet another country defying the norms and rules. Opponents make their own three main points: that military action might set the Iranian nuclear program back but wouldn't destroy it, and instead would make Iran even more defiant and determined to get nuclear weapons; that risks of escalation include the incitement to terrorism, whether directed by Iran and/or from sympathizer groups angered by yet another Western attack on a Muslim country (even if done by Israel alone, the U.S. would likely be deemed complicit); and that there would be discrediting of the United States across the Arab world, Sunni countries included, amid the political dynamics set off by the 2011 Arab Spring.[68]

The argument for the grand bargain option is that the nuclear issue is part of broader Iranian-American tensions and can only be resolved in the context of a fundamental improvement in relations akin to the U.S.-Soviet détente that helped end the Cold War. Just as Americans have their own historical grievances rooted in the 1979 hostage affair, Iranians have theirs going back to the 1953 CIA role in the overthrow of the Mossadegh government (Chapter 5) and U.S. support for the shah and his secret police.

Human rights and democracy promotion also have been issues. They were especially salient when the June 2009 Iranian presidential election was hotly disputed over substantial evidence of fraud in Mahmoud Ahmadinejad's claim to re-election. Iranians protested in numbers not seen since the fall of the shah, rallying in what became known as the "Green Movement" (for the official color of opposition presidential candidate, Mir Hossein Musavi). The Ahmadinejad regime and the Supreme (religious) Leader Ayatollah Ali Khamenei responded with brutal repression, yet protests continued. Calculating that speaking out too much would play into the regime's effort to blame the unrest on the United States and other foreigners, the Obama administration was initially restrained in its support for the Green Movement. This strategy was supported by some as pragmatic, criticized by others as weak and not true to American principles.

The debate over Iran policy extends to regime change and echoes the debate over Iraq. Many of those who supported the Iraq War make comparable arguments about Iran. Opponents see the Iraq War as exactly why regime change should not be pursued in Iran.

The Arab-Israeli Conflict

The Arab-Israeli conflict (see Map 11.2) has gone through four major regional wars (1948, 1956, 1967, 1973), two Palestinian *intifadas* (1987–93 and 2000–2004), two Israeli-Lebanon wars (1982, 2006), two Israel-Gaza wars (2008, 2012), and other violence and instability. The core issue has been "land for peace," meaning recognition by the Arabs of Israel's right to exist and a genuine commitment to peaceful coexistence with Israel, Israel's return of territories captured in the 1967 war, and creation of a Palestinian state. Intensive U.S. peace brokering in the Middle East goes back at least to Secretary of State Henry Kissinger's *shuttle diplomacy* during and following the 1973 Arab-Israeli war, working out ceasefires and other agreements among Israel, Egypt, Jordan, Syria, and others in the region. The main breakthrough came in the 1979 *Camp David Accords* between Egypt and Israel, negotiated by the Egyptian president Anwar Sadat, the Israeli prime minister Menachem Begin, and the U.S. president Jimmy Carter. Egypt became the first Arab state to make peace with Israel, and consistent with the land-for-peace formula, it regained territories such as the Sinai Peninsula, which it had lost in the 1967 war.

One of the main reasons the Middle East peace process took off in the early 1990s was the transformed regional context caused by the end of the Cold War and the U.S.-led victory in the Gulf War. Without the Soviet Union, Middle East "rejectionists" (those who reject peace with Israel) such as the PLO were bereft of a superpower patron. In contrast, with the United States' profound political victory in the Cold War and overwhelming military victory in the Gulf War, the country's prestige was at an all-time high. Seeking to capitalize on this, the first Bush administration called a Middle East peace conference for October 1991, held in Madrid, Spain.[69]

The major breakthrough came in 1993 with the Israeli-Palestinian Declaration of Principles (DOP), signed by Israel's prime minister Yitzhak Rabin and the Palestine Liberation Organization (PLO) leader Yasir Arafat alongside President Bill Clinton. "It is time to put an end to decades of confrontation and conflict," the DOP stated, "and strive to live in peaceful coexistence and mutual dignity and security and achieve a just, lasting and comprehensive peace." Since the negotiations actually had been conducted during secret talks in Oslo, Norway, the agreement was dubbed the *"Oslo agreement."* Once the talks were completed, though, the signing ceremony took place in Washington. The United States played the major diplomatic role in brokering the follow-up agreements,

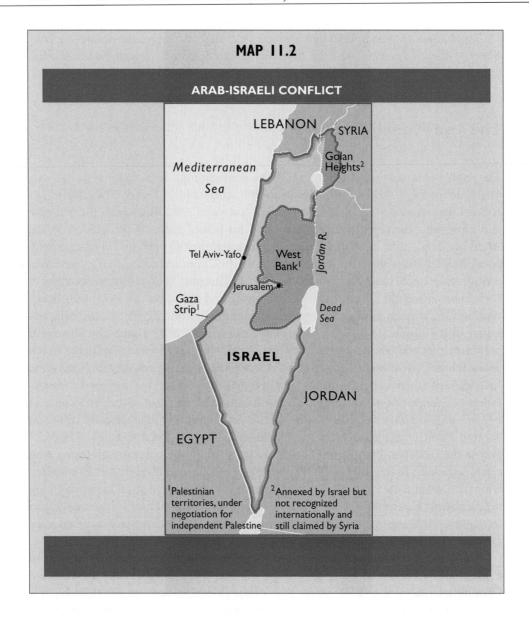

MAP 11.2

ARAB-ISRAELI CONFLICT

LEBANON

SYRIA

Golan
Heights[2]

Mediterranean

Sea

Tel Aviv-Yafo

West
Bank[1]

Jordan R.

Jerusalem

Gaza
Strip[1]

*Dead
Sea*

ISRAEL

JORDAN

EGYPT

[1]Palestinian
territories, under
negotiation for
independent Palestine

[2]Annexed by Israel but
not recognized
internationally and
still claimed by Syria

including the 1994 Israel-Jordan treaty, and in trying to move the process along toward a comprehensive peace.

Prior to 1993, Arafat and the PLO considered the United States an enemy, and the United States condemned and opposed them as terrorists. But for a number of reasons those views changed. For Arafat, although other world leaders had received him for many years, the invitation to the White House conferred a degree of legitimacy and status that could come only from Washington. The United States also was the key to unlocking international economic assistance. Arafat also knew that if there ever was to be peace and independence for his people, only the United States could provide the combination of reassurance, persuasion, and pressure that was necessary for Israel to agree.

The 1993 DOP set a five-year timetable for final status agreement on a just, lasting, and comprehensive peace. It failed to fulfill this. The Clinton administration called its own Camp David summit in July 2000, and then a last-ditch effort in Taba, Egypt, in January 2001 just before President Clinton left office.[70]

On the ground, violence again raged. The Palestinians launched a second *intifada* marked by suicide bombings and other terrorist acts. The Israeli military, with Ariel Sharon as prime minister, reoccupied many parts of the West Bank and Gaza. The Bush administration refused to meet with Yasir Arafat and struck common chords with Sharon about fights against terrorism. A peace plan known as the "road map" was proposed by the "quartet" of the United States, the European Union, Russia, and the United Nations. But it did not have much impact.

Some progress was made in 2004–05. In late 2004, Arafat died. Many attributed to Arafat a major part of the responsibility for the breakdown of the peace process. Arafat also had been losing standing with the Palestinian people because of corruption and human rights violations. He was succeeded by Mahmoud Abbas, the new leader of Arafat's political organization, Fatah, and generally viewed as more pragmatic. On the Israeli side, Prime Minister Sharon was shifting his approach and strategy. Sharon had been elected on a platform of peace with security. Yet he too saw that although there was no guarantee that peace would bring security, Israel could never have real security without peace. In 2005 Sharon took the bold step of unilaterally withdrawing from Gaza, meaning both pulling out the Israeli military and disbanding Israeli settlements. He ran for reelection on a much more pro-peace platform than he'd originally been elected on, including withdrawals and settlement disbandment in the West Bank.

In January 2006, however, two events halted whatever momentum had been building. Ariel Sharon had an incapacitating stroke. He was replaced by Ehud Olmert, whose positions on key issues were largely the same as Sharon's but who lacked Sharon's personal credibility. On the Palestinian side, parliamentary elections were held. The winner was Hamas, an Islamic fundamentalist group that had been a major perpetrator of terrorism and a staunch opponent of peace, but which also had been gaining popular support through its domestic agenda of fighting corruption within the Palestinian government and providing social services to the Palestinian people. Outside observers deemed the elections free and fair.

This posed a dilemma for the Bush administration. It had been strongly advocating democracy in the Arab world, yet in this election the winner was a group that was on the U.S. terrorism list and whose charter called for the destruction of Israel. The Bush policy, and also that of much of Europe, was to suspend financial aid to the Hamas government.

Tensions increased, not only between Palestinians and Israelis but also between Hamas and Fatah. Violence, both Israeli-Palestinian and Palestinian-Palestinian, was again on the rise.

In mid-July 2006, Hezbollah, the Lebanese Islamic terrorist and political force closely allied with Iran, crossed the border and kidnapped two Israeli soldiers. Over the next month, war intensified between Israel and Hezbollah. In one sense, everyone lost. Hezbollah and Lebanon suffered massive damage, many lives were lost, and much of the Lebanese economy and infrastructure, which had been reconstructed after decades of war, were again in ruins. Israel not only suffered damage to several northern cities and a relatively large number of deaths for such a small population, but also experienced further erosion of its security. Its military, which had been formidable in previous wars, performed poorly. Part of the problem could be traced to failures in planning and execution. Much had to do with the difference between the more conventional combat methods of taking on Arab state armies and air forces, which the Israelis were well equipped and trained for, and the asymmetric warfare required against an enemy such as Hezbollah. This problem was similar to that encountered by U.S. forces in Iraq and Afghanistan. Notwithstanding the damage the Israeli armed forces did inflict, Hezbollah ended up with greater political power within Lebanon and enhanced prestige in the Arab world for having stood up to Israel.

In late December 2008, the Gaza war broke out. Citing increased rocket attacks by Hamas on Israeli populations in nearby towns, Israel invaded Gaza. This war was even more controversial than the 2006 Lebanon war. On the one hand, Israelis felt they had a stronger claim to acting in self-defense, given Hamas's attacks on Israeli towns. Israel also received a degree of tacit support, or at least less overt opposition and criticism, from such surrounding Arab states as Egypt, Jordan, and Saudi Arabia, which were concerned about Hamas's fundamentalism and links to Iran. On the other hand, numerous reports of civilian casualties and humanitarian emergencies among the Gazan people, including some accusations of war crimes, had damaging international political effects and raised ethical questions. Assessments of the war's impact on the ground varied. Some saw Israeli success in the killing or capture of Hamas leaders and members and the Israeli military's demonstration of its will and capacity to respond. Others questioned whether even this degree of military success left Israel more secure in a sustainable way, considering the political damage of the humanitarian consequences.

The Gaza war came during the Bush-Obama transition. If the Obama transition team had any doubt about the need to engage quickly in Arab-Israeli diplomacy, the Gaza war dispelled it. This was a shift from the Bush policy, which had relegated the Arab-Israeli peace process to a lower priority. Through much of the first year of the Obama administration, U.S.-Israeli relations were tense. Benjamin Netanyahu had returned to office as the Israeli prime minister, leading a largely right-wing coalition. Netanyahu and Obama clashed over the issue of Israeli settlements. The Obama administration pushed hard for a full freeze on settlements. The Netanyahu government resisted. Amid this and other issues, Israeli public opinion polls showed Obama's approval at below 10 percent. On the

U.S. side, controversies over the "Israel lobby" were exacerbated. Still, cooperation continued on a number of fronts, including joint military exercises, continued diplomatic consultations, and President Obama's reiteration that despite policy differences, U.S. support for Israel's security and survival remained firm.

On the Palestinian side, along with and related to the peace process with Israel, were the economic and security challenges of moving toward a viable state. In June 2009, along with colleagues from a number of American universities, I met in Ramallah with Palestinian prime minister Salam Fayyad. Though we did discuss the peace process, most of the focus was on economic and security policies geared to making life better for the Palestinian people. There was recognition that while economic and security progress could not go past a certain point unless peace was achieved, making that progress would help the move toward peace. Such progress would also strengthen Fatah in its internal competition with Hamas and other forces.

But no significant progress was made on an Israeli-Palestinian peace. The 2011 "Arab Spring" further compounded the issues. While Israelis often criticized Egypt and President Hosni Mubarak for confining their 1979 Camp David treaty to a "cold peace," they now worried whether the new Egyptian government led by the Muslim Brotherhood would even abide by the treaty. Others felt that the Muslim Brotherhood's Islamist credentials would give them more credibility than Mubarak among the Palestinians and other Arab peoples for helping broker a peace.

In November 2012 stepped-up violence broke out between Israel and Gaza. This came close to another war but a ceasefire was worked out through Egyptian and American diplomacy. President Obama made Israel the destination for the first foreign trip of his second term (March 2013). The goals were to get off to a better start with the Netanyahu government (also recently re-elected, though with less of a margin than many anticipated) and connect more to the Israeli public. The following month major new arms sales to Israel were announced.* Part of the strategy was to see if such affirmations of U.S. support for Israel would help get Israeli-Palestinian peace talks going again. Secretary of State Kerry made trips before and after, as well as with President Obama, signaling that he was intent on engaging more directly and consistently in peace process diplomacy than Secretary Clinton had been. Meanwhile, the Palestinians were going through their own political dynamics, as Prime Minister Salam Fayyad resigned and Hamas-Fatah tensions persisted.

Amid these and other uncertainties, two things are clear. One is that as difficult as peace is today, it will be even more difficult tomorrow. More children on both sides will grow up socialized into hatred. More violence will be perpetrated. More distrust will build up. More windows of opportunity will slam shut.

---

*Arms sales to Saudi Arabia and the United Arab Emirates were included in the same package, as part of strengthening defense and deterrance against Iran.

The other is that American interests will continue to be significantly affected by the Arab-Israeli conflict. The strategies for peace brokering are not necessarily the same as those used by Secretary of State Kissinger after the 1973 war, or by President Carter at Camp David, or by President Clinton in the Oslo process. But the history of recent decades has been that progress in Middle East peace requires the United States to play a central role.

Arab Spring: Power and Principles

It started with a vegetable vendor. That last insult and last extortion by a Tunisian municipal official was too much for twenty-six-year-old vendor Mohammed Bouazizi. On December 17, 2010, he set himself on fire.[71]

His one-man protest spread. Within weeks, Zine El Abidine Ben Ali, the Tunisian dictator for almost a quarter century, fell and fled. In mid-February 2011 Egyptian president Hosni Mubarak, in office even longer than Ben Ali, was brought down. So, too, was the even-longer-serving president Ali Abdullah Saleh in Yemen. Then Muammar Qaddafi in Libya. Protests shook the Bahraini monarchy. There were stirrings in Saudi Arabia, Jordan, Morocco, the United Arab Emirates, and Oman. Syria was torn by brutal civil war.

Much has been made of the role of technology in the "*Arab Spring*," which has come to be called the "Facebook-Twitter" revolution. There's some truth to that. Information and communication always are key to reform and revolution. During the Cold War, Soviet dissidents like Andrei Sakharov and Alexsandr Solzhenitsyn, as well as Soviet Jews, improvised their *samizdat* (clandestine circulation) by reproducing documents with carbon paper, xeroxing however they could. Facebook and Twitter are samizdat on steroids, so much faster and with such wider reach.

But while new technologies have been crucial to the protests and changes in the Arab world, other deep societal dynamics were also being tapped into (Reading 11.3):

11.3

"Wizard of Oz" effect: Recall the scene when Dorothy pulls back the curtain and reveals that the great Oz is nothing more than an unimposing man? The fall of the first Arab dictator punctured the aura of invincibility surrounding political leaders and countered the sense of popular powerlessness. "Generations believed we could do nothing," one protester in Jordan affirmed, "and now, in a matter of weeks, we know that we can."[72]

Political repression: While Mubarak long had rigged elections, his party "winning" almost 95 percent of the seats in the fall 2010 Egyptian parliamentary elections took this to an extreme. While Qaddafi long had been repressive, his prisons were getting ever fuller, the torture more severe. While Assad long had ruled with an iron hand, when the police responded to the slogan "The people want the regime to fall"—written on a wall

in the small city of Deraa—by arresting the children who'd done the scrawling, a resonant chord was struck.

Socioeconomic inequality: Egypt, for example, was 109th in the world in GDP per capita,
and 101st on the Human Development Index (including education, life expectancy, and
other social indicators). Moreover, the gap between the rich and poor had been widening
in recent years, a fact highlighted by the spate of gated communities being built in and
around Cairo and other major Egyptian cities.

Corruption: The need to continually pay small-scale bribes to local officials was what
drove Bouazizi to suicide. But the corruption was systemic. Ben Ali's family and cronies
lived in luxury, as did Mubarak's and the others. While Tunisia and Egypt were "only"
59th and 98th on the NGO Transparency International's corruption index, Syria was
127th and Yemen and Libya were tied for 146th.

Generational change: About 60 percent of the population in the Arab world is under
thirty. The median age is around twenty-six. This "youth bulge" was not finding anything
close to the economic, political, or personal opportunities that it sought. This generation
didn't buy as much into the narrative of heroic anticolonialism that partially palliated
their parents and grandparents. In these and other ways, the gap between the aspirations
of Arab youth and the actualities of their lot was wide and getting wider.

Gender: In 2002, the *Arab Human Development Report*, written by a group of prominent
Arab intellectuals and policy experts, stressed the gender gap as particularly acute in their
countries. Only one-fourth of women were in the labor force. There is not a single Arab
country in which women have political rights equal to men's. Political change presented
an opportunity to narrow that gap, starting at the most basic level of how technology
empowered young women in traditional villages, allowing them "to bypass the men—
fathers, brothers, husbands—who circumscribed their worlds and their ability to communicate. They cannot go to the park unaccompanied and meet friends, but they can
join a chat room or send instant messages."[73]

For U.S. foreign policy, which while espousing Principles has historically followed the
Power-based adage "He may be an SOB but he's our SOB,"[74] the Arab Spring has posed
major challenges. "For sixty years," Bush administration secretary of state Condoleezza
Rice acknowledged, "my country, the United States, pursued stability at the expense of
democracy in this region here in the Middle East—and we achieved neither."[75] Yet while
the Bush administration spoke about its freedom agenda, it largely kept to the "he's our
SOB" strategy of supporting the U.S.-friendly dictators in the region. The Obama administration was slow to shift, but at the key moment did withdraw support from longtime
U.S. ally Mubarak. But in other cases involving U.S. allies, such as Bahrain, the Obama
administration's policy was more mixed, with pressure for political reform limited by concern about continued access for the U.S. Navy's Fifth Fleet to a military base in Bahrain.

Some argue that political reform should be supported not just as a matter of values but also for strategic reasons, that is, as Power-Principles complementarity.[76] The Arab Spring has shown that autocratic rulers do not bring stability, and that the supposed security benefits of supporting them are not sustainable. In a sense, the situation goes back to another old adage: "Those who make peaceful change impossible make violent revolution inevitable."[77]

Further complicating the U.S. policy debate is the prevalence of political Islam among the movements and groups gaining power in the Arab world. With different forms and different political strengths in different Arab countries, political Islam is part of the mix more often than not. A key is to not make the same mistake that U.S. foreign policy did during the Cold War of lumping together as part of the Soviet orbit leaders, parties, and movements that in any way smacked of radicalism. This was a central factor in many U.S. foreign policy failures during the Cold War in the then-Third World. While transnational links to Al Qaeda, Iran, or others need to be taken into account, they must not automatically subsume national differentiations. Within those national differentiations, further assessments must be made of the goals, strategies, visions, and leadership of the respective parties and movements. Blithe generalizations, binary thinking, and fear-mongering distort both the political dialogue and the analytic capacity needed to pursue policies differentiated according to the particular political dynamics of the different countries of the Arab world and the strategic challenges posed.[78]

All told, political instability of an unprecedented scope, severity, and duration is likely to continue. Democracy does not spring forth like Athena from Zeus's head. It takes a long time to build. "It's an entire country that needs to be remade," as a Tunisian mayor put it. "It's not going to be one year, or two years, or three years. It's going to be an entire generation."[79] Even after the initial Arab Spring changes, the Middle East-North Africa region still is the least free region in the world, with 72 percent of the countries and 85 percent of the people still denied basic political rights and civil liberties.[80] Nor is sustainable political stability only about elections and political process. Democracy must deliver on the economic and social-justice issues that underlie the revolts, and on which the internal political competition and overall stability of the system depend. That means more than just GDP growth rates and larger amounts of foreign investment; it also has to be about greater equity and penetrating beyond elites into societies to alleviate problems.

Foreign Policy Politics Case Study: Counter-Terrorism and the National Security–Civil Liberties Great Debate

September 11, 2001, transformed foreign policy politics no less than foreign policy strategy. For the first time since the end of the Cold War, there was an Enemy. Not just a number of "small-e" enemies, or the possibility that a major one might emerge down the road; Osama bin Laden, Al Qaeda, and terrorism writ large—together these constituted a "capital-e" Enemy.

The stakes now were higher than at any point since the Cuban missile crisis in 1962. The threat was here at home, not just out there. The terrorists could target average citizens in their daily lives, anywhere, anytime. As bad as the September 11 attack was, the next one could be much worse.

Initially, consistent with the historical pattern of "politics stopping at the water's edge" during crises and times of war, foreign policy politics was characterized by broad domestic consensus. Congress overwhelmingly voted to support the Afghanistan war. The 2001 USA PATRIOT Act* was passed by near unanimous votes. The Department of Homeland Security (DHS) was created. Congress voted overwhelmingly in support of the Iraq War.

But although this new political consensus had its foreign policy benefits, it also raised difficult issues, just as consensuses had in the past. Moreover, the consensus began to crack over some counter-terrorism issues that re-raised the tensions between national security and civil liberties.

National Security, the Bill of Rights, and the War on Terrorism

As in the past, one of the toughest balances to strike is between national security and the Bill of Rights. How can the United States make security against terrorism a priority in this new and threatening age, while safeguarding the freedoms and rights on which it was founded and that have been fundamental to American democracy for more than two hundred years?

Such debates did not split along standard liberal and conservative, Democratic and Republican lines. For example, William Safire, a noted conservative columnist and outspoken hawk on national security issues, warned about the dangers of greater government surveillance: "Is this the kind of world we want? The promise is greater safety; the tradeoff is government control of individual lives. Personal security may or may not be enhanced by this all-seeing eye and ear, but personal freedom will surely be sharply curtailed."[81] Yet Democrats in Congress voted overwhelmingly for the USA PATRIOT Act and other laws that prioritized national security over civil liberties.

Two sets of questions lie at the heart of the various national security–civil liberties issues. First, what should the scope of governmental and especially presidential powers be? How much power is justified in the name of national security? Second, how is accountability in the exercise of those powers to be ensured? How can checks and balances, judicial review, freedom of the press, and other political mechanisms be assured?

---

*USA PATRIOT Act was the cleverly derived acronym for *Uniting and Strengthening America* (USA) by *Providing Appropriate Tools Required to Intercept and Obstruct Terrorism* (PATRIOT) Act of 2001. The USA PATRIOT Act was reauthorized with some changes in 2006.

DOMESTIC POWERS OF THE MILITARY AND INTELLIGENCE AGENCIES   In the aftermath of September 11, Americans began hearing about the Posse Comitatus Act of 1878. This law was passed during the Reconstruction era in reaction to President Ulysses S. Grant's use of federal troops to monitor elections in the former Confederate states. It prohibited the armed forces from engaging in police activities such as search, seizure, and arrest within the borders of the United States. In the century and a half since, this issue had rarely arisen. Even during World War II, domestic security against German and Japanese espionage and infiltration was maintained within these bounds. Now, given the nature of the terrorist threat, genuine debate arose about the military's role in homeland security.

One step toward more of a homeland defense role for the military was the creation of the Northern Command. The American military is organized globally into regional commands: the Southern Command covers Latin America, the European Command covers NATO and Europe, the Central Command covers the Middle East and Central Asia, the African Command covers Africa, and the Pacific Command covers South and East Asia. Never before had there been a command structure to cover the United States or the rest of North America. As an organizational issue, the creation of the Northern Command generally was seen as a necessary enhancement of national defense. What role, though, would it play and what powers would it exercise? Could it fulfill its mission within the no-policing restrictions of the Posse Comitatus law? Should this law be changed?

Even more than for the military, debate intensified over the roles of the CIA, the FBI, and the rest of the intelligence community. One of the main controversies was over application of the *Foreign Intelligence Surveillance Act (FISA)* and a secret Bush program through which the *National Security Agency (NSA)* monitored the international phone calls and e-mails of "hundreds, perhaps thousands, of people inside the United States to search for evidence of terrorist activity without the court-approved warrants ordinarily required for domestic spying."[82] The Bush administration claimed that this domestic surveillance program was necessary to track down possible terrorists linked to Al Qaeda. According to President Bush, "one of the ways to protect the American people is to understand the intentions of the enemy. . . . If they're making phone calls into the United States, we need to know why."[83] The administration also argued that the domestic surveillance program was legal, citing not only FISA but the president's inherent authority under Article II of the Constitution as the commander in chief of the military, and implicit authority in the post–9/11 bill passed by Congress authorizing the president "to use all necessary and appropriate force against those nations, organizations, or persons he determines planned, authorized, committed, or aided the terrorist attacks that occurred on September 11, 2001, or harbored such organizations or persons, in order to prevent any future acts of international terrorism against the United States by such nations, organizations or persons."

Critics saw the NSA program as a major threat to the Fourth Amendment prohibition of unreasonable searches and seizures, applied here to wiretaps and other forms of electronic eavesdropping. Before a search, the government is required to show probable cause that the items being searched for are connected with criminal activity and will be found in the place being searched—mere suspicion is not enough. With certain exceptions, a warrant must be issued by a neutral and detached magistrate before a search is conducted, and notice of the search must be given. Because it did not go through this process of oversight by the courts, the Bush NSA program raised concerns that citizens might be monitored even if they had no connection to terrorism or other criminal activity. Supporting these concerns was the Bush administration's own track record and the historical abuses by U.S. intelligence agencies during the 1960s (spying on civil rights groups and protesters against the Vietnam War). Indeed, FBI counterterrorism agents were reported to have "conducted numerous surveillance and intelligence-gathering operations that involved, at least indirectly, groups active in causes as diverse as the environment, animal cruelty, and poverty relief"—although officials said that investigators had no interest in monitoring political or social activities and that if these investigations touched on advocacy groups, they were based on evidence of criminal or violent activity at public protests or in other settings.[84]

The program's counterterrorism effectiveness also has been debated. Supporters have cited cases such as the breaking up of a planned bombing of the New York City subway system in 2004, accomplished in part through electronic surveillance. In a 2006 Canada case, the terrorist suspects were tracked through Internet chat rooms, e-mail, and telephone communications. But critics saw investigators being swamped by a "vacuum cleaner approach" that brought in much information that "led to dead ends or innocent Americans. . . . 'We'd chase a number, find it's a schoolteacher with no indication they've ever been involved in international terrorism,' said one former FBI official, who was aware of the program and the data it generated for the bureau. 'After you get a thousand numbers and not one is turning up anything, you get some frustration.'"[85]

Controversies continued into the Obama administration. In April 2009 the press reported e-mail and phone call intercepts "that went beyond the broad legal limits." The NSA responded that its operations were "in strict accordance with U.S. laws and regulations." The director of national intelligence raised the possibility that some mistakes may have been made "inadvertently," and if so, were being corrected.[86] Civil liberties advocates continued to criticize the Obama policy as more continuity with than change from the Bush policy. A 2010 investigative journalism report in the *Washington Post* showed in great detail that "the top-secret world the government created in response to the terrorist attacks of September 11, 2001, has become so large, so unwieldy and so secretive that no one knows how much money it costs, how many people it employs, how many programs exist within it or exactly how many agencies do the same work."[87] In December 2012, with strong support from the Obama administration and over the objections of civil liberties advocates, Congress approved legislation extending the electronic intercept program and making only minor changes in executive accountability.

TORTURE   The debate over torture has focused on two main issues: Did the United States torture? If so, was torture justified?

The debate over whether torture has been conducted has revolved around how torture is defined. This involves interpretations of both the U.S. Constitution and the Geneva Conventions and other international laws. President George W. Bush, Vice President Dick Cheney, and other key administration officials contended that their methods, though harsh, were not torture. The "torture memos" written by the Bush Justice Department acknowledged such practices as forced nudity, slamming detainees into walls, prolonged sleep deprivation, and dousing with ice-cold water but claimed that these "enhanced techniques" were short of torture and thus consistent with U.S. and international law.[88] They also claimed that the information gained had been vital both to apprehending the 9/11 perpetrators and to preventing another terrorist attack on the United States. This was how America captured Khalid Sheikh Mohammed, the lead planner of the 9/11 attacks. Other examples have been kept classified but show "the success of the effort," former vice president Cheney argued.[89]

Critics disagreed, strongly. How could the administration claim that waterboarding was not torture when the United States had held it to be so when Japanese soldiers inflicted it on American prisoners during World War II? Was enclosing a suspect known to be afraid of insects in a small box full of insects not torture? What about shackling a suspect to a chair for two to three weeks? Some critics acknowledged that valuable security information had been gained, but still objected on legal and ethical grounds. Others questioned the very claims of security gains. According to a former FBI agent, the information from and about Khalid Sheikh Mohammed was gained through "traditional interrogation methods . . . before the harsh techniques were introduced." Other confessions made under torture were inaccurate, even intentionally deceptive, a gambit by the tortured to tell the torturers what they wanted to hear so that the torture would stop.[90]

On his first day in office, President Obama signed an executive order banning torture. But over the course of his administration, ambivalence has been evident. He closed the CIA "black sites"—secret prisons where much of the torture was conducted—but continued to allow renditions of suspected terrorists to countries with jurisdiction which might or might not have their own prohibitions on torture. His Justice Department worked against civil suits brought by past torture victims. The 2012 Oscar-nominated movie *Zero Dark Thirty* and its portrayal of the role torture played in getting some of the information that led to the capture and killing of Osama bin Laden set off further controversy. Its "unflinching portrayal of the CIA's brutal interrogation of Al Qaeda prisoners hews close to the official record," as a *New York Times* journalist put it. "What has divided the critics, journalists and activists . . . is the suggestion that the calculated infliction of pain and fear, graphically shown in the first 45 minutes of the film, may have produced useful early clues to find" bin Laden. Senators Dianne Feinstein and Carl Levin, chairs of the Senate Intelligence and Armed Services Committees respectively, cited a

6,000 page report by their committees that while classified and unable to be released, found little evidence that information gained through torture was what led to bin Laden. Michael Morell, then the acting CIA Director, stated that the movie "creates the strong impression that the enhanced interrogation techniques that were part of our former detention and interrogation program were the key to finding bin Laden. That impression is false. . . . The truth is that multiple streams of intelligence led C.I.A. analysts to conclude that bin Laden was hiding in Abbottabad [the city in Pakistan where a Navy SEAL team found him]. Some came from detainees subjected to enhanced techniques. But there were many other sources as well. . . . Whether enhanced interrogation techniques were the only timely and effective way to obtain information from those detainees, as the film suggests, is a matter of debate that cannot and never will be definitively resolved."[91]

JUDICIAL PROCESSES   A number of issues have arisen regarding due process of the law.

Indefinite Detentions and Secrecy in the Courts   Suspicion of providing "substantial support" of Al Qaeda or "associated forces" has been grounds for indefinite detention and especially tight secrecy in the courts. Some of these cases have involved American citizens, some non-citizens within U.S. borders. "The courtroom must be closed for these cases," said Judge Michael J. Creppy, the nation's top immigration judge. "No visitors, no family and no press." This secrecy even included "confirming or denying whether such a case is on the docket." Judge Gladys Kessler of the Federal District Court in Washington, D.C., saw it differently: "The court fully understands and appreciates that the first priority of the executive branch in a time of crisis is to ensure the physical security of its citizens. By the same token, the first priority of the judicial branch must be to ensure that our government always operates within the statutory and constitutional constraints which distinguish a democracy from a dictatorship."[92] Another district court made a different ruling, saying the press and public do not have a First Amendment right to have access to such hearings. "Since the primary national policy must be self-preservation, it seems elementary that, to the extent open . . . hearings might impair national security, that security" must be taken into account.[93]

This issue also has carried over throughout the Obama administration. In early 2013 President Obama signed legislation passed by Congress which, along with sections dealing with the overall defense budget, included a provision continuing to authorize indefinite detention including of American citizens on grounds of suspicion of support for Al Qaeda and associated forces. On the one hand, President Obama stated that he would not use these powers, that he signed the bill because of the need for the other defense-related provisions. On the other hand, his Justice Department has continued to advocate for these powers, including appealing court decisions that restricted them.

Guantánamo and Military Tribunals Despite conflicts with Cuba, the United States has maintained a military base at Guantánamo Bay for over one hundred years. Since September 11, the Guantánamo base ("Gitmo") has been used as a prison for hundreds of suspected terrorists. Since Guantánamo was not within the United States, the Bush administration claimed that prisoners held there were not protected by the right of *habeas corpus* and other constitutional provisions that applied within America's own borders. They also claimed limited applicability of international laws, such as the 1949 Geneva Convention protecting prisoners of war. Human rights groups condemned the Guantánamo "legal black hole."[94] International criticism has been widespread, even from Great Britain. The Supreme Court made a number of rulings during the latter years of the Bush administration that ran counter to the administration's legal claims and practices. These somewhat constrained the use of military tribunals and affirmed *habeas corpus* rights for detainees. As a candidate, Barack Obama had campaigned on a pledge to close the Gitmo prisons and detention centers. Soon after his inauguration, he announced a plan for doing so within a year. Two years later, though, after congressional debate about such issues as relocating Gitmo prisoners to prisons in local communities and the risks of releasing the most dangerous prisoners, Obama signed an order to keep Gitmo open. Some changes were made, specifically the granting of some prisoners' civil procedures, but military tribunals were retained at the government's discretion. This set of policy decisions only kicked the issues down the road. In early 2013 reports emerged of "chaos" amidst hunger strikes by many detainees.[95]

PRESIDENTIAL POWERS The Supreme Court addressed the broad question of presidential powers in the post-9/11 world in a 2004 Guantánamo-related case, *Hamdi v. Rumsfeld.* The majority opinion, written by Justice Sandra Day O'Connor, was strong in its statement that even a state of war "is not a blank check for the President when it comes to the rights of the Nation's citizens." Citing the 1952 *Youngstown Steel* case, in which the Court had restrained powers being exercised by President Truman during the Korean War (see Chapter 2), Justice O'Connor continued: "Whatever power the United States Constitution envisions for the Executive in its exchanges with other nations or with enemy organizations in times of conflict, it most assuredly envisions a role for all three branches when individual liberties are at stake."[96]

FREEDOM OF THE PRESS The freedom of the press questions raised within the United States by aspects of the war on terrorism were in many respects even more complex and difficult than war-reporting issues had been. The Persian Gulf, Afghanistan, and Iraq wars largely stayed "over there." World War II had had an "in here" dimension because of German and Japanese espionage. But the sense of penetration of American society by the enemy in the war on terrorism is much greater. It can be exaggerated, but it is a very real concern. Should the press be restricted, for example, from breaking a story about an FBI operation aimed at an Al Qaeda cell in the United States? Perhaps a cell planning to launch a biological weapons attack might escape or evade capture if it knew it was under surveillance. Yet what if the FBI were wrong and the suspects were innocent? Breaking a story in such a situation could ensure that civil liberties are not violated and that other unwarranted consequences are not inflicted on individuals and their families.

There also were controversies over leaks. During the 2012 presidential campaign the Obama administration was accused of leaking key classified information concerning the bin Laden assassination raid and the Stuxnet virus, which was used against the Iranian nuclear weapons complex. The administration denied the charges and countercharged that the accusers were playing their own politics. At the same time the administration began cracking down internally, prosecuting and firing leakers to such an extent that freedom of the press advocates raised concerns.

DISTORTIONS OF DOMESTIC POLITICS   We've seen a number of times in American history the distorting effects on domestic politics when national security concerns run high. The national security rationale sometimes is invoked to justify policy choices for which its application is a real stretch. Take, for example, the claim made by President Bush that agricultural subsidies paid to American farmers to keep prices up were not just a farm policy or budget policy issue but a matter of national security. "This nation has got to eat," President Bush told a cheering crowd at the 2002 convention of the National Cattlemen's Beef Association in Denver, Colorado, at a time when Congress was considering a bill that would provide $172 billion in farm subsidies over ten years. "It's in our national security interests that we be able to feed ourselves. Thank goodness, we don't have to rely on somebody else's meat to make sure our people are healthy and well-fed."[97] Bush's political strategy aimed to trump economic and budgetary arguments by invoking the national security rationale as a justification. This is tried-and-true politics, but is it good policy? If eating beef is a matter of national security, then what isn't?

When the domestic consensus is too restrictive, a distorting effect occurs that cuts even deeper to fundamental questions about democracy: the equating of dissent with disloyalty. Manifesting national solidarity is one thing, the delegitimization of debate and dissent quite another. The war on terrorism has not produced repressive trends as dangerous to democracy as 1950s McCarthyism was, but it has produced some worrisome political dynamics. In the immediate aftermath of the September 11 attacks, Attorney General John Ashcroft accused critics of his domestic security policies of using tactics that "aid terrorists" and "give ammunition to America's enemies" by "erod[ing] our national unity."[98] Statements such as this were one thing that led to the concern cited earlier of the terrorism threat being overblown and the response overwrought.

OPEN SOCIETY   In a certain sense, the openness of American society is a source of vulnerability. The very values that Americans have cherished for so long, the freedoms that come with being a democracy, create opportunities for terrorism. An Al Qaeda manual told its operatives that they could find much of the information and equipment they needed in libraries, magazines, shopping malls, and other everyday parts of American life. The September 11 hijackers visited the World Trade Center a number of times, going up with the throngs of tourists to the observation deck. They bought portable global-positioning-system equipment in electronics stores. They used toll-free phone numbers to buy videotapes of the instrument panels of the jets they would hijack. They took flight lessons in American flight schools.

But how can the vulnerabilities of openness be reduced without threatening the essence of American democracy and freedom? The war on terrorism has been called a war to preserve freedom. How is it to be fought so that freedom at home is not compromised, or worse? This is the essence of the tension between national security and the Bill of Rights, one that we have seen before in American history but that may well now pose even greater dilemmas and challenges.

Summary

Since the end of the Cold War, the Middle East has posed some of the most difficult choices for American foreign policy. Its threats have presented formidable challenges to American Power. Its prospects for Peace have been hard to achieve. Its oil remains crucial to America's economy (Prosperity). Its issues test America's Principles.

The foreign policy politics issues raised by September 11 and continuing threats of terrorism have been highly contentious. They manifest some of the toughest recurring debates American democracy has seen, particularly over the balance between national security and civil liberties.

Notes

[1]Bruce W. Jentleson, *With Friends Like These: Reagan, Bush, and Saddam, 1982–1990* (New York: Norton, 1994).

[2]Dan Caldwell, *Vortex of Conflict: U.S. Policy Toward Afghanistan, Pakistan, and Iraq* (Stanford: Stanford University Press, 2011), 71 and Chapter 5.

[3]National Commission on Terrorism, *Countering the Changing Threat of International Terrorism*, report issued in 2001, http://govinfo.library.unt.edu/911/report/index/htm (accessed 3/2/13).

[4]Richard K. Betts, "The Soft Underbelly of American Primacy: Tactical Advantages of Terror," *Political Science Quarterly* 117.1 (Spring 2002): 25.

[5]Keith B. Richburg and William Branigin, "Attacks from Out of the Blue," *Washington Post*, November 18, 2001, A24.

[6]David Johnston, Don Van Natta, Jr., and Judith Miller, "Qaeda's New Links Increase Threats from Global Sites," *New York Times*, June 16, 2002, A1.

[7]Carlotta Gall, "Taliban Threat Is Said to Grow in Afghan South," *New York Times*, May 3, 2006.

[8]Dexter Filkins, "Bribes Corrode Afghans' Trust in Government," *New York Times*, January 2, 2009.

[9]Cited in Editorial, "Running Out of Time," *New York Times*, September 22, 2008.

[10]Defense Secretary Leon Panetta, "Submitted Statement on Afghanistan and Iraq," Senate Armed Services Committee, September 22, 2011, www.armed-services.senate.gov/statemnt/2011/09%20September/Panetta%2009-22-11.pdf (accessed 3/2/13).

[11]Vali Nasr, "A Deeply Disillusioning Experience," *Foreign Policy* 199 (March/April 2013), 42–51.

[12]Amir Ahmed and Chelsea J. Carter, "Panetta to Karzai: Thank U.S. for Sacrifices Rather Than Criticize," *CNN .com*, October 6, 2012, www.cnn.com/2012/10/06/world/asia/afghanistan-karzai-panetta (accessed 3/2/13).

[13]Alissa J. Rubin, "In Old Taliban Strongholds, Qualms on What Lies Ahead," *New York Times*," January 9, 2013, A1; Defense Department, Report to Congress, "Progress Toward Security and Stability in Afghanistan," December 12, 2012, www.defense.gov/news/1230_Report_final.pdf (accessed 3/2/13).

[14]Chicago Council on Global Affairs, "Americans Question War in Afghanistan," www.thechicagocouncil.org/files/Studies_Publications/POS/Survey2012/Afghanistan.aspx (accessed 3/2/13).

[15]David E. Sanger, *The Inheritance: The World Obama Confronts and the Challenges to American Power* (New York: Harmony Books, 2009), 245.

[16]Sanger, *The Inheritance,* 213–14.

[17]Andrew F. Krepinevich, "The Collapse of Pakistan," in *7 Deadly Scenarios: A Military Futurist Explores War in the 21st Century* (New York: Bantam Books, 2009), 30–62.

[18]Fred Kaplan, "Rumsfeld's Pentagon Papers: His Leaked Memo Is the Most Astonishing Document of This War So Far," *Slate*, October 23, 2003, www.slate.com/id/2090250/ (accessed 3/2/13).

[19]George W. Bush, Commencement Address, U.S. Military Academy, West Point, New York, December 9, 2008, www.clipsandcomment.com/2008/12/10/transcript-bush-delivers-defenseterrorism-speech-at-west-point-december-9/ (accessed 3/2/13).

[20]Andrew Bacevich, "Raising Jihad," *National Interest* 100 (March/April 2009), 95.

[21]Barack Obama, Inaugural Address, January 20, 2009, www.whitehouse.gov/the_press_office/President_Barack_Obamas_Inaugural_Address/ (accessed 3/2/13).

[22]Barack Obama, remarks to the Turkish Parliament, April 6, 2009, www.whitehouse.gov/the_press_office/Remarks-By-President-Obama-To-The-Turkish-Parliament/ (accessed 3/2/13); President Obama, "A New Beginning," Speech in Cairo, Egypt, June 4, 2009, www.whitehouse.gov/blog/NewBeginning (accessed 3/2/13).

[23]Elise Labott, "Global War on Terror—No More," *AC360°*, March 30, 2009, http://ac360.blogs .cnn.com/2009/03/30/global-war-on-terror-no-more/ (accessed 3/2/13).

[24]See, for example, Lawrence Freedman, *Deterrence* (Cambridge: Polity Press, 2004); Robert F. Trager and Dessislava P. Zagorcheva, "Deterring Terrorism: It Can Be Done," *International Security* 30.3 (Winter 2005/06): 87–123; Audrey Kurth Cronin, *How Terrorism Ends: Understanding the Decline and Demise of Terrorist Campaigns* (Princeton: Princeton University Press, 2009); Andrew H. Kydd and Barbara F. Walter, "The Strategies of Terrorism," *International Security* 31.1 (Summer 2006): 49–80; Bruce W. Jentleson, "Military Force against Terrorism: Questions of Legitimacy and Efficacy," in *Beyond Preemption: Force and Legitimacy in a Changing World,* Ivo H. Daalder, ed., 40–58 (Washington, D.C.: Brookings Institution, 2007).

[25]Speech to the Council on Foreign Relations, cited in Dan Robinson, "U.S. Official Defends Strategy in Yemen," *Voice of America News*, August 8, 2012, www.voanews.com/content/us-strategy-yemen-drone-strikes/1476716.html (accessed 3/2/13).

[26]Gregory D. Johnsen. "The Wrong Man for the CIA," *New York Times*, November 19, 2012, A27; Micah Zenko, "Addicted to Drones," *FP.com*, October 1, 2010, www.foreignpolicy.com/articles/2010/10/01/addicted_to_drones?page=0,0 (accessed 3/2/13).

[27]John Mueller and Mark G. Stewart, "The Terrorism Delusion: America's Overwrought Responses to September 11," *International Security* 37 (Summer 2012), 4 and 81–110; and Mueller, *Overblown: How*

Politicians and the Terrorism Industry Inflate National Security Threats and Why We Believe Them (New York: Simon and Schuster, 2006).

[28]George W. Bush, War Message, Washington, D.C., March 19, 2003, www.presidentialrhetoric.com/speeches/03.19.03.html (accessed 3/2/13).

[29]"President Bush's Message to the Iraqi People," April 10, 2003, www.gpo.gov/fdsys/pkg/WCPD-2003-04-14/pdf/WCPD-2003-04-14-Pg424-2.pdf (accessed 3/2/13).

[30]"Commander-in-Chief Lands on *USS Lincoln*," May 2, 2003. Available at www.cnn.com/2003/ALLPOLITICS/05/01/bush.carrier.landing/ (accessed 3/2/13).

[31]George W. Bush, remarks at the United Nations General Assembly, September 12, 2002, www.presidentialrhetoric.com/speeches/09.12.02.html (accessed 3/2/13).

[32]Dick Cheney, Remarks by the Vice President to the Veterans of Foreign Wars 103rd National Convention, August 27, 2002, www.nationalreview.com/document/document082702.asp (accessed 3/2/13).

[33]George W. Bush, State of the Union Address, January 28, 2003, www.presidentialrhetoric.com/speeches/01.28.03.html (accessed 3/2/13).

[34]Bob Woodward, *Plan of Attack* (New York: Simon and Schuster, 2004), 249.

[35]Transcript of Colin Powell's U.N. Presentation, February 6, 2003, www.cnn.com/2003/US/02/05/sprj.irq.powell.transcript/index.html (accessed 3/2/13).

[36]Commission on the Intelligence Capabilities of the United States Regarding Weapons of Mass Destruction [Robb-Silberman Commission], *Report to the President of the United States*, March 31, 2005, www.gpoaccess.gov/wmd/pdf/full_wmd_report.pdf (accessed 3/2/13); see also U.S. Senate, Select Committee on Intelligence, *Report on Whether Public Statements Regarding Iraq by U.S. Government Officials Were Substantiated by Intelligence Information, Together with Additional and Minority Views,* July 9, 2004, http://intelligence.senate.gov/080605/phase2a.pdf (accessed 3/2/13); Central Intelligence Agency, *Comprehensive Revised Report with Addendums on Iraq's Weapons of Mass Destruction* (Duelfer Report), rev. ed., September 2004, www.gpoaccess.gov/duelfer/index.html (accessed 3/2/13); Douglas Jehl and David E. Sanger, "The Struggle for Iraq: Intelligence; Powell's Case, a Year Later: Gaps in Picture of Iraq Arms," *New York Times,* February 1, 2004, 1.

[37]National Intelligence Council, "NIC Mission," www.dni.gov (accessed 3/2/13).

[38]Woodward, *Plan of Attack,* 194–99.

[39]Bob Drogin and John Goetz, "The Curveball Saga: How U.S. Fell Under the Spell of 'Curveball,'" *Los Angeles Times,* November 20, 2005, A1.

[40]Murray Waas, "What Bush Was Told About Iraq," *National Journal,* March 2, 2006; Waas, "Insulating Bush," *National Journal,* March 30, 2006.

[41]Senate Select Committee on Intelligence, 18.

[42]Paul R. Pillar, *Intelligence and U.S. Foreign Policy: Iran, 9/11 and Misguided Reform* (New York: Columbia University Press, 2011), 43, 47, 56. See also Dan Caldwell, *Vortex of Conflict: U.S. Policy Toward Afghanistan, Pakistan and Iraq* (Stanford: Stanford University Press, 2011), 139–47.

[43]George Packer, *The Assassins' Gate: America in Iraq* (New York: Farrar, Straus and Giroux, 2005) 45.

[44]George W. Bush, Remarks on Iraq at Cincinnati Museum Center–Cincinnati Union Terminal, Cincinnati, Ohio, October 7, 2002, www.presidentialrhetoric.com/speeches/10.7.02.html (accessed 3/2/13).

[45]Packer, *The Assassins' Gate,* 107.

[46]Cited in Frank Rich, "The Banality of Bush White House Evil," *New York Times,* April 26, 2009; see also Jonathan S. Landay, "Report: Abusive Tactics Used to Seek Iraq–al Qaida Link," McClatchy Washington Bureau, April 22, 2009, www.mcclatchydc.com/2009/04/21/report-abusive-tactics-used-to.html (accessed 3/2/13).

[47]Richard A. Clarke, *Against All Enemies: Inside America's War on Terror* (New York: Free Press, 2004), 32.

[48]Walter Pincus and Dana Milbank, "Al Qaeda–Hussein Link Is Dismissed," *Washington Post,* June 17, 2004, A1.

[49]Cheney statement on March 16, 2003, videotape shown and discussed on *Meet the Press,* September 14, 2003, www.msnbc.msn.com/id/3080244 (accessed 3/2/13); Rumsfeld cited in Bob Herbert, "The Army's Hard Sell," *New York Times,* June 27, 2005; Ken Adelman, "Cakewalk in Iraq," *Washington Post,* February 13, 2002, A27.

[50]Eric Schmitt and Joel Brinkley, "The Struggle for Iraq: Planning; State Dept. Study Foresaw Trouble Now Plaguing Iraq," *New York Times,* October 19, 2003, 1.

[51]Statements by Paul R. Pillar, CIA National Intelligence Officer for the Near East and South Asia, cited in Walter Pincus, "Ex-CIA Official Faults Use of Data on Iraq," *Washington Post,* February 10, 2006, A1.

[52]Packer, *The Assassins' Gate,* 118.

[53]James Fallows, "Blind into Baghdad," *Atlantic Monthly* (January/February 2004), 57.

[54]Packer, *The Assassins' Gate,* 114; Michael R. Gordon and General Bernard E. Trainor, *Cobra II: The Inside Story of the Invasion and Occupation of Iraq* (New York: Pantheon Books, 2006), 102–3.

[55]Iraq Coalition Casualty Count, http://icasualties.org/Iraq/index.aspx (accessed 3/2/13).

[56]Gordon Trowbridge, "Troops Sound Off: Military Times Poll Finds High Morale, But Less Support for Bush, War Effort," *Military Times,* January 5, 2006, www.militarycity.com/polls/2005_main.php (accessed 3/2/13).

[57]Gen. Barry McCaffrey (ret.), cited in Mark Danner, "The War on Terror: Four Years On; Taking Stock of the Forever War," *New York Times Magazine,* September 11, 2005, 45.

[58]George W. Bush, "The New Strategy in Iraq," address to the nation, January 10, 2007, www.presidentialrhetoric.com/speeches/01.10.07.html (accessed 3/2/13).

[59]Frederick W. Kagan, "Out of Conflict, A Partnership," *New York Times,* November 22, 2008.

[60]Lawrence J. Korb and Sean Duggan, "A Very Quiet Surge," *Guardian,* September 9, 2008.

[61]Stephen Biddle, Jeffrey A. Friedman, and Jacob N. Shapiro, "Testing the Surge: Why Did Violence Decline in Iraq in 2007?," *International Security* 37 (Summer 2012), 3 and 7–40.

[62]George W. Bush, The National Security Strategy, March 2006, 12–13, http://georgewbush-whitehouse.archives.gov/nsc/nss/2006/ (accessed 3/2/13).

[63]Francis Fukuyama, *America at the Crossroads: Democracy, Power and the Neoconservative Legacy* (New Haven: Yale University Press, 2006), 2.

[64]Kishore Mahbubani, *Beyond the Age of Innocence: Rebuilding Trust Between America and the World* (New York: Public Affairs, 2005), xvii.

[65]Bruce W. Jentleson, *With Friends Like These: Reagan, Bush, and Saddam, 1982–90* (New York: W. W. Norton, 1994).

[66]Joseph Cirincione, "Bombs Won't 'Solve' Iran," Issue Brief, *Washington Post,* May 11, 2005, www.washingtonpost.com/wp-dyn/content/article/2005/05/10/AR2005051001185.html (accessed 3/2/13).

[67]"Transcript of Obama's AIPAC speech," *Politico,* March 4, 2012, www.politico.com/news/stories/0312/73588.html

[68]In September 2012 I participated in a crisis simulation sponsored by the Brookings Institution. I was asked to play the role of National Security Advisor. See the coverage in *Newsweek* and *The Daily Beast,* October 8, 2012 www.thedailybeast.com/newsweek/2012/10/07/newsweek-s-iran-war-game.html and www.thedailybeast.com/newsweek/2012/10/07/newsweek-s-war-game-players.html

[69]The venue was symbolic because both Jews and Muslims (Moors) had been driven out of Spain in the fifteenth century during the Spanish Inquisition.

[70]Dennis Ross, *The Missing Peace: The Inside Story of the Fight for Middle East Peace* (New York: Farrar, Straus and Giroux, 2004).

[71]This draws from my article "The Remaking of the Middle East," *Duke Magazine* (May–June 2011), 37–41.

[72]Michael Slackman, "Bullets Stall Youthful Push for Arab Spring," *New York Times,* March 17, 2011, www.nytimes.com/2011/03/18/world/middleeast/18youth.html?pagewanted=all (accessed 3/2/13).

[73]Idem.

[74]While there is some debate about who first said this about whom, most historians attribute it to President Franklin D. Roosevelt about the Nicaraguan dictator Anastasio Somoza.

[75]Goodreads, "Condoleezza Rice Quotes," http://www.goodreads.com/author/quotes/48389.Condoleezza_ Rice (accessed 3/2/13).

[76]Bruce W. Jentleson, Andrew M. Exum, Melissa G. Dalton, and J. Dana Stuster, *Strategic Adaptation: Toward a New U.S. Strategy in the Middle East* (Washington, D.C.: Center for a New American Security, 2012).

[77]This is attributable to President John F. Kennedy, "Address on the First Anniversary of the Alliance for Progress," March 13, 1962, www.presidency.ucsb.edu/ws/?pid=9100#axzz1LrGlsDJa (accessed 3/2/13).

[78]Bruce W. Jentleson, "Beware the Duck Test," *Washington Quarterly* (Summer 2011), 137–49.

[79]Scott Sayare, "Zarzis Journal: Now Feeling Free, But Still Without Work, Tunisians Look to Europe," *New York Times,* March 24, 2011, http://query.nytimes.com/gst/fullpage.html?res=9B00E7DA1331F937A1 5750C0A9679D8B63&&scp=1&sq=It's%20an%20entire%20coutnry%20that%20needs%20to%20be%20r emade&st=cse.

[80]Cited in Seth G. Jones, "The Mirage of the Arab Spring," *Foreign Affairs* 92 (January/February 2013), 56.

[81]William Safire, "The Great Unwatched," *New York Times,* February 18, 2002, A19.

[82]James Risen and Eric Lichtblau, "Bush Lets U.S. Spy on Callers without Courts," *New York Times,* December 16, 2005, A1. Risen and Lichtblau were awarded the Pulitzer Prize for this and related articles.

[83]George W. Bush, "The War on Terror: At Home and Abroad," Kansas State University, Manhattan, Kansas, January 23, 2006, www.presidentialrhetoric.com/speeches/01.23.06.html (accessed 3/5/13).

[84]Eric Lichtblau, "F.B.I. Watched Activist Groups, New Files Show," *New York Times,* December 20, 2005, A1.

[85]Lowell Bergman, Eric Lichtblau, Scott Shane, and Don Van Natta Jr., "Spy Agency Data After Sept. 11 Led FBI to Dead Ends," *New York Times,* January 17, 2006, A1.

[86]Eric Lichtblau and James Risen, "N.S.A.'s Intercepts Exceed Limits Set by Congress," *New York Times,* April 16, 2009, A1.

[87]Dana Priest and William A. Arkin, "Top Secret America," *Washington Post,* July 19, 2010, http://projects .washingtonpost.com/top-secret-america/ (accessed 3/5/13).

[88]"Justice Department Torture Memos," redacted text, *New York Times,* April 16, 2009, http://documents .nytimes.com/justice-department-memos-on-interrogation-techniques#p=1 (accessed 3/5/13).

[89]Mark Silva, "Cheney: Torture Memos Miss 'Success,'" *The Swamp,* April 21, 2009, http://politicalticker .blogs.cnn.com/2009/04/21/cheney-i-dont-think-weve-got-much-to-apologize-for-2/ (accessed 3/5/13).

[90]Ali Soufan, "My Tortured Decision," *New York Times,* April 23, 2009; Peter Finn and Joby Warrick, "Detainee's Harsh Treatment Foiled No Plots," *Washington Post,* March 29, 2009, A1.

[91]Scott Shane, "Portrayal of CIA Torture in Bin Laden Film Reopens a Debate," *New York Times,* December 12, 2012, A1; "Senators Say Torture Scenes in Movie on Bin Laden are Misleading," December 19, 2012, A25; "Acting CIA Director, Michael J. Morell, Criticizes 'Zero Dark Thirty,'" December 22, 2012, A33.

[92]Adam Liptak, Neil A. Lewis, and Benjamin Weiser, "After September 11, A Legal Battle on the Limits of Civil Liberty," *New York Times,* August 4, 2002, 1, 16; Linda Greenhouse, "The Imperial Presidency vs. the Imperial Judiciary," *New York Times,* September 8, 2002, WK 3.

[93]*North Jersey Media Group, Inc., v. Ashcroft,* 308 F.3d 198 (3rd Cir. 2002).

[94]Amnesty International, "Guantánamo Bay—A Human Rights Scandal," www.amnestyen/library/info/ AMR51/159/2006 (accessed 3/5/13).

[95]Charlie Savage, "Officials Describe Chaos at Guantanamo in Weeks Before Raid on Prison," *New York Times,* April 17, 2013, A10.

[96]*Hamdi v. Rumsfeld,* 542 U.S. 507, 536 (2004).

[97]Mike Allen, "Bush Calls Farm Subsidies a National Security Issue," *Washington Post,* February 9, 2002, A4. The article also notes that the rural areas and business interests that stood to benefit most from the farm subsidies were key Bush supporters in the 2000 presidential election.

[98]Neil A. Lewis, "Ashcroft Defends Antiterrorism Plans and Says Criticism May Aid Foes," *New York Times,* December 7, 2001, A1.

12 Old Friends, Old Enemy: Twenty-First-Century Relations with Europe and Russia

Introduction: Post–Cold War Transitions in U.S. Relations with Europe and Russia

U.S. relations with Europe and Russia, each in its own way, have had to adapt to the end of the Cold War and the beginning of this new twenty-first-century era. For the United States and Europe, the challenge has been to prove wrong the geopolitical dictum that "alliances are against, and only derivatively for, someone or something."[1] It was the Soviet enemy that prompted the United States and Western Europe to create **NATO (North Atlantic Treaty Organization)** and other aspects of the Western alliance. Yet the alliance has held together even with the Soviet enemy gone—not without tensions, to be sure, but with the fundamentals still intact. The reason is that on balance it continues to serve U.S. national interests as well as those of Europe. NATO remains the most capable military alliance in the world (Power). Working together the United States and Europe can be more effective forces for Peace than each on their own. The United States and the European Union (EU) are each other's largest trade partners (Prosperity). And, as liberal democracies with shared political values, the United States and Western Europe are societies thickly interlinked both through formal institutions and more informal networks, and peoples with affinity for one another based on common culture and heritage (Principles). There is no guarantee that interests will stay this aligned. Keeping them so requires dealing effectively with key issues such as those discussed in this chapter.

With Russia, for over forty years the number-one enemy (when it was still the Soviet Union), the challenge has been transitioning to a new relationship. Will relations improve to the point that Russia genuinely could be considered a friend or even an ally? Does

MAP 12.1

EUROPE

U.S.–Russian cooperation have limits based on differences in national interests and other factors that may lead even a noncommunist, non–Soviet Russia to reemerge as a great-power competitor of the United States? Or might foreign policy differences become so great, or might Russian domestic politics take such a turn, that the two end up again as adversaries?

This chapter's foreign policy politics case study examines the U.S. domestic politics of nuclear arms control. We go back over how these politics played out over major nuclear arms–control agreements with the Soviet Union during the Cold War as well as in the post–Cold War era.

The Atlantic Alliance in the Post–Cold War Era

From a historical perspective, an enormous amount was achieved in Europe in the second half of the twentieth century. The continent which set off both world wars as well as the Cold War avoided becoming again torn by war. The Atlantic Alliance brought the United States and Western Europe together in the greatest peacetime alliance in modern history. Europe itself began to unify. It's easy to forget how profound all three of these changes were in their time.

Since the Cold War ended, though, there were the brutal 1990s wars in three republics that were once part of the former Yugoslavia—Bosnia, Croatia, and Kosovo. The Atlantic Alliance has undergone strains over such issues as the 2003 Iraq War and more generally over NATO and its membership and mission. And the European Union (EU) has been experiencing its greatest crisis since its inception.

The 1990s Balkans Wars

BOSNIA 1992–95   During the Cold War, Yugoslavia was a communist country but much more independent of the Soviet Union than the USSR's Warsaw Pact satellites. It was held together amid ethnic and other differences by Josep Tito, who ruled until his death in 1980. Over the next decade, as internal tensions intensified and support for independence increased in constituent republics such as Slovenia, Croatia, and Bosnia, the Serbian leader Slobodan Milosevic cracked down first with political repression and then with outright warfare in order to maintain Serbian dominance. The wars that ensued in Croatia and especially Bosnia (1991–95) led to the worst bloodshed in Europe since the Nazi Holocaust during World War II—close to a million people dead or wounded and almost 2 million displaced. And these wars added a chilling new term, so-called *ethnic cleansing*, to the lexicon of warfare.

Yet the George H. W. Bush administration did not intervene. "We don't have a dog in that fight," was how Secretary of State James Baker offhandedly put it.[2] These conflicts were largely seen as a European problem, and the verdict was that the Europeans should take the lead along with the UN. During the 1992 presidential campaign, candidate Bill Clinton was harshly critical of the Bush policy and promised to be more assertive by, among other things, lifting the arms embargo against the Bosnian Muslims and launching air strikes against the Bosnian Serbs ("lift and strike"). But once in office, Clinton backed off, showing indecisiveness and succumbing to political concerns about the risks involved. "It's really a tragic problem," Secretary of State Warren Christopher stated in early 1993 amid the horrors of "ethnic cleansing" in Bosnia. "The hatred between all these groups—the Bosnians and the Serbs and the Croatians—is . . . centuries old. That really is a problem from hell."[3]

If this were true, then, whatever the stakes, both American foreign policy and the United Nations really had little chance of having much impact. But there was reason to doubt whether the problem was as intractable as Secretary Christopher portrayed it. At its core the debate was between ***primordialist*** and ***purposive*** theories of the sources of ethnic conflict.

The so-called primordialist view sees ethnicity as a fixed and inherently conflictual historical identity; thus the 1990s wars were primarily continuations of conflicts going back hundreds of years—"Balkan ghosts" going back to the fourteenth century, as one book called them.[4] In reality, though, the histories are not nearly so deterministic. A number of studies have shown that ethnic identities are much less fixed over time, and the frequency and intensity of ethnic conflict much more varied over both time and place, than primordialist theory would have it. In Bosnia, for example, the ethnic intermarriage rate in 1991 was around 25 percent, and there were very few ethnically "pure" urban residents or ethnically homogeneous smaller communities. As a Bosnian Muslim schoolteacher put it, "We never, until the war, thought of ourselves as Muslims. We were Yugoslavs. But when we began to be murdered because we are Muslims things changed. The definition of who we are today has been determined by our killing."[5]

An alternative explanation of the sources of ethnic conflict is the "purposive" view. This view acknowledges the deep-seated nature of ethnic identifications and the corresponding animosities and unfinished agendas of vengeance that persist as historical legacies. But the purposive view takes a much less deterministic view of how, why, and whether or not these identity-rooted tensions become deadly conflicts. Historically shaped, yes; historically determined, no. The focus is on factors that activate and intensify historical animosities into policies and actions reflecting conscious, deliberate choices for war and violence. Milosevic's ethnic cleansing was not the playing out of historical inevitability but was instead "the purposeful actions of political actors who actively create violent conflict" to serve their own domestic political agendas by "selectively drawing on history in order to portray [events] as historically inevitable."[6]

By mid-1995 the urgency of the situation no longer could be denied. The UN and EU forces were unable to prevent the ethnic cleansing, most graphically seen in the mass killings of more than seven thousand Bosnian Muslims in a supposed safe haven, the town of Srebrenica. The Bosnian Serbs had become so brash as to take several hundred UN peacekeepers hostage. Congress was threatening to cut off aid to the UN peacekeeping mission. This not only endangered what was left of any semblance of peacekeeping and humanitarian assistance, but also threatened a crisis within NATO, because British and French troops were among the UN forces that would be endangered by such an abandonment. Then three top American officials were killed in Bosnia when their jeep hit a land mine. Realizing that it no longer had a middle option, and that the choices now were give up or get serious, the Clinton administration finally asserted American leadership. NATO air strikes were launched against Bosnian Serb forces, and with more firepower than earlier "pinprick" strikes. Military support was given to the Croatian army for a major offensive against the Serbs. Economic sanctions were ratcheted up. And diplomacy was stepped up, culminating in the peace conference convened in Dayton, Ohio.

Skilled peace brokering by President Clinton and his lead diplomat, Richard Holbrooke, helped the negotiations succeed. The warring parties signed the **Dayton Accord** in November 1995. The agreement ended the war and established terms for a political settlement. NATO was mandated to provide a peacekeeping force, and the Organization on Cooperation and Security in Europe (OSCE, formerly the CSCE) was given principal responsibility for establishing free and fair elections and for taking other political measures such as protecting human rights.

The original NATO force had about sixty thousand troops, of which about twenty thousand were American. By 2004 the peacekeeping mission was handed over to the European Union, leaving only a few U.S. troops to hunt war-crimes suspects and help train the Bosnian army. Elections were held on numerous occasions, generally meeting the criteria of free and fair. Still, almost twenty years after the outbreak of war, tensions remained high and stability was uncertain, with continuing concern that Bosnia could lapse into "a severe crisis."[7] Bosnia showed that even when much is done to build post-conflict peace, the memories of war and mass atrocities make real reconciliation extremely difficult.

KOSOVO 1999   In Kosovo, a Serbian province populated largely by Albanian Muslims against whom Milosevic had unleashed another round of ethnic cleansing, the United States and NATO acted sooner than they had in Bosnia, but still not soon or effectively enough to prevent mass killings and displacements. The threat of air strikes was made only in late 1998, many months after the first wave of Serbian aggression and despite numerous warnings and calls for earlier preventive action. When the air campaign was launched in March 1999, some argued that the United States and NATO could have prevailed more quickly, more overwhelmingly, and prevented more ethnic killing had ground troops also been sent in. Concerned that "casualty phobia" would undermine American public support, however, President Clinton had stated from the start that ground troops were "off the table." At a minimum, critics argue, the ground troops option should have been left open as a threat that could have coerced Milosevic into surrendering sooner.

Similarly mixed lessons came from Kosovo as a case of "war by alliance." This was the first time NATO had fought a war. It had trained, prepared, positioned, and formulated strategies for war throughout the Cold War, but had never actually had to fight one. To its credit, NATO did hold together politically and did carry out generally well-coordinated and effectively executed military operations in Kosovo. But this did not happen without a great deal of political pulling and tugging. As the British scholar Michael Cox put it, "Friends were politically necessary but militarily problematic."[8] Within a general consensus of common interests in defending Kosovo, different NATO members had different particular interests at stake. Yet NATO decision-making rules required unanimity, or at least no dissenting votes (some states might choose to abstain). Some in the United States saw the internal NATO politics as little more than cumbersome, getting in the way of military planning. So one aspect of Kosovo was that although the United States and NATO won, they "won ugly."[9]

The Kosovo case also brought to a head the question of who in the international community should be able to decide to use military force for humanitarian interventions? Can the United States and other major countries make this decision on their own or through alliances such as NATO? Or must it be a decision of the UN Security Council (UNSC)? In the case of Kosovo, Chinese and Russian opposition prevented UNSC action, and the United States and NATO decided on their own to intervene. Secretary-General Kofi Annan criticized the U.S.–NATO action on the grounds that the UNSC is "the sole source of legitimacy on the use of force." Yet he also acknowledged the failure of the Security Council to act as it should have done in this crisis, noting that it did not "unite around the aim of confronting massive human rights violations and crimes against humanity on the scale of Kosovo," thereby "betray[ing] the very ideals that inspired the founding of the United Nations."[10] For all the invocations of Serbian sovereignty and claims of principle made by Russia and China as reasons for opposing intervention in Kosovo, their positions were based more on their concerns about precedents that might later be applied to Chechnya, Russia's rebellious Muslim area, and to Taiwan and Tibet for China.[11] Kosovo also led to an unusual distinction when an independent international commission called the U.S.–NATO intervention illegal in the sense of not having followed the letter of the UN Charter, but legitimate in being consistent with the norms and principles that the charter embodies.[12]

Kosovo's post-conflict stability has been tenuous. The NATO peacekeeping force established at the end of the war by a UN mandate had to remain amid recurring outbreaks of violence. UN-authorized peace negotiations headed by Martti Ahtisaari, the former prime minister of Finland, led to independence for Kosovo in February 2008.* The United States

---

*Ahtisaari won the 2008 Nobel Peace Prize for his role in Kosovo negotiations as well as for other diplomacy.

and most member states of the European Union were supportive. As of early 2013 101 countries have granted Kosovo diplomatic recognition. Serbia, as well as Russia and some others, have remained opposed. Russia has used the threat of its Security Council veto to block Kosovo's membership into the UN.

Iraq War and U.S.–European Relations

Even before the Iraq War, Robert Kagan, a conservative American analyst and columnist, postulated a deep and fundamental European–American divergence: "It is time to stop pretending that Americans and Europeans share a common view of the world," he wrote. "On major strategic and international questions Americans are from Mars and Europeans from Venus: They agree on little and understand one another less and less."[13] Kagan put most of the blame on the Europeans for their naiveté regarding the need for power and force in international affairs, for lapsing further into military weakness, and for not pulling their weight in NATO, especially on global security threats.

Many Europeans saw the problems quite differently. In their view the United States had fallen into a "cult of unilateralism," characterized by an "instinctive refusal to admit to any political restraint on its action . . . placing itself above international law, norms, and restraints when they do not suit its objectives." There was some acknowledgment of "European legalistic fervour" as going too far in its own right, and of both sides' contributing to "a dialogue of the deaf."[14] But the main source of intra-alliance tensions was seen as emanating from the United States' side of the Atlantic.

Whatever one's view of the causes, it was clear by 2001–2002 that the list of issues on which the United States and western Europe were in conflict had been growing longer. That list included the Kyoto global warming treaty, the International Criminal Court, the multilateral land mines treaty, relations with Iran, the Israeli–Palestinian conflict, and a number of international trade issues. And then came the Iraq War, over which tensions ran extremely high and conflicts cut quite deep. Britain was front and center in supporting the United States, as were some other European countries. But France, Germany, and others were strongly opposed. The foreign minister of France, Dominique de Villepin, went so far as to threaten to use France's veto in the UN Security Council to try to block U.S. military action against Iraq.

Although the U.S.–French conflict over Iraq was particularly intense, tensions in this relationship were hardly new. It was in 1966, right in the middle of the Cold War, that President Charles de Gaulle took France out of the NATO military command. U.S. leaders often see France as an irksome ally, a country that hasn't come to grips with its faded imperial status. The French, in turn, often view the United States as both naive and arrogant. "For my part," Foreign Minister Hubert Vedrine stated, "I believe that since 1992 the word 'superpower' is no longer sufficient to describe the United States. That's why I use the term 'hyperpower.' . . . We cannot accept either a politically unipolar world, nor a culturally uniform world, nor the unilateralism of a single hyperpower. And that is why we are fighting for a multipolar, diversified, and multilateral world."[15] Still, despite such views and the differences over Iraq, there has been significant French–American cooperation on some issues, such as some major covert-action operations in the war on terrorism.[16]

British–American relations, though not the "special relationship" of Roosevelt and Churchill during World War II, had been close under Clinton as well as George H. W. Bush. During the Persian Gulf War, the 1990s "no-fly zone" containment strategy against Iraq, the Kosovo war, the Afghanistan war, and especially the Iraq War, British and American interests were sufficiently aligned to provide the basis for joint military action. British prime minister Tony Blair was the key ally for the George W. Bush administration during the Iraq War. In Blair's view, on Iraq and more broadly, "There never has been a time when the power of America was so necessary; or so misunderstood." Europe and America needed partnership, not rivalry, "a common will and a shared purpose in the face of a common threat. . . . [I]f we split, all the rest will play around, play us off, and nothing but mischief will be the result of it. . . . We should not minimize the differences. But we should not let them confound us either."[17]

As for Germany, one of the old sayings about NATO was that, in addition to keeping the Russians out of Europe and the Americans in, its tacit purpose was also to keep the Germans down. Germany's "traumatic past" and the determination "never again to allow German militarism and nationalism to threaten European stability" defined the parameters of Germany's foreign policy as that of a "civilian power."[18] The toughest post–Cold War issues for Germany have involved military intervention. The United States and other NATO countries deployed peacekeeping forces in Bosnia and then fought the war in Kosovo, but the former Yugoslavia had been an area of Nazi brutalization during World War II. In light of this, how would Germany balance historical memory and its present alliance obligation in deciding what role its military should take on? German troops did join in the Bosnia peacekeeping effort, and the German air force participated in the Kosovo war in ways that struck a balance and marked an evolution of, but not a departure from, the "civilian power" role. This issue came up again during the 2001 Afghanistan war, when Chancellor Gerhard Schroeder proposed committing almost four thousand German troops to the war effort. The sensitivity and complexity of the issue was evident in the fact that the bill authorizing the participation of the Bundeswehr (the German army) passed the Bundestag (the German parliament) by only two votes. Later when the Iraq War loomed, Schroeder was in the midst of a tough reelection campaign. He seized on the issue of Iraq as a way of gaining support from those German voters who had become the most anti-American. This was a striking contrast with the way pro-American positions had been good politics in Germany for decades.

American–European relations improved during President George W. Bush's second term, but only partially. Whereas in 2002, 64 percent of Europeans had viewed U.S. leadership as desirable, by 2008 only 36 percent did. Approval of President Bush's handling of international affairs was at 18 percent. Some saw the tensions as having become even more fundamental. As one group of scholars writes in *The End of the West? Crisis and Change in the Atlantic Order*, issues of "the logic and character of the Atlantic political order and its future" run deeper than just who the American president is. Indeed, whether we are *Growing Apart?*—as another book on the subject was titled—is a matter not just of the particulars of the foreign policy agenda but of social forces and other dynamics within European and American political systems and overall societies.[19] These questions still pertain even with improved European–American relations during the Obama years.

The Future of NATO

Time and again during the Cold War and at its end, pundits sounded warnings about the decline and possible death of NATO. But when the Berlin Wall fell, the Warsaw Pact (the Soviet Union's counterpart alliance to NATO) was torn up, and the Soviet Union came asunder, NATO was still standing. Its central goal—to "safeguard the freedom, common heritage and civilization of [its] peoples, founded on the principles of democracy, individual liberty, and the rule of law"—had been achieved without a single shot having been fired in anger. No wonder NATO has been touted as the most successful peacetime alliance in history.

The ensuing question has been whether NATO's very success would lead to its demise—one possible result of the aforementioned adage that "alliances are against, and only derivatively for, someone or something." With the Soviet enemy gone, did NATO really have a strong enough reason to continue? Given budgetary costs and other factors, should it just be showered with testimonials, given its "gold watch," and sent into retirement? All these questions boil down to two issues about NATO's future: its membership and its mission.

THE EXPANSION OF NATO MEMBERSHIP   At the end of the Cold War, NATO faced a problem that was the fruit of its success: its former adversaries had been defeated. Indeed, their major alliance, the Warsaw Pact, had fallen apart; their major empire, the Soviet Union, had crumbled. Confrontation had ended, and cooperation was now possible. The challenge for NATO now was how to build new cooperative relationships with these former adversaries, and with Russia in particular.

The initial transitional strategy, started by the first Bush administration and furthered by the Clinton administration, was to create new institutional mechanisms linked to NATO but not fully part of it. In 1991 all of the former Soviet and Soviet-bloc states were invited to join the North Atlantic Cooperation Council, later renamed the Euro-Atlantic Partnership Council. This was to be a mechanism for consultation on political and security issues. In 1994 the Partnership for Peace (PFP) was created, also involving most Soviet and Soviet-bloc states and geared toward building cooperation among the members' militaries and defense establishments.

In 1998 the first three ex–Warsaw Pact countries were brought into NATO: Poland, Hungary, and the Czech Republic (see Table 12.1). The expansion process for the second group of prospective members began in late 2002. This group included additional ex-Soviet-bloc countries (Bulgaria, Romania, and Slovakia), part of the former Yugoslavia (Slovenia), and—for the first time—countries that had been part of the Soviet Union itself (the Baltic states of Estonia, Latvia, and Lithuania). Two more countries, Albania and Croatia, joined in 2009. Others may follow according to the official NATO policy statement of "an open-door policy on enlargement. Any European country in a position to further the principles of the North Atlantic Treaty and contribute to the security in the Euro-Atlantic area can become a member of the Alliance, when invited to do so by the existing member countries."[20] Most controversial are Ukraine and Georgia, two former Soviet republics that have had major tensions with Russia over issues including Moscow's interference in the 2004 Ukrainian election and the 2008 Russia–Georgia war.

Three principal arguments are made in favor of ***NATO expansion***. The first is based on the concept of a ***security community***, defined as an area "in which strategic rivalries are attenuated and the use of force within the group is highly unlikely."[21] NATO expansion

---

TABLE 12.1   NATO: Its Evolution, Cold War to Post–Cold War

Charter Members	Joined during the Cold War	Joined after the Cold War
Belgium	Greece (1952)	Czech Republic (1999)[‡]
Canada	Turkey (1952)	Hungary (1999)[‡]
Denmark	Federal Republic of Germany	Poland (1999)[‡]
France[*]	(1955)[†]	Bulgaria (2004)[‡]
Iceland	Spain (1982)	Estonia (2004)[§]
Italy		Latvia (2004)[§]
Luxembourg		Lithuania (2004)[§]
Netherlands		Romania (2004)[‡]
Norway		Slovakia (2004)[‡]
Portugal		Slovenia (2004)[**]
United Kingdom		Albania (2009)[‡]
United States		Croatia (2009)[**]

[*]Withdrew from NATO military command in 1965 but maintained political membership; rejoined the NATO military command in 2009.
[†]As a condition of German reunification in 1990, NATO agreed not to station military forces in the territory of the former German Democratic Republic (East Germany)
[‡]Former Warsaw Pact members.
[§]Formerly part of the Soviet Union.
[**]Part of the former Yugoslavia.

has enlarged the area of Europe in which this sense of security and stability prevails. Once a country is a member of NATO, it gives the assurance that it will not threaten the security of other members, and it gets the assurance that other countries in the security community will help ensure its security.

The second rationale for NATO expansion is the reinforcement of democratization. Free elections and the building of other democratic political institutions and practices, including civilian control of the military, are prerequisites to NATO membership. This provides an incentive to choose and then stay on the democratic path. The Czech president Vaclav Havel, who spent years in prison as a dissident during the communist era, took this concept further, stressing the political, cultural, and even psychological benefits for the countries of Eastern Europe once they finally became genuine and full members of the Western community.

The third pro-expansion argument stresses the continued, albeit altered, need for deterrence. NATO doctrine still calls for a deterrence posture to ensure collective security against a potential aggressor. The main concern, mostly left implicit, is a resurgent Russia. It is not so much a fear that the Soviet Union may be reconstituted, although this possibility is not totally dismissed. The more salient concerns about Russia run deeper, historically speaking—Russia does have a pre-communist history of regional expansionism—and grow out of the uncertainties and instabilities of Russia's own post-communist transition and the possibility of more aggressively nationalist leaders coming to power.

Critics of NATO expansion stress two chief points. One is that NATO has still not figured out what to do about Russia. The first round of NATO expansion to former Soviet-bloc countries included an agreement for closer NATO–Russia consultation. Russia was to be given a voice in NATO, but not such a strong voice as to constitute veto power. This agreement was heralded at the time but did not prove very meaningful in actual practice. The same is true of other agreements since then. The 2008 Russia–Georgia war left both sides in the NATO expansion debate claiming validation. Russia remains expansionist and aggressive, proponents say—not ready to live in peace with its neighbors. Now more than ever, Georgia and Ukraine need to be brought into NATO. NATO's own credibility is even more at stake. NATO expansion opponents contend that we've ended up with the self-fulfilling prophecy we warned about. NATO expansion did not strengthen deterrence so much as provoke Russia. The Russians expressed their concerns all along, and now that they have recovered economically and these issues are hitting closer to home, what analysts are seeing is less of a shift than a culmination in what had been building all along as NATO expanded.[22]

A second argument against NATO expansion is the concern that adding new members will dilute the cohesion that has made NATO function so effectively. This is less a criticism of any specific new members than a basic organizational precept: as the number of members goes up, making decisions and carrying out policies becomes that much harder. "If one country after another is admitted," a former U.S. ambassador to NATO argued, "it will no longer be today's functioning and cohesive NATO that the new members will be joining but rather a diluted entity, a sort of [L]eague of [N]ations."[23] The intra-alliance tensions that were exposed during the Kosovo war could be even worse with even more members. A bigger NATO may not be a better NATO if member states take seriously the importance of being able to function effectively first and foremost as a military alliance.

NATO's POST–COLD WAR MISSION   During the Cold War, NATO focused on deterring and defending against the threat posed by the Soviet Union and the Warsaw Pact. Its central mission was to meet this threat with the necessary forces, weapons, and doctrine. In the immediate aftermath of the Cold War, NATO doctrine recognized that security threats were now less likely to come from "classical territorial aggression" than from "the adverse consequences that may arise from the serious economic, social, and political difficulties, including ethnic rivalries and territorial disputes, which are faced by many countries in Central and Eastern Europe."[24] This meant both that deterrence strategy needed to be reformulated and that peace operations needed to be a new and major part of NATO's mission.

The wars in the former Yugoslavia posed the first test of how well NATO would handle this new mission of peace operations. These wars—first in Croatia and Bosnia, and then in Kosovo—posed a number of difficult issues for NATO, and the results were decidedly mixed. The former Yugoslavia was "out of area" in terms of the North Atlantic Treaty's provisions pertaining to attacks on or within the territory of member countries. On the other hand, the underlying purpose of the alliance was to keep the peace in Europe, and these wars in the former Yugoslavia were the most gruesome and destructive conflicts in Europe since World War II. They also were a different type of conflict than NATO had been formed to fight. NATO doctrine, training, deployments, battle plans, and equipment were all geared to conventional warfare against the Warsaw Pact forces—armies against armies, along demarcated battle lines, relying on technology and classical strategy. In Bosnia and Kosovo, though, the wars were driven by ethnic cleansing, not classical invasion.

From 1992 until late 1995, while the Bosnia war raged, the United States and western Europe mostly hurled accusations and counteraccusations across the Atlantic—"three years of collective buck-passing," as Joseph Lepgold put it.[25] NATO finally did intervene in Bosnia following the signing of the Dayton accord in December 1995. It did so with a sixty-thousand-troop Implementation Force (IFOR), which was followed about a year later by a somewhat smaller Stabilization Force (SFOR). IFOR and SFOR succeeded in restoring stability to Bosnia, demonstrating that NATO could play an important peace-keeping role. Both NATO forces operated much more efficiently and conveyed much more of a deterrent threat than had the crazy-quilt UN force that had preceded them. They also were noteworthy in including Russian and other former-Soviet-bloc troops. In 2001, when Macedonia, another part of the former Yugoslavia, began sliding into its own ethnic violence, NATO did act sooner and was able to prevent the conflict from escalating or spreading. But it left NATO with the burden of maintaining three simultaneous peacekeeping missions in the former Yugoslavia.

Terrorism has posed yet another set of issues about NATO's mission. When the United States was attacked on September 11, 2001, its NATO allies invoked Article 5 of the North Atlantic Treaty. This was the first time that this collective security provision, had actually been invoked, and it was done by the allies to help the United States rather than the reverse. NATO's action reflected the new reality of terrorism as a shared threat.

Within that general perception of threat, though, lie other differences over how best to deal with terrorism. The United States originally chose to conduct the war in Afghanistan with some assistance from European allies in their individual national capacities, but outside of their NATO membership, in order to have greater control over wartime command and strategy than it had during the Kosovo war. The United States later turned to NATO to take over the International Security Assistance Force (ISAF) and its peacekeeping mission in Afghanistan. This was not only a further instance of NATO's new mission of peacekeeping; it also was the first time that NATO had taken on a major ongoing mission outside the Euro-Atlantic geographic area. In the Iraq War, the Bush administration again opted to fight outside of NATO auspices. The ad hoc coalition included some NATO members acting in their individual national capacities. (Britain again was the main partner, along with Poland, the Czech Republic, and some others.) Unlike with Afghanistan, though, there were major policy differences that led to open and intense confrontations with France and Germany.

A personal anecdote: In February 2003, on the eve of the Iraq War, I was at a major conference in Germany. One evening I was talking with an American military officer serving with NATO. Although he steered clear of a position on Iraq, his concern was that the bitter intra-NATO conflicts over Iraq not spill over to other aspects of the fight against terrorism in which NATO cooperation was working well. Activities such as intelligence sharing, force transformation, and small counterterrorism operations needed to be kept going, as they had their own crucial roles to play in the comprehensive strategy. The overall objective, as reflected in a NATO policy statement, was "a far-reaching transformation of its forces and capabilities to better deter and defend against terrorism. [NATO] is working closely with partner countries and organizations to ensure broad cooperation in the fight against terrorism."[26]

The Afghanistan war continued to bring out intra-alliance differences. The Bush administration wanted greater commitments from allies. But only a few countries—Britain, France, Canada, the Netherlands—were willing to make substantial troop commitments. Others, such as Germany, constrained their personnel from being assigned to the riskiest areas. Some of this reluctance reflected genuine differences over approach and how best to balance the military operations with civil-society building, economic assistance, and other components of the overall strategy. Some also reflected differing domestic politics.

Polls showed similar views in Europe and America on some dimensions of the mission. For example, in a 2008 poll 73 percent of Americans and 79 percent of Europeans were in favor of providing security for economic reconstruction projects, 76 percent and 68 percent were in favor of assisting training of Afghan police and military forces, and 70 percent and 76 percent were in favor of antinarcotics measures. But as for conducting combat operations, support ranged from 76 percent of Americans to only 43 percent of Europeans.[27] Some countries, such as Canada, had made substantial troop commitments. But other NATO countries' domestic political pressures to cut back had increased to the extent that they were becoming reluctant to share more of the burden. The intra-NATO debate carried over into the Obama administration.

In 2010 NATO issued its new "Strategic Concept." This was to be NATO 3.0 (the original Cold War mission being 1.0, the Balkans wars 2.0) It gave even greater emphasis to threats that emanated beyond NATO's borders but affected NATO security. In its first test, in Libya in 2011, NATO got a mixed review. On the one hand it did take on the bulk of the military operations and performed them effectively. On the other hand the alliance was split, with only some members agreeing to be part of the operation while others, including Germany, refused.

Differences over relative shares of the budget burden also have grown sharper. The Europeans have their debt crisis and the United States its deficit crisis. "If current trends in the decline of European defense capabilities are not halted and reversed," Defense Secretary Robert Gates warned in 2011, "future U.S. political leaders—those for whom the Cold War was not the formative experience that it was for me—may not consider the return on America's investment in NATO worth the cost."[28] As of early 2013 the United States was financing almost three-quarters of NATO's budget, up from 63 percent in 2001. No European country is meeting NATO's spending guidelines of 2 percent GDP. The Europeans have their own critique of the U.S. position as making too many and too flawed military commitments.

All told, although some answers about NATO's post–Cold War mission have been worked out, many questions remain.

The European Union (EU), the Euro Crisis, and U.S.–EU Economic Relations

For all the problems the European Union has been facing, it's important to recall how much success it has had in its fifty-plus years of formal existence. The intra-European rivalries that set off two world wars and countless other wars in history have been tamed. The original six-member European Economic Community, formed in 1957, has grown by 2013 to the 28-member European Union, with other countries possibly joining in future

MAP 12.2

EUROPEAN UNION

GREENLAND

ARCTIC OCEAN

Barents
Sea

ICELAND

Norwegian
Sea

SWEDEN   FINLAND

NORWAY

ESTONIA   RUSSIA

LATVIA

North   DENMARK   LITHUANIA
Sea   RUSSIA
IRELAND   UNITED
          KINGDOM   NETHERLANDS   BELARUS

ATLANTIC   GERMANY   POLAND
OCEAN   BELGIUM
                                                          UKRAINE
          LUXEMBOURG   CZECH REP.
                              (CZECHIA)
          FRANCE   LIECHTENSTEIN   SLOVAKIA
          SWITZERLAND   AUSTRIA   MOLDOVA
                                    HUNGARY
                    SLOVENIA
                              CROATIA   ROMANIA
                    SAN   BOSNIA AND
          PORTUGAL   ANDORRA   MARINO   HERZEGOVINA SERBIA   Black Sea
                    MONACO   BULGARIA
          SPAIN   MONTENEGRO   KOSOVO
                    VATICAN CITY   ITALY   MACEDONIA
                                    ALBANIA   TURKEY
                              GREECE

                    M e d i t e r r a n e a n   S e a
MOROCCO   CYPRUS   SYRIA
                         MALTA   LEBANON
          TUNISIA

                                                          ISRAEL

ALGERIA

                    LIBYA   EGYPT

European Union

░ EU member states
▒ EU new members 2004
▓ EU new members 2007
░ EU candidates
■ EFTA member states

          NIGER   CHAD   SUDAN

Source: http://www.nationsonline.org/oneworld/europe_map.htm

years. National economies have integrated to a far greater extent than in any other region in the world. Students have the opportunity to study in universities across the continent as well as in Britain and Ireland. Far more people speak more than one language than in the United States. And the euro became the first common currency in modern history.

But beginning in late 2009, major debt problems in member countries such as Ireland and Greece, coming on top of the U.S.-driven 2007–8 financial crisis and with other factors, created a crisis in the euro zone. Many challenging issues and questions were involved. Was austerity—imposing tight fiscal conditions on Greece, Spain, and other debtor countries—the best policy? Or, with unemployment already so high (more than double the very high rate in the United States), was austerity economically counterproductive and politically risky (in that it could stoke extremist politics)? Was Germany, as the largest and most successful European economy, being asked to bear unfair bailout burdens, or was this in its own best interest, since the countries to be bailed out were some of its major markets? Would the euro survive? Should it survive? While answers to these questions are pending, immediate political effects could be seen with leadership changes (electoral defeats, retirements) in fifteen of the twenty-seven EU member states between 2009 and 2012.

The euro crisis affects the United States in a number of ways. The American and European economies are highly integrated. Europe felt the shock of the 2007–8 Wall Street financial meltdown, and the United States has been feeling the effects of the Euro crisis. At $646 billion (2012), the U.S.–EU trade relationship is the largest in the world. Much of this is intra-company transfer, meaning exports and imports between American and European subsidiaries of the same large corporation. Total U.S. investment in the EU is three times more than in all of Asia. EU investment in the U.S. is about eight times more than EU investment in China and India combined. Together the U.S. and EU economies amount to almost half the entire world GDP. In his 2013 State of the Union address President Obama called for a free trade agreement to even more tightly integrate the American and EU economies. This was not a totally new idea: it has had many advocates for a number of years. Its politics are complicated with potential benefits to some interest groups and costs to others. It's another issue to keep an eye on.

While economic integration has always been the priority, the EU has also sought to develop a "common foreign and security policy" (CFSP). As discussed in Reading 12.1, the EU's goal is to establish itself as a stronger and more independent foreign-policy player in its own right. The CFSP, however, has been slow to develop. Foreign policy is still made primarily in individual national capitals such as London, Paris, and Berlin rather than at EU headquarters in Brussels. "The idea that the European Union should speak with one voice in world affairs is as old as the European integration process itself. But," the EU acknowledges on its own Web site, "the Union has made less progress in forging a common foreign and security policy over the years than in creating a single market and a single currency."[29] The defeat of a proposed new EU constitution in 2005, which was supposed to strengthen collective action in this and other areas, raised even further doubts about the future of CFSP. Even now that the new constitution has been adopted, there are no signs that the EU foreign minister will supplant the British, French, and German foreign ministers anytime soon.

Turkey

Turkey literally and figuratively bridges East and West. Istanbul, Turkey's capital city, is split by the Straits of Bosporous, with part lying on the edge of the European continent and part, along with most of the rest of Turkey, in an area geographers call Asia Minor. In Cold War strategic configurations Turkey was principally considered part of the West: a charter member of NATO, grouped within the United Nations alongside western European countries. Yet many in Europe have opposed Turkey's entry to the EU. The main reason is that it while it is not an Arab country (Turks are distinct ethnically and historically), Turkey is a majority Muslim country. Now, though, with the EU mired in its economic crisis while the Turkish economy has been doing well, and with some nationalist resentment within Turkey over European prejudice, there has been increasing questioning whether Turkey itself really wants EU membership. Whereas 73 percent of Turks favored EU membership in 2004, only 38 percent did in 2010.

Turkey has also been more active in taking its own initiatives in its Middle East policy. In 2007–8, when the United States was doing very little to push Arab–Israeli peace talks ahead, Turkey convened talks between Israel and Syria and between Israel and the Palestinians. Its relations with Israel shifted from extensive military, economic, and political cooperation in the 1990s and 2000s to diplomatic confrontation following the 2008 Gaza war and a 2010 incident at sea. Turkey has supported sanctions against Iran but has also pursued its own diplomacy as it seeks to break the deadlock over nuclear proliferation. It has been among the lead countries in supporting the opposition fighting Syrian president Bashar Assad.

These and other issues have fed debate over whether Turkey is turning east instead of west. There is no question that Turkey has been less automatically supportive of U.S. policies than in the past. Such dichotomous framing, though, misses the ways in which Turkey is charting its own course. As a Turkish foreign ministry official expressed the nationalist logic, "We [used to wait] for the big powers to make up their minds on big issues and we just follow them. For the past several years we have made up our own minds." A Turkish university student interviewed in an Istanbul café put it similarly: "Turkey is neither East nor West. We are moving in our own direction."[30] Substantial economic growth has made Turkey the fifteenth largest economy in the world. It has been playing a more active global diplomatic role in the Middle East and at the United Nations. It has been showing its own soft power as others admire its blend of democracy and Islam. Polls conducted during the Arab Spring showed Recep Tayyip Erdogan, Turkish prime minister and head of the Islamist Justice and Development Party (AKP are its initials in Turkish), to be the most admired regional leader among Arab publics. Turkey's cultural influence also has spread; for example, Turkish television series such as

"Magnificent Century" and "Forbidden Love" (their English names) have been breaking viewer records across the Middle East.[31]

With these and other dynamics at work, U.S.–Turkish relations have been going through a transition from the old Cold War "leader-follower" model to one more like U.S. relations with other emerging powers such as India and Brazil.

Russia: Friend, Competitor, Adversary?

The great uncertainty about Russia and its future should not surprise us. Think about it: Russia has not gone through a change just of policy, or of leadership, or of ruling party. The Union of Soviet Socialist Republics (USSR), heralded in 1922 by Vladimir Ilyich Lenin as a new and revolutionary model that would transform the entire world, collapsed and fell apart in 1991. Democracy was proclaimed, capitalism replaced socialism: change swept through every part of Russian society. The first free elections in Russian history were held. A stock market opened in Moscow. Cultural freedom came out of the shadows. Western influences were let in, including even the Rolling Stones, who played a live concert in Moscow in the summer of 1998.

Fundamentally, no matter the particular nature or pace of ups and downs, the central post–Cold War issue for Russia has been, as Stanford University's Gail Lapidus posed it, "defining a new Russian identity and place in the world after the Soviet collapse." Russia "was attempting to come to grips with a profound and traumatic set of losses." It had lost territory, its alliance system, much of its power, and even its superpower status:

> The sudden transformation of a country that had once controlled the fate of millions to a country that perceived itself to have lost control of its own fate created a radical sense of vulnerability that deeply influenced the ongoing Russian struggle to define its identity and place in the post–Cold War international system. How to manage the fundamental asymmetry of power, interests, and priorities had become and would long remain the central challenge of the Russian–American bilateral relationship.[32]

The key question in the U.S.–Russian relationship is, Which of three scenarios noted earlier will prevail: friend, competitor, or adversary?

Russia as Friend

"Ron and Mikhail," "Bill and Boris," "George and Vladimir"—the end of the Cold War brought quite a bit of chumminess between American and Soviet/Russian leaders. There was much mutual praise, many amiable photo ops, plenty of pledges to work together.

Andrei Kozyrev, Boris Yeltsin's first foreign minister, spoke in 1992 of Russia's becoming "a reliable partner in the community of civilized nations."[33] Warren Christopher, President Clinton's first secretary of state, reciprocated with numerous affirmations of his own about the new Russian–American friendship. The administration of George W. Bush initially was much harsher in its rhetoric and approach, but President Bush left his first summit with Russian president Vladimir Putin speaking of a newfound friend. "I looked the man in the eye," Bush went so far as to say. "I found him to be very straightforward and trustworthy. . . . I was able to get a sense of his soul."[34]

A number of genuine and substantive areas of foreign policy cooperation did emerge in the post–Cold War Russian–American relationship.

U.S. FOREIGN AID TO RUSSIA AND OTHER EX-SOVIET STATES   American aid to Russia and the other ex-Soviet states exceeded $13 billion during the 1990s. These programs included food aid, medical and health care aid, business development, a first-time Peace Corps presence, funding for the development of the rule of law and other democratization initiatives, military cooperation, and even the construction of housing for former Soviet troops returning from East Germany and elsewhere in Eastern Europe. All this was quite a change from the preceding half-century, when the Soviet threat was the principal rationale for U.S. foreign aid programs to other states. It was somewhat reminiscent of World War II, when, as part of the anti-Hitler alliance, Russia was second only to the United Kingdom as a beneficiary of Lend-Lease and other U.S. aid programs.

NUCLEAR ARMS CONTROL   The first of the post–Cold War U.S.–Soviet nuclear arms-control agreements, known as **START** (the Strategic Arms Reduction Treaty), was signed in 1991 by President George H. W. Bush and the Russian president, Mikhail Gorbachev. It cut strategic nuclear weapons from Cold War levels of 13,000 U.S. and 11,000 Soviet warheads to 6,000 on each side. START I was ratified by both the U.S. Senate and the Russian Duma (parliament). A follow-up treaty, START II, was signed in 1993 and ratified by the U.S. Senate in 1996 but not by the Russian Duma, so it never took effect. The Moscow Treaty on Strategic Offensive Reductions was signed by Presidents George W. Bush and Vladimir Putin in May 2002, making additional cuts over the ensuing ten years. The momentum toward further nuclear arms–control negotiations slowed amid other Russian–American tensions during the Bush–Putin years. President Obama and the Russian president, Dmitri Medvedev, re-initiated negotiations and in 2010 agreed to the New START by which long-range nuclear weapons are to be cut to 1550 on each side by 2017. Senate ratification was contentious but came later that year, as discussed in our foreign policy politics case study later in this chapter.

As significant as these cuts have been, some argue that they can go much further. "It is more than two decades since the end of the Cold War," the Arms Control Association argues, "yet the United States maintains—and is poised to rebuild—a costly strategic nuclear triad that is sized to launch far more nuclear weapons than necessary to deter nuclear attack against the U.S. or its allies."[35] U.S.–Russian negotiations continue over another possible treaty.

COOPERATIVE THREAT REDUCTION   Many analysts stress the threat from Russian *"loose nukes."* Given Russia's economic instability and broader societal dislocation, these analysts have expressed grave concerns about the safety and security of the country's remaining nuclear weapons, about the plutonium and other components from dismantled weapons, and about Russian weapons scientists who might be tempted to sell their expertise on the "WMD market" to rogue states or terrorists. The Nunn-Lugar Cooperative Threat Reduction program was named for its key congressional bipartisan sponsors, Senators Sam Nunn (D-Georgia) and Richard Lugar (R-Indiana). Originally established in 1991, this program has provided U.S. funds, expertise, and other assistance on a cooperative basis with the Russian government to reduce these dangers. Its list of accomplishments is quite impressive: almost 8,000 strategic nuclear warheads deactivated, over 900 intercontinental ballistic missiles (ICBMs) destroyed, more than 30 submarines capable of launching ballistic missiles destroyed, 24 nuclear-weapons storage sites provided with upgraded security. To put all this into perspective, the Nunn-Lugar program has dismantled more nuclear weaponry than Great Britain, France, and China combined currently possess. From another viewpoint, though, few if any experts believe that the program has sufficed to ensure that terrorists or others won't get their hands on ex-Soviet "loose nukes."

TERRORISM   Then-president Vladimir Putin was the first foreign leader to phone President Bush with condolences and support following the September 11 terrorist attacks. Russian cooperation has been especially important in the war in Afghanistan. It included Russian aid to the anti-Taliban Northern Alliance in the initial months, and consent to ground and air transit through Russia. This was indicative of the underlying shared interest in working against a re-radicalized Afghanistan. There also appeared to be at least a tacit quid pro quo whereby Washington would not actively oppose Russia's effort to quell the separatist insurgency in Chechnya, a largely Muslim part of the Russian Federation, an effort that the Russian government portrays as its own war on terrorism.

Russia as Geopolitical Competitor

One of the axioms of international relations is that major powers often seek to counterbalance whichever state is the most powerful in the international system. Even as Russia was being weighed down with economic and other problems, many analysts felt that its sheer size, resource endowments (especially oil and natural gas), geography, and history ensured that it again would be a great power. Even when Russian–American friendship was at its peak in the early 1990s, there remained a degree of geopolitical competition and even conflict. This was evident on the U.S. side in the 1992 Pentagon "primacy" document discussed in Chapter 7. On the Russian side, it comes through in the 2000 National Security Concept, which delineated two potential future directions for twenty-first-century geopolitics (see also Reading 12.2). One was the cooperative direction of "the strengthened economic and political positions of a significant number of states and their integrative associations and in improved mechanisms for multilateral management of international processes." The other was the more competitive direction of "attempting to create an international relations structure based on domination by developed Western countries in the international community, under U.S. leadership and designed for unilateral solutions." Such "attempts to ignore Russia's interests . . . are capable of undermining international security, stability, and the positive changes achieved in international relations."[36]

Whereas the Clinton administration was split between the friend and competitor approaches, the Bush administration came to office emphasizing the latter almost exclusively. "In some ways," Bush's secretary of state Colin Powell stated, "the approach to Russia shouldn't be terribly different than the very realistic approach we had to the old Soviet Union in the late 1980s. We told them what bothered us. We told them where we could engage on things. We tried to convince them of the power of our values and our system. They argued back."[37] Others in the administration were even more caustic. Secretary of Defense Donald Rumsfeld accused Russia of being "an active proliferator . . . helping Iran and others develop nuclear and other weapons of mass destruction." Paul Wolfowitz, the deputy secretary of defense (and a lead author of the 1992 primacy strategy), was even blunter, saying that the Russians "seem to be willing to sell anything to anyone for money." The Russian response to such statements was to accuse the Bush administration of reverting to "the spirit of the Cold War."[38]

"It's time to press the reset button," Vice President Joe Biden suggested in a speech early in the Obama administration, "and to revisit the many areas where we can and should be working together with Russia." Biden acknowledged that "we will not agree with Russia on everything."[39] Given history, geography, and other factors, the two countries would still have different interests but they could also increase cooperation where interests are more shared. This is pretty much how U.S.–Russian relations have played out in the Obama administration, with cooperation greater in some areas (e.g., nuclear arms control, Iran) than others (e.g., Syria).

THE 1990s BALKAN WARS Both because they are fellow Slavs and also for their own geopolitical reasons, Russia and Serbia historically have had close relations. Serbia thus had pretty solid Russian support in its aggressive struggle for dominance as Yugoslavia was breaking up. During the war in Bosnia and Herzegovina (1992–95), the United States sided with the Bosnian Muslims, and Russia sided with the Eastern Orthodox Christian

Serbs. These differences were bridged following the 1995 Dayton accord that ended the Bosnian war. The Russian military was even brought into the NATO-led peacekeeping effort that followed.

The 1999 Kosovo war, though, was a much greater source of tension. Again, Russian sympathies and political allegiances were with the Serbs; the United States and NATO sided with the Muslim Kosovars. This time, the United States and NATO actually intervened militarily in the conflict, not just after the fact as a peacekeeping force. Although U.S.–NATO forces intervened in reaction to Serbian aggression, from the Russian perspective the key issues were that the military action was taken against a sovereign state (whereas Bosnia was an independent state, Kosovo was a province of Serbia) and without UN Security Council authorization. This "fed into an already heightened sense of Russia's own vulnerability and fueled highly implausible anxieties about Kosovo as a precedent for possible Western intervention in Russia's internal affairs, particularly in Chechnya."[40] When the war reached the point when NATO was about to move from air strikes to ground troops, Russia assisted with the diplomacy, helping convince the Serbian leader Slobodan Milosevic to concede and withdraw. Even then, though, Russia's peacekeeping cooperation was much less than in Bosnia. U.S.–Russian tensions over the Balkans persisted, as they did over broader multilateral issues of sovereignty and intervention. When in 2008 Kosovo declared its independence, the United States and most of western Europe recognized the new nation, but Russia did not.

CHECHNYA   Russia's wars and its antiterrorism campaign against Chechnya have posed a Power-Principles tension between, on the one hand, American strategic interests in maintaining good relations with Russia, and, on the other, American condemnation of the atrocities and other blatant human rights violations that Russian troops have committed in Chechnya. In 1996, during the first Chechen war, Bill Clinton drew stinging criticism from human rights advocates and others for drawing an analogy to the U.S. Civil War, with Russian president Boris Yeltsin as Russia's Abraham Lincoln seeking to preserve the Union. The Clinton administration was a bit more critical of the Russians in the Chechnya war that began in 1999. So, too, was the Bush administration, initially. But after September 11, the Russians cast Chechnya as their own war on terrorism. The Russian national security adviser, Sergei Ivanov, went so far as to declare that the Russian war in Chechnya was in the West's interest, with Russia serving as "a frontline warrior fighting international terrorism . . . saving the civilized world [from] the terrorist plague in the same way as it used to save Europe from the Tatar-Mongol invasions in the twelfth century."[41]

The Chechen insurgents, too, have definitely been guilty of atrocities. In the 2002 siege of a theater in Moscow, terrorists took more than eight hundred people hostage. In the 2004 seizure of a schoolhouse in the town of Beslan, hundreds of children and adults died. But many analysts also blame Putin for botched rescue attempts that increased the casualties in both incidents, for brutal policies in Chechnya that have fed support for the insurgents and the terrorists, and for making Chechnya a magnet and a rallying cry for Al Qaeda and other global terrorist groups. This view sees American interests and not just American principles as threatened by Russia's Chechnya policies. The Chechnya issue is still simmering, albeit with less visibility and prominence. Russian troops have remained in Chechnya. Moscow has continued to choose Chechnyan presidents. Human rights groups have continued to report repression and killings, such as the July 2009 assassination of Natalia Estemirova, a leading human rights activist and critic of the Russian role in Chechnya.

THE RUSSIAN "NEAR ABROAD"   The "near abroad" is the term Russia uses to refer to the other former Soviet republics. To Russia, this is its traditional sphere of influence, an area in which it claims a right to exert political pressure and even to intervene militarily to protect its interests, as it already has done in Georgia, Estonia, Moldova, Tajikistan, Armenia, and Azerbaijan. Putin cited the precedent of the Bush administration's doctrine of preemption when he asserted Russia's right to intervene in other states if it determines that terrorism or some other serious threat exists. In the case of Ukraine, Russia intervened not militarily but covertly and politically in an effort to rig the 2004 presidential election in favor of the pro-Russian but highly unpopular presidential candidate Viktor Yanukovich over the reformist Viktor Yushchenko. This attempt backfired and sparked the "orange revolution" of mass protests by Ukrainians demanding a fair election, which Yushchenko won. But then, amid economic discontent and other factors—including Russian support—Yanukovich won the next presidential election. Once he was in power, trade with Russia increased 70 percent, more-liberal leaders were arrested, and Ukraine became more pro-Russia and more like Russia.

NATO EXPANSION   As noted before, although proponents of expanding NATO to include former Soviet allies and even former Soviet republics claimed that this would strengthen Peace, Russia saw it as strengthening American Power. As Richard K. Betts writes, "One need not be an apologist for the regime in Moscow or its behavior, or sympathetic to Russia's national interests, to empathize with its resentments of this revolutionary overturning of the balance of power. . . . Washington, and with its prodding other NATO governments, succumbed to victory and kept kicking Russia while it was down."[42] NATO and Russia did reach their own agreements for consultation that defused tensions but did not eliminate them, particularly as NATO began considering major former Soviet republics such as Ukraine and Georgia for membership. Missile defense was another issue. While the United States claimed the new Europe-based missile defense system was for protection against Iran, Russia saw it as directed against itself. The Obama administration modified the design in order to strengthen its argument that the system was not directed against Russia. But tensions remained.

RUSSIA–GEORGIA 2008 WAR   In Georgia, tensions went past a war of words to outright war. Georgia had been one of the closest U.S. allies among the former Soviet republics. It received U.S. military aid. It sent troops to Iraq. In 2004 it elected a charismatic and strongly pro-U.S. and anti-Russia president, Mikhail Saakashvili. In 2005 George W. Bush, the first U.S. leader to visit Georgia, proclaimed it a "beacon of liberty" and pledged continued U.S. support.[43] Since its independence in 1991, though, Georgia had experienced tensions and violence with South Ossetia and Abkhazia, two regions with ethnic and cultural differences whose peoples had been pushing first for greater autonomy and then for independence of their own. Both were getting support from Russia, especially after Saakashvili was elected.

When war did break out in August 2008, each side has its own version of how much of the responsibility lay with Russian aggression and how much with Georgian provocation. Russian actions, Secretary of State Condoleezza Rice stated, were unprovoked and aggressive: "We have to deny Russian strategic objectives, which were clearly to undermine Georgia's democracy, to use its military capability to damage, and in some cases, destroy Georgian infrastructure, and to try and weaken the Georgian state."[44] Russia's foreign minister, Sergei Lavrov, argued that Russia was responding to atrocities committed by Georgian troops against its citizens and peacekeepers in the region, saying, "[T]he Georgian leadership gave an order which led to an act of genocide, which resulted in war crimes, ethnic cleansing. And this, of course, cannot go unanswered."[45]

The fighting lasted about two weeks. A ceasefire was worked out, requiring an end to military action, a pullback to prewar positions, and access for humanitarian and monitoring missions from the United Nations and the Organization for Security and Cooperation in Europe (OSCE). The ceasefire, though, was a tenuous one. Russia did not comply with the troop withdrawal provisions. It used its UN Security Council veto to deny renewal of the UN observer mission. It also pressed for ending the OSCE mission. The claims to independence by Abkhazia and South Ossetia were recognized only by Russia and a few other countries, such as Hugo Chávez's Venezuela. Meanwhile, NATO deferred the issue of Georgian and Ukrainian membership rather than resolving it, keeping their candidacies on the agenda but not taking significant steps toward acting on them.

THE MIDDLE EAST AND THE PERSIAN GULF   During the Cold War, U.S.–Soviet rivalry was deep and recurring in these regions. In this context, the Russian–American cooperation of the early 1990s was quite significant. During the 1990–91 Persian Gulf War, although Russia did not join the U.S.-led military coalition, it did give unprecedented diplomatic cooperation to the war effort. Russia and the United States co-chaired the Middle East multilateral peace negotiations of the 1990s, involving Israel and most Arab countries, on issues ranging from arms control and regional security to regional economic cooperation, water, and the environment. This cooperation continued through the "Quartet" of the United States, Russia, the European Union, and the United Nations, which sought to get the Israeli–Palestinian peace process back on track after the renewed violence of 2000–2002 through a peace plan called the "road map."

Iraq, though, was a very divisive issue. Throughout the 1990s Russia had been a consistent opponent within the UN Security Council of U.S. efforts to tighten economic sanctions and get UN weapons inspectors back into Iraq. In 2002–3, when the Bush administration was pushing for war, Russia joined France in threatening to use its UN Security Council veto to try to block American military action. Putin labeled the war "some new form of colonialism."[46] Russian motivations were in part economic: the $7 billion debt Saddam Hussein's regime owed Russia, plus the stakes that the rising Russian oil industry had in potential investment opportunities in Iraq. Russian motivations were also geopolitical, in two respects. One was in the Middle East–Persian Gulf, as this crucial region entered yet another period of historic transformation. The other was in a broader global context. "The future international security architecture must be based on a multipolar world," Putin stressed during the Iraq debate. "I am absolutely confident that the world will be predictable and stable only if it is multipolar."[47]

In contrast, the United States and Russia have been largely cooperative on the Iran issue. Russia's official position has been opposition to Iranian nuclear proliferation: "We are categorically opposed to the enlargement of the club of nuclear states," Putin stated.[48] Russia has supported numerous rounds of economic sanctions imposed by the UN Security Council. It called off some of its arms sales to Iran. Also, as part of the "P5 + 1" (all five permanent members of the UN Security Council plus Germany) negotiations with Iran, and through some specific proposals seeking to work out how to ensure Iran's rights to peaceful nuclear energy while ending the proliferation threat, Russia has had a key role in the overall diplomacy.

On Libya in 2011, it abstained rather than use its veto on UN Security Council Resolution 1973 authorizing military intervention against the Qaddafi regime. But as the intervention went on, Russia claimed that the United States and NATO had exceeded their mandate by using force not just to protect civilians but to engineer regime change. When Syria reached a crisis later that year, official statements from Moscow pulled no punches in citing retaliation for western intervention in Libya as a driver of their pro-Assad position on Syria. "The international community unfortunately did take sides in Libya," Foreign Minister Sergey Lavrov stated, "and we would never allow the Security Council to authorize anything similar." A source close to the Kremlin put it more bluntly: "We were naive and stupid. . . . Trust this: That was the last mistake of such type."[49] It may well be that Russian interests in arms sales, its only Mediterranean naval base, and hanging on to one of its few allies left in the Middle East may have led them to the same or a similar position on Syria. Whatever the internal causality, Russian opposition to UN action was a key factor constraining efforts to end the violence in Syria.

LEVERAGING ITS OIL AND NATURAL GAS   Russia is the world's second largest oil producer. Its oil reserves are the world's ninth largest. Natural gas reserves and natural gas exports both are the largest in the world. At the peak price of the 2008 oil boom, Russia was taking in $1.25 billion *a day* in energy-export revenue. Even when prices have fallen, oil and natural gas exports have constituted an enormous share of Russian hard-currency earnings. As such, while not a member of OPEC, Russia is well served when OPEC takes steps to limit production and keep prices up.

Further, Russia has not been shy about exerting "energypolitik" leverage. Natural gas is especially manipulable since it flows through directed pipelines and is harder to replace with alternative sources than oil, which often can be obtained in open global markets. Russia has turned off the natural gas spigot in recent years in disputes with Germany, Ukraine, Belarus, and other customers with which it has had political and policy differences.

Russia as Adversary

Columbia University scholar Robert Legvold has raised concern about an "alienated and combative Russia. . . . It would take only a mishandling of the mounting issues in contention between the United States and Russia to turn Russia into the odd man out among great powers, a spoiler in the sphere of great-power cooperation, and a state with a grudge looking for ways to inflict damage on U.S. interests."[50]

Russia could become an adversary in one of two ways. One would be through the rise of a nationalist leader who might go beyond normal great-power competition and seek to rebuild an empire and regain global influence through an aggressive and militaristic foreign policy. Expansionism is rooted deep in Russian history, some historians argue; it did not just start with Lenin and the communists. Moreover, the instabilities of Russian politics raise concerns that, as with Hitler in Weimar Germany during the 1930s, an aggressively nationalist leader could rise to power by promising to restore the motherland's greatness. The extremist Vladimir Zhirinovsky, promising to restore the old Russian empire (including taking back Alaska!), caused a scare with the gains he and his party made in the December 1993 Duma elections. While Putin is not as extreme as that, and while his relations with the United States have had some areas of cooperation, there is some concern that his long-term strategy has become more geopolitically zero-sum, with gains for the United States calculated as losses for Russia, and vice versa.

Especially since his return to the Russian presidency in 2012, Putin has been articulating fervently nationalist themes tapping Russian history and traditional values. In policies such as the 2013 ban on Americans from adopting Russian children (after more than 60,000 such adoptions over the prior two decades), and in granting Russian citizenship to the French actor Gérard Depardieu, who was locked in a tax dispute with his government, there has been a greater anti-Western tone than in recent times.

The other scenario involves Russia's becoming a major threat due to weakness rather than due to strength—if, for example, Russia becomes less and less able to govern itself effectively. Russia has "unanswered questions," Legvold also observes, "about its ability to avoid a basic breakdown of its domestic order and maybe even its demise as a state."[51] This specter of societal disorder has many aspects, perhaps most significantly (from a U.S. perspective) the "loose nukes" issue raised earlier: an accidental launching after a false alarm that is not checked out properly amid the breakdown of discipline or of equipment; an intentional but unauthorized launching by disgruntled officers; a terrorist group's stealing or buying a nuclear weapon. Such scenarios have been depicted in Hollywood movies and Tom Clancy novels, but any one of them could become all too real.

RUSSIAN DEMOCRATIZATION   What Russia has achieved in its transition from almost a century of authoritarian communism to at least some elements of democracy should not be underestimated. Still, Russia's road has been anything but straight and smooth. It has faced the challenge of moving from the initiation of democracy toward the consolidation and institutionalization of democracy, and real questions persist about whether in recent years it has been backsliding in the authoritarian direction.

An early and graphic example of this challenge occurred in October 1993. Boris Yeltsin, who led the anti-Soviet revolution and became the first president of post-communist Russia, was pushing hard for political and economic reform. His main opposition came from the Duma, where the communists and other hard-line and anti-reform political parties had sufficient strength to block many of these reforms. Amid political deadlock Yeltsin resorted to a military attack on the parliament building. The image of the man who in August 1991 had stood defiantly on a Soviet army tank, personifying the democratic revolution, now commanding Russian army tanks in an attack on the national legislature, captured the dilemmas of democratization. This posed a difficult policy choice for the Clinton administration: although Clinton strongly supported Yeltsin, he was painfully aware that a military attack on an elected legislature was not exactly an exemplary display of democracy.

Yeltsin also faced growing discontent arising from the deepening economic crisis. The transition from the Soviet command economy to market-based capitalism initially proved to be a "great leap backward."[52] The Russian GDP fell below those of Mexico, Brazil, and Indonesia. The standard of living for the average Russian was lower in 2000 than it had been in 1990, with 40 percent of the population living below the poverty line. Government employees, Russian soldiers, and others went months without receiving paychecks. Social services were cut back dramatically in the name of fiscal responsibility. Corruption was rampant, with "robber-baron capitalism" creating a new economic elite of billionaires. In 1998 the Russian government defaulted on its debt, setting off a major financial crisis. The ruble (the Russian unit of currency) collapsed, and investment plummeted.

Yeltsin's own behavior added to the problems. He always had been mercurial, but now he became even more unpredictable and unstable. He resorted to measures having questionable constitutionality, did not govern very effectively, and periodically disappeared from the scene due to health problems (some related to his alcoholism). On December 31, 1999, Yeltsin announced his resignation as president, and he appointed Putin as his successor. At first this appointment was provisional, but in March 2000 Putin was elected with slightly over 50 percent of the vote. (The communist candidate was again the leading challenger, with 29 percent.)

Putin mitigated some of the drift of Yeltsin's last years by strengthening the state in ways that, as reported in the *New York Times*, "managed to produce a measure of order and even modest prosperity that his embattled predecessor [Yeltsin] could only dream of." Yet the question, as the *Times* went on to say, was "where a strong state ends and a strongman begins."[53] Putin himself is a former agent of the KGB (the Soviet spy agency). As president he strengthened the KGB's successor agencies, reversing the breakup into separate departments begun by Yeltsin. He gave their leaders more power within the Kremlin and a mandate for stepping up internal security measures. "I see only one aim in reuniting all the security services into one large monster," stated the noted dissident Sergei Kovalev: "The creation of a more authoritarian state."[54] Newspapers and television stations were shut down for criticizing the Putin government. Their owners were arrested and forced into exile. In 2000 sixteen journalists were killed and seventy-three attacked, many of them badly beaten. The Committee to Protect Journalists, a major free-press NGO, named Putin in its list of the "ten worst enemies of the press" in 2001.[55] In 2003 the government shut down Russia's last independent national television network, replacing it with a state-run sports channel.

Putin won reelection in 2004 with 71 percent of the vote. Part of his appeal was having gotten the economy going again, with a 6.5 percent annual economic growth rate. Still, the election observer group from the Organization for Security and Cooperation in Europe (OSCE) gave the election a mixed assessment—not fixed but also not fully fair. The OSCE observers cited heavily biased media coverage and suspiciously high voter turnout. Legislative elections were held in 2007, but their legitimacy was questioned on a number of counts, including the charge that, according to the Council of Europe, "the media showed strong bias in favour of President Putin and the ruling United Russia party. The new election code makes it extremely difficult for new and smaller parties to develop and compete effectively. There were widespread reports of harassment of opposition parties."[56]

In this and other ways, Putin did much to personalize power around himself and his small circle, prompting questions about whether he would abide by the two-term limit in the Russian constitution and not run again in 2008. In fact, he did abide by the limit—at least technically. His hand-picked candidate, Dmitri Medvedev, was elected president while Putin became prime minister. But four years later, rather than having

Medvedev run for a second term, Putin engineered a constitutional interpretation of the limit being two *consecutive* terms as president and so he became the party's candidate; he won in elections even more severely criticized by international monitors than earlier ones. These really fit the pattern of "electoralism with authoritarian institutions and values."[57] Some protests were mounted, with thousands turning out even in the extreme cold of the Moscow winter. But Putin ratcheted up repression. He continued to do so once back in office.

What priority should the United States put on pushing for democratic reform and human rights in Russia? How high should Principles rank in relation to other issues on the U.S.–Russian agenda? And to the extent that Principles are a priority, how best to have an impact? Russian civil society and nonprofit groups, which for many years had received American funding (government and foundation), now were being required to register as foreign agents if they continued to receive any non-Russian funding—and there was very little Russian funding. The Putin government also ordered official U.S. democracy-promotion programs, both official governmental ones and ones run by NGOs, to be terminated.

Organization for Security and Cooperation in Europe (OSCE)

The Conference on Security and Cooperation in Europe (CSCE) was established in 1975 during détente as the only European institution with full East–West regional membership. With thirty-five members drawn from NATO, the Warsaw Pact, and the neutral states of Europe, the conference made its principal impact through the Helsinki Final Act, whose most important sections established norms and principles for human rights within, and peaceful conflict resolution among, member countries. For the most part the CSCE was just that—a conference that met from time to time as a forum for consultation and discussion. But when the East European revolutions came in 1989, it became clear in retrospect how important the CSCE had been in providing a political platform and moral support for the champions of democratic change, such as Solidarity in Poland and Charter 77 in Czechoslovakia, that brought communism down.

In the post–Cold War era, the CSCE expanded its membership to fifty-six states, enhanced its role, and changed its name. Made in 1994, the name change to the ***Organization for Security and Cooperation in Europe (OSCE)***, was intended to imply greater institutionalization. The rationale for the larger role lay in increased recognition of the link between regional security and the peaceful resolution of ethnic and other internal conflicts. On this basis the OSCE has taken on a greater role in preventive diplomacy and other types of political and diplomatic conflict management, as well as in conflict resolution. It does so through structures such as its Office for Democratic Institutions and Human Rights, which monitors elections, provides assistance in the drafting of constitutions and other laws, and promotes the development of civil society; the High Commissioner on National Minorities, which seeks to protect the rights of ethnic minorities through human rights monitors and other measures; and third-party mediators to help resolve conflicts.

The OSCE's record has been mixed. One major study concludes that it has its greatest success "in relatively low-level situations."[58] These tend to be cases in which tensions have not yet crossed the Rubicon of widespread violence: in Estonia and Latvia in the early 1990s, over the issues of the withdrawal of Russian troops and also human rights protections for Russian ethnic minorities; and in Macedonia, like Bosnia a former Yugoslav republic with deep ethnic splits but one which has managed to limit ethnic violence. But in cases such as Bosnia, Croatia, Kosovo, and Nagorno-Karabakh (an enclave with a large Armenian population that is geographically separate from but ruled by Azerbaijan), the conflicts ran too deep and had degenerated too much for the limited tools of the OSCE. Still, it remains the most important European multilateral regional organization working on conflict prevention and resolution, as well as democracy promotion and human rights protection.

Foreign Policy Politics Case Study: U.S. Domestic Politics of Nuclear Arms Control

To get a sense for the foreign policy politics of nuclear-arms control with the Soviet Union/Russia, we look at two sets of cases: the Strategic Arms Limitation Treaties (SALT) in the 1970s, and the Strategic Arms Reduction Treaties (START) in the 1990s and 2000s.

Politics of SALT I and SALT II

SALT I   Nuclear arms control was a main part of the 1970s U.S.–Soviet détente discussed back in Chapter 6. No issue was more important to détente, the overall relaxation in Cold War relations, than reducing the chance of nuclear war. Towards that objective, in May 1972—after almost three years of negotiations—U.S. president Richard Nixon and Soviet president Leonid Brezhnev signed the first Strategic Arms Limitation Treaty, also known by its acronym SALT I.

SALT I set limits on strategic nuclear weapons according to a formula known as "essential equivalence," whereby the Soviets were allowed a larger quantity of missiles because the United States had technological advantages that allowed it to put more bombs on each missile.* The idea was that if the Soviets had a quantitative edge and the United States a qualitative one, both would be assured of deterrence. SALT I also severely limited ABM defense systems on the grounds that such defensive systems were destabilizing: if one side knew it could defend itself against nuclear attack, then mutual destruction would no longer be assured and that side might be more likely to launch a first strike.

As we know, treaties require ratification by the U.S. Senate by a two-thirds majority. The Senate did ratify SALT I by the healthy margin of 88–2. But the politics along the way were more contentious than the final vote margin might indicate.

SALT I had two parts. One was a near total ban on ABM systems. While these are defensive systems intended to protect from a nuclear attack, there were two reasons for banning them. One was the point made above that in the logic of nuclear deterrence, if one side believes that it can defend against the other side's retaliatory attack, it may be more likely to launch a first strike. In that sense, too good a defense can be destabilizing, making nuclear war more likely, not less. The other reason was that a few years earlier (in 1969) when Nixon had proposed building an ABM system, Congress nearly voted it down. Opposition was based on its high costs, doubts about the reliability of the technology ("hitting a bullet with a bullet," as some put it) and a consequent false sense of security, and the general antiwar and anti–defense spending atmosphere amid growing opposition to the Vietnam War. The Senate vote was actually tied, resulting in a rare instance in which Vice President Spiro Agnew exercised his office's power as *president pro tempore* of the Senate and cast the tie-breaking vote. So with concern that there would be insufficient political support to match the Soviets if they built their own ABM systems, it seemed better simply to ban them.

SALT I's other provision was an agreement to limit the growth of offensive nuclear missiles so that both sides had equal strength, as per the principle of essential equivalence. Some senators, led by Senator Henry Jackson (D-Washington), questioned whether the limits agreed to in the treaty might actually give the Soviets an advantage. While no one was accusing the Nixon administration of doing this intentionally, the debate was over different ways of analyzing the treaty provisions. Two steps were taken to overcome this opposition. One was approval of the Jackson Amendment, which called on the president to ensure that any future treaty—what would eventually become SALT II—did "not limit the United States to levels of [strategic nuclear] forces inferior to the limits provided for the Soviet Union." The other was linking approval of SALT I to increased spending on new U.S. strategic nuclear-weapons systems such as the Trident submarine,

---

*The technical term is MIRVs, or multiple independently targeted re-entry vehicles. Think of missiles as delivery vehicles on which nuclear bombs are put. A MIRVed missile is one that can hold multiple bombs, each aimed at its own target.

the B-1 bomber, and strategic cruise missiles. In effect, in order to get some nuclear arms control there also had to be some increased nuclear-arms development.

There were also politics within the Nixon administration itself. Treaty negotiation was one of those issues on which National Security Advisor Henry Kissinger maneuvered to ensure his own control of the intra–executive branch policy process. As one author puts it, Kissinger "circumvented" the bureaucracy and "centralized" policy development in the White House and his National Security Council staff.[59] Gerard Smith, Director of the Arms Control and Disarmament Agency (ACDA) and officially the principal SALT negotiator dealing with the Soviets, was unaware of the "back-channel" negotiations that Kissinger was conducting with the Soviets at the same time.[60]

SALT II   President Jimmy Carter and Soviet president Brezhnev signed the SALT II Treaty on June 18, 1979. Four days later President Carter submitted it to the Senate for its advice and consent. Consent never came. Even before the Soviet invasion of Afghanistan in late December 1979, there were signs that Carter did not have sufficient support in the Senate to get the necessary two-thirds margin for ratification. Once the Soviets invaded Afghanistan, Carter withdrew the treaty from Senate consideration.

SALT II negotiations had actually begun back in 1973, the year after SALT I took effect. While the expectation was that these talks would go quickly, they clearly did not. The Watergate scandal and impeachment pressures brought the Nixon administration to an abrupt end in 1974. Détente generally was running into increasing criticism at home. The terms of the treaty were even more complicated than those of SALT I as they included both quantitative and qualitative limits, the latter being more complex to calculate for balance given the differences in the types of weapons in the two sides' nuclear arsenals. Carter's overall foreign policy had been running into a great deal of opposition on issues including the Panama Canal Treaties, reduced support for some traditional allies due to greater emphasis on human rights, and defense cuts such as cancellation of the B-1 bomber project.

Carter also had strained relations with Congress generally, even with members of his own party. He was seen by many on Capitol Hill as having a disdain for legislators and not being approachable. William Perry, a high-ranking Defense Department official, is quoted as saying that "the Carter administration did not have a good working relationship with Congress, partly because the president didn't recognize the importance of that and didn't work at it hard enough, and partly for reasons out of his control."[61]

The Senate Foreign Relations Committee began its hearings on SALT II a few weeks after the Carter-Brezhnev treaty signing. Hearings went on for twenty-seven days, quite a lot by usual standards, dragging out until that October. Some opponents tried to undermine the treaty by attaching amendments that they knew would make the treaty no longer acceptable to the Soviet Union. Other senators attached conditions that complicated the treaty. After all this wrangling, the committee vote was only 9–6 in favor, a proportion (three-fifths) less than the two-thirds that would be needed from the full Senate, and with two Democrats (members of the president's own party) as part of the opposition. While the Senate Armed Services Committee did not have formal jurisdiction, it held its own hearings and issued its own report denouncing the treaty as "not in the national security interest of the United States."[62] At this point, still months before the Soviet invasion of Afghanistan, vote counters estimated that only fifty-seven senators were prepared to vote for ratification, with twenty-seven opposed and sixteen undecided.

The intra–executive branch politics had started back in the Nixon administration. After his reelection in 1972, Nixon asked for the resignations of all appointed officials in the executive branch. Some were submitted and rejected, but in the Arms Control and Disarmament Agency nearly all were accepted. Gerard Smith, the ACDA director, stated that he wanted to leave government after SALT I, but many recognized the White House political motivation for appeasing the hawks through a "mini-purge in a deliberate attempt to start SALT II with a new team of officials unsullied by association with SALT I."[63] Fred Iklé, the new ACDA director, was much more hawkish than Smith.

The Carter administration had its own hawks-and-doves splits, particularly the one between National Security Advisor Zbigniew Brzezinski and Secretary of State Cyrus Vance, respectively. Both did support SALT II, although Brzezinski was more concerned with improving relations with China and gaining leverage over the Soviets that way. There had also been tensions with Paul Warnke, Carter's original ACDA director and lead SALT II negotiator, who was attacked in Congress and the media as being "too soft." Indeed, the conservative pressure on Warnke was so great that he resigned in late 1978, even before the SALT II negotiations were completed.

The lead anti–SALT II interest group was the Committee on the Present Danger. It was led by conservatives such as Paul Nitze, a prominent figure in U.S. policy since the early days of the Cold War. He and others in the group had opposed détente under Nixon and Ford and were even more concerned now that Carter was president. They had been against SALT I when it was first proposed, and they were all the more convinced now that the Soviets had taken advantage of SALT I to make strategic gains. They saw SALT II as even more imbalanced and dangerous. Their public communications campaign was quite impressive especially for its times, with almost five hundred television commercials and radio spots as well as press conferences, op-eds, debates, public forums, and speaking engagements.

The Committee on the Present Danger both played on and pushed along shifts in public opinion. At the height of détente in 1972–73, over 40 percent of Americans had come to have a favorable view of the Soviet Union, the highest since the Soviets had been a World War II ally against Hitler. By 1976 this approval was down to about 16 percent, and it fell even lower during the Carter years. Similarly, whereas between 1973 and 1978 the percentage saying defense spending was too much was about equal to those saying it was too little, by 1980 over 50 percent took the "too little" view. Declining support for

SALT II from over 40 percent in 1978 to about 25 percent by the end of 1979 was a reflection of this broader context as well as a manifestation of views particular to the treaty.[64]

In sum, SALT II had generated conflictual inter-branch politics, intra–executive branch splits, intensive interest-group opposition, and unfavorable public opinion.

Politics of the START Treaties, 1990s and 2000s

Even though SALT II had failed to be ratified, both the United States and the Soviet Union tacitly agreed to abide by its proposed limitations on strategic nuclear arms for a number of years. In 1982 President Ronald Reagan proposed an approach to nuclear arms control that he called the Strategic Arms Reduction Talks, or START. The "L" in SALT had been about *limiting* the growth of nuclear arsenals; the "R" in START was to signify *actual cuts.*

START I   The first Strategic Arms Reduction Treaty was signed in 1991 by President George H. W. Bush and Soviet president Mikhail Gorbachev. It called for a one-third reduction in the number of nuclear warheads on each side. With the Cold War having just ended, U.S. foreign policy politics were marked by a stronger sense of bipartisan consensus than in many years. START I was ratified 93–6 by a Democratic-controlled Senate. While not quite the 88–2 margin that SALT I had had back in 1972, START I was ratified with much less amending and other tinkering.

Another example of bipartisanship during these years was the Nunn-Lugar Cooperative Threat Reduction Program. This was created in 1992 at the initiative of Georgia senator Sam Nunn, a Democrat and chairman of the Senate Armed Services Committee, and Indiana senator Richard Lugar, the highest-ranking Republican on the Senate Foreign Relations Committee and, once his party held the majority, the committee chairman. This program provided U.S. funding as well as technical and scientific expertise to assist Russia and the other republics that had been left with nuclear weapons in the safe, secure dismantling of the weapons and associated infrastructure. Amid so much partisanship on so many issues, the Nunn-Lugar program maintained support for many years.

START II   In January 1993, just before leaving office, President George H. W. Bush signed START II with Russian president Boris Yeltsin. In the intervening years the Soviet Union had fallen apart. Ukraine, Belarus, and Kazakhstan, now independent countries, agreed to destroy or turn over the nuclear weapons that had been stationed in their territory while they still were parts of the Soviet Union. It was thus Russia that was the sole possessor of nuclear weapons among the former Soviet republics. While there were some issues on which President Bill Clinton broke with Bush's foreign policy, he did support START II. And when the Republicans won majorities in both the House and Senate in

1994, the many issues on which they opposed the Clinton administration did not include START II. In January 1996 the Senate ratified START II by an 87–4 vote.

But the treaty never actually went into force. First the Russian Duma (Russia's national legislature) delayed its ratification in protest against the expansion of NATO. Then, when the George W. Bush administration withdrew from the SALT I ABM treaty, Russia countered by linking START II ratification to continuation of the ABM treaty. Just as the United States had its foreign policy politics, so too did Russia.

NEW START   Seeking some reinvigoration through a partial renaming, while sticking with the START acronym, the Obama administration called the next treaty "New START." President Obama and Russian president Dmitri Medvedev signed it in April 2010. The principal provisions were a reduction of nuclear missiles by about half, further cuts in the number of deployed nuclear warheads to a level nearly two-thirds below that of arsenals before the first START treaty, and other cuts to be achieved by 2021.

In May 2010 President Obama submitted the treaty to the Senate for ratification. In September 2010 the Senate Foreign Relations Committee voted 14–4 in favor. This was above the two-thirds margin that would be needed from the full Senate. And it included three Republicans, including Senator Lugar. Still, with many Republicans still in opposition, the White House and the Senate leadership calculated that ratification would be more likely if postponed until the "lame duck" session after the November 2010 midterm congressional elections, when senators would be more willing to buck the anti-START political pressure from conservative groups. On December 22, New START did get ratified by 71–26, with all fifty-six Democrats, the two Independents, and thirteen Republicans voting in favor.

In sum, from SALT to START, across the forty-plus years of nuclear arms control treaties with the Soviet Union/Russia, we see both similarities and differences in the politics over time. As the next round of nuclear arms control negotiations continues, it will be interesting to see what mix of change and continuity will prevail in the foreign policy politics.

Summary

Without question, Europe is not as central to twenty-first-century American foreign policy as it was in the twentieth century. But that hardly means it is unimportant. We share many interests. We are democracies. Our economies are intertwined. Our peoples connect at many levels. The challenge is adapting relations so that old friends stay friends.

Relations with Russia are likely to continue to be a mix of cooperation and conflict. The challenge is seeking to expand the former, limit the latter, and manage domestic politics on both sides so as not to further complicate the agenda.

Notes

[1]George Liska, *Nations in Alliance: The Limits of Interdependence* (Baltimore: Johns Hopkins University Press, 1962), 12.

[2]Samantha Power, *"A Problem from Hell": America and the Age of Genocide* (New York: Basic Books, 2002), 267.

[3]Cited in Power, *"A Problem from Hell,"* xii.

[4]Robert D. Kaplan, *Balkan Ghosts: A Journey Through History* (New York: Vintage, 1993).

[5]Chris Hedges, "War Turns Sarajevo Away from Europe," *New York Times*, July 28, 1995, A4.

[6]V. P. Gagnon, "Ethnic Nationalism and International Conflict: The Case of Serbia," *International Security* 19.3 (Winter 1994–95) 130–166. The Carnegie Commission for Preventing Deadly Conflict makes its own strong statement of the purposive view in its *Final Report*: "Mass violence invariably results from the deliberately violent response of determined leaders and their groups to a wide range of social, economic, and political conditions that provide the environment for violent conflict, but usually do not independently spawn violence" (39).

[7]International Crisis Group, *Bosnia's Incomplete Transition: Between Dayton and Europe*, Europe Report No. 198, March 9, 2009, 3, www.crisisgroup.org/en/regions/europe/balkans/bosnia-herzegovina/198-bosnias-incomplete-transition-between-dayton-and-europe.aspy (accessed 3/7/13).

[8]Michael Cox, "American Power Before and After September 11: Dizzy with Success?" *International Affairs* 78.2 (2002): 290.

[9]Ivo H. Daalder and Michael E. O'Hanlon, *Winning Ugly: NATO's War to Save Kosovo* (Washington, D.C.: Brookings Institution Press, 2000).

[10]United Nations, "Secretary-General Says Renewal of Effectiveness and Relevance of Security Council Must Be Cornerstone of Efforts to Promote Peace in Next Century," United Nations Press Release SG/SM/6997, May 18, 1999.

[11]Statement by Tang Jiaxuan, Minister of Foreign Affairs of the People's Republic of China, at the 54th Session of the UN General Assembly, September 22, 1999, www.fmprc.gov.cn/eng/wjdt/zyjh/t24963.htm (accessed 3/7/13); Bates Gill and James Reilly, "Sovereignty, Intervention, and Peacekeeping: The View from Beijing," *Survival: Global Politics and Strategy* 42.3 (Autumn 2000): 41–59.

[12]Independent International Commission on Kosovo, *The Kosovo Report: Conflict, International Response, Lessons Learned* (Oxford: Oxford University Press, 2000).

[13]Robert Kagan, "Power and Weakness," *Policy Review* 113 (June 2002): 1.

[14]Nicole Gnesotto, "Reacting to America," *Survival: Global Politics and Strategy* 44.4 (Winter 2002–3): 100, 102.

[15]Craig R. Whitney, "France Presses for a Power Independent of the U.S.," *New York Times*, November 7, 1999, sec. 1, p. 9.

[16]Dana Priest, "Help From France Key in Covert Operations," *Washington Post*, July 3, 2005, A1.

[17]Tony Blair, speech to the U.S. Congress, July 18, 2003, www.cnn.com/2003/US/07/17/blair. transcript (accessed 3/7/13).

[18]Hans W. Maull, "Germany and the Use of Force: Still a 'Civilian Power'?" *Survival: Global Politics and Strategy* 42.2 (Summer 2000): 56–80.

[19]Jeffrey Anderson, G. John Ikenberry, and Thomas Risse, eds., *The End of the West? Crisis and Change in the Atlantic Order* (Ithaca, N.Y.: Cornell University Press, 2008). See also: Dana H. Allin, Gilles Andreani, Philippe Errera, and Gary Samore, *Repairing the Damage: Possibilities and Limits of Transatlantic Consensus*, Adelphi Paper 389 (London: International Institute for Strategic Studies, 2007); Jeffrey Kopstein and Sven Steinmo, eds., *Growing Apart? America and Europe in the Twenty-First Century* (New York: Cambridge University Press, 2008).

[20]NATO, "Enlargement," www.nato.int/cps/en/natolive/official_texts_24733.htm?selectedLocale-en.html (accessed 3/7/13).

[21]Joseph Lepgold, "NATO's Post–Cold War Collective Action Problem," *International Security* 23 (Summer 1998): 84–85.

[22]Bruce W. Jentleson, "The Atlantic Alliance in a Post-American World," *Journal of Transatlantic Studies* 7.1 (March 2009): 61–72.

[23]David Abshire, "A Debate for 16 Parliaments," *Washington Post*, February 19, 1997, A21.

[24]Lepgold, "NATO's Post–Cold War Collective Action Problem," 81.

[25]Lepgold, "NATO's Post–Cold War Collective Action Problem," 91.

[26]"NATO and the Fight Against Terrorism," www.nato.int/cps/en/natolive/76706.htm (accessed 3/7/13).

[27]*Transatlantic Trends Report: Key Findings 2008*, 4, http://trends.gmfus.org/files/archived/doc/2008_english_key.pdf (accessed 3/7/13).

[28]Ira Trainor, "US defence chief blasts Europe over NATO," *The Guardian*, June 10, 2011 www.guardian .co.uk/world/2011/jun/10/nato-dismal-future-pentagon-chief (accessed 3/7/13).

[29]European Union, Activities of the European Union, Foreign and Security Policy, http://europa.eu/pol/cfsp/index_en.htm (accessed 3/7/13).

[30]*New Republic*, April 29, 2010; Dan Bilefsky, "For Turkey, Lure of Tie to Europe Is Fading," *New York Times*, December 4, 2011, A4.

[31]Here I draw on the 2012 Master's thesis by Matthew Gullo, a Duke graduate student in Political Science.

[32]Gail W. Lapidus, "Transforming Russia: American Policy in the 1990s," in *Eagle Rules? Foreign Policy and American Primacy in the Twenty-First Century,* Robert J. Lieber, ed. (Upper Saddle River, N.J.: Prentice-Hall, 2002), 108-09.

[33]Andrei Kozyrev, "Russia: A Chance for Survival," *Foreign Affairs* 71.2 (March/April 1992): 9–10.

[34]Press Conference by President Bush and Russian Federation president Putin, Brdo Castle, Brdo Pri Kranju, Slovenia, June 16, 2001, http://georgewbush-whitehouse.archives.gov/news/releases/2001/06/20010618.html (accessed 3/7/13).

[35]Arms Control Association, "Nuclear and Missile Systems We Can't Afford, Don't Need," July 18, 2012 www.armscontrol.org/issuebriefs/Nuclear-and-Missile-Systems-We-Cant-Afford-Dont-Need%20 (accessed 3/7/13).

[36]"Russia's National Security Concept," *Arms Control Today* (January/February 2000), www.armscontrol.org/act/2000_01-02/docjf00 (accessed 8/14/09).

[37]Jane Perlez, "U.S. Scolds Russia for Plans to Resume Arms Sales to Iran," *New York Times*, March 15, 2001, A15.

[38]Patrick E. Tyler, "Moscow Says Remarks by U.S. Resurrect 'Spirit of Cold War,'" *New York Times*, March 21, 2001, www.nytimes.com/2001/03/21/world/21RUSS.html?searchpv-site02 (accessed 3/7/13).

[39]Remarks by Vice President Biden at 45th Munich Conference on Security Policy, Munich, Germany, February 7, 2009, www.whitehouse.gov/the_press_office/RemarksbyVicePresidentBidenat45thMunich ConferenceonSecurityPolicy/ (accessed 3/7/13).

[40]Lapidus, "Transforming Russia," 126.

[41]Sergei Ivanov, speech at the Wehrkunde Security Conference, Munich, Germany, February 4, 2001, http://belfercenter.kgg.harvard.edu/files/rw03.pdf (accessed 3/7/13)

[42]Richard K. Betts, "The Three Faces of NATO," *National Interest Online*, April 10, 2009, www.nationalinterest .org/Article.aspx?id=20944 (accessed 3/7/13).

[43]Bush Addresses Tens of Thousands in Georgia's Freedom Square, Tbilisi, May 10, 2005, www.america .gov/st/washfile-english/2005/May/20050510114027btruevecer0.9125635.html (accessed 3/7/13).

[44]Condoleezza Rice, Remarks en Route to Brussels, Belgium, August 18, 2008, http://2001–2009.state.gov/secretary/rm/2008/08/1085552.htm (accessed 3/7/13).

⁴⁵BBC News Europe, "Russia and Georgia Agree on a Truce," August 13, 2008, http://news.bbc.co.uk/2/hi/europe/7557457.stm (accessed 3/7/13).

⁴⁶Jim Hoagland, "Three Miscreants," *Washington Post*, April 13, 2003, B7.

⁴⁷Cited in Stephen M. Walt, *Taming American Power: The Global Response to U.S. Primacy* (New York: Norton, 2005), 111.

⁴⁸Putin: "Iran Does Not Need Nuclear Weapons," Globalsecurity.org, September 25, 2004, www.globalsecurity.org/wmd/library/news/iran/2004/iran-040925-irna01.htm (accessed 3/7/13).

⁴⁹Neil MacFarquhar, "At UN, Pressure Is on Russia for Refusal to Condemn Syria," *New York Times*, February 1, 2012; and Ellen Barry, "As Nations Line Up against Syrian Government, Russia Sides Firmly with Assad," *New York Times*, January 27, 2012.

⁵⁰Robert Legvold, "The Three Russias: Decline, Revolution, and Reconstruction," in *A Century's Journey: How the Great Powers Shape the World*, ed. Robert A. Pastor (New York: Basic Books, 1999), 188–89.

⁵¹Legvold, "The Three Russias," 189.

⁵²Lapidus, "Transforming Russia," 120

⁵³Michael Wines, "Russia's Latest Dictator Goes by the Name of Law," *New York Times*, January 21, 2001, sec. 4, p. 3.

⁵⁴Mark Franchetti, "Putin Resurrects Spectre of KGB," *Sunday Times* (London), February 4, 2001.

⁵⁵Ellen Mickiewicz, *Changing Channels: Television and the Struggle for Power in Russia* (New York: Oxford University Press, 1997); Kathy Lally, "Battle over Free Press Intensifies in Russia," *Baltimore Sun*, February 3, 2001, 1A; "A Moscow Media Magnate Urges a Definition of Limits for Russia," *New York Times*, May 4, 2001.

⁵⁶Council of Europe, "Russian Duma Elections 'Not Held on a Level Playing Field,' Say Parliamentary Observers," December 3, 2007, https://wcd.coe.int/ViewDoc.jsp?id=1221469&Site=DC&BackColorInternet=F5CA75&BackColorIntranet=F5CA75&BackColorLogged=A9BACE (accessed 3/7/13).

⁵⁷Lapidus, "Transforming Russia," 117.

⁵⁸Abram Chayes and Antonia Handler Chayes, *Preventing Conflict in the Post-Communist World: Mobilizing International and Regional Organizations* (Washington, D.C.: Brookings Institution Press, 1996), 10.

⁵⁹Alan Platt, *The U.S. Senate and Strategic Arms Policy, 1969–1977* (Boulder, Colo.: Westview Press, 1978), 10.

⁶⁰Platt, *U.S. Senate and Strategic Arms Policy*, 99.

⁶¹Dan Caldwell, *The Dynamics of Domestic Politics and Arms Control: The SALT II Treaty Ratification Debate* (Columbia, S.C.: University of South Carolina Press, 1991), 127.

⁶²Caldwell, *SALT II Treaty Ratification Debate*, 145.

⁶³Platt, *U.S. Senate and Strategic Arms Policy*, 29.

⁶⁴Caldwell, *SALT II Treaty Ratification Debate*, 91, 81.

13 *The Americas: Relations with Latin America and Canada*

Introduction: 4 Ps Tensions

U.S. policy toward Latin America has long been defined by tensions regarding the 4 Ps. In chapter 4 we saw how frequently the United States intervened militarily in various Latin American countries in the late nineteenth and early twentieth centuries, in large part to protect foreign investment and export interests: Prosperity in tension with Principles. In Chapters 5 and 6 we saw many examples of covert action, military intervention, and other "ABC" (anything but communism) policies during the Cold War in the name of Power yet in tension with Principles.

Americans* tend to be much less conscious of such historical legacies than are Latin Americans. We thus start this chapter with historical background. We then turn to the current agenda with three sections on region-wide issues—regional diplomacy, democracy promotion, and the "drug wars"—and then three on major bilateral relations with Mexico, Haiti, and Cuba. We also look at relations with Canada, the neighbor to the north with which relations have been mostly but not fully cooperative. This chapter's foreign policy politics case study turns back to Latin America and the politics of immigration.

---

*I use *Americans* to refer to the people of the United States. Latin Americans often use the term *norteamericanos*, indirectly making the point that they, too, are part of the Americas. *Norteamericanos*, though, has its own ambiguity, either encompassing or excluding Canadians. *Yanquis* is an alternative but it is both slang and carries a negative connotation. *Americans* and *Latin Americans*, while presenting their own problems, still seem the best terminology to use.

MAP 13.1

WESTERN HEMISPHERE

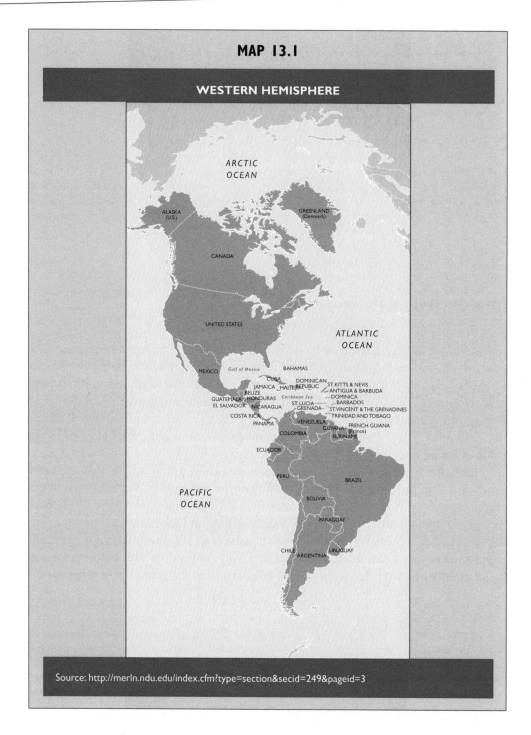

Source: http://merln.ndu.edu/index.cfm?type=section&secid=249&pageid=3

Historical Legacies

The Monroe Doctrine is a good example of varying U.S. and Latin American perspectives. In 1823, with concern mounting that Britain, Spain, and other "Old World" European powers were eager to re-intervene against Latin American independence movements (like that led by Simón Bolívar in Colombia and Venezuela), President James Monroe declared that the United States would stand by its hemispheric neighbors. "We could not view any interposition for the purpose of oppressing them, or controlling in any other manner their destiny, by any European power," Monroe stated in the language of the day, "in any other light than as the manifestation of an unfriendly disposition toward the United States." Initially, as historian Gaddis Smith has written, some Latin American countries saw this very positively as a U.S. pledge to help them maintain their independence, and even proposed "that the Doctrine be transformed into a binding inter-American alliance." But Secretary of State John Quincy Adams "said no. He emphasized that the Doctrine was a unilateral American statement and that any action taken under it would be for the United States alone to decide."[1] Historian Richard Van Alstyne goes even further, terming it "an official declaration fencing in the 'western hemisphere' as a United States sphere of influence."[2] There was little altruism in this policy; it was much more the self-interest of a regional power seeking to preserve its dominant position against outside challengers.

In 1904, President Theodore Roosevelt added his "corollary" claiming broad U.S. intervention rights in the Western Hemisphere. The United States only desired, Roosevelt maintained, "to see the neighboring countries stable, orderly, and prosperous." Countries that conducted themselves in this manner "can count upon our hearty friendship." But

> Chronic wrongdoing, or an impotence which results in a general loosening of the ties of civilized society, may . . . ultimately require intervention by some civilized nation, and in the Western Hemisphere the adherence of the United States to its Monroe Doctrine may force the United States, however reluctantly, in flagrant cases of such wrongdoing or impotence, to the exercise of an international police power.[3]

Indeed, over the ensuing thirty years the United States repeatedly intervened militarily in Mexico, Cuba, the Dominican Republic, Haiti, Honduras, Nicaragua, and Panama.

Cuba was a particularly flagrant case. One of the reasons given for the Spanish-American War was supporting Cuban independence from its colonial master, Spain. But while Cuba did gain formal independence, the United States insisted that an amendment be attached to the Cuban constitution granting the United States rights to veto treaties between Cuba and other governments and to intervene militarily. On this basis "the United States exercised sweeping control over Cuban internal affairs, which included three military interventions (1906–9, 1912, 1917–22), political meddling and supervision of Cuban fiscal and budgetary affairs."[4] It also provided for the acquisition of a naval base on the eastern end of the island, the Guantánamo Naval Station, with an open-ended lease that could only be terminated by mutual agreement.

The 1930s "Good Neighbor Policy" of President Franklin D. Roosevelt shifted to more cooperative relations with Latin America. Under this policy, existing military occupations were ended and no new military intervention was undertaken. When U.S. oil companies were nationalized (taken over) by the governments in Mexico and Bolivia, FDR negotiated compensation rather than sending troops in. The efforts that were made to impact politics and economic policy within Latin American countries consisted largely of diplomacy and trade. The United States still looked to preserve its interests and manifest a power imbalance in its favor, but did so in more of a "good neighborly" way. This approach, however, as evidenced by support for such military dictators as Batista in Cuba and Somoza in Nicaragua, did not include much support for democracy. Some historians trace the old adage "He may be an SOB, but he's our SOB" to an FDR statement about Somoza.

With the onset of the Cold War, U.S. policy shifted back to a highly interventionist mode. Ensuring that governments in the region remained anticommunist was the priority. In some instances this was done through military intervention—for example, in the Dominican Republic in 1965. In other instances it was done through covert action, including against democratically elected governments (such as Guatemala in 1954 and Chile from 1970 to 1973). In still other instances it was through support for military coups (such as Brazil in 1964 and Argentina in the 1970s). And in yet other instances it was through continued support for longtime dictators, including the Somozas in Nicaragua. With Cuba, where Fidel Castro led the revolution that in 1959 toppled the U.S.-backed Batista regime and brought communism to the country, U.S. policy has included the 1961 Bay of Pigs invasion, assassination plots against Castro, fifty-plus years' worth of economic sanctions, and other elements, as we discuss in greater detail later in the chapter.

The Carter administration early on signaled its change in U.S. policy by negotiating a new Panama Canal Treaty ending U.S. control of the Panama Canal. Not only was this gesture important to Panama, it was symbolic to much of Latin America as a manifestation of a more cooperative U.S. attitude. Carter also brought a greater emphasis on human rights and resorted less to the "ABC" definition of democracy. This meant less support for military governments in countries such as Argentina and Chile. With Nicaragua, the decline in U.S. support, for reasons of human rights, was a key factor in weakening the Somoza government, which eventually fell to the Sandinistas, a leftist social revolutionary group.

The Reagan administration shifted support in Nicaragua to the "contras" (a Spanish word meaning "those against") in their fight against the Sandinistas, using both military assistance and covert operations. It also supported the right-wing military government in El Salvador, even as human rights violations grew worse. In these and other ways, Reagan took U.S. policy back in the Cold War direction. He also, though, did start to reduce U.S. support for the military regimes in Argentina and Chile and provide some support efforts for transitions back to democracy.

An editorial cartoon depicting a Latin American *campesino* (peasant) trying to get the attention of Uncle Sam captured the gist of U.S. policy in the Cold War era. "Uncle Sam, Uncle Sam," the *campesino* says in the first frame, "I have no job." Uncle Sam looks the other way. The second frame: "Uncle Sam, Uncle Sam, my children are hungry." Uncle Sam still looks the other way. Then in the third frame: "Uncle Sam, Uncle Sam, I just saw a communist." Now Uncle Sam pays attention, and in the last frame chases after the *campesino*.

Post–Cold War: Eroding Regional Hegemony

While the United States remains the most powerful country in the hemisphere, it is no longer a hegemon. This shift is evident in three main respects.

First, the United States is less able to get its way in regional organizations. During the Cold War, the ***Organization of American States (OAS)***, the principal hemispheric regional multilateral organization, was seen largely as being under the U.S. thumb. It dutifully supported the 1954 U.S. covert action in Guatemala and the 1965 military intervention in the Dominican Republic, as well as the expulsion of Cuba following Fidel Castro's revolution in 1959. But over a decade after the Cold War ended, the OAS was less willing to side with the United States in its conflicts with President Hugo Chávez of Venezuela. Chávez, an ex-military officer, was first elected Venezuelan president in 1999 and reelected repeatedly. Although he delivered on some promised social programs, once in power his rule became increasingly repressive politically and had very mixed economic results. He forged close ties with Cuba and in other ways pursued an anti-American foreign policy. In 2002 a coup was attempted. Whether or not the Bush administration actively supported the coup is a matter of debate; even if it did not, it certainly did nothing to oppose it and appeared to welcome it. While few Latin American leaders were very pro-Chávez, they also were leery of the antidemocratic precedent that the coup set. Just a few months earlier—in fact, coincidentally, on September 11, 2001—the OAS had approved its new Inter-American Democratic Charter, which affirmed member countries' shared commitment to defending democracy. In that context, rather than criticize Chávez the OAS instead condemned the coup as an "alteration of the constitutional order" and invoked the new Democratic Charter as the basis for threats to impose economic sanctions and perhaps take other actions if the coup were not reversed.

To be sure, the United States still exerts substantial power and leverage within the OAS, including through providing about 60 percent of the budget. U.S. influence remains substantial; it's just not the hegemonic dominance it used to be. We also see this in other issues, such as the re-admission of Cuba to the OAS, as discussed below.

Moreover, a new regional organization called **UNASUR (Union of South American Nations)**, excluding the United States, was established in 2008. It has its own secretariat, its own agenda and its own summits. It is not anti-American but it is independent of the United States, a mechanism for South American countries to cooperate on issues that pertain most directly to them. For example, UNASUR played a valuable role in settling border disputes among Ecuador, Colombia, and Venezuela. Its 2012 summit called for developing a common South American citizenship similar to that of the European Union.

The rise of Brazil is a second key factor in hemispheric power shifts. When emerging powers are discussed, Brazil is one of those most often included. It's the "B" in BRICS (Brazil, Russia, India, China, South Africa), a commonly used shorthand for the world's notable rising powers. Brazil's land mass covers more than half of South America, and two of its cities are among the world's most populous—Sao Paulo (20 million) and Rio de Janeiro (13 million). Its recent president, Luiz Inácio Lula da Silva (2003–10), gained enormous prestige regionally and globally for his charisma, as well as for his success in implementing progressive policies that helped the poor (40 million Brazilians moved out of poverty) while also fostering a favorable climate for business. So, too, has the country as a whole, as evidenced by its winning bids for the 2014 World Cup and 2016 Olympics.

As with much of Latin America, U.S. relations with Brazil have had a mixed history. The United States had a hand in the 1964 military coup, and then supported the military regime for most of its two-plus decades. When Lula was first elected president, his left-leaning ideas and his role as a labor leader were looked on suspiciously by the Bush administration. Relations later did improve somewhat and have continued to do so during the Obama administration. But even without major disputes, Brazil has been moving toward a more independent foreign policy, measured less by whether it is pro– or anti–United States than by its desire to get its own seat at the table and pursue its own national interests.

Brazil's rising diplomatic position is evident globally and regionally. It is a member of the G20. It is on the short list for a new permanent seat should the UN Security Council expand. It has been playing a lead role in UNASUR. It has been building up its own military and pursuing discussions with other countries about the creation of a South American defense council. These initiatives, too, are less about opposition to the United States than about lessened dependence on it. Relations could become more problematic, but even if they don't, Brazil's trend is toward a more independent foreign policy.

The third factor in the hemispheric power shift is the lessened dependence of Latin American economies on the United States. There are some exceptions, such as Mexico (to be discussed later) and countries such as Colombia and Panama, with which the United States has made free-trade agreements. But the Free Trade Area of the Americas proposed in the late Clinton and early Bush years did not come to fruition. It ran into opposition both at home, from labor unions and others who feared job losses, and from some within Latin America who feared domination by large U.S. corporations and local elites without any significant reduction of economic inequality. The Central American Free Trade Agreement met a similar fate. Meanwhile, Latin American trade with China increased from only $10 billion in 2000 to $240 billion in 2011—still second to U.S.-Latin American trade but by much less. Trade also has been increasing within regional trade organizations such as Mercosur, often called the Common Market of the South, with Argentina, Brazil, Paraguay, and Uruguay as longtime members and Venezuela added in 2012.

In sum, as also comes through in Reading 13.1, while the United States continues to have substantial influence in Latin America, political, diplomatic, and economic forces have been making this influence less prominent than in the past.

13.1

Democracy Promotion: Scopes and Limits

What is the state of democracy today in Latin America? Has the United States been truer to its Principles as a democracy promoter than it was during the Cold War?

The main shift towards democracy started in the 1980s with the fall of military regimes in countries such as Brazil, Argentina, and Chile that had been supported by the United States as part of Cold War containment. In Nicaragua, a Marxist government gave way to democracy. In Mexico, competitive elections ended decades-old one-party rule. Overall, democracy has become more widespread in Latin America than ever before in its history.

This has not, however, been a straightforward process. Argentina had musical-chair presidents, five in fewer than four years between 1999 and 2003. In Bolivia, one president was forced to resign in 2003; another tried to resign in early 2005 but had his resignation rejected by Congress and then was pressured by public protests to call early elections. In Ecuador, one president was forced to resign in 2000 and another in 2005. In Venezuela, Hugo Chávez survived coup attempts and rigged elections, and his rule became increasingly autocratic until his death in March 2013. In Honduras in 2009 and Paraguay in 2012, military coups ousted democratically elected governments. All told, while Cuba was the only country ranked by Freedom House as not free in 2012, ten were ranked as only partly free while eighteen were ranked as free.[5] Even more mixed is the "democracy index" published by the Economist Intelligence Unit, which lists only two Latin American countries as full democracies, fourteen as flawed democracies, seven as "hybrid regimes" (containing some elements of democracy but also significant repression), and one (Cuba) as authoritarian.[6]

One issue has been the continued weakness of political institutions. As assessed by one prominent analyst, "severe deficiencies mark political life—weak capacity and performance of government institutions, widespread corruption, irregular and often arbitrary rule of law, poorly developed patterns of representation and participation, and large numbers of marginalized citizens."[7] Because of both its economic impact of wasted resources and its political effects of delegitimization, corruption has been especially corrosive. Indeed, a survey of eighteen countries by a Chilean public opinion firm found that the Latin American people see corruption as one of their severest problems. The World Bank concurs, saying that "official graft and nepotism are so powerful that they are rotting governmental institutions and stunting economic growth." An American government analysis estimated "that official corruption might shave as much as 15 percent off annual growth in Latin America, as public funds are pilfered and wary foreign investors shy away."[8]

Economic inequality is another factor. Some progress is being made: a report by the Economic Commission for Latin America and the Caribbean shows poverty rates down from 48.4 percent of the population in 1990 to 31.4 percent in 2010.[9] This is still a high poverty rate, though, reflecting masses of urban poor and rural *campesinos*. In Bolivia, for example, while the national average for basic subsistence is reasonably high, "the entire populations of some municipalities are unable to satisfy at least one basic need, such as adequate sanitation or sufficient caloric intake." In Mexico, despite the notable wealth in some segments of the population, the national literacy rate still hovers at around only 15 percent.[10]

During the Cold War, Latin America was one of the regions where socialism had its greatest appeal as a popular movement. Although socialism itself may not reemerge, the question remains whether other competing ideologies and political-economic models may develop. In their fundamentals, socialism and communism were efforts to address the problem of social, political, and economic inequality. While these particular remedies largely failed, the core problem of inequality remains. If democracy and capitalism do not more effectively deal with these fundamental problems, it stands to reason that other ideologies will be articulated and other political models advanced with at least the promise of addressing real concerns. "The logic of the market does not resolve all problems," Chile's then-president Michelle Bachelet stated. "You need strong and powerful social policies by the state to resolve the problems of income and equality of opportunity."[11] The wave of electoral victories by left-of-center presidential candidates—Lula and his successor Dilma Rousseff in Brazil, Rafael Correa in Ecuador, Daniel Ortega in Nicaragua, Evo Morales in Bolivia, Alan García in Peru, and Bachelet in Chile—demonstrated the political appeal of this "social market" approach. But the trend is not unidirectional. More traditional pro-business candidates have won presidential elections in Chile, Paraguay, Honduras, and elsewhere.

In terms of U.S. policy, much has been done to support Latin American democracy. This includes foreign aid, initiatives by NGOs, and other programs and policies. With Guatemala, the Obama administration tied military aid to greater commitment to meet the Guatemalan public's demand for justice in addressing the political killings and human rights abuses of past military governments. But in the case of the 2009 Honduras coup, the

Obama policy was sharply criticized for not prioritizing democracy and human rights. Another democratically elected left-of-center leader pushing social and economic reform at home and with close relations with Venezuela's Hugo Chávez and Castro's Cuba, Honduran president José Manuel Zelaya, was thrown out of office. While "Obama's initial instinct was to side with the consensus in the region to restore Zelaya to power," as Council on Foreign Relations scholar Julia Sweig argues, "the organizers of Zelaya's ouster and their lawyers pushed hard in the U.S. Congress and the media to promote an alternative narrative. . . . American conservatives in Congress who had vowed to make Obama a one-term president . . . [and were] eager to pin the scarlet letter of national-security weakness on [him] . . . argued that Zelaya deserved his fate, given his affinity with Hugo Chávez in particular."[12] Under this political pressure the Obama administration went along with the election of a new president a few months later despite the protests of most Latin American countries and claims by many international observers that the election was not free and fair. In the years since, human rights groups have reported killings of journalists, opposition leaders, and *campesino* activists in land struggles as well as other state-sponsored repression.[13]

Drug "Wars"

Three caveats to start: First, calling these policy challenges "wars" has been controversial since the term started being commonly used back in the 1970s. Second, while many aspects involve Latin America, the issues are global in scope. Third, the problem is not just a matter of foreign policy—that is, concerned purely with the supply side of drugs flowing into the United States from other countries—but also a matter of domestic demand.

In the 1990s and 2000s, Colombia was a major case. Drug cartels assassinated government officials who sought to crack down on them, including supreme court justices and a popular presidential candidate. Plan Colombia, initiated by the Clinton administration and continued by the Bush administration, entailed over $7.3 billion in military, economic, and other assistance to the Colombian government for drug interdiction. By some measures Plan Colombia was considered a success. U.S. assistance enabled the training of large numbers of additional Colombian military and police personnel, and the United States provided helicopters and other advanced equipment for penetrating the drug lords' hideouts in the mountains and jungles. Cocaine production was cut by about 35 percent. Homicides decreased from around 29,000 in 2002 to around 16,000 in 2009. Guerrillas operating in the country were estimated to be half the 2000 level. Kidnappings fell. In these and other ways, the everyday sense of security in the country markedly improved.

However, these gains have not been free of human cost. Combat deaths were estimated at over 20,000. Civilian casualties and victims of extrajudicial killings were in the many thousands. Since 2000, over 3 million Colombians have fled their homes due to violence, a number of refugees and internally displaced people exceeding that of Iraq and surpassed only by the Sudan. Human rights violations by Colombian security forces were widely reported, but the first human rights–based conviction in Colombian courts did not occur until 2010. Moreover, the crackdown on Colombian cocaine production had only a partial global supply-reduction effect, as some was simply shifted to neighboring countries Peru and Bolivia.

The Mexican drug wars began getting a great deal of attention in the mid-2000s. Close to 90 percent of the cocaine heading to the United States was now transiting through Mexico. The drug cartels were armed like paramilitaries with platoon-size units of trained fighters, antitank rockets, heavy machine guns, encrypted communications, and fleets of helicopters and submarines. Between 2006 and 2012 almost 50,000 people were killed; to put that in perspective, it is almost twelve times greater than the number of U.S. casualties in the Iraq war.

The effects were quite tangible within the United States. In Tucson, Arizona, three-quarters of the two hundred home invasions investigated by the police were linked to the drug trade. Violent incidents even farther from the border in Atlanta, Georgia, and Shelby County, Alabama, were linked to the Mexican drug cartels. The Drug Enforcement Administration (DEA) arrested over seven hundred people linked to Mexican cartels in one hundred and twenty American cities. In early 2009 the State Department issued a travel alert warning of the risks of travel to Mexico—its timing geared in no small part to college students about to head out on spring break.

The Mérida Initiative, a program similar to Plan Colombia, was launched late in the Bush administration and continued in the Obama administration to provide financing and training for Mexican security forces. In addition, some CIA and DEA agents were deployed, and surveillance drones were used. Some success was registered: arrests increased, some of the cartels were broken up, and thousands of pounds of cocaine and other drugs were seized. But violence still raged and corruption remained rampant. In May 2012, three Mexican generals were arrested for involvement in drug trafficking. The corruption also extended to the lower ranks of the army, where cartels find it easy to bribe junior soldiers. These troops have come to be perceived in certain areas as armed thugs known for the use of excessive force, intimidation tactics, and human rights violations. Some Mexicans see little difference between enforcers of the cartels and certain elements of the armed forces.

The diversion-deflection market-supply effect that we saw between Colombia and its neighbors was also occurring between Mexico and Central America. In Guatemala in May 2012, twenty-seven people were brutally murdered by drug gangs, the worst violence in that country since 1996. One of my own former students serving as a Peace Corps volunteer in Guatemala e-mailed me in April 2012 that she was being forced to leave because of drug-related violence.

The impact was especially great in Honduras. According to DEA estimates, over 300 tons of cocaine are smuggled out of or flown into Honduran territory every year, representing almost one-third of all global supply.[14] This new importance as a critical waypoint for cocaine traffickers, due to its huge swaths of ungoverned territory, was a key factor in a surge in violent crime that brought Honduras the dubious distinction of being named the deadliest country in the world, and one of its cities—San Pedro Sula—being named the deadliest city in the world.[15] In response, U.S. policy has blurred the line even further between law enforcement and the military, what one commentator called "fusing of elements of the 'War on Drugs' with the 'War on Terror'."[16] American military forces, CIA operatives, and DEA agents have helped Honduras set up counter-narcotic bases at various strategic locations in the country, drawing directly on the lessons of the Afghan War. Joint Task Force-Bravo, based in a remote airfield, became "the largest concentration of American military forces south of the Rio Grande."[17] The DEA has also been "quietly deploying" commando-style squads comprised of former Navy SEALs, who provide support and training to the Honduran police force and anti-drug authorities.[18]

These have not been the only elements of U.S. policy. Numerous diplomatic initiatives continue to be undertaken. Border patrols have been ramped up. Civil society initiatives, officially and through NGOs, also are important components. But we call special attention to the military aspects of U.S. policy because they have brought policy closer to the literal meaning of a drug *war*. As one Honduran activist put it, "Helicopters and soldiers are not development."[19]

Moreover, the United States has not just been the bearer of consequences. Its domestic policies, such as lax gun control, and societal habits that create much of the demand for illegal drugs are both substantial causes of the problem. At a December 2011 regional summit, speaking for a broad coalition of Latin American presidents, then president of Guatemala Álvaro Colom did not mince words: "Our region is seriously threatened by organized crime, but there is very little responsibility taken by the drug-consuming countries."[20] The hemisphere was paying the price for drug consumption in the United States, he said, with "our blood, our fear and our human sacrifice." There has been at least some recognition of this by the United States, as in the statement by then-secretary of state Hillary Clinton that "our insatiable demand for illegal drugs fuels the drug trade. Our inability to prevent weapons from being illegally smuggled across the border to arm these criminals causes the death of police officers, soldiers, and civilians."[21] While some progress has been made in recent years, clearly much remains to be done.

Mexico

No country in Latin American plays a larger role in U.S. foreign policy than Mexico. As the State Department observes, "The two countries share a 2,000-mile border, and relations between the two have a direct impact on the lives and livelihoods of millions of

Americans—whether the issue is trade and economic reform, homeland security, drug control, migration, or the environment."[22] More than 32 million U.S. residents are of Mexican origin, equivalent to about 60 percent of all Latinos and 10 percent of the total U.S. population.

Along with the drug issue, discussed above, and immigration, which will be the focus of this chapter's domestic politics case study, economic relations have been another major policy area. Mexico is second only to Canada as a market for U.S. exports, and third only to Canada and China as an overall trade partner. It also is the United States' second largest supplier of oil (Saudi Arabia is first). Moreover, Mexico sends about 80 percent of its exports to the United States. It also relies heavily on remittances (U.S. dollars sent home from family and friends in the United States) totaling over $22 billion (2011) and growing as a major source of foreign currency. The NAFTA has been a key part of U.S.-Mexican economic relations. NAFTA was originally signed in 1992 by President George H. W. Bush and brought to approval by President Clinton. At the time it was seen as a test case in the free trade–protectionism debate. Proponents stressed the value of creating the world's largest free-trade area, linking 444 million people and economies producing $17 trillion worth of goods and services. Opponents were concerned about job losses as well as such related issues as environmental regulations, labor standards, and other parts of what has become the broader globalization agenda, as discussed back in Chapter 8. In the end, the margin of approval, 61–38 in the Senate and 234–200 in the House, was larger than expected. In terms of the party breakdown, Republicans were strongly supportive, voting 132–43 in the House and 34–10 in the Senate in favor of the agreement, while Democrats were overall narrowly opposed in the Senate (27–28) and widely against the agreement in the House (102–157).

Since it's implementation, there has been much debate over NAFTA's actual impact. Trade has surely increased; for example, U.S. exports to Mexico have tripled. How much of this is attributable to NAFTA and how much is a function of factors that would have been operating anyway is hard for economists to determine. There are studies, such as one conducted by two Yale economists, that credit NAFTA with having raised wages in the United States, Mexico, and Canada—all three countries that are party to the treaty. On the negative side are studies that find major U.S. job losses; the Economic Policy Institute reported that as of 2010, 600,000 American jobs had been lost due to NAFTA.[23]

Overall diplomatic relations between the U.S. and Mexico have been largely positive. As neighbors, the two countries work together on an enormous number of issues on a daily basis. While these affect the daily lives of the citizens of both countries, they do not make the headlines in the way that disputes between the countries do.

One longstanding dispute has been over Cuba. Mexico was the only Latin American country not to break relations with Cuba in the aftermath of Castro's rise to power, and throughout the Castro years Mexico has maintained closer relations to that country than the United States has preferred. Mexico's opposition to the 2003 Iraq War was another example of tension between the U.S. and Mexico. And Mexicans naturally have the sensitivities that come with the power imbalance and what Mexicans at times see as U.S. meddling in their politics and domestic affairs. In 2011, for example, the U.S. ambassador to Mexico was forced to resign following the publicizing by Wikileaks of a cable he sent back to Washington criticizing the Mexican government's anti–drug cartels policies. Indeed, optimal strategies for the drug wars have long been a mix of cooperation and tension in U.S.-Mexican relations. The only issue which has been more controversial is immigration, as we shall see at the end of this chapter.

As to Mexican politics, in December 2012 a new president, Enrique Peña Nieto, took office for a six-year term. His election marked the return to power of the Institutional Revolutionary Party (PRI in its Spanish acronym). Until the National Action Party (PAN) and its candidate Vicente Fox won the presidency in 2000, the PRI had been in office for over 70 years. Corruption and economic mismanagement had so tarnished its reputation that its historical claims as the embodiment of Mexican nationalism were no longer enough for it to hold onto power. The PAN recaptured the presidency in 2006, but the rise in drug-related violence and other issues weakened its stature, and the PRI's own reforms and re-imaging helped Peña Nieto win the election back for his party in 2012. In his early speeches and initiatives Peña Nieto prioritized more effective policies against the drug cartels, expanded social programs, economic growth, and progress on immigration to the United States.

Cuba

As we've seen, the U.S.-Cuban relationship was troubled long before Fidel Castro came to power. For decades, the U.S. generally supported one dictator after another, including Fulgencio Batista, a former sergeant in the Cuban army who led a coup in 1934 and ruled for most of the period until 1959. Batista was among the most corrupt rulers of his day. Among other things, he had such close relations with the Mafia as to turn Cuba into "a criminal state." Mafia don Charles "Lucky" Luciano, whom the United States had deported back to Sicily, "quietly made his way to Cuba, a country whose government did not interfere with criminal business interests." Batista also had Meyer Lansky, another major Mafia kingpin, on his payroll as "gambling adviser."[24]

It was in this context that the revolution led by Castro had broad appeal to the Cuban people. Scholars debate whether it was inevitable that Castro would be as anti-American and as autocratic as he became, or whether less antagonistic U.S. policies could have made the relationship less adversarial. On the one hand, Castro was consolidating personal power. Early on he purged even many of those who had been comrades. He nationalized U.S. businesses and turned to the Soviet Union for economic assistance. On the other hand, the United States imposed its first round of economic sanctions a little more than a year after Castro came to power, and just a year later, in April 1961, launched the Bay of Pigs invasion to topple his government and re-install officials from the Batista era. The October 1962 Cuban missile crisis, which brought the world closer to a nuclear showdown than ever before, thrust Cuba into the center of the Cold War. In other parts of Latin America, Castro and Ernesto "Che" Guevara sought to spread revolution while the United States supported anticommunist military governments. All the while the United States also hatched various assassination plots against Castro, some of which were revealed by congressional and journalist investigations in the 1970s.

As part of its hard line on Cuba, the Reagan administration established "Radio Martí," a U.S.-government-sponsored radio station based in Miami that broadcast Spanish-language programming into Cuba. The station was named after Jose Martí, the leader of the Cuban independence movement against Spain in the 1890s. Modeled after Radio Free Europe and used for analogous purposes (broadcasting into the Soviet bloc), Radio Martí sought to break the hold of Cuban censors and provide information more favorable to the United States and critical of the Castro regime. In 1990, Radio Martí was complemented by TV Martí. According to a study by the Broadcasting Board of Governors, 72 percent of those surveyed stated that they had listened to Radio Martí and 30 percent reported that they listened to it daily.[25] Some, though, saw irony if not hypocrisy in invoking Jose Martí's name for a pro-U.S. initiative, given how disillusioned Martí became with the United States in his day for being less interested in Cuban independence than in advancing its own interests.[26]

In its initial years, the Cuban revolution did produce significant achievements for the Cuban people. Public health care exceeded that available in much of Latin America. So too did literacy rates. Over time, though, economic problems increased. These were in part a consequence of the U.S. embargo and in part a consequence of the Castro regime's economic mismanagement. With the collapse of the Soviet Union in the early 1990s and the end of the vast economic subsidies it had been providing, the Cuban economy reached crisis stage. The Soviet Union and its allies had accounted for 85 percent of Cuba's trade, including 80 percent of its sugar exports and much of its oil imports. In order to jump start its flagging economy, the Cuban government allowed some partial economic liberalization, which included the partial legalization of the U.S. dollar. The government also transformed several of its state farms into hybrid public-private cooperatives and legalized some private enterprises.

At the same time, the Clinton administration took steps to partially open up relations. It reached some emigration agreements seeking to avoid another mass "boat people" exodus like the one in 1980 that had caused a major crisis for the Carter administration.

It allowed some travel from the United States to Cuba. It opened the flow of remittances from Cuban Americans to their families back in Cuba. But pressure from the Cuban American lobby and within Congress led to passage in 1996 of the Helms-Burton Act, which tightened economic sanctions even further. Then came a major controversy in 1999–2000: the Elián Gonzáles case involved a young boy who fled Cuba and was found off the Florida coast after the boat he had traveled in had capsized, killing his mother and stepfather. U.S. immigration authorities placed Elián with other family members living in Miami. But Elián's father, who was still in Cuba, asserted his custody rights, claiming that he had never given permission for the boy to leave Cuba. This became a high-intensity courtroom drama combining U.S.-Cuban relations and parental custody rights. The U.S. courts ruled in favor of the father's custody rights, and Clinton administration attorney general Janet Reno ordered Elián to be returned to his father in Cuba. The Cuban American community protested vociferously, with local confrontations and full-bore media coverage. Many analysts pointed to the Elián case as a key factor in the 2000 presidential election, prompting the Cuban American community to vote against Vice President Al Gore in numbers that made the vote in Florida as close as it was, ultimately leading to the Supreme Court decision that made George W. Bush the victor. Once in office, President Bush re-tightened the trade, travel, and remittance rules.

In 2006 Fidel Castro became too ill to maintain control, and by 2008 he had handed power over to his brother Raúl. In 2009, partly in response to some changes by Raúl Castro, President Obama re-liberalized trade, travel, and remittances. This included allowing cultural exchanges and travel by educational groups, such as a group I went with as professor-in-residence in November 2012. The established Cuban American lobby strongly opposed even such partial openings of relations. Yet 2012 election exit polls showed President Obama having won the Cuban American vote. The margin was small but quite significant compared to the huge margins that Republican candidates had piled up in prior elections. Analysts saw it as indicative of demographic change within the Cuban American community towards a younger generation that, while hardly pro-Castro or pro-communist, was more supportive of some engagement. Whereas in 2003, 53 percent of Cuban Americans opposed American citizens being able to travel to Cuba, and 61 percent supported continuing the embargo, in 2009 the numbers were down to 29 percent and 42 percent, respectively—and 22 percent and 33 percent for the younger Cuban American generation.[27]

The main debate in U.S. policy toward Cuba, as reflected in Readings 13.2 and 13.3 is over the embargo and other economic sanctions. Those who favor maintaining them make four main arguments:

- Ending the embargo will strengthen the Castro government.
- Ending the embargo will not guarantee an ease in levels of Cuban repression.

13.2

13.3

- Ending the embargo sends the wrong message to human rights and democracy advocates.
- Cuba still is a security threat.

There are four main arguments on the other side:

- The embargo has been in effect for decades and hasn't worked.
- The embargo hurts civilians more than the regime.
- The embargo prevents Americans from reaping the benefits of trade with and investment in Cuba.
- The embargo only strengthens Castro's power.

The Cuba policies of other countries provide some context for the U.S. debate. Europe, Canada, and Latin American nations all have diplomatic relations with Cuba, while the United States only maintains an "interests section," which is not a full embassy and is headed by a diplomat below the rank of ambassador. European countries use these relations to bring their own pressure on human rights and democratization issues, at times with better results than the U.S. achieves, as in 2012 when the Spanish government joined with the Catholic Church to gain the release of 52 political prisoners. Canadian and European companies have been investing in the Cuban tourism industry, Brazil in the construction of a major new commercial port, and South Korea in exporting automobiles.

Latin American countries have also been pressuring to bring Cuba into the major regional organizations. In 2009 the OAS voted to re-admit Cuba (it had been suspended back in 1962). Seeing that it could not block the vote, the United States worked in some compromises, such as requiring Cuba to show that "its participation meets the purposes and principles of the organization, including democracy and human rights," as then-secretary of state Hillary Clinton put it.[28] Cuba rejected these preconditions and put off beginning the process of reentry. Similar pressures have been brought for inclusion of Cuba in the Summit of the Americas.

Much depends on what choices the Cuban government makes both diplomatically and domestically. Over the past few years it has allowed some private enterprise; for example, many of the best restaurants in Havana are small, family-owned *paladers*. Rules for selling autos and homes have been partially relaxed. Restrictions on travel abroad by Cubans have been loosened. Will such changes continue? At a pace fast enough and with sufficient impact to meet the pressures for change? Will there also be political liberalization? Who will succeed Raúl Castro, who, while younger than Fidel, is also in his eighties and announced that his current presidential term ending in 2018 will be his last? One gets a sense of Cuba being very much at an inflection point, a country with dramatic change coming but with great uncertainty about what path change will take. U.S. policy will not be determinative but it will have an impact one way or another.

Haiti

Haiti is actually the second oldest republic in the Western Hemisphere, after the United States. A slave rebellion in 1791 started the breakdown of French colonial rule, and independence came in 1804. But for fear that diplomatic recognition might spur a slave revolt in the United States, it wasn't until 1862, during the Civil War, that President Abraham Lincoln established official relations with Haiti.

In 1915 the United States intervened militarily in Haiti, claiming the need to restore order and citing the risk of foreign powers gaining a foothold in the tumult of World War I. Military occupation continued until 1934. There was some semblance of democracy with periodic elections, but political and economic control rested largely with the military and economic elites. In 1957 François Duvalier, also known as "Papa Doc," came to power. His rule was brutal and corrupt. But as elsewhere in Latin America, U.S. Cold War containment policies prioritized Power over Principles, and Papa Doc was another U.S.-supported Latin American dictator. When he died in 1971, his son Jean-Claude Duvalier ("Baby Doc") took over.

In the 1970s Congress and the Carter administration shifted policy toward greater emphasis on human rights. Economic aid was targeted more directly to the poor in order to get around government corruption. Military aid was cut. But the Reagan administration reduced such pressures.

In the early 1980s Haitian "boat people," fleeing economic deprivation and political repression, began heading to the United States. But unlike Cubans—many of whom were deemed political refugees and were thus granted asylum—Haitians were categorized as undocumented aliens. As the historian Brenda Gayle Plummer notes,

> Many of the Haitians, who set sail in all sorts of unseaworthy crafts, died en route; other vessels were intercepted by the U.S. Coast Guard and repatriated; Haitians fortunate enough to arrive in safely in the United States remained in legal limbo. The AIDS pandemic also affected Haitian refugees. The Centers for Disease Control considered Haitian immigrants a special risk because of the large proportion of Haitians suffering from AIDS.[29]

In February 1986 a popular revolt overthrew Baby Doc. The ensuing years were unstable amidst struggles for power among the military, economic elites, and emerging leaders of the masses of poor people. Elections were attempted in 1987 and 1988, but the results had little credibility. In December 1990, with international observers supervising what would be Haiti's first free and fair elections, Jean-Bertrand Aristide, a charismatic Roman Catholic priest who had emerged as a key figure in the resistance against the Duvalier regime, was elected president with 70 percent of the vote. Aristide enacted a series of reforms designed to reorganize the army, abolish an oppressive system of rural section chiefs, and drastically reduce human rights violations. Many of these reforms angered members of the military and threatened elites among the business class, leading to a coup in September 1991. Aristide fled the country and a military junta led by General Raoul Cédras took power. The United States suspended military aid and joined with other members of the Organization of American States (OAS) in imposing sanctions and diplomatically isolating the Cédras regime. The UN Security Council took the sanctions further with a global oil and arms embargo.

Sanctions hit Haiti so hard that per capita GDP fell 25 percent, unemployment leaped to 70 percent, and inflation rose to 60 percent, all in a country that already was the poorest in the Western Hemisphere. When sanctions were first imposed, the Haitian people generally supported them, showing a willingness to bear some costs in the expectation that the military regime and its supporters would be brought down. Instead, largely because the sanctions were poorly enforced and targeted, the coup leaders were so little affected that in Creole (the Haitian language), the word for "embargo," *anbago*, gave way to *anba gwo*, meaning "under the heels of the rich and powerful."[30] As such, the Haiti case demonstrated the "political gain–civilian pain" dilemma, in which sanctions risk hurting most the very people they seek to help.[31]

In July 1994 the UN Security Council authorized military intervention under the moniker Operation Uphold Democracy. As a last-ditch diplomatic effort, the Clinton administration sent the high-level team of former president Jimmy Carter, former senator Sam Nunn, and former chairman of the Joint Chiefs of Staff Colin Powell. With the threat of military intervention imminent—naval ships were on their way and planes were in the air—Cédras agreed to cede power and allow Aristide to return.

The UN and OAS established peacekeeping missions which, as of this writing, are still in Haiti. Political stability and economic progress have been difficult to achieve. While maintaining support among many Haitians, Aristide was a divisive leader who committed his own human rights abuses during his presidency (1990–91, 1994–96, 2001–04). Natural disasters further compounded the problems. In 2004 Hurricanes Ivan and Jeanne hit Haiti hard. Nearly 3,000 people were killed and almost 250,000 displaced. In 2008 a succession of two tropical storms and two hurricanes wiped out nearly 25 percent of the country's already struggling economy. Early in 2010 a major earthquake registering 7.0 on the Richter scale killed over 230,000 people, decimated the capital city Port-au-Prince, and destroyed roughly 80 percent of the Haitian economy. In October 2010 a cholera epidemic broke out, spreading across all of Haiti's ten provinces, with nearly 600,000 cases and almost 7,000 deaths reported. And in 2012 a devastating one-two punch came from Tropical Storm Isaac in August and Hurricane Sandy in November.

Relief efforts got bipartisan support in the United States, with former presidents George H. W. Bush, Bill Clinton, and George W. Bush playing leadership roles, and the Red Cross, Doctors Without Borders, and other NGOs active in raising money and providing in-country assistance. The UN, OAS, and other countries in the Western Hemisphere and around the world also responded with humanitarian aid. Still, for a country that already was one of the world's poorest, the cumulative toll was catastrophic.

Canada

In many respects, relations with Canada are the most important the United States has. At over 5,500 miles, our land border is the longest in the world. Canada is our foremost trade partner, supporting millions of jobs. It is our foremost energy supplier (all sources taken together). Over 300,000 people cross the border by plane, auto, bus, train, and ship every day. Since air and water pollution doesn't stop at national boundaries, we have to cooperate on environmental protection. The U.S. attorney general and secretary of homeland security co-chair with their Canadian counterparts the Cross-Border Crime Forum. Defense cooperation includes the North American Aerospace Defense Command (NORAD) and the Permanent Joint Board on Defense as well as membership in NATO. Yet U.S.-Canadian relations get little attention.*

Back in the eighteenth and nineteenth centuries there were plenty of tensions. As one historian put it, "Feeling of hatred and mistrust toward the new United States character- ized the attitudes of some 40,000 loyalists (supporters of Great Britain during the American Revolution) who had migrated to the Canadian wilderness after the war."[32] (Canada was still a British colony then.) During the War of 1812, when Britain invaded the United States from Canada, some Americans pushed to take over Canada. U.S. forces did invade Canada a number of times during this war, but were unsuccessful. In 1817–18 the United States and Canada signed treaties resolving most of their border disputes.

In more recent times, while there have been few major tensions, U.S.-Canadian rela- tions have had their issues. Canadians at times have been wary of economic relations becoming too close. This was an issue in the 1980s in the bilateral free-trade agreement that preceded NAFTA. While the pre-NAFTA agreement eventually was signed and approved by the Canadian parliament, this came only after extensive debate about whether, for all the benefits of freer trade, the influx of U.S. money, products, and adver- tising would damage Canada's economic sovereignty and cultural identity.

In international diplomacy, Canada has carved out its own role as a country known for its commitment to multilateralism. Lester Pearson, a Canadian diplomat who later would become prime minister, won the 1957 Nobel Peace Prize for his role in defusing

---

*True confessions: this is the first of the five editions of this book to have even a short section on Canada.

the 1956 Suez crisis through crisis diplomacy and the deployment of one of the first UN peacekeeping forces. Over ensuing decades, Canada has been one of the leading proponents of UN peacekeeping and political mediation. It was a Canadian general, Roméo Dallaire, who in 1993–94 bravely tried to convince the international community to take action to prevent the genocide in Rwanda. Later in the 1990s Canadian Foreign Minister Lloyd Axworthy played a key role in establishing the commission that developed "Responsibility to Protect" as a principal norm and strategy for preventing further mass atrocities. The key global conferences that led to the treaty banning landmines were held in Montreal. Much of the scholarly work on multilateralism, peacekeeping, and related subjects takes place in Canadian universities and think tanks. Despite Canada's overall support for U.S. policies, a strong orientation towards multilateralism came through in Canada's refusal to join the 2003 U.S. invasion of Iraq, in sharp contrast to its commitment of troops for the 1990–91 Gulf War and the 2000s Afghanistan war, which were much more multinational efforts.

Foreign Policy Politics Case Study: Politics of Immigration Reform

Immigration has been controversial at many points in American history. Our focus here is on the politics of immigration from Mexico and elsewhere in Latin America over the last few decades.

By the early 1980s, illegal immigration, particularly from Mexico, had reached unprecedented levels. Among the issues being debated were whether to grant amnesty to those illegal immigrants already in the United States, how much to increase border security, and whether to impose financial penalties on employers who knowingly hired illegal immigrants. Business groups, especially agricultural associations whose member companies relied heavily on low-paid seasonal workers, feared that not being able to hire undocumented workers or having to pay a penalty for doing so would drive their costs up. Some human rights groups and Hispanic rights groups, while also concerned about labor exploitation, feared that even legal Hispanic immigrants would be subjected to discrimination and possibly unfair arrest. In 1986 there was sufficient bipartisan support for Congress to pass and President Ronald Reagan to sign a modified Immigration Reform and Control Act. The law's amnesty provision applied to any illegal immigrant who had come to the United States before 1982; approximately three million people took advantage of this opportunity. Some employer sanctions were imposed, although these got watered down over time. Border security was tightened.

The 1986 law's impact was limited. Critics argued that the amnesty provision had the unintended consequence of creating a new incentive for additional illegal immigrants, who might think that down the road they too would be granted amnesty. By the early 2000s, illegal immigration had climbed to an estimated 850,000 per year and 12 million total, equivalent to about 5 percent of the U.S. workforce. Not only did controversy swirl in Washington, but at the local level there appeared groups such as the Minutemen, armed civilians self-appointed to patrol the border. "We shall not allow our nation to be invaded and we shall not allow our freedom to be given away," said Steve Eichler, executive director for the Minuteman Project.[33] In the wake of the 9/11 attacks, porous borders heightened security concerns about the entry into the United States of terrorists, not just those seeking work.

In 2005–6 another effort was made to pass substantive legislation. This, too, had bipartisan support from President George W. Bush, some congressional Republicans such as Senator John McCain (R-Arizona), and Democrats such as Senator Ted Kennedy (D-Massachusetts). But no bill ever made it all the way through the legislative process. The bill passed by the Senate was a comprehensive reform similar to what the Bush administration had proposed. It had numerous provisions for border security and enforcement, including expanding the fence along the U.S.-Mexican border and beefing up the Border Patrol. It also had a conditional amnesty for illegal immigrants who had been in the United States for more than five years and were willing to pay fines and back taxes, a guest worker program with a limited amnesty provision allowing illegal aliens to work for two years before having to return home, and protections for the rights of legal immigrants. It passed the Senate by a wide margin, 62–36.

The bill passed by the House was much more about enforcement, and indeed was quite punitive in some of its provisions. It required more than double the miles of border fence then in place, made illegal immigration a felony, made criminals of those who aid illegal immigrants (including churches and charities), and stiffened the penalties on employers who hire illegal immigrants. This bill passed the House by 239–182. And its proponents were uncompromising. Some were from districts near the border but many were not, including one bill sponsor from Wisconsin and another from Iowa. The issue for them was a mix of economics, law and order, and—as many believed—prejudice. Differences between the House and Senate bills could not be reconciled. In December 2006 the 109th Congress ended without passing a new immigration policy.

Interest-group politics were an important factor. The U.S. Chamber of Commerce, representing business interests—particularly those with needs for unskilled labor (such as hotels, restaurants, nursing homes, and fruit growers)—supported the Senate bill. Civil liberties and Hispanic groups did have concerns about the Senate bill but were much more opposed to the House bill. Wade Henderson, president of the Leadership Conference on Civil Rights, said, "This deeply flawed bill [the House version] attempts to criminalize undocumented immigrants without providing any safe, legal alternatives for people who simply want to share in the American Dream."[34] Other organizations such as the American Civil Liberties Union and the National Council of La Raza took similar positions. The AFL-CIO supported some aspects of the bill but pushed for changes in provisions that they felt most threatened the jobs of their members.

Groups on the other side showed little such ambivalence. "These are immigrants who are here illegally," said Susan Wysoki, spokeswoman for the Federation for American Immigration Reform. "They are demanding that they be given rights U.S. citizens have when their first act was to break the law by coming into this country illegally."[35] "We have to get this under control," Jack Clark of the American Immigration Control Foundation said. "This is the occupation of the United States of America by a foreign country. We have to put a stop to it."[36]

Public opinion showed two main patterns. One was that concern about the issue varied by ethnicity and region. Nationally, only 4 percent of respondents cited immigration as one of the most important issues facing the country. In areas with large Hispanic populations, the percentage was much higher: 55 percent in Phoenix, for example. Second was the split as to what should be done. A 2006 poll by the Pew Hispanic Center found that 32 percent of respondents thought illegal immigrants should be granted amnesty, another 32 percent favored a temporary guest-worker program under the condition that they leave after that, and 27 percent took the position that all illegal immigrants should be required to go home right away.[37]

The politics of immigration continued to roil the country. The Great Recession that began in 2007 gave more political weight to the economic arguments about job loss. At the local level, the small city of Hazleton, Pennsylvania, passed its own ordinances making English the official language, suspending business permits of employers who hired illegal workers, and requiring renters to obtain occupancy permits and conditioning those permits on proof of citizenship. These ordinances were overturned on appeal: "The genius of our Constitution is that it provides rights even to those who evoke the least sympathy from the general public," the federal district court ruled.[38] Sheriff Joe Arpaio of Maricopa County, Arizona, got wide attention for what he claimed was strict enforcement of the law in aggressively pursuing undocumented immigrants and demanding, "Show me your papers." Many saw his actions, including such denigrating practices as holding suspects in tent cities and making them wear pink underwear, as racial profiling that affected Latinos broadly.[39] A 2012 Supreme Court decision overruled some of these practices but not all of them.

The immigration issue was a huge factor in the 2012 election. During the Republican presidential primaries, candidates tried to outdo one another to show who would be tougher on immigration. Consider excerpts from some of the Republican candidates' debates:

> Representative Michelle Bachman of Minnesota: "I would build a fence on America's southern border on every mile, on every yard, on every foot, on every inch of the southern border. . . . And here's the other thing I would do. I would not allow taxpayer-funded benefits for illegal

aliens or for their children. That's a madness. End the madness for illegal aliens to come into the United States of America."

Former senator Rick Santorum of Pennsylvania: "People who have come to this country illegally have broken the law repeatedly. If you're here, unless you're here on a trust fund, you've been working illegally. You've probably stolen someone's Social Security number, illegally. And so it's not just one thing that you've done wrong, you've done a lot of things wrong. And as a result of that, I believe that people . . . should not be able to stay here."

Former Massachusetts governor Mitt Romney: "Our problem is 11 million people getting jobs that many Americans, legal immigrants, would like to have. It's school kids in schools that districts are having a hard time paying for. It's people getting free health care because we are required under the law to provide that health care."[40]

In the 2012 general election the Hispanic vote was a key factor in President Obama's reelection. He won 71 percent of the Hispanic vote, while Governor Romney won only 27 percent. This 44 percent margin was eight points greater than Obama's margin over John McCain in 2008. Moreover, the number of Hispanics voting now comprised 10 percent of the total electorate, compared to only 6 percent in 2000. Opinion polls reinforced this pattern; 70 percent of Republicans said controlling and reducing illegal immigration was an important issue but only 48 percent of independents and 43 percent Democrats said so.[41]

Obama helped his own cause by having combined enforcement and opportunity in his first-term immigration policy. His administration had increased the U.S. Border Patrol to 20,000 agents, two times the level of a decade earlier. It had deported an estimated 1.2 million illegal immigrants. He also had created the DREAM program through executive order after it had been stalled in Congress. Standing for ***Development, Relief and Education for Alien Minors (DREAM),*** this program gave legal status and a path to citizenship to Hispanics under the age of thirty-one who had come to the United States when they were under the age of sixteen; who were currently in school, had earned a high school diploma, or had been honorably discharged from the military; who did not have a criminal record; and who had been in the country continually for at least five years, even if they had come illegally.

Hispanic groups were emboldened by the political power they demonstrated in the 2012 election. The National Council of La Raza, the largest Latino political organization in the country, "warned Congress . . . that they will keep a report card during the immigration debate."[42] The United We Dream network, the largest national movement of young immigrants, mobilized in support of immigration reform. A Pew Hispanic Center analysis found that Latinos will account for as much as 40 percent of the growth in the number of eligible voters between now and 2013. By that year an estimated 40 million Hispanics will be eligible to vote, nearly double the 2012 total.[43] With such political pressure and trends in mind, some Republican leaders tried to shift the party away from being so identified as anti-immigration. "Look at the last election," Senator McCain candidly put it. "We are losing dramatically the Hispanic vote, which we think should be ours." He and some other Republican senators worked with Democratic counterparts on a bipartisan plan that would further strengthen border enforcement while also set a pathway to citizenship for the estimated 11 million illegal immigrants already in the country. This approach "puts the Republican Party closer to alignment with the moderate, pragmatic approach to immigration that most Americans accept."[44] Resistance remained, though, among House Republicans. "When you legalize those who are in the country illegally," Rep. Lamar Smith of Texas said, "it costs taxpayers millions of dollars, costs American workers thousands of jobs and encourages more illegal immigration."[45] As of mid-2013 when we went to press, no bill had been passed.

It may be that on this issue, foreign policy politics and foreign policy strategy are starting to point in the same direction. For many years the anti-immigration dynamic in U.S. domestic politics compounded the foreign policy problems in relations with Mexico and other Latin American countries. With the growing potency of the Hispanic American vote, pro-immigration positions may now be good politics as well as good policy. We will see.

Summary

U.S.-Latin American relations are going through their own twenty-first-century transition. Even in an age of globalization, geography still matters. Those countries with which the United States shares the Western Hemisphere will continue to have their own importance, regardless of whatever else happens in the Middle East, Asia, and elsewhere. Some of the foreign policy issues have been problematic historically. Some carry over from the Cold War. And some reflect political, economic, diplomatic, and ideological changes of the contemporary era.

Notes

[1]Gaddis Smith, "Monroe Doctrine," in *Encyclopedia of U.S. Foreign Relations*, ed. Bruce W. Jentleson and Thomas G. Paterson (New York: Oxford University Press, 1997), 3:159–67.

[2]Richard Van Alstyne, *The Rising American Empire* (Chicago: Quadrangle Books, 1965), 99.

[3]Theodore Roosevelt, "Fourth Annual Message," December 16, 1904, *A Compilation of the Messages and Papers of the Presidents* (New York: Bureau of National Literature, 1923), 14:6894–930.

[4]Louis A. Perez Jr., "Platt Amendment," in Jentleson and Paterson, *Encyclopedia of U.S. Foreign Relations*, 3:400.

[5]Freedom House, *Freedom in the World 2012*, www.freedomhouse.org/report-types/freedom-world (accessed 3/8/13).

[6]Economist Intelligence Unit (EIU), *Democracy Index 2011: Democracy Under Stress*, www.eiu.com/public/thankyou_download.aspx?activity=download&campaignid=DemocracyIndex2011 (accessed 3/8/13).

[7]Thomas Carothers, "Democracy without Illusion," *Foreign Affairs* 76.1 (January/February 1997): 89.

[8]Larry Rohter and Juan Forero, "Unending Graft Is Threatening Latin America," *New York Times*, July 30, 2005, A1.

[9]UN News Centre, "Latin American Poverty Levels Fall to Lowest in Two Decades," November 30, 2011, www.democraticunderground.com/discuss/duboard.php?az=view_all&address=102×5076267 (accessed 3/8/13).

[10]Jo Tuckman, "Latin America's Poverty Data Masks Great Inequalities, Report Says," *The Guardian*, April 25, 2012, www.guardian.co.uk/global-development/2012/apr/25/latin-america-poverty-data-inequalities (accessed 3/8/13).

[11]Larry Rohter, "Visit to U.S. Isn't a First for Chile's First Female President," *New York Times*, June 8, 2006, A3.

[12]Julia E. Sweig, "Getting Latin America Right," *The National Interest* 123 (January/February 2013), 26–27.

[13]Dana Frank, "In Honduras, a Mess Made in the U.S.," *New York Times*, January 26, 2012, A27.

[14]Nick Miroff, "Grim Toll as Cocaine Trade Expands in Honduras," *Washington Post*, December 26, 2011, http://articles.washingtonpost.com/2011-12-26/world/35287206_1_honduras-central-america-drug-flights (accessed 3/8/13).

[15]James Verini, "Dispatch: Prisoners Rule," *Foreign Policy*, November 2012, 36–39.

[16]Charlie Savage, "D.E.A. Squads Extend Reach of Drug War," *New York Times*, November 7, 2011, A1.

[17]Eric Schmitt and Thom Shanker, *Counterstrike: The Untold Story of America's Secret Campaign Against Al Qaeda* (New York: St. Martin's Griffin, 2011), 291.

[18]Savage, "D.E.A. Squads Extend Reach of Drug War."

[19]Damien Cave, "Honduran Villages Caught in Drug War's Cross-Fire," *New York Times*, May 23, 2012, A1.

[20]William Booth, "Latin American Leaders Assail U.S. Drug 'Market,'" *Washington Post*, December 19, 2011, www.washingtonpost.com/world/latin-american-leaders-assail-us-drug-market/2011/12/16/gIQAjyy63O_story.html (accessed 3/8/13).

[21]Mark Landler, "Clinton Says U.S. Feeds Mexico Drug Trade," *New York Times*, March 26, 2009, A6.

[22]U.S. State Department, Bureau of Western Hemisphere Affairs, "Fact Sheet: U.S. Relations with Mexico," June 25, 2012, www.state.gov/r/pa/ei/bgn/35749.htm (accessed 3/8/13).

[23]Lorenzo Caliendo and Fernando Parra, "Estimates of the Trade and Welfare Effects of NAFTA," National Bureau of Economic Research Working Paper No. 18508, November 2012, http://data.nber.org/papers/w18508; Economic Policy Institute, "Heading South: U.S.–Mexico Trade and Job Displacement after NAFTA," May 3, 2011, http://epi.3cdn.net/fdade52b876e04793b_7fm6ivz2y.pdf (both accessed 3/8/13).

[24]Tom Gjelten, *Bacardi and the Long Fight for Cuba: The Biography of a Cause* (New York: Viking, 2008), 144, 146, 170.

[25]*Report of Inspection: U.S. Interests Section Havana, Cuba*, Rep. no. ISP-I-07-27A, US Department of State, July 2007, http://oig.state.gov/documents/organization/121798.pdf (accessed 3/8/13).

[26]Gjelten, *Bacardi and the Long Fight for Cuba*, 52–53.

[27]Poll was published April 21, 2009, in the *New York Times*.

[28]Arthur Brice, "OAS Lifts 47-Year-Old Suspension of Cuba," CNNWorld.com, June 3, 2009, http://articles.cnn.com/2009-06-03/world/cuba.oas_1_oas-organization-of-american-states-purposes-and-principles?_s=PM:WORLD (accessed 3/8/13).

[29]Brenda Gayle Plummer, "Haiti," in *Encyclopedia of U.S. Foreign Relations*, ed. Bruce W. Jentleson and Thomas G. Paterson (New York: Oxford University Press, 1997), 2:276.

[30]Claudette Antoine Werleigh, "The Use of Sanctions in Haiti: Assessing the Economic Realities," in *Economic Sanctions: Panacea or Peacebuilding in the Post–Cold War World?* ed. David Cortright and George Lopez (Boulder, Colo.: Westview, 1995), 169.

[31]Thomas G. Weiss, David Cortright, George A. Lopez, and Larry Minear, eds., *Political Gain and Civilian Pain: Humanitarian Impact of Economic Sanctions* (Lanham, Md.: Rowman and Littlefield, 1997).

[32]J. L. Granatstein, "Canada," in Jentleson and Paterson, *Encyclopedia of U.S. Foreign Relations*, 1:211.

[33]Fox News, "Bush to Address Nation Monday Night on Immigration," May 12, 2006, www.foxnews.com/story/0,2933,195244,00.html (accessed 3/8/13).

[34]Leadership Conference, "The Immigration Debate," Fall 2006, www.civilrights.org/monitor/fall2006/art2p1.html (accessed 3/8/13).

[35]OneNews, "Immigration Rallies Sweep through the United States," April 11, 2006, http://tvnz.co.nz/view/page/411749/699184 (accessed 3/8/13).

[36]Fox News, "Bush to Address Nation Monday Night on Immigration."

[37]Pew Hispanic Center, "America's Immigration Quandary," March 30, 2006, www.pewhispanic.org/2006/03/30/americas-immigration-quandary/ (accessed 3/8/13).

[38]Julianna Goldman, "Pennsylvania Town's Anti-Immigrant Laws Struck Down by Judge," *Bloomberg News*, July 27, 2007, www.bloomberg.com/apps/news?pid=newsarchive&sid=aRVJ1nLjSTaY (accessed 3/8/13).

[39]Sarafina Wright and Amanda Terkel, "Joe Arpaio Believes He Can 'Get Along Great with Hispanics,'" *Huffington Post*, November 29, 2012, www.huffingtonpost.com/2012/11/28/joe-arpaio-hispanics_n_2208267.html (accessed 3/8/13).

[40]Bachman quote from FoxNews-Google debate, September 22, 2011, www.foxnews.com/politics/2011/09/22/fox-news-google-gop-2012-presidential-debate/; Santorum and Romney quotes from CNN debate, January 26, 2012, http://blogs.suntimes.com/sweet/2012/01/gop_cnn_florida_debate_jan_26_.html (both accessed 3/8/13).

[41]Chicago Council on Global Affairs, *Foreign Policy in the New Millennium: Results of the 2012 Chicago Council Survey of American Public Opinion and U.S. Foreign Policy* (Chicago: Chicago Council on Global Affairs, 2012), Table 5.2, p. 43.

[42]Julia Preston, "Latino Groups Warn Congress to Fix Immigration, or Else," *New York Times*, December 12, 2012, A24.

[43]Pew Hispanic Center, "An Awakened Giant: The Hispanic Electorate is Likely to Double by 2030," November 14, 2012, www.pewhispanic.org/2012/11/14/an-awakened-giant-the-hispanic-electorate-is-likely-to-double-by-2030/ (accessed 3/8/13).

[44]Julia Preston, "Senators Offer a Bipartisan Blueprint for Immigration," and Editorial, "Now We're Talking," *New York Times*, January 28, 2013, A1, A22.

[45]Michael D. Shear, "Bipartisan Plan faces Resistance in G.O.P.," *New York Times*, January 28, 2013, A12.

14 *Africa: Persisting Old Issues, Pressing New Ones*

Introduction: More and Better Attention to Africa?

Over the years, U.S. foreign policy has paid less attention to Africa than to any other region. Historically, it was the Europeans, not the U.S., who were the principal colonial powers. During the Cold War, Africa did achieve greater prominence on the U.S. geopolitical radar, albeit for Cold War reasons that largely led to U.S. support for Africa's version of "ABC" (anybody but communists) dictators and repressive political systems like South Africa's *apartheid*—another example of Power over Principles. As Africa has been devastated by ethnic and related conflicts in the post–Cold War era, the United States' involvement has been limited, with some exceptions.

From early in his tenure, President Obama pledged to make Africa a higher priority, and indeed it was the destination of one of his first foreign trips as president. "I do not see the countries and peoples of Africa as a world apart," he declared in a speech in Ghana in June 2009. "I see Africa as a fundamental part of our interconnected world—as partners with America on behalf of the future that we want for all our children."[1] This chapter examines the extent to which the Obama administration has followed through on this pledge (see Reading 14.1 for an overview of the Obama Africa policy). Has the United States in fact been giving more attention to Africa? If so, has the attention been successful in terms of balancing the 4 Ps, both with regard to U.S. national interests and the impact on the countries and peoples of Africa?*

We first assess the historical context. We then examine a range of issues on the U.S.-Africa foreign policy agenda: genocide, ethnic conflict and civil wars; counterterrorism in Africa;

14.1

---

*Our focus in this chapter is on sub-Saharan Africa, excluding for the most part the North African Arab countries Egypt, Tunisia, Algeria, and Morocco, which were included in Chapter 11, on the Middle East.

MAP 14.1

AFRICA

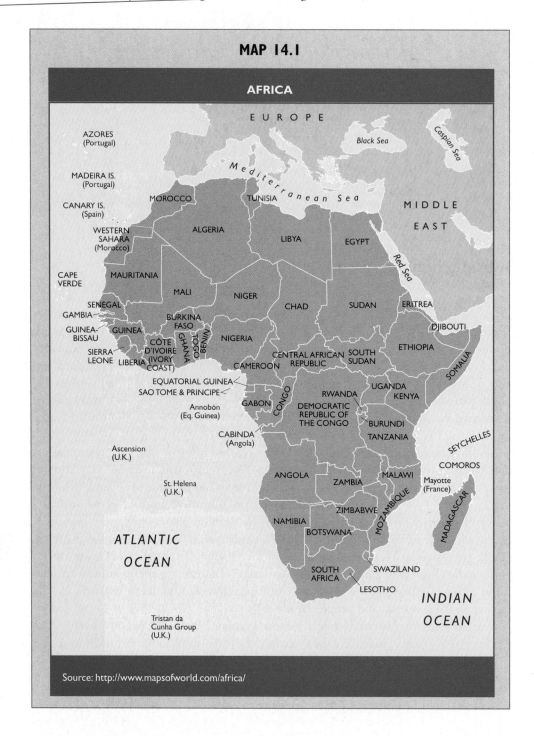

EUROPE

AZORES
(Portugal)

Black Sea

Caspian Sea

MADEIRA IS.
(Portugal)

Mediterranean Sea

CANARY IS.
(Spain)

MOROCCO

TUNISIA

MIDDLE
EAST

WESTERN
SAHARA
(Morocco)

ALGERIA

LIBYA

EGYPT

CAPE
VERDE

MAURITANIA

Red Sea

MALI

NIGER

CHAD

SUDAN

ERITREA

SENEGAL

GAMBIA

BURKINA
FASO

DJIBOUTI

GUINEA-
BISSAU

GUINEA

CÔTE
D'IVOIRE
(IVORY
COAST)

GHANA

TOGO

BENIN

NIGERIA

CENTRAL AFRICAN
REPUBLIC

SOUTH
SUDAN

ETHIOPIA

SOMALIA

SIERRA
LEONE

LIBERIA

CAMEROON

EQUATORIAL GUINEA

SAO TOME & PRINCIPE

Annobón
(Eq. Guinea)

GABON

CONGO

DEMOCRATIC
REPUBLIC OF
THE CONGO

RWANDA

BURUNDI

UGANDA

KENYA

TANZANIA

SEYCHELLES

Ascension
(U.K.)

CABINDA
(Angola)

COMOROS

Mayotte
(France)

St. Helena
(U.K.)

ANGOLA

ZAMBIA

MALAWI

MADAGASCAR

ATLANTIC

OCEAN

NAMIBIA

ZIMBABWE

MOZAMBIQUE

BOTSWANA

SOUTH
AFRICA

SWAZILAND

LESOTHO

INDIAN

OCEAN

Tristan da
Cunha Group
(U.K.)

Source: http://www.mapsofworld.com/africa/

geopolitical implications of China's growing role in Africa; democracy and good-governance issues; and trade, development, and HIV/AIDS. The foreign policy politics case study focuses on the economic sanctions imposed in the 1980s against apartheid in South Africa.

Historical Context

Map 14.2 shows the pattern of European colonization of Africa as it developed over centuries and was finalized in the late 1800s. Mainly because the divvying up was done before the United States became a global player, the United States did not have any African colonies.

In 1957 Ghana became the first sub-Saharan African country to go from European colony to independent country and member of the United Nations. By 1960 another seventeen had become independent and joined the UN; by 1965, another 12. Decolonization continued until, by 1976, there were no European colonies left in Africa.

The "founding fathers" of African independence held great aspirations. Decolonization was "the dawn of a new era," as Kwame Nkrumah, the first president of Ghana, proclaimed at the United Nations (see "International Perspectives" p. 571). Leaders such as Julius Nyerere, president of Tanzania from 1961 to 1985, envisioned regional unification of all the newly independent African states into "a continent-wide . . . all-African government" (also in "International Perspectives"). Such aspirations, though, were at best only partially achieved. Leaders such as Nkrumah, heroes to their own people in the struggle for independence, often became politically repressive autocrats. The *Organization of African Unity (OAU)* was established in 1963, but more as a loose regional organization than as an integrated all-African government.

Africa also became another front in the playing out of Cold War geopolitics. The Soviet Union and the United States both supported movements and leaders that served their particular interests. The United States, for example, supported Joseph Mobutu (more commonly known as Mobutu Sese Seko), dictator of Zaire (known as the Belgian Congo while a colony, and in its initial independence as The Congo) for over thirty years. Mobutu came to power in the 1960s as a leader of two military coups that overthrew Patrice Lumumba, an independence leader and the first elected prime minister, who had some links to the Soviet Union. As in Latin America and Southeast Asia, U.S. policy was driven largely by a global containment strategy. Despite political repression and corruption on such a massive scale that his regime was known as a "kleptocracy," Mobutu's Zaire became the largest African recipient of U.S. military aid.[2] While the relationship fluctuated somewhat amidst various disputes and some human rights pressures during the Carter years, it was only with the end of the Cold War that U.S. support for Mobutu really ended. After Mobutu's fall in 1996, the country changed its name to the Democratic

MAP 14.2

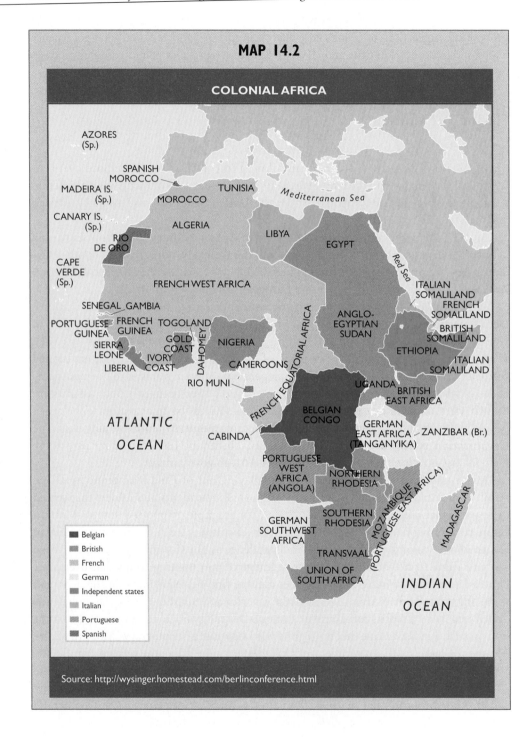

COLONIAL AFRICA

AZORES
(Sp.)

SPANISH
MOROCCO

MADEIRA IS.
(Sp.)

TUNISIA

MOROCCO

Mediterranean Sea

CANARY IS.
(Sp.)

ALGERIA

RIO
DE ORO

LIBYA

EGYPT

CAPE
VERDE
(Sp.)

FRENCH WEST AFRICA

Red Sea

ITALIAN
SOMALILAND

FRENCH
SOMALILAND

SENEGAL GAMBIA

ANGLO-
EGYPTIAN
SUDAN

BRITISH
SOMALILAND

PORTUGUESE
GUINEA

FRENCH
GUINEA

TOGOLAND

GOLD
COAST

SIERRA
LEONE

DAHOMEY

NIGERIA

ETHIOPIA

ITALIAN
SOMALILAND

IVORY
COAST

LIBERIA

CAMEROONS

RIO MUNI

FRENCH EQUATORIAL AFRICA

UGANDA

BRITISH
EAST AFRICA

ATLANTIC

OCEAN

BELGIAN
CONGO

GERMAN
EAST AFRICA
(TANGANYIKA)

ZANZIBAR (Br.)

CABINDA

PORTUGUESE
WEST
AFRICA
(ANGOLA)

NORTHERN
RHODESIA

MOZAMBIQUE
(PORTUGUESE EAST AFRICA)

MADAGASCAR

GERMAN
SOUTHWEST
AFRICA

SOUTHERN
RHODESIA

■	Belgian
▨	British
▒	French
░	German
▨	Independent states
▒	Italian
▨	Portuguese
▨	Spanish

TRANSVAAL

UNION OF
SOUTH AFRICA

INDIAN

OCEAN

Source: http://wysinger.homestead.com/berlinconference.html

INTERNATIONAL PERSPECTIVES

INTERNATIONAL PERSPECTIVES

AFRICAN LEADERS' VIEWS

The following quotes from two major African leaders reflect their views of U.S. policy and of international affairs generally in the immediate post-colonial years.

Kwame Nkrumah was the first president of Ghana, the first modern African country to gain independence from colonial rule. This excerpt is from a 1960 speech to the United Nations in which Nkrumah addressed anticolonialism, opposition to the Cold War, and belief in the UN.

The flowing tide of African nationalism . . . constitutes a challenge to the colonial powers to make a just restitution for the years of injustice and crime committed against our continent. . . . For years and years Africa has been the foot-stool of colonialism and imperialism, exploitation and degradation. From the north to the south, the east to the west, her sons languished in the chains of slavery and humiliation. . . . Those days are gone and gone forever, and now I, an African, stand before this august Assembly of the United Nations and speak with a voice of peace and freedom, proclaiming to the world the dawn of a new era. . . .

Preoccupation with armaments prevents the big powers from perceiving what are the real forces in the world today. If world population continues to grow, and if inequality between the so-called developed and underdeveloped countries is allowed to remain . . . then however great the armaments piled up, an international explosion cannot in my view be averted. . . .

Julius Nyerere, president of Tanzania from 1961 to 1985, was a leading proponent of African continental unity.

The requirements of African Unity necessitate the establishment of a new international entity to replace the present small international entities which now exist in our continent. Until we have achieved that we shall not be in a position to utilize the resources of Africa for the people of Africa, and we shall not be free from fear of the rest of the world. A continent-wide state, single and indivisible, must be established. . . .

And it must be quite clear to everyone that the achievement of unity will not itself solve the problems of Africa. It will merely enable them to be solved by Africa. At the beginning, the effectiveness of the all-African government will be limited; it will have more responsibility than power. It will have to inch forward, organizing and arguing every step of the way, and gradually growing in stature—just as the federal government of the United States is still growing in relation to the states' governments because of the necessities of the people and the world. . . .

These preliminary steps need not be daydreaming. If we have courage and intelligence they can become reality in the immediate future. And certainly they are essential if the ordinary African citizen is ever really to overcome the poverty which at present grips him and if he is to increase his degree of personal safety. For this is, and must be, the purpose of greater unity in Africa and elsewhere. Not size for its own sake, but strength and power used to defend the real freedoms of the ordinary man and to help him progress in his freedom.

Sources: Nkrumah, www.nkrumah.net/un-1960/kn-at-un-1960-cvrfrn.htm; Nyerere, www.worldbeyond borders.org/africanunity.htm (both accessed 3/8/13).

Republic of the Congo. In the years since, it has been torn by the worst civil war of our current era, with a death toll of over five million people and sexual crimes so widespread and heinous that the United Nations labeled Congo "the rape capital of the world."[3] While some of these struggles are rooted in deep-seated historical ethnic conflicts and other causes, the Mobutu legacy of a politically emasculated and economically stripped-down state has been a key factor.

The Cold War context was also the main reason that the United States was slow to end its support for apartheid in South Africa. Under apartheid, the white minority controlled the South African political and economic systems, politically repressing the majority of black South Africans and largely keeping them in abject poverty. The few links that anti-apartheid leader Nelson Mandela and the African National Congress party had to communists were deemed sufficient during the Cold War for another "ABC" rationale justifying U.S. support even for this apartheid regime, an international pariah. The policy shifts that finally did occur in the mid-1980s, including the imposition of economic sanctions, helped bring apartheid to an end; we will examine this in the case study later in the chapter.

Genocide, Ethnic Conflict, Civil Wars

Some of the worst recent cases of mass atrocities have occurred in Africa. We focus on three: Somalia, Rwanda, and the Sudan (Darfur as well as other aspects).

Somalia

In December 1992 the United States intervened in Somalia with twenty-seven thousand troops (**Operation Restore Hope**) in the largely humanitarian mission of helping restore order and get food to the Somali people, who were starving amid the chaos of warring militias. This mission, as launched by the George H. W. Bush administration, initially had a 90-day timetable and was coordinated with a UN peacekeeping force already in Somalia. By March 1993, though, it was clear to the newly inaugurated Clinton administration that if the U.S. forces withdrew before Somalia's own political institutions were strong enough to keep order, starvation would spread again. Yet staying, too, presented its own dilemma, often referred to as "nation-building." The risks and costs of this broader mission were driven home when, in October 1993, eighteen U.S. soldiers were killed in urban battles in the capital city of Mogadishu (an incident best known from the book and movie *Black Hawk Down*). Amidst intense political pressure at home and abroad, the Clinton administration abruptly withdrew U.S. forces.

Broader U.S. policy was also affected. During the Somalia mission, the Clinton administration had been conducting a comprehensive review of U.S. policy on UN peacekeeping. It's worth recalling that just a few years earlier, the 1988 Nobel Peace Prize had been awarded to the UN Peacekeeping Forces in recognition of their many successes. It was a "top priority," U.S. ambassador to the UN Madeleine Albright told Congress in May 1993, "to ensure that the UN is equipped with a robust capacity to plan, organize, lead, and service peacekeeping activities."[4] Initial reports on the administration's policy review were leaked to the press; these reports mentioned increased U.S. funding for UN peacekeeping and a willingness to put American troops "under the 'operational control' of UN commanders 'on a regular basis.'"[5] Despite such sentiments in the private reports, the Black Hawk Down incident was ultimately blamed on U.S. troops' being under foreign command, both by critics and to an extent by a Clinton White House seeking to deflect criticism. But this was simply untrue—"not only disingenuous but factually inaccurate," as one noted expert put it.[6] Still, when the overall peacekeeping policy review was finished a few months later, the thrust had shifted: "The U.S. does not support a standing UN army, nor will we earmark specific U.S. military units for participation in UN operations. . . . It is not U.S. policy to expand either the number of UN peace operations or U.S. involvement in such operations."[7]

Meanwhile, in the decades since then, Somalia has continued to suffer from weak governance and recurring humanitarian crises amid food shortages, disease outbreaks, pervasive unemployment, and the absence of law and order. Various Islamic fundamentalist groups have fed off such turmoil. In 2006 one such group, the Islamic Courts, came to power. A few months later Ethiopia invaded Somalia, ousting the Islamic Courts government. Ethiopia claimed to have been acting in its own national defense—as a largely Christian country against which the Islamist regime was issuing threats—as well as in the interest of the Somali people. The United States supported the Ethiopian invasion with intelligence and some military cooperation. A little over two years later, though, Ethiopia was forced to withdraw due to military losses and failure to impose stability, leaving behind what the NGO Refugees International called the world's worst humanitarian crisis. Even more-radical Islamist groups, such as the Al Qaeda–affiliated Al-Shabab, grew stronger. It also was during the Ethiopian intervention that some Somali Americans living in Minneapolis returned to their homeland to join the *jihad*, or holy war.

Somalia has also been the principal locus for piracy in the eastern Indian Ocean. Professor Ken Menkhaus, a leading expert on Somalia, traces the rise of piracy there back to the early 1990s, "when the state first collapsed and warlords sought new ways to parlay their firepower into profit."[8] As such, while it happened at sea, "the Somali piracy epidemic is unquestionably an on-shore crisis demanding an on-shore solution. Naval operations to interdict and apprehend pirates will help, but cannot possibly halt the daily quest of over a thousand gunmen in such vast waters when the risks are so low, the rewards so high and alternatives so bleak."[9]

In 2011 the worst drought in six decades further exacerbated the situation. The international community provided some relief, but still only in very limited amounts and with difficulties in getting it past Al-Shabab and other obstacles. An *African Union (AU)**[*] peacekeeping force played the leading role in these operations. The AU force also regained control of Mogadishu and other key cities from Al-Shabab. In 2012, for the first time in 20 years, the Somali parliament met and a new president was chosen, raising hopes for further progress.

Rwanda

"In one hundred days," reported Samantha Power in her Pulitzer Prize–winning book, *"A Problem From Hell:" America and the Age of Genocide*, referring to the period that began in April 1994, "some eight hundred thousand Tutsi and politically moderate Hutu were murdered. . . . The Rwandan genocide would prove to be the fastest, most efficient killing spree of the twentieth century." Yet, Power continues, "the United States did almost nothing to try to stop it."[10] Nor did the UN, or Europe, or any other major actor in the international community. This was not even "just" ethnic cleansing: it was *genocide*.

A strong argument can be made that while all this killing could not have been prevented, atrocities on the scale that occurred—an estimated 850,000 dead, millions displaced, thousands raped—could have been deterred or stopped if there had not been such a failure of political will by the international community, the United States included. This argument has three distinct components. First was the failure to deter the Hutu extremists effectively because of the weaknesses of the United Nations Assistance Mission in Rwanda (UNAMIR), which had been established the year before to help support a

---

*The African Union (AU) was the successor to the Organization of African Unity (OAU).

peace agreement that had been reached between the two main Rwandan ethnic groups, Hutus and Tutsis. Astri Suhrke and Bruce Jones saw the formation and deployment of UNAMIR as a "critical juncture" that was not taken advantage of. Instead, because of its small size, inadequate equipment, narrow mission, and highly circumscribed mandate, UNAMIR became counterproductive. It was not only a very weak deterrent to those planning the genocide, and at best a tepid signal to Hutu extremists that the international community was fully invested in the accords, but once the genocide was ultimately unleashed, UNAMIR was in a very poor position to do anything effective in response. "A more decisive and robust demonstration of international force at that time," Suhrke and Jones contend, "might have restrained the extremist forces directly, or at any rate sent signals to the effect that the international community was fully behind the peace accords."[11]

Second was the failure to act on the warning that UNAMIR received in January 1994 from a Hutu informant about the mass killings being planned and the arms being stockpiled by Hutu extremists. Not only was the information borne out by later events, but the level of detail and other aspects of the information made it highly credible at the time. The UNAMIR commander, General Roméo Dallaire, passed it back to UN headquarters in a coded cable that included his plan to raid the arms caches and break up the genocide planning. He was not asking for additional troops. He was not even asking for permission. He saw such action as consistent with the existing UNAMIR peacekeeping mandate, and he was doing what he thought was responsible in informing UN headquarters. But UN headquarters turned him down. General Dallaire repeated his requests the next month but again was turned down.

This was a crucial moment for possibly preventing the Rwandan genocide. "At the Source" (p. 576) provides General Dallaire's account. It is an important testimony on what was proposed in real time and what could have been done. Although we cannot be certain that such actions would have prevented the Rwandan genocide, the same is true of any "what-if"—and the case General Dallaire makes is entirely credible.

Then there was the response to the April 1994 crisis. Again General Dallaire sent requests for a strengthening of UNAMIR, but again they were rebuffed, with the blame to be shared by key UN officials and Security Council member nations, including the United States. A 1998 study by the Carnegie Commission on Preventing Deadly Conflict set the last week of April 1994 as the closing of the window of opportunity for an emergency intervention short of massive force. By that time mass violence had spread to the countryside.[12] Yet one of the reasons that the Hutu "crisis committee" decided to expand the massacre to the countryside, reported the Commission, was "the failure of the international community to respond forcefully to the initial killings in Kigali and other regions." Choices and calculations were being made. Violence was not spreading just by its own momentum. The evidence of divisions within the Hutu military, as cited by

AT THE SOURCE
AT THE SOURCE

"SAVE US FROM CATASTROPHE"

General Roméo Dallaire, Force Commander, United Nations Assistance Mission in Rwanda (UNAMIR):

Late in the afternoon of January 10, Faustin [a Rwandan government official] came to my office and insisted on a private meeting. He was shaking with excitement and fear. I took him out onto the balcony where we could talk without being overheard. Almost breathlessly, he told me that he was in contact with someone inside the Interahamwe [a Hutu paramilitary organization] who had information he wanted to pass on to UNAMIR. I had a moment of wild exhilaration as I realized we might finally have a window on the mysterious third force, the shadowy collection of extremists that had been growing in strength ever since I had arrived in Rwanda. . . .

He [Jean-Pierre, the code name for the informer] and others like him were ordered to have the cells under their command make lists of the Tutsis in their various communes. Jean-Pierre suspected that these lists were being made so that, when the time came, the Tutsis, or the *Inyenzi* as Rwandan hate radio called them—the word means "cockroaches" in Kinyarwanda—could easily be rounded up and exterminated. Jean-Pierre said he hated the RPF [the Tutsi Rwandan Patriotic Front] and saw them as the enemy of Rwanda, but he was horrified that he had been drawn into a plan to create a series of highly efficient death squads that, when turned loose on the population, could kill a thousand Tutsis in Kigali within twenty minutes of receiving the order. He described in detail how the Interahamwe were being trained at army bases and by army instructors in several locations around the country, and that on a weekly basis a number of young men would be collected and transported for a three-week weapons and paramilitary training course that placed special emphasis on killing techniques. Then the young men were returned to their communes and ordered to make lists of Tutsis and await the call to arms.

I was silent, hit by the depth and reality of this information. It was as if the informant, Jean-Pierre, had opened the floodgates on the hidden world of the extremist third force, which until this point had been a presence we could sense but couldn't grasp.

Luc [a UN peacekeeping force officer] told us that until now the only weapons the Interahamwe possessed were traditional spears, clubs, and machetes, but Jean-Pierre had claimed that the army had recently transferred four large shipments of AK-47s, ammunition, and grenades to the militia. These weapons were stored in four separate arms caches in Kigali. He offered to show us one of the caches to confirm the information he was giving us. . . .

Jean-Pierre warned that the leadership was about to make a decision to distribute the arms caches to every Interahamwe cell in Kigali. If that happened, he said, there would be no way to stop the slaughter.

I made the decision to go after the weapons caches. I had to catch these guys off guard, send them a signal that I knew who they were and what they were up to, and that I fully intended to shut them down. . . .

After Luc left, I decided to inform the SRSG [Special Representative of the UN Secretary-General] first thing in the morning. . . .

I needed New York [UN headquarters] to realize that, even though I wanted to move quickly, I was not blind to the possibility that this could be a well-laid trap to force UNAMIR onto the offensive and jeopardize our role as keepers of a fragile peace. I also wanted to make it clear in the cable that I was not asking permission to raid the caches but was informing New York of my intentions, as was my responsibility as force commander. I was finally going to be able to wrest the initiative from the hard-liners. . . .

When I woke up the next morning after a few fitful hours of sleep, I was convinced that we were on the verge of regaining the initiative or at least of throwing the extremists off balance, making them vulnerable to defections, to panic, to making foolish mistakes. Little did I realize as I waved to the local kids on the side of the dirt road on my way to work, that New York was already shooting my plan of action out of the water. . . . Something had to be done to save us from catastrophe. For the rest of the week, I made phone call after phone call to New York, arguing over the necessity of raiding the arms caches. During these exchanges, I got the feeling that New York now saw me as a loose cannon and not as an aggressive but careful force commander. . . .

My failure to persuade New York to act on Jean-Pierre's information still haunts me. . . . I was presenting a reasonable, carefully laid-out plan that was consistent with the approach I had adopted from the very beginning: to maximize our rules of engagement in order to ensure the atmosphere of security demanded by the peace agreement. . . . In my view the inside information offered us by Jean-Pierre represented a real chance to pull Rwanda out of the fire. The DPKO's [UN Department of Peacekeeping Operations] response whipped the ground out from under me. . . .

The genocide in Rwanda was a failure of humanity that could easily happen again.

Source: General Roméo Dallaire, *Shake Hands with the Devil: The Failure of Humanity in Rwanda* (New York: Carroll and Graf, 2003), xxv, 141–47.

Suhrke and Jones, suggests that "a more determined international response against the extremists would have found allies within."[13]

The Clinton administration played a large part in this pattern of inaction. Although the same can be said of others, including the UN and major European nations, it remains true that if the United States had spoken out and pushed for action it is likely that the UN would have responded or that, as in other cases, a coalition of nations could have been put together to intervene. But the Rwanda crisis came just six months after the October 1993 debacle in Somalia, and the Clinton administration balked at confronting potential domestic political opposition to any new peacekeeping initiative in Africa. The administration expressed its empathy but contended that the U.S. national interest was not sufficiently at stake. Indeed, people working in the State Department at the time recall being told to avoid using the word *genocide* because doing so could invoke obligations under the international genocide treaty to take action, and the Clinton administration did not want to get involved in any significant way.

Sudan: Darfur and South Sudan

Over 300,000 dead, according to the United Nations. Around 4 million in internal refugee camps and camps across the border in Chad. Countless villages burned or otherwise devastated. The conflict in **Darfur**, a mainly desert region of Sudan, caught the world's attention—but did not prompt much action.

Darfur is in the western part of Sudan. It is large, about the size of France. Historically, there have been tensions with the central government based in the city of Khartoum, hundreds of miles to the east. There also are ethnic differences. Much of Darfur's population is Muslim but is ethnically distinct from the dominant Arab population of the rest of Sudan. These tensions were exacerbated by the devastating 1980s drought, which left the various tribal and religious groups competing for shrinking resources of water, grassland, and arable soil. The Sudanese government teamed up with Arab tribesmen (dubbed *janjaweed* from an old epithet meaning "devils on horseback") for a concerted offensive assault, consisting of "killing, burning villages and farms, terrorizing people, confiscating property from members of African tribes and forcing them from Darfur."[14]

Although some details surfaced only over time, the first warning was sounded in early 2003, when Darfur refugees escaping to Chad reported the scorched-earth attacks of the Sudanese army and the *janjaweed*. When UN agencies, NGOs, and journalists finally were able to get into Darfur in early 2004, the scope and scale of the conflict were very heavily reported.[15] After seeing the crisis for themselves, both UN secretary-general Annan and U.S. secretary of state Colin Powell used the term *genocide*. So did President Bush in his own statement, as well as the U.S. Congress in a condemnatory resolution.

But the *janjaweed* militias continued to kill, rape, and destroy, with the Sudanese government's support and complicity.

The international community did little, and what it did do was too weak to be effective. Various resolutions were passed by the UN Security Council, but only after they were watered down to meet Russian and Chinese opposition. Russia actually completed a sale of military aircraft to the Sudanese government—the same aircraft that were being used to bomb villages in Darfur—"even as Security Council members deliberated over how to address the crisis."[16] For China the issue was Sudanese oil. At the time, Sudan was supplying 6 percent of China's oil needs, with projections very much on an upward curve. China also had approximately $3 billion invested in Sudan's oil sector, had been awarded hundreds of millions of dollars in additional contracts for the construction of pipelines and port facilities, and was the principal financer of a $200 million hydroelectric plant. It had also been (and continues to be) Sudan's largest arms supplier.

To its credit, the Bush administration did work with the international community on Darfur. This was "genocide," Secretary of State Colin Powell bluntly told Congress in September 2004, "and the Government of Sudan and the *janjaweed* bear responsibility."[17] The following year his successor as secretary of state, Condoleezza Rice, made a dramatic visit to Darfur, making a point to meet with rape victims. The United States was a major donor of humanitarian aid. Deputy Secretary of State Robert Zoellick became the administration's point man, making numerous trips of his own, including one during which he broke free of diplomatic niceties and pushed back against Sudanese government obstructionism and disingenuousness.[18] Zoellick also played a key role in peace negotiations, brokering an agreement, albeit one that did not hold on the ground.

U.S. domestic politics were less of a political constraint than is often the case for humanitarian intervention. In Congress, a bipartisan coalition was led by then-senators Barack Obama (D-Illinois) and Sam Brownback (R-Kansas). The Christian right, which had been very involved in the southern Sudan conflict in defense of the Sudanese Christians, also weighed in on Darfur. On the left, various NGOs were generating at least a degree of attention and action. Socially entrepreneurial college students started the Genocide Intervention Fund and had raised $250,000 by late 2005. The Rally to Stop Genocide, held in April 2006 in Washington, D.C., featured a range of speakers rarely found on the same podium, including Richard Land, president of the Southern Baptist Convention; the actor George Clooney; the Holocaust survivor Elie Wiesel; and Paul Rusesabagina, the Rwandan humanitarian made famous by the movie *Hotel Rwanda*. Although overall media attention was limited, journalist Nicholas Kristof made Darfur a recurring focus, using a creative blend of his *New York Times* column and Internet resources, for which he received a 2006 Pulitzer Prize. A June 2005 public opinion poll showed strong and broad support for more U.S. leadership and tougher policies, albeit short of sending American ground forces.[19]

Those who expected a major initiative from President Obama based on his record as a senator and the positions he had taken in the 2008 presidential campaign were disappointed. When the International Criminal Court (ICC) issued an arrest warrant against Sudanese President Omar al-Bashir for crimes against humanity and genocide, and al-Bashir not only refused to comply but retaliated by kicking out NGOs that had been providing food and medical care to the Darfuri people, the Obama administration protest was less than full-throated. Press reports highlighted splits within the administration during its overall first-year policy review over balancing pressures and incentives.[20]

Hopes were raised in early 2012 when, amid a decline in the violence, over 100,000 refugees returned home. But as the year went on reports came in of attacks on villages and on the UN-African Union peacekeeping force.

Civil war between the central Sudanese government and **South Sudan** predated the Darfur conflict. South Sudan was largely African Christian and animist (a religious worldview that stresses spirituality in nature rather than in a monotheistic God), while northern Sudan was largely Muslim and Arab. In 2005 a peace agreement was negotiated seeking to end the civil war. The Bush administration, the UN, European countries, and the African Union (AU) each played a role in helping the parties reach this accord.

Violence was reduced but tensions remained. In 2011 a referendum was held in which the South Sudanese people voted for full independence. In this instance as well, U.S., UN, European and AU diplomacy helped limit the violence and pressure Sudanese President al-Bashir to accept the results. Diplomatic measures included making sure the referendum was held on time, deploying additional multilateral peacekeeping forces, tapping conflict-assessment officers from the State Department, and prepositioning additional humanitarian supplies in the event that conflict reemerged.

But while the independence ceremonies were "pulsating with pride and jubilation," within months the country was "exploding in violence."[21] Some of the violence involved conflict between Sudan and newly independent South Sudan, fueled by disputes over oil and unresolved implementation of the 2005 peace agreement that ended the civil war. Some of the new violence was intercommunal within South Sudan; by early 2012 atrocities between the Lou Nuer and the Murle tribes were estimated to have left thousands killed and more than 50,000 displaced. In early February 2012 a UN team trying to mediate got caught in the crossfire, with one UN employee among those killed. In Sudan to the north, President Omar al-Bashir has added to his long record of abusing human rights by ordering his security forces to crack down on political dissent, leading to aerial attacks against civilians, hundreds of thousands of displaced people, and untold suffering due to the obstruction of international efforts to provide humanitarian aid. The UN Security Council responded by increasing the size and strengthening the mandate of the peacekeeping force deployed there. As with earlier UN and African Union peacekeeping efforts in the region, however, the current force is handicapped by the country's large size and limited infrastructure.

Africa in U.S. Counterterrorism Strategy

One of Al Qaeda's first direct attacks on the United States took place in Africa. In 1998 truck bombs planted at the U.S. embassies in Nairobi, Kenya, and Dar es Salaam, Tanzania, killed hundreds of Americans and Africans working at the embassies and in the vicinity. Indeed, it was these incidents that caused the FBI to put Osama bin Laden on its Ten Most Wanted Fugitives list for the first time.

Counterterrorism was one of the main missions for which the U.S. African Command (AFRICOM) was created in 2007, the first time that the American military had a regional command focused on Africa. AFRICOM also had other missions, such as helping African states strengthen their militaries, engaging in antipiracy efforts, and helping prevent mass atrocities. But counterterrorism was the first priority mentioned when AFRICOM Commander General Carter Ham testified to Congress in early 2012.[22] News reports focused on a base in Djibouti, a country in the Horn of Africa, said to be "the busiest Predator drone base outside the Afghan war zone." While its location in eastern Africa allows it to also serve counterterrorism operations in Yemen and elsewhere in the Middle East, its main role is as "the centerpiece of an expanding constellation" of half a dozen U.S. drone and surveillance bases in Africa, created to combat a new generation of terrorist groups across the continent."[23] In early 2013 another such base was established in Niger, a western African country bordering Mali.

Al-Shabab in Somalia, as already mentioned, is one of the Islamist terrorist groups linked to Al Qaeda. Another is Al Qaeda in the Islamic Maghreb (AQIM), which has been active since the late 1990s in countries of the northern African region known as the Maghreb, including Algeria, Morocco, and Libya. AQIM was involved in the September 2012 attack on the U.S. consulate in Benghazi, Libya, in which U.S. ambassador Chris Stevens and three other Americans were killed.

In 2012 attention turned to Mali. In earlier editions of *American Foreign Policy*, this country in western Africa was one of the few African countries listed as a democracy. Indeed, as recently as early 2012 the State Department called Mali "a leading regional partner in U.S. efforts against terrorism."[24] But extreme poverty, continuing ethnic conflict, and other factors undermined stability, particularly in the northern part of the country among the ethnic Tuareg minority. In March 2012 a military coup overthrew the elected government and installed one weak regime after another. Meanwhile, AQIM, which had been gaining foothold among the Tuareg in the north working with an indigenous Islamist group called Ansar Dine (Defenders of the Faith), took over the entire region, effectively splitting it from the rest of the country. They imposed strict *sharia* law (based on traditional Islamic teachings) and quickly set out to "terrorize the population, particularly women, with amputations, stonings, whippings, and other abuses."[25] They also set up terrorist training camps not only for operations in Mali but also to aid AQIM terrorism in other countries, as well as to support other extremist groups such as Boko Haram in Nigeria.

This was not only a concern for the United States but also for the western African region and the broader international community. "Northern Mali is at risk of becoming a permanent haven for terrorists and organized criminal networks where people are subjected to a very strict interpretation of *shariah* law and human rights are abused on a systematic basis," UN secretary-general Ban Ki-moon stated. In January 2013 France (Mali had once been a French colony) headed a military intervention force along with troops from Chad and other countries neighboring Mali that succeeded in blunting the Islamist momentum, including liberating the historic city of Timbuktu. In the following April the UN Security Council voted to establish a peacekeeping force building on the French and African forces while also seeking to broker political dialogue among the Malian factions. No American troops ("boots on the ground") were to be involved, but U.S. military advisers have been sent to Mali and AFRICOM is providing some other assistance. Still, doubts remain about whether these and other initiatives would succeed.

While not yet as violent and unstable as Mali, Nigeria also is of increasing concern. It is a major oil producer. As Africa's most populous country, it also is often looked to for regional leadership. Nigeria has had a long history of civil war and other internal conflict. The threat from Boko Haram has to be understood both for its transnational terrorist links to AQIM and for its national roots. Despite substantial oil revenues, poverty has been increasing in Nigeria: in the northern areas where Boko Haram is strongest, over 60 percent of the people live on less than $1 a day.[26] There may be "a veneer of democratic institutions," as a former U.S. ambassador puts it, but "Nigeria has suffered from dysfunctional governance for decades. . . . Crime is ubiquitous in the cities and on the highways. . . . Nigeria's fundamental problem is a system of institutionalized corruption that channels public money into the pockets of a few Nigerian 'big men.'"[27] Reports in April 2013 of a massacre of villagers by the Nigerian military, for the alleged killing of a soldier (and additionally justified as part of the struggle against Islamist insurgents), exacerbated such concerns.

Is Chinese Influence in Africa a Geopolitical Threat to U.S. Interests?

"China Pledges $20 Billion in Loans to African Countries"
"China's Arms Exports Flooding Sub-Saharan Africa"
"Pursuing Soft Power, China Puts Stamp on Africa's News"
"The Next Empire"[28]

News headlines such as these reflect the concern that China is becoming the dominant global power in Africa. There surely are bases for closer Chinese-African relations.

Economically, at a time when the United States and Europe are fiscally constrained, the Chinese government has plenty of money for aid and investment. Estimates of Chinese investment in Africa between 2002 and 2012 run to about $15 billion spent on dams, airports, luxury hotels, mines, wind farms, and infrastructure. Two-way trade grew from about $14 billion to over $80 billion in the same period. The $20 billion in new loans announced in 2012 include agriculture, infrastructure, cultural exchanges, and scholarships to study in China. Howard French, the journalist who wrote the article "The Next Empire," captures the broad extent of the economic relationship:

> Chinese companies have muscled in on lucrative oil markets in places like Angola, Nigeria, Algeria, and Sudan. But oil is neither the largest nor the fastest-growing part of the story. Chinese firms are striking giant mining deals in places like Zambia and the Democratic Republic of the Congo, and building what is touted as the world's largest iron mine in Gabon. They are prospecting for land on which to build huge agribusinesses. And to get these minerals and crops to market, they are building major new ports and thousands of miles of highway.[29]

And China does all this without what many African governments consider those annoying human rights and democracy stipulations that the United States and Europe often insist on. "It's not China's policy to make regime change," as one Chinese ambassador put it. "Who is the king, who is the president should be the decision of the people of that country. You have no right to interfere with the internal affairs of a peaceful country and its set of laws. Only the people have the right to decide, not outsiders. To interfere in sovereignty is against international law."[30]

China also has been active diplomatically on a continent-wide basis. In 2000 it hosted a first China-Africa Forum in Beijing, with leaders and other top officials from forty-four African states participating. These have continued once every three years, alternating between Beijing and an African capital. No such Africa-wide conferences are held by the United States.

In these and other ways, one can see bases for U.S. concerns about Chinese gains of geopolitical influence. But the United States has its own diplomatic, security, economic, and other relations with Africa. AFRICOM's presence has already been discussed. Even with the growth in China-Africa trade, it is still much less than U.S.-Africa trade ($80 billion compared to $120 billion). Moreover, there are checks on Chinese influence coming from African leaders and peoples who, after centuries of European colonialism and then decades of Cold War machinations, are not about to allow another global power to dominate them. While many aspects of China-Africa economic relations are beneficial, South African President Jacob Zuma struck a note of caution: "This trade pattern is unsustainable in the long term. Africa's past economic experience with Europe dictates a need to be cautious when entering into partnerships with other economies."[31] The 2011 Zambia presidential election was a case in point. Incumbent President Rupiah Banda and his political party had been pushing for expanded economic relations with China, and by 2010 China had invested over $2 billion, particularly in the copper industry. Opposition candidate Michael Sata made criticism of China a central part of his campaign. He contended that China had been taking most of the profits out of the country, not creating jobs at the levels promised, and was imposing hard working conditions and polluting the environment. Despite his party never having won a presidential election before, Sata was the victor.

The results were widely interpreted as a sign that an African country was affirming its own national interest, pushing back against the latest non-African power potentially seeking domination. Sata's victory did not negate concerns about China's influence in Africa, but it did provide a check against overstating the threat. Moreover, much depends on the United States' own policy and the extent to which it establishes shared interests with African partners.

Democracy and Good Governance

In his July 2009 Ghana speech, besides pledging shifts in U.S.-Africa policy, President Obama delivered a "tough love" message about what Africans needed to do in their own politics and societies:

> Development depends on good governance. That is the ingredient which has been missing in far too many places, for far too long. That is the change that can unlock Africa's potential. And that is a responsibility that can only be met by Africans. . . .
>
> Africa doesn't need strongmen, it needs strong institutions. . . .
>
> It is still far too easy for those without conscience to manipulate whole communities into fighting among faiths and tribes.
>
> These conflicts are a millstone around Africa's neck. We all have many identities—of tribe and ethnicity, of religion and nationality. But defining oneself in opposition to someone who belongs to a different tribe, or who worships a different prophet, has no place in the twenty-first century. Africa's diversity should be a source of strength, not a cause for division.[32]

These were not totally new themes. The Bush administration had more closely linked U.S. foreign aid to good governance practices. The World Bank had developed good governance criteria. Various studies had shown a strong relationship between good governance and economic development, despite disagreement about sequencing and causal direction. Although most of these studies were global in scope, applying across regions, Africa was a principal focus.

The free/partly free/not free rankings by Freedom House, based on elections, civil liberties, and other political freedom measures (also cited in earlier chapters for other regions), are one measure of democracy. In the decade between 2002 and 2012, these show democracy in Africa having fallen back a bit. The percentage of countries ranked free or partly free dropped from 64 percent to 61 percent, while the percentage ranked not free rose from 36 percent to 39 percent. Another ranking system specific to Africa is the Ibrahim Index of African Governance. Named for Mo Ibrahim, a Sudanese-born British businessman-philanthropist, the "governance" scope of this index also includes measures of policy performance such as sustainable economic opportunity and human development. The fact that the results are similar—for example, in 2012, Mauritius, Botswana, South Africa, and Ghana were among the highest-ranked countries in both indices—reinforces the interconnection of effective political systems and socioeconomic progress. The Ibrahim Foundation also gives an award to former African leaders who were democratically elected, served only their constitutionally mandated term, and "developed their countries, lifted people out of poverty, and paved the way for future prosperity and success."[33] In some years the Foundation has not given the award, as a signal that it takes the criteria seriously and is not going to award the honor just to award it.

The United States provides some foreign aid and other assistance for promoting democracy in Africa. These programs are principally run by the Agency for International Development (AID). They include programs for rule of law, anticorruption, elections, civil society, and governance. Some involve direct AID roles, others are in partnership with NGOs. They are not, though, a major share of the U.S. foreign aid budget.

The greatest African democratization success story is South Africa. The apartheid system had ensured the white minority's total control of the government and the economy, and condemned the black majority to oppression, injustice, and poverty. Yet in 1994 Nelson Mandela, the leader of the anti-apartheid movement who had been held as a political prisoner for twenty-seven years until his release in 1990, was elected president. Black majority rule was established, with protections for white minority rights.

One of the lessons of South Africa was how important national leaders are to democratization. Despite having been held for all those years as a political prisoner, Mandela did not do unto his old enemies as they had done unto him. As president, he displayed extraordinary statesmanship and ruled in a spirit of reconciliation, not retribution. It is no wonder that Mandela won the Nobel Peace Prize, sharing it with F. W. de Klerk, the white former president of South Africa, who led the dismantling of apartheid from within. Other cases in Africa and elsewhere are less historically dramatic but also involve leaders and groups opting for peaceful and democratic transitions over narrow self-interest. When the opposite choice prevails, though, the effects are devastating. Ethnic conflict in recent years often has resulted when leaders foment political violence, when they play to and play up the historical roots of hatreds, and when they seek to mobilize groups around these divisions rather than seek reconciliation.

Another lesson, though, is that even a leader of Mandela's caliber is not sufficient to ensure the future of a new democracy. Thabo Mbeki, Mandela's successor as president, confounded other leaders as well as the public health community with his opposition to science-based AIDS policies. The next president, Jacob Zuma, came to power already tainted by ethics scandals. Meanwhile, the South African economy has been hit by high unemployment and other economic problems even worse than those in many other countries in the region. An estimated one-third of South Africans earn less than $2 per day. Half of those under age 24 are unemployed. The average income of black households is one-sixth that of whites.'[34] Will the political system remain stable amid mounting socioeconomic problems? The gap between rich and poor has been widening. Crime rates have been very high. The HIV/AIDS crisis continues to tear at the social fabric. In these and other ways, challenges continue.

Trade, Development, and HIV/AIDS

First the good news: African economic growth has generally been on the upswing. Between 2000 and 2010, real GDP growth averaged 5.7 percent annually, up from only 2.4 percent in the prior two decades. During that same period six of the ten fastest-growing economies in the world were in Africa. Per capita income was rising by 3 percent per year, almost two times the global average.[35] This economic progress came despite the negative effects of the global financial crisis precipitated by the U.S. financial meltdown and then the euro crisis. A 2012 World Bank report (excerpted in Reading 14.2) went so far as to speculate that "Africa could be on the brink of an economic takeoff, much like China was thirty years ago, and India twenty years ago."[36]

Social indicators also were moving in the right direction. The percentage of people living below the $1.25-a-day poverty line fell below 50 percent for the first time. Maternal deaths decreased 26 percent between 1990 and 2009. Child mortality rates were falling as well. Primary school completion rates were increasing more rapidly than anywhere else in the world. HIV infection rates were leveling off.[37]

Such progress, though, exists in the context of continuing huge socioeconomic challenges. The 47 percent poverty rate, while lower than before, is still the highest regional rate in the world. So, too, are the maternal and child mortality rates. The percentage of students enrolled in primary schools is still the world's lowest; indeed, more than half of all the children in the world not in primary school live in Africa. Life expectancy (fifty-eight years) is the world's lowest. Population increase is the world's fastest. Food insecurity has been particularly acute in recent years amidst price spikes, along with continuing hunger and malnutrition problems.

U.S. policy in response to these challenges includes both trade and aid. The Africa Growth and Opportunity Act (AGOA), first passed in 2000, provides trade preferences for African countries that reform their economies consistent with free-market principles. Foreign aid programs include technical assistance and training for greater agricultural productivity, improved sanitation, literacy and education, and women's empowerment.

Numerous environmental issues pose their own challenges. A combination of short-sighted national policies and global climate change has worsened desertification and deforestation. Biodiversity is being lost. Rapid urbanization exacerbates water, sewage, and related problems. Climate change has been bringing rising sea levels and consequent coastal erosion and flooding, more frequent and severe droughts, and other environmental and economic impacts. Some U.S. foreign aid programs are targeted at these and other environmental issues.

HIV/AIDS is one of the most troubling problems. Here, too, the record is mixed. Between 2005 and 2011, sub-Saharan African countries reduced deaths from AIDS-related causes by 32 percent. Some countries made exceptional progress; Botswana, for example, cut AIDS-related deaths by 71 percent, and Rwanda cut such deaths by 68 percent. But sub-Saharan Africa still has much higher death rates than any other region. It also has the highest new-infection rate; at 0.59 per 100 people aged 15–49, this amounts to 70 percent of new HIV infections for a region that is home to just 12 percent of the global population. The 1.92 sub-regional new-infection rate for Southern Africa is especially striking. The South African government, especially under former president Thabo Mbeki (1999–2008), has faced particular criticism for its resistance to science-based policies. One study estimated that 365,000 deaths could have been prevented if the Mbeki government had not refused to provide antiretroviral drugs to AIDS patients and other widely administered drugs to pregnant women at risk of infecting their babies. As a result, only 23 percent of those in need were reached, compared with 85 percent in neighboring Botswana and 71 percent in Namibia.[38] The post-Mbeki government has been shifting toward more science-based policies that have achieved encouraging results, such as a 75 percent increase (2010–12) in the number of patients added to treatment programs.[39]

AIDS continues to be a deeply disturbing humanitarian crisis. It also has a major impact on economic development. How can a country succeed in its economic development when it is losing such large numbers of citizens, often at the most productive stages of their working lives? As then-UN secretary-general Kofi Annan stated in a speech to the African summit on HIV/AIDS:

> Disease, like war, is not only a product of underdevelopment. It is also one of the biggest obstacles preventing our societies from developing as they should. This is especially true of HIV/AIDS, which takes its biggest toll among young adults—the age group that normally produces most, and has the main responsibility for rearing the next generation. That is why AIDS has become not only the primary cause of death on this continent, but our biggest development challenge.[40]

Even more immediate are the added costs of dealing with the consequences; consider, for example, the over 12 million children orphaned by AIDS in sub-Saharan Africa alone. HIV/AIDS is also a factor in worsening famines, having left so many farm workers unable to work the fields that the amount of cultivated land has declined by almost 70 percent in some countries.

The George W. Bush administration received credit for substantially increasing funding for combating global AIDS. The President's Emergency Plan for AIDS Relief (PEPFAR) increased funding from $2.3 billion in 2004 to $6 billion in 2008. The State Department billed this as "the largest international health initiative any nation has ever undertaken directed at a single disease."[41] A Stanford University Medical School study credited Bush's PEPFAR with reducing global AIDS death rates by 10 percent.[42] But although garnering praise, the Bush AIDS policy also was criticized for its overemphasis on sexual abstinence. As with population control, this was seen as an extension of American domestic politics and as running counter to more-effective global strategies.

Obama's de-emphasizing of abstinence as a component of U.S. AIDS policy was greeted positively by many global HIV/AIDS activists. Although, in his first term, Obama proclaimed the goal of an "AIDS-free generation," his policy was criticized for providing less funding than he had pledged when first running for president.[43]

Foreign Policy Politics Case Study: Anti-Apartheid Economic Sanctions

The baseline for presidential–congressional cooperation on cases of economic sanctions is the provision of the Constitution granting Congress the power "to regulate commerce with foreign nations." Sanctions are like tariffs in this respect. Although sanctions are motivated more by politics and tariffs are motivated more by economics, both constitute regulation of international trade. Presidents do have some powers to impose sanctions, granted through the International Economic Emergency Powers Act and other legislation. Executive-branch politics is also often evident: different departments and agencies have different perspectives and interests at stake, for in bureaucratic politics, where you stand depends on where you sit.

All five types of interest groups in our interest-group typology from chapters 3 and 9 can exert pressure in sanctions cases: economic interest groups, motivated by their trade and investment interests; identity groups, motivated by their ethnic, racial, national, religious, and other links to targeted countries; political issue groups, including many NGOs engaged in democracy promotion and human rights protection; state and local governments, drawing on their purchasing power, pension funds, and other economic levers to pursue their own sanctions; and foreign governments, through contracts with Washington, D.C., law firms, public relations firms, and other lobbyists. The media may also be engaged, depending on the salience and drama of the case. The extent to which public opinion is activated varies in similar ways.

Of all the recent sanctions cases, the 1985–86 anti-apartheid sanctions against South Africa stand out as an example in which the foreign policy politics was especially intense—and, for our purposes, very instructive.[44] Since 1948, South Africa had been governed by a system known by the Afrikaans word *apartheid*. Literally meaning "separateness," apartheid gave the white minority power over the black African majority. The black majority was denied meaningful political participation, relegated to economic inequality, confined to living in designated areas, and repressed overall. The apartheid system was viewed as the most unequal and racist in the world.

Prior to the mid-1980s, the United States had done little to oppose or seek to change the apartheid system. The Kennedy administration had imposed an arms embargo (economic sanctions on military weapons). The Carter administration had signed on to the United Nations arms embargo and added some other selected sanctions. The Reagan administration, however, shifted back in the other direction: Secretary of State Alexander Haig spoke of "old friends . . . who are getting together again."[45] By 1984 American exports of aircraft, computers, communications equipment, and other military-related goods had increased 100 percent over Carter administration levels.

But things grew worse in South Africa. ***Anti-apartheid*** protests intensified and by late 1985, as the situation became increasingly violent, the reported death toll was more than three people every day. In January 1986 President P. W. Botha declared a state of emergency, cracking down on political demonstrations, school boycotts, labor stoppages, and rent strikes. His regime arrested key black leaders, including the leaders of the largest black political organization, the African National Congress (ANC). These leaders joined the already-imprisoned Nelson Mandela, the ANC leader who had been arrested and held in prison since the early 1960s.

The anti-apartheid movement in the United States responded to these events with a political impact greater than that of any protest movement since the Vietnam War. It was led by TransAfrica, a small political issue group that until then was little known. TransAfrica came up with the very effective initial strategy of dramatizing the issue and demonstrating outrage by having political leaders and celebrities protest at the South African embassy in Washington, D.C., in ways that would intentionally get them arrested. By mid-December 1985 the "celebrity arrests" included American civil rights leaders, Hollywood movie stars, religious leaders of many faiths, and fifteen members of Congress. This public protest in turn led to greater press coverage; before long the average American "was gaining an unprecedented awareness of South Africa."[46] Public opinion was strongly opposed to apartheid. College campuses were seized with this issue.

Teach-ins, demonstrations, and other manifestations of student activism were reminiscent of such activities on campuses during the Vietnam era.

The principal policy issue was whether to impose economic sanctions and, if so, how comprehensive to make those sanctions. Some proposals included sanctioning all U.S. trade with and investment in South Africa. This was controversial, as American companies had extensive economic interests in South Africa. The United States was South Africa's leading trade partner, supplying 15 percent of its imports, including 70 percent of its computer equipment, 45 percent of its oil, and 33 percent of its cars. Imports from South Africa were only 8 percent of total U.S. imports but included 75 percent of the U.S. supply of chromium, vital for manufacturing stainless steel and aircraft engines; 67 percent of its platinum, used in automobile catalytic converters, fertilizer, explosives, and purified glass; and $140 million in diamonds. In terms of investments, about 350 American firms had operations in South Africa, including fifty-seven of the Fortune 100 companies. American banks had about $7.5 billion in loans out to South African companies. It thus was no surprise that most of the American business community opposed sanctions.

The strong support from Democrats in Congress for an anti-apartheid sanctions bill was no surprise either. What was a surprise was the support that started to come from Republicans. The Republican Reagan administration was opposed to sanctions, as Republicans in Congress had long been. But a group of young conservative House members saw this issue as one that could be politically beneficial in broadening the party's popular base. "South Africa has been able to depend on conservatives in the United States . . . to treat them with benign neglect," said Representative Vin Weber (R-Minnesota), a leader of this group. "We served notice that, with the emerging generation of conservative leadership, that is not going to be the case."[47] Senator Richard Lugar (R-Indiana), chair of the Senate Foreign Relations Committee, also became a supporter of at least some sanctions. Lugar was generally seen as a moderate on foreign policy issues, and was emerging through this and other issues as a more prominent foreign policy figure.

The Anti-Apartheid Act of 1985 was approved by huge margins, 380–48 in the House and 80–12 in the Senate, despite continued opposition from the Reagan administration. When the White House threatened to veto the bill, Weber and Lugar were among those warning the White House that on this issue the two-thirds majorities needed for veto override would be there, with many Republicans joining in.

Congress still had to go through the final steps of a conference committee to work out differences between the House and Senate bills, and then bring that bill to a final vote in each chamber. The Reagan administration took advantage of this delay to shift tactics. It issued an executive order imposing its own sanctions, which were more than it had previously favored but less than those mandated by the congressional bills. Party loyalty prevailed at that point, and House and Senate Republicans blocked final passage of the congressional bills.

But the issue was taken up again the following year. In May 1986 Democrats in the House introduced a new bill, the Comprehensive Anti-Apartheid Sanctions Act, which called for even more extensive sanctions. This bill was approved on the floor with an amendment by Representative Ron Dellums (D-California) that not only prohibited new investments by American companies in South Africa but also required divestment (i.e., selling off of existing investments). The Senate then passed its own bill, which went further than the 1985 Reagan executive order but not so far as the House bill. Lugar kept the Senate coalition together amid opposition to any sanctions bill from conservatives such as Jesse Helms (R-North Carolina) and pressure from liberals such as Edward Kennedy (D-Massachusetts) to make the Senate bill as tough as the House one.

Largely on the basis of a commitment by Senator Lugar to stand by the bill even if President Reagan vetoed it, House Democratic leaders agreed to bypass the negotiations of a conference committee and accept the Senate version of the bill. President Reagan did veto it. But by votes of 313–83 in the House and 78–21 in the Senate, well beyond the necessary two-thirds majorities, the veto was overridden and the Comprehensive Anti-Apartheid Sanctions Act became law.

This was the first foreign policy veto override since President Richard Nixon's veto of the War Powers Resolution was overruled by Congress in 1973. It showed how politically strong the anti-apartheid forces had become. All along, groups such as TransAfrica had been keeping up their pressure, as had businesses and other interests on the other side. State and local governments were coming out against apartheid, passing their own versions of sanctions through prohibitions on purchases from and investments in American companies doing business with South Africa. Public opinion showed ever larger majorities in favor of sanctions. Campuses stayed active. Meanwhile, the press and television kept covering the South African government's violent and repressive tactics.

In this case, the foreign policy politics were strong enough to push the U.S. government to give priority to Principles over Prosperity.

Summary

On the one hand, with the increased emphasis on Asia, the continuing threats from the Middle East, longstanding ties to Europe, and the proximity to the United States of Latin America, the U.S. foreign policy agenda is already quite full. But in bringing together issues that persist from earlier periods and ones that are especially pressing in our twenty-first-century world, Africa makes strong claims to its own importance for the U.S. national interest in all its elements: Power, Peace, Prosperity, and Principles.

Notes

[1]Barack Obama, Remarks by the President to the Ghanaian Parliament, July 11, 2009, www.whitehouse .gov/the_press_office/Remarks-by-the-President-to-the-Ghanaian-Parliament/ (accessed 3/9/13).

[2]Adam Hochschild, *King Leopold's Ghost: A Story of Greed, Terror and Heroism in Colonial Africa* (New York: Houghton Mifflin, 1998); Odd Arne Westad, *The Global Cold War* (Cambridge, U.K.: Cambridge University Press, 2007).

[3]Jeffrey Gettleman, "Congo's Never-Ending War," *New York Times*, December 15, 2012, SR1.

[4]Cited in Mats R. Berdahl, "Fateful Encounter: The United States and UN Peacekeeping," *Survival* 36 (Spring 1994): 32.

[5]Cited in Berdahl, "Fateful Encounter," 34.

[6]Cited in Berdahl, "Fateful Encounter," 40–41; see also: Walter Clarke and Jeffrey Herbst, "Somalia and the Future of Humanitarian Intervention," *Foreign Affairs* 75 (March/April 1996): 70–85.

[7]U.S. Department of State, *The Clinton Administration's Policy on Reforming Multilateral Peace Operations*, May 1994; see also the follow-up report put out by the White House, *A Time for Peace, Promoting Peace: The Policy of the United States*, February 1995.

[8]Ken Menkhaus, "Dangerous Waters," *Survival: Global Politics and Strategy* 51 (February–March 2009): 22.

[9]Donna Nincic, "State Failure and the Re-emergence of Maritime Piracy in Africa," paper delivered at the International Studies Association 49th Annual Convention, San Francisco, March 2008, www.allacademic .com//meta/p_mla_apa_research_citation/2/5/4/3/2/pages254325/p254325-1.php (accessed 12/26/12).

[10]Samantha Power, *"A Problem from Hell": America and the Age of Genocide* (New York: Basic Books, 2002), 334.

[11]Astri Suhrke and Bruce Jones, "Preventive Diplomacy in Rwanda: Failure to Act or Failure of Actions?" in *Opportunities Missed, Opportunities Seized: Preventive Diplomacy in the Post–Cold War World*, ed. Bruce W. Jentleson (Lanham, Md.: Rowman and Littlefield, 2000), 247.

[12]Suhrke and Jones, "Preventive Diplomacy in Rwanda," 257–58; Charles Truehart, "UN Alerted to Plans for Rwanda Bloodbath," *Washington Post*, September 25, 1997, A1, A28; Philip Gourevitch, *We Wish to Inform You That Tomorrow We Will Be Killed with Our Families: Stories from Rwanda* (New York: Farrar, Straus, and Giroux, 1998); Scott R. Feil, *Preventing Genocide: How the Early Use of Force Might Have Succeeded in Rwanda* (Washington, D.C.: Carnegie Commission on Preventing Deadly Conflict, 1998), 22.

[13]Suhrke and Jones, "Preventive Diplomacy in Rwanda," 259. See also: Alison Des Forges, *Leave None to Tell the Story* (New York: Human Rights Watch, 1999). The viability of a late intervention is questioned by Alan J. Kuperman, "Rwanda in Retrospect," *Foreign Affairs* 79 (January/February 2000): 94–118. Kuperman argues that even a force of 13,500 troops could have reduced the death toll by only 25 percent. Even if his analysis is accurate regarding what a *late* intervention could have achieved, however, his argument only further underscores the importance of acting early and decisively.

[14]Nicholas Kristof, "The Secret Genocide Archive," *New York Times*, February 23, 2005. See also: Human Rights Watch, *Entrenching Impunity: Government Responsibility for International Crimes in Darfur*, December 2005, www.hrw.org/en/reports/2005/12/08/entrenching-impunity (accessed 7/28/09).

[15]Scott Anderson, "How Did Darfur Happen?" *New York Times Magazine*, October 17, 2004; International Crisis Group (ICG), *Darfur Rising: Sudan's New Crisis*, ICG Africa Report No. 76, March 25, 2004; Amnesty International, "Sudan: Crisis in Darfur—Urgent Need for International Commission of Inquiry and Monitoring," press release, April 28, 2003, www.amnesty.org/en/library/asset/AFR54/026/2003/en/094fac27 -d6f9-11dd-b0cc-1f0860013475/afr540262003en.html (accessed 7/28/09).

[16]Cheryl O. Igiri and Princeton Lyman, *Giving Meaning to "Never Again": Seeking an Effective Response to the Crisis in Darfur and Beyond*, Council on Foreign Relations, CSR No. 5, September 2004, 24.

[17]Rebecca Hamilton, "Inside Colin Powell's Decision to Declare Genocide in Darfur, The Atlantic.com, August 17, 2011, http://www.theatlantic.com/international/archive/2011/08/inside-colin-powells-decision-to-declare-genocide-in-darfur/243560/ (accessed 3/9/13).

[18]Joel Brinkley, "Violence and Refugee Numbers Grow in Sudan," *New York Times*, November 11, 2005, http://travel.nytimes.com/2005/11/11/international/africa/llsudan.html.

[19]International Crisis Group, *Do Americans Care About Darfur? An International Crisis Group / Zogby International Opinion Survey*, Africa Briefing No. 26, June 1, 2005.

[20]Nichols Kristof, "Has Obama Forgotten Darfur?" *New York Times*, June 11, 2010, http://kristof.blogs.nytimes.com/2010/06/11/has-obama-forgotten-darfur/; "Obama and Darfur," *Wall Street Journal*, October 22, 2009, http://online.wsj.com/article/SB10001424052748704597704574485761817446056.html (both accessed 3/9/13).

[21]Jeffrey Gettleman, "Raid on Rivals in South Sudan Shows Escalating Violence," *New York Times*, January 5, 2012, A10.

[22]Statement of General Carter Ham to the House Armed Services Committee, February 29, 2012, www.africom.mil/NEWSROOM/Article/8832/2012/-posture-statement-statement-of-general-carter (accessed 3/9/13).

[23]Craig Whitlock, "Remote U.S. Base at Core of Secret Operations," *Washington Post*, October 25, 2012, www.washingtonpost.com/world/national-security/remote-us-base-at-core-of-secret-operations/2012/10/25/a26a9392-197a-11e2-bd10-5ff056538b7c_story.html (accessed 3/9/13). See also: Eric Schmitt and Thom Shanker, *Counterstrike: The Untold Story of America's Secret Campaign against Al Qaeda* (New York: St. Martin's Griffin, 2012), 190–94.

[24]Cited in Council on Foreign Relations, "Backgrounder: Al Qaeda in the Islamic Maghreb (AQIM)," October 15, 2012, www.cfr.org/north-africa/al-qaeda-islamic-maghreb-aqim/p12717 (accessed 3/9/13).

[25]Eric Schmitt, "American Commander Details Al Qaeda's Strength in Mali," *New York Times*, December 4, 2012, A14.

[26]Adam Nossiter, "In Nigeria, A Deadly Group's Rage Has Local Roots," *New York Times*, February 26, 2012, A6.

[27]John Campbell, "Nigeria's Battle for Stability," *The National Interest* 118 (March/April 2012), 31–32.

[28]Jane Perlez, "With $20 Billion Loan Package, China Strengthens Its Ties to African Nations," *New York Times*, July 19, 2012, A6; Colum Lynch, "China's Arms Exports Flooding Sub-Saharan Africa," *Washington Post*, August 25, 2012, www.washingtonpost.com/world/national-security/chinas-arms-exports-flooding-sub-saharan-africa/2012/08/25/16267b68-e7f1-11e1-936a-b801f1abab19_story.html?wpisrc=emailtoafriend (accessed 3/9/13); Andrew Jacobs, "Pursuing Soft Power, China Puts Stamp on Africa's News," *New York Times*, August 17, 2012, A1; Howard W. French, "The Next Empire," *The Atlantic*, May 2010.

[29]French, "The Next Empire."

[30]David Smith, "China's Booming Trade with Africa Helps Tone Its Diplomatic Muscle," *The Guardian*, March 22, 2012, www.guardian.co.uk/world/2012/mar/22/chinas-booming-trade-africa-diplomatic (accessed 3/9/13).

[31]Leslie Hook, "Zuma Warns on Africa's Trade Ties to China," *Washington Post*, July 19, 2012, www.washingtonpost.com/world/asia_pacific/zuma-warns-on-africas-trade-ties-to-china/2012/07/19/gJQAFgd7vW_story.html (accessed 3/9/13).

[32]President Obama, Speech to the Ghanaian Parliament; July 2009.

[33]Mo Ibrahim Foundation, www.moibrahimfoundation.org/ibrahim-prize/ (accessed 3/9/13).

[34]Eve Fairbanks, "You Have All the Reasons to Be Angry," *The New Republic*, March 11/2013, 28–30.

[35]"The Lion Kings?" *The Economist*, January 6, 2011, www.economist.com/node/17853324?zid=295&ah=0bca374e65f2354d553956ea65f756e0 (accessed 3/9/13).

[36]Lydia Polgreen, "U.S., Too, Wants to Bolster Investment in a Continent's Economic Prospects," *New York Times*, August 9, 2012, A9.

[37]World Bank, "Africa Regional Brief," http://web.worldbank.org/WBSITE/EXTERNAL/COUNTRIES/AFRICAEXT/0,,menuPK:258652~pagePK:146732~piPK:146828~theSitePK:258644,00.html;   United

Nations, *Millennium Development Goals Report 2012,* www.un.org/millenniumgoals/pdf/MDG%20Report%202012.pdf (both accessed 3/9/13).

[38]Celia W. Dugger, "Study Cites Toll of AIDS Policy in South Africa," *New York Times,* November 26, 2008.

[39]UNAIDS, *World AIDS Day Report 2012,* 15–17, www.unaids.org/en/media/unaids/contentassets/documents/epidemiology/2012/gr2012/JC2434_WorldAIDSday_results_en.pdf (accessed 3/9/13).

[40]Kofi Annan, address to the African Summit on HIV/AIDS, Tuberculosis and Other Infectious Diseases, Abuja, Nigeria, April 26, 2001, www.un.org/News/Press/docs/2001/SGSM7779R1.doc.htm (accessed 3/9/13).

[41]U.S. Department of State, Office of the U.S. Global AIDS Coordinator, "Action Today, a foundation for Tomorrow: Second Annual Report to Congress on PEPFAR (2006)," www.state.gov/s/gac/rl/c16742.htm (accessed 3/9/13).

[42]Ali Gharib and Jim Lobe, "U.S.: Obama's Global Health Plan Disappoints Activists," May 5, 2009, http://ipsnews.net/news.asp?idnews=46734 (accessed 3/9/13).

[43]John Donnelly, "Activists: In the Fight Against AIDS, Obama Doesn't Measure Up to Bush," Talking Points Memo (TPM), http://tpmdc.talkingpointsmemo.com/2012/06/aids-policy-public-health-barack-obama-george-w-bush-presidents-emergency-plan-for-aids-relief-pepfar.php (accessed 3/9/13).

[44]This section draws on Bruce W. Jentleson, "American Diplomacy: Around the World and Along Pennsylvania Avenue," in *A Question of Balance: The President, the Congress and Foreign Policy,* ed. Thomas E. Mann (Washington, D.C.: Brookings Institution Press, 1990), 146–200; and Jentleson, ed., *Perspectives on American Foreign Policy: Readings and Cases* (New York: Norton, 2000), chap. 2, and the Kennedy School of Government (Harvard University) case study, "The United States and South Africa: The Anti-Apartheid Sanctions Debate of 1985," by Pamela Varley for Gregory Treverton (1989).

[45]Cited in Jentleson, "American Diplomacy," 157.

[46]Jentleson, *Perspectives,* 42.

[47]Cited in Jentleson, *Perspectives,* 42.

Readings for Part II: American Foreign Policy in the Twenty-First Century: Choices and Challenges

American Primacy

7.1

ROBERT J. LIEBER
Anti-Declinism*

The idea that the United States is in a state of rapid, fundamental decline is now widely proclaimed. . . .

The description is driven by America's difficulties overseas and at home. The frustrations and costs of long wars in Afghanistan and Iraq, a continuing campaign against radical Islamist terrorism, the rise of China and of other emerging powers, and the challenges of coping with globalization and growing economic competition suggests that the United States has become overextended and is no longer capable of playing a leading role in world affairs. At home, the collapse of the real estate bubble, followed by financial crisis and a great recession, a lagging recovery, and destructive partisanship in the face of deepening problems of debt and deficit have led to gloomy assessments about America's economy, politics and society. . . .

The problems are real and serious. Nevertheless, if we take a longer view, the picture looks rather different, and much of the discourse about decline appears exaggerated, hyperbolic, and ahistorical. Why? For two broad reasons. First, because of the deep underlying strengths of the United States. These include not only size, population, demography, and resources, but also the scale and importance of its economy and financial markets, its scientific research and technology, its competitiveness, military power, and absorptive capacity, and its unique attractiveness to talented immigrants. Second, there is the weight of history and of American exceptionalism, or what social scientists like to call path dependency. Throughout its history, the United States has repeatedly faced and eventually overcome daunting challenges and crises, many of which gave rise to weighty and dire predictions. The most dangerous of these experiences have included the Civil War, repeated financial crises during the nineteenth century, the Great Depression of the 1930s, and the geopolitical and ideological threats posed by Nazi Germany, Imperial Japan, and the Soviet Union. . . .

To be sure, there can be no certainty about America's ability to overcome current problems, and contingency and human agency

---

*From Robert J. Lieber, *Power and Willpower in the American Future: Why the United States Is Not Destined to Decline* (New York: Cambridge University Press, 2012), 1–5.

come into play. Ultimately, elite and popular beliefs, policy choices, and leadership remain critical in shaping outcomes. In this sense, the challenges facing the United States are at least as much ideational as they are material. Here, however, there may be a paradox working in America's favor. It is that the worse the crisis, the greater the sense of urgency and the more likely that policy makers, regardless of their prior inhibitions and beliefs, will find themselves having to respond effectively.

The stakes are immense, and not only for America itself. Since World War II, the United States has been the world's principal provider of collective goods. The leading international institutions of today and much of the existing international order have been a product of American leadership. Evidence from recent decades suggests that the alternative is not that some other institution or major power (the UN, the EU, China, India, Russia, or Japan) will take its place, but that none will. Some have argued that the effects of globalization are leading the world toward greater cooperation and even collective security. This may be a comforting view about the implications or even desirability of American disengagement, but practical experience suggests otherwise. In dealing with failed states, ethnic cleansing, human rights, the environment, trade liberal-ization, regional conflict, and nuclear proliferation, emerging powers such as the BRICS (Brazil, Russia, India, China, and South Africa) have been largely unhelpful, and others in Europe, Asia, Africa, or Latin America have more often than not lacked the will or capacity to act collectively on common tasks.

For the United States, as I argue here, the maintenance of its leading role matters greatly. The alternative would not only be a more disorderly and dangerous world in which its own economic and national security would be adversely affected, but also regional conflicts and the spread of nuclear weapons would be more likely. In addition, allies and those sharing common values, especially liberal democracy and the market economy, would increasingly be at risk. Ultimately, America's ability to avoid serious decline and the significant international retrenchment that would be a result of severely reduced resources becomes a matter of policy and political will. There is nothing inevitable about decline, and both past experience and national attributes matter greatly. Flexibility, adaptability, and the capacity for course correction provide the United States with a resilience that has proved invaluable in the past and is likely to do so in the future.

*   *   *

Liberal Internationalism

G. John Ikenberry
Liberal Internationalism 3.0*

Over the past century, the liberal international "project" has evolved and periodically reinvented itself. The liberal international ideas championed by Woodrow Wilson were extended and reworked by Franklin Roosevelt and Harry Truman. Today's liberal internationalist agenda is evolving yet again.

* * *

The liberal imagination is vast, and the ideas and design for liberal international order are also extraordinarily wide ranging.[1] At its most basic, liberal internationalism offers a vision of an open, rule-based system in which states trade and cooperate to achieve mutual gains.[2] Liberals assume that peoples and governments have deep common interests in the establishment of a cooperative world order organized around principles of restraint, reciprocity, and sovereign equality. There is an optimist assumption lurking in liberal internationalism that states can overcome constraints and cooperate to solve security dilemmas, pursue collective action, and create an open, stable system. There is also an optimistic assumption that powerful states will act with restraint in the exercise of their power and find ways to credibly convey commitments to other states. Across the decades, liberal internationalists have shared the view that trade and exchange have a modernizing and civilizing effect on states, undercutting illiberal tendencies and strengthening the fabric of international community. Liberal internationalists also share the view that democracies are—in contrast to autocratic and authoritarian states—particularly able and willing to operate within an open, rule-based international system and to cooperate for mutual gain. Likewise, liberal internationalists have shared the view that institutions and rules established between states facilitate and reinforce cooperation and collective problem solving.[3]

* * *

As in the past, the liberal international project is evolving. The old American-led liberal hegemonic order is giving way to something new. But what sort of new order? . . . Three sets

---

*From G. John Ikenberry, "Liberal Internationalism 3.0: America and the Dilemmas of Liberal World Order," *Perspectives on Politics* (March 2009), 71–86.

of issues are particularly important in shaping what comes next. One set of issues concerns scope and hierarchy.

One set of issues concerns scope and hierarchy. A reformed liberal international order will need to become more universal and less hierarchical—that is, the United States will need to cede authority and control to a wider set of states and give up some of its hegemonic rights and privileges. But a "flatter' international order will also be one in which the United States plays a less central role in providing function services—generating public goods, stabilizing markets, and promoting cooperation. So the questions are several. What is the logic of a post-hegemonic liberal order—and is it viable? Can these functional services be provided collectively? Will the United States agree to relinquish the special rights and privileges built into liberal internationalism 2.0. Of course, it is possible for more incremental shifts away from liberal hegemony. The United States could continue to provide functional services for liberal order but do so in wider concert with other major states? Liberal order can be endangered if there is too much hierarchy—indeed hierarchy in its extreme form is empire. But it might also be endangered if there is too little hierarchy, as the Wilsonian-era experiment in liberal order revealed.

A second issue concerns legitimate authority and post-Westphalian sovereignty. A reformed liberal international order will need to find ways to reconcile more intrusive rules and institutions with legitimate international authority. The human rights revolution makes the international community increasingly concerned with the internal workings of states. So too does the new international-threat environment—a situation where growing "security interdependence" is making each country's security increasingly dependent on what goes on elsewhere, including elsewhere inside of states. The international community is going to need capacities and legitimate authority to intervene in weak and troubled states.[4] . . . Nonetheless, finding consensus on the norms of intervention in a post-Westphalian world is deeply problematic—yet short of establishing such legitimate authority, the international order will continue to be troubled and contested.

A third issue relates to democracy and the international rule of law. Here the question is: how do you build up authority and capacity at the international level—international bodies and agreements—without jeopardizing popular rule and accountability built into liberal democratic states? Can the authority and capacity of the international community to act be strengthened without sacrificing constitutional democracy at home?

* * *

The way in which liberal order evolves will hinge in important respects on the United States—and its willingness and ability to make new commitments to rules and institutions while simultaneously reducing its rights and privileges within the order. The United States is deeply ambivalent about making institutional commitments and binding itself to other states—ambivalence and hesitation that has been exacerbated by the end of the Cold War, American unipolarity, and new security threats. But the United States still possesses profound incentives to build and operate within a liberal rule-based order. Just as importantly, that order is now not simply an extension of American power and interests—it has taken on a life of its own. American power may rise or fall and its foreign policy ideology may wax and wane between multilateral and imperial impulses—but the wider and deeper liberal global order is now a reality that America itself must accommodate to.

Notes

[1]International order refers to the settled arrangements between states that define the terms of their interaction. Liberal international order refers to international order that is open and rule-based. As noted, the more specific features of liberal international order—in particular the character and location of sovereignty and political authority—can vary widely within liberal orders.

[2]For surveys of liberal international theory, see Doyle 1997; Russett and Oneal 2001; Deudney and Ikenberry 1999; and Keohane, in John Dunn 1990.

[3]No single modern theorist captures the whole of liberal international theory, but a variety of theorists provide aspects. On the democratic peace, see Doyle 1983. On security communities, see Adler and Barnett 1998, and Deutsch, Burrell, and Kann 1957. On the interrelationship of domestic and international politics, see Rosenau 1969. On functional integration theory, see Haas 1964. On international institutions, see Keohane 1984; and Krasner 1981. On the fragmented and complex nature of power and interdependence, see Keohane and Nye 1977. On domestic preferences and foreign policy, see Moravcsik 1997. On transgovernmentalism and networks, see Slaughter 2004. On the modernization theory underpinnings of the liberal tradition, see Morse 1976 and Rosenau 1991.

[4]For discussions of post-Westphalian forms of international supervision and management of weak or collapsed states, see Krasner 2005; Fearon and Laitin, 2004; and Keohane in Holzgrefe and Keohane 2003. See also Ferguson 2004.

Multipolarity

Charles A. Kupchan
No One's World*

* * *

The twenty-first century marks not the ultimate triumph of the West, but the emergence of a global landscape that is headed toward a turning point rather than an end point. The West is losing not only its material primacy as new powers rise, but also its ideological dominance. The world's autocracies, far from being at their last gasp, are holding their own. China has been enjoying rates of economic growth triple those of Western democracies, and its surpluses remain critical to underwriting America's pendulous debt. The global downturn took a heavy toll on the Russian economy, but the Kremlin has nonetheless maintained firm control over the state and is pursuing a muscular foreign policy. The oil-rich sheikdoms of the Persian Gulf, although shaken by the contagion of unrest that has recently spread through much of the Arab world, have continued autocratic ways. Moreover, should participatory governments spread in the Middle East, the regimes that emerge may well be much tougher customers than the autocra-

cies they replace. Even rising powers that are democratic, such as India and Brazil, are hardly stalwart supporters of the Western camp. On the contrary, they regularly break with the United States and Europe on geopolitics, trade, the environment, and other issues, preferring to side with ascending states, whether democratic or not. Interests matter more than values. . . .

The emerging landscape is one in which power is diffusing and politics diversifying, not one in which all countries are converging toward the Western way. Indeed, the world is on the cusp of a global turn. Between 1500 and 1800, the world's center of power moved from Asia and the Mediterranean Basin to Europe and, by the end of the nineteenth century, North America. The West then used its power and purpose to anchor a globalized world—and has been at the leading edge of history ever since. But the West's rise was a function of time and place, and history is now moving on. East Asia has been anointed as the candidate most likely to assume the mantle of leadership.

---

*Charles A. Kupchan, *No One's World: The West, the Rising Rest and the Coming Global Turn* (New York: Oxford University Press, 2012), 2–5.

It is doubtful, however, that any country, region, or model will dominate the next world. The twenty-first century will not be America's, China's, Asia's, or anyone else's; it will belong to no one. The emergent international system will be populated by numerous power centers as well as multiple versions of modernity.[1] For the first time in history, an interdependent world will be without a center of gravity or global guardian. A global order, if it emerges, will be an amalgam of diverse political cultures and competing conceptions of domestic and international order. . . .

Most strategists are, however, misconstruing the nature of the fundamental challenge posed by the global diffusion of power. The prevailing wisdom holds that the Western powers should capitalize on the twilight hours of their primacy to corral countries into the liberal international order that they have constructed. According to G. John Ikenberry, the West should "sink the roots of this order as deeply as possible," thereby ensuring that "the international system the United States leads can remain the dominant order of the twenty-first century."[2] While it still has the power to do so, the West must complete the process of extending its values and institutions to the rest of the globe. Even Fareed Zakaria, who has recognized that a "post-American world" lies ahead, falls into the same intellectual trap. "The power shift . . . is good for America, if approached properly," Zakaria writes. "The world is going America's way. Countries are becoming more open, market-friendly, and democratic."[3]

To cast the grand strategic challenge of the era in such terms may be reassuring to Americans and their democratic allies, but it is wishful thinking. The Chinese ship of state will not dock in the Western harbor, obediently taking the berth assigned to it. Rather than embracing the rules of the current international system, rising powers will as a matter of course seek to adjust the prevailing order in ways that advantage their own values and interests. They have been doing so since the beginning of time, and the coming era will be no different. The task at hand is not guiding rising powers into the Western harbor. Rather, it is establishing a new order whose fundamental terms will have to be negotiated by Western powers and newcomers alike. The West will have to give as much as it gets to fashion a new international order that includes the rest.

The world is barreling toward not just multipolarity, but also multiple versions of modernity—a politically diverse landscape in which the Western model will offer only one of many competing conceptions of domestic and international order. Not only will well-run autocracies hold their own against liberal democracies, but rising power that are democratic will also regularly part company with the West. Perhaps *the* defining challenge for the West and the rising rest is managing this global turn and peacefully arriving at the next world by design. The alternative is a competitive anarchy arrived at by default as multiple centers of power and the differing conceptions of order they represent vie for primacy.

* * *

Notes

[1] On the concept of multiple versions of modernity, see Shmuel Eisenstadt, ed., *Multiple Modernities* (Piscataway: Transaction Publishers, 2002).

[2] G. John Ikenberry, "The Rise of China and the Future of the West," *Foreign Affairs*, Vol. 87, no. 1 (January/February 2008), pp. 25, 37.

[3] Fareed Zakaria, *The Post-American World* (New York: Norton, 2008), p. 218.

Globalization

JOSEPH STIGLITZ
Making Globalization Work*

Reforming Globalization

The globalization debate has gone from a general recognition that all was not well with globalization and that there was a real basis for at least some of the discontent to a deeper analysis that links specific policies with specific failures. . . .

Six areas where the international community has recognized that all is not well illustrate both the progress that has been made and the distance yet to go.

The pervasiveness of poverty

Poverty has, at last, become a global concern. The United Nations and multinational institutions such as the World Bank have all begun focusing more on poverty reduction. In September 2000, some 150 heads of state or government attended the Millennium Summit at the United Nations in New York and signed the Millennium Development Goals pledging to cut poverty in half by 2015. They recognized the many dimensions to poverty—not just inadequate income, but also, for instance, inadequate health care and access to water. . . .

The need for foreign assistance and debt relief

. . . In tandem with the recognition that aid should be increased has come a broad agreement that more assistance should be given in the form of grants and less in loans—not surprising given the constant problems in repaying the loans. Most telling of all, however, is the altered approach to conditionality. Countries seeking foreign aid are typically asked to meet a large number of conditions; for instance, a counry may be told that it must quickly pass a piece of legislation or reform social security, bankruptcy, or other financial systems if it is to receive aid. The enormous number of conditions often distracted governments from more vital tasks. Excessive conditionality was one of the major complaints against the IMF and World Bank. Both institutions now admit that they went overboard, and in the last five years they have actually greatly reduced conditionality.

---

*Joseph E. Stiglitz, *Making Globalization Work* (New York: Norton, 2006), 13–18.

Many developing countries face a huge burden of debt. In some, half or more of their governmental spending or foreign exchange earnings from exports has to be used to service this debt—taking away money that could be used for schools, roads, or health clinics. Development is difficult as it is; with this debt burden, it becomes virtually impossible. . . .

The aspiration to make trade fair

Trade liberalization—opening up markets to the free flow of goods and services—was supposed to lead to growth. The evidence is at best mixed. Part of the reason that international trade agreements have been so unsuccessful in promoting growth in poor countries is that they were often unbalanced: the advanced industrial countries were allowed to levy tariffs on goods produced by developing countries that were, on average, four times higher than those on goods produced by other advanced industrial countries. While developing countries were forced to abandon subsidies designed to help their nascent industries, advanced industrial countries were allowed to continue their own enormous agricultural subsidies, forcing down agricultural prices and undermining living standards in developing countries. . . .

The limitations of liberalization

. . . Trade and capital market liberalization were two key components of a broader policy framework, known as the Washington Consensus—a consensus forged between the IMF (located on 19th Street), the World Bank (on 18th Street), and the U.S. Treasury (on 15th Street)—on what constituted the set of policies that would best promote development.[1] It emphasized downscaling of government, deregulation, and rapid liberalization and privatization. By the early years of the millennium, confidence in the Washington Consensus was fraying, and a post–Washington Consensus consensus was emerging. The Washington Consensus had, for instance, paid too little attention to issues of equity, employment, and competition, to pacing and sequencing of reforms, or to how privatizations were conducted. There is by now also a consensus that it focused too much on just an increase in GDP, not on other things that affect living standards, and focused too little on sustainability—on whether growth could be sustained economically, socially, politically, or environmentally. . . .

Protecting the environment

A failure of environmental stability poses an even greater danger for the world in the long run. . . . Unless we lessen environmental damage, conserve on our use of energy and other natural resources, and attempt to slow global warming, disaster lies ahead. Global warming has become a true challenge of globalization. The successes of development, especially in India and China, have provided those countries the economic wherewithal to increase energy usage, but the world's environment simply cannot sustain such an onslaught. There will be grave problems ahead if everybody emits greenhouse gases at the rate at which Americans have been doing so. The good news is that this is, by now, almost universally recognized, except in some quarters in Washington; but the adjustments in lifestyles will not be easy.

A flawed system of global governance

There is now also a consensus, at least outside the United States, that something is wrong with the way decisions are made at the global level; there is a consensus, in particular, on the dangers of unilateralism and on the "democratic deficit" in the international economic institutions. Both by structure and process, voices that ought to be heard are not. Colonialism is dead, yet the developing countries do not have the representation that they should.

∗   ∗   ∗

Note

[1]The term "Washington Consensus" was originally coined by a distinguished economist, John Williamson, to describe policy reforms in Latin America. His list was longer (including ten points) and more nuanced. See John Williamson, "What Washington Means by Policy Reform," chapter 2 in *Latin American Adjustment: How Much Has Happened?*, ed. John Williamson (Washington, DC: Institute for International Economics, 1090); and Joseph E. Stiglitz, "The Post Washington Consensus Consensus," IPD Working Paper Series, Columbia University, 2004, presented at the From the Washington Consensus Towards a New Global Governance Forum, Barcelona, September 24–25, 2004.

Global Health

UNAIDS Report on Global AIDS Epidemic*

This global community has embarked on an historic quest to lay the foundation for the eventual end of the AIDS epidemic.

This effort is more than merely visionary. It is entirely feasible. Unprecedented gains have been achieved in reducing the number of both adults and children newly infected with HIV, in lowering the numbers of people dying from AIDS-related causes and in implementing enabling policy frameworks that accelerate progress. A new era of hope has emerged in countries and communities across the world that had previously been devastated by AIDS.

However, a world in which AIDS has been eliminated can only be achieved through renewed and sustained commitment and solidarity and only if the available evidence and limited resources are used as efficiently and effectively as possible.

Recognizing the genuine opportunity to plan for the end of AIDS, countries pledged in the 2011 United Nations Political Declaration on HIV and AIDS: Intensifying Our Efforts to Eliminate HIV and AIDS to take specific steps to achieve ambitious goals by 2015. Drawing from the 2011 Political Declaration, UNAIDS has articulated 10 specific targets for 2015 to guide collective action.

1. Reduce sexual transmission by 50%
2. Reduce HIV transmission among people who inject drugs by 50%
3. Eliminate new infections among children and substantially reduce the number of mothers dying from AIDS-related causes.
4. Provide antiretroviral therapy to 15 million people.
5. Reduce the number of people living with HIV who die from tuberculosis by 50%.
6. Close the global AIDS resource gap and reach annual global investment of US$ 22 billion to US$ 24 billion in low- and middle-income countries.
7. Eliminate gender inequalities and gender-based abuse and violence and increase the capacity of women and girls to protect themselves from HIV.
8. Eliminate stigma and discrimination against people living with and affected by HIV by promoting laws and policies

---

*United Nations, UNAIDS *Report on Global* AIDS *Epidemic 2012*, 6–12, http://www.unaids.org/en/media/unaids/contentassets/documents/epidemiology/2012/gr2012/20121120_UNAIDS_Global_Report_2012_en.pdf

that ensure the full realization of all human rights and fundamental freedoms.
9. Eliminate restrictions for people living with HIV on entry, stay and residence.
10. Eliminate parallel systems from HIV-related services to strengthen the integration of the AIDS response in global health and development efforts. . . .

The results summarized here are encouraging, since progress achieved to date conclusively demonstrates the feasibility of achieving the targets set in the 2011 Political Declaration However, the findings also reveal that, to reach most of those targets by 2015, a significant additional effort is required.

State of the Epidemic

* * *

The number of people newly infected globally is continuing to decline, but national epidemics continue to expand in many parts of the world. Further, declines in the numbers of children dying from AIDS-related causes and acquiring HIV infection, although substantial, need to be accelerated to achieve global AIDS targets.

The Global Epidemic at a Glance

Globally, 34 million people [31.4 million–35.9 million] were living with HIV at the end of 2011. An estimated 0.8% of adults aged 15-49 years worldwide are living with HIV, although the burden of the epidemic continues to vary considerably between countries and regions.

Sub-Saharan Africa remains most severely affected, with nearly 1 in every 20 adults (4.9%) living with HIV and accounting for 69% of the people living with HIV worldwide. Although the regional prevalence of HIV infection is nearly 25 times higher in sub-Saharan Africa than in Asia, almost 5 million people are living with HIV in South, Southeast and East Asia combined. After sub-Saharan Africa, the regions most heavily affected are the Caribbean and Eastern Europe and Central Asia, where 1% of adults are living with HIV in 2011.

New Infections Declining

Worldwide, the number of people newly infected continues to fall: the number of people (adults and children) acquiring HIV infection in 2011 (2.5 million) was 20% lower than in 2001. Here, too, variation is apparent. The sharpest declines in the number of people acquiring HIV infection since 2001 have occurred in the Caribbean (42%) and sub-Saharan Africa (25%).

In some other parts of the world, HIV trends (for children and adults) are cause for concern. Since 2001, the number of people newly infected in the Middle East and North Africa has increased by more than 35% (from 27,000 [22,000–34,000] to 37,000 [29,000–46,000]). Evidence indicates that the incidence of HIV infection in Eastern Europe and Central Asia began increasing in the late 2000s after having remained relatively stable for several years.

Reductions in Deaths from Aids-Related Causes

The number of people dying from AIDS-related causes began to decline in the mid-2000s because of scaled-up antiretroviral therapy and the steady decline in HIV incidence since the peak in 1997. In 2011, this decline continued, with evidence that the drop in the number of people dying from AIDS-related causes is accelerating in several countries.

In 2011, 1.7 million people died from AIDS-related causes worldwide. This represents a 24% decline in AIDS-related mortality compared with 2005 (when 2.3 million deaths occurred).

The number of people dying from AIDS-related causes in sub-Saharan Africa declined by 32% from 2005 to 2011, although the region still accounted for 70% of all the people dying from AIDS in 2011. The Caribbean (48%) and Oceania (41%) experienced significant declines in AIDS-related deaths between 2005 and 2011. More modest declines occurred during the same period in Latin America (10%), Asia (4%) and Western and Central Europe and North America (1%). Two other regions, however, experienced significant increases in mortality from AIDS— Eastern Europe and Central Asia (21%) and the Middle East and North Africa (17%). . . .

The scaling up of antiretroviral therapy in low- and middle-income countries has transformed national AIDS responses and generated broad-based health gains. Since 1995, antiretroviral therapy has saved 14 million life-years in low- and middle-income countries, including 9 million in sub-Saharan Africa. . . .

Global Climate Change

U.S. NATIONAL RESEARCH COUNCIL
Climate Change as a National Security Concern*

It is now clear from an accumulation of scientific evidence that the risks of potentially disruptive climate events are increasing. The scientific evidence on this point is aptly summarized in this conclusion from a recent major review of the science by National Research Council: "Climate change is occurring, is caused largely by human activities, and poses significant risks for—and in many cases is already affecting—a broad range of human and natural systems". These increased risks will not be reduced anytime soon: "Human-induced climate change and its impacts will continue for many decades, and in some cases for many centuries. Individually and collectively, these changes pose risks for a wide range of human and environmental systems, including national security." . . .

In short, it is becoming increasingly likely that the world will experience climate-related conditions it has not seen before. The frequency of natural disasters related to weather and climate has been increasing for at least three decades, as have losses from these events.

Temperature trends at the local level show both increasing average temperatures and increasingly frequent occurrences of high temperatures that were quite rare in the 1951–1981 period.

* * *

Potential Climate–Security Connections

Over the past decade, several groups within the U.S. security policy community, both within and outside the government, have given increasing attention to the potential risks that climate change could pose for national as well as international security. . . .

Taken together, the most commonly cited climate–security scenarios in these reports result from failures or shortcomings of human systems in adapting to a changing climate; that is, they turn on the vulnerabilities of theses

---

*U.S. National Academies of Sciences, National Research Council, *Climate and Social Stress: Implications for Security Analysis* (Washington, D.C.: National Academies Press, 2012), 1–1 to 1–5.

systems to climate events. In these scenarios climate events cause harm to various support systems for human life and well-being by exceeding the ability of these systems to cope. Depending on other social, economic, political, and environmental factors, the harm may result in larger scale political and social outcomes that are of concern for U.S. national security. All of the reports include some scenarios of this sort, although different reports emphasize the effects of climate change on different support systems. Declines in food and water security are among the most frequently cited kinds of harm. . . .

In some of the scenarios increasing food and water insecurity interact to increase risks of health. In others health risks result from changes in weather patterns that shift the ranges for vector-borne diseases. Several scenarios see such declines in food or water security or disease outbreaks as likely drivers of population migrations, both within and across borders, that result in political or social stress, usually in the countries that receive the immigration population. Two of the most-often cited scenarios are increasing flooding or a rise in sea level forcing millions of Bangladeshis into India and an increasing desertification and drought forcing people from northern and sub-Saharan Africa into Europe. In both scenarios immigration issues are already a source of major tension. . . .

The paths envisioned from climate events to specific security consequences are often complicated. For example, tensions could increase over access to increasingly scarce resources, and that escalation, especially if it led to overt conflict, could in turn further limit access to resources so that people who had not previously been affected would now face shortages. Some scenarios suggest that diminished national capacity or outright state failure would create increasing opportunities for extremism or terrorism. Again, sub-Saharan Africa is often cited as the most vulnerable region.

In addition to these specific scenarios, many of the reports foresee increasingly frequent and increasingly severe natural disasters that will strain the capacity to cope with the resulting humanitarian emergencies, both in the United States and overseas. . . .

Perhaps the most frequently cited security risk from climate change is the possibility of melting Arctic sea ice leading to increased international tensions over newly accessible sea routes and natural resources in the Arctic.

＊　＊　＊

Democratic Peace?

Edward D. Mansfield and Jack Snyder
Democratization and the Danger of War*

One of the best-known findings of contemporary social science is that no democracies have ever fought a war against each other, given reasonably restrictive definitions of democracy and of war.[1] This insight is now part of everyday public discourse and serves as a basis for American foreign policymaking. President Bill Clinton's 1994 State of the Union address invoked the absence of war between democracies as a justification for promoting democratization around the globe. In the week following the U.S. military landing in Haiti, National Security Adviser Anthony Lake reiterated that "spreading democracy . . . serves our interests" because democracies "tend not to abuse their citizens' rights or wage war on one another."[2]

It is probably true that a world where more countries were mature, stable democracies would be safer and preferable for the United States. However, countries do not become mature democracies overnight. More typically, they go through a rocky transitional period, where democratic control over foreign policy is partial, where mass politics mixes in a volatile way with authoritarian elite politics, and where democratization suffers reversals. In this transitional phase of democratization, countries become more aggressive and war-prone, not less, and they do fight wars with democratic states.

The contemporary era shows that incipient or partial democratization can be an occasion for the rise of belligerent nationalism and war.[3] Two pairs of states—Serbia and Croatia, and Armenia and Azerbaijan—have found themselves at war while experimenting with varying degrees of partial electoral democracy. Russia's poorly institutionalized, partial democracy has tense relationships with many of its neighbors and has used military force brutally to reassert control in Chechnya; its electorate cast nearly a quarter of its votes for the party of radical nationalist Vladimir Zhirinovsky.

This contemporary connection between democratization and conflict is no coincidence. Using the same databases that are typically used to study the democratic peace, we find considerable statistical evidence that democratizing

*From *International Security* 20.1 (Summer 1995).

states are more likely to fight wars than are mature democracies or stable autocracies. States like contemporary Russia that make the biggest leap in democratization—from total autocracy to extensive mass democracy— are about twice as likely to fight wars in the decade after democratization as are states that remain autocracies. However, reversing the process of democratization, once it has begun, will not reduce this risk. Regimes that are changing toward autocracy, including states that revert to autocracy after failed experiments with democracy, are also more likely to fight wars than are states whose regime is unchanging.

Moreover, virtually every great power has gone on the warpath during the initial phase of its entry into the era of mass politics. Mid-Victorian Britain, poised between the partial democracy of the First Reform Bill of 1832 and the full-fledged democracy of the later Gladstone era, was carried into the Crimean War by a groundswell of belligerent public opinion. Napoleon III's France, drifting from plebiscitary toward parliamentary rule, fought a series of wars designed to establish its credentials as a liberal, popular, nationalist type of empire. The ruling elite of Wilhelmine Germany, facing universal suffrage but limited governmental accountability, was pushed toward World War I by its escalating competition with middle-class mass groups for the mantle of German nationalism. Japan's "Taisho democracy" of the 1920s brought an era of mass politics that led the Japanese army to devise and sell an imperial ideology with broad-based appeal.[4] In each case, the combination of incipient democratization and the material resources of a great power produced nationalism, truculence abroad, and major war.

Why should democratizing states be so belligerent? The pattern of the democratizing great powers suggests that the problem lies in the nature of domestic political competition after the breakup of the autocratic regime. Elite groups left over from the ruling circles of the old regime, many of whom have a particular interest in war and empire, vie for power and survival with each other and with new elites representing rising democratic forces. Both old and new elites use all the resources they can muster to mobilize mass allies, often through nationalist appeals, to defend their threatened positions and to stake out new ones. However, like the sorcerer's apprentice, these elites typically *find* that their mass allies, once mobilized, are difficult to control. When this happens, war can result from nationalist prestige strategies that hard-pressed leaders use to stay astride their unmanageable political coalitions.[5]

The problem is not that mass public opinion in democratizing states demonstrates an unvarnished, persistent preference for military adventure. On the contrary, public opinion often starts off highly averse to war. Rather, elites exploit their power in the imperfect institutions of partial democracies to create *faits accomplis*, control political agendas, and shape the content of information media in ways that promote belligerent pressure-group lobbies or upwellings of militancy in the populace as a whole.

Once this ideological connection between militant elites and their mass constituents is forged, the state may jettison electoral democracy while retaining nationalistic, populist rhetoric. As in the failure of Weimar and Taisho democracy, the adverse effects of democratization on war-proneness may even heighten after democracy collapses. Thus, the aftershock of failed democratization is at least one of the factors explaining the link between autocratization and war. * * *

How Democratization Causes War

Why are democratization and autocratization associated with an increased chance of war? What causal mechanism is at work?* Based on case studies of four great powers during their initial phases of democratization, we argue that threatened elites from the collapsing autocratic regime, many of whom have parochial interests in war and empire, use nationalist appeals to compete for mass allies with each other and with new elites. In these circumstances, the likelihood of war increases due to the interests of some of the elite groups, the effectiveness of their propaganda, and the incentive for weak leaders to resort to prestige strategies in foreign affairs in an attempt to enhance their authority over diverse constituencies. Further, we speculate that transitional regimes, including both democratizing and autocratizing states, share some common institutional weaknesses that make war more likely. At least in some cases, the link between autocratization and war reflects the success of a ruling elite in using nationalist formulas developed during the period of democratization to cloak itself in populist legitimacy, while dismantling the substance of democracy. In explaining the logic behind these arguments,

we draw on some standard theories about the consequences of different institutional arrangements for political outcomes.

We illustrate these arguments with some contemporary examples and with cases drawn from four great powers at early stages in the expansion of mass political participation: mid-Victorian Britain, the France of Napoleon III, Bismarckian and Wilhelmine Germany, and Taisho Japan. * * *

Democratic versus Democratizing Institutions

Well-institutionalized democracies that reliably place ultimate authority in the hands of the average voter virtually never fight wars against each other. Moreover, although mature democracies do fight wars about as frequently as other types of states, they seem to be more prudent: they usually win their wars; they are quicker to abandon strategic overcommitments; and they do not fight gratuitous "preventive" wars.[6] Explanations for these tendencies focus variously on the self-interest of the average voter who bears the costs of war, the norms of bargaining and conflict resolution inherent in democracy, the moderating impact of constitutional checks and balances, and the free marketplace of ideas.[7]

However, these happy solutions typically emerge only in the very long run. In the initial stages of expanding political participation, strong barriers prevent the emergence of full-fledged democratic processes and the

---

*Editor's Note: Autocratization is shifting away from democracy toward autocracy or other nondemocratic rule.

foreign policy outcomes associated with them. The two main barriers are the weakness of democratic institutions and the resistance of social groups who would be the losers in a process of full-fledged democratization.

Popular inputs into the policymaking process can have wildly different effects, depending on the way that political institutions structure and aggregate those inputs.[8] It is a staple of political science that different institutional rules—for example, proportional representation versus single-member districts, or congressional versus executive authority over tariffs—can produce different political outcomes, even holding constant the preferences of individual voters. In newly democratizing states, the institutions that structure political outcomes may allow for popular participation in the policy process, but the way they channel that input is often a parody of full-fledged democracy. As Samuel Huntington has put it, the typical problem of political development is the gap between high levels of political participation and weak integrative institutions to reconcile the multiplicity of contending claims.[9] In newly democratizing states without strong parties, independent courts, a free press, and untainted electoral procedures, there is no reason to expect that mass politics will produce the same impact on foreign policy as it does in mature democracies.

* * *

Competitive mass mobilization

In a period of democratization, threatened elite groups have an overwhelming incentive to mobilize allies among the mass of people, but only on their own terms, using whatever special resources they still retain. These have included monopolies of information (e.g., the German Navy's unique "expertise" in making strategic assessments); propaganda assets (the Japanese Army's public relations blitz justifying the invasion of Manchuria); patronage (British Foreign Secretary Palmerston's gifts of foreign service postings to the sons of cooperative journalists); wealth (Krupp steel's bankrolling of mass nationalist and militarist leagues); organizational skills and networks (the Japanese army's exploitation of rural reservist organizations to build a social base); and the ability to use the control of traditional political institutions to shape the political agenda and structure the terms of political bargains (the Wilhelmine ruling elite's deal with the Center Party, eliminating anti-Catholic legislation in exchange for support in the Reichstag on the naval budget).[10]

* * *

Ideology takes on particular significance in the competition for mass support. New participants in the political process may be uncertain of where their political interests lie, because they lack established habits and good information, and are thus fertile ground for ideological appeals. Ideology can yield particularly big payoffs, moreover, when there is no efficient free marketplace of ideas to counter false claims with reliable facts. Elites try out all sorts of ideological appeals, depending on the social position that they need to defend, the nature of the mass group that they want to recruit, and the type of appeals that seem plausible in the given political setting. A nearly universal element in these ideological appeals is nationalism, which has the advantage of positing a community of interest that unites elites and masses, thus distracting attention from class cleavages.

Nationalist appeals have often succeeded even though the average voter was not consistently pro-war or pro-empire.

∗   ∗   ∗

Implications for Policy

In light of these findings, it would be hard to maintain a naive enthusiasm for spreading peace by promoting democratization. Pushing nuclear-armed great powers like Russia or China toward democratization is like spinning a roulette wheel, where many of the potential outcomes are likely to be undesirable. However, in most cases the initial steps on the road to democratization will not be produced by the conscious policy of the United States, no matter what that policy may be. The roulette wheel is already spinning for Russia, and perhaps China, regardless of what the West does. Moreover, reversals of democratization are nearly as risky as democratization itself. Consequently, the international community needs a strategy not so much for promoting or reversing democratization as for managing the process in ways that minimize its risks and facilitate smooth transitions.

What might be some of these mitigating conditions, and how might they be promoted? The association of democratization with war is probabilistic. Democratization can lead either to war or to peace, depending on a variety of factors, such as the incentives facing the old elites during the transition process, the structure of the marketplace of foreign policy ideas, the speed and thoroughness of the democratic transition, and the character of the international environment in which democratization occurs. Some of these features may be subject to manipulation by astute democratic reformers and their allies in the international community.

One of the major findings of scholarship on democratization in Latin America is that the process goes most smoothly when elites that are threatened by the transition, especially the military, are given a "golden parachute."[11] Above all, they need a guarantee that if they relinquish power they will not wind up in jail. The history of the democratizing great powers broadens this insight. Democratization was least likely to lead to imprudent aggression in cases where the old elites saw a reasonably bright future for themselves in the new social order. British aristocrats, for example, had more of their wealth invested in commerce and industry than they did in agriculture, so they had many interests in common with the rising middle classes. They could face democratization with relative equanimity. In contrast, Prussia's capital-starved, small-scale Junker landholders had no choice but to rely on agricultural protection and military careers.

In today's context, finding benign, productive employment for the erstwhile Communist *nomenklatura*, military officer corps, nuclear scientists, and smoke stack industrialists ought to rank high on the list of priorities. Policies aimed at giving them a stake in the privatization process and subsidizing the conversion of their skills to new, peaceful tasks in a market economy seem like a step in the right direction. According to some interpretations, Russian Defense Minister Pavel Grachev was eager to use force to solve the Chechen confrontation in order to show that Russian military power was still useful and that increased investment in the Russian army would pay big dividends. Instead of pursuing this reckless path, the Russian military elite needs to be convinced that its prestige, housing, pensions, and technical competence will rise if and only if it transforms itself into a western-style military, subordinate to civilian authority and resorting to force only in accordance with prevailing international norms. Moreover, though old elites need to be kept happy, they also need to be kept weak. Pacts should not prop up the remnants of the authoritarian system, but rather create a niche for them in the new system.

A top priority must also be placed on creating a free, competitive, yet responsible marketplace of ideas in the newly democratizing states. Most of the war-prone democratizing great powers had pluralistic public debates, but the terms of these debates were skewed to favor groups with money, privileged access to the media of communication, and proprietary control over information, ranging from historical archives to intelligence about the military balance. Pluralism is not enough. Without an even playing field, pluralism simply creates the incentive and opportunity for privileged groups to propound self-serving myths, which historically have often taken a nationalist turn. One of the rays of hope in the Chechen affair was the alacrity with which Russian journalists exposed the true costs of the fighting and the lies of the government and the military about it. Though elites should get a golden parachute in terms of their pecuniary interests, they should be given no quarter on the battlefield of ideas. Mythmaking should be held up to the utmost scrutiny by aggressive journalists who maintain their credibility by scrupulously dis-

tinguishing fact from opinion and tirelessly verifying their sources. Promoting this kind of journalistic infrastructure is probably the most highly leveraged investment that the West can make in a peaceful democratic transition.

Our research offers inconclusive results about the wisdom of speed and thoroughness in transitions to democracy. On the one hand, we found that states making the big jump from autocracy to democracy were much more war-prone than those moving from autocracy to anocracy. This would seem to favor a strategy of limited goals. On the other hand, the experience of the former Communist states suggests that those that have gone farthest and fastest toward full democracy are less nationalistic and less involved in militarized quarrels. This is a question that needs more research.

Finally, what kind of ruling coalition emerges in the course of democratization depends a great deal on the incentives that are created by the international environment. Both Germany and Japan started on the path toward liberal, stable democratization in the mid-1920s, encouraged in part by abundant opportunities for trade and investment from the advanced democracies and by credible security treaties that defused nationalist scare-mongering in domestic politics. But when the international supports for free trade and democracy were yanked out in the late 1920s, their liberal coalitions collapsed. Especially for the case of contemporary China, whose democratization may occur in the context of sharply expanding economic ties to the West, the steadiness of the Western commercial partnership and security presence is likely to play a major role in shaping the incentives of proto-democratic coalition politics.

In the long run, the enlargement of the zone of stable democracy will probably enhance the prospects for peace. But in the short run, there is a lot of work to be done to minimize the dangers of the turbulent transition.

Notes

[1]Michael Doyle, "Liberalism and World Politics," *American Political Science Review*, Vol. 80, No. 4 (December 1986), pp. 1151–1169; Bruce Russett, *Grasping the Democratic Peace* (Princeton: Princeton University Press, 1993). For skeptical views, see David E. Spiro, "The Insignificance of the Liberal Peace," *International Security*, Vol. 19, No. 2 (Fall 1994), pp. 50–86; and Christopher Layne, "Kant or Cant: The Myth of the Democratic Peace," *International Security*, Vol. 19, No. 2 (Fall 1994), pp. 5–49. They are rebutted by Bruce Russett, "The Democratic Peace: 'And Yet It Moves,'" *International Security*, Vol. 19, No. 4 (Spring 1995), pp. 164–175.

[2]"Transcript of Clinton's Address," *New York Times*, January 26, 1994, p. A17; Anthony Lake, "The Reach of Democracy: Tying Power to Diplomacy," *New York Times*, September 23, 1994, p. A35.

[3]Zeev Maoz and Bruce Russett, "Normative and Structural Causes of the Democratic Peace, 1956–1986," *American Political Science Review*, Vol. 87, No. 3 (September 1993), pp. 630, 636; they note that newly created democracies, such as those in Eastern Europe today, may experience conflicts, insofar as their democratic rules and norms are not adequately established. See also Russett, *Grasping the Democratic Peace*, p. 134, on post-Soviet Georgia.

[4]Asa Briggs, *Victorian People*, rev. ed. (Chicago: University of Chicago, 1970), chaps. 2–3; Geoff Eley, *Reshaping the German Right* (New Haven: Yale University Press, 1980); Alain Plessis, *De la fête impériale au mur des fédérés,*

1852–1871 (Paris: Editions du seuil, 1973), translated as *The Rise and Fall of the Second Empire, 1852–1871* (Cambridge: Cambridge University Press, 1985); Jack Snyder, *Myths of Empire: Domestic Politics and International Ambition* (Ithaca: Cornell University Press, 1991), chaps. 3–5.

[5]Hans Ulrich Wehler, *The German Empire, 1871–1918* (Dover, N.H.: Berg, 1985); Jack S. Levy, "The Diversionary Theory of War: A Critique," In Manus Midlarsky, ed., *Handbook of War Studies* (Boston: Unwin-Hyman, 1989), pp. 259–288.

[6]David Lake, "Powerful Pacifists," *American Political Science Review*, Vol. 86, No. 1 (March 1992), pp. 24–37; Snyder, *Myths of Empire*, pp. 49–52; Randall Schweller, "Domestic Structure and Preventive War: Are Democracies More Pacific?" *World Politics*, Vol. 44, No. 2 (January 1992), pp. 235–269.

[7]Russett, *Grasping the Democratic Peace*; Miles Kahler, "Introduction," in Miles Kahler, ed., *Liberalization and Foreign Policy* (forthcoming); Jack Snyder, "Democratization, War, and Nationalism in the Post-Communist States," in Celeste Wallander, ed., *The Sources of Russian Conduct after the Cold War* (Boulder: Westview, forthcoming).

[8]Kenneth Shepsle, "Studying Institutions: Some Lessons from the Rational Choice Approach," *Journal of Theoretical Politics*, Vol. 1, No. 2 (April 1989), pp. 131–147.

[9]Samuel Huntington, *Political Order in Changing Societies* (New Haven: Yale University Press, 1968).

[10]Snyder, *Myths of Empire*, pp. 103, 140–141, 205; Louise Young, "Mobilizing for Empire: Japan and Manchukuo, 1930–1945," Ph.D. dissertation, Columbia University, 1992.

[11]On the importance of bargaining with and co-opting old elites (giving them incentives, a "golden parachute," to depart from power), see the literature summarized in Doh Chull Shin, "On the Third Wave of Democratization: A Synthesis and Evaluation of Recent Theory and Research," *World Politics*, Vol. 47, No. 1 (October 1994), pp. 135–170, esp. 161–163.

Domestic Institutions and War Powers

NATIONAL WAR POWERS COMMISSION
President, Congress and War Powers*

* * *

Few would dispute that the most important decisions our leaders make involve war. Yet after more than 200 years of constitutional history, what powers the respective branches of government possess in making such decisions is still heavily debated. The Constitution provides both the President and Congress with explicit grants of war powers, as well as a host of arguments for implied powers. How broadly or how narrowly to construe these powers is a matter of ongoing debate. Indeed, the Constitution's framers disputed these very issues in the years following the Constitution's ratification, expressing contrary views about the respective powers of the President, as "Commander in Chief," and Congress, which the Constitution grants the power "To declare War."

Over the years, public officials, academics, and experts empaneled on commissions much like this one have expressed a wide range of views on how the war powers are allocated—or could best be allocated—among the branches of government. One topic on which a broad consensus does exist is that the War Powers Resolution of 1973 does not provide a solution because it is at least in part unconstitutional and in any event has not worked as intended.

Historical practice provides no decisive guide. One can point to examples of Presidents and Congresses exercising various powers, but it is hard to find a "golden age" or an unbroken line of precedent in which all agree the Executive and Legislative Branches exercised their war powers in a clear, consistent, and agreed-upon way.

Finally, the courts have not settled many of the open constitutional questions. Despite opportunities to intervene in several inter-branch disputes, courts frequently decline to answer the broader questions these war powers cases raise, and seem willing to decide only those cases in which litigants ask them to protect individual liberties and property rights affected by the conduct of a particular war.

Unsurprisingly, this uncertainty about war powers has precipitated a number of calls for reform and yielded a variety of proposals over the years. These proposals have largely been

---

*From National War Powers Commission Report, University of Virginia, Miller Center of Public Affairs (2008), Executive Summary, http://web1.millercenter.org/reports/warpowers/report.pdf

rejected or ignored, in many cases because they came down squarely on the side of one camp's view of the law and dismissed the other.

However, one common theme runs through most of these efforts at reform: the importance of getting the President and Congress to consult meaningfully and deliberate before committing the nation to war. Gallup polling data throughout the past half century shows that Americans have long shared this desire for consultation. Yet, such consultation has not always occurred.

No clear mechanism or requirement exists today for the President and Congress to consult. The War Powers Resolution of 1973 contains only vague consultation requirements. Instead, it relies on reporting requirements that, if triggered, begin the clock running for Congress to approve the particular armed conflict. By the terms of the 1973 Resolution, however, Congress need not act to disapprove the conflict; the cessation of all hostilities is required in 60 to 90 days merely if Congress fails to act. Many have criticized this aspect of the Resolution as unwise and unconstitutional, and no President in the past 35 years has filed a report "pursuant" to these triggering provisions.

This is not healthy. It does not promote the rule of law. It does not send the right message to our troops or to the public. And it does not encourage dialogue or cooperation between the two branches.

In our efforts to address this set of problems, we have been guided by three principles:

- First, that our proposal be practical, fair, and realistic. It must have a reasonable chance of support from both the President and Congress. That requires constructing a proposal that avoids clearly favoring one branch over the other, and leaves no room for the Executive or Legislative Branch justifiably to claim that our proposal unconstitutionally infringes on its powers.

- Second, that our proposal maximize the likelihood that the President and Congress productively consult with each other on the exercise of war powers. Both branches possess unique competencies and bases of support, and the country operates most effectively when these two branches of government communicate in a timely fashion and reach as much agreement as possible about taking on the heavy burdens associated with war.

- Third, that our proposal should not recommend reform measures that will be subject to widespread constitutional criticism. It is mainly for this reason that our proposal does not explicitly define a role for the courts, which have been protective of defining their own jurisdiction in this area.

Consistent with these principles, we propose the passage of the War Powers Consultation Act of 2009. The stated purpose of the Act is to codify the norm of consultation and "describe a constructive and practical way in which the judgment of both the President and Congress can be brought to bear when deciding whether the United States should engage in significant armed conflict."

The Act requires such consultation before Congress declares or authorizes war or the country engages in combat operations lasting, or expected to last, more than one week ("significant armed conflict"). There is an "exigent circumstances" carve-out that allows for consultation within three days after the beginning of combat operations. In cases of lesser conflicts—*e.g.*, limited actions to defend U.S. embassies abroad, reprisals against terrorist groups, and covert operations—such advance consultation is not required, but is strongly encouraged.

Under the Act, once Congress has been consulted regarding a significant armed conflict, it too has obligations. Unless it declares war or otherwise expressly authorizes the conflict, it must hold a vote on a concurrent resolution within 30 days calling for its approval. If the concurrent resolution is approved, there can be little question that both the President and Congress have endorsed the new armed conflict. In an effort to avoid or mitigate the divisiveness that commonly occurs in the time it takes to execute the military campaign, the Act imposes an ongoing duty on the President and Congress regularly to consult for the duration of the conflict that has been approved.

If, instead, the concurrent resolution of approval is defeated in either House, any member of Congress may propose a joint resolution of disapproval. Like the concurrent resolution of approval, this joint resolution of disapproval shall be deemed highly privileged and must be voted on in a defined number of days. If such a resolution of disapproval is passed, Congress has several options. If both Houses of Congress ratify the joint resolution of disapproval and the President signs it or Congress overrides his veto, the joint resolution of disapproval will have the force of law. If Congress cannot muster the votes to overcome a veto, it may take lesser measures. Relying on its inherent rule making powers, Congress may make internal rules providing, for example, that any bill appropriating new funds for

all or part of the armed conflict would be out of order.

In our opinion, the Act's requirements do not materially increase the burdens on either branch, since Presidents have often sought and received approval or authorization from Congress before engaging in significant armed conflict. Under the Act, moreover, both the President and the American people get something from Congress—its position, based on deliberation and consideration, as to whether it supports or opposes a certain military campaign. If Congress fails to act, it can hardly complain about the war effort when this clear mechanism for acting was squarely in place. If Congress disapproves the war, the disapproval is a political reality the President must confront, and Congress can press to make its disapproval binding law or use its internal rule-making capacity or its power of the purse to act on its disapproval.

We recognize the Act we propose may not be one that satisfies all Presidents or all Congresses in every circumstance. On the President's side of the ledger, however, the statute generally should be attractive because it involves Congress only in "significant armed conflict," not minor engagements. Moreover, it reverses the presumption that inaction by Congress means that Congress has disapproved of a military campaign and that the President is acting lawlessly if he proceeds with the conflict. On the congressional side of the ledger, the Act gives the Legislative Branch more by way of meaningful consultation and information. It also provides Congress a clear and simple mechanism by which to approve or disapprove a military campaign, and does so in a way that seeks to avoid the constitutional infirmities that plague the War Powers

Resolution of 1973. Altogether, the Act works to gives Congress a seat at the table; it gives the President the benefit of Congress's counsel; and it provides a mechanism for the President and the public to know Congress's views before or as a military campaign begins. History suggests that building broad-based support for a military campaign—from both branches of government and the public—is often vital to success.

To enable such consultation most profitably to occur, our proposed Act establishes a Joint Congressional Consultation Committee, consisting of the majority and minority leaders of both Houses of Congress, as well as the chairmen and ranking members of key committees. We believe that if the President and Committee meet regularly, much of the distrust and tension that at times can characterize inter-branch relationships can be dissipated and overcome. In order that Congress and the Committee possess the competence to provide meaningful advice, the Act both requires the President to provide the Committee with certain reports and establishes a permanent, bipartisan congressional staff to facilitate its work. Given these resources, however, our proposed Act limits the incentives for Congress to act by inaction—which is exactly the course of conduct that the default rules in the War Powers Resolution of 1973 often promoted.

To be clear, however, in urging the passage of War Powers Consultation Act of 2009, we do not intend to strip either political branch of government of the constitutional arguments it may make about the scope of its power. As the Act itself makes plain, it "is not meant to define, circumscribe, or enhance the constitutional war powers of either the Executive or Legislative Branches of government, and neither branch by supporting or complying with this Act shall in any way limit or prejudice its right or ability to assert its constitutional war powers or its right or ability to question or challenge the constitutional war powers of the other branch."

In sum, the nation benefits when the President and Congress consult frequently and meaningfully regarding war and matters of national security. While no statute can guarantee the President and Congress work together productively, the Act we propose provides a needed legal framework that encourages such consultation and affords the political branches a way to operate in this area that is practical, constructive, fair, and conducive to the most judicious and effective government policy and action.

NGOs

9.2

Margaret E. Keck and Kathryn Sikkink

Transnational Networks in International Politics: An Introduction*

World politics at the end of the twentieth century involves, alongside states, many nonstate actors that interact with each other, with states, and with international organizations. These interactions are structured in terms of networks, and transnational networks are increasingly visible in international politics. Some involve economic actors and firms. Some are networks of scientists and experts whose professional ties and shared causal ideas underpin their efforts to influence policy.[1] Others are networks of activists, distinguishable largely by the centrality of principled ideas or values in motivating their formation.[2] We will call these *transnational advocacy networks*.

Advocacy networks are significant transnationally and domestically. By building new links among actors in civil societies, states, and international organizations, they multiply the channels of access to the international system. In such issue areas as the environment and human rights, they also make international resources available to new actors in domestic political and social struggles. By thus blurring the boundaries between a state's relations with its own nationals and the recourse both citizens and states have to the international system, advocacy networks are helping to transform the practice of national sovereignty.

* * *

Major actors in advocacy networks may include the following: (1) international and domestic nongovernmental research and advocacy organizations; (2) local social movements; (3) foundations; (4) the media; (5) churches, trade unions, consumer organizations, and intellectuals; (6) parts of regional and international intergovernmental organizations; and (7) parts of the executive and/or parliamentary branches of governments. Not all these will be present in each advocacy network. Initial research suggests, however, that international and domestic NGOs play a central role in all advocacy networks, usually initiating actions

*From *Activists Beyond Borders: Advocacy Networks in International Politics* (Ithaca, N.Y.: Cornell University Press, 1998), ch. 1.

and pressuring more powerful actors to take positions. NGOs introduce new ideas, provide information, and lobby for policy changes.

Groups in a network share values and frequently exchange information and services. The flow of information among actors in the network reveals a dense web of connections among these groups, both formal and informal. The movement of funds and services is especially notable between foundations and NGOs, and some NGOs provide services such as training for other NGOs in the same and sometimes other advocacy networks. Personnel also circulate within and among networks, as relevant players move from one to another in a version of the "revolving door."

Relationships among networks, both within and between issue areas, are similar to what scholars of social movements have found for domestic activism.[3] Individuals and foundation funding have moved back and forth among them. Environmentalists and women's groups have looked at the history of human rights campaigns for models of effective international institution building. Refugee resettlement and indigenous people's rights are increasingly central components of international environmental activity, and vice versa; mainstream human rights organizations have joined the campaign for women's rights. Some activists consider themselves part of an "NGO community."

* * *

Advocacy networks are not new. We can find examples as far back as the nineteenth-century campaign for the abolition of slavery. But their number, size, and professionalism, and the speed, density, and complexity of international linkages among them have grown dramatically in the last three decades. As Hugh Heclo remarks about domestic issue networks, "If the current situation is a mere outgrowth of old tendencies, it is so in the same sense that a 16-lane spaghetti interchange is the mere elaboration of a country crossroads."[4]

We cannot accurately count transnational advocacy networks to measure their growth over time, but one proxy is the increase in the number of international NGOs committed to social change. Because international NGOs are key components of any advocacy network, this increase suggests broader trends in the number, size, and density of advocacy networks generally.

* * *

Transnational advocacy networks appear most likely to emerge around those issues where (1) channels between domestic groups and their governments are blocked or hampered or where such channels are ineffective for resolving a conflict, setting into motion the "boomerang" pattern of influence characteristic of these networks; (2) activists or "political entrepreneurs" believe that networking will further their missions and campaigns, and actively promote networks; and (3) conferences and other forms of international contact create arenas for forming and strengthening networks. Where channels of participation are blocked, the international arena may be the only means that domestic activists have to gain attention to their issues. Boomerang strategies are most common in campaigns where the target is a state's domestic policies or behavior; where a campaign seeks broad procedural change involving dispersed actors, strategies are more diffuse.

Political Entrepreneurs

Just as oppression and injustice do not themselves produce movements or revolutions, claims around issues amenable to international action do not produce transnational networks. Activists—"people who care enough about some issue that they are prepared to incur significant costs and act to achieve their goals"[5]—do. They create them when they believe that transnational networking will further their organizational missions—by sharing information, attaining greater visibility, gaining access to wider publics, multiplying channels of institutional access, and so forth. For example, in the campaign to stop the promotion of infant formula to poor women in developing countries, organizers settled on a boycott of Nestlé, the largest producer, as its main tactic. Because Nestlé was a transnational actor, activists believed a transnational network was necessary to bring pressure on corporations and governments.[6] Over time, in such issue areas, participation in transnational networks has become an essential component of the collective identities of the activists involved, and networking a part of their common repertoire. The political entrepreneurs who become the core networkers for a new campaign have often gained experience in earlier ones.

The Growth of International Contact

Opportunities for network activities have increased over the last two decades. In addition to the efforts of pioneers, a proliferation of international organizations and conferences has provided foci for connections. Cheaper air travel and new electronic communication technologies speed information flows and simplify personal contact among activists.[7]

Underlying these trends is a broader cultural shift. The new networks have depended on the creation of a new kind of global public (or civil society), which grew as a cultural legacy of the 1960s.[8] Both the activism that swept Western Europe, the United States, and many parts of the third world during that decade, and the vastly increased opportunities for international contact, contributed to this shift. With a significant decline in air fares, foreign travel ceased to be the exclusive privilege of the wealthy. Students participated in exchange programs. The Peace Corps and lay missionary programs sent thousands of young people to live and work in the developing world. Political exiles from Latin America taught in U.S. and European universities. Churches opened their doors to refugees, and to new ideas and commitments.

Obviously, internationalism was not invented in the sixties. Religious and political traditions including missionary outreach, the solidarity traditions of labor and the left, and liberal internationalism have long stirred action by individuals or groups beyond the borders of their own state. While many activists working in advocacy networks come out of these traditions, they tend no longer to define themselves in terms of these traditions or the organizations that carried them. This is most true for activists on the left who suffered disillusionment from their groups' refusal to address seriously the concerns of women, the environment, or human rights violations in eastern bloc countries. Absent a range of options that in earlier decades would have competed for their commitments, advocacy and activism through either NGOs or grassroots movements became the most likely alternative for those seeking to "make a difference."

* * *

How Do Transnational Advocacy Networks Work?

Transnational advocacy networks seek influence in many of the same ways that other political groups or social movements do. Since they are not powerful in a traditional sense of the word, they must use the power of their information, ideas, and strategies to alter the information and value contexts within which states make policies. The bulk of what networks do might be termed persuasion or socialization, but neither process is devoid of conflict. Persuasion and socialization often involve not just reasoning with opponents, but also bringing pressure, arm-twisting, encouraging sanctions, and shaming. * * *

* * *

Our typology of tactics that networks use in their efforts at persuasion, socialization, and pressure includes (1) *information politics,* or the ability to quickly and credibly generate politically usable information and move it to where it will have the most impact; (2) *symbolic politics,* or the ability to call upon symbols, actions, or stories that make sense of a situation for an audience that is frequently far away;[9] (3) *leverage politics,* or the ability to call upon powerful actors to affect a situation

where weaker members of a network are unlikely to have influence; and (4) *accountability politics,* or the effort to hold powerful actors to their previously stated policies or principles.

* * *

Information Politics

Information binds network members together and is essential for network effectiveness. Many information exchanges are informal—telephone calls, E-mail and fax communications, and the circulation of newsletters, pamphlets and bulletins. They provide information that would not otherwise be available, from sources that might not otherwise be heard, and they must make this information comprehensible and useful to activists and publics who may be geographically and/or socially distant.[10]

* * *

Nonstate actors gain influence by serving as alternate sources of information. Information flows in advocacy networks provide not only facts but testimony—stories told by people whose lives have been affected. Moreover, activists interpret facts and testimony, usually framing issues simply, in terms of right and wrong because their purpose is to persuade people and stimulate them to act. How does this process of persuasion occur? An effective frame must show that a given state of affairs is neither natural nor accidental, identify the responsible party or parties, and propose credible solutions. These aims require clear, powerful messages that appeal to shared principles, which often have more impact on state policy than advice of technical experts. An important part of the political struggle over information is precisely whether an issue is defined primarily as technical—and thus subject to consideration by "qualified" experts—or as something that concerns a broader global constituency.

* * *

Networks strive to uncover and investigate problems, and alert the press and policymakers. One activist described this as the "human rights methodology"—"promoting change by reporting facts."[11] To be credible, the information produced by networks must be reliable and well documented. To gain attention, the information must be timely and dramatic. Sometimes these multiple goals of information politics conflict, but both credibility and drama seem to be essential components of a strategy aimed at persuading publics and policymakers to change their minds.

* * *

Symbolic Politics

Activists frame issues by identifying and providing convincing explanations for powerful symbolic events, which in turn become catalysts for the growth of networks. Symbolic interpretation is part of the process of persuasion by which networks create awareness and expand their constituencies. Awarding the 1992 Nobel Peace Prize to Maya activist Rigoberta Menchú and the UN's designation of 1993 as the Year of Indigenous Peoples heightened public awareness of the situation of indigenous peoples in the Americas.

Indigenous people's use of 1992, the 500th anniversary of the voyage of Columbus to the Americas, to raise a host of issues well illustrates the use of symbolic events to reshape understandings.[12]

* * *

Leverage Politics

Activists in advocacy networks are concerned with political effectiveness. Their definition of effectiveness often includes some policy change by "target actors" such as governments, international financial institutions like the World Bank, or private actors like transnational corporations. In order to bring about policy change, networks need to pressure and persuade more powerful actors. To gain influence the networks seek leverage (the word appears often in the discourse of advocacy organizations) over more powerful actors. By leveraging more powerful institutions, weak groups gain influence far beyond their ability to influence state practices directly. The identification of material or moral leverage is a crucial strategic step in network campaigns.

Material leverage usually links the issue to money or goods (but potentially also to votes in international organizations, prestigious offices, or other benefits).

* * *

Although NGO influence often depends on securing powerful allies, their credibility still depends in part on their ability to mobilize their own members and affect public opinion via the media. In democracies the potential to influence votes gives large membership organizations an advantage over nonmembership organizations in lobbying for policy change; environmental organizations, several of whose memberships number in the millions, are more likely to have this added clout than are human rights organizations.

Moral leverage involves what some commentators have called the "mobilization of shame," where the behavior of target actors is held up to the light of international scrutiny. Network activists exert moral leverage on the assumption that governments value the good opinion of others; insofar as networks can demonstrate that a state is violating international obligations or is not living up to its own claims, they hope to jeopardize its credit enough to motivate a change in policy or behavior. The degree to which states are vulnerable to this kind of pressure varies, and will be discussed further below.

Accountability Politics

Networks devote considerable energy to convincing governments and other actors to publicly change their positions on issues. This is often dismissed as inconsequential change, since talk is cheap and governments sometimes change discursive positions hoping to divert network and public attention. Network activists, however, try to make such statements into opportunities for accountability politics. Once a government has publicly committed itself to a principle—for example, in favor of human rights or democracy—networks can use those positions, and their command of information, to expose the distance between discourse and practice. This is embarrassing to

many governments, which may try to save face by closing that distance.

* * *

Domestic structures through which states and private actors can be held accountable to their pronouncements, to the law, or to contracts vary considerably from one nation to another, even among democracies. The centrality of the courts in U.S. politics creates a venue for the representation of diffuse interests that is not available in most European democracies.[13] It also explains the large number of U.S. advocacy organizations that specialize in litigation. * * *

Under What Conditions Do Advocacy Networks Have Influence?

To assess the influence of advocacy networks we must look at goal achievement at several different levels. We identify the following types or stages of network influence: (1) issue creation and agenda setting; (2) influence on discursive positions of states and international organizations; (3) influence on institutional procedures; (4) influence on policy change in "target actors" which may be states, international organizations like the World Bank, or private actors like the Nestlé Corporation; and (5) influence on state behavior.

Networks generate attention to new issues and help set agendas when they provoke media attention, debates, hearings, and meetings on issues that previously had not been a matter of public debate. Because values are the essence of advocacy networks, this stage of influence may require a modification of the "value context" in which policy debates takes place. The UN's theme years and decades, such as International Women's Decade and the Year of Indigenous Peoples, were international events promoted by networks that heightened awareness of issues.

Networks influence discursive positions when they help persuade states and international organizations to support international declarations or to change stated domestic policy positions. The role environmental networks played in shaping state positions and conference declarations at the 1992 "Earth Summit" in Rio de Janeiro is an example of this kind of impact. They may also pressure states to make more binding commitments by signing conventions and codes of conduct.

The targets of network campaigns frequently respond to demands for policy change with changes in procedures (which may affect policies in the future). The multilateral bank campaign is largely responsible for a number of changes in internal bank directives mandating greater NGO and local participation in discussions of projects. It also opened access to formerly restricted information, and led to the establishment of an independent inspection panel for World Bank projects. Procedural changes can greatly increase the opportunity for advocacy organizations to develop regular contact with other key players on an issue, and they sometimes offer the opportunity to move from outside to inside pressure strategies.

A network's activities may produce changes in policies, not only of the target states, but also of other states and/or international institutions. Explicit policy shifts seem to denote success, but even here both their causes and meanings may be elusive. We can point with some confidence to network impact where human rights network pressures have achieved cut-offs of military aid to repressive regimes, or a curtailment of repressive practices. Sometimes human rights activity even affects regime stability. But we must take care to distinguish between policy change and change in behavior; official policies regarding timber extraction in Sarawak, Malaysia, for example, may say little about how timber companies behave on the ground in the absence of enforcement.

We speak of stages of impact, and not merely types of impact, because we believe that increased attention, followed by changes in discursive positions, make governments more vulnerable to the claims that networks raise. (Discursive changes can also have a powerfully divisive effect on networks themselves, splitting insiders from outsiders, reformers from radicals.) A government that claims to be protecting indigenous areas or ecological reserves is potentially more vulnerable to charges that such areas are endangered than one that makes no such claim. At that point the effort is not to make governments change their position but to hold them to their word. Meaningful policy change is thus more likely when the first three types or stages of impact have occurred.

* * *

Issue Characteristics

Issues that involve ideas about right and wrong are amenable to advocacy networking because they arouse strong feelings, allow networks to recruit volunteers and activists, and infuse meaning into these volunteer activities. However, not all principled ideas lead to network formation, and some issues can be framed more easily than others so as to resonate with policymakers and publics. * * *

* * *

As we look at the issues around which transnational advocacy networks have organized most effectively, we find two issue characteristics that appear most frequently: (1) issues involving bodily harm to vulnerable individuals, especially when there is a short and clear causal chain (or story) assigning responsibility; and (2) issues involving legal equality of opportunity. The first respond to a normative logic, and the second to a juridical and institutional one.

* * *

Actor Characteristics

However amenable particular issues may be to strong transnational and transcultural messages, there must be actors capable of transmitting those messages and targets who are vulnerable to persuasion or leverage. * * *

Target actors must be vulnerable either to material incentives or to sanctions from outside actors, or they must be sensitive to pressure because of gaps between stated commitments and practice. Vulnerability arises both from the availability of leverage and the target's sensitivity to leverage; if either is missing, a campaign may fail.

* * *

Notes

[1] Peter Haas has called these "knowledge-based" or "epistemic communities." See Peter Haas, "Introduction: Epistemic Communities and International Policy Coordination," *Knowledge, Power and International Policy Coordination*, special issue, *International Organization* 46 (Winter 1992), pp. 1–36.

[2] Ideas that specify criteria for determining whether actions are right or wrong and whether outcomes are just or unjust are shared principled beliefs or values, Beliefs about cause-effect relationships are shared causal beliefs, Judith Goldstein and Robert Keohane, eds., *Ideas and Foreign Policy: Beliefs, Institutions, and Political Change* (Ithaca: Cornell University Press, 1993), pp. 8–10.

[3] See John D. McCarthy and Mayer N. Zald, "Resource Mobilization and Social Movements: A Partial Theory," *American Journal of Sociology* 82:6 (1977): 1212–41. Myra Marx Feree and Frederick D. Miller, "Mobilization and Meaning: Toward an Integration of Social Psychological and Resource Perspectives on Social Movements," *Sociological Inquiry* 55 (1985): 49–50; and David S. Meyer and Nancy Whittier, "Social Movement Spillover," *Social Problems* 41:2 (May 1994): 277–98.

[4] Hugh Heclo, "Issue Networks and the Executive Establishment," in *The New American Political System*, ed. Anthony King (Washington, D.C.: American Enterprise Institute, 1978), p. 97.

[5] Pamela E. Oliver and Gerald Marwell, "Mobilizing Technologies for Collective Action," in *Frontiers in Social Movement Theory*, ed. Aldon D. Morris and Carol McClurg Mueller (New Haven: Yale University Press, 1992), p. 252.

[6] See Kathryn Sikkink, "Codes of Conduct for Transnational Corporations: The Case of the WHO/UNICEF Code," *International Organization* 40 (Autumn 1986): 815–40.

[7] The constant dollar yield of airline tickets in 1995 was one half of what it was in 1966, while the number of international passengers enplaned increased more than four times during the same period. Air Transport Association home page, June 1997, http://www.airtransport.org/data/traffic.htm. See James Rosenau, *Turbulence in World Politics* (Princeton: Princeton University Press, 1990), pp. 12, 25.

[8] See Sidney Tarrow, "Mentalities, Political Cultures, and Collective Action Frames: Constructing Meanings through Action," in *Frontiers in Social Movement Theory*, p. 184.

[9]Alison Brysk uses the categories "information politics" and "symbolic politics" to discuss strategies of transnational actors, especially networks around Indian rights. See "Acting Globally: Indian Rights and International Politics in Latin America," in *Indigenous Peoples and Democracy in Latin America*, ed. Donna Lee Van Cott (New York: St. Martin's Press/Inter-American Dialogue, 1994), pp. 29–51; and "Hearts and Minds: Bringing Symbolic Politics Back In," *Polity 27* (Summer 1995): 559–85.

[10]Rosenau, *Turbulence*, p. 199, argues that "as the adequacy of information and the very nature of knowledge have emerged as central issues, what were once regarded as the petty quarrels of scholars over the adequacy of evidence and the metaphysics of proof have become prominent activities in international relations."

[11]Dorothy Q. Thomas, "Holding Governments Accountable by Public Pressure," In *Ours by Right: Women's Rights as Human Rights*, ed. Joanna Kerr (London: Zed Books, 1993), p. 83. This methodology is not new. See, for example, David H. Lumsdaine, *Moral Vision*, in *International Politics: The Foreign Aid Regime* (Princeton: Princeton University Press, 1993), pp. 187–88, 211–13.

[12]Brysk, "Acting Globally."

The Media, Public Opinion, and Foreign Policy

9.3

MATTHEW A. BAUM
Soft News and Foreign Policy*

People who are not interested in politics often get their news from sources quite different from those of their politically engaged counterparts. While alternative news sources for the politically uninvolved have been available, the last two decades have witnessed a dramatic expansion in the number and diversity of entertainment-oriented, quasi-news media outlets, sometimes referred to collectively as the soft news media.

Political scientists, including public opinion scholars, have mostly ignored the soft news media. And, indeed, most of the time these media eschew discussion of politics and public policy, in favor of more "down-market" topics, such as celebrity gossip, crime dramas, disasters, or other dramatic human-interest stories. Yet, as I shall demonstrate, on occasion, the soft news media do convey substantive information concerning a select few high-profile political issues, prominently among them foreign policy crises. This suggests the proliferation of soft news may have meaningful implications for politics, including foreign policy.

Scholars have long pondered the barriers to information and political participation confronting democratic citizens. The traditional scholarly consensus has held that the mass public is woefully ignorant about politics and foreign affairs, and hence, with rare exceptions, only relatively narrow segments of the public—the so-called "attentive public" or "issue publics"—pay attention to public policy or wield any meaningful influence on policymakers. By, in effect, broadening access to information about some political issues, soft news coverage of politics may challenge this perspective, at least in part. If a substantial portion of the public that would otherwise remain aloof from politics is able to learn about high-profile political issues, such as foreign crises, from the soft news media, this may expand the size of the attentive public, at least in times of crisis. And a great deal of research has shown that intense public scrutiny, when it arises, can influence policymakers, both in Congress and the White House.

*Matthew A. Baum, "Sex, Lies, and War: How Soft News Brings Foreign Policy to the Inattentive Public," *American Political Science Review* 96 (March 2002), 91–106.

This possibility raises a number of questions. First, to what extent and in what circumstances do the entertainment-oriented, soft news media convey information about serious political issues? Second, what types of political topics appeal to such media outlets? Third, how might their coverage differ from that found in traditional news sources? Finally, who is likely to consume political news presented in this entertainment-oriented media environment, and why? These are the primary questions motivating the present study.

I argue that for many individuals who are not interested in politics or foreign policy, soft news increasingly serves as an alternative to the traditional news media as a source of information about a select few political issues, including foreign policy crises. This is because the soft news media are in the business of packaging human drama as entertainment. And, like celebrity murder trials and sex scandals—the usual fare of soft news outlets—some political issues, prominently among them foreign crises, are easily framed as compelling human dramas. As a result, the soft news media have increased many politically inattentive individuals' exposure to information about select high-profile political issues, primarily those involving scandal, violence, heroism, or other forms of human drama. Yet public opinion scholars have largely failed to consider how this might influence public views of politics. . . .

The Soft News Media

Since the early 1980s, the growth of cable—and, more recently, satellite television and the Internet—has created a highly competitive media environment, especially in television. Rising competition for viewers has forced broadcasters to find new ways to raise their profit margins, such as increasing the audience for news and lowering production costs. To do so, they have, in part, repackaged certain types of news into inexpensively produced forms of entertainment, sometimes referred to as soft news. This is because soft news is far less expensive to produce, and in many cases far more profitable, than original entertainment programming. . . .

How Soft News Programs Cover Foreign Crises

While, like traditional news outlets, soft news programs do appear to cover foreign crises regularly, they do not necessarily do so in the same manner. Where traditional news outlets typically cover political stories in manners unappealing—either too complex or too arcane—to individuals who are not intrinsically interested in politics, the soft news media self-consciously frame issues in highly accessible terms—which I call "cheap framing"—emphasizing dramatic and sensational human-interest stories, intended primarily to appeal to an entertainment-seeking audience.

Neuman, Just and Crigler identify five common frames readily recognized and understood by most individuals. These include "us vs. them," "human impact," "powerlessness," "economic," and "morality." To this list, Powlick and Katz add an "injustice" frame. Graber found that several of these frames—"human impact," "morality," and "injustice"—resonated strongly with her interview subjects. Not surprisingly, these are the prevalent themes found in soft news media. . . . By making news about foreign crises, or other high-profile political issues, accessible, soft news programs increase the likelihood that politically uninterested individuals will pay attention to, and learn about, them.

A review of the content of soft news coverage of several 1990s foreign crises offers support for the findings of the aforementioned studies. In each case, rather than focus on the more arcane aspects of these crises, such as military tactics or geopolitical ramifications, the soft news media tended to focus on highly accessible themes likely to appeal to viewers who were not necessarily watching to learn about military strategy or international diplomacy. For instance, during the Persian Gulf War, while CNN and the major networks filled the airwaves with graphic images of precision bombs and interviews with military experts, the daytime talk shows hosted by Oprah Winfrey, Geraldo Rivera, and Sally Jesse Raphael, as well as A Current Affair, focused on the personal hardships faced by spouses of soldiers serving in the gulf and on the psychological trauma suffered by families of Americans being held prisoner in Iraq as "human shields."

Similarly, in mid-1995, in covering the escalating U.S. military involvement in Bosnia, a review of the nightly news broadcasts of the three major networks indicates that they addressed a broad range of issues—including international diplomacy, military tactics, the role of NATO, "nation building," and ethnic cleansing, to name only a few. In contrast, the soft news media devoted most of their coverage to a single dramatic story: the travails of U.S. fighter pilot Scott O'Grady, who was shot down over enemy territory on June 2, 1995. Captain O'Grady's heroic story of surviving behind enemy lines for 5 days on a diet of insects and grass, before being rescued by NATO forces, represented ideal made-for-soft-news of human drama. . . .

Conclusion

Through cheap framing, the soft news media have successfully piggybacked information about foreign crises to entertainment-oriented information. Soft news consumers thereby gain information about such issues as an incidental by-product of seeking entertainment. My statistical investigations demonstrated that individuals do learn about these types of issues—but not other, less accessible or dramatic issues—from the soft news media, without necessarily tuning in with the intention of doing so. . . .

My findings further suggest that some of the barriers to information and political participation confronting democratic citizens may be falling. Where America's foreign policy was once the domain of a fairly small "foreign policy elite," the soft news media appear to have, to some extent, "democratized" foreign policy. This represents both a challenge and an opportunity for America's political leaders. It is a challenge because leaders can no longer count on communicating effectively with the American people solely through traditional news outlets. To reach those segments of the public who eagerly reach for their remotes any time traditional political news appears on the screen, leaders must reformulate their messages in terms that appeal to programs preferred by these politically uninterested individuals.

The rise of the soft new media also offers an opportunity, because to the extent that they are able to adapt their messages accordingly, soft news outlets allow leaders to communicate with segments of the population that have traditionally tuned out politics and foreign affairs entirely. This may allow future leaders to expand their support coalitions beyond the traditionally attentive segments of the population. Broader support coalitions, in turn, may translate into more effective leadership, particularly in difficult time.

Finally, from the citizens' perspective, one might be tempted to take heart from the apparent leveling-off of attentiveness to foreign policy across differing groups of Americans. After all, a more broadly attentive public might yield more broad-based participation in the political process. Many democratic theorists would likely consider this a desirable outcome. Yet it is unclear whether more information necessarily makes better citizens, particularly if the quality or diversity of that information is suspect. Indeed, one might also be tempted to wonder about the implications of a citizenry learning about the world through the relatively narrow lens of the entertainment-oriented soft news media.

U.S.-China Relations

KENNETH LIEBERTHAL AND WANG JISI

U.S.-China Strategic Distrust*

The issue of mutual distrust of long-term intentions—termed here "strategic distrust"—has become a central concern in U.S.-China relations. . . .

Both Beijing and Washington seek to build a constructive partnership for the long run. U.S.-China relations are, moreover, mature. The two sides understand well each others' position on all major issues and deal with each other extensively. The highest level leaders meet relatively frequently, and there are more than sixty regular government-to-government dialogues between agencies in the two governments each year. This history and these extensive activities have not, however, produced trust regarding long-term intentions on either side, and arguably the problem of lack of such trust is becoming more serious. Distrust is itself corrosive, producing attitudes and actions that themselves contribute to greater distrust. Distrust itself makes it difficult for leaders on each side to be confident they understand the deep thinking among leaders on the other side regarding the future U.S.-China relationship. . . .

Understanding Strategic Distrust: The Chinese Side

Since the end of the Cold War, the PRC leadership has consistently demonstrated the desire to "increase trust, reduce trouble, develop cooperation, and refrain from confrontation" in U.S.-China relations. Beijing realizes that China-U.S. cooperation must be based on mutual strategic trust. Meanwhile, in Beijing's view, it is U.S. policies, attitude, and misperceptions that cause the lack of mutual trust between the two countries.

Chinese strategic distrust of the United States is deeply rooted in history. Four sentiments reflecting recent structural changes in the international system contribute to this distrust: the feeling in China that since 2008 the PRC has ascended to be a first-class global power; the assessment that the United States, despite ongoing great strength, is heading for decline; the observation that emerging powers like India, Brazil, Russia and South Africa are increasingly challenging Western dominance

---

*Kenneth Lieberthal and Wang Jisi, *Addressing U.S.-China Strategic Distrust* (Brookings Institution, 2012).

and are working more with each other and with China in doing so; and the notion that China's development model of a strong political leadership that effectively manages social and economic affairs provides an alternative to Western democracy and market economies for other developing countries to learn from.

In combination, these views make many Chinese political elites suspect that it is the United States that is "on the wrong side of history." Because they believe that the ultimate goal of the U.S. in view of these factors is to maintain its global hegemony, they conclude that America will seek to constrain or even upset China's rise.

America's democracy promotion agenda is understood in China as designed to sabotage the Communist Party's leadership. The leadership therefore actively promotes efforts to guard against the influence of American ideology and U.S. thinking about democracy, human rights, and related issues. This perceived American effort to divide and weaken China has been met by building increasingly powerful and sophisticated political and technological devices to safeguard domestic stability.

U.S. arms sales to Taiwan despite vastly improved cross-Strait relations—and close-in surveillance activities off China's coasts—contribute to Beijing's deepening distrust of U.S. strategic intentions in the national security arena. Washington's recent rebalancing toward Asia further contributes to this sense of threat. American diplomatic positions spanning North Korea, Iran, and countries in Southeast Asia are discomfiting and increase Chinese suspicions of U.S. intentions.

China also views the U.S. as taking advantage of the dollar as a reserve currency and adopting various protectionist measures to disadvantage the PRC economically.

China's criticisms of, and resistance to, some of America's international policies and actions toward the Korean Peninsula, Iran, Syria, and elsewhere reflect the suspicion that they are based on injustice and narrow U.S. self-interest that will directly or indirectly affect China's interests.

Understanding Strategic Distrust: The U.S. Side

Strategic distrust of China is not the current dominant view of national decision makers in the U.S. government, who believe it is feasible and desirable to develop a basically constructive long-term relationship with a rising China. But U.S. decision makers also see China's future as very undetermined, and there are related worries and debates about the most effective approach to promote desired Chinese behavior. Underlying concerns of American leaders are as follows:

Various sources indicate that the Chinese side thinks in terms of a long-term zero-sum game, and this requires that America prepare to defend its interests against potential Chinese efforts to undermine them as China grows stronger. PLA aspirations for dominance in the near seas (*jinhai*) potentially challenge American freedom of access and action in international waters where such freedom is deemed vital to meet American commitments to friends and allies. The context for this is that, as China's strength in Asia grows, it is more important for America to maintain the credibility of its commitments to friends and allies in the region.

Economically, the United States worries that China's mercantilist policies will harm the chances of American economic recovery. China-based cyber theft of American trade secrets and technology further sharpens these concerns.

China's one-party governing system also induces distrust in various ways. Americans believe democratic political systems naturally understand each other better and that authoritarian political systems are inherently less stable and more prone to blaming others for their domestic discontent. Authoritarian systems are also intrinsically less transparent, which makes it more difficult to judge their sincerity and intentions. What Americans view as human rights violations (especially violations of civil rights) make it more difficult for the U.S. to take actions targeted at building greater mutual trust.

While the U.S. welcomes a wealthier, more globally engaged China, it no longer regards China as a developing country that warrants special treatment concerning global rules. Washington also looks to Beijing to take on some of the responsibilities for international public goods that major powers should assume, and it worries when Beijing declines to do so. Given the U.S. view that Asia is the most important region in the world for future American interests, American leaders are especially sensitive to Chinese actions that suggest the PRC may be assuming a more hegemonic approach to the region. . . .

On the economic and trade side, America is especially sensitive to Chinese policies that impose direct costs on the U.S. economy. These include intellectual property theft, keeping the value of the RMB below market levels, serious constraints on market access in China, and China's 2010-2011 restrictions on exports of rare earth metals, which appeared to be strategically designed to acquire sensitive foreign technologies—especially in clean energy.

Recent developments have increased suspicions among relevant American agencies. The U.S. military sees the PLA apparently prioritizing development of weapons systems particularly targeted at American platforms, and it worries about lack of transparency in China's military plans and doctrines. The scope and persistence of China-based cyber attacks against U.S. government, military, and private sector targets has alarmed American officials in charge of cyber efforts and raised very serious concerns about Chinese norms and intentions. And U.S. intelligence officials see increased evidence of zero-sum thinking in Beijing regarding the U.S. and also increased Chinese espionage efforts in the United States.

Analysis

Drawing from the above, there are three fundamental sources of growing strategic distrust between the United States and China: different political traditions, value systems and cultures; insufficient comprehension and appreciation of each others' policymaking processes and relations between the government and other entities; and a perception of a narrowing gap in power between the United States and China.

The first highlights structural and deep-rooted elements in the United States and China that are not likely subject to major change. It is more realistic for Washington and Beijing to address instead the second and third sources of strategic distrust by improving their understanding of each other's domestic situations and working together more effectively in international endeavors both bilaterally and with other players. In so doing, readers should be mindful that strategic distrust appears to be more the accepted wisdom in Beijing than in Washington, possibly reflecting China's memories of the "100 years of humiliation" and the recognition of its disadvantageous power position vis-à-vis the United States.

* * *

U.S.-India Relations

INDIAN INSTITUTE FOR DEFENSE STUDIES AND ANALYSES
India's Grand Strategy*

Six and a half decades ago, a remarkable experiment in democracy and nation building was launched in India that has fundamentally altered the world as we know it today. India, an economically impoverished, continent-sized, vastly diverse nation, resolved to meet its tryst with destiny on the basis of democratic values, secularism, inclusive nationalism and internationalism. Despite possessing limited material resources in the early decades of its independence, India played a key role in redefining the nature of international relations in the aftermath of the Second World War. It emerged as a significant player in global struggles against imperialism, colonialism and racism. In the first decades of independence, India also emerged as a third pillar in the international system—a pillar that stood for principled opposition to military blocs, while simultaneously demonstrating its willingness to contribute to the maintenance and expansion of world peace and security. The imagination and commitment of the national leadership ensured that India's freedom from oppressive colonial rule was translated into an opportunity to build a world without imperialism and war.

In the past two decades, India has undergone dramatic transformations in the economic, social and political spheres. The country has radically transformed its economy and is now projected to be on course to become the third largest economy in the world by 2030. Besides this spectacular economic growth, Indian democracy has steadily consolidated and expanded its scope and remit in the post-independence era. The recent successes of civil society groups in mobilising public support for various causes are testimony to the power and resilience of democratic India's ability to negotiate conflicts within the society through peaceful methods. However, despite its numerous successes, India faces enormous challenges at the domestic, regional and global levels.

India's economic growth has not been matched by the evolution of its governance structures and institutional competence

---

*From "Introduction", Krishnappa Venkatshamy and Princy George, *Grand Strategy for India: 2020 and Beyond* (New Delhi, India: Institute for Defence Studies and Analyses, 2012), 1–12.

resulting in higher expectations of political institutions to bridge the gap between promise and performance. India's growth story has not yet translated into the economic democracy envisioned by the country's leaders. This may cause greater social and political stresses than those that India has had to contend with during the first six decades after its independence. The rise in Maoist violence in large areas of India is one such challenge, and tackling it would require 'a concerted effort to bridge the development deficit.' Besides radical left movements, India also has to manage manifestations of violent political dissent in some states, including the Naga insurgency in northeast India and the Kashmir issue in north. A number of insurgent groups that are involved in such conflicts are at times aided and abetted by institutions in neighboring countries, as is the case with some groups in Kashmir. India is also home to a number of terrorist groups that are motivated by religious or ethnic grievances. Addressing these and other related domestic security concerns will preoccupy India's leaders in the coming decade.

India's security in next decades will also depend on how the broader regional situation evolves. Much of the world is wary of China's rise. India, in particular, is concerned about China's continuing support to Pakistan and its growing footprint in regions that are of strategic interest to India. Many of India's neighbours face instability. Experts are increasingly questioning Pakistan's ability to craft a policy for a stable and functioning polity. The instability in Afghanistan and adjoining areas of Pakistan make that region one of the most volatile in the world. Moreover, the presence of nuclear weapons in the region makes it an area of particular concern for global security planners. This

situation is unlikely to change in the coming decade. In addition, it is unlikely that India will achieve significant breakthroughs in border negotiations with China or Pakistan in the next decade. However, India could make progress on other less contentious issues with both of these states. India will have increasing opportunities to reinforce and expand existing confidence building measures (CBMs) thereby greatly enhancing crisis management and war-avoidance mechanisms. While India's security planners will need to strengthen defence capabilities to counter challenges to territorial integrity and internal cohesion, India, in its enhanced role as a global player, will also be expected to contribute to global public goods such as protection of global commons, humanitarian assistance, peacekeeping and environmental mitigation.

The contemporary strategic environment is marked by several systemic transformations—the emergence of India, China, Brazil and Turkey among others; the relative decline of the United States and Europe; the relative shift of economic power to emerging economies; instability in West Asia and North Africa; the increasing agency of non-state actors; an expanding population and pressing demands for food, water and energy; growing concerns about planetary safety due to climate change; revolution in military affairs and technology diffusion; the proliferation of weapons of mass destruction; and dispersed terrorism. The leaders from government, society, business and the military will face the challenges that emerge from complex interactions between economic, technological, social and ideological forces that may be difficult to disaggregate.

Given the complex policy environment of the coming decade, rife with challenges that emerge out of the interface of crosscutting and dynamically interacting domains, a renewed focus on rethinking India's security strategy is imperative. . . .

India's security in the coming decades will be influenced largely by its economic growth, and the benefits derived from this to remove poverty, improve educational and health services for the country's growing population. Rapid economic growth would require radical and unprecedented structural reforms.

Given the critical role that higher education can play in a globalising world where the knowledge economy is occupying an increasingly large space, there exists a direct correlation between important national objectives such as rapid poverty reduction and exploitation of India's demographic advantages, and the role of education. Human capital leads to a build up of the labour force of a country that can result in an increase in labour productivity, subsequently impacting economic development. Education also has a large number of non-measurable, non-economic returns such as reduction of infant mortality, fertility rates, and crimes. Its role is vital in the promotion of democracy, human rights and political stability. Even though India has the world's third largest scientific and technical manpower pool, the figure is quite low in relation to the country's total population.

Framing a grand strategy necessitates a holistic view of security and a forward-looking vision for the country that accounts for both threats and opportunities. . . .

In the next two decades, the US will still be the most predominant power, China the second power, trying to close its gap with the US, and India as the third 'swing' power. Three options are identified for India to deal with the challenges of such a new world order. The Indo-US partnership will be the key to India's strategy in the coming years. . . .

India cannot afford to ignore 'global issues which affect the prospects of territorial integrity, the sanctity of national political and social life, the increase of economic well-being, and a balance of power relative to other major actors'. Global public goods that are considered most vital include safety of the planet from natural disasters; the prevention of deadly epidemics; stability of the world economy; and, control of weapons of mass destruction. . . .

Indians believe that they are best served by an international order marked by peace, stability and liberal norms that will allow India to focus on economic development and political consolidation; however, if it encounters aggression or humiliation in this quest for prosperity and status, then calls to enhance India's military power are likely to grow louder. Four competing visions of India's place in the international system are advanced: *moralists* wish for India to serve as an exemplar of principled action; *Hindu nationalists* want Indians to act as muscular defenders of Hindu civilisation; *strategists* advocate cultivating state power by developing strategic capabilities; and *liberals* seek prosperity and peace through increasing trade and interdependence. . . .

Tanvi Madan in her essay on the China-India-US triangle, argues that the manner in which India deals with these challenges and opportunities will not just affect India's relations with China and the US, but its foreign relations across the entire spectrum, including the internal dimension of India's strategy. India can choose from several options to manage this strategic triangle: Trust No One (keep both China and the US at arm's length and engaging when appropriate, while minimising their impact on India); Yankee Go Home (India should work with China to limit the role and influence of the US in their relationship, in Asia and more broadly in the world); The Dynamic Democratic Duo (India should seek a *de facto* or *de jure* alliance with the US to counter China); Why Can't We All Just Get Along (China, India and the US cooperate to maintain stability and prosperity in the region and beyond), and; Hedgemony (India should hedge its bet and even strive to play a key part in Beijing and Washington's hedging strategies). . . .

In an increasingly militarised global environment, the role of nuclear weapons in ensuring a state's national security is a highly debated one. . . . Though the minimum deterrence strategy is optimal for national security, there is a growing tension between its political (how political decision makers think about nuclear weapons) and technical components (professionals who think about strategy and/or operate the weapons, and represent the

possible use of the weapons) resulting from too much reliance on concepts developed elsewhere and in different strategic environments, particularly in the United States. . . .

We are of the view that sustainable national security will emerge as a result of India's defence preparedness, the competence of its diplomatic institutions, and the social, economic and cultural well being of the society. We believe it is crucial that a grand strategy for India be formulated keeping in view the mutually reinforcing relationship between defence, diplomacy and development. The grand strategy should also be integrative given an interconnected regional and global environment. In such an environment, keeping in view its enlightened national interests, India should focus on promoting stability and security in its neighbourhood and in the world community. We hope that this volume of work along with efforts undertaken elsewhere will provide a basis for future debate and discussion on important elements of India's grand strategy.

Bush Doctrine on Pre-Emption

GEORGE W. BUSH
Pre-Emption and National Security Strategy*

For much of the last century, America's defense relied on the Cold War doctrines of deterrence and containment. In some cases, these strategies still apply. But new threats also require new thinking. Deterrence—the promise of massive retaliation against nations—means nothing against shadowy terrorist networks with no nation or citizens to defend. Containment is not possible when unbalanced dictators with weapons of mass destruction can deliver those weapons on missiles or secretly provide them to terrorist allies. * * *

If we wait for threats to fully materialize, we will have waited too long. * * * [O]ur security will require all Americans to be forward-looking and resolute, to be ready for pre-emptive action when necessary to defend our liberty and to defend our lives.

* * *

The great struggles of the twentieth century between liberty and totalitarianism ended with a decisive victory for the forces of freedom— and a single sustainable model for national success: freedom, democracy, and free enterprise. In the twenty-first century, only nations that share a commitment to protecting basic human rights and guaranteeing political and economic freedom will be able to unleash the potential of their people and assure their future prosperity. People everywhere want to be able to speak freely; choose who will govern them; worship as the please; educate their children—male and female; own property; and enjoy the benefits of their labor. These values of freedom are right and true for every person, in every society—and the duty of protecting these values against their enemies is the common calling of freedom-loving people across the globe and across the ages.

Today, the United States enjoys a position of unparalleled military strength and great economic and political influence. In keeping with our heritage and principles, we do not use our strength to press for unilateral advantage. We seek instead to create a balance of

---

*First two paragraphs are from George W. Bush, Commencement Address, U.S. Military Academy, West Point, New York, June 1, 2002, http://georgewbush-whitehouse.archives.gov/news/releases/2002/06/20020601-3.html (accessed 9/23/09); rest from George W. Bush, "The National Security Strategy of the United States of America," September 17, 2002, http://georgewbush-whitehouse.archives.gov/nsc/nss/2002/index.html (accessed 9/23/09).

power that favors human freedom: conditions in which all nations and all societies can choose for themselves the rewards and challenges of political and economic liberty. In a world that is safe, people will be able to make their own lives better. We will defend the peace by fighting terrorists and tyrants. We will preserve the peace by building good relations among the great powers. We will extend the peace by encouraging free and open societies on every continent.

Defending our nation against enemies is the first and fundamental commitment of the Federal Government. Today, that task has changed dramatically. Enemies in the past needed great armies and great industrial capabilities to endanger America. Now, shadowy networks of individuals can bring great chaos and suffering to our shores for less than it costs to purchase a single tank. Terrorists are organized to penetrate open societies and to turn the power of modern technologies against us.

To defeat this threat we must make use of every tool in our arsenal—military power, better homeland defenses, law enforcement, intelligence, and vigorous efforts to cut off terrorist financing. The war against terrorists of global reach is a global enterprise of uncertain duration. America will help nations that need our assistance in combating terror. And America will hold to account nations that are compromised by terror, including those who harbor terrorists—because the allies of terror are the enemies of civilization. The United States and countries cooperating with us must not allow the terrorists to develop new home bases. Together, we will seek to deny them sanctuary at every turn.

The gravest danger our nation faces lies at the crossroads of radicalism and technology. Our enemies have openly declared that they are seeking weapons of mass destruction, and evidence indicates that they are doing so with determination. The United States will not allow these efforts to succeed. We will build defenses against ballistic missiles and other means of delivery. We will cooperate with other nations to deny, contain, and curtail our enemies' efforts to acquire dangerous technologies. And, as a matter of common sense and self-defense, America will act against such emerging threats before they are fully formed. We cannot defend America and our friends by hoping for the best. So we must be prepared to defeat our enemies' plans, using the best intelligence and proceeding with deliberation. History will judge harshly those who saw this coming danger but failed to act. In the new world we have entered, the only path to peace and security is the path of action. * * *

The struggle against global terrorism is different from any other war in our history. It will be fought on many fronts against a particularly elusive enemy over an extended period of time. Progress will come through persistent accumulation of successes—some seen, some unseen. * * *

While the United States will constantly strive to enlist the support of the international community, we will not hesitate to act alone, if necessary, to exercise our right of self-defense by acting preemptively against such terrorists, to prevent them from doing harm against our people and our country. * * *

In the war against global terrorism, we will never forget that we are ultimately fighting for our democratic values and way of life. Freedom and fear are at war, and there will be no quick or easy end to this conflict. In leading the campaign against terrorism, we are forging new, productive international relationships and redefining existing ones in ways that meet the challenges of the twenty-first century.

Lessons and Legacies of the Afghanistan and Iraq Wars

Dan Caldwell
U.S. Policy Toward Afghanistan, Pakistan, and Iraq*

* * *

Never underestimate the enemy

Like most nationalities, Americans tend to be ethnocentric, if not arrogant, concerning the capabilities of the United States relative to other states. In 1957 when the Soviet Union, which most Americans at the time considered backward, launched *Sputnik*, the world's first satellite orbiting the earth, Americans were shocked, surprised, and alarmed. President Lyndon Johnson dismissed North Vietnamese guerillas as "little men in black pajamas" and was shocked and surprised when they were able to defeat U.S. forces. . . .

The quick, decisive victory of American forces over Iraqi forces in both January 1991 and March 2003 led some Americans to conclude that Iraqi forces were comparatively weak and ineffective; however once defeated on the conventional battlefield, many of those forces adopted a different approach for challenging U.S. control of their country. They adopted an asymmetrical approach, which proved to be relatively effective against the military forces of the most powerful country in the world until the U.S. modified its strategy for fighting the insurgents. . . .

Make assumptions about the enemy and military operations that are based on facts and not wishful thinking

The assumptions underlying the invasion of Iraq were based on wishful thinking rather than facts and hard analysis. American soldiers were welcomed in the initial days of the invasion, but soon thereafter, most Iraqis wanted the Americans to leave. They stayed, and the insurgency developed.

---

*From Dan Caldwell, *Vortex of Conflict: U.S. Policy Toward Afghanistan, Pakistan, and Iraq* (Stanford: Stanford University Press, 2011), 251–259, 263–265.

In Afghanistan and Iraq, American policy-makers made best-case as opposed to worst-case assumptions. This was a curious reversal of the practice throughout the cold war, when U.S. leaders assumed the worst case with regard to the Soviet Union and its military capabilities. . . .

It is essential that American leaders make realistic, plausible assumptions prior to going to war. . . .

Key U.S. decision-makers assumed that ex-patriate Iraqi leaders such as Ahmad Chalabi and Ali Allawi would be accepted and even wel-comed by Iraqis. This assumption grossly sim-plified the complex reality of Iraqi politics, which was based on complex connections among families, clans, and tribes, in addition to the fundamental split between Sunnis and Shia. In addition, accepting the facile assur-ances of neoconservatives, American policy-makers assumed that once Saddam Hussein was overthrown, democracy and the rule of law would take hold in Iraq and then spread throughout the Middle East. . . .

Obtain the support of other states, nongovernmental organizations, and intergovernmental organizations

In the days and weeks following the 9/11 attacks on the U.S., there was substantial inter-national support for and cooperation with the United States in identifying and taking down individual terrorists and their networks. . . .

The contrast between the first and sec-ond Gulf wars is instructive. In the first Gulf War, President George Herbert Walker Bush worked tirelessly to convince close American

allies to support the coalition in opposing and reversing Iraq's takeover and occupation of Kuwait. In the end, more than thirty countries supported the coalition with both military and economic support. Although the first Gulf War cost a total of $55 billion, American allies—principally Kuwait, Saudi Arabia, and Japan—reimbursed the U.S. $50 billion. As a result, the first Gulf War cost the U.S. a total of $5 billion, which is equivalent to the cost of the wars in Afghanistan and Iraq for two weeks in 2009. . . .

Faced with a new and unknown threat fol-lowing 9/11, George W. Bush chose to almost "go it alone" in Afghanistan and with only the United Kingdom and several other close allies in Iraq. This almost unilateral approach was costly to the U.S. in both human and eco-nomic terms. It is worth remembering that in those cases in which the United States had a legitimate cause and genuine coalition (World War II, Korea, Afghanistan), it was successful. When the U.S. went it alone or had a weak coalition (Iraq), it had serious problems or it failed (Vietnam). . . .

Do not ask too much from the members of the military and their families compared to the rest of American society

In the aftermath of 9/11, Americans experi-enced a wave of patriotic feelings and many responded to defend their country that had been attacked. . . . People in the military today have paid a grossly disproportionate price for the wars in Afghanistan and Iraq. Almost all members of the Army or the Marines during their first four-year enlistment have been deployed to Afghanistan or Iraq for one tour of duty; many have been deployed for two tours; and some for three tours. In contrast, civilians are not directly involved or affected by the wars unless they have a loved one overseas. Of course, all Americans, civilian and military alike, will be paying for these wars for several generations, given the deficits that have been run up in order to pay for them. And, of course, those who have lost loved ones will never fully recover.

In fighting the enemy, maintain and observe fundamental ideals

Soon after the al Qaeda attacks on the United States of September 11, 2001, a number of Americans worried that the fear engendered by the attacks would cause the United States to weaken its traditional support for and observance of fundamental individual and human rights. The George W. Bush administration's response to the attacks in some significant ways confirmed these fears by weakening rights of privacy with warrantless wiretaps and the passage of the Patriot Act. In addition, the long-standing prohibition on torture was violated by different government agencies, most dramatically in Abu Ghraib prison in Iraq. The weakening of the U.S. observance of international and domestic laws regarding privacy and the prohibition of torture underscores the need to observe American values and ideals assiduously so that these values do not appear hypocritical or even meaningless. . . .

Relearn the lessons of the past

At the end of the first Gulf war, a number of commentators, including President George H.W. Bush, indicated that the United States had at long last kicked the "Vietnam syndrome" and had shown that the "U.S. was back." It had taken a decade for the U.S. military to recover from Vietnam, and by 1990, it was clear that the U.S. military had recovered, and its impressive performance in the first Gulf War clearly proved this. The generation of military leaders who had served as junior officers in Vietnam came into prominence in the 1990s, and, having experienced the trauma of Vietnam, they worked assiduously to avoid the mistakes that the earlier military leaders had made. First they supported the creation and the building of the all-volunteer force consisting of those who wanted to be in the military rather than those who, many against their will, were drafted into service. Second, they believed in the massive application of military force. Third, they criticized the limited application of force such as counterinsurgency and believed that the purpose of war was, first and foremost, to defeat the enemy. Lost in pursuing this objective, of course, was winning the support of the local people.

The irony of the wars in Afghanistan and Iraq from the military's perspective is that the effect was similar to Vietnam; namely, the war in Afghanistan supplanted Vietnam as "America's longest war."

* * *

Challenges of the Arab Spring

11.3

MARC LYNCH
The Big Think Behind the Arab Spring*

"Why does every nation on Earth move to change their conditions except for us? Why do we always submit to the batons of the rulers and their repression? How long will Arabs wait for foreign saviors?" That is how the inflammatory Al Jazeera talk-show host Faisal al-Qassem opened his program in December 2003. On another Al Jazeera program around that same time, Egyptian intellectuals Saad Eddin Ibrahim and Fahmy Howeidy debated whether it would take American intervention to force change in the Arab world. Almost exactly seven years later, Tunisians erupted in a revolution that spread across the entire region, finally answering Qassem's challenge and proving that Arabs themselves could take control of their destiny.

Throughout this year of tumult, Arabs have debated the meaning of the great wave of popular mobilization that has swept their world as vigorously as have anxious foreigners. There is no single Arab idea about what has happened. To many young activists, it is a revolution that will not stop until it has swept away every remnant of the old order. To wor-

ried elites, it represents a protest movement to be met with limited economic and political reforms. Some see a great Islamic Awakening, while others argue for an emerging cosmopolitan, secular, democratic generation of engaged citizens. For prominent liberals such as Egypt's Amr Hamzawy, these really have been revolutions for democracy. But whatever the ultimate goal, most would agree with Syrian intellectual Burhan Ghalyoun, who eloquently argued in March that the Arab world was witnessing "an awakening of the people who have been crushed by despotic regimes.". . .

So while the Arab uprisings generated a marvelous range of innovative tactics (uploading mobile-camera videos to social media like Facebook and Twitter, seizing and holding public squares), they did not introduce any particularly new ideas. The relentless critique of the status quo, the generational desire for political change, the yearning for democratic freedoms, the intense pan-Arab identification—these had all been in circulation for more than a decade. What changed with the fall of Zine el-Abidine Ben Ali in Tunisia was

---

*Marc Lynch, "The Big Think Behind the Arab Spring," *Foreign Policy* (November 28, 2011).

the recognition that even the worst tyrants could be toppled. It shattered the wall of fear. That is why hundreds of thousands of Egyptians came into the streets on Jan. 25. It's why protests broke out in Yemen, Bahrain, Morocco, and Jordan. It's why Syrians and Libyans took unfathomable personal risks to rise up against seemingly untouchable despots despite the near certainty of arrests, torture, murder, and reprisals against their families.

The uprisings came in the wake of years of institutional political decay diagnosed acutely by Arab intellectuals such as Egyptian jurist Tariq al-Bishri, by the prescient 2002 Arab Human Development Report, and by nascent political leaders like former International Atomic Energy Agency chief Mohamed ElBaredei. Beneath the edifice of stability, they warned, state institutions were crumbling, their legitimacy faded in the relentless drift of corruption, nepotism, casual brutality, and indifference towards their people. Elections became ever more fraudulent (with the Egyptian and Jordanian elections of late 2010 among the worst), security services more abusive, graft more flagrant.

All this greatly contributed to the economic underpinnings of this year's discontent. The previous decade saw neoliberal economic reforms that privatized industries to the benefit of a small number of well-connected elites and produced impressive rates of GDP growth. But, as ruthlessly dissected by Arab economists like Egypt's Galal Amin, the chasm between the rich and poor grew and few meaningful jobs awaited a massive youth bulge. . . .

But the uprisings were not only about jobs and bread; as Sudanese intellectual Abdelwahab El-Affendi wrote in January, echoing a famous slogan of the 1950s, the revolutions were needed so that the people would deserve bread. The theme of restoring the dignity of the people pervaded the Arab uprisings. The police abuse that drove Tunisian fruit vendor Mohamed Bouazizi's self-immolation and killed the young Egyptian Khaled Said struck a chord with populations who experienced daily the depredations of uncaring sates. The gross corruption of Ben Ali's in-laws and Hosni Mubarak's efforts to groom his son for the presidency simply insulted many Tunisians and Egyptians—and they were ever less afraid to say so. A fiercely independent and articulate rising generation would no longer tolerate brazen corruption, abusive police, indifferent bureaucracy, a stagnant economy, and stage-managed politics. . . .

But it would be a mistake to portray the enthusiasm for revolution as universal in the Arab world. Saudi and Gulf intellectuals, in particular, argued fiercely against the spread of the revolutions to their own lands, insisting that the Gulf monarchies were different. Many, such as Emirati writer Sultan Al Qassemi, argued that the monarchical regimes would prove more resilient than the republics, whether due to greater legitimacy or simply greater wealth. Most have indeed avoided significant internal challenges. For now. . . .

And then there is the contested role of religion in the Middle East's new politics. Islamist political movements such as the Egyptian Muslim Brotherhood and Jordan's Islamic Action Front have long participated in elections, citing the fatwas of Doha-based cleric Yusuf al-Qaradawi to avoid seeing democracy as an un-Islamic innovation. In Tunisia and Egypt, such movements rapidly demonstrated their mastery of the techniques of political competition, out-organizing and out-campaigning their secular rivals. Even more tellingly, their longtime

Salafi critics—who had spent decades denouncing them for joining an un-Islamic political game—now rushed to form their own political parties. But as their power grows, these Islamists have struggled to reassure their domestic critics and the West of their commitment to democratic principles—and, given their first opportunity to actually exercise power, to figure out for themselves how deep those commitments run.

The uprisings were also about America—just not in the way most Americans would have it. Arabs found the idea that Iraq's liberation had inspired their democracy struggle laughable; if anything, it was the protests against the Iraq war that taught them the value of public dissent. Americans cheered themselves with the thought that the protesters in Tahrir Square were not burning Americans flags—and that Libyans in Benghazi were waving them. But this was a dangerous misunderstanding. Many Arab analysts directly equated dictatorial regimes at home with a foreign policy they considered subservient to Israel and the United States. The Arab uprisings called for independence, national sovereignty, and respect for the will of the people—all of which pointed to less eager cooperation with Washington and frostier relations with Tel Aviv.

None of that, however, means that Arabs are flocking to join a new anti-American axis. Indeed, groups such as Hamas and Hezbollah, which inspired many Arabs over the last decade with their perceived success and anti-American defiance, have lost appeal, equivocating as their patrons in Damascus and Tehran preside over the slaughter of unarmed protesters in the streets. . . .

So it's early days yet. But as Palestinian intellectual Khaled Hroub wrote in February, "the fundamental change is the return of the people" to the region's politics. And that—the idea that the opinions of Arabs matter and can never again be ignored—may be the most potent new idea of all.

The European Union

GIOVANNA GREVI
Renewing EU Foreign Policy*

* * *

[T]he EU will need to show the world that it means business, or the world may be excused for thinking that it is drifting out of business.

The standard line of defence to counter the diagnosis of waning EU influence consists of boasting the—still—remarkable Union share of world Gross Domestic Product (GDP), trade and investment, development aid and defence spending. While technically correct, this is a statistical answer to a political question. Besides, it fails to take into account that, on these and other indicators, time is probably not on Europe's side. Like a supernova, absent renewed ambition, the Union may continue to shine beyond its expiration date, but its economic engines and political drive might become exhausted. . . .

[W]hile EU resources may be shrinking relative to others, it is how and to what ends they are mobilised that matters most. The added-value of EU foreign policy depends on what the Union stands for in global politics, and whether it is prepared to take action in a more pragmatic and effective fashion, adapting to a changing world.

The international system is fluid, ever more diverse and turbulent but—overall—not yet adversarial. It is an arena where political authority depends on ideas and innovation as much as on generating record growth rates. On this account, the EU has much to be proud of. . . . Europe's 'brand' based on democracy, peace, cooperation, sustainable growth and solidarity is an attractive one for many worldwide. This is not a vain claim of righteousness but a sober reminder that Europe's values and experience are still relevant well beyond its borders, and should be a platform for international engagement.

The profile of the Union is not tainted because others are threatening it or advancing alternative, more viable political or economic models. What chiefly dents the credibility of the EU is that Europeans have not been practicing what they preach as consistently and effectively as they committed to do, at home and abroad. For example, they have left their monetary union incomplete

---

*From Giovanna Grevi, "Introduction: Renewing EU Foreign Policy," in FRIDE, *Challenges for EU Foreign Policy in 2013: Renewing the EU's Role in the World* (Madrid, Spain: FRIDE, 2013).

for ten years, letting economic imbalances grow within the eurozone; they have not invested in a common defence policy; they have not prevented turmoil in the EU's Southern neighbourhood by supporting political change in authoritarian countries; and they have not empowered EU bodies to work with major rising powers across the vast policy spectrum from economics to security.

* * *

Values as influence

The cornerstone of EU influence and foreign policy are its founding values and principles, which the Lisbon treaty says should inform its external action. The economic crisis has not drastically sapped the EU's commitment to democracy and human rights. In fact, following the Arab uprisings, the EU has upgraded its commitment to 'deep democracy', has taken a tougher line on illiberal drifts in Ukraine and Russia, has stepped up democracy-related sanctions, and has appointed a high representative for human rights equipped with a new human rights strategy. From the EU's neighbourhood to Latin America, Europe's championing of these political values is still regarded as central to its (blurring) attractiveness. But new approaches and instruments will need to be implemented and prioritised . . . to deliver on this commitment.

Overall, the EU will need to focus less on governments and more on citizens, whether in the Eastern neighbourhood, the Mediterranean or Central Asia. The 'Neighbourhood Civil Society Facility' helps in this direction but broader efforts should be made to engage civil society, which would also strengthen the accountability

and effectiveness of democracy-related assistance programmes. Next year will see the launch of the European Endowment for Democracy (EED)—an opportunity to increase resources for democracy promotion, initially focusing the new tool on supporting reform in selected countries. Opening up societies also depends on intensified people-to-people contacts and human mobility at large. This is a pressing priority in relations with Eastern neighbours, but also a defining (if so far atrophied) feature of a renewed relationship with Southern partners. On top of this, the EU will have to avoid complacency on the double-standards that crippled its reputation in North Africa, trading false stability for stagnating reform in the Gulf, Central Asia and elsewhere.

Multi-level engagement

The Union is well placed to pursue multiple levels of engagement at once, which requires a strategic approach upstream to connect different initiatives downstream. From Asia to Latin America, the EU has been shifting emphasis from inter-regional relations to bilateral partnerships with major actors such as the BRICS (Brazil, Russia, India, China and South Africa). The pursuit of bilateral free trade agreements (FTAs) with a range of Asian and Latin American countries has paralleled or replaced stalled negotiations with the Association of Southeast Asian Nations (ASEAN) and the Southern Common Market (Mercosur). With the Doha round stagnant, the EU and the United States (US) are edging closer to a major trade deal. . . . However, the EU should not mimic the balance-of-power approach of other large powers. It should continue to invest in regional cooperation and integration where there is demand for it, playing to its strengths as a rules-based regional actor. . . .

A whole-of-the-Union approach

The EU is a unique catalyst of resources, networks and experience, drawing on its different institutions and member states. But this variety of tools can turn from an asset into a liability if not framed by an overarching approach based on a shared analysis. Institutional segmentation and different national agendas have often hampered the coherence of EU external action, and the credibility of the Union. More than three years since the entry into force of the Lisbon Treaty, it is imperative for EU institutions and member states to upgrade their policy-making software and move to a 'whole-of-the-Union' approach. This approach rests on three pillars, namely the collective definition of the EU's interests, the framing of a policy mix that draws on the many instruments of the Union, and the leveraging of the clout of EU member states for common goals. A truly joined-up approach should also be flexible, as various policy tools should be mobilised based on needs, and different member states can take the lead on different issues depending on their priorities and expertise. . . .

Foreign policy starts at home

Size may not suffice but it does matter, notably in a world of heavyweights like the US, China, Russia and, in perspective, Brazil and India. The EU gives scale to internal policies with important external implications, thereby strengthening the collective clout of its member states and helping shape the terms for international cooperation. Of course, the connection between internal policies and the external projection of the EU is nowhere as crucial as when addressing the economic crisis. . . . The legitimacy and prosperity of the Union are at stake. But other internal policies can have a significant impact abroad. For example, completing the internal energy market is a core dimension of EU energy security, alongside a shared approach to the diversification of supply and transit options. . . .

The EU should develop a more coherent position on energy and resource issues . . . taking into account the medium-term implications of the hydrocarbon revolution in the Atlantic basin (shale gas in the US, deepwater oil and gas in the South Atlantic). Besides, the EU should show the way on developing and deploying low carbon technologies. . . .

Conclusion

The EU is a power unlike any other but whether this is a strategic advantage or a disadvantage is up to Europeans themselves. Member states have a choice: to seriously invest in EU foreign policy as a springboard for global influence, or use it as an occasional platform for joint initiatives when national or other options are precluded or less profitable. That means pursuing a foreign policy that is consistent with its values, but also suited to match challenges and opportunities with pragmatic initiatives, leveraging the scale of the EU where relevant. It also requires EU institutions to overcome untenable bureaucratic divides, and make a sharper contribution to the shared strategic assessment and implementation of common priorities.

U.S.-Russia Relations

Yevgeny Primakov
Russia in a Polycentric World*

Russia's place in today's world is determined primarily by two factors: domestic development (economic, social, political, and military) and the nature of the international environment of which the country is a member. The book you are holding was prepared by the Russian Academy of Sciences' newly created Department of Global Problems and International Relations. The book's main topic is the international conditions of the Russian state's continued existence and development.

The monograph's very name [*Russia in a Polycentric World*] tells us that its authors consider today's world to be polycentric. It must be said that a great many political scientists did not come to this conclusion immediately after the collapse of the bipolar world order, foreordained by the end of the Cold War. Many people, both abroad and in Russia, thought then that a transition to a unipolar world was under way. In support of this thesis, they offered what seemed to be convincing arguments: the Soviet Union, the Warsaw Pact and COMECON had all ceased to exist, while the United States remained in the global arena as the strongest nation in the world, and the NATO bloc binding the United States and its allies retained and even strengthened its capabilities.

All of this was indeed true; however, new centers of world development emerged simultaneously and this objective process continued apace. In the period preceding the current economic crisis (i.e., up to 2008), China's share in world GDP growth was six times greater than that of the United States. The economies of India, Brazil and Russia were growing faster than the US economy.

It must be stressed that the unevenness of economic development affected another important field, that of technological innovation. The United States continues to lead the world in this field, but China has begun to catch up with it. If we extrapolate current trends in world scientific and technological progress, the People's Republic of China has an excellent chance of drawing even with the

---

*Foreword by Yevgeny Primakov (former Russian Prime Minister and Foreign Minister), in *Russia in a Polycentric World*, eds. Alexander Dynkin and Natalia Ivanona (Moscow: Institute of World Economy and International Relations [IMEMO], Russian Academy of Sciences, 2012), 7–8.

United States as early as the mid-21st century, in the opinion of many experts.

The financial and economic crisis that unfolded in the first decade of the 21st century confirmed the hopelessness of the unipolar world order. This crisis, the consequences of which are far from being overcome, has demonstrated the unviability of a world financial system controlled from one center. The US dollar's dominant position in it is obvious. Under the conditions of the absence or relative weakness of other reserve currencies, however, the instability of such a system has been revealed. The future likely lies in the creation of regional financial centers. Everything points to both China and Russia following such a path. This in no way means we should minimize the role of the US dollar, but we can foresee that the pegging of other nations' currencies to it will abate.

The reality of the transition to a polycentric world is also founded on comprehending that the formation of a new world order is, on the one hand, an objective process; on the other hand, it is or should be the result of the efforts of different nations, aimed at satisfying the world community's need for stability and security in the international arena. It is quite characteristic that among the arguments of those who initially favored a unipolar world order (and their numbers have now clearly dwindled) was the assertion (expressed, for example, by former US Secretary of State Condoleezza Rice) that a multipolar system was incompatible with the need to pool national efforts in the interests of stabilizing the world situation. I know of no politician or political scientist who feels nostalgia for the multipolarity of the past, before the First or Second World War. But can we really ignore the indisputable fact that the present change in

the structure of the world order, the transition to a multipolar world, is taking place under new conditions? At this new stage of globalization, a strong interdependence of different world centers is developing along polycentrism. Business relations are becoming largely transnational in nature.

Globalization cannot lead to a *volte face* into the past. The multipolarity of the 21st century in and of itself is not pushing us toward confrontation between nations or to the creation of military alliances hostile to one another. Nations are being integrated into groupings, especially in the sphere of economics, and the number of political agreements aimed at stabilizing the situation in one region or another is growing.

So, whereas the history of the 20th century testifies to the inability of different nations to propagate their ideology on a worldwide scale, the 21st century demonstrates that a unipolar world order cannot be imposed even if one world power, stepping out of line becomes the strongest nation in the world.

Polycentrism of the world order will not, however, lead to an international situation free of conflict. The transition to a multipolar system is not a one-time event; the continuous development of the system and the changing of its form is an ongoing process during which various conflicts can emerge and be exacerbated. These are due mainly to the unevenness of development among nations and the success or failure of integration groupings. The instable relationship between, let us say, a policy of "rebooting" relations and the inertial lines of national behavior that took root in the time of open confrontation during the Cold War also affects the course of political, military, and economic affairs. Neither is the desire to establish palatable regimes in the

Asian and African countries, by force or otherwise, receding into the past.

Under such conditions, control over the international agenda is vital. One of the main mechanisms of such control ought to be the United Nations, the role of which is undoubtedly growing. Events sometimes push the united Nations to adopt resolutions on exerting force full pressure on countries whose leaders take large-scale armed actions against their own people. But when such forceful methods go beyond the UN mandate, as happened in Libya, the situation becomes fraught with legalizing NATO intervention in a civil war on the side of anti-government forces. This cannot and should not become the international standard in a polycentric world.

Russia is of course one pole of a multipolar world. Even after the collapse of the Soviet Union, Russia remains the largest country on Earth in terms of territory—straddling two continents—Europe and Asia. More than one-third of the world's natural mineral resources lie under the soil of Russia. In addition, Russia inherited all of the Soviet Union's nuclear missile capability and remains the only nation in the world comparable to the United States in the field of nuclear missile weapons.

Russia's place in today's world is also defined by our nation's sincere desire to play a leading role in key affairs while maintaining security and stability in the world arena, and to continue integrating itself into the world economic system more effectively. Without Russia it would be difficult (even impossible) to confront the challenges and threats facing humanity in the 21st century. The country's active participation in international affairs undoubtedly will make it easier to deal with its domestic problems as well.

★　★　★

U.S.-Latin American Relations

JULIA E. SWEIG
U.S.-Latin American Relations*

During the Cold War, the United States generally aligned itself with and underwrote a repressive status quo, or was instrumental in rolling back popular, even democratic, challenges to the status quo in the region. America's Cuba obsession had poisoned the atmosphere and substance of U.S. policies more than even Fidel Castro's support for revolution there. With the exception of the militaries, mercenaries, oligarchies, and now discredited political parties that benefited from their alliances with the United States, Latin Americans by and large regard the Cold War as having exacted a high human and political cost. Latin Americans thus greeted the end of the Cold War with relief, hopeful that the United States might no longer find cause to compress its regional policies into the politically deadening and socially destructive shackles of anticommunism and containment. . . .

Indeed, in the 1990s the United States set forth a positive agenda for the region, supporting civil society after decades of authoritarian rule and civil war, promoting economic prosperity and political democracy. U.S. security preoccupations did not subside: The ideological and geopolitical emphasis on fighting communists and guerrillas yielded to a new war—the war on drugs. Yet the new U.S. agenda was a far and refreshing cry from the tired saws of the previous four decades, and Latin America welcomed the new U.S. approach. The region was not a priority for the United States, but the message from the North was largely positive, inclusive and respectful. An era of summitry—breathless meetings of heads of state committing to critical goals of democracy, development and the rule of law—generated momentum, energy, and hope. . . .

By the turn of the century, despite the perception that U.S. economic prescriptions of trade integration and market liberalization were to blame for widening inequality and poverty, Latin American public opinion toward the United States remained largely positive. . . .

As the war in Iraq dragged on, without the international legal authority Latin America had insisted upon, whatever well of goodwill the United States might have drawn upon for its post–Cold War embrace of democracy in the

---

*Julia E. Sweig, *Friendly Fire: Losing Friends and Making Enemies in the Anti-American Century* (New York: Public Affairs, 2006), 149–151, 160–164.

hemisphere had run virtually dry. On the eve of a World Trade Organization ministerial meeting in Cancún in fall 2003, the governments of Brazil, Argentina, Mexico and ten other Latin American countries joined with India, South Africa, China, and even U.S. war-on-terror allies Colombia and Pakistan to form the "Group of Twenty". Though the Cancun summit was aimed at achieving an agreement on agricultural issues, the draft proposals, heavily influenced by the United States, Europe and Japan, kept the agricultural subsidies in place. The Group of Twenty's collective demand that developed countries first eliminate their agricultural subsidies effectively scuttled the U.S. European and Japanese negotiating position, which held that they would cut subsidies only in return for guarantees that developing countries would grant improved market access. Although the developing countries' opposition also was directed at the European Union and Japan, coming on the heels of the failed diplomacy around the Iraq war, the show of defiance represented a significant diplomatic defeat for the United States. . . .

A fundamental realignment is under way in Latin America. The nonviolent left–some with a history of insurgency or involvement in military coups–is coming to power within government and gaining a voice outside of it. . . .

Save [Hugo] Chavez [Venezuela] and [Evo] Morales [Bolivia], none of the new left-leaning elected Latin leaders are talking revolution: They are pragmatic, understand firsthand the risks of unmanageable domestic conflict and the U.S. temptation to step in and fill the breach, and are searching for a middle way somewhere between the heavily state-dominated economic model of their authoritarian pasts and the politically unsustainable market orthodoxy of the Washington Consensus. . . .

Regionally and internationally, under Brazil's and Chile's leadership, Latin America is reorienting its historic trade and diplomatic habit of looking first to the United States to set the hemisphere's agenda. With the exception of Colombia, Peru, and Central America—the small island-states of the Caribbean essentially broke with the United States over Haiti—U.S. influence is diminishing. The Free Trade Area of the Americas, planned for 2005, was dead on arrival. New regional organizations have been created and old ones strengthened with an eye to deepening market integration in order to better leverage an eventual trade deal with the United States, particularly once U.S. agricultural subsidies are eliminated. . . . In the meantime, individually and collectively, the major countries of South America and Mexico have diversified their trade substantially, reaching agreements with the European Union, Japan, China and India. . . .

These realignments have pulled the rug out from under America's historic sway in the region. Neither the Alliance for Progress of the 1960s, the North American Free Trade Agreement (NAFTA), the summitry of the 1990s, the Free Trade Area of the Americas at the end of the American Century, the billions of dollars in military assistance and training, nor even the largely sincere but at times half-hearted embrace of democracy at the end of the Cold War could bring the United States lasting goodwill. But even by a colder calculus, these U.S. investments have not yielded their expected returns. Just as the United States seeks to extend the power and influence it once exercised over Latin America to much of the rest of the globe, save China, Latin America can no longer be relied on to support the U.S. global trade, market, and security agenda.

* * *

Debate on U.S. Cuba Policy (I)

13.2

José R. Cárdenas
Beware Appeasement*

Critics of current U.S. policy towards Cuba have already begun speculating what unilateral changes may be in store for that contentious relationship during President Obama's second term. By winning the state of Florida—home to the highest concentration of Cuban exiles—despite implementing some initiatives in his first term that were opposed by Cuban Americans in Congress, President Obama, in their view, can be aggressive in further liberalizing policy without fear now of any political fallout (although widely reported exit polls that suggested up to 48 percent of Cuban Americans voted for Obama have been debunked by CapitolHillCubans.com).

Yet however the numbers play out in Florida, frankly it is no more than irrational exuberance to expect any significant change in U.S.-Cuba relations over the next four years—that is, barring the deaths of both Fidel and Raul Castro.

In the first place, the Cuban American bloc remains solid in Congress. In the Senate, the formidable duo of Sens. Bob Menendez (D-NJ) and Marco Rubio (R-FL) has been augmented by Senator-Elect Ted Cruz (R-TX) to keep the administration honest on policy. In the House, anyone who believes newly elected Joe Garcia (D-FL) is going to carry the banner of appeasement is sorely mistaken. He favors family contact, not overturning the embargo.

Secondly, critics have convinced themselves that if it weren't for the Cuban American lobby, the U.S. would have long ago reached an accommodation with the Castro dictatorship. What they refuse to recognize is that the biggest impediment to any fundamental change in the relationship is the absolute unwillingness of the dictatorship to undertake significant reforms that would put pressure on U.S. policymakers to reciprocate with policy changes.

That said, to contemplate any serious re-evaluation of relations on the U.S. part as long as the regime systematically represses the Cuban people—to say nothing of the continued unjust incarceration of U.S. development worker Alan Gross—and relentlessly continues to thwart U.S. interests in international fora is just self-delusion.

---

*José R. Cárdenas, "Cuba Policy in a Second Obama Term", *Shadow Government: Notes from the Loyal Opposition*, FP.com, November 13, 2012, http://shadow.foreignpolicy.com/posts/2012/11/13/cuba_policy_in_a_second_obama_term.

Moreover, even in the space the administration thinks it may have some flexibility on the issue—expanded travel, supporting micro-enterprises, and increased agricultural sales—there are complications. The 1996 Cuban Liberty & Democratic Solidarity Act (a.k.a., Helms-Burton) is still on the books and it states that anyone improperly using property illegally confiscated from U.S. citizens (including naturalized citizens of Cuban descent) can be sued in a U.S. court of law. While it is true that the "right of action" has been suspended by successive administrations, the law still holds that anyone using or accessing those properties is liable.

Will a U.S. administration sanction activity that might violate the letter and spirit of U.S. law? For example, what happens when a U.S. tour group traveling under a license as part of the administration's expanded travel program entertains itself at a venue illegally confiscated from its original owners? Or, what happens when a U.S. agricultural company sells its products to Cuba and has to utilize a port, a dock, or otherwise come into some contact with what U.S. law considers stolen property?

It matters little what anyone thinks about the matter; the law is the law. I'm not a lawyer, but one has to wonder how long U.S. law can recognize a wrong was committed against U.S. citizens without giving them the opportunity to redress it. No doubt some creative attorneys are thinking about the same thing.

So, advice to critics of U.S. policy towards Cuba is to re-cork the bubbly. Absent any significant change in Havana, including the earthly expiration of Fidel and Raul Castro, the Holy Grail of unilateral change in U.S. policy is unlikely to be forthcoming. Their energies should instead be directed towards convincing Cuban leaders to establish a concrete rationale as to why any U.S. administration would need to re-evaluate the relationship.

Debate on U.S. Cuba Policy (II)

LARRY BIRNS AND FREDERICK MILLS
End the Anachronistic Policy*

The Obama Administration should be prepared to take, in quick progression, three important initial steps to trigger a speedy rapprochement with Cuba: immediately phase out the embargo, free the Cuban five, and remove Havana from the spurious State Department roster of nations purportedly sponsoring terrorism. These measures should be seen as indispensable if Washington is to ever mount a credible regional policy of mutual respect among nations and adjust to the increased ideological diversity and independence of the Latin American and Caribbean regions. Washington's path towards an urgently needed rehabilitation of its hemispheric policy ought to also include consideration of Cuba's own pressing national interests. A thaw in US—Cuba relations would enhance existing security cooperation between the countries, amplify trade and commercial ties, and guarantee new opportunities for citizens of both nations to build bridges of friendship and cooperation. For this to happen, the Obama Administration would have to muster the audacity to resist the anti-Castro lobby and their hardline allies in Congress, whose Cuba bashing has no limits. Nevertheless, it is time to replace belligerency with détente.

This essay argues that the embargo against Cuba is blatantly counterproductive, immoral, and anachronistic. If the initial purpose of this measure was to punish Havana for expropriating U.S. property and to bring about fundamental political and economic reforms, Washington has had more than 50 years to see that the *status quo* is flawed. Over the years, invasion, embargo, and covert psychological operations against Cuba have only served to reinforce a 'circle the wagons' mentality in Havana. The island also has been subject to a relentless barrage of propaganda and terrorist assaults organized by militant anti-Castro zealots to advance their cause. . . .

Besides being counter-productive, there are also strong moral arguments for ending the embargo. From a utilitarian point of view, the policy is objectionable because it has brought

---

*"Best Time for U.S.-Cuba Rapprochement Is Now", Council on Hemispheric Affairs, January 30, 2013, www.coha.org/best-time-for-u-s-cuba-rapprochement-is-now/.

about needless suffering without convincing evidence of praiseworthy results. . . .

A more recent report by *Human Rights Watch* also points to the needless suffering caused by the embargo: "The United States' economic embargo on Cuba, in place for more than half a century, continues to impose indiscriminate hardship on Cubans, and has failed to improve human rights in the country." (2012 Report on Cuba). The embargo, then, has harmed those whom it purportedly meant to benefit—the average Cuban.

In addition to being counter-productive and immoral, U.S. policy towards Havana is also anachronistic. During the excesses of the Cold War, the U.S. sought to use harsh and unforgiving measures to isolate Cuba from its neighbors in order to limit the influence of the Cuban revolution on a variety of insurgencies being waged in the region. That narrative did not sufficiently recognize the homegrown causes of insurgency in the hemisphere. Some argue that it inadvertently drove Cuba further into the Soviet camp. Ironically, at the present juncture of world history, the embargo is in some ways isolating the U.S. rather than Cuba. Washington is often viewed as implementing a regional policy that is defenseless and without a compass. At the last Summit of the Americas in Cartagena in April 2012, member states, with the exception of Washington, made it clear that they unanimously want Cuba to participate in the next plenary meeting or the gathering will be shut down. There are new regional organizations, such as the Community of Latin American and Caribbean States (CELAC), that now include Cuba and exclude the U.S. Not even America's closest allies support the embargo. Instead, over the years, leaders in NATO and the OECD member nations have visited Cuba and, in some cases, allocated lines of credit to the regime. So it was no surprise that in November of 2012, the United Nations General Assembly voted overwhelmingly (188–3), for the 21st year in a row, against the US embargo. . . .

Despite the basic intransigence of US policy towards Cuba, in recent years, important changes have been introduced by Havana: state control over the economy has been diminished; most travel restrictions affecting both Americans and Cubans on the island have been lifted; and the "group of 75" Cuban dissidents detained in 2003 have been freed. Washington has all but ignored these positive changes by Havana, but when it comes to interacting with old foes such as those of Myanmar, North Korea, and Somalia, somehow constructive dialogue is the order of the day. One reason for this inconsistency is the continued opposition by the anti-Castro lobby to a change of course by Washington.

The anti-Castro lobby and their allies in the US Congress argue that the reforms coming out of Havana are too little too late and that political repression continues unabated. They continue to see the embargo as a tool for coercing either more dramatic reforms or regime change. It is true that the reformist tendency in Cuba does not include a qualitative move from a one party system to political pluralism. Lamentably, Cuba reportedly continues to use temporary detentions and the occasional jailing of non-violent dissidents to limit the parameters of political debate and total freedom of association. The authors agree that no non-violent Cuban dissident should be intimidated, detained or jailed. But continuing to maliciously turn the screws on Havana has never provided an incentive for more democracy in any sense of the word nor has it created a political opening into which Cuba, with confidence, could enter. The easing of tensions between Washington and Havana is more likely to contribute to the evolution of a more democratic form of socialism on the island, the early stages of which we may presently be witnessing. In any case *the precise form of such change inevitably should and will be decided in Cuba, not in Washington or Miami.*

* * *

U.S.-Africa Relations

OBAMA ADMINISTRATION
U.S. Strategy Toward Sub-Saharan Africa*

The Four Pillars of the U.S. Strategy Toward Sub-Saharan Africa

The United States will partner with sub-Saharan African countries to pursue the following interdependent and mutually reinforcing objectives: (1) strengthen democratic institutions; (2) spur economic growth, trade, and investment; (3) advance peace and security; and (4) promote opportunity and development. Across all objectives, we will: deepen our engagement with Africa's young leaders; seek to empower marginalized populations and women; address the unique needs of fragile and post-conflict states; and work closely with the U.N. and other multilateral actors to achieve our objectives on the continent.

I. Strengthen Democratic Institutions

As the President said in Ghana, "Africa doesn't need strong men, it needs strong institutions."

We will work to advance democracy by strengthening institutions at every level, supporting and building upon the aspirations of Africans for more open and accountable governance, promoting human rights and the rule of law, and challenging leaders whose actions threaten the credibility of democratic processes. As the National Security Strategy states, our support for democracy is critical to U.S. interests and is a fundamental component of American leadership abroad. We will pursue the following actions:

■ **Promote Accountable, Transparent, and Responsive Governance.** The United States will expand efforts to support and empower key reformers and institutions of government at all levels to promote the rule of law, strengthen checks on executive power, and incorporate responsive governance practices. We will also seek to expand African membership in the Open Government Partnership and the Extractive Industries Transparency Initiative, which promote sound governance, transparency, and accountability.

*From The White House, *U.S. Strategy Toward Sub-Saharan Africa* (June 2012), 2–7.

- **Bolster Positive Models.** The United States recognizes that Africans must forge lasting solutions, and build their own democracies. To this end, we will support those leaders and actors who are creating vibrant democratic models, including elected leaders as well as young Africans who are leaders in civil society and entrepreneurship. . . .
- **Promote and Protect Human Rights, Civil Society, and Independent Media.** The United States will amplify and support voices calling for respect for human rights, rule of law, accountability and transitional justice mechanisms, and independent media. Further, we will continue to focus on empowering women and marginalized populations, and opposing discrimination based on disability, gender, or sexual orientation.
- **Ensure a Sustained Focus on the Credibility of Democratic Processes.** The United States will take a strong and consistent stand against actions that undermine democratic institutions or the legitimacy of democratic processes. We will evaluate elections against the highest possible standards of fairness and impartiality. The United States will seek to expand adherence to the principle of civilian control of the military, and will support strong measures against individuals or groups that threaten legitimately elected governments.
- **Promote Strong Democratic Norms.** The United States will support efforts by regional and international bodies to enforce the consistent application of democratic practices, particularly the African Union's African Charter on Democracy, Elections, and Governance and other multilateral standards. We will

support basic and civic education to ensure future generations are active, informed, and committed to the rights and responsibilities of democratic citizenship.

II. Spur Economic Growth, Trade, and Investment

It is in the interest of the United States to improve the region's trade competitiveness, encourage the diversification of exports beyond natural resources, and ensure that the benefits from growth are broad-based. We will pursue the following actions as we seek to accelerate inclusive economic growth, including through trade and investment:

- **Promote an Enabling Environment for Trade and Investment.** Building on U.S. programs such as the Partnership for Growth and New Alliance for Food Security and Nutrition, as well as international programs such as the Open Government Partnership and the Extractive Industries Transparency Initiative, we will encourage legal, regulatory, and institutional reforms that contribute to an environment that enables greater trade and investment in sub-Saharan Africa. We will also encourage sub-Saharan Africa's private sector to engage governments to undertake these necessary reforms.
- **Improve Economic Governance.** We will help to build the public sector's capacity to provide services and improve protections against illicit financial activity. . . .
- **Promote Regional Integration.** Increased African regional integration would create larger markets, improve

economies of scale, and reduce transaction costs for local, regional, and global trade. . . .

■ **Expanding African Capacity to Effectively Access and Benefit from Global Markets.** . . . To increase Africa's capacity to produce goods for export that are diverse, competitive, and meet global standards, we will (1) work with the Congress to extend the unilateral preferences under the African Growth and Opportunity Act beyond 2015 and extend the Generalized System of Preferences beyond 2013 . . . (2) increase cooperation and technical assistance on a range of issues, including building Africa's capacity to meet product standards, food safety and sanitary and phytosanitary requirements, product testing, and certification requirements. . . .

■ **Encourage U.S. Companies to Trade with and Invest in Africa.** . . . In harmony with the National Export Initiative, we will develop a "Doing Business in Africa Campaign" to harness the resources of the United States Government to assist U.S. businesses in identifying and seizing opportunities in sub-Saharan Africa. We will also engage with members of the sub-Saharan African Diaspora in the United States, who are showing an increasing level of interest in investing in their countries of origin.

III. Advance Peace and Security

African states are showing increasing capacity to take the lead on security issues on the continent. Nonetheless, international and domestic conflict and the inability of some governments to meet the basic security needs of their people continue to be key obstacles to effective democratic governance, economic growth, trade and investment, and human development. Only Africa's governments and people can sustainably resolve the security challenges and internal divisions that have plagued the continent, but the United States can make a positive difference. Recognizing this fact, we will pursue the following actions:

■ **Counter al-Qa'ida and Other Terrorist Groups.** . . . Consistent with the National Strategy for Counterterrorism, we will concentrate our efforts on disrupting, dismantling, and eventually defeating al-Qa'ida and its affiliates and adherents in Africa to ensure the security of our citizens and our partners. In doing so, we will seek to strengthen the capacity of civilian bodies to provide security for their citizens and counter violent extremism through more effective governance, development, and law enforcement efforts.

■ **Advance Regional Security Cooperation and Security Sector Reform.** We will deepen our security partnerships with African countries and regional organizations and their stand-by forces by expanding efforts to build African military capabilities through low-cost, small-footprint operations. . . . Moreover, U.S. military and civilian agencies will help establish effective partner nation security forces, intelligence organizations, and law enforcement and border control agencies that are subordinate to and operating jointly with their constitutional civil authorities.

■ **Prevent Transnational Criminal Threats.** We will build comprehensive partnerships that leverage our land border, maritime, aviation, cybersecurity, and financial sector expertise to counter illicit movement of people, arms, drugs, and money, as well as guard against the criminal facilitation of weapons of mass destruction material and technology. We will work to curb armed robbery at sea and protect fisheries, and continue to implement our Counter-Piracy Action Plan off the coast of Somalia. . . .

- **Prevent Conflict and, Where Necessary, Mitigate Mass Atrocities and Hold Perpetrators Accountable.** . . . [W]e will address atrocity risks at the earliest stage possible to help prevent violence before it emerges, and bolster domestic and international efforts to bring perpetrators to justice. . . .

- **Support Initiatives to Promote Peace and Security.** We will support U.N. peacebuilding and peacekeeping missions in sub-Saharan Africa, including by working to ensure that peacekeeping missions are well-led, well-supported, and appropriately resourced in order to maximize their effectiveness. Within African countries, we will support those who work to overcome communal divisions in pursuit of sustainable and peaceful political processes.

IV. Promote Opportunity and Development

. . . We will pursue the following actions as we strive to further accelerate development progress:

- **Address Constraints to Growth and Promote Poverty Reduction.** We will

leverage our engagement via multilateral financial institutions to advocate for increased financing for poorer countries, and will focus on addressing constraints to growth. We will encourage governments to use revenues, particularly from energy sources, to more broadly benefit their populations, and we will continue to support the expansion and improvement of sub-Saharan Africa's education services.

- **Promote Food Security.** Food security will remain a priority, consistent with the commitments made by the United States at the L'Aquila Summit, through the Feed the Future Initiative, and the New Alliance for Food Security and Nutrition launched at the 2012 G-8 Summit. . . .

- **Transform Africa's Public Health.** We will work through the Global Health Initiative and our disease-specific programs, including the President's Emergency Plan for AIDS Relief and the President's Malaria Initiative, to tackle other diseases and malnutrition while strengthening health systems for sustainable impact. We will continue to leverage the leadership being demonstrated by a growing number of African countries on global health in order to bolster our efforts to promote good governance, development, and economic growth, including as we pursue the expanded AIDS prevention targets announced on World AIDS Day in 2011 and through the June 2012 Child Survival Call to Action.

- **Increase Opportunities for Women and Youth.** We will continue to use our diplomacy and assistance programs to empower women, including through the African Women Entrepreneurship Program, implementing the U.S. National Action Plan on Women, Peace, and Security, and focusing on maternal and child health as a centerpiece of the Global Health Initiative. This includes enhancing efforts to protect women in the context of conflict and humanitarian emergencies. . . .

- **Respond to Humanitarian Crises While Promoting Resilience.** While continuing to lead the world in response to humanitarian crises in Africa, we will promote and bring to scale resilience policies and programs. In that context, we will work to prevent the weakening or collapse of local economies, protect livestock, promote sustainable access to clean water, and invest in programs that reduce community-level vulnerability to man-made and natural disasters.

- **Promote Low-emissions Growth and Sustainable Development, and Build Resilience to Climate Change.** We will continue promoting resilience and adaptation to impacts of climate change on food, water, and health in vulnerable African countries, supporting the adoption of low-emissions development strategies, and mobilizing financing to support the development and deployment of clean energy. We will also work to protect and encourage sustainable use of Africa's natural resources.

Development in Africa

WORLD BANK
Africa's Future*

The 10-year vision of the strategy is an Africa where, for at least 20 countries, per capita income would be 50 percent higher than today—implying per capita GDP growth rates of 3–4 percent a year. Another 20 countries would grow at an average rate of 1–2 percent. The poverty rate would have declined by 12 percentage points. At least five countries will achieve middle-income status. This growth will be achieved with a production mix that is considerably more diversified, with manufacturing and services growing rapidly and absorbing labor at a rapid clip. Meanwhile, agricultural productivity will increase, with 15 countries— up from the current 8—registering at least 5 percent average annual agricultural GDP growth. The continent's share in world trade will double (to 8 percent), with regionally integrated infrastructure providing services at globally competitive costs and human development indicators going beyond the MDGs to achieve quality goals in health and education. Access to infrastructure will have doubled so that at least half of households have power. Women's legal capacity and property rights will

have increased significantly. Climate change adaptation measures will have been put in place. Finally, governance indicators will be rising, with the ICT revolution strengthening accountability in the public sector. . . .

To realize this vision, the strategy must be transformative. It cannot rely on a single sector or product to trigger rapid growth and poverty reduction. Even if consensus exists that a particular ingredient is fundamental, such as education—without which nothing can be achieved—realizing the desired level of education requires the coordination of a number of sectors, such as health, education, transport, and communication. Accordingly, the proposed strategy does not divide itself neatly into individual sectors. Instead, it attempts to exploit the synergies among these sectors by organizing around critical themes. This strategy does not mean that individual sectors are not important. Indeed, some, such as health and education, are important in their own right. But achieving health and education goals requires a multidimensional approach, including achieving goals in other sectors.

---

*From The World Bank, *Africa's Future and the World Bank's Support to It* (World Bank, 2011), 8–11, 13–16, 20, 22.

Conversely, infrastructure is not a goal in itself, but rather a critical ingredient in achieving almost all other development objectives, most importantly economic growth. . . .

*   *   *

The strategy has two pillars, (a) competitiveness and employment and (b) vulnerability and resilience, and a foundation—governance and public sector capacity. . . .

Pillar 1: Competitiveness and Employment

The first pillar, competitiveness and employment, represents the way to harness private sector growth for sustainable poverty reduction and, ultimately, wealth creation. . . .

Africa's weak investment climate is caused by three main factors: (a) poor infrastructure, (b) poor business environment (policies and access to finance), and (c) insufficient technical skills. Africa's infrastructure seriously lags that of other developing regions, and the gap is widening over time. Moreover, because of their small scale and limited competition, Africa's infrastructure services are typically several times more expensive than those in other parts of the developing world. This factor lies behind the cost disadvantage African exports suffer in world markets and is one of the obstacles to the productive development of rural and urban areas. . . .

Agriculture, which is Africa's largest private sector, faces the same problems as well as some that are distinctive to the sector. Farms, including family-run ones, are businesses and have needs similar to small enterprises, such as mar-

ket stability, access to finance, and information. Yet a large number of government interventions exist, such as extension services and fertilizer subsidies, whose effectiveness is being questioned. Recent experience demonstrates the constraints that African agriculture faces in diversifying. Family enterprises have difficulty taking advantage of higher food prices and expanding domestic market demand. Furthermore, because 93 percent of African agriculture is rain-fed, improving resilience to the harmful effects of climate change (including floods and droughts) is particularly challenging, given the limited installed water storage capacity across the region, among other things. Improved agricultural water management, better transport, and access to cheaper energy are essential conditions to securing access to markets and improving the competitiveness of farming businesses. . . .

Microfinance, while growing, has huge, untapped potential in Africa. It is not all about credit, however: households have a large demand for low-cost payment services (Mpesa in Kenya), savings accounts (Mzansi in South Africa), and insurance (weather insurance in Kenya). . . . On the demand side, financial (and overall business) literacy has come into focus as a key constraint. Because most enterprises are informal (often due to burdensome business registration and operation procedures, high indirect costs, especially energy, and restrictive labor regulations), policies aimed at the informal sector could reap high returns. . . .

More generally, mobile phones are becoming the most valuable asset of the poor. The widespread adoption of this technology—largely because of the sound regulatory environment and entrepreneurship—opens the possibility that it could serve as a vehicle for transforming the lives of the poor.

The empowerment of women to accelerate economic development—critical because, as one participant at a consultation put it, "[T]he future of Africa is in the hands of African women"—involves many cross-cutting challenges, from poor access to potable water to disadvantaged health and nutrition status. Women in Africa spend a considerable portion of their day fetching water and fuelwood, which leaves little time for family care, education, and production. Identification and prioritization of such issues will help women better integrate and contribute to their economies. Education of women will be especially important in expanding the continent's skilled labor base and securing a better education for its youth. Empowerment entails making regulations and other business conditions more conducive to women entrepreneurs. Women farmers in particular would benefit from support and training in marketing products that women produce. Property rights and other protection of women can also yield high benefits. . . .

Pillar 2: Vulnerability and Resilience

Although Africa faces unprecedented opportunities for transformation and growth, countries in the region and their people are subject to a large number of shocks, such as droughts and floods; food shortages; microeconomic crises; HIV/AIDS, malaria, and other diseases; conflict; and climate change. These shocks by themselves have an immediate effect of lowering living standards. Worse, because few possi-

bilities exist to insure against these shocks, poor Africans adopt risk-averse behaviors, such as accumulating livestock even if the returns are low or taking their children out of school in the face of financial shocks, which keep them in poverty now and for future generations. Reducing vulnerability and building resilience to these shocks is therefore the second pillar of the Bank's strategy. . . .

Conflict and political violence have a myriad of effects at the national and household levels. According to a 2007 report, between 1990 and 2005 the cost of conflict in Africa was equivalent to the funds granted to the continent in international aid over the same period—both the cost of conflicts and aid from 1990 to 2005 amounted to $284 billion. Conflicts in Burundi and Rwanda have cost their governments an annual economic loss of 37 percent and 32 percent of GDP, respectively. A conflict is estimated to turn the development clock back by 10–15 years. As economic activity falters or grinds to a halt, the country suffers from inflation, debt, and reduced investment, while its people suffer from unemployment, lack of public services, and trauma. . . .

* * *

Foundation: Governance and Public Sector Capacity

[U]nderlying Africa's many development problems is the challenge of governance and political leadership. Competitiveness is constrained by restrictive business regulations that are difficult to remove because of vested interests. Infrastructure—often considered another binding constraint—is itself impeded by poor public investment choices, weak budget management, corrupt or lethargic procurement practices, inefficient public utilities, and regulations that prohibit entry into the trucking industry or keep electricity tariffs below sustainable levels. The poor quality of public services—reflected in absent doctors and teachers, and leakage of public funds—is the result of failures in accountability of civil servants and politicians to the public.

But these problems are found in other developing regions. The governance challenge in Africa is particularly acute for three reasons. The first is the large number of fragile states—20 of the world's 33, using the World Bank's definition of fragile and conflict-affected states (FCSs). The Center for Systemic Peace classifies 23 African countries as "extreme" or "high" in terms of state fragility, with another in the "serious" classification. The problem of fragility is exacerbated by the exceptionally weak capacity of the public sector in these countries.

Second, political instability continues to bedevil many countries. Contested elections are followed by post-electoral crises and ethnic or political conflict, as in Kenya, Zimbabwe, and most recently, Côte d'Ivoire. Coups and nondemocratic transfers of power occur with disturbing frequency, as in Guinea, Mauritania, Niger, and Madagascar in 2008–09.

Third, Africa's resource-rich countries have experienced especially severe governance problems, including widespread corruption and civil conflict, giving rise to the term "resource curse." . . .

A reasonable question to ask is why, when so many African countries are electoral democracies, it is necessary to work on the demand for good governance. Why is accountability of politicians to citizens not addressed at the ballot box? The answer is that most African countries are making an uneven political and institutional transition toward more open democratic political systems. In 1988, Sub-Saharan Africa had more than 30 dictatorships; these have declined sharply since 1989 to less than a handful. However, because democracies require a complex set of institutions to develop and be functional, the decline of dictatorships has not seen a commensurate increase in the number of democracies but a growth in intermediate systems, termed *anocracies*, which in some have features of democratic systems and in others are reminiscent of dictatorships. Anocracies lack some of the institutional capabilities to manage conflict. They are typically more vulnerable to misgovernance, armed societal conflict, and political instability. The relatively large number of anocracies in Sub-Saharan Africa is thus a relevant factor in understanding the governance challenge posed by political instability.

Credits

Graham T. Allison: "Conceptual Models and the Cuban Missile Crisis" by Graham T. Allison from *American Political Science Review* 62.3 (September 1969). Copyright © 1969 American Political Science Association. Reprinted with the permission of Cambridge University Press.

Matthew Baum: "Sex, Lies and War: How Soft News brings Foreign Policy to the Inattentive Public," *American Political Science Review*, Vol. 96, No. 1, 2002, pp. 91–92, 94–96, 105–106. Copyright © 2002 American Political Science Association. Reprinted with the permission of Cambridge University Press.

Larry Birns and Frederick Mills: "Best Time for U.S.-Cuba Rapprochement is Now," Council on Hemispheric Affairs online – www.coha.org (January 30, 2013). Reprinted with permission.

Bernard Brodie: *Strategy in the Missile Age.* © 1959 The Rand Corporation. Published by Princeton University Press. Reprinted by permission of Princeton University Press.

Dan Caldwell: Excerpts from *Vortex of Conflict: U.S. Policy Toward Afghanistan, Pakistan, and Iraq* by Dan Caldwell. Copyright © 2011 by the Board of Trustees of the Leland Stanford Jr. University. All rights reserved. Used with the permission of Stanford University Press, www.sup.org.

José R. Cárdenas: "Cuba Policy in a Second Obama Term," Shadow Government: Notes from the Loyal Opposition, *Foreign Policy*, Nov. 13, 2012. Reproduced with permission of Carnegie Endowment for International Peace in the format Republish in a book via Copyright Clearance Center.

John Byrne Cooke: From *Reporting the War: Freedom of the Press from the American Revolution to the War on Terrorism*, by John Byrne Cooke, pp. 1–3. Copyright © John Byrne Cooke, 2007. Reprinted by permission of Macmillan Publishers Ltd.

John Lewis Gaddis: From *The United States and the End of the Cold War: Implications, Reconsiderations, Provocations* by John Lewis Gaddis. Copyright © 1992 by John Lewis Gaddis. Reprinted by permission of Oxford University Press.

Leslie H. Gelb: "Vietnam: The System Worked," *Foreign Policy* 3 (Summer 1971). Reproduced with permission of Carnegie Endowment for International Peace in the format Republish in a book via Copyright Clearance Center.

Mikhail Gorbachev: From Mikhail Gorbachev, et al., *Essays on Leadership* (Washington, D.C.: Carnegie Commission on Preventing Deadly Conflict, 1998). Reprinted by permission of the Carnegie Corporation of New York.

Giovanni Grevi: "Introduction: Renewing EU Foreign Policy" from *Challenges for EU Foreign Policy in 2013: Renewing the EU's Role in the World*, © FRIDE 2013. Reprinted by permission of FRIDE.

Ole R. Holsti: Excerpts from "Public Opinion and Foreign Policy: Challenges to the Almond-Lippmann Consensus" by Ole R. Holsti, International Studies Quarterly, Vol. 36, No. 4, Dec. 1992. Copyright © 1992 International Studies Association. Reproduced with permission of Blackwell Publishing Ltd.

Glossary

administrative trade remedies   Actions by executive-branch agencies when relief from import competition is warranted under the rules of the international trading system.

Afghanistan war   Ongoing U.S. military action against the Taliban and the Al Qaeda terrorist network in Afghanistan that began in October 2001.

African Union (AU)   The major African regional organization, with fifty-three member states, founded in 2002 to replace the Organization for African Unity.

Alien and Sedition Acts (1798)   Legislation that silenced opponents of the war with France by limiting their freedom of speech and of the press.

Alliance for Progress   Foreign aid program established by the Kennedy administration in 1961, ostensibly to promote democracy and enhance economic cooperation with Latin America, but these policies gave way to support for military coups.

alliances   Associations of states for collective security or other mutual interest. Alliances against a common enemy are key components of both defense and deterrence strategies.

Al Qaeda   Osama bin Laden's terrorist network, which emerged during the 1990s and was responsible for 9/11 and a number of other attacks on the United States and other nations.

American exceptionalism   The belief that the United States has a uniqueness and special virtue that ground our foreign policy in Principles much more than the foreign policies of other countries.

anti-apartheid   An international movement, including economic sanctions, against South Africa's system of apartheid; strongly supported on American college campuses during the 1980s and by other activists in the United States, other countries, and within South Africa. (Also see *apartheid*.)

anti-ballistic missile (ABM) defense systems   Defense systems that use missiles to counter ballistic missiles. Concerns that such systems were destabilizing because they meant mutual destruction was no longer assured led to the 1972 ABM treaty as part of SALT I, committing both the United States and the Soviet Union to a limited number of systems.

apartheid   South African system of systematic discrimination by the white minority against the black African majority, depriving black Africans of political rights, economic opportunity, and social justice. (Also see *anti-apartheid*.)

Arab Spring   A series of popular revolutions and uprisings beginning in December 2010 that deposed or challenged the dictatorships in a number of Middle Eastern countries, including Tunisia, Egypt, Libya, Yemen, Bahrain, Syria, and others.

Asian financial crisis   The crisis that struck in mid–1997, starting in Thailand and spreading to Indonesia, South Korea, and then throughout East Asia; also had a significant impact on American banks, companies, and exporters.

A-4

Atlantic Charter   A joint statement by FDR and Churchill in August 1941 in which they described the principles and values that should define the post–World War II world.

"axis of evil"   The name given to Iraq, Iran, and North Korea by President George W. Bush in his 2002 State of the Union speech.

Baruch Plan   A U.S. proposal to the UN Atomic Energy Commission for establishing international control of nuclear weapons; rejected by the Soviet Union.

Bay of Pigs invasion   A U.S.-engineered invasion of Cuba in 1961 by exiled forces seeking to overthrow Fidel Castro. The invasion failed miserably and is one of the most often cited cases of flawed executive-branch decision making.

belief system   Worldview, made up of the analytic component of the conception of the international system, the normative component of the national-interest hierarchy, and the instrumental component of a basic strategy.

bipolar system   An international system in which there are two major powers.

bureaucratic politics   The way in which the positions of executive-branch departments and agencies on an issue depend on the interests of that particular department or agency; "where you stand depends on where you sit."

Camp David Accord   A major breakthrough in Middle East peace brokering in 1979 between Egypt and Israel, negotiated by the Egyptian president Anwar Sadat, the Israeli prime minister Menachem Begin, and the U.S. president Jimmy Carter.

cap and trade   A policy for combating global climate change whereby companies and others agree to emission-cuts targets and can sell emissions permits to those who have trouble meeting their targets.

Carter Doctrine   A doctrine proclaimed by President Carter in January 1980 following the Soviet invasion of Afghanistan. The doctrine stated that the United States would use any means, including military force, to defend the Persian Gulf region.

catastrophic terrorism   The use of nuclear, chemical, or other weapons of mass destruction by terrorists.

China lobby   During the Cold War, the anticommunist lobby supporting Taiwan and opposing "Red China." The term is still used, although now in reference to lobbies in current issues of U.S.-China relations.

city on a hill   The image related to American exceptionalism that the United States was to play a highly principled role in the world that would be both good for us and good for others; can be traced back to John Winthrop, governor of the Massachusetts Bay colony, in 1630.

coercive diplomacy   Measures used to exert power and influence without military force. These range from low-level actions, such as the filing of an official protest or issuing a public condemnation; to withdrawing an ambassador and suspending diplomatic relations; to imposing economic sanctions; and other, tougher measures.

Cold War   A period of political and military tension, including risks of nuclear war, between the Soviet Union and the United States with their respective allies. The Cold War lasted more than four decades after World War II, from 1945 to 1989 in some analyses, 1991 in others.

collective defense   An agreement between an organization of states to commit support in defense of a member state if it is attacked by an outside state.

compellence   The act of getting another state to take a particular action that it otherwise would not.

Comprehensive Test Ban Treaty (CTBT)   Treaty building on prior limited bans that now seeks to ban all tests of nuclear weapons.

containment   A Cold War doctrine whereby the United States would counter any attempt by the Soviet Union to expand its sphere of influence or to spread communism beyond its own borders.

covert action   The secret operations of intelligence agencies to overthrow another nation's government or achieve other foreign policy objectives.

credibility gap   The sense of skepticism that caused the public to lose faith in the truthfulness of its leaders about Vietnam.

Cuban missile crisis   A major confrontation in 1962 between the United States and the Soviet Union over Soviet missiles in Cuba in which the world came close to nuclear war. It is one of the most often cited cases of effective executive-branch decision making.

Darfur   A region in the western part of Sudan in which the Sudanese government was accused of genocide in the 1980s.

Dayton Accord   A peace agreement that ended the 1990s wars in the former Yugoslavia, named for the American city where the agreement was reached by the leaders of Bosnia, Serbia, and Croatia facilitated by Clinton administration diplomacy.

declaratory commitments   Foreign policy commitments derived from speeches and statements by presidents, such as the Monroe Doctrine.

Democratic Idealism   An international relations theory that emphasizes Principles and is rooted in two central tenets: in a tradeoff, "right" is to be chosen over "might," and in the long run, "right" makes for "might."

democratic peace   An international relations theory that asserts that promoting democracy also promotes peace because democracies do not go to war against each other. In other words, this theory claims that the world could be made safe *by* democracy.

Department of Defense (DOD)   The federal department created in 1947, combining previous separate Departments of War (including the Army) and the Navy, now also including the Air Force and Marines, headed by a civilian Secretary of Defense, with headquarters at the Pentagon.

détente   Literally, a "relaxation of tensions," the principal term used to characterize efforts during the 1970s to break out of the Cold War and improve relations between the United States and the Soviet Union.

deterrence   The prevention of war by credibly communicating sufficient will and capacity to retaliate as a second strike if attacked.

Development, Relief and Education for Alien Minors (DREAM) An Obama administration program giving legal status and a path to citizenship to Hispanics under the age of 31 who came to the United States under the age of 16; were currently in school, had earned a high school diploma, or had been honorably discharged from the military; did not have a criminal record; and had been in the country continually for at least five years, even if they came illegally.

diplomacy The process by which states conduct official relations, most often through ambassadors or other diplomatic representatives.

Doha Round Multilateral trade negotiations launched in late 2001, which placed a greater emphasis than did past rounds on the issues most affecting developing countries.

economic sanctions Restrictions on trade, finance, and/or other economic relations, imposed by one country to exert power or influence over another country.

energy security Concerns about U.S. economic and overall security due to threats from the supply side (price hikes by the OPEC cartel, wars, or other political instability) and the demand side (the insatiable global demand for energy).

Espionage and Sedition Acts Legislation passed during 1917–18 that imposed broad prohibitions on speech and made it a crime to express dissent against World War I.

executive agreements International commitments made by the president that do not require a two-thirds Senate majority and usually do not require congressional approval.

Export-Import Bank of the United States The government bank that provides credit and other financing for foreign customers to buy American exports.

fast track A U.S. legislative mechanism that guaranteed that trade agreements negotiated by the president would receive expedited consideration in Congress. The fast track was developed during the 1970s to ensure passage of the Tokyo Round.

Foreign Intelligence Surveillance Act (FISA) A law passed in 1978 that authorizes and regulates the use of electronic surveillance to obtain foreign intelligence information. It has been amended several times since 9/11.

Four Freedoms Proclaimed by FDR as the values underlying the war against Hitler and Nazism: freedom of religion, freedom of speech, freedom from fear, and freedom from want.

free trade Trade between countries without tariffs or other barriers from government intervention.

General Agreement on Tariffs and Trade (GATT) Established in 1944 as a mechanism for managing trade disputes so as to prevent their escalation to trade wars. GATT moved the world gradually toward freer trade through periodic "rounds" of negotiations. In 1995 GATT was folded into the newly created World Trade Organization (WTO).

genocide The deliberate and intentional effort to eliminate a people, as in Nazi Germany during World War II or Rwanda in 1994.

glasnost   Literally, "openness," it meant greater political freedoms in the Soviet Union, including a degree of freedom of the press, the release of prominent dissidents, and an end to the Communist party's "leading role" in society.

globalization   The increasing interconnectedness of the world across nation-state boundaries; affects governments, businesses, communities, and people in a wide range of policy areas.

Great Depression   The worldwide economic depression that began with the crash of the U.S. stock market on October 29, 1929 (Black Tuesday) and soon affected nearly every country in the world.

groupthink   A concept from social psychology that refers to the pressures within small groups for unanimity that work against individual critical thinking.

Gulf of Tonkin Resolution   Passed by Congress in 1964 in response to alleged North Vietnamese attacks on U.S. naval ships; gave the president an open-ended authorization to use military force, without any formal declaration of war by Congress.

guns and butter strategy   President Lyndon B. Johnson's attempt to pursue major domestic social programs while also escalating the Vietnam War, which caused the federal budget deficit to grow and led to stagflation.

hegemon   A leading power that can exert its influence and values throughout the world.

Helsinki Accords   Adopted in 1975 by the Conference on Security and Cooperation in Europe; gave the Soviets the recognition they wanted of territorial borders in central and Eastern Europe, but also established human rights and other democratic values as the basic tenets that the members agreed to respect.

hydrogen bomb (H-bomb)   A nuclear weapon that is vastly more destructive than the atomic bomb (A-bomb). Its development was seen as necessary to maintain nuclear deterrence because the Soviets developed the A-bomb more quickly than expected.

imperialism   The subordination of a weaker state by a stronger political entity, frequently through conquest or territorial occupation.

interagency process   The part of the executive branch policy process that brings together the State Department, Defense Department, and other relevant executive branch officials, usually chaired by the National Security Council staff.

International Atomic Energy Agency (IAEA)   An agency created in 1957 to ensure that as nations develop nuclear energy, it would be used only for peaceful purposes such as nuclear power plants.

International Criminal Court (ICC)   A permanent criminal tribunal, founded in 2002 to prosecute individuals who commit the most serious crimes against the international community, including crimes against humanity, war crimes, and genocide.

International Institutionalism   A school of international relations theory that emphasizes both the possibility and the value of international institutions and other forms of cooperation for reducing the chances of war and other conflict.

International Monetary Fund (IMF) The global organization that oversees the international monetary system, promotes international monetary cooperation and exchange-rate stability, and provides resources to help members in balance of payments difficulties or to assist with poverty reduction.

International Trade Commission (ITC) An independent regulatory agency with six members, evenly divided between Republicans and Democrats, all appointed by the president (subject to Senate confirmation), that rules on certain cases of competition from imports.

interservice rivalry Tensions among the Army, Navy, Air Force, and Marines over budgets, strategy, and other defense policy matters.

Intifada Palestinian uprisings, the first of which was against Israeli occupation of the West Bank in Gaza from 1987 to 1993 and the second of which was from 2000 to 2004.

Iran-contra scandal A secret deal worked out by Reagan administration officials whereby the United States would provide arms to Iran in exchange for Iran's help in getting the American hostages in Lebanon released. The profits from the arms sales were then used to fund the Nicaraguan contras, thereby circumventing congressional prohibitions.

Iraq War The invasion of Iraq in March 2003, led by the United States along with Great Britain and a coalition of about forty countries. The invasion was based on the claim that Iraq possessed weapons of mass destruction.

isolationist Engaging in a foreign policy in which the country minimizes its involvement in world affairs.

Jackson-Vanik Amendment Passed by Congress in 1974, linking most-favored-nation status for the Soviet Union to a prescribed increase in emigration visas for Soviet Jews.

Janjaweed "Devils on horseback," the name given to the Arab tribesmen who, along with the Sudanese government, have burned villages and farms and killed and terrorized the people of Darfur.

Japanese-American internment The imprisonment of 120,000 Japanese Americans during World War II, often cited as an example of civil liberties violations in the name of national security.

jihad Translated from Arabic as "struggle," often interpreted as "holy war" and linked to Al Qaeda.

Joint Chiefs of Staff Established during World War II to coordinate the military services; made up of the chairman, the vice chairman, the Chief of Staff of the army, the Chief of Naval Operations, the Chief of Staff of the air force, and the commandant of the Marine Corps.

just war An ethical doctrine with bases in all major religions that claims war must meet certain criteria, including a just cause, proportionality of the military means, a strong possibility of success, and the use of force as a last resource.

Kyoto Treaty The 1997 United Nations Framework on Climate Change; went into effect in February 2005 despite American opposition and has had a mixed record.

League of Nations An international institution created after World War I as a result of the Treaty of Versailles. Its failure was due to two crucial errors: U.S. nonmembership and the weakness of its institutional design.

liberal international economic order (LIEO)   The relatively open, market-based, free-trade system created after World War II with a minimum of tariffs and other government-initiated trade barriers, and with international economic relations worked out through negotiations.

loose nukes   Nuclear weapons and materials, particularly from Russia, that could fall into the hands of rogue states or terrorists.

Louisiana Purchase   The acquisition of the western territory of the United States from France for $15 million in 1803.

Ludlow Amendment   A constitutional amendment proposed in 1938 that would have required a national referendum before any decision to go to war.

manifest destiny   A term coined in 1845 that refers to the "right" claimed by the United States to continental expansion.

Marshall Plan   The first major U.S. Cold War foreign-aid program, for the reconstruction of Western Europe after World War II and during the Cold War.

massive retaliation   A nuclear strategy doctrine pursued during the Eisenhower administration whereby the United States threatened to resort to nuclear weapons to counter any Soviet challenge anywhere of any kind.

Mayaguez incident   A 1975 incident involving the limited use of force against Cambodia to rescue an American merchant ship and its crew.

McCarthyism   Widespread public accusations of procommunist activity that gripped the country in the early 1950s, based on little evidence and often in violation of civil liberties.

Mexican Revolution   Civil war in Mexico that began in 1910, caused by corruption and social unrest, and in which the United States intervened militarily.

Mexican War   War between the United States and Mexico, 1846–48, that focused on the annexation of Texas, which had declared its independence from Mexico in 1836.

military assistance   The provision of weapons, advisers, financing, and/or other forms of aid to a government or rebel group.

Military intervention   The "small wars," or the use of military force in a relatively limited fashion, as in the overthrow of governments considered hostile to U.S. interests and the protection or bringing to power of pro-U.S. leaders.

multilateralism   An approach to foreign policy that emphasizes acting with other nations (three or more is what distinguishes multilateral from bilateral) through processes that are more consultative and consenual as structured by international institutions, alliances, and coalitions.

multipolar system   An international system in which there are three or more major powers.

Munich analogy   A reference to the negotiations in Munich leading up to World War II; invokes the need to confront dictators and aggressors, using force if necessary, rather than making concessions and pursuing "appeasement."

mutually assured destruction (MAD)   A Cold War nuclear doctrine based on the fact that the United States and the Soviet Union had enough nuclear weapons to destroy one another. MAD was considered potentially stabilizing because neither country could launch a "first strike" without risking devastation by a "second strike."

National Intelligence Estimate (NIE)   Officially defined as "the coordinated judgments of the Intelligence Community regarding the likely course of future events," written with the goal of providing "policymakers with the best, unvarnished and unbiased information—regardless of whether analytic judgments conform to U.S. policy."

national security adviser   Appointed by the president as the principal national security policy advisor within the White House.

National Security Agency (NSA)   The nation's cryptologic intelligence organization, dating back to the Cold War. The NSA gained attention for its role in a secret Bush program of warrantless wiretapping and electronic surveillance of hundreds or thousands of people within the United States.

National Security Council (NSC)   The president's principal forum for considering national security and foreign policy matters with senior national security advisors and Cabinet officials.

NATO expansion   Post–Cold War opening of NATO to former Soviet-bloc states.

neocolonialism   Extensive power exercised by one country over another through less direct control than colonialism.

neoconservatism   A belief system prevalent in the George W. Bush administration that strongly links Power and Principles and holds that America's role is to advance freedom through the exercise of its superior power, including military force.

nongovernmental organization (NGO)   An unofficial, nonprofit organization; NGOs have grown in numbers and roles as actors in foreign policy and international affairs.

Nixon shock   President Nixon's announcement on August 15, 1971 that the United States was unilaterally devaluing the dollar, suspending its convertibility to gold, and imposing a 10 percent special tariff on imports.

North American Free Trade Agreement (NAFTA)   Approved in 1993, created a free-trade area among the three North American countries: Canada, Mexico, and the United States.

North Atlantic Treaty Organization (NATO)   The first peacetime military alliance in American history. Created in 1949, NATO ensured a military commitment to keeping U.S. troops in Europe and the collective defense pledge that the United States would defend its European allies if they were attacked.

Nonproliferation Treaty (NPT)   Approved by the UN General Assembly in 1968, allowing the five states that already had nuclear weapons—the United States, the Soviet Union, Britain, France, and China—to keep them, and prohibiting all other states from acquiring or developing them.

NSC-68   An influential security-planning paper developed in early 1950 by President Truman's National Security Council. NSC-68 called for three important shifts in U.S. strategy: globalization of containment, militarization of containment, and the development of the hydrogen bomb.

nuclear deterrence Prevention of nuclear war by credibly communicating sufficient will and capacity to retaliate as a second strike if attacked.

nuclear freeze movement A movement during the early 1980s based on widespread fear that the nuclear buildup had gone too far.

Nuclear Nonproliferation Treaty (NPT) Approved by the UN General Assembly in 1968, allowing the five states that already had nuclear weapons—the United States, the Soviet Union, Britain, France, and China—to keep them, and prohibiting all other states from acquiring or developing them.

nuclear utilization targeting strategy (NUTS) In contrast with the doctrine of mutually assured destruction (MAD), this theory argued that only if the United States alone had the capacity to fight a "limited" nuclear war would deterrence be strengthened—and only then would the United States be in a position to "win" should it come to that.

"One China" policy Established by Nixon and Kissinger as part of détente; signified that American policy shifted from its traditional support for Taiwan and supported the peaceful reunification of China.

Open Door policy A demand made on the major European powers in the 1890s that the United States not be closed out of spheres of trade and influence in China; the United States claimed to be helping China against the encroachments of European colonialism, but was also self-interested.

Operation Desert Shield Response to the 1990 invasion of Kuwait by Iraq, the most rapid buildup of U.S. military forces since World War II to protect Saudi Arabia from an invasion by the Iraqi armies of Saddam Hussein.

Operation Desert Storm Followed Desert Shield, the U.S.-led coalition operation launched in January 1991 to drive the Iraqi armies of Saddam Hussein out of Kuwait; it was a formidable military victory, with Iraqi forces withdrawing from Kuwait in little more than a month and with few American and coalition casualties.

Operation Restore Hope A largely humanitarian mission in which the United States sent twenty-seven thousand troops to Somalia in December 1992 to help restore order and bring food to the Somali people.

Organization for Security and Cooperation in Europe (OSCE) The new name given to the CSCE in 1994, which expanded its membership to fifty-six states, enhanced its role in diplomacy and conflict management and resolution, and implied greater institutionalization.

Organization of African Unity (OAU) A major regional organization for Africa, created in 1963, succeeded by the Africa Union in 2002.

Organization of American States (OAS) The major regional organization of the Western Hemisphere, which currently has thirty-five member states; dominated by the United States during the Cold War, but less so since then.

Organization of Petroleum Exporting Countries (OPEC) An organization that led an oil embargo in 1973, targeted at the United States and the Netherlands for their support of Israel in the Yom Kippur War, and a global price hike, actions that forever changed the economics of oil. OPEC led a second oil shock in 1979 during the Iranian Revolution.

Oslo agreement   Officially the Israeli-Palestinian Declaration of Principles, it was signed by Israel's prime minister Yitzhak Rabin and the Palestine Liberation Organization leader Yasir Arafat alongside President Bill Clinton in 1993 and marked a major breakthrough toward resolution of the Israeli-Palestinian conflict.

Overseas Private Investment Corporation (OPIC)   The government corporation that provides insurance and financing for foreign investments by U.S. companies that will create jobs back home and increase exports.

Pearl Harbor   A U.S. naval base in Hawaii, the site of a surprise attack by the Japanese on on December 7, 1941 that precipitated U.S. entry into World War II.

perestroika   Literally, "restructuring," it meant changes in the Soviet economy, allowing for more open markets with some private enterprise and foreign investments.

Platt Amendment (1901)   An amendment attached to the Cuban constitution to protect U.S. special interests in Cuba.

policy enhancement   Argues that the freedom of action the United States gives up by acting multilaterally tends to be outweighed by the capacity gained to achieve shared objectives.

political institutions   The ongoing governing structure essential for maintaining political stability, accountability, and good governance.

Powell Doctrine   A term named after General Colin Powell that refers to the decisive use of force to end conflict quickly and minimize U.S. casualties, as in the 1990–91 Persian Gulf War.

power transition   A situation in which a dominant global power is at least somewhat declining and a new global power is rising. During a power transition, risks of conflict and even war can run high.

preemptive war   The use of military force anticipatorily against imminent threats.

prerogative encroachment   The concern that actions by the UN and other multilateral institutions infringe on American power and freedom of action.

preventive war   In general, action to reduce chances of a future conflict; in military terms, the anticipatory use of force against a prospective but not an imminent threat.

primacy   The dominant position of a major power.

primordialist   Refers to an explanation of the sources of ethnic conflict that sees ethnicity as a fixed and inherently conflictual historical identity.

procedural legislation   Process-specific legislation that spells out the procedures and structures through which foreign policy will be made.

proliferation   The spread of nuclear weapons to states that are banned from having them by the Nuclear Nonproliferation Treaty.

Proliferation Security Initiative (PSI)   A global coalition initiated by the G.W. Bush administration aimed at stopping trafficking of WMD, missiles and other delivery systems, and related materials to and from states and nonstate actors of concern.

protectionism   An economic policy of restricting trade to protect businesses in one country from foreign competition, often through the use of tariffs.

purposive   Refers to an explanation of the sources of ethnic conflict that acknowledges how history shapes ethnic tensions but stresses the ways in which demagogic leaders and others intentionally exploit, exacerbate, and escalate such tensions.

Reagan Doctrine   A U.S. foreign policy strategy developed by the Reagan administration as the basis for going beyond containment to seek to oust communist regimes that had come to power.

Realism   A school of international relations theory that emphasizes power as the objective of the state and conceives the international system as a competition for power.

Reciprocal Trade Agreements Act   First passed by Congress in 1934, delegating to the president authority to cut tariffs by as much as 50 percent if he could negotiate reciprocal cuts with other countries. This act laid the basis for a fundamental shift away from protectionism and toward free trade.

Red Scare   The period 1919–20 when the Wilson administration, led by Attorney General A. Mitchell Palmer, grossly overreacted to fears of internal subversion linked to "world communism'" with heavy-handed repression and blatant disregard for civil liberties.

responsibility to protect (R2P)   Emerging norm stressing that individuals must be protected from mass killings and other gross violations of their rights within states, the corresponding limits to claims of sovereignty by offending states, and the legitimacy of certain types of international intervention.

revolution in military affairs   A mastery of electronic and information technologies that gave the United States unprecedented conventional military capabilities during Operation Desert Storm.

ripeness   Refers to points(s) in the life cycle of a conflict at which that conflict is more conducive to possible resolution than at other times.

rogue state   Describes a state that is considered an extreme security threat and is not very susceptible to negotiations for ideological or other essential reasons.

Roosevelt Corollary   Set forth in 1904, claimed for the United States the "international police power" to intervene when instability within a Latin American country risked creating the pretext for an Old World power to act.

Russian Revolution   The series of revolutions in 1917 against the Czarist government which led to the creation of the Soviet Union and the world's first communist state.

Secretary of the Treasury   The head of the Department of the Treasury and one of the president's principal economic advisers.

security community   An area in which strategic rivalries are attenuated and the use of force within the group is highly unlikely.

self-defense   Military action taken in response to already having been attacked.

shuttle diplomacy   Secretary of State Henry Kissinger's method of intensive U.S. peace brokering during and following the 1973 Arab-Israeli war, working out cease-fires and other agreements among Israel, Egypt, Jordan, Syria and others in the region.

Six-Party Talks   A series of negotiations involving the United States, China, Russia, Japan, South Korea, and North Korea to peacefully resolve the nuclear proliferation threat posed by North Korea.

Smoot-Hawley Tariff   A protectionist tariff of 1930 that had disastrous effects, including contributing to the Great Depression.

soft power   The ways in which the values for which a nation stands—its cultural attractiveness and other aspects of its reputation—can be sources of influence in the world.

South Sudan   Formerly the region of the Republic of Sudan, created as an independent country in 2011.

Spanish-American War   War in 1898 between Spain and the United States in which the United States gained dominance over Cuba and took the Philippines as a colony, and that also marked the beginning of the emergence of the United States as a world power.

START (Strategic Arms Reduction Treaty)   The first of the post–Cold War U.S.-Soviet nuclear arms control agreements, signed by President George H. W. Bush and the Russian president, Mikhail Gorbachev, in 1991. It cut strategic nuclear weapons from Cold War levels of 13,000 U.S. and 11,000 Soviet warheads to 6,000 on each side.

Strategic Arms Limitation Treaty (SALT I)   Negotiations during the 1970s to limit U.S. and Soviet nuclear weapons. SALT I was signed and ratified during the Nixon administration.

Strategic Arms Limitation Talks (SALT II)   The follow-up agreement to limit U.S. and Soviet nuclear weapons. It was never finalized amid controversies over détente and then the Soviet invasion of Afghanistan.

Strategic Defense Initiative (SDI)   A Reagan-initiated program to build a nationwide defense umbrella against nuclear attack; also known as "Star Wars."

structural adjustment   Policies required by the International Monetary Fund as a key condition for financial assistance to debtor countries that stressed fiscal austerity, including major cuts in safety nets.

substantive legislation   Policy-specific legislation that spells out what the details of what foreign policy should or should not be.

surge   A major shift in strategy during the Iraq war, which involved a buildup of another thirty thousand troops combined with a revised counterinsurgency strategy; led by General David Petraeus.

Sustainable development   A policy approach that meets the needs of the present without compromising the ability of future generations to meet their own needs.

Taiwan   An island off the coast of mainland China to which the Jiang Jeishi (Chiang Kai-shek) government retreated after its defeat in the 1949 Chinese revolution; a strong U.S. ally during the Cold War, still backed by the United States but in the context of overall U.S. relations with Beijing and support for peaceful reunification.

Tibet   The home of the Tibetan people, who seek greater autonomy from China and possibly secession from China itself; a major human rights issue in U.S.-China relations.

Tokyo Round   A round of GATT global trade negotiations during the 1970s that not only lowered tariffs but also brought down some "nontariff barriers"—various governmental policies and practices that discriminated against imports and thus impeded free trade.

Trade and Development Agency   An agency that helps American companies put together business plans and feasibility studies for new export opportunities.

transitional justice   The set of judicial and non-judicial measures, including criminal prosecutions, truth commissions, and reparations programs, implemented in order to instill accountability for and rectify the effects of past human rights abuses.

Truman Doctrine   A U.S. commitment proclaimed in March 1947 to aid Greece and Turkey against Soviet and Soviet-assisted threats; key basis for containment.

Uighurs   A Turkic ethnic group living in China that has had tensions with the Han, China's ethnic majority. Those tensions exploded into violent riots in July 2009.

unilateralism   An approach to foreign policy that emphasizes actions that a nation takes largely on its own, or acting with others but mainly on its own terms.

Union of South American Nations (UNASUR)   A new regional organization established in 2008 including South American nations but not the United States, Canada, Central American, or Caribbean nations.

unipolarity   An international system in which there is one major power.

United Nations (UN)   The principal global institution founded on June 26, 1945 by fifty-one countries to ensure peace. The UN now includes 192 countries and plays a key, often controversial, role in world affairs.

U.S. Trade Representative (USTR)   The president's principal trade advisor, negotiator and spokesperson on trade issues.

veto   The constitutional right of the president to refuse to approve legislation passed by the legislature.

Vietnam War   A hugely controversial war in Southeast Asia, fought mostly between 1965 and 1975, in which the United States allied with South Vietnam against communist North Vietnam and the Viet Cong. The war was a major defeat for the United States, the reasons for which are hotly debated.

War of 1812   The war between the United States and Britain along the Canadian border, the Atlantic coast, the Gulf of Mexico and on the oceans. British forces burned the White House.

war powers   The constitutional power given to the president to serve as "commander in chief" and given to Congress to "declare war" and "provide for the common defense." Because these are not separate powers but rather shares of the same power, war powers have been a topic of recurring debate in foreign policy politics.

War Powers Resolution (WPR) of 1973 An act seeking to limit presidential war powers by tightening requirements for consulting with Congress; based on the lessons of Vietnam but has not had much actual impact.

Watergate The political scandal which began with the arrest of five men for breaking into Democratic party offices at the Watergate complex in June 1972. The resulting investigation revealed that President Nixon and his cronies had lied and committed crimes, and led to Nixon's resignation.

weapons of mass destruction Weapons, including nuclear, biological, and chemical weapons, that can kill very large numbers of people and cause other massive destruction.

Weinberger criteria Six criteria laid out by Defense Secretary Caspar Weinberger in November 1984 that set the threshold for when and how to use military force; prompted by the failure of American troops in Lebanon.

World Bank Formally named the International Bank for Reconstruction and Development, it initially focused on European reconstruction and later became a major source of development aid for Third World countries.

World War I A major world conflict, from 1914 to 1918, that the United States entered in 1917. The world powers organized into two opposing camps: the Triple Entente and the Triple Alliance. This war resulted in over 15 million casualties.

World War II A major world conflict, from 1939 to 1945, in which the Allied powers fought against Hitler's Nazi Germany and imperial Japan, engaging in a war that resulted in 70 million deaths. The war was fought in both the European and Pacific theaters. The United States and the Soviet Union emerged as the world's superpowers.

Index